CRIMINAL JUSTICE:

INTRODUCTORY CASES AND MATERIALS

FIFTH EDITION

By

JOHN KAPLAN
Late Jackson Eli Reynolds Professor of Law,
Stanford University

JEROME H. SKOLNICK, Ph.D.
Claire Clements Dean's Professor of Law
University of California, Berkeley

MALCOLM M. FEELEY, Ph.D.
Professor of Law (Jurisprudence and Social Policy)
University of California, Berkeley

Westbury, New York
THE FOUNDATION PRESS, INC.
1991

Library of Congress Cataloging-in-Publication Data

Kaplan, John.
    Criminal justice : introductory cases and materials / by John
Kaplan, Jerome H. Skolnick, and Malcolm M. Feeley. — 5th ed.
        p.   cm.
    Includes bibliographical references and index.
    ISBN 0-88277-873-0
    1. Criminal justice, Administration of—United States—Cases.
I. Skolnick, Jerome H. II. Feeley, Malcolm. III. Title.
KF9223.A7K35 1991
345.73'05—dc20
[347.3055]   90-27563

INTRODUCTORY NOTE

John Kaplan began this book more than a decade ago. John, who was Jackson Eli Reynolds Professor of Law at Stanford University, was a premier criminal law scholar and a leading criminologist. He was also a legendary teacher and treasured colleague. With deep regret and sadness I must inscribe that John, who was born in 1929, succumbed to cancer on November 23, 1989. This edition is dedicated to his memory.

No one can ever duplicate or replace John Kaplan's unique contribution to any enterprise in which he was engaged. Much of what he contributed to this book remains—from the basic organization, to the funniest and most apt selections, to the cleverest commentary and questions.

Nevertheless, I was fortunate to bring on board as accessory after the fact my colleague Malcolm Feeley, a political scientist and University of California, Berkeley, law professor. Professor Feeley is a distinguished author of prizewinning books and articles on various aspects of criminal justice—particularly the criminal courts, court reform and plea bargaining. His participation in this and future editions will be most welcome.

JEROME H. SKOLNICK

*

PREFACE

This book has been in print for more than a decade and has been used in more than 300 colleges and university courses. We believe that the book's wide acceptance is attributable to six features, which we retain and expand upon in this edition:

First, the book has a coherent organization. It begins with an introduction to the concept of crime, addresses major issues surrounding that concept—such as how we measure criminality, its variety, the justifications we employ punishing it. We follow this with an introduction to processing institutions—police, prosecutor, defense attorney, courts, sentencing and corrections. The book stresses the relations among these institutions and illustrates them with examples.

Second, the book is up-to-date. We have undertaken an extensive search of cases, books, journals, magazines, and newspapers to find the latest and most interesting material on the topics covered.

Third, criminal justice topics and concerns do not stand still. In this edition, as in previous ones, we have, in various parts of the book, introduced new cases and materials on important issues: acquaintance rape, feminist theory and criminal law, the drug legalization debate, plea-bargaining and white collar crime. And in a shrinking world, we have introduced materials which emphasize comparative law and legal organization.

Fourth, the book is interdisciplinary and varied. The materials in the book include cases and statutes, the writings and commentary of legal scholars, articles by social scientists, humanists, newspaper editorials; and reports by criminal justice practitioners. The best from a multiplicity of sources.

Fifth, the book is readable. Criminal justice is written at several levels. Some technical writings are accessible primarily to the legal or social science professionals, beyond the reach of most undergraduates. We diligently searched for accurate, analytically challengeable, but nevertheless understandable levels of writing. We have especially edited cases for clarity.

Sixth, the book is teachable. We try throughout to capture the student's and the teacher's interest, partly through issues implied by the book's organization; more directly by comments and questions that highlight the meaning of the excerpts. We seek only partly to describe. Our larger aspiration is to clarify issues and the implications of criminal justice policy choices, so as to advance the quality of the discussion of them.

JEROME H. SKOLNICK
MALCOLM M. FEELEY

January, 1991

*

ACKNOWLEDGEMENTS

We thank Susan Poser for superior assistance. She helped organize the manuscript, contributed valuable suggestions, read proofs and formulated the index. We wish her well in what will undoubtedly be a successful career. Rod Watanabe, as usual, monitored the secretarial resources at the Center for the Study of Law and Society with grace and good cheer.

*

SUMMARY OF CONTENTS

TABLE OF CONTENTS

Page

Page

TABLE OF CONTENTS

xix

TABLE OF CONTENTS

*

TABLE OF CASES

Principal cases are in italic type. Non-principal cases are in roman type. References are to Pages.

*

CRIMINAL JUSTICE:

INTRODUCTORY CASES AND MATERIALS

*

Chapter I

CRIME

Introduction

Most of this book will be concerned with how our criminal justice system actually works, and with our ideal of how it should work. To understand the theory, operations, and contradictions of our criminal justice system, however, one must know something about the phenomenon of crime. This chapter explores some of that complexity.

A. WHAT DISTINGUISHES CRIME?

1. NOTE ON THE CRIMINOLOGICAL DEFINITION OF CRIME

Criminologists generally agree that there is no clear cut, compelling definition of crime. However, most would subscribe to a legally based definition. Thus, crime is defined as conduct, prohibited by a legislature, to which such penalties as fine and imprisonment are attached. Since the criminal law varies from time to time, and from place to place, actions which may be crimes in one place or time may not be crimes in another.

Some people equate the idea of crime more broadly with social wrongdoing. The problem with using such a definition is that citizens and legislatures do not always agree about right and wrong. Some citizens, for example, believe that abortion is a serious crime, tantamount to murder. Others believe that it is a socially necessary form of birth control or at least an inalienable right of women who do not wish to bear children.

Under the social wrong-doing view, "crime" is a socially, not a legally, defined concept—subject to the fact that different sections of society might look at the matter differently. Under the more legal view, it would simply be said that there are some actions which are not crimes, but which one might argue are anti-social or dangerous. And there are some crimes which are arguably not very dangerous or anti-social.

Yet another view regards crime not as legally or socially defined, but rather as a moral or even religious wrong. Thus some people equate crime with sin. Again, in a society with widely differing views of proper behavior, it may be difficult to apply such a concept. After all, about half of the commands of the Ten Commandments are not enforced by the criminal law.

1

Before we move on to the precise ways in which the law defines crime, we must first consider whether there is any essential quality—other than being the object of the exercise of power by the legislature—which distinguishes conduct which should be made criminal from other conduct.

2. THE NATURE OF CRIME

a. WHAT IS DISTINCTIVE ABOUT A CRIME?*

Can crimes be distinguished from civil wrongs on the ground that they constitute injuries to society generally which society is interested in preventing? The difficulty is that society is interested also in the due fulfillment of contracts and the avoidance of traffic accidents and most of the other stuff of civil litigation. The civil law is framed and interpreted and enforced with a constant eye to these social interests. Does the distinction lie in the fact that proceedings to enforce the criminal law are instituted by public officials rather than private complainants? The difficulty is that public officers may also bring many kinds of "civil" enforcement actions—for an injunction, for the recovery of a "civil" penalty, or even for the detention of the defendant by public authority.** Is the distinction, then, in the peculiar character of what is done to people who are adjudged to be criminals? The difficulty is that, with the possible exception of death, exactly the same kinds of unpleasant consequences, objectively considered, can be and are visited upon unsuccessful defendants in civil proceedings.

If one were to judge from the notions apparently underlying many judicial opinions, and the overt language even of some of them, the solution of the puzzle is simply that a crime is anything which is *called* a crime, and a criminal penalty is simply the penalty provided for doing anything which has been given that name. So vacant a concept is a betrayal of intellectual bankruptcy. Moreover, it is false to popular understanding. Conviction for crime is a distinctive and serious matter—a something, and not a nothing. What is that something?

What distinguishes a criminal from a civil sanction and all that distinguishes it, it is ventured, is the judgment of community condemnation which accompanies and justifies its imposition.

Questions

Does the above selection argue that all actions that are worthy of condemnation are crimes? Does it argue that all actions worthy of condemnation should be made crimes by the legislature? Does it argue that all actions which are made crimes by the legislature would be

* Henry M. Hart, Jr. "The Aims of the Criminal Law," *Law and Contemporary Problems* Vol. 23, No. 3 (Summer 1958), pp. 403–404, Copyright 1958, Duke University School of Law. (Reprinted with permission).

** This would be the case where a person is held for "civil commitment" to a mental institution.

worthy of condemnation even if the legislature had not made them crimes?

Is not anyone who deliberately violates the law blameworthy and deserving of condemnation—at least so long as the law itself does not recognize some justification or excuse for his conduct? Is it important to emphasize that if, for some reason, a particular person does not deserve condemnation for violating the legislative command, he should not be guilty of a crime?

b. THE DISTINCTION BETWEEN TORTS * AND CRIMES **

. . . Nozick contends that there are certain actions, typically those that inflict personal injury, that we fear even though we may know that we will be compensated fully for the injury if and when it is inflicted. Thus, for example, if I know that sometime in the coming month my arm will be broken, I will be nervous and fearful despite my knowledge that I will receive full compensation for this injury. By contrast, I will not suffer any fear from the knowledge that my car will be damaged and that I will be fully compensated. If I believe that the system in which I live permits people to break my arm provided that they pay compensation, I will suffer fear: I will fear being victimized by such actions.

Thus, the prohibition against fear-producing acts is not addressed to the fear of a person who is actually injured. That fear could be compensated. Rather, it seeks to protect the other members of society from the fear that they will suffer if such actions are allowed subject to the requirement of compensation. This fear cannot be compensated: it would be unfair to extract compensation from the transgressor in any individual case (e.g., an assault) for the general fear suffered by those not directly involved, since the individual transgressor did not cause that fear. Rather, it is the knowledge that the system allows such acts that causes the fear. Thus, the uncompensated general fear gives rise to a "legitimate public interest" in prohibiting fear-producing actions. It provides, Nozick says:

> one dimension of a distinction between private wrongs and wrongs having a public component. Private wrongs are those where only the injured party need be compensated; persons who know they will be compensated fully do not fear them. Public wrongs are those people are fearful of, even though they know they will be compensated fully if and when the wrongs occur.

---

* Torts are sometimes called "civil wrongs." They consist, as a first approximation, of automobile accident injuries, medical malpractice, libel or any other kind of violation of legal rights for which the law gives a remedy in money damages. Tort suits seeking a remedy in damages for legal wrongs form a large portion of our civil litigation. Some torts, such as as-sault, are also crimes, and most crimes injuring someone's person or property are also torts.

** Robert W. Drane and David J. Neal, "On Moral Justifications for the Tort/ Crime Distinction," *California Law Review* Vol. 68, No. 2, © March 1980, p. 409. (Reprinted with permission).

Questions

Is it clear that calling a harmful act a "crime" cannot be justified simply on the basis of the extent of harm produced? Which of the justifications—moral condemnation or capacity to induce fear—do you find more persuasive? Why? Do you find neither of the justifications persuasive? If not, what would you substitute?

B. HOW THE LAW DEFINES CRIMES

1. NOTE ON THE DEFINITION OF CRIMES

Crimes are usually defined by the legislature to provide for punishment of persons who perform specific acts in the presence of certain "attendant circumstances" while possessing certain states of mind.* Each of these, the act, the attendant circumstance, and the state of mind (or *mens rea*) is called an "element" of a crime. Thus the elements of common-law ** burglary are the breaking and entering (acts) into a dwelling house by night (attendant circumstances) with intent to commit a felony therein (a state of mind).

2. STATE OF MIND

Introduction

It is important to note that a crime is not merely a physical act. The law recognizes a great difference between, on one hand, running down and killing a pedestrian who happens to stagger into one's path while one is driving carefully, and, on the other, committing premeditated murder by purposely driving one's car over someone. In other words, it is not only physical acts we are concerned with but the mental states with which they are performed. In Justice Holmes' famous phrase, "Even a dog distinguishes between being stumbled over and being kicked."

a. PEOPLE v. STRONG
Court of Appeals of New York, 1975.
37 N.Y.2d 568, 376 N.Y.S.2d 87, 338 N.E.2d 602.

JASEN, Judge.

Defendant was charged, in a one-count indictment, with manslaughter in the second degree for causing the death of Kenneth Goings. At the trial, the defense requested that the court submit to the jury, in addition to the crime charged, the crime of criminally negligent homicide. The court refused, and the jury found defendant guilty as charged.

---

* In a relatively small number of crimes, a particular specified result is also necessary. The most notable of these are the homicidal crimes, murder and manslaughter where a particular result—the death of a human being—is necessary.

** Common-law burglary is burglary as it was originally defined.

The sole issue upon this appeal is whether the trial court erred in refusing to submit to the jury the lesser crime of criminally negligent homicide.

In determining whether the defendant in this case was entitled to the charge of the lesser crime, the focus must be on the evidence in the record relating to the mental state of the defendant at the time of the crime. The record discloses that the defendant, 57 years old at the time of trial, had left his native Arabia at the age of 19, emigrating first to China and then coming to the United States three years later. He had lived in Rochester only a short time before committing the acts which formed the basis for this homicide charge. He testified that he had been of the Sudan Muslim religious faith since birth, and had become one of the sect's leaders, claiming a sizable following. Defendant articulated the three central beliefs of this religion as "cosmic consciousness, mind over matter and physiomatic psychomatic consciousness." He stated that the second of these beliefs, "mind over matter", empowered a "master," or leader, to lie on a bed of nails without bleeding, to walk through fire or on hot coals, to perform surgical operations without anesthesia, to raise people up off the ground, and to suspend a person's heartbeat, pulse, and breathing while that person remained conscious. In one particular type of ceremony, defendant, purportedly exercising his powers of "mind over matter," claimed he could stop a follower's heartbeat and breathing and plunge knives into his chest without any injury to the person. There was testimony from at least one of defendant's followers that he had successfully performed this ceremony on previous occasions. Defendant himself claimed to have performed ths ceremony countless times over the previous 40 years without once causing an injury. Unfortunately, on January 28, 1972, when defendant performed this ceremony on Kenneth Goings, a recent recruit, the wounds from the hatchet and three knives which defendant had inserted into him proved fatal.

We view the record as warranting the submission of the lesser charge of criminally negligent homicide since there is a reasonable basis upon which the jury could have found that the defendant failed to perceive the risk inherent in his actions. The defendant's conduct and claimed lack of perception, together with the belief of the victim and defendant's followers, if accepted by the jury, would justify a verdict of guilty of criminally negligent homicide. There was testimony, both from defendant and from one of his followers, that the victim himself perceived no danger, but in fact volunteered to participate. Additionally, at least one of the defendant's followers testified that the defendant had previously performed this ritual without causing injury. Assuming that a jury would not believe that the defendant was capable of performing the acts in question without harm to the victim, it still could determine that this belief held by the defendant and his followers was indeed sincere and that defendant did not in fact perceive any risk of harm to the victim.

On the particular facts of this case, we conclude that there is a reasonable view of the evidence which, if believed by the jury, would support a finding that the defendant was guilty only of the crime of criminally negligent homicide, and that the trial court erred in not submitting, as requested, this lesser offense to the jury.

Accordingly, we would reverse and order a new trial.

GABRIELLI, Judge (dissenting).

I dissent and conclude that there is no justification in the record for the majority's holding that "defendant's conduct or claimed lack of perception, together with the belief of the victim and defendant's followers, if accepted by the jury, would justify a verdict of criminally negligent homicide". The Appellate Division was correct in holding that "Defendant's belief in his superhuman powers, whether real or simulated, did not result in his failure to perceive the risk but, rather, led him consciously to disregard the risk of which he was aware".

Simply stated, a reckless offender (manslaughter) is aware of the risk and consciously disregards it; whereas, on the other hand, the "criminally negligent" offender is *not* aware of the risk created and cannot thus be guilty of disregarding it.

Can it be reasonably claimed or argued that, when the defendant inflicted the several stab wounds, one of which penetrated the victim's heart and was four and three-quarter inches deep, the defendant failed to perceive the risk? The only and obvious answer is simply "no".

This case might profitably be analogized to one where an individual believing himself to be possessed of extraordinary skill as an archer attempts to duplicate William Tell's feat and split an apple on the head of another individual from some distance. However, assume that rather than hitting the apple, the archer kills the victim. Certainly, his obtuse subjective belief in his extraordinary skill would not render his actions [merely] criminally negligent. The archer was unquestionably reckless and would, therefore, be guilty of manslaughter in the second degree. The present case is indistinguishable.

There being no proper evidentiary basis for the lesser charge here, the order of the Appellate Division should be affirmed.

Order reversed, etc.

b. NOTE ON THE STRONG CASE

There are several possible states of mind, with respect to the death of Kenneth Goings, which Strong might conceivably have had when stabbing him with a knife.

(1) *Purpose:* His desire might have been to kill Goings—perhaps for his insurance. He then would have acted purposefully—and would everywhere be guilty of murder.*

---

* Some jurisdictions divide murder into two degrees. First degree murder, the more serious, may require not only knowl- edge or purpose, but some degree of calm reflection on the killing before going through with it. This degree of reflection

(2) *Knowledge:* Strong might have known that plunging a knife into Goings' chest would kill him. Most of us would have known this. This could have been the case even if Strong had not desired Goings' death. Thus, Strong might have felt a need to do something very dramatic, regretting all the while that it would kill his follower. In this case, too, he would be guilty of murder everywhere, just as if he had acted purposefully.

(3) *Recklessness:* Strong might have thought that the knife might possibly kill Goings but decided that it was worth taking a chance. Here, it would be important not only that, in his own mind, he had adverted to the risk of death, but also that the risk itself was unjustified. Of course, there is no criminal liability on the doctor who performs an operation involving serious risk to the patient, if the operation is justifiable on medical grounds. In the normal case involving recklessness, there is usually no argument that the risk somehow was justified. Typically, the accused either argues that the risk was not a very serious one or else that he did not realize that he was taking such a risk. A reckless killing is usually held to be manslaughter.

(4) *Criminal Negligence:* According to the majority at the court, it is possible, under the facts of the case, that Strong did not even think about any possible harm to his follower. Whether or not it was true, the question, then, would be whether a reasonable man in Strong's position would have known of the unreasonable risk he was taking with his follower's life. The majority assumes that this is at least the case.

Negligence is typically a basis of liability in civil cases, such as automobile accidents, but criminal negligence is generally held to be a much higher degree of negligence. To be criminally negligent, the accused must overlook an especially serious risk under circumstances where it was grossly careless to do so.

Questions

1. Is it fair to punish someone who does something stupid if he does the best he can?

2. Do you believe that Strong did think there was any risk that Goings would be killed?

3. Do you believe that Strong really had done this sort of thing before without injuring anyone?

c. DEUTERONOMY 19:4, 5 *

This is the kind of homicide who may take sanctuary there and save his life: the man who strikes another without intent and with no previous enmity between them; for instance, the man who goes into a wood with his mate to fell trees, and, when cutting a tree, he relaxes his grip on the axe, the head glances off the tree, hits the other man

and thought is generally referred to as   * The New English Bible.
"premeditation and deliberation."

and kills him. The homicide may take sanctuary in any one of these cities, and his life shall be safe.

3. ABSOLUTE LIABILITY

a. NOTE

How would the law treat Strong if it were determined that he had killed Goings but that he was not purposeful, knowledgeable, reckless or even negligent with respect to her death? This would be the case if he were carrying his knife carefully and Goings stumbled into it. In this case, we would simply treat the homicide as accidental and impose no criminal liability upon Strong.

b. THE DECLINE OF INNOCENCE **

It is no answer that under the Wootton proposal, *mens rea* would not be eliminated but simply taken into account, albeit with many other factors, after conviction rather than before. What is crucial is that it would cease to be relevant on the issue of guilt or innocence. That is the point at which it functions to distinguish the responsible from the irresponsible, the blameworthy from the blameless. To use *mens rea* simply as additional data in manipulating deviants is no concession at all. . . . There are objections also on another level. The proposed reconstitution of the criminal law would create insecurity in the general community when the central function of the criminal law is to create that security. The Wootton fallacy is to see only the negative side of the criminal law—the punishment of persons found guilty of criminal conduct. But it is crucial to keep in mind as well the positive side of the criminal law. It not only provides for the punishment of the guilty, it also protects the rest of us against official interference in the conduct of our lives and does so primarily through the much maligned concept of innocence. Where a person has behaved as well as a human being can behave, the requirement of *mens rea,* in its special sense, protects him. To abandon *mens rea* and to substitute a Wootton code—in which, as I tried to show, the occurrence of the harm as a purely factual consequence of a person's physical movements suffices for conviction—removes this essential safeguard. Even the best of us may be swept into the net, for the test of our eligibility for sanctions is not our responsible acts and the consequences for which we may fairly be held responsible, but sheer accident; and accident, by definition, may befall us all. Nor is it any comfort that we will no longer be exposed to condemnation and punishment as such. Whatever it is called we will be exposed to coercive intervention by the state in our daily lives regardless of our most dutiful efforts to comply with what is required of us. Even if the proposal would more effectively deal with the threat of crime (which, as I said, there is no reason to

** Sanford Kadish, "The Decline of Innocence," *Cambridge Law Journal,* 26 (1968), pp. 286–289, Copyright 1968 (Reprinted with permission).

believe) it would do so by substituting what most of us would consider a greater threat to our security and liberty. . . .

Questions

Is it just to make the mental state of a criminal defendant irrelevant? Assume that someone is so unfortunate as to run over and kill a small child who dashes into the street in front of his car. If he is driving carefully, should he nonetheless be convicted of a crime? Why? Does not the requirement of some kind of culpable mental state follow from the idea that in order to commit a crime one must be blameworthy? Is it any answer to this to say that the judge can consider the absence of blameworthiness and not sentence the convicted criminal to any punishment?

c. THE IMPORTANCE OF CULPABILITY *

MIK.** (*looking at paper*). Dear, dear, dear! this is very tiresome. (To KO–KO ***.) My poor fellow, in your anxiety to carry out my wishes you have beheaded the heir to the throne of Japan!

KO. I beg to offer an unqualified apology.

POOH. I desire to associate myself with that expression of regret.

PITTI. We really hadn't the least notion—

MIK. Of course you hadn't. How could you? Come, come, my good fellow, don't distress yourself—it was no fault of yours. If a man of exalted rank chooses to disguise himself as a Second Trombone, he must take the consequences. It really distresses me to see you take on so. I've no doubt he thoroughly deserved all he got. (*They rise.*)

KO. We are infinitely obliged to your Majesty—

PITTI. Much obliged, your Majesty.

POOH. Very much obliged, your Majesty.

MIK. Obliged? Not a bit. Don't mention it. How *could* you tell?

POOH. No, of course we couldn't tell who the gentleman really was.

PITTI. It wasn't written on his forehead, you know.

KO. It might have been on his pocket-handkerchief, but Japanese don't use pocket-handkerchiefs! Ha! ha! ha!

MIK. Ha! ha! ha! I forget the punishment for compassing the death of the Heir Apparent.

KO.
POOH.   } Punishment. (*They drop down on their knees again.*)
PITTI.

* W.S. Gilbert, *The Mikado*.   *** The Lord High Executioner.

** The Emperor of Japan.

MIK. Yes. Something lingering, with boiling oil in it, I fancy. Something of that sort. I think boiling oil occurs in it, but I'm not sure. I know it's something humorous, but lingering, with either boiling oil or melted lead. Come, come, don't fret—I'm not a bit angry.

KO. (*in abject terror*). If your Majesty will accept our assurance, we had no idea—

MIK. Of course—

PITTI. I knew nothing about it.

POOH. I wasn't there.

MIK. That's the pathetic part of it. Unfortunately, the fool of an Act says "compassing the death of the Heir Apparent." There's not a word about a mistake—

KO., PITTI., *and* POOH. No!

MIK. Or not knowing—

KO. No!

MIK. Or having no notion—

PITTI. No!

MIK. Or not being there—

POOH. No!

MIK. There should be, of course—

KO., PITTI., *and* POOH. Yes!

MIK. But there isn't.

KO., PITTI., *and* POOH. Oh!

MIK. That's the slovenly way in which these Acts are always drawn. However, cheer up, it'll be all right. I'll have it altered next session. Now, let's see about your execution—will after luncheon suit you? Can you wait till then?

. . . I'm really very sorry for you all, but it's an unjust world, and virtue is triumphant only in theatrical performances.

Questions

Do people generally know what conduct is prohibited by the criminal law, and what penalties are attached? Does it matter whether they know? Is the point that they can find out, and that so long as they keep their conduct within the requirements of the law they will be safe from criminal punishment? And if they violate the law with a mental state that makes them blameworthy, shouldn't they be punished?

What would it be like to live in a place which had no explicit criminal law, but instead punished citizens for committing socially dangerous or undesirable acts? Should not both the requirement of an explicit criminal law and of a culpable mental state be seen as protections for the individual against the power of the government?

C. THE EXTENT OF CRIME

1. WHY MEASURE CRIME RATES? *

There appear to be four main reasons:

1.   Historically, the first purpose for collecting statistics on crime and criminals appears to have been the measurement of the "moral health" of nations, cities, etc. The names given by the earliest demographers and statisticians to their measures of crime—Moralstatistik, statistique morale—give a sufficient indication of this objective; if the numbers of crimes or criminals increased, then in some sense the moral "health" of the nation was growing worse. Something of this concern appears to linger on in popular interpretations of crime statistics: a rising crime rate is not infrequently seen as an indication of increased depravity or decreased probity, or as a sign of a usually ill-defined "social pathology." Somewhat similarly, Taylor, Walton, and Young have argued that from a radical perspective crime statistics can be used as an "examination of the extent of compliance in industrial society (in quite the same way . . . as it is possible to use statistics on strikes as an index of dissensus in direct class relations at the work-place)."

2.   A second purpose for measuring crime has been the evaluation of the effectiveness of the machinery of social control. Bentham (1778) was one of the first to urge that accurate measurement of crime was a necessary adjunct for the legislator; he urged the collection of statistics on convictions and prisoners as "a kind of political barometer, by which the effects of every legislative operation relative to the subject may be indicated and made palpable."

3.   A third reason for measuring crime is the estimation of the risk of becoming a victim.

As victimization surveying has developed over the past decade, the assessment of risk has become increasingly prominent; indeed, it appears to have been one of the main objectives of the National Crime Surveys now being conducted by the Census Bureau.

4.   Finally, the measurement of crime has been a necessary preliminary to the development and testing of criminological theories. Typically the testing of such theories has involved comparisons of crime rates in different places or types of place (for example, cities versus suburbs), or over time, or attempts at correlating changes in candidate independent or explanatory variables with changes in crime rates.

2. COUNTING CRIMES *

Few of our social problems command as much public attention or evoke as much public concern as does crime. From the daily news

* Richard F. Sparks, Indicators of Crime and Criminal Justice Quantitative Studies, U.S. Department of Justice, Bureau of Justice Statistics, 1980, Edited by Stephen E. Fienberg and Albert J. Reiss, Jr. © 1980 (Reprinted with permission).

* What Do We Know About Crime?, Albert J. Reiss, Jr., from Reflections of

story to the periodic statistical report, information about crime and criminal matters is central to a number of issues and questions that the public and policymakers want answered. How much crime is there? How many criminals are there? Over the years, are we getting more crimes and more criminals? Is the behavior of criminals becoming more violent and are we at greater risk of being victimized by "crime in the streets"? . . . A moment's reflection will make the reader aware that the answers to these questions depend in part upon statistical information and analyses about numbers of crimes and criminals to determine how and in what ways these may be changing.

Despite decades of collecting and reporting crime statistics, we cannot provide satisfactory answers to any of these questions. There are a number of reasons why this is so.

Our Crime Reporting System

First, we do not systematically collect information on many of the different types of criminal law violations, and when we do, there often is no provision for systematic collation and reporting. The public's concern and attention about crime is statistically focused on only a relatively small proportion of all known crimes, the seven index crimes in our Uniform Crime Reporting System/(UCR). The UCR index crimes are murder and nonnegligent manslaughter, forcible rape, robbery, aggravated assault, burglary, larceny-theft, and motor vehicle theft. Soon UCR will also report on arson, but although there is information on many white-collar and a large number of other common crimes, such as vandalism, this is not systematically collated and reported.

Second, the separation of government into Federal, State, and local domains and into executive, legislative, and judicial branches within each of these domains makes the statistical job difficult. The nationally centralized systems of collection or reporting that exist—such as those on crimes, offenders, and incarcerated persons—are based on voluntary cooperation and lack completeness. UCR, for example, is such a system for local and State police agencies, with the Federal Bureau of Investigation (FBI) serving as the national clearinghouse. Local police agencies report their aggregate statistics to the FBI, so that the kind and amount of information available is limited by its standardization into aggregate forms. We can know either the age and sex or the race and sex of offenders, for example, but not their race, age, and sex, because the three-way combination is not required for aggregate reporting. Despite the UCR, which was founded 50 years ago, there still are police departments that do not report to the FBI. During 1978, the figures the law enforcement agencies sent to the UCR represented 99 percent of the people living in SMSA's (standard metropolitan statistical areas), 96 percent of the inhabitants of other cities, and 94 percent of the rural population. Statistics for the United States as a whole include estimates for nonreporting areas that assume crime rates much like those of comparable reporting areas.

The only way we can know about crime and criminals is in terms of some socially organized way of detecting and reporting on these matters. As of now, the amount and accuracy of our detection and reporting depends upon the capacity of police departments to detect criminal offenses on their own and upon victims' and witnesses' voluntary reports of offending behavior through complaints to a law enforcement agency. Most police departments have a very limited capacity to detect major crimes and rely almost entirely on voluntary reporting from citizens to know about them.

A great deal of crime goes unreported to the police, however, so that their statistics substantially underestimate the kind and amount of crime that victimizes persons and organizations. To provide some estimate of underreporting and additional information on the victims and the characteristics of major offenses, another organized means of knowing about crime was developed. The National Crime Survey (NCS) currently reports on household and personal victimizations from crimes.

UCR crime and NCS victimization rates are based on different concepts for property crime rates: UCR calculates the property crime rates for burglary, larceny from a household or organization, and motor vehicle theft by using the U.S. population as the base, while the NCS treats these as household crimes, using the number of households or privately owned motor vehicles as the base and excluding all property crimes against businesses and other organizations. Clearly, household rates are much higher than population rates simply because there are fewer than half as many households as people. For the same reason, the rates for businesses or other organizations, when reported, are even higher than those for households.

Each of these organized ways of knowing has its limits for obtaining information on crimes and criminals. The victimization survey, for example, has distortions arising from self-reports of crimes and can tell us little about offenders. Law enforcement agency statistics tend to substantially underreport the less serious victimizations and provide information mainly on persons the victims or police report as offenders or who are arrested and charged with the commission of crimes.

In addition there are certain limitations in the data-collection system. These arise in part because the means used to detect crimes are circumscribed and partly because we do not know how to acquire important kinds of information. We are particularly restricted in what we can know about offenders and their careers in crime because of problems in detecting offenses and collating information about them. There are few organized ways of tracking the careers of criminals systematically.

Selected Crime Rates,
Selected Years: 1970-1979

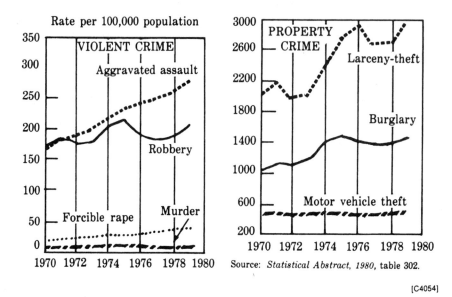

Source: *Statistical Abstract, 1980*, table 302.

[C4054]

[The amount of] crime we measure in our UCR system is far less than that reported from the NCS, then, for two major reasons: First, victims fail to report many crimes to law enforcement agencies such as police departments. A very substantial proportion of all victimizations from index crimes, except for homicides, are not reported to the police. The NCS for 1977 estimated that only 46 percent of all crimes of violence, 25 percent of all personal larceny, 49 percent of all burglary, and 68 percent of all motor vehicle theft were reported to the police. Generally, the more serious the crime, the more likely it is to be reported. Two examples may illustrate the effect of this: Although 56 percent of all robberies in the 1977 survey were reported to the police, 75 percent of the most serious ones (robberies with injury from serious assaults) were, compared with but 55 percent of the less serious ones (robberies with injury from minor assaults). In household crime, 72 percent of all burglaries with forcible entry were reported, as compared with 39 percent of those by unlawful entry and 32 percent of all attempted burglary in 1977.

Second, the victimization rate is based on different kinds of populations at risk—although those currently reported measures are at best very crude. The NCS, for example, excludes persons under 12 years of age from its survey of victims. Rates of amount of crime are much higher for the NCS than for the UCR (although they are not strictly comparable). UCR is based on the complaints that police receive from citizens, any change in the latter's behavior can affect the crime rate. The NCS estimates, for example, that between 1973 and 1977 there was an increase in the proportion of burglaries reported. The trend was most significant for homeowners, an increase of about 7 percent. Such a change in citizen reporting behavior can increase police estimates of crime rates, provided they find citizens are notifying them about bona fide victimizations. It has often been noted that police organizations can affect the kind and amount of crime reported in other ways, primarily because they control the allocation of personnel for detecting crimes and processing crime matters, including their classification as offenses. Thus they can downgrade many kinds of crime from index to less serious ones, such as classifying an aggravated assault as a simple one or rape as another, lesser sex offense.

The National Crime Survey of victimizations also is subject to reporting problems; one of the more serious is that of counting repeat victimizations for certain kinds of crime. Victims of repeated, particularly domestic, assaults, for example, often have difficulty recalling the actual number and details. Victimizations that occur in series of three or more and where the victim is unable to describe the details of each event separately are excluded from the analysis and data tables. Crude estimates of their numbers are provided in an appendix to each report.

We still lack information on repeat victimization over time; we know that households and persons vary considerably in this rate. Studies of NCS panel data disclose that some households have a rate of victimization of more than one per month, while the majority of households do not report any incidents during a 6–month period.

3. VICTIMS OF CRIMES

a. BLACK VICTIMS *

Data from the National Crime Survey (NCS) show that between 1979 and 1986 blacks had higher rates of violent and household crime victimization than whites. In addition, violent crimes committed against blacks tended to be more serious than those committed against whites.

Major findings of this report include—

> •During 1979 to 1986 the violent crime victimization rate for persons age 12 or older was 44 per 1,000 blacks and 34 per 1,000 whites. Blacks experienced higher rates of rape, robbery, and aggravated assault, but whites had higher rates of simple assault and personal theft.

> •Blacks had higher robbery rates than whites for both males and females. Robbery rates per 1,000 persons were 18 robberies for black males, 7 for white males, 9 for black females, and 4 for white females. Robbery rates were higher for blacks than for whites for all age and marital status categories and nearly all levels of family income. Robbery rates for blacks

---

* Catherine J. Whitaker, "Black Victims," U.S. Department of Justice, Bureau of Justice Statistics. Special Report. April 1990.

and whites with family incomes of $50,000 or more did not differ.

•In central cities, blacks had higher robbery and household burglary rates than whites regardless of the age or family income of the victim or household head. In the suburbs and nonmetropolitan areas, blacks had higher rates than whites for these crimes but there were fewer measurable differences when age, family income, and home ownership were taken into account.

•Offenders were more likely to have weapons in violent crimes committed against blacks than in those against whites. The percentage of violent crimes against blacks in which the offender had a gun was nearly twice the percentage of violent crimes in which whites were the victims (11% versus 20%).

•Of all crimes of violence committed by single offenders against white or black victims, 69% involved a white offender and a white victim, 15% involved a black offender and a white victim, 11% involved a black offender and a black victim, and 2% involved a white offender and a black victim. (About 3% involved offenders of other races.)

•Robbery was the violent crime most likely to have an offender and victims of different races—about 37% of all robberies committed by a single offender and involving white or black victims.

•Black victims were more likely than white victims to be physically attacked during a violent crime. Although white robbery victims were more likely than black robbery victims to be physically attacked, offenders were more likely to attack black victims of aggravated assault than white victims (48% versus 41%). In aggravated assaults, black victims were more likely than white victims to be injured. Black victims injured in violent crimes were more likely to sustain serious injuries than white victims.

b. VICTIM INTIMIDATION*

A survey of crime victims and witnesses in the Bronx, N.Y. has found that intimidation by criminal defendants is common, and often has the effect of causing the victims to drop charges.

Thirty-two percent of crime victims interviewed in the complaint room of the Bronx Criminal Court said they had been threatened by the defendant, according to the New York City Victim Services Agency, the nonprofit organization that conducted the study. Most of the victims reported being threatened more than once. In another 5 percent of the

* Criminal Justice Newsletter, Vol. 21, No. 20, October 15, 1990.

cases, the defendant had tried to dissuade the victim from pressing charges but had not made any overt threat.

The researchers speculated that actual rates of intimidation were higher. "Threats by their very nature are likely to be underreported, since, if the intimidation was successful, the respondent is unlikely to report it," they said in a report.

The Victim Services Agency tracked the cases and found that 32 percent of the victims who had been threatened dropped the charges at some time during the course of the case, compared to 12 percent of the victims who had not been threatened. "It is patently clear that defendants' threats are sometimes having their desired effect," the researchers said. "Our study found a positive correlation between victims who were intimidated and their desire to drop charges."

In 90 percent of the cases, the reported intimidation took the form of threats of violence against the victim or his property. "He threatened to set fire to my house," one victim said. "He told me I was going to pay for having him arrested," another said. In 6 percent of the cases, the victim reported that retaliatory physical attacks already had occurred. The remaining 4 percent of the cases involved "menacing looks or gestures."

The study found that victims who had close ties to the defendant were twice as likely to report intimidation as those who were strangers to the defendant.

D. VARIETIES OF CRIMINAL ACTIVITY

1. VIOLENT CRIME

Although comparative crime statistics are notoriously complex, according to 1990 figures, the United States murder rate is about five times that of Japan and seven times that of Great Britain. The robbery rate is seventeen times higher than Japan and eighteen times larger than Great Britain; and the rate of forcible rape in the United States is ten times higher than Japan and twelve times higher than Great Britain. Is it any wonder that two criminologists, Norval Morris and Gordon Hawkins have commented, "whether or not the United States is the land of the free, it is certainly the home of the brave."?

2. STREET CRIME

a. FEAR OF CRIME *

Why are people as afraid as they are? The answer cannot lie in the number of violent crimes alone; from an actuarial standpoint, street crime is a lot less dangerous than riding in an automobile, working around the house, going swimming, or any number of other activities in which Americans engage without apparent concern. The

* Charles E. Silberman, *Criminal Violence, Criminal Justice*, Random House, New York, © 1978 pp. 6–7 (Reprinted with permission).

chances of being killed in an automobile accident are ten times greater than those of being murdered by a stranger, and the risk of death from a fall—slipping in the shower, say, or tumbling from a ladder—are three times as great.

Accidents also cause far more nonfatal injuries than do violent crimes. Yet radio and television newscasts are not filled with accident reports, as they are with crime news; people do not sit around their living rooms trading stories about the latest home or auto accident, as they do about the latest crime; nor has any candidate for high office promised to wage war on accidents or restore safety to our highways and homes.

In fact, it is perfectly rational for Americans to be more concerned about street crime than about accidents, or, for that matter, about white-collar crime. Violence at the hand of a stranger is far more frightening than a comparable injury incurred in an automobile accident or fall; burglary evokes a sense of loss that transcends the dollar amount involved.

b. PUBLIC PERCEPTIONS OF CRIME **

Americans [in 1990] continue to say that crime is increasing rather than decreasing, something the majority has been saying since 1972. Fifty-one percent said crime was on the increase in their area as long ago as 1972 (53 percent said crime was on the increase last year).

Only 10 percent of Americans say that they don't feel safe and secure at home at night—a considerably smaller number than the 20 percent registered in 1975, and the 16 percent measured in 1981 and 1983 (the number is unchanged from 1989).

There has also been a small uptick in confidence in the police's ability to protect Americans from violent crime—52 percent say they have a great deal or quite a lot of confidence in the police, compared to 48 percent in 1989 and 49 percent in 1981.

Asked what can be done to curb crime, Americans talk about eliminating drugs, and imposing harsher and surer punishment. The majority also favors spending more money on social and economic problems rather than simply increasing police and punishment.

c. THE ADVANTAGES OF STREET CRIME *

. . . The street thieves tabulated in the pages of the Uniform Crime Reports run the gamut from the rankest amateur who steals from time to time to buy things he sees others enjoying, to the professional who earns a comfortable livelihood exclusively from steal-

** George Gallup, Jr. and Dr. Frank Newport; Support for Gun Control at all Time High, Gallup Poll News Service, September 26, 1990 (Reprinted with permission).

* Erich Goode, *Deviant Behavior*, Prentice-Hall, Inc., Englewood Cliffs, New Jersey pp. 440–442. © 1978 Reprinted by permission of Prentice-Hall, Inc., Englewood Cliffs, N.J.

ing. For both, stealing tends to be a *rational* activity: it is a means to an end that most of us seek, though in a somewhat different fashion. Whatever other benefits that are derived from stealing ("kicks," fun, excitement, etc.) are secondary to the monetary function. A nation with high rates of theft . . . is one that: (1) emphasizes material values; (2) manifests great material differences between rich and poor; (3) prominently displays the possessions of the affluent; (4) portrays the possessions of the affluent as attainable for everyone; (5) deemphasizes the means of attaining these possessions; (6) makes it difficult, if not impossible, for a large number of the members of that nation to attain these possessions legally. *It is these features that almost guarantee that a given society or nation will have high rates of theft.* They make for "the rip-off" society.

Among the tugs and pulls inducing people to attempt thievery as a means of earning money, certainly two stand out as most prominent. The first would be the choice between poverty and cash. In a nation with an unemployment rate close to one worker in ten, with a black unemployment twice that of whites, and with a teenage unemployment rate over three times that of adults, many people are induced to steal because they literally have no other means of earning any money at all. Even holding down a job doesn't guarantee many of us enough cash to move in the world with much dignity or comfort. Poverty has to be counted as a major inducement to thievery. We have a great deal of theft in this society because the economy does not guarantee enough people a decent livelihood. But remember, it is not poverty alone that does it; theft tends to be rare in the nations of the world in which people are *the most* improverished, partly because the rule of the rich is far more tyrannical than is true here, and partly because the poor do not dream that they could, through acts of theft, acquire what the rich have.

The second factor that induces people to steal is the fact that most jobs, even if one is able to work at one, are not very interesting. In fact, most are boring, alienating, even demeaning. So the choice, for some, isn't simply between poverty and cash, but between working at a regular job that one despises and doing something that is illegal but is perhaps less humiliating, or at least that doesn't consume eight or ten hours a day. Stealing from others involves being one's own boss, choosing one's working hours, and doing the jobs one decides to do. It is difficult to imagine an inducement more persuasive than this one.

. . .

Let's listen to what a professional armed robber has to say about what led him to pick up a revolver and earn a livelihood using it:

> I've never had any trouble getting a job. Anybody can work, but of course I don't dig working. I mean, not that type of manual work. And then when we got together and talked it over and decided that in order to get the amount of money we wanted in the shortest time, that crime was the way to get it.

And crime, we feel, is just like any other business. In other words, there's setbacks in crime and there's deficits, just like you run a business and there's a chance that you might burn down or you might go bankrupt or your employee might have embezzled everything you got without the insurance to cover it, and it's the same way with crime. Of course the penalty for going bankrupt in crime is much stiffer, but at the same time your material gain is much more than it is in a regular business.

A journalist, James Willwerth, talked to, followed around, and hung out with, a young man, Jones, who made a living out of mugging people on the street, usually with a knife, sometimes with a gun, occasionally with his fists. Willwerth wrote a "portrait of a mugger" from the information he gathered (1976):

Jones is a violent man; he knows the streets may kill him. He looks over his shoulder every moment of his life. He hates the tension of this, while knowing it comes with the life he chooses to lead. For the streets allow him to run away from himself, and from the demands and limitations of ghetto life. The alternative is a job; years of dreary work and grinding semi-poverty. The people uptown have good-paying jobs, houses and cars and good clothes. It doesn't happen to anyone in Jones's neighborhood. The way to get over is to stay in the street. If you stay alive, you can be *anything*—sooner or later the "big sting" comes your way and you can have all the women, clothes, cars, and penthouses you need, right? In the meantime, keep moving. . . . When Jones works regularly [at mugging], he says he makes more than a hundred dollars a day. . . . It is tax free. . . . So he has the equivalent of a $25,000 job. . . . "Fear is just another emotion" [Jones explains]. "You are taught from birth you will be punished if you do something wrong. Dig it: pulling a rip is against the law, and you are taught fear of the law. But then you say, if this can help *me,* it's right. . . . I won't lie to you. What I do is wrong. . . . *But man, it gives me life*".

Comment and Questions

Do you think that the explanation of street thievery and robbery offered by Erich Goode would be applicable to other street crimes such as forcible rape?

d. THE MEANING OF RAPE

For the purpose of the Uniform Crime Reports, forcible rape is defined as:

The carnal knowledge of a female forcibly and against her will. Assaults or attempts to commit rape by force or threat of force are also included; however, statutory rape (without force) and other sex offenses are not included in this category.

We actually know very little about the causes of forcible rape, or even of the true motives of the rapist. A study of forcible rape found that in 43 percent of the cases, the victim was raped by two or more persons. The author concluded that the criminological literature on this crime was inadequate because it was "dominated by the clinical approach and the survey method, which deals with the individual offender or (rarely) the victim, rather than with the act of rape as a social and group event." What might the author be suggesting?

Finally, can you think of reasons other than victims' fear or their embarrassment over the incidents that might inhibit women from reporting to the police that they had been forcibly raped? Is it because women think the law will not recognize the validity of their claims?

(1) Boys' Rules *

Sexism in the law of rape is no matter of mere historical interest; it endures, even where some of the most blatant testaments to that sexism have disappeared. Corroboration requirements unique to rape may have been repealed, but they continue to be enforced as a matter of practice in many jurisdictions. The victim of rape may not be required to resist to the utmost as a matter of statutory law in any jurisdiction, but the definitions accorded to force and consent may render "reasonable" resistance both a practical and a legal necessity. In the law of rape, supposedly dead horses continue to run.

The study of rape as an illustration of sexism in the criminal law also raises broader questions about the way conceptions of gender and the different backgrounds and perspectives of men and women should be encompassed within the criminal law. In one of his most celebrated essays, Oliver Wendell Holmes explained that the law does not exist to tell the good man what to do, but to tell the bad man what not to do. Holmes was interested in the distinction between the good and bad man; I cannot help noticing that both are men. Most of the time, a criminal law that reflects male views and male standards imposes its judgment on men who have injured other men. It is "boys' rules" applied to a boys' fight. In rape, the male standard defines a crime committed against women, and male standards are used not only to judge men, but also to judge the conduct of women victims. Moreover, because the crime involves sex itself, the law of rape inevitably treads on the explosive ground of sex roles, of male aggression and female passivity, of our understandings of sexuality—areas where differences between a male and a female perspective may be most pronounced.

* Susan Estrich, "Rape," The Yale Law Journal, May 1986, Vol. 95, Issue 6, p. 1091 (Reprinted with Permission).

(2) Force and Resistance *

The requirement of force is not unique to the law of rape. But rape is different in two critical respects. First, unlike theft, if "force" is not inherent in noncriminal sex, at least physical contact is. Certainly, if a person stripped his victim, flattened that victim on the floor, lay down on top, and took the other person's wallet or jewelry, few would pause before the conclusion of a forcible robbery. Second, rape does not involve "one person" and "another person." It involves, in practice if not everywhere by definition, a male person using "force" against a female person. The question of whose definition of "force" should apply, whose understanding should govern, is therefore critical.

The distinction between the "force" incidental to the act of intercourse and the "force" required to convict a man of rape is one commonly drawn by courts. Once drawn, however, the distinction would seem to require the courts to define what additional acts are needed to constitute prohibited rather than incidental force. This is where the problems arise. For many courts and jurisdictions, "force" triggers an inquiry identical to that which informs the understanding of consent. Both serve as substitutes for a *mens rea* requirement. Force is required to constitute rape, but force—even force that goes far beyond the physical contact necessary to accomplish penetration—is not itself prohibited. Rather, what is required, and prohibited, is force used to overcome female nonconsent. The prohibition is defined in terms of a woman's resistance. Thus, "forcible compulsion" becomes the force necessary to overcome reasonable resistance. When the woman does not physically resist, the question becomes then whether the force was sufficient to overcome a reasonable woman's will to resist. Prohibited force turns on the judge's evaluation of a reasonable woman's response.

(3) People v. Barnes
Supreme Court of California, 1986.
42 Cal.3d 284, 228 Cal.Rptr. 228, 721 P.2d 110.

BIRD, Chief Justice.

Was the Court of Appeal correct in relying on a rape complainant's lack of "measurable resistance" to overturn convictions of rape and false imprisonment as unsupported by sufficient evidence?

I.

Since the sufficiency of evidence to support the convictions is in issue, it is necessary to present a somewhat detailed statement of the factual circumstances of this case.

Marsha M. had known appellant about four years as of May of 1982. They were neighbors and acquaintances. She had been to his

* Id., pp. 1107–1108.

house briefly once before to buy some marijuana. A couple of weeks before the present incident, they had drunk wine together at her house.

Around 10 p.m. on May 27, 1982, appellant called Marsha and invited her over for some drinks to celebrate his parents' having come into a sum of money. Marsha was undecided and told appellant to call back or she would call him.

Over the next two hours, appellant called twice to see what Marsha had decided to do. She finally told him she would come over and that she wanted to buy a little marijuana from him. She asked him to meet her outside his house.

Marsha arrived at appellant's house around 1 a.m. Appellant was waiting for her outside the front gate. It was cold. Appellant suggested they go inside and smoke some marijuana. At first Marsha refused. She told appellant she had to get up early and wanted to buy the marijuana and go home. However, after a couple of minutes, appellant persuaded her to come inside.

Marsha followed appellant through the house to a room off the garage. At first, they carried on a conversation which Marsha described as "normal chatter." Appellant provided some marijuana and they both smoked it. Appellant offered some cocaine, but she refused. She kept telling appellant she wanted to hurry up and leave.

After 10 or 15 minutes, appellant began to hug Marsha. She pushed him away and told him to stop. She did not take him seriously as he was "just coming on."

Appellant continued his advances despite Marsha's insistence that she only wanted to buy marijuana and leave. When appellant asked her why she was in such a hurry, she reiterated she just wanted him to give her the marijuana and let her go since she had to get up early in the morning. Appellant told her he did not want her to leave. Marsha finally said good-bye and walked out of the room. Until this point, things between them had been "decent and friendly."

As Marsha approached the front gate, appellant, who was behind her and appeared angry, stated, "No, you don't go leaving. You don't just jump up and leave my goddamn house." He began "ranting and raving" and arguing with her. He wanted to know why she was "trying to leave." He told her that she made him feel as if he had stolen something; that she was acting like he was "a rapist or something." Marsha characterized appellant's behavior as "psychotic."

When she reached the front gate, Marsha did not try to open it because she did not know how. She asked appellant to open it, but he just stood looking at her. This behavior made her nervous. When she asked appellant what was wrong, he "reared back" as if he were going to hit her.

They argued at the gate for about 20 minutes. Marsha told appellant she did not understand what he was arguing with her about and that he seemed to be trying to find a reason to be angry with her.

She told him, "I came to your house to get some grass. Now, I want to leave. You won't let me leave."

Appellant replied that he was going to let her leave but needed to put his shoes on first. He then returned to the room and Marsha followed. She said she returned to the room because she felt she could not get out the front gate by herself.

As she was following appellant, the door leading to the stairs closed behind her, prompting him to shout that she was "slamming the goddamn door" in his house. After they entered the room, appellant closed the door behind them. He was "fussing" at Marsha, talking and "carrying on" the whole time he was putting on his shoes. He stated, "I don't know what the hell you bitches think you want to do." Marsha was confused and concerned about what was happening and about what appellant was going to do. Several times, appellant stopped talking and looked at her "funny."

Appellant then stood up and began to "lecture" Marsha. He was angry. He began to threaten her, telling her he was a man and displaying the muscles in his arms. He grabbed her by her sweater collar and told her he could pick her up with one hand and throw her out. Flexing his muscles, he stated, "You see this? I am a man. You respect me like a man. I am no kid."

Appellant also told Marsha of his past sexual exploits. He stated: "I had bitches do anything I want. I have had bitches suck me . . . I have had them do that. I can make you do anything I want. You understand me?" Occasionally, appellant would stop talking, "rear back," look at her and tell her how much she upset him.

At one point appellant said, "You're so used to see [*sic*] the good side of me. Now you get to see the bad." Then he became quiet and stared at her. This statement again made Marsha believe he was going to hit her.

Marsha asked appellant whether he wanted to hit her. She told him she could not fight him. Appellant responded by lecturing her. Marsha began to move toward the door. When appellant noticed her, he said, "I don't know why you're standing by the door. What are you looking at the door for?" Marsha thought appellant pushed the door closed a little tighter.

Appellant continued talking but then suddenly turned and started hugging Marsha "affectionately." He told her he did not mean to "fuss" at her. By now, Marsha felt she was in the room with a "psychotic person" who had again changed personalities. Approximately 40 minutes had elapsed since they entered the room a second time. It was at this juncture that Marsha began to "play along" and feign compliance with appellant's desires.

In an effort to get out of appellant's house, Marsha suggested they go to her house where they could be alone. Appellant told her not to worry about his parents coming home. He continued to hug and talk to her. After a few minutes, appellant stated, "I have to have some of this right now," and told Marsha to remove her clothes. Marsha refused. Appellant reacted by telling her she was going to upset him and by making some type of gesture. In response, Marsha removed her clothes. An act of sexual intercourse ensued which lasted about one hour and included the exchange of kisses. Afterward, both appellant and Marsha fell asleep.

Marsha testified she engaged in sexual intercourse with appellant because she felt if she refused, he would become physically violent. She based this assessment on appellant's actions and words, including his statements that she was about to "see the bad side" of him and that he could throw her out if he wanted.

Marsha awoke around 4 a.m. She cajoled appellant into walking her to the front gate and opening it so she could leave. She returned home and immediately called Kaiser Hospital to request an examination. She was eventually referred to the sexual trauma center and examined for venereal disease.

Marsha did not report the incident to the police that day because she was confused and felt "it was my word against his." She had been told at the sexual trauma center that she had three days within which to make a report. After discussing the incident with a coworker, she reported it to the police the following day.

Appellant telephoned Marsha the morning of the incident and a couple of days later. On both occasions she hung up on him.

The defense was consent. Appellant's testimony was substantially similar to Marsha's regarding the events prior to her arrival at his house. However, the versions differed markedly as to the subsequent events.

Appellant testified that the first time they were in the room together he gave Marsha some marijuana and refused payment for it. They smoked some marijuana. Appellant told Marsha he had "feelings for her," he was sexually attracted to her and did not want her to leave so quickly. According to appellant, they did not argue over anything. He was surprised that she was in such a rush to leave.

At the front gate, they continued to talk. He again expressed feelings of sexual attraction for her. According to appellant, it was Marsha who first returned to the room. There, she told him she would stay a little while longer. Then, without being asked, she started removing her clothes. Consensual sexual intercourse ensued during which Marsha returned appellant's hugs and kisses. Appellant testified he did not threaten Marsha in any way, make gestures toward her, display his muscles or force her to stay. He confirmed the fact that he had telephoned Marsha twice afterwards. However, he testified they talked briefly each time.

Appellant was convicted after a jury trial of one count each of rape and false imprisonment (Pen.Code, §§ 261, subd. (2), 236) as to Marsha

M. The Court of Appeal reversed these convictions as unsupported by substantial evidence. This court granted the Attorney General's petition for review in order to clarify the requirements for conviction under section 261, subdivision (2) as amended by the Legislature in 1980.

II.

Until its amendment in 1980, former section 261, subdivisions 2 and 3 defined rape as an act of sexual intercouse under circumstances where the person resists, but where "resistance is overcome by force or violence" or where "a person is prevented from resisting by threats of great and immediate bodily harm, accompanied by apparent power of execution. . . ."

The Legislature amended section 261 in 1980 to delete most references to resistance. (Stats.1980, ch. 587, § 1, p. 1595.) In pertinent part, the statute now defines rape as "an act of sexual intercourse accomplished with a person not the spouse of the perpetrator, under any of the following circumstances: . . . [¶](2) Where it is accomplished against a person's will by means of force or fear of immediate and unlawful bodily injury on the person or another."

.   .   .

The Court of Appeal proceeded to review the evidence in light of certain facts which bore mainly on the existence of resistance by Marsha and of threats by appellant. It concluded that (1) "at no time did [appellant] specifically threaten physical harm to Marsha unless she consented to an act of intercourse"; (2) "Marsha removed her clothes and acceded to his demands *without any explicit protestation or measurable resistance* to appellant's advances"; (3) the record does not contain "credible evidence of solid value from which an inference can be made beyond a reasonable doubt that appellant intended to have intercourse with Marsha *irrespective of her protestations or passive resistance*"; and (4) the record shows only "Marsha's *bare assertion* of an *uncommunicated resistance* to the act in question." (Emphasis added.) On this basis, the Court of Appeal reversed appellant's conviction of rape.

.   .   .

It is clear that in a rape prosecution involving force or violence under former section 261, subdivision 2, resistance *was* a crucial and necessary circumstance to be proved before the trier of fact.

The importance of resistance lay in its relationship to the issues of force and consent. The accused's conduct became criminal only if the complainant failed to consent, exhibited resistance, and was overcome in this will by the accused's use of force or violence. By establishing resistance, the state was able to prove the key elements of the crime: the accused's intent to use force in order to accomplish an act of sexual intercourse, and the woman's nonconsent. Thus, even assuming appellant is semantically correct that resistance was not an "element" of the offense of rape, this court cannot, as he urges, dismiss its elimination in the 1980 amendment to subdivision (2) as unnecessary or insignificant.

. . .

. . . Insight into the purpose of Assembly Bill No. 2899 can be garnered from the analysis by the Assembly Committee on Criminal Justice (now called the Assembly Committee on Public Safety): "The main purpose of this bill is to eliminate the 'resistance' requirement in rape. Under current law, a woman must either resist or be prevented from resisting because of threats. According to the proponents, victims who resist are injured by the rapist twice as often as victims who don't resist. The proponents also indicate that prosecutors are unable and unwilling to file cases when the victim does not resist."

. . .

Moreover, appellant is incorrect in asserting that the amendment made no change insofar as the significance of resistance is concerned. For the amendment has effected a crucial change in the fact-finding process. Prior to 1981, when an accused was charged with rape by means of force or violence, the jury was instructed, in accordance with the language of former section 261, subdivision 2, that the "element" of resistance must be proved. By contrast, the 1982 revision mirrored the statutory change and now allows the jury to convict of rape by force or fear without proof of victim resistance.

Appellant's minimization of the 1980 amendment also ignores the crucial role the resistance requirement has played in the history of rape laws. That the Legislature's elimination of resistance represents a profound change in the law is evident from a review of its historical evolution.

At common law, the crime of rape was defined as "the carnal knowledge of a woman forcibly and against her will." (4 Blackstone, Commentaries 201.) Historically, it was considered inconceivable that a woman who truly did not consent to sexual intercourse would not meet force with force. The law originally demanded "utmost resistance" from the woman to ensure she had submitted rather than consented. Not only must she have resisted to the "utmost" of her physical capacity, the resistance must not have ceased throughout the assault.

California long ago rejected this "primitive rule" of utmost resistance. "A woman who is assaulted need not resist to the point of risking being beaten into insensibility. If she resists to the point where further resistance would be useless or, . . . until her resistance is overcome by force or violence, submission thereafter is not consent." In our state, it had long been the rule that the resistance required was only that which would reasonably manifest refusal to consent to the act of sexual intercourse.

Nevertheless, courts refused to uphold a conviction of rape by force where the complainant had exhibited little or no resistance.

The requirement that a woman resist her attacker appears to have been grounded in the basic distrust with which courts and commentators traditionally viewed a woman's testimony regarding sexual assault. According to the 17th century writings of Lord Matthew Hale, in order to be deemed a credible witness, a woman had to be of good fame, disclose the injury immediately, suffer signs of injury and cry out for help.

This distrust was formalized in the law in several areas. For example, juries were traditionally advised to be suspect and cautious in evaluating a rape complainant's testimony, particularly where she was "unchaste."

In most jurisdictions, corroboration of the complaining witness was necessary for a conviction of rape. Skeptical of female accusers, the majority of courts and commentators considered it appropriate that the "prosecutrix" in all sexual assault cases undergo psychiatric examination before trial.

Such wariness of the complainant's credibility created "an exaggerated insistence on evidence of resistance." As an objective indicator of nonconsent, the requirement of resistance insured against wrongful conviction based solely on testimony the law considered to be inherently suspect. In our state, it supplied a type of intrinsic corroboration of the prosecuting witness's testimony, a collateral demanded even when extrinsic corroboration was not required. . . .

Recently, however, the entire concept of resistance to sexual assault has been called into question. It has been suggested that while the presence of resistance may well be probative on the issue of force or nonconsent, its absence may not.

For example, some studies have demonstrated that while some women respond to sexual assault with active resistance, others "freeze." One researcher found that many women demonstrate "psychological infantilism"—a frozen fright response—in the face of sexual assault. The "frozen fright" response resembles cooperative behavior. Indeed, as Symonds notes, the "victim may smile, even initiate acts, and may appear relaxed and calm." Subjectively, however, she may be in a state of terror. Symonds also reports that the victim may make submissive signs to her assailant and engage in propitiating behavior in an effort to inhibit further aggression. These findings belie the traditional notion that a woman who does not resist has consented. They suggest that lack of physical resistance may reflect a "profound primal terror" rather than consent.

Additionally, a growing body of authority holds that to resist in the face of sexual assault is to risk further injury.

. . .

On the other hand, other findings indicate that resistance has a direct correlation with *deterring* sexual assault. . . .

. . .

In sum, it is not altogether clear what the absence of resistance indicates in relation to the issue of consent. Nor is it *necessarily* advisable for one who is assaulted to resist the attack. It is at least arguable that if it fails to deter, resistance may well increase the risk of bodily injury to the victim. This possibility, as well as the evolution in societal expectations as to the level of danger a woman should risk when faced with sexual assault, are reflected in the Legislature's elimination of the resistance requirement. . . . For the first time, the Legislature has assigned the decision as to whether a sexual assault should be resisted to the realm of personal choice.

. . .

By removing resistance as a prerequisite to a rape conviction, the Legislature has brought the law of rape into conformity with other crimes such as robbery, kidnapping and assault, which require force, fear, and nonconsent to convict. In these crimes, the law does not expect falsity from the complainant who alleges their commission and thus demand resistance as a corroboration and predicate to conviction. Nor does the law expect that in defending oneself or one's property from these crimes, a person must risk injury or death by displaying resistance in the face of attack.

This court therefore concludes that the Legislature's purposes in amending section 261 were (1) to relieve the state of the need to establish resistance as a prerequisite to a rape conviction, and (2) to release rape complainants from the potentially dangerous burden of resisting an assailant in order to substantiate allegations of forcible rape.

As noted, it is no longer proper to instruct the jury that it must find the complainant resisted before it may return a verdict of guilt. Nor may lack of resistance be employed by courts—like the Court of Appeal here—to support a finding of insufficient evidence of rape.

For these reasons, the Court of Appeal's reliance upon any absence of resistance by Marsha was improper.

III.

. . .

Under prior law, forcible rape required that the accused employ that degree of force necessary under the circumstances to overcome the victim's resistance. Although resistance is no longer the touchstone of the element of force, the reviewing court still looks to the circumstances of the case, including the presence of verbal or nonverbal threats, or the kind of force that might reasonably induce fear in the mind of the victim, to ascertain sufficiency of the evidence of a conviction under section 261, subdivision (2). Additionally, the complainant's conduct must be measured against the degree of force manifested or in light of whether her fears were genuine and reasonably grounded.

Marsha's testimony constitutes substantial evidence of rape by means of force or fear of immediate and unlawful bodily injury. From the moment she arrived at appellant's house, she communicated to him that she did not want to stay and intended to leave after purchasing marijuana. She initially refused appellant's suggestion that they go inside, but ultimately agreed so that she could obtain the marijuana. Once inside, she repeated her desire to proceed with the drug transaction so she could leave. She rebuffed the first round of appellant's physical advances by pushing him away and telling him to stop. When appellant disregarded this rebuff and continued his advances, Marsha left the room and went to the front gate. At this point, appellant's demeanor changed markedly. He cursed and berated Marsha for leaving, apparently in an effort to intimidate her.

At the front gate, Marsha repeatedly requested that appellant "let me leave," a plea which fell on deaf ears. Significantly, on at least one such occasion, appellant "reared back"—a gesture which made Marsha believe he was going to hit her. Appellant created the impression, even if it were untrue, that the outside gate was locked and that Marsha would not be able to open it. He reinforced this impression by telling her he would *let* her leave after he returned to the room for his shoes.

Back in the room, appellant shouted at Marsha, cursing the fact she had caused the door to slam. He interrupted his angry, verbal onslaught only to stop all activity and look at Marsha in a "funny" manner. He threatened her by displaying his muscles, grabbing her by the collar, and claiming he could pick her up with one hand and throw her out.

Most importantly, he ominously informed her he could make her do "anything he wanted" and that she was about to see the "bad side" of him. These statements were made in conjunction with his boasting of having had other women perform sex acts upon him and with Marsha's statement to him that she could not fight him. Appellant's response of pressing the door closed when he saw Marsha's movement toward it also suggested coercion. Finally, when Marsha initially refused to remove her clothes, appellant warned her—both physically and verbally—that her refusal "was going to make him angry."

In light of the totality of these circumstances, the jury, having observed the witnesses and their demeanor, could reasonably have concluded that Marsha's fear of physical violence from appellant if she did not submit to sexual intercourse was genuine and reasonable. Under these facts, a reasonable juror could have found that Marsha's subsequent compliance with appellant's urgent insistence on coitus was induced either by force, fear, or both, and, in any case, fell short of a consensual act.

Additionally, Marsha several times communicated her unwillingness to stay and have sexual intercourse with appellant. Appellant should have realized that his threatening conduct, combined with Marsha's rejection of his sexual advances and repeated requests to leave, created a situation where he was able to overcome rather than respect her will. That appellant may have deluded himself into believing her eventual submission represented a consensual act could have been rejected by a rational trier of fact as an unreasonable response to Marsha's conduct. Therefore, the jury's rejection of appellant's defense that he reasonably believed she consented was proper given the totality of these circumstances.

Appellant contended in the Court of Appeal that Marsha's testimony was inherently improbable because (1) she returned to appellant's room after the argument at the front gate; (2) she returned appellant's kisses during the sex act; and (3) she fell asleep after having intercourse.

. . .

. . . It cannot be said that Marsha's testimony was inherently improbable. She testified she returned to the room because she felt she could not leave without appellant's aid. The jury may well have concluded her return was a reasonable response, especially since it was cold outside and at that point the situation had not so grossly deteriorated.

Marsha also explained that she pretended to be a willing partner and to invite appellant to her house in an attempt to extricate herself from the situation. She testified that she engaged in sexual intercourse to avoid physical violence. A reasonable juror could have concluded that her subsequent act of exchanging kisses was part of a similar effort to avoid physical violence by simulating reciprocation. Marsha was not required to display either active or passive resistance in order to save her testimony from inherent improbability, or to "develop corroborative evidence."

Finally, the fact that Marsha fell asleep after sexual intercourse was of little consequence. Her failure to stay alert and awake was at least susceptible of the conclusion that she was physically exhausted after having spent almost two hours attempting to extricate herself from an escalating and potentially dangerous situation. Moreover, the jury could have reasonably concluded that in Marsha's judgment, the danger of physical violence had passed with the violation of her physical integrity and that, therefore, she could temporarily relax. Although the record is not clear, it appears that any slumber to which she succumbed lasted but a brief period of time—perhaps only minutes.

When she awoke, she renewed her efforts to leave by cajoling appellant into letting her out of the gate. Thereafter, she called Kaiser Hospital and reported to the sexual trauma center for an examination. At most, her falling asleep was an unusual circumstance and does not render the entirety of her testimony inherently improbable.

Under these circumstances, this court holds that the evidence was sufficient to sustain appellant's conviction of rape. The false imprisonment conviction must also be affirmed, as its commission was attendant to the rape.

Question

Do you agree with Justice Bird that Marsha was raped?

3. WHITE COLLAR CRIME

a. NOTE ON WHITE COLLAR CRIME

Criminologists have focused on another type of criminal activity that takes a form very different from street crime and which is perpetrated by different participants. Sometimes that activity is called "white collar" crime and sometimes business or corporate crime.

The general public does not feel as threatened by illegal corporate activity as by robbery or burglary. That is understandable since robberies or burglaries encompass more than a loss of property or experience of pain. They produce fear because they violate the integrity of the self and of genuinely personal property.

One reason, then, for the public's relative complacency toward business crime is its subtlety. The victim usually does not know that he or she is being victimized. Another factor is that it is often difficult to pin down who is responsible for the criminal activity occurring in a business organization. In addition, business offenders are often otherwise respectable and socially attractive.

White collar crime is important for various reasons. First, it costs the nation in money terms far more than do robbery and burglary. Second, the fact that it is often committed with impunity causes disrespect for law among many people. Third, the lenient treatment of white-collar criminals, though explainable, causes many to regard the criminal justice system as basically unfair. For criminologists a study of white-collar crime is important because it sheds light on those causes of crime having no connection with poverty, poor housing, broken homes, inadequate education and the like.

b. THE NATURE OF WHITE COLLAR CRIME *

The definition of "white-collar crime" is not purely an academic matter but, as noted later, has a very significant bearing on how best to combat the offense. White-collar crimes are illegal acts characterized by guile, deceit, and concealment—and are not dependent upon the application of physical force or violence or threats thereof. They may be committed by individuals acting independently or by those who are part of a well-planned conspiracy. The objective may be to obtain money, property, or services; to avoid the payment or loss of money, property, or services; or to secure business or personal advantage.

And by focusing on the nature of the violation, rather than on the nature of the violator, this definition of white-collar crime is considera-

---

* U.S. Chamber of Commerce, "White Collar Crime, The Problem and its Import," *A Handbook on White Collar Crime,* Washington, U.S. Chamber of Commerce, pp. 3–11. Copyright 1974 (Reprinted with permission).

bly more encompassing than the traditional one, which tends to concentrate exclusively on top management and "crime in the executive suite." As one observer comments, "White collar crime is democratic. It can be committed by a bank teller or the head of his institution. . . . The character of white-collar crime must be found in its modi operandi and its objectives [not] in the nature of the offenders."

Looked at in this light, embezzlement of $100,000 by a "white-collar" vice president who manipulated accounts payable records is not substantively different from the pilferage of $100,000 worth of merchandise by a "blue-collar" warehouse clerk who tried to cover up by falsifying inventory records or engaging in other forms of concealment. The same can be said about the offense committed by the housewife who fraudulently tries to use someone else's credit card—or about the young "phone freak" who is guilty of toll fraud by utilizing a "blue box" in a phone booth to bypass the telephone company's billing mechanism while he places a $1,000 around-the-world call to the adjoining booth.

Obviously, what this is leading up to is not justification of white-collar crime at the executive level on the grounds that others also engage in the same type of offense. Rather, the point is that an eyes-open approach to white-collar crime does not limit its focus to the executive suite but is geared to counteract white-collar illegalities originating from a wide range of sources, within *and* outside of the organization.

For example, white-collar crime can be committed by, and perpetrated against, (1) corporations, partnerships, professional firms, non-profit organizations, and governmental units and/or (2) their executives, principals, and employees as well as such "outsiders" as customers, clients, suppliers and other organizations or individuals. Failure to review and evaluate this range of possibilities is likely to result in countermeasures about as effective as baseball players whose manager has trained them to cover all bases except home plate.

How Much Does It Cost?

White-collar crime not only results in an immediate and direct financial impact but also, and even more important, generates nonfinancial and long-term consequences. Careful consideration of these effects will help demonstrate that the response to white-collar illegalities should be considerably more than writing them off as just another cost of doing business.

Although white-collar crimes, if and when detected, are among the most underreported offenses, a reasonable approximation of their economic impact is possible. One way to assess the financial consequences is to reflect upon the implications of the following:

1. The yearly cost of embezzlement and pilferage reportedly exceeds by several billion dollars the losses sustained throughout the nation from burglary and robbery.

2. Fraud was a major contributing factor in the forced closing of about 100 banks during a 20–year period.

3. An insurance company reported that at least 30 percent of all business failures each year are the result of employee dishonesty.

4. The annual bill for all purchases by a state is said to have dropped an estimated 40 percent following exposure and prosecution of businessmen and government officials for bribery and kickbacks.

5. Dishonesty by corporate executives and employees has increased the retail cost of some merchandise by up to 15 percent and, in the case of one company, caused shareholders to suffer a paper loss of $300-million within just a few days.

6. Restitution in the amount of $696,000 was obtained by a state for its residents who were victims of a single consumer fraud scheme which operated nationwide.

7. Distribution of untaxed bootleg cigarettes throughout one eastern state during a recent six-year period resulted in a loss of $384-million in state and local revenue and in a loss of about $2-billion in gross sales to the legitimate cigarette industry.

8. Internal dishonesty, in addition to the adverse effect on profits represented by the amount of the pilferage or embezzlement, may result in costs associated with the loss of one or more trained employees; the training of replacements; higher insurance rates and/or deductibles; reconstruction of destroyed, stolen, or altered records; contamination of other employees who pick up where the apprehended thief left off; and lowered productivity when honest and valued employees feel they are under suspicion. . . .

A total dollar figure for white-collar crimes is estimated at not less than $40-billion annually, which *excludes* the cost to the public and business of price-fixing illegalities and industrial espionage (satisfactory measures of these offenses were not found).

Question

Can "white-collar" crime cause physical injury as well as financial loss? How?

c. CORPORATE CRIME *

A look at the record since 1970 shows that a surprising number of big companies have been involved in blatant illegalities.

No single answer accounts for the variety of corporate misbehavior. One generalization often invoked plays on the distinction between *malum in se*—a crime in itself, like the immemorial offenses of the common law—and *malum prohibitum*—purely statutory crimes that vary with the society. As a celebrated corporate defense counsel

---

* By Irwin Ross, "How Lawless Are Big Companies?," FORTUNE, December 1, 1980, p. 58. © 1980 Time, Inc. All rights reserved (Reprinted with permission).

recently put it, "These business crimes are perceived by individual actors as victimless. We all grew up in an environment in which we learned that thou shalt not murder, rape, rob, probably not pay off a public official—but not that it was a crime to fix prices."

d. CIVIL vs. CRIMINAL ENFORCEMENT *

There are compelling reasons to use civil rather than criminal sanctions in order to deter illegal corporate activity. First, the rationale for imposing criminal penalties on such activity is problematic. The criminal law is being used to regulate behavior that is not in and of itself morally blameworthy, and indeed in some cases to impose sanctions in the absence of fault. The use of criminal sanctions for purely regulatory purposes represents a severe departure from the traditional aims of the criminal law—deterrence *and* retribution. In addition, the type of activity which results in criminal liability in the corporate setting is different from other criminal activity; the primary concern is often with the supervisors and managers rather than with the direct actors. Thus corporate officials may be held liable for acquiescing in, or for recklessly or negligently tolerating, the illegal activity of subordinates. Finally, imposing criminal sanctions on a corporation, an artificial entity wich can possess no state of mind, seems questionable in the absence of some theory which ascribes fault to the corporation itself, rather than only to its officers, directors, and employees. And the use of criminal procedures for corporate prosecutions has raised troubling questions regarding the applicability of constitutional protections to such artificial entities.

e. SANCTIONS AGAINST THE CORPORATION *

The *Harvard Law Review* commentary on corporate crime rejected retribution as a goal of corporate criminal sanctions, and focused on deterrence as the sole goal. It concluded that corporations cannot be punished in a stigmatic manner; that if stronger deterrents are needed, they should come in the form of heavier fines; and that since criminal fines have no advantage over civil fines, they should come in the form of heaver civil fines.

But the overwhelming evidence from scholars, prosecutors, and judges is that fines, often small and well below authorized ceilings, do not deter corporate crime. Criminologist John Braithwaite has called them "license fees to break the law." Fines in the typical antitrust case rarely reach the authorized ceiling. W. Breit and K. Elzinger, in a study of antitrust violations between 1967 and 1970, found that the Justice Department recommended imposing the maximum fine in less

* Developments in the Law—Corporate Crime: Regulating Corporate Behavior Through Criminal Sanctions, Harvard Law Review, April 1979, Vol. 92, No. 6, p. 1369 (Reprinted with Permission).

* Russell Mokhiber, *Corporate Crime and Violence,* Sierra Club Books, San Francisco (1988), p. 29–31.

than one-third of the cases where it obtained convictions. Braithwaite, in a recent study of law enforcement in the mine safety area, found that about 90 percent of the mine operators stated that civil penalties assessed or paid did not affect their production or safety activities. "Penalty dollar amounts were not considered of sufficient magnitude to warrant avoidance of future penalties and improvements in safety procedure," he observed. Operators contemptuously classified the fines as a "cost of doing business" or as a royalty paid to the government to continue in business. Producers who were fined saw no connection between penalties and safety.

Christopher Stone's study of laws governing corporations, *Where the Law Ends*, came to similar conclusions. "The overall picture," according to Stone, "is that our strategies aimed to control corporations by threatening their profits are a very limited way of bringing about the internal changes that are necessary if the policies behind the law are to be effectuated." The trouble with using fines to control corporate crime, according to Clinard, is that the amount paid is more than offset by the financial gain from the offense. In his study of more than 500 major U.S. corporations, Clinard found that four-fifths of the penalties levied against corporations were $5,000 or less, 11.6 percent were between $5,000 and $50,000, 3.7 percent were between $50,000 and $1,000,000, and 0.9 percent were over $1,000,000.

A major criticism of using fines to control corporate crime has been described by New York University Law School Professor John C. Coffee, Jr. and others as "the deterrence trap." The corporation contemplating the commitment of a crime will be deterred only if the expected punishment cost of the illegal activity exceeds the expected gain. Coffee gives the following example: If the expected gain were $1 million and the risk of arrest were 25 percent, then the penalty would have to be $4 million in order to make the expected punishment cost equal to the expected gain. Coffee observes that "the maximum meaningful fine that can be levied against any corporate offender is necessarily bound by its wealth." For example,

> if a corporation having $10 million of wealth were faced with an opportunity to gain $1 million through some criminal act or omission, such conduct could not logically be deterred by monetary penalties directed at the corporation if the risk of apprehension were below 10%. That is, if the likelihood of apprehension were 8%, the necessary penalty would have to be $12.5 million (i.e., $1 million times 12.5, the reciprocal of 8%). Yet such a fine exceeds the corporation's ability to pay. In short, our ability to deter the corporation may be confounded by our inability to set an adequate punishment cost which does not exceed the corporation's resources.

Since corporate crimes are easy to conceal and all indications are that rates of apprehension are exceedingly low, most major corporations will not be deterred by the types of fines that federal sentencing officials currently arc imposing.

Questions

Is business crime the same as white-collar crime? Do you think that the public's complacency toward crime by businesses contributes to its growth and persistence? Is not the public's complacency justified? After all, aren't business crimes clearly less dangerous and destructive than street crimes? If you believe that business crimes are as dangerous as street crimes, is there any reason why higher-class criminals should be treated less severely than lower-class ones?

4. CRIMES WITHOUT VICTIMS

a. NOTE ON CONSENSUAL CRIME

The idea of victimless crime means not so much that those who engage in them are not victims, but rather that they consent to the acts which the law defines as a crime. As a result, "victims" of drug dealers, bookmakers, and prostitutes do not relate to their so-called victimizers as do the victims of robbers, burglars, and rapists to those who victimize them. Whether or not they are prey, the victims of victimless crimes consider themselves customers. Hence they do not complain to the police.

Victimless crimes usually involve the sale of a goods or services and constitute a form of illegal commerce. Some such crimes enjoy more commercial potential than others. For instance, although prostitution is widespread, it does not lend itself as easily to the sort of industry-wide organization as do various forms of gambling and the production and sale of such drugs as beverage alcohol, heroin, marijuana, and cocaine.

The term victimless crime also suggests that the act in question is only socially offensive rather than seriously harmful, either to an individual or the social system. Obviously this need not be the case for all crimes usually regarded as victimless. In addition, profits from such activities as illegal drug trafficking, gambling, and prostitution may funnel into broad criminal conspiracies—organized crime—which may therefore become as socially destructive as counterfeiting or armed robbery.

Despite this, the more remote the harm is from the act to be outlawed, the more difficult it is to provide justification for outlawing it. Thus, a variety of scholars and other commentators have questioned how far the criminal law ought to be extended to control victimless crime.

b. JOHN STUART MILL—THE CLASSIC STATEMENT *

[T]he sole end for which mankind are warranted, individually or collectively, in interfering with the liberty of action of any of their number, is self-protection. That the only purpose for which power can be rightfully exercised over any member of a civilized community, against his will, is to prevent harm to others. IIis own good, either physical or moral, is not a sufficient warrant. He cannot rightfully be compelled to do or forbear because it will be better for him to do so, because it will make him happier, because, in the opinions of others, to do so would be wise, or even right. These are good reasons for remonstrating with him, or reasoning with him, or persuading him, or entreating him, but not for compelling him, or visiting him with any evil in case he do otherwise. To justify that, the conduct from which it is desired to deter him must be calculated to produce evil to some one else. The only part of the conduct of any one, for which he is amenable to society, is that which concerns others. In the part which merely concerns himself, his independence is, of right, absolute. Over himself, over his own body and mind, the individual is sovereign.

Comment and Questions

Is it not clear that "no man is an island," and that even what we do to ourselves affects others? Is Mill oblivious to this, or is he saying:

1. that the injury to others must be substantial before society should restrict a person's freedom; or

2. that the injury to others must be the real reason why we prohibit conduct, and not merely a cloak for our feelings of moral disapproval; or

3. that regardless of its effects on others, what one does to oneself is none of society's business?

c. MORALS AND VICTIMLESS CRIME

(1) CONVENTIONAL MORALITY **

. . . A position demanding enforcement of conventional morality through criminal law typically involves a claim that convention coincides with custom. "Immorality," contends Sir Patrick Devlin "is what every right-minded Christian person presumes to be immoral." According to this position, the behavior in question, whether it be homosexuality, adultery, fornication, gambling, or drinking, cannot be a matter of individual choice, because conventional morality is the glue holding

* John Stuart Mill, "On Liberty", in *On Liberty and Other Essays* (E. Neff. ed., 1926). New York, Columbia University Press.

** Jerome H. Skolnick, "Coercion to Virtue: The Enforcement of Morals," *University of Southern California Law Review*, 41 (1968) p. 608, Copyright 1968 (Reprinted with permission).

society together. Therefore it must be enforced by the use of "those instruments without which morality cannot be maintained. The two instruments are those of teaching, which is doctrine, and of enforcement, which is the law."

One serious problem of this position is its assumption of customary morality in a differentiated society composed of groups having primary identification along ethnic, religious, racial, educational, occupational, and status lines. There are some behaviors which, in line with a traditional conception of *mala in se,* are customarily regarded as immoral, e.g., murder, robbery, theft. Thus, for those who advocate criminal enforcement on moral grounds the problem is to demonstrate to the society at large that the behavior to be proscribed is indeed inherently evil. In so doing, there is usually reference both to fact and to custom. Suppose, however, that the argument from fact is distorted or overstated. One response is simply to dismiss such argument out of hand. . . .

. . .

But that would be missing the sociological significance of these sorts of contentions. If we wish to achieve a deeper understanding of the relation between societal consensus and the legislation of morals, the arguments of those whose evidence does not fit the facts should not be merely dismissed. Their position may represent an identifiable kind of political response which does not stem solely from a psychological base or a failure of reasoning. A sociological analysis requires that we distinguish among different kinds of motives and examine what a position on morals may represent to its holders. Or, why is there a claim of public support for the position?

Comment and Questions

The excerpt on conventional morality considers the problem of attempting to translate a majority's view of the morality of an action into the law of the state. How relevant to this issue are questions of fact concerning the harmfulness of the activity in question? Does it often turn out that what appear to be questions of fact, on examination, become value judgments?

To what extent is this applicable to each of the most commonly discussed victimless crimes: gambling, obscenity, prostitution, "deviant" sexual activity and drug use?

(2) SHOULD DRUGS BE LEGAL? *

As numbers of thoughtful people despair of controlling drugs through criminal-law enforcement, decriminalization is increasingly proposed as an alternative. Would it be a good idea? It might, but we need to think through how decriminalization would play out if imple-

* Jerome Skolnick, "Drugs, More or Fewer Controls?" Los Angeles Times, January 22, 1988 (Reprinted with Permission).

mented; what the benefits and costs would be and to whom, and whether decriminalization can be reconciled with a positive moral message.

Let's consider two possibilities of how decriminalization would work. Under the least restrictive, the free-market, model, psychoactive drugs would be freely available. Such substances would be treated as we now treat aspirin and over-the-counter drugs. Supermarkets could sell, and anyone could purchase, unlimited supplies. Considerable benefits would flow: Since all drugs would be legal, we could reasonably speculate that nobody would be interested in buying street-corner drugs. With one stroke we could eradicate smuggling, organized drug gangs, street sales, street violence and, since drug prices presumably would be reduced, most crime undertaken to purchase drugs.

An alternative legalization example implies much more formal control. Drugs would be regulated as we currently supervise the content and sale of alcoholic beverages. Administrators might try to monitor purity, potency of product and age of buyers. The more controls, however, the more incentives for illegal markets. If we prohibited cocaine or crack sales to minors but made the drugs freely available to adults at low prices, we would stimulate an illegal cocaine-crack market for minors. Thus, regulation would predictably reduce some of the benefits of decriminalization.

Decriminalization advocates assume that benefits would outweigh costs. But how to measure costs and to whom? To be persuasive, decriminalization advocates will have to persuade skeptics that easier availability of drugs would neither trigger significantly more use nor stimulate more intensive use by current users.

We can only speculate about what would really happen. One theory holds that drugs are already so easily available that anyone who wants to use them does and would not be interested in using significantly larger amounts. That speculation probably holds best for the 1960s generation of affluent and educated drug users. There are of course plenty of them—but their drugs of choice are alcohol, cigarettes, marijuana and nasal cocaine. Crack, heroin and PCP are ghetto and barrio favorites. More important, affluent users rarely commit crimes to buy drugs, don't sell drugs on street corners and don't fire off Uzis in housing projects. On the whole, decriminalization would benefit affluent, recreational drug users.

The crime-violence-drug link is a problem of the inner city, the jobless, the poor. Those who speak on behalf of this constituency are concerned that decriminalization would generate a sharp rise in drug use among the truly disadvantaged, especially teen-agers who have tough lives and bleak futures. Since they are not saying "no" to expensive illegal drugs, why should they say "no" to less expensive legal ones?

So decriminalization may entail two heavy costs: an explosion of drug use, especially in the inner cities, and a long-run symbolic defeat, with decriminalization signaling a surrender to drugs.

To prevail, decriminalization advocates will have to address these serious concerns. Some responses are possible. Those who fear a surge of inner-city drug use might be moved by a promise of a sharp reduction in crime and violence. Thus, decriminalization would heighten the safety of inner-city streets and involve fewer inner-city youngsters in crime and in the criminal-justice system as felons.

What about the symbolic meaning of decriminalization? Legalization of "vice" is often equated with a third model—approval, even promotion, of the formerly forbidden activity. When governments have legalized gambling—lotteries, casinos and off-track betting—they have also condoned and shamelessly promoted it.

But decriminalization need not imply approval. When the British legalized casinos in 1968, their purpose was to control organized crime. They didn't permit casinos to advertise at all—not even with matchbooks or ads in the telephone book.

Similarly, if drugs are to be legalized, advocates must ensure that the purpose will not be to pump money into state treasuries, but rather to control a major social and public-health problem.

To be acceptable, decriminalization would need to be grounded in a larger moral purpose—to reduce crime, to enhance public health and safety, to invigorate a sense of community. Decriminalization would need to be part of a bigger package, including social programs for the truly disadvantaged, strict licensing of sellers, increased enforcement against those who sell to the young (even at the risk of losing some of decriminalization's benefits), major anti-drug education programs and adequate resources for rehabilitation of users. Proposals for decriminalization that fail to put drug use in context with other social problems and fail to advocate a powerful anti-poverty, anti-drug strategy will likely be rejected—and should be.

(3) SHOULD PORNOGRAPHY BE CRIMINAL? *

Pornography, in the feminist view, is a form of forced sex, a practice of sexual politics, an institution of gender inequality. In this perspective, pornography is not harmless fantasy or a corrupt and confused misrepresentation of an otherwise natural and healthy sexuality. Along with the rape and prostitution in which it participates, pornography institutionalizes the sexuality of male supremacy, which fuses the erotization of dominance and submission with the social construction of male and female. Gender is sexual. Pornography constitutes the meaning of that sexuality. Men treat women as who they see women as being. Pornography constructs who that is. Men's

* Catharine A. MacKinnon, *Feminism Unmodified*, Harvard University Press, 1987, p. 148 (Reprinted with Permission).

power over women means that the way men see women defines who women can be. Pornography is that way.

In pornography, women desire dispossession and cruelty. Men, permitted to put words (and other things) in women's mouths, create scenes in which women desperately want to be bound, battered, tortured, humiliated, and killed. Or merely taken and used. This is erotic to the male point of view. Subjection itself, with self-determination ecstatically relinquished, is the content of women's sexual desire and desirability. Women are there to be violated and possessed, men to violate and possess them, either on screen or by camera or pen, on behalf of the viewer.

(a) AMERICAN BOOKSELLERS ASSOCIATION, INC. v. HUDNUT

United States Court of Appeals, Seventh Circuit, 771 F.2d 323, 1985.

EASTERBROOK, Circuit Judge.

Indianapolis enacted an ordinance defining "pornography" as a practice that discriminates against women. "Pornography" is to be redressed through the administrative and judicial methods used for other discrimination. The City's definition of "pornography" is considerably different from "obscenity," which the Supreme Court has held is not protected by the First Amendment.

[1] To be "obscene" under *Miller v. California*, 413 U.S. 15, (1973), "a publication must, taken as a whole, appeal to the prurient interest, must contain patently offensive depictions or descriptions of specified sexual conduct, and on the whole have no serious literary, artistic, political, or scientific value." Offensiveness must be assessed under the standards of the community. Both offensiveness and an appeal to something other than "normal, healthy sexual desires" are essential elements of "obscenity."

"Pornography" under the ordinance is "the graphic sexually explicit subordination of women, whether in pictures or in words, that also includes one or more of the following:

(1) Women are presented as sexual objects who enjoy pain or humiliation; or

(2) Women are presented as sexual objects who experience sexual pleasure in being raped; or

(3) Women are presented as sexual objects tied up or cut up or mutilated or bruised or physically hurt, or as dismembered or truncated or fragmented or severed into body parts; or

(4) Women are presented as being penetrated by objects or animals; or

(5) Women are presented in scenarios of degradation, injury, abasement, torture, shown as filthy or inferior, bleeding,

bruised, or hurt in a context that makes these conditions sexual; or

(6) Women are presented as sexual objects for domination, conquest, violation, exploitation, possession, or use, or through postures or positions of servility or submission or display."

The statute provides that the "use of men, children, or transsexuals in the place of women in paragraphs (1) through (6) above shall also constitute pornography under this section." The ordinance as passed in April 1984 defined "sexually explicit" to mean actual or simulated intercourse or the uncovered exhibition of the genitals, buttocks or anus. An amendment in June 1984 deleted this provision, leaving the term undefined.

The Indianapolis ordinance does not refer to the prurient interest, to offensiveness, or to the standards of the community. It demands attention to particular depictions, not to the work judged as a whole. It is irrelevant under the ordinance whether the work has literary, artistic, political, or scientific value. The City and many amici point to these omissions as virtues. They maintain that pornography influences attitudes, and the statute is a way to alter the socialization of men and women rather than to vindicate community standards of offensiveness. And as one of the principal drafters of the ordinance has asserted, "if a woman is subjected, why should it matter that the work has other value?" Catherine A. MacKinnon, *Pornography, Civil Rights, and Speech,* 20 Harv.Civ.Rts.—Civ.Lib.L.Rev. 1, 21 (1985).

Civil rights groups and feminists have entered this case as amici on both sides. Those supporting the ordinance say that it will play an important role in reducing the tendency of men to view women as sexual objects, a tendency that leads to both unacceptable attitudes and discrimination in the workplace and violence away from it. Those opposing the ordinance point out that much radical feminist literature is explicit and depicts women in ways forbidden by the ordinance and that the ordinance would reopen old battles. It is unclear how Indianapolis would treat works from James Joyce's *Ulysses* to Homer's *Iliad;* both depict women as submissive objects for conquest and domination.

We do not try to balance the arguments for and against an ordinance such as this. The ordinance discriminates on the ground of the content of the speech. Speech treating women in the approved way—in sexual encounters "premised on equality"—is lawful no matter how sexually explicit. Speech treating women in the disapproved way—as submissive in matters sexual or as enjoying humiliation—is unlawful no matter how significant the literary, artistic, or political qualities of the work taken as a whole. The state may not ordain preferred viewpoints in this way. The Constitution forbids the state to declare one perspective right and silence opponents.

Comment and Question

In the law of libel, defamation is a *false* assertion which tends to injure a person's reputation by lowering the community's estimation of the person. Thus, to say of someone that they are a thief or a rapist is to make a defamatory statement about them. If the statement is true—that is, if the person has been convicted of theft or rape, there is no libel.

Several legal commentators have considered pornography as a form of "group defamation." It is to be considered like defamation of an ethnic group or of a profession. Thus, to write, for instance, that all Irishmen are drunkards; or that all lawyers are crooked, is to make a statement that is defamatory of a group.

Neither of those statements is actionable in law under the theory that the group defamed is so large that no individual will be harmed. Similarly, it is thought that pornographic movies do not harm the reputation of women generally, only of those who appear in them. Do you agree?

5. ORGANIZED CRIME

a. THE BEGINNINGS *

Prohibition set the moral, economic, and political stage for the emergence of organized crime on a large scale in American society. The Volstead Act, which in 1919 restricted the sale and manufacture of alcoholic beverages, provided the young, undercapitalized and ambitious gangs with a new and rich market. Fitting almost naturally into the nation's capitalist tradition of commercial enterprise—in fact, drawing on two simultaneous drives for vice and profit—the bootlegging engendered by the Volstead Act opened the way for full flowering of entrepreneurial crime, under the guidance of ambitious young gangsters.

Several factors in American society converged to prompt this prospering of entrepreneurial crime. The success of the bootleggers was due in large part to the unpopularity and unenforceability of the Prohibition laws. The desire for alcoholic beverages among the public, resistance to government interference in spheres of morality, and the lure of the profit motive combined to produce a breeding ground for organized criminal activity.

The low capital outlay required to become a minor bootlegger, and the potential for high financial return were strong inducements for formerly law-abiding citizens, as well as the gangsters, to get into the bootlegging business. John Landesco, a University of Chicago student of organized crime, wrote that "Prohibition opened up a new criminal occupation . . . with less risk of punishment, with more certainty of gain and with less social stigma than the usual forms of crime, like

* John Dombrink; Unpublished doctoral Dissertation, University of California at Berkeley, Department of Sociology, 1981, *Outlaw Businessmen: Organized Crime and the Legalization of Casino Gambling,* (Reprinted with permission).

robbery, burglary and larceny." The early 1920s were a period of intense competition among criminal entrepreneurs attracted by Prohibition's economic opportunities. Those urban residents who had opposed the Volstead Act still craved available alcoholic beverages. "Everyone" seemed to be breaking the law, and the gangster was seen as performing a public service. Minor bootlegging and distilling became a source of added income for working class families, in this way intertwining in a distribution and production network of operators and consumers. Since the unenforceability of the Prohibition laws encouraged widespread flaunting of the Volstead Act, police officers were inspired to "look the other way" when confronting otherwise law-abiding citizens who might be cooking mash in their backyards for the production of alcohol.

Criminals could speak of their value to society and the business world because bootlegging provided a service that Americans wanted. Al Capone is reported to have said:

> "Prohibition is a business . . . Whatever else they may say, my booze has been good and my games have been on the square. Public service is my motto. I've always regarded it as a public benefaction if people were given decent liquor and square games."

In addition, Prohibition provided for the entrenchment of organized criminal enterprises, and their expansion through investment of profits earned during Prohibition. One author notes, "Prohibition was giving the gangster an opportunity that might never come again, a chance to walk at least part way through the door to respectability and a measure of social acceptance as good businessmen nonetheless." . . .

b. THE EXPANSION *

How big is the Syndicate? The most famous appraisal is that of Meyer Lansky back in the late 1950s: "We are bigger than U.S. Steel." As *Time* pointed out a decade later, the usual official estimates of income place the Syndicate bigger than U.S. Steel, American Telephone and Telegraph, General Motors, Exxon, General Electric, Ford, IBM, Chrysler, and RCA put together. Such estimates are impossible to make accurately, however. The Mafia doesn't file an annual financial statement with the Securities and Exchange Commission, and the individuals who make the money hide it. As much as possible, they even hide it from their fellow Mafiosi. Normal costs of most businesses, such as executive salaries and overhead, are subtracted before profits are determined, but they aren't subtracted from the usual estimates of the income of the Mafia, since nobody really knows what they are. Nevertheless, there is adequate evidence to presume that the Syndicate is incredibly big, certainly the biggest business in America in terms of gross *or* net.

* Jonathan Kwitny, *Vicious Circles: The Mafia in the Marketplace*, Norton, New York, pp. 49–50, 65–67. Copyright 1979 (Reprinted with permission).

c. THE DECLINE *

Battered by aggressive investigators and weakened by incompetent leadership, most of America's traditional Mafia families appear to be fading out of existence, law-enforcement officials and independent experts say.

The Mafia remains potent in the New York City area, where officals say it is hard to uproot because it has five separate and large crime families, and in the suburbs of Chicago. But in most other areas, where prosecutors have to contend with only a single family, the legendary mob that once controlled whole labor unions, city governments and criminal enterprises has clearly lost its grip.

Officials say the convictions of top Mafia leaders and their hierarchies have dismantled thriving underworld organizations in Philadelphia, New Jersey, New England, New Orleans, Kansas City, Detroit, Milwaukee and St. Louis.

'The Geritol Gang'

Here in Los Angeles, investigators speak of the "Mickey Mouse Mafia," saying the mob is so enfeebled that illegal bookmakers refuse to pay it for the right to operate. In Cleveland and Denver, where Mafia gangs once flourished, officials of the Federal Bureau of Investigation say each city is left with a lone mobster who was "made," or formally inducted in a secret ritual. And in New Jersey, Col. Justin Dintino, the State Police Superintendent, calls the Bruno–Scarfo group the "Geritol gang," so aged and ineffective does he find its leaders.

Many experts and officials say it is premature to write the Mafia's obituary, and they emphasize that its decline does not mean that organized crime has been banished: other groups are moving in to take the Mafia's place. In particular, Chinese international gangs called the Triads are making a strong bid to succeed the Mafia in the sophisticated crimes of large-scale gambling, loan sharking and labor racketeering.

Causes of Decline

But experts say the recent defeats of the Mafia will nevertheless mean real gains for the public, reducing the financial and social costs of rigged public contracts, of domination of labor unions like the teamsters and longshoremen, and of influence in the construction, trucking, trash-collection and garment-manufacturing industries.

While there is wide agreement that the Mafia is declining, there is much disagreement on the causes. Law-enforcement officials generally credit a long-term strategy adopted by the Justice Department and the Federal Bureau of Investigation in the early 1980's: developing cases

---

* Selwyn Raab, "A Battered and Ailing Mafia Is Loosing Its Grip on America," New York Times, October 22, 1990 (Reprinted with Permission).

against the top leaders of organized-crime families and relying largely on the Racketeer Influenced and Corrupt Organizations Act, or RICO, as a courtroom tool.

By concentrating on enteprises rather than individuals, Federal prosecutors in the last five years have removed the high commands of families through the convictions and long prison sentences of almost 100 top Cosa Nostra leaders.

The chief architect of the RICO act, G. Robert Blakey, a professor of law at the University of Notre Dame, admits he was surprised by its impact. "It was sort of like George Kennan's containment policy of the Soviet Union," he said. "We tried it and by God it worked."

But two other experts, Peter A. Lupsha and Howard Abadinsky, say demographic changes, too, have helped undermine the Mafia. Mr. Lupsha, a political scientist at the University of New Mexico who is a consultant on organized-crime matters for Federal and state agencies, and Mr. Abadinsky, founder of the International Association for the Study of Organized Crime, a research organization, cite these factors:

• The dispersal of white populations away from urban neighborhoods. This diminished both the Mafia's political influence, which was strongest in Italian–American sections of big cities, and the surreptitious protection that organized-crime bosses often got from the local police and political machines.

• A new generation of Mafia leaders who took control after the convictions or deaths of previous bosses and capos, or captains, but were less competent than their predecessors.

• The disintegration of traditional Mafia loyalties, with members breaking the code of silence to become informers against leaders.

• The emergence of rival crime groups controlled by Asians, Colombians, black Americans and the Sicilian Mafia, a powerful unit that operates independently of America's Mafia or Cosa Nostra. These new groups dominate drug trafficking and illegal gambling, especially in the inner cities.

A Multinational Trend

"The real trend in organized crime today is transnational with the ability to move drugs and money across borders," Mr. Lupsha said. "The old Italian–American organized crime groups were too content with what they had and too slow to think globally."

E.   RECOMMENDED READING

Braithwaite, John, *Crime, Shame and Reintegration.* Cambridge University Press, New York, 1989.

Currie, Elliott, *Confronting Crime: An American Challenge.* Pantheon, New York, 1985.

Gottfredson, Michael R., Hirschi, and Travis. *A General Theory of Crime.* Stanford University Press, Stanford, CA., 1990.

Hart, H.L.A. *Law, Liberty and Morality.* Stanford University Press, Stanford, Calif., 1963.

Katz, Jack, *Seductions of Crime: Moral and Sensual Attractions in Doing Evil.* Basic Books, New York, 1988.

Kinsey, Richard, Lea John and Young, Jock. *Losing the Fight Against Crime.* Blackwell, Oxford, 1986.

Morris, Norval and Hawkins, Gordon. *The Honest Politician's Guide to Crime Control.* University of Chicago Press, Chicago, 1970.

Nettler, Gwynn. *Explaining Crime.* McGraw-Hill Book Co., San Francisco, 2d ed. 1978.

Silberman, Charles. *Criminal Violence, Criminal Justice.* Random House, New York, 1978.

Sykes, Gresham. *Criminology.* Harcourt Brace Javanovich, Inc., New York, 1978.

Taylor, Ian; Walton, Paul and Young, Jock. *The New Criminology: For a Social Theory of Deviance.* Harper and Row, New York, 1974.

Wilson, James Q. *Thinking About Crime.* Vintage Books, New York, 1977.

Wilson, James Q. and Herrnstein, Richard. *Crime and Human Nature.* Simon and Schuster, New York, 1985.

Chapter II

WHY PUNISH CRIMES?

Introduction

This chapter focuses on the issue of what society expects to accomplish through categorizing conduct as criminal. Typically we do not devote much attention to this question. In most cases the criminality of the act—if the defendant did it—is clear. Despite this, the differing reasons why we use the criminal law against those who engage in certain kinds of conduct—in other words, the justifications for criminal punishment—are extremely important at many stages of the criminal process.

A. SPECIFIC CASES

1. MURDER

THE QUEEN v. DUDLEY AND STEPHENS
14 Q.B.D. 273 (1884).

LORD COLERIDGE, C.J. The two prisoners, Thomas Dudley and Edwin Stephens, were indicted for the murder of Richard Parker on the high seas on the 25th of July in the present year. They were tried . . . and . . . the jury returned a special verdict, the legal effect of which has been argued before us, and on which we are now to pronounce judgment.

The special verdict . . . settled before us is as follows.

". . . that on July 5, 1884, the prisoners, Thomas Dudley and Edwin Stephens, with one Brooks, all able-bodied English seamen, and the deceased also an English boy, between seventeen and eighteen years of age, the crew of an English yacht, a registered English vessel, were cast away in a storm on the high seas 1600 miles from the Cape of Good Hope, and were compelled to put into an open boat belonging to the said yacht. That in this boat they had no supply of water and no supply of food, except two 1 lb. tins of turnips, and for three days they had nothing else to subsist upon. That on the fourth day they caught a small turtle, upon which they subsisted for a few days, and this was the only food they had up to the twentieth day when the act now in question was committed. That on the twelfth day the remains of the turtle were entirely consumed, and for the next eight days they had nothing to eat. That they had no fresh water, except such rain as they from time to time caught in their oilskin capes. That the boat was drifting on the ocean, and was probably more than 1000 miles away from land. That on the eighteenth day, when they had been seven days without food and five without water, the prisoners spoke to Brooks as to what should be done if no succour came, and suggested that some one should be sacrificed to save the rest, but Brooks dissented, and the boy, to whom they were understood to refer, was not consulted. That on the 24th of July, the day before the act now in question, the prisoner Dudley proposed to Stephens and Brooks that lots should be cast who should be put to death to save the rest, but Brooks refused to consent, and it was not put to the boy, and in point of fact there was no drawing of lots. That on that day the prisoners spoke of their having families, and suggested it would be better to kill the boy that their lives should be saved, and Dudley proposed that if there was no vessel in sight by the morrow morning the boy should be killed. That next day, the 25th of July, no vessel appearing, Dudley told Brooks that he had better go and have a sleep, and made signs to Stephens and Brooks that the boy had better be killed. The prisoner Stephens agreed to the act, but Brooks dissented from it. That the boy was then lying at the bottom of the boat quite helpless, and extremely weakened by famine and by drinking sea water, and unable to make any resistance, nor did he ever assent to his being killed. The prisoner Dudley offered a prayer asking forgiveness for them all if either of them should be tempted to commit a rash act, and that their souls might be saved. That Dudley, with the assent of Stephens, went to the boy, and telling him that his time was come, put a knife into his throat and killed him then and there; that the three men fed upon the body and blood of the boy for four days; that on the fourth day after the act had been committed the boat was picked up by a passing vessel, and the prisoners were rescued, still alive, but in the lowest state of prostration. That they were carried to the port of Falmouth, and committed for trial at Exeter. That if the men had not fed upon the body of the boy they would . . . within the four days have died of famine. That the boy, being in a much weaker condition, was likely to have died before them. That at the time of the act in question there was no sail in sight, nor any reasonable prospect of relief. That under these circumstances there appeared to the prisoners every probability that unless they then fed or very soon fed upon the boy or one of themselves they would die of starvation. That there was no appreciable chance of saving life except by killing some one for the others to eat. That assuming any necessity to kill anybody, there was no greater necessity for killing the boy than any of the other three men. But whether, upon the whole matter by the jurors found, the killing of Richard Parker by Dudley and Stephens be felony and murder the jurors are ignorant, and pray the advice of the Court thereupon, and if upon the whole matter the Court shall be of opinion that the killing of Richard Parker be felony and murder, then the jurors say that Dudley and Stephens were each guilty of felony and murder as alleged in the indictment."

From these facts, stated with the cold precision of a special verdict, it appears sufficiently that the prisoners were subject to terrible temptation, to sufferings which might break down the bodily power of the strongest man, and try the conscience of the best. Other details yet more harrowing, facts still more loathsome and appalling, were presented to the jury, and are to be found recorded in my learned Brother's notes. But nevertheless this is clear, that the prisoners put to death a weak and unoffending boy upon the chance of preserving their own lives by feeding upon his flesh and blood after he was killed, and with the certainty of depriving *him* of any possible chance of survival. The verdict finds in terms that "if the men had not fed upon the body of the boy they would *probably* not have survived," and that "the boy being in a much weaker condition was *likely* to have died before them." They might possibly have been picked up next day by a passing ship; they might possibly not have been picked up at all; in either case it is obvious that the killing of the boy would have been an unnecessary and profitless act. It is found by the verdict that the boy was incapable of resistance, and, in fact, made none; and it is not even suggested that his death was due to any violence on his part attempted against, or even so much as feared by, those who killed him. Under these circumstances the jury say that they are ignorant whether those who killed him were guilty of murder, and have referred it to this Court to determine what is the legal consequence which follows from the facts which they have found.

. . . [T]he real question in the case [is] whether killing under the circumstances set forth in the verdict be or be not murder. The contention that it could be anything else was, to the minds of us all, both new and strange, and we stopped the Attorney General in his negative argument in order that we might hear what could be said in support of a proposition which appeared to us to be at once dangerous, immoral, and opposed to all legal principle and analogy. All, no doubt, that can be said has been urged before us, and we are now to consider and determine what it amounts to. First it is said that it follows from various definitions of murder in books of authority, which definitions imply, if they do not state, the doctrine, that in order to save your own life you may lawfully take away the life of another, when that other is neither attempting nor threatening yours, nor is guilty of any illegal act whatever towards you or any one else. But if these definitions be looked at they will not be found to sustain this contention.

It is . . . clear . . . that the doctrine contended for receives no support from the great authority of Lord Hale. . . . Hale himself has made it clear. For in the chapter in which he deals with the exemption created by compulsion or necessity he thus expresses himself:—"If a man be desperately assaulted and in peril of death, and cannot otherwise escape unless, to satisfy his assailant's fury, he will kill an innocent person then present, the fear and actual force will not acquit him of the crime and punishment of murder, if he commit the fact, for he ought rather to die himself than kill an innocent; but if he cannot otherwise save his own life the law permits him in his own defence to kill the assailant, for by the violence of the assault, and the offence committed upon him by the assailant himself, the law of nature, and necessity, hath made him his own protector cum debito moderamino inculpatae tutelae." * (Hale's Pleas of the Crown, vol. i. 51.)

But, further still, Lord Hale in the following chapter deals with the position asserted by the casuists, and sanctioned, as he says, by Grotius and Puffendorf, that in a case of extreme necessity, either of hunger or clothing; "theft is no theft, or at least not punishable as theft, as some even of our own lawyers have asserted the same." "But," says Lord Hale, "I take it that here in England, that rule, at least by the laws of England, is false; and therefore, if a person, being under necessity for want of victuals or clothes, shall upon that account clandestinely and animo furandi steal another man's goods, it is felony, and a crime by the laws of England punishable with death." (Hale, Pleas of the Crown, i. 54.) If, therefore, Lord Hale is clear—as he is—that extreme necessity of hunger does not justify larceny, what would he have said to the doctrine that it justified murder? . . .

Is there, then, any authority for the proposition which has been presented to us? Decided cases there are none. . . .

The one real authority of former time is Lord Bacon, who, in his commentary on the maxim, "necessitas inducit privilegium quoad jura privata," ** lays down the law as follows:—"Necessity carrieth a privilege in itself. Necessity is of three sorts—necessity of conservation of life, necessity of obedience, and necessity of the act of God or of a stranger. First of conservation of life; if a man steals viands to satisfy his present hunger, this is no felony nor larceny. So if divers be in danger of drowning by the casting away of some boat or barge, and one of them get to some plank, or on the boat's side to keep himself above water, and another to save his life thrust him from it, whereby he is drowned, this is neither se defendendo nor by misadventure, but justifiable." On this it is to be observed that Lord Bacon . . . cites no authority for it, and it must stand upon his own. . . . Now it is admitted that the deliberate killing of this unoffending and unresisting boy was clearly murder, unless the killing can be justified by some well-recognised excuse admitted by the law. It is further admitted that there was in this case no such excuse, unless the killing was justified by what has been called "necessity." But the temptation to the act which existed here was not what the law has ever called necessity. Nor is this to be regretted. Though law and morality are not the same, and many things may be immoral which are not necessarily illegal, yet the absolute divorce of law from morality would be of fatal consequence; and such divorce would follow if the temptation to murder in this case were to be held by law an absolute defence of it. It is not so. To preserve one's life is generally speaking a duty, but it may be the plainest and the highest duty to sacrifice it. War is full of instances in which it is a man's duty not to live, but to die. The duty, in case of

* With the privilege to apply moderate force.

** "necessity grants a privilege in respect of a private right."

shipwreck, of a captain to his crew, of the crew to the passengers, of soldiers to women and children, as in the noble case of the *Birkenhead;* these duties impose on men the moral necessity, not of the preservation, but of the sacrifice of their lives for others, from which in no country, least of all, it is to be hoped, in England, will men ever shrink, as indeed, they have not shrunk. It is not correct, therefore, to say that there is any absolute or unqualified necessity to preserve one's life. . . . Who is to be the judge of this sort of necessity? By what measure is the comparative value of lives to be measured? Is it to be strength, or intellect, or what? It is plain that the principle leaves to him who is to profit by it to determine the necessity which will justify him in deliberately taking another's life to save his own. In this case the weakest, the youngest, the most unresisting, was chosen. Was it more necessary to kill him than one of the grown men? The answer must be "No"—

"So spake the Fiend, and with necessity,

The tyrant's plea, excused his devilish deeds."

It is not suggested that in this particular case the deeds were "devilish," but it is quite plain that such a principle once admitted might be made the legal cloak for unbridled passion and atrocious crime. There is no safe path for judges to tread but to ascertain the law to the best of their ability and to declare it according to their judgment; and if in any case the law appears to be too severe on individuals, to leave it to the Sovereign to exercise that prerogative of mercy which the Constitution has intrusted to the hands fittest to dispense it.

It must not be supposed that in refusing to admit temptation to be an excuse for crime it is forgotten how terrible the temptation was; how awful the suffering; how hard in such trials to keep the judgment straight and the conduct pure. We are often compelled to set up standards we cannot reach ourselves, and to lay down rules which we could not ourselves satisfy. But a man has no right to declare temptation to be an excuse, though he might himself have yielded to it, nor allow compassion for the criminal to change or weaken in any manner the legal definition of the crime. It is therefore our duty to declare that the prisoners' act in this case was wilful murder, that the facts as stated in the verdict are no legal justification of the homicide; and to say that in our unanimous opinion the prisoners are upon this special verdict guilty of murder.

THE COURT then proceeded to pass sentence of death upon the prisoners.[1]

Question

What reason is there to hold the defendants guilty of murder—or is the court's point that there does not have to be a reason?

1. This sentence was afterwards commuted by the Crown to six months' imprisonment.

2. ANTI–TRUST VIOLATIONS *

In a tense and packed Philadelphia courtroom last week, a drama took place that U.S. business will long remember—to its shame. The cases before him, said Federal District Judge J. Cullen Ganey, were "a shocking indictment of a vast section of our economy." . . .

Up for sentencing were 29 electrical-equipment companies, headed by the industry's two "competitive" giants, General Electric and Westinghouse, and 44 of their executives. Long ago, faced with incontrovertible evidence gathered by the Eisenhower Administration's relentless trustbusters, the companies and individuals had pleaded guilty or *nolo contendere* (no contest) to charges that they conspired over the past seven years to fix prices and rig bids in the sale of some $7 billion worth of heavy electrical equipment. . . . Now the moment of reckoning had come. First before the court came the lawyer for . . . a vice president of Westinghouse, to plead for mercy. His client, said the lawyer, while [his client] bowed his head, was a vestryman of St. John's Episcopal Church in Sharon, Pa. and a benefactor of charities for crippled children and cancer victims. "These men," the lawyer pleaded, "are not grasping, greedy, cut-throat competitors."

In antitrust cases, executives may be fined but are rarely jailed. Judge Ganey sentenced [him] to 30 days in jail. He began automatically to return to his seat, but was startled to be seized by two armed deputy U.S. marshals and hustled off to the marshal's office to be fingerprinted.

One by one, as the sentencing went on, lawyers rose to describe their clients as pillars of the community. [One defendant], vice president of General Electric, was the director of a boys' club in Schenectady, N.Y. and the chairman of a campaign to build a new Jesuit seminary in Lenox, Mass. His lawyer pleaded that [he] not be put "behind bars with common criminals who have been convicted of embezzlement and other serious crimes." Judge Ganey thought the company appropriate, gave [him] 30 days in jail. The lawyer for [a] Westinghouse division sales manager and a man prominent in charitable and community affairs in Drexel Hill, Pa., asked: "What difference does it make if the Government recommends 30 days or 60 days or more? What matters is crossing the prison door at all." Judge Ganey recommended 30 days behind the door.

Despite other pleas attesting to the public usefulness and position of the defendants, the federal judge handed out the greatest number of jail terms ever in an antitrust proceeding.

. . .

* "The Great Conspiracy," *Time*, 17 Feb. 1961, p. 84. Reprinted by permission from   TIME, The Weekly Newsmagazine; © Time Inc.

Question

What possible reason could there be for sending such fine men to jail?

B. THE REASONS FOR CRIMINAL PUNISHMENT

1. DETERRENCE

a. DEUTERONOMY 19:16–22 *

When a malicious witness comes forward to give false evidence against a man, and the two disputants stand before the LORD, before the priests and the judges then in office, if, after careful examination by the judges, he be proved to be a false witness giving false evidence against his fellow, you shall treat him as he intended to treat his fellow, and thus rid yourselves of this wickedness. The rest of the people when they hear of it will be afraid: never again will anything as wicked as this be done among you. You shall show no mercy: . . .

b. HOLMES ON DETERRENCE **

If I were having a philosophical talk with a man I was going to have hanged (or electrocuted) I should say, "I don't doubt that your act was inevitable for you but to make it more avoidable by others we propose to sacrifice you to the common good. You may regard yourself as a soldier dying for your country if you like. But the law must keep its promises." I fear that the touch of sentiment that I notice in your political writing will be revolted at this, but personally I feel neither doubt nor scruple. . . .

c. COMMONSENSE ON DETERRENCE †

Few social norms are so deeply implanted that they enforce themselves completely with no help from the law. The taboo against cannibalism may be one of these. In most societies, the very thought is disgusting. Violations are rare—almost unknown. When they occur, people assume, almost automatically, that the violator must be insane. . . . Murder, rape, and arson are repellent to the average man; but they do occur and must be guarded against. No doubt, if the penal code through some technical error were suddenly suspended, people would not rush out to butcher their enemies. Strong moral chains would keep people in control, at least for a while, but not everyone and not in every respect. Occasionally, laws *do* take a holiday—when police go on strike, for example—and what happens sheds indirect light on the matter. Johannes Andenaes has recounted

---

* The New English Bible.

** Mark DeWolfe Howe ed., *Holmes-Laski Letters* (Cambridge, Harvard University Press. 1953) p. 806.

† Friedman, Lawrence M., *The Legal System.* New York, Russell Sage Foundation 1975, pp. 68–78. © Reprinted with permission of the publisher.

one such episode. In occupied Denmark in 1944, the Germans arrested the entire police force. During the rest of the occupation, an unarmed watch corps served as makeshift police, but they were not very effective. Robbery increased tremendously, rising from ten cases a month to a hundred. Other crimes, such as embezzlement and fraud, did not increase, but these were crimes "where the criminal is usually known if the crime itself is discovered."

The case is clearer for minor, detailed rules of modern law which lack strong moral supports—the precise time limit on a parking meter, for example. Unenforcement leads to wholesale violation.

Scholars generally agree, however, that a theory of legal behavior must be multiple; legal acts work on the minds of subjects in various ways. These ways, we repeat, can be grouped into three main categories. First, there are *sanctions*—threats and promises. Second, there is the influence, positive or negative, of the social world: the *peer group*. Third, there are internal values: *conscience* and related attitudes, the sense of what is and is not legitimate and what is or is not worthy to be obeyed.

We begin with the model of legal behavior that stresses reactions of subjects to sanctions. In one form or another, this idea is basic to law. People comply with rules or use the law for their own benefit or to avoid punishments, penalties, and pains. These do not always come from the government. One of the most powerful motives for obeying speed limits is that people are afraid of an accident. This is self-interest, pure and simple, but it is as potent as any sanction offered by the state.

[T]he study of legal sanctions and their effect on behavior is barely beginning. Only in recent years has there grown up a substantial body of research. Most of it has focussed on one particular point, the question, crudely put, whether punishment deters. Almost all of the studies deal with deterrence of crime or other blameworthy acts, such as cheating on exams. One overpowering subquestion has been whether capital punishment is of much use as a deterrent. People feel strongly about capital punishment. They would like to prove that it does not work. Some go on to doubt whether punishment deters at all.[1]

Any theory of sanctions, however, must start out by accepting the fact that the threat of punishment tends to deter, just as rewards tend to encourage rewarded behavior. As a general rule, people want what is pleasant and rewarding, and they avoid costs, punishments, and pains. These propositions are basic to learning theory and to the study of human behavior. Skepticism about legal punishments arises out of the fact that under *some* circumstances, *some* kinds of sanction do not seem to produce much effect, but the basic proposition must be taken as unassailable.

1. The thesis that punishment is inefficient, once bolstered by studies largely confined to rats, has now been abandoned by psychologists.

Another proposition must also be taken as true. Suppose a rule of law threatens behavior X with a sanction. If we increase the sanction, behavior X will decrease, all other things being equal. The *rate* of change may not be predictable, of course. Some kinds of behavior are elastic, some inelastic. There is no way to say crudely and flatly that 10 percent more punishment buys 10 percent more deterrence, ounce for ounce. What one can say is that more units of genuine punishment will discourage, not encourage, whatever behavior is the target of the sanction.

Are there exceptions to the basic propositions? Are there cases where, if one threatens to punish behavior, the behavior will actually be encouraged? In rare situations, the sanction may give conduct some symbolic meaning that increases its importance. The United States Congress passed a law, during the war in Vietnam, which made it a crime to burn one's draft card. There was only one reason to burn a draft card: as a symbol of defiance toward the war. It is possible that Congress heightened the meaning of the act by passing the law, making it more attractive to people looking for some way to express their disgust for the war. At least such cases are *theoretically* possible.

The basic propositions assume a certain degree of rational, or cost-benefit, behavior. They do not assume that people are nothing but unfeeling machines. People do act unselfishly at times, and at times irrationally, in every sense of the word. But social science deals with group or mass behavior—with general, typical, modal tendencies. It does not matter if a few people murder, pillage, and rape, regardless of punishment, and are incapable of responding to threats. Some of these people will be considered insane—not legally responsible for their acts. Most *potential* murderers and rapists are not outside the reach of sanctions. And one cannot leap from murder to less "expressive" crimes—crimes without passion (except the passion for money), economic crimes, regulatory crimes, or violations of small rules of order— overtime parking, walking on the grass, or littering the streets.

The deterrent effect of sanctions means, first of all, *general deterrence,* that is, the likelihood that the population or part of it, hearing about a sanction or perhaps seeing it in operation, will modify its behavior accordingly. *General deterrence* is distinguished from *special deterrence* which means the [deterrence through threat to the individual being punished that he will suffer again should he again transgress.] The idea of general deterrence is, for example, that the law against armed robbery will frighten people into thinking twice about committing armed robbery for fear of arrest, conviction, and jail; special deterrence means that a robber, once sent to jail, may think twice about robbing again. In either case, the deterrence lies mainly in the threat.

It goes without saying that it does not deter to make punishment more severe—on paper. Many people who argue that punishment is futile mean that words in a book are futile in themselves. This is correct. An unenforced sanction is a poor deterrent, because it is so weak and so flabby a threat. It may work, but only if people do not know that the threat is an empty one.

It has been often said that what is important about a sanction is its certainty. This is what makes surveillance so strong. No one parks in a "No Parking" zone under the policeman's nose. It seems likely that fewer people would drive when drunk, if they were sure that they would be caught and given a year in jail. A five-year penalty would be even more effective. How effective, we cannot tell, but suppose that as the penalty increased to five years, the chance of arrest and conviction retreated to one out of five. We are now unsure whether we have increased the punishment at all. Perhaps we have only changed its form. Deterrence depends on the perceived *risk* that a sanction will actually fall on a person's head. By raising the level of enforcement, one gets more deterrence out of the same formal punishment. If every thief was caught and jailed and this fact became known, a small fine and a week in jail might provide as much general and specific deterrence as harsher but less certain punishments. In the nineteenth century, penal laws became more humane, prison terms shorter, and the death penalty shriveled to a shadow of itself. But perhaps techniques of enforcement improved. Society could then afford to inflict mild penalties on the many who were caught instead of great cruelty on the few.

In short, then, for deterrence to work, a sanction must be real or *seem* real. Paper tigers do not bite or deter, unless their weakness is kept secret. In one study, students in a Florida college were asked what they thought the penalties were for possession of marijuana, whether they thought offenders were likely to be caught, whether they knew people who had been arrested, and whether they themselves were violators. Nonviolators tended to assess the risks as greater than violators. This is what deterrence theory would expect. In general, we know little about perceptions of risk. It is a promising area for study. Jonathan Casper, who interviewed convicted burglars in Connecticut, quoted one as saying that "you can . . . get a lot of breaking and entering, and it's very hard to catch you on one." Most burglars, Casper felt, "assume that for any given job they will not be caught, though in the long run they will."

We are also not sure how to affect perceptions of risk. Some communities boldly mark their police cars. The idea is to make the police as visible as possible, increasing the perceived risk to bad drivers. One could also make an argument for unmarked cars; drivers might then imagine police lurking everywhere and over-assess the risk of getting caught. A study of the effect on crime of increasing subway police in New York found a "phantom effect"—"deterrence caused by a police activity that is not actually present." Crime on the subway decreased even during times when the police were not there, probably because of "an incorrect perception of the threat of apprehension."

The *speed* with which a punishment or reward is delivered is as important as its certainty and severity. An immediate punishment or reward has more impact than a delayed one. . . . Experiments show that "the effect of a delay is to lessen severity, and manipulations of severity have little effect at long delays." Laboratory experiments call it "delay," if the punishment comes thirty seconds later than the act to be punished. The lag in the legal system may be years. Still, it seems logical that "a five-year sentence beginning a year after the commission of a crime may not be as effective as a six-month sentence administered without delay."

d. DETERRENCE IN ACTION

(1) DRUNKEN DRIVING *

The political climate of the 1980s in America has led to the view that drunk driving is a violent crime, properly punishable with time served in jail. This evolving viewpoint has led to a little-recognized confrontation between the branches of government. Legislatures, influenced by groups like Mothers Against Drunk Driving (MADD) to view the behavior as extremely dangerous, have tried to force this perception on a resistant judiciary. The judicial belief that in most cases drunk driving is a none-too-dangerous traffic infraction results from the experience of processing numerous cases in which no harm resulted. Furthermore, judges face imperative demands to move cases through the system by agreeing to reduced penalties for guilty pleas. One outcome of this confrontation has been for legislatures to mandate jail sentences for convicted drunk drivers and to prohibit plea bargaining as a means to avoid these sentences.

As of late 1988, mandatory jail for convicted drunk drivers had become law in forty-two states in the case of repeat offenders and in fourteen states for first offenders. Typically, the mandatory incarceration is for relatively brief periods, and some statutes permit substitution of community service. Despite the brevity of the jail sentences and the occasional possibility of substituting community service, these laws have been strongly supported as providing the severity necessary for effective deterrence of drunk driving.

This support relies on the conventional belief in deterrence that the threat of swift, certain, and severe punishment can reduce undesirable behavior. The empirical evidence for the deterrent effectiveness of severe penalties such as jail is, however, inconsistent at best. In Norway and Sweden, where drunk driving laws carrying jail penalties have been in place for a half-century, there appears to be less impaired driving than in many other Western countries, but Ross has shown that the causal connection between these laws and low rates of impaired

* H. Laurence Ross, Richard McCleary, and Gary LaFree, "Can Mandatory Jail Laws Deter Drunk Driving? The Arizona Case," *The Journal of Criminal Law &* *Criminology*, Spring 1990, Vol. 81, No. 1, pp. 156–159, 163–164 (Reprinted with Permission).

driving is unproved in Scandinavia. Votey and Shapiro, in work
intended to criticize Ross's position, conclude that fines and license
actions have been more effective than jail in producing the Scandinavian results. In the United States, early studies of severity-based drunk
driving interventions all produced negative findings. More recently, an
evaluation of mandatory jail for first offenders in the state of Tennessee
found that, although implementation was relatively good, there was no
significant change in either awareness of the law or measures of the
extent of drunk driving. Similarly, a case study of an Ohio jurisdiction
where the judge routinely sentences first-offense drunk drivers to jail
found no evidence of reduced drinking and driving even though the
penalties were well known among the citizens.

Two recent United States studies claim to have found evidence for
a deterrent effect of mandatory jail laws. One instance involved two
independent analyses by Falkowski and by Cleary and Rodgers of the
impact of a policy by judges in Minneapolis which led to the brief
jailing of the vast majority of convicted drunk drivers in that city. The
evaluations found that nighttime fatal crashes—a generally accepted
indicator of drunk driving—declined significantly near the time of
implementation of the jailing policy. Although reductions were also
found statewide and in neighboring Ramsey County (St. Paul), these
were smaller than those in Hennepin County, where the jailing policy
was in effect. Confidence in these results must be tempered by the fact
that numerous other changes were made in the drunk driving law at
about the same time, which could have caused the change. Moreover,
in the Falkowski study, the crash reductions appeared following an
unexplained two-month delay beyond the policy's inception.

A different kind of evidence favoring the deterrent effectiveness of
jail comes from a cross-sectional study of state laws. The types of law
found effective by the research team included "illegal per se" laws,
administrative license-revocation laws, and mandatory-jail laws. The
laws providing for mandatory jail terms were credited with producing a
six percent reduction in late-night fatal crashes. Although negative
results were found in a similarly designed study by Joksch, the study by
Zador and his colleagues seems to have utilized more appropriate
comparisons, and its results are more credible.

In sum, the question of whether the threat of a mandatory brief jail
sentence can be effective in deterring drunk driving is an open one. A
majority of the individual case studies failed to find evidence for
effectiveness of jail, but two independent teams concluded that the
Minneapolis judges may have achieved their goal, and the better-
designed of the national correlational analyses supports the deterrence
predictions. This report adds to the literature evidence from experience in another mandatory-jail jurisdiction, the state of Arizona, since
1982.

II. THE ARIZONA CASE

In the context of drunk-driving laws prevailing at the time, the Arizona law of 1982 appears to have been exceptionally severe. A first-time offender, whether guilty of impaired driving (Section A) or driving with a blood-alcohol level concentration (BAC) of more than .10% (Section B, the illegal per se provision), was subject to a sentence including a mandatory twenty-four hours in jail as well as a $250 fine and a ninety-day license suspension. Further, second-time offenders within three years faced sixty days in jail along with fines and license actions, and third-time offenders faced six months in jail along with other penalties. The law also prohibited plea bargaining: if convicted, persons accused of drunk driving were to be found guilty on the original charges. This would prevent an offender's being charged merely with a first offense if arrested for drunk driving on a subsequent occasion.

The legislature indeed meant business. In the words of the Arizona drivers license manual: "Get caught driving drunk in Arizona and you're going to spend at least 24 hours in jail. . . . You'll have your license suspended for 90 days, too." Initial news stories assumed that jail would be the routine penalty for drunk drivers, and we based our theoretical expectation of deterrence on perceptions prevailing at the inception of the law. We expected no delay for the deterrent effect, if an effect did occur. Moreover, people we spoke with in the Phoenix legal community believed that most members of the public expected to be treated severely when convicted of drunk driving. As one person put it: "It's pitiful to hear them beg and plead. . . . They believe they've had it—they're going to jail."

The failure to incarcerate, though notorious among informed people, is probably not well known by ordinary drivers in Arizona even today, and it was certainly not suspected in the early days of the 1982 law. It cannot explain the law's failure to deter.

A more reasonable explanation lies in the possibility that the public disregards threats when it perceives a negligible likelihood of these threats being applied. The actual chances of apprehension for a drunk driver in an American jurisdiction are estimated to range between 1 in 200 and 1 in 2000. Hence, drivers who perceive a severe punishment if caught, but a near-zero chance of being caught, are being rational in ignoring the threat. We were unable to find Maricopa County data directly on point, but a survey taken in two rural Arizona counties in November 1982, shortly after the legislature enacted the law, found that 25% of the respondents described the probability of their being caught by the police when driving drunk as either low or very low, and 15% thought that the probability of being punished even if caught was low or very low.

Although the majority professed other beliefs, it is possible that the optimistic (and realistic) minority seeing relatively little risk might ignore the new law. Moreover, this minority may be comprised of those people who are most in need of having their impulses controlled by deterrent threats, yet who are at the same time the most immune to the threats. Some research has found that drunk drivers are disproportionately likely to be problem drinkers and alcoholics, as well as young working-class men whose attitudes towards compliance with law in general may be casual. As one state safety official noted: "The thinking class drinks less, but the blue-collar areas are untouched now." A traffic court judge added: "The major effect has been on people who don't cause that many accidents anyway. . . . [F]or the real problem drinker, nothing deters."

Another possible explanation for the failure of the law is that members of the target population did not perceive it as severe. Jail may be symbolically important to middle-class people, including the vast bulk of members of citizen activist groups like MADD. However, defense attorneys in Phoenix often told us that the punishment most threatening to their clients was not jail, but license suspension. The effect of the 1982 law on this component of punishment for drunk drivers is unclear, and it was not highlighted in publicity. Many habitual drunk drivers may have viewed the 1982 law as constituting less of a change than did the law's initiators and supporters.

(2) RIOT *

Montrealers discovered last week what it is like to live in a city without police and firemen. The lesson was costly: six banks were robbed, more than 100 shops were looted, and there were twelve fires. Property damage came close to $3,000,000; at least 40 carloads of glass will be needed to replace shattered storefronts. Two men were shot dead. At that, Montreal was probably lucky to escape as lightly as it did.

The immediate cause of the outburst was a strike for more pay staged by the city's cops and firemen.

One morning last week, the 8 a.m. police shift went off to the Paul Sauvé Arena to argue strike tactics instead of reporting to their beats. Suddenly the city was left unguarded. By 11:20 a.m., the first bank robbery had occurred. By noon shops began to close, and banks shut their doors to all except old customers. Early in the evening, a group of taxi drivers added to the confusion. Protesting the fact that they are prohibited from serving Montreal's airport, they led a crowd of several hundred to storm the garage of the Murray Hill Limousine Service Ltd., which has the lucrative franchise. Busses were overturned and set ablaze. From nearby rooftops, snipers' shots rang out. A handful of frightened Quebec provincial police, called in to help maintain order, stood by helplessly. One was shot in the back by a sniper and died.

The crowd, augmented by other opportunists, moved through downtown Montreal, burning and looting. Rioters stormed into the swanky

* "City Without Cops," *Time,* 17 October 1969, p. 47. Reprinted by permission from   TIME, The Weekly Newsmagazine; © Time Inc.

Queen Elizabeth Hotel, then moved on to the nearby Windsor Hotel and nearly wrecked Mayor Jean Drapeau's newly opened restaurant. Expensive shops along St. Catherine Street were hit by looters. On the city's outskirts, burglars went to work; one was shot dead by a doctor in his suburban home.

Belatedly, the Quebec provincial government called out 600 infrantrymen and 300 Royal Canadian Mounted Police [and brought the situation under control.]

e. DETERRENCE CRITICIZED *

An additional purpose of punishment is to deter potential wrongdoers from the commission of similar or worse crimes. This is simply a derived rationalization of revenge. Though social revenge is the actual psychological basis of punishment today, the apologists for the punitive regime are likely to bring forward in their argument the more sophisticated, but equally futile, contention that punishment deters from crime. In this concept of *deterrence* there is a childlike faith in punishment. . . .

With the development of the biological sciences and the growth of new philosophies regarding life and social responsibility, other concepts of crime and criminals developed. These concepts sharply challenged the doctrine of free will, notably a shift from theories of revenge, retribution, expiation, and deterrence, to the goal of the reformation of the offender and protection of society. The emphasis became focused on the individual who committed the crime rather than on the crime itself.

It is plain that, however futile it may be, social revenge is the only honest, straightforward, and logical justification for punishing criminals. The claim for deterrence is belied by both history and logic. History shows that severe punishments have never reduced criminality to any marked degree. It is obvious to anyone familiar with the activities of criminals that the argument for deterrence cannot be logically squared with the doctrine of the free moral agent, upon which the whole notion of punishment is based. If a man is free to decide as to his conduct, and is not affected by his experiences, he cannot be deterred from crime by the administration of any punishment, however severe.

f. THE UNDETERRABLE **

[T]he belief in the value of deterrence rests on the assumption that we are rational beings who always think before we act, and then base our actions on a careful calculation of the gains and losses involved.

* Harry Elmer Barnes and Negley K. Teeters, NEW HORIZONS IN CRIMINOLOGY, 2nd ed., © 1951, pp. 337–338. Reprinted by permission of Prentice-Hall. Inc., Englewood Cliffs, N.J.

** Gerald Gardiner, "The Purpose of Criminal Punishment," *Modern Law Review* 21, 1958, pp. 122–125. Copyright 1958 (Reprinted with permission).

These assumptions, dear to many lawyers, have long since been abandoned in the social sciences. No economist would seriously maintain them today, and even to the uninformed the movements of shares on the stock exchange—where one might expect to see Bentham's principle of "enlightened self-interest" vindicated most clearly—demonstrate that men's actions are governed quite as much by fear or greed as by reason; and that the ability to ignore hard facts, and to see only what you want to see, is shared by a surprisingly large and influential section of the community.

Amongst criminals, foresight and prudent calculation is even more conspicuous by its absence. John Gittens, a very experienced Headmaster of an Approved School, and also of a special Classifying School (which allows him to see a very wide range of young delinquents between the ages of eight and seventeen), has some pertinent remarks to make on the subject. In his "Approved School Boys"—a Government publication issued by the Stationery Office—he underlines the boys'

> "inability to foresee the consequences of their actions. Most of the troubles that the boys get into are just like running one's head against a brick wall. In boys of a very low intelligence, this is sometimes the result of a genuine inability to look ahead and it may reach dramatic proportions—as with the boy *who pushed his hand through a pane of glass* to punch another boy."

Even though there is no consensus amongst doctors about the exact description of the so-called "psychopaths," experienced Prison Medical Officers, and for that matter, Prison Governors, are agreed that there is a type of prisoner who is quite incapable of foresight, who cannot learn even from the experience of punishment, much less from the threat of it. Yet other offenders, notably some sex-offenders (but also others subject to compulsive behaviour) are sometimes at the mercy of their impulses, and unable, without proper help and treatment, to control themselves adequately. Such persons are frequently in conflict, not only with society, but also with themselves. . . .

g. THE SEAMY SIDE OF DETERRENCE *

Let us now see what are the objections to the Deterrent or Terrorist system.

It necessarily leaves the interests of the victim wholly out of account. It injures and degrades him; destroys the reputation without which he cannot get employment; and when the punishment is imprisonment under our system, atrophies his powers of fending for himself in the world. Now this would not materially hurt anyone but himself if, when he had been duly made an example of, he were killed like a vivisected dog. But he is not killed. He is, at the expiration of his

* Used by permission of the Philosophical Library, Inc., from *The Crime of Imprisonment* by George Bernard Shaw (Copyright 1946 by Philosophical Library, Inc., New York), pp. 32–34.

sentence, flung out of the prison into the streets to earn his living in a labor market where nobody will employ an ex-prisoner, betraying himself at every turn by his ignorance of the common news of the months or years he has passed without newspapers, lamed in speech, and terrified at the unaccustomed task of providing food and lodging for himself. There is only one lucrative occupation available for him; and that is crime. He has no compunction as to Society: why should he have any? Society having for its own selfish protection done its worst to him, he has no feeling about it except a desire to get a bit of his own back. He seeks the only company in which he is welcome: the society of criminals; and sooner or later, according to his luck, he finds himself in prison again. The figures of recidivism show that the exceptions to this routine are so few as to be negligible for the purposes of our argument. The criminal, far from being deterred from crime, is forced into it; and the citizen whom his punishment was meant to protect suffers from his depredations.

It is, in fact, admitted that the deterrent system does not deter the convicted criminal. Its real efficacy is sought in its deterrent effect on the free citizens who would commit crimes but for their fear of punishment. The Terrorist can point to the wide range of evil-doing which, not being punished by law, is rampant among us; for though a man can get himself hanged for a momentary lapse of self-control under intolerable provocation by a nagging woman, or into prison for putting the precepts of Christ above the orders of a Competent Military Authority, he can be a quite infernal scoundrel without breaking any penal law.

h. DETERRENCE CAUSES PAIN *

. . . [I]f the offender's suffering is not taken into account as a cost, the usual result of comparing the cost of extra offender suffering and alternative crime reduction methods will be to opt for the extra suffering. The situation is reminiscent of the stranger who had just been advised that the best method of increasing his horse's efficiency was to violently castrate the animal with two bricks. When the stranger asked, "Doesn't that hurt?," his mentor responded, "Not if you don't get your thumbs in the way."

i. NOTE ON DETERRENCE

We have a sizable and rapidly growing literature based on econometric studies which purport to show the effectiveness of deterrence. These studies use gross data on criminality and arrest and imprisonment rates in various jurisdictions and, through the use of sophisticated mathematical and statistical techniques, attempt to deter-

* Franklin E. Zimring, Perspectives on Deterrence, Public Health Service Publication, No. 2056 (Chevy Chase Maryland National Institute for Mental Health, January, 1971), pp. 24–25. Copyright 1971 (Reprinted with permission).

mine whether increasing likelihood of arrest and punishment actually work to reduce crime.

Such studies are questionable on methodological grounds since the data as to crimes perpetrated are quite unreliable. And the problem of untangling cause from effect is a difficult one. The correlation between lower arrest rates and higher crime may simply mean that as the crime rate goes up, the percentage of crimes solved by arrest decreases simply because the police and other organs of the criminal justice system become overloaded.

Despite these problems, the unanimity of such studies in finding a deterrent effect in the likelihood of arrest are impressive. (The results on the issue of increased punishment are less clear, however.)

Deterrence works, in its classic form, where the potential criminal, in deciding whether to commit a criminal act, weighs the likelihood that he might be caught and subjected to criminal punishment and is, therefore, dissuaded from committing the crime. It is likely that such a simple mechanism works in cases such as overtime parking and tax evasion.

Deterrence, however, can take far more complex and indirect forms. One might think that drunken drivers, who risk their own death or serious injury and who, additionally, are befuddled by drink, would be very unlikely to be deterred by the criminal law. Nonetheless, as the excerpt on pp. 55–56 indicates, this does not appear to be the case. Moreover, in Scandinavia, where drunken driving is rigorously prosecuted and uniformly punished by jail terms, the law does seem to work to deter drunken driving. It is very common in Scandinavia for a husband and wife about to attend a cocktail party to decide that one of them will not drink so as to be able to drive the other— presumably quite intoxicated—home.

A similar indirect mechanism may also act to reduce husband-wife homicides. These killings are classically the result of increasing domestic friction over a period of years, until one spouse reaches his or her breaking point. Though we cannot be sure, it is unlikely that the deterrent effect of the criminal law exerts an influence at the very moment of the fatal assault. Nonetheless, one spouse will occasionally leave another to avoid the likelihood that their continued living together would, sooner or later, end in homicide.

Other, even more indirect, aspects of deterrence can be important. Often, young delinquents, who are not deterred noticeably from crimes committed in the company of their fellows, gradually notice that a higher and higher percentage of their fellows have gotten into legal trouble and ended up in prison. Some, at this point, conclude that running around with that gang sooner or later is going to get them into the same kind of trouble, and reduce the associations which were leading them into delinquency.

Deterrence also works when the criminal law provides an excuse or rationalization for not committing a crime: a member of a juvenile gang may sometimes be able to use his fear of criminal punishment as a reason he can give both his friends and himself for not engaging in criminal conduct. This might be especially important if his real moral grounds would be even less acceptable to the group culture.

The ways in which deterrence may work are considerably more varied than these examples indicate. There are, however, a great many things about deterrence that we do not know. For instance, we cannot measure its overall effectiveness in the real world, and we are even less able to assign any share of the total effect to any particular mechanism. Most practically, we do not know with any degree of precision how to weigh the variables which determine, in any particular case, whether deterrence will be effective. These include the personality of the individual to be deterred, his knowledge of the law, the situation he finds himself in, the rewards of the crime contemplated, the perceived likelihood of being caught and punished and the severity of the punishment.

It should be noted that the issue of whether, and to what extent, criminal punishment deters the commission of crime does not automatically determine the deterrent effects of different punishments. Thus, the battle over capital punishment is waged in great part over whether the threat of the death penalty deters murder better than does the threat of life imprisonment. Merely believing that the criminal law has a deterrent function does not obligate one to believe that the deterrence can be endlessly increased by increasing the penalties.

Indeed, it is arguable that, after a certain point, increases in the penalties provided for those convicted of crimes do not significantly—or even at all—increase the deterrent effect of the law. At this point, even a firm believer in deterrence might weigh the additional costs of increased penalties. Thus, in addition to asking whether capital punishment deters more than life imprisonment, he might then ask which punishment was more expensive to implement (at least under today's conditions, capital punishment seems to be) and whether it makes sense to teach reverence for human life by executing those who have taken it.

Similarly, where capital punishment is not in issue, even one convinced of the deterrent value of the criminal law might be opposed to increasing criminal penalties for two other reasons. First, incarceration is expensive, and second, he may believe that in all those cases where the convict is eventually released into society, the longer the term of imprisonment, the less likely will be his future assimilation into a non-criminal lifestyle.

2. INCAPACITATION

a. RESTRAINT *

Most serious crime is committed by repeaters. What we do with first offenders is probably far less important than what we do with habitual offenders. . . .

After tracing the history of nearly ten thousand Philadelphia boys born in 1945, Marvin Wolfgang and his colleagues at the University of Pennsylvania found that over one-third were picked up by the police for something more serious than a traffic offense, but that 46 per cent of these delinquents had no further police contact after their first offense. Though a third started on crime, nearly half [of these] seemed to stop spontaneously— . . .   Out of the ten thousand boys, however, there were six hundred twenty-seven—only 6 per cent—who committed five or more offenses before they were eighteen. Yet these few chronic offenders accounted for *over half* of all the recorded delinquencies and about *two-thirds* of all the violent crimes committed by the entire cohort.

Only a tiny fraction of all serious crimes lead immediately to an arrest, and only a slightly larger fraction are ultimately "cleared" by an arrest, but this does not mean that the police function is meaningless. Because most serious crime is committed by repeaters, most criminals eventually get arrested. The Wolfgang findings and other studies suggest that the chances of a persistent burglar or robber living out his life, or even going a year, with no arrest are quite small. Yet a large proportion of repeat offenders suffer little or no loss of freedom. Whether or not one believes that such penalties, if inflicted, would act as a deterrent, it is obvious that they could serve to incapacitate these offenders and thus, for the period of the incapacitation, prevent them from committing additional crimes. . . .

Shlomo and Reuel Shinnar have estimated the effect on crime rates in New York State of a judicial policy other than that followed during the last decade or so. Given the present level of police efficiency and making some assumptions about how many crimes each offender commits per year, they conclude that the rate of serious crime would be only *one-third* what it is today if every person convicted of a serious offense were imprisoned for three years. This reduction would be less if it turned out (as seems unlikely) that most serious crime is committed by first-time offenders, and it would be much greater if the proportion of crimes resulting in an arrest and conviction were increased (as also seems unlikely). The reduction, it should be noted, would be solely the result of incapacitation, making no allowance for such additional reductions as might result from enhanced deterrence or rehabilitation.

* James Q. Wilson, *Thinking About Crime* (New York: Basic Books, 1975) pp. 199–201. Excerpted from chapter 10, "Some Concluding Thoughts" © 1975 Basic Books, Inc. Publishers, New York. Reprinted with permission.

b. NOTE ON THE PROBLEM OF PREDICTION

Incapacitation is a mode of punishment that uses the fact that a person has committed a crime of a particular sort as the basis for assessing his personality and then predicting that he will commit further crimes of that sort. It is an empirical question in every case whether the prediction is a valid one. To the extent that the prediction is valid, utilitarian ethics can approve the use of punishment for incapacitative purposes, on the view that the pain inflicted on persons who are punished is less than the pain that would be inflicted on their putative victims and on society at large if those same persons were left free to commit further offenses.

c. A STUDY *

What would happen to the crime rate if we followed the hard-line "lock 'em up" strategy?

Theorists such as James Q. Wilson have based much of their punishment-oriented philosophies on the principle of *incapacitation*.

By incapacitation, the hard-liners mean the mandatory imprisonment of career and repetitively violent offenders for lengthy periods. Assuming that most violent crimes are committed by a relatively small group of "career criminals", taking such persons out of circulation for long periods ought to reduce crime rates.

[Stephen] Van Dine used official data on all adults indicted for violent crimes in Franklin County (Columbus), Ohio in 1973 to test various sentencing options. He asked how many of the 1973 offenses would have been prevented had the offenders still been incarcerated for their last previous offenses.

Under the most stringent sentencing policy—a five year net mandatory prison term for any felony, violent or not—the result was that at most 4% of the 1973 violent felonies would have been prevented.

The next most stringent sentencing policy—a five year net mandatory prison term for a *second* or following felony, violent or not— would have produced a maximum violent crime reduction of 1.5%.

These results generally coincide with the low estimates of [some] analysts but they are in stark contrast to the 80% crime reduction figure computed by [others].

Van Dine avers: "The implication of this analysis is clear. . . . Incapacitation is a much less effective tool in the reduction of crime than some believe."

* Criminal Justice Newsletter (*National Council on Crime and Delinquency*) Dec. 6,   1976, p. 3. © 1976 (Reprinted with permission of the publisher).

Among the reasons suggested for this rather small impact are:

(1) the study excluded juveniles (except those sentenced as adults);

(2) the pool of violent recidivists who would have been immobilized through incapacitation is comparatively small; only 31% of the [indicted] population—more than two thirds of the violent offenders studied were first-time felony offenders;

(3) the rate of repetition for the recidivist group was too infrequent to be blocked by even five-year prison terms because the average interval between violent crimes was 5.6 years.

Question

Is it correct that by imprisoning criminals we lessen their opportunities for further crime? Or do we merely make it more likely that the crimes of convicts will be directed against each other?

d. NOTE ON INCAPACITATION

It has been asserted—mostly for dramatic effect—that the crime rate would not rise perceptibly if all those presently imprisoned were released at once. The theory of this is that the great majority of potential criminals at any one time are not in prison and, therefore, that the release even of those who might repeat their transgressions would hardly be noticed in the total criminal picture. If this statement is correct, does it shed any light on the actual importance of incapacitation in the criminal system? Second, is it possible that the statement is correct simply because a great many of those who would be most likely to commit serious crimes are handled by society in other ways, such as in mental institutions (from which the statement does not contemplate their release)? Third, it should be noted that the statement presumably contemplates that the deterrent effect of the law would not be compromised and that criminals convicted in the future would be imprisoned. Also, it is, of course, possible that the statement is simply not true.

3. REHABILITATION

a. CHANGE IN THE OFFENDER *

The most immediately appealing justification for punishment is the claim that it may be used to prevent crime by so changing the personality of the offender that he will conform to the dictates of law; in a word, by reforming him . . . .

[W]hat we do to the offender in the name of reform is being done to him by compulsion and for *our* sake, not for his. Rehabilitation may be the most humane goal of punishment, but it is a goal of *punishment* so

---

* Herbert Packer, *The Limits of the Criminal Sanction*, Stanford, Stanford University Press, p. 50, Copyright 1968. (Reprinted with permission).

long as its invocation depends upon finding that an offense has been committed, and so long as its object is to prevent the commission of offenses. . . .

If rehabilitation is the goal, the nature of the offense is relevant only for what it tells us about what is needed to rehabilitate the offender. . . . The rehabilitative ideal teaches us that we must treat each offender as an individual whose special needs and problems must be known as fully as possible in order to enable us to deal effectively with him. Punishment, in this view, must be forward-looking. The gravity of the offense, however measured, may give us a clue to the intensity and duration of the measures needed to rehabilitate; but it is only a clue, not a prescription. There is, then, no generally postulated equivalence between the offense and the punishment, as there would be in the case of the retributive or even the deterrent theory of punishment.

It follows from this offender-oriented aspect of the rehabilitative ideal that the intensity and duration of punishment are to be measured by what is thought to be required in order to change the offender's personality. Unlike the related goal of incapacitation, the inquiry is not into how dangerous the offender is but rather into how amenable to treatment he is. If a writer of bad checks can be cured of his underlying disorder only by five years of intensive psychotherapy, then that is what he is to receive. And, of course, no one knows at the outset how much of what kind of therapy will be needed in his or anyone else's case, so it cannot be said in advance what the duration of his punishment will be. It ends whenever those in authority decide that he has been rehabilitated. Of course, if he does not yield to treatment and is thought to present a danger, he will not be released.

[There is a] major objection to making rehabilitation the primary justification for punishment [which] probably comes very close to settling the matter for present purposes. It is, very simply, that we do not know how to rehabilitate offenders, at least within the limit of the resources that are now or might reasonably be expected to be devoted to the task. The more we learn about the roots of crime, the clearer it is that they are nonspecific, that the social and psychic springs lie deep within the human condition. To create on a large scale the essentials of a society that produced no crime would be to remake society itself.
. . .

b. DEBASEMENT OF THE REHABILITATIVE IDEAL *

Now permit me to turn to another sort of difficulty that has accompanied the rise of the rehabilitative ideal in the areas of corrections and criminal justice. It is a familiar observation that an idea once propagated and introduced into the active affairs of life undergoes

* Francis A. Allen, "Criminal Justice, Legal Values and the Rehabilitative Ideal," *Journal of Criminal Law, Criminology and* *Police Science,* 50 (1950), pp. 226–232. Copyright 1950 (Reprinted with permission).

change. The real significance of an idea as it evolves in actual practice may be quite different from that intended by those who conceived it and gave it initial support. An idea tends to lead a life of its own; and modern history is full of the unintended consequences of seminal ideas. The application of the rehabilitative ideal to the institutions of criminal justice presents a striking example of such a development. My second proposition, then, is that the rehabilitative ideal has been debased in practice and that the consequences resulting from this debasement are serious and, at times, dangerous.

This proposition may be supported, first, by the observation that, under the dominance of the rehabilitative ideal, the language of therapy is frequently employed, wittingly or unwittingly, to disguise the true state of affairs that prevails in our custodial institutions and at other points in the correctional process. Certain measures, like the sexual psychopath laws, have been advanced and supported as therapeutic in nature when, in fact, such a characterization seems highly dubious. Too often the vocabulary of therapy has been exploited to serve a public-relations function. Recently, I visited an institution devoted to the diagnosis and treatment of disturbed children. The institution had been established with high hopes and, for once, with the enthusiastic support of the state legislature. Nevertheless, fifty minutes of an hour's lecture, delivered by a supervising psychiatrist before we toured the building, were devoted to custodial problems. This fixation on problems of custody was reflected in the institutional arrangements which included, under a properly euphemistic label, a cell for solitary confinement. Even more disturbing was the tendency of the staff to justify these custodial measures in therapeutic terms. Perhaps on occasion the requirements of institutional security and treatment coincide. But the inducements to self-deception in such situations are strong and all too apparent. In short, the language of therapy has frequently provided a formidable obstacle to a realistic analysis of the conditions that confront us. And realism in considering these problems is the one quality that we require above all others.

There is a second sort of unintended consequence that has resulted from the application of the rehabilitative ideal to the practical administration of criminal justice. Surprisingly enough, the rehabilitative ideal has often led to increased severity of penal measures. This tendency may be seen in the operation of the juvenile court. Although frequently condemned by the popular press as a device of leniency, the juvenile court, is authorized to intervene punitively in many situations in which the conduct, were it committed by an adult, would be wholly ignored by the law or would subject the adult to the mildest of sanctions. The tendency of proposals for wholly indeterminate sentences, a clearly indentifiable fruit of the rehabilitative ideal, is unmistakably in the direction of lengthened periods of imprisonment. A large variety of statutes authorizing what is called "civil" commitment of persons, but which, except for the reduced protections afforded the parties proceeded against, are essentially criminal in nature, provide for absolutely indeterminate periods of confinement. Experience has demonstrated that, in practice, there is a strong tendency for the rehabilitative ideal to serve purposes that are essentially incapacitative rather than therapeutic in character.

4. OTHER UTILITARIAN JUSTIFICATIONS FOR THE CRIMINAL LAW

Although punishment through the criminal law is generally defended in terms of deterrence, incapacitation and rehabilitation, a number of other utilitarian justifications for criminal punishment are also heard.

a. NOTE ON AVOIDANCE OF BLOOD FEUDS

Historically, there is some evidence that the criminal law began as a method of removing the taking of revenge from private hands. It was felt that, unless the law found and punished a murderer, the family of his victim would kill whomever they believed to be the murderer— prompting the late suspect's family to take their revenge, and so on. Viewed this way, criminal punishment is an effort to socialize the deeply felt impulse for revenge (whether it is right or wrong to feel such an impulse) and to limit the damage it can do in society. According to the classic analogy of Sir James Stephen, one of the great Victorian authorities on the criminal law, the criminal law bears the same relation to the urge for revenge as marriage does to the sexual urge.

It is hard to imagine that for most crimes short of murder and perhaps sex crimes this is a serious justification today. Moreover, this justification has historically been used to perpetrate many serious kinds of injustice. Thus, the Spanish inquisition was justified in part as a device to provide orderly procedures for the determination of heresy, lest the mob violence of the righteous be illegally inflicted upon those under suspicion.

On the other hand, this type of reasoning cannot be completely ignored today. The growth of vigilante movements at various times in our history should remind us that if the criminal law fails to perform what are felt to be its functions, other groups will try, often illegally, to do the job themselves. And in the extreme case, a government that cannot enforce its criminal law may be replaced by one which can.

b. NOTE ON THE EDUCATIONAL EFFECT

The criminal law may have an important and valuable educational effect entirely apart from deterrence. In many borderline areas—and some that many of us would not consider borderline at all—there are those who doubt the moral wrongfulness of certain types of criminal conduct. Thus, a significant number of young people feel it is all right to engage in shoplifting and other petty thefts so long as the victim is a large corporation. It is possible that our schools could make them understand that, as a practical matter, the loss due to such thefts will usually be merely reflected in the price charged to the individual customers—whom the thief presumably did not wish to injure. Where the schools have failed, however, one suitable way of emphasizing the wrongfulness of this conduct is to administer criminal punishment to those caught engaging in it. This not only may cause public debate, but also can bring home to people the seriousness with which society takes such behavior.

It should be noted, with respect to serious crimes such as murder and rape, that this educational benefit is not really necessary for the great majority of the population. It can, of course, be argued that one of the reasons why this is so is because we do, in fact, prosecute and punish those guilty of such offenses. In any event, our experience with marijuana is some proof that the mere declaration of wrongfulness by the law, even accompanied by widespread prosecution and punishment, may not be enough to educate the population that the conduct prohibited is wrongful unless certain underlying conditions are met.

c. NOTE ON THE PEACE–KEEPING FUNCTION

Another reason for the criminal law, distinct from all previous ones, is unrelated even to trial and criminal punishment. As we will see in Chapter IV, our society requires the police to handle a large number of troublesome situations. In many of these, a simple arrest, with no real thought of prosecution, will handle the matter. This may explain in part the laws against attempting suicide, which might otherwise seem to fit into none of the other purposes of the criminal law. In this case, the criminal law gives the police a right to intervene in any suicide attempts, arresting the attemptor so that he may be subjected to psychiatric treatment.

This type of reason for the criminal law, is a controversial one, since it envisions police action separate from that of the courts. Nonetheless, it is probably the major justification for the much debated vagrancy laws and for the types of police action taken when political demonstrations threaten to get out of hand.

Often, indeed, arrest is not necessary in these situations since the threat of an arrest will prove sufficient. Thus, when a householder telephones the police to complain that a drunk is asleep on his steps, the police may simply wake the drunk and, using the threat of an arrest, convince him to move on.

5. RETRIBUTION

a. AS A JUSTIFICATION FOR PUNISHMENT

(1) LEVITICUS 24:17–22 *

When one man strikes another and kills him, he shall be put to death. Whoever strikes a beast and kills it shall make restitution, life for life. When one man injures and disfigures his fellow-countryman, it shall be done to him as he has done; fracture for fracture, eye for eye, tooth for tooth; the injury and disfigurement that he has inflicted upon another shall in turn be inflicted upon him.

(2) THE RETRIBUTIVE VIEW **

The retributive view rests on the idea that it is right for the wicked to be punished: because man is responsible for his actions, he ought to receive his just desserts. The view can take either of two main versions: the revenge theory or the expiation theory. Revenge as a justification for punishment is deeply ingrained in human experience, and goes back at least as far as the *lex talionis:* an eye for an eye, a tooth for a tooth, and, we might add, a life for a life. Its marks on the criminal process are similarly deep, the most conspicuous example today being the death penalty for murder. . . .

The other principal version of the retributive view is that only through suffering punishment can the criminal expiate his sin. Atonement through suffering has been a major theme in religious thought through the ages, and it doubtless plays a role in thought about secular punishment as well. In this view the emphasis is shifted from our demands on the criminal and becomes a question of demands that the criminal does or should make on himself to reconcile himself to the social order. In the absence of assurance that his sense of guilt is equal to the demands made upon it, we help to reinforce it by providing an external expression of guilt.

It hardly matters which aspect of the theory is espoused. The result is the same. The criminal is to be punished simply because he has committed a crime. It makes little difference whether we do this because we think we owe it to him or because we think he owes it to us. Each theory rests on a figure of speech. Revenge means that the criminal is paid back; expiation means that he pays back. The revenge theory treats all crimes as if they were certain crimes of physical violence: you hurt X; we will hurt you. The expiration theory treats all crimes as if they were financial transactions: you got something from X; you must give equivalent value.

---

* The New English Bible.

** Herbert Packer, *The Limits of the Criminal Sanction* (Stanford: Stanford University Press, 1968) pp. 37–38. ©1968. Reprinted with permission of the publisher.

(3) Retribution is Revenge *

The desire to hurt the thing that hurt you is as old as mankind itself and can be shown to have existed throughout the history of punishment. It applies to animals and inanimate objects as well as to human beings. It is what makes us kick the table-leg on which we stub our toe. Seagle, in his *History of Law,* tells of the old Hebrew rule of stoning an ox to death if it killed a man. In ancient Athens, an axe which had injured a man could be tried, and if found guilty, punished by being hurled over the city boundary. According to Herodotus, Xerxes whipped the Hellespont with 300 lashes because a storm wrecked his bridge. Calvert quotes a case in 1386, at Falaise, where a sow was "sentenced to be mangled in the head and forelegs and then hanged for having torn the face and arms of a child, and thus caused its death." And in 1685, the church bell of La Rochelle was whipped and buried in the earth for having assisted heretics.

(4) Vengeance Disguised **

There remains to be mentioned the affirmative argument in favor of the theory of retribution, to the effect that the fitness of punishment following wrong-doing is axiomatic, and is instinctively recognized by unperverted minds. I think that it will be seen, on self-inspection, that this feeling of fitness is absolute and unconditional only in the case of our neighbors. It does not seem to me that any one who has satisfied himself that an act of his was wrong, and that he will never do it again, would feel the least need or propriety, as between himself and an earthly punishing power alone, of his being made to suffer for what he had done, although, when third persons were introduced, he might, as a philosopher, admit the necessity of hurting him to frighten others. But when our neighbors do wrong, we sometimes feel the fitness of making them smart for it, whether they have repented or not. The feeling of fitness seems to me to be only vengeance in disguise. . . .

(5) Note on Retribution

Probably the most serious problem with retribution as a justification for punishment in our criminal system is that the idea works well wholesale, but not at retail. In other words, from a distance, when one knows very little about the criminal and knows only the details of what he has done, retribution may—and usually does—seem very appropriate. The closer one comes to the case and to the criminal, the less appropriate retribution appears. The more we learn of the background of the criminal and the forces which shaped him, the more dangerous we may feel him to be, but the less we may desire to spend resources

* Gerald Gardiner, "The Purposes of Criminal Punishment," *Modern Law Review,* 21 (1958), p. 119. Copyright 1958 (Reprinted with permission).

** Oliver W. Holmes, *The Common Law,* M. Howe, ed. (Cambridge: Belknap Press of Harvard University Press, 1963), p. 39.

simply to make him suffer because he has committed a crime. Even if one does not go so far as the French proverb—"to know all is to forgive all"—one may nonetheless believe that retribution itself is not a sufficient justification for our criminal system.

We will shortly examine several other justifications for the criminal law which seem to have a more utilitarian rationale, before doing this however, we must remind ourselves about a facet of retribution which we have already considered, in different terms, in Chapter I.

b. RETRIBUTION AS A LIMITING PRINCIPLE

As we have seen in Chapter I, a basic requirement of criminal conduct is that the accused must be blameworthy in violating the criminal law. In a sense he must be worthy of retribution. Thus, even if one decided that retribution was not a reason to punish someone through the criminal law, it might still be felt that retribution is a necessary condition—a limiting principal—for punishment. In simple terms, then, if someone is not blameworthy, he does not deserve retribution and should not be punished. Our rules on state of mind help accomplish this end, but there are other consequences of this principle, as well.

(1) The Importance of Culpability *

The view I take of the role of culpability in the justification for punishment is an instrumental one. I see this limitation on the utilitarian position as desirable not for any inherent quality that it possesses but because it serves ends that I think require attention in a criminal system. It does so in several different ways. First, it establishes a firm basis for resisting the attenuation of the offense as a component in the definition of punishment. Without an offense—a more or less specifically defined species of conduct—there can be no basis for imputing blame. A man may be a danger to others, or in need of help, or any other equivalent in the current cant that denotes an inconvenient human being whom we would like to get out of the way; but unless he has committed an offense, unless he has done something rather than merely been something, we cannot say that he has been culpable. And, it follows from the view taken of culpability as a necessary condition, that he cannot be found guilty through the criminal process and subjected to criminal punishment. A strictly preventive view would rightly see this limitation to offenses actually committed as nonsense. If we have solid grounds for thinking that a person is disposed to the commission of offenses, why wait until he has done so to punish (i.e., rehabilitate and/or restrain) him? The instrumental use of culpability through the ascription of legal guilt prevents this dissolution of the nexus between offense and punishment. Of course, the important practical question is not whether the nexus is to be dissolved,

* Herbert Packer, *The Limits of the Criminal Sanction*, Stanford, Stanford University Press, 1968, pp. 67–69. Copyright 1968 (Reprinted with permission).

but rather how far and in what ways it may be relaxed. It is enough now to note that there are solid arguments for keeping the offense in sharp focus, and the culpability restriction is a good means of doing this.

Another aspect of this instrumental case for culpability is that there is a rough correspondence between the dictates of the culpability limitation and aspects of the desirable operation of the criminal sanction. People ought in general to be able to plan their conduct with some assurance that they can avoid entanglement with the criminal law; by the same token the enforcers and appliers of the law should not waste their time lurking in the bushes ready to trap the offender who is unaware that he is offending. It is precisely the fact that in its normal and characteristic operation the criminal law provides this opportunity and this protection to people in their everyday lives that makes it a tolerable institution in a free society. Take this away, and the criminal law ceases to be a guide to the well-intentioned and a restriction on the restraining power of the state. Take it away is precisely what you do, however, when you abandon culpability as the basis for imposing punishment. While it may often serve the state's purposes not to interfere with its citizens unless they have acted with foresight, on many occasions their foresight or lack of it may seem immaterial. If we leave to a purely utilitarian calculus the decision whether a man's innocence or ignorance shall count for him, the answer on any given occasion will be uncertain. Only by providing the shield of a culpability requirement can this desirable aspect of the criminal law be preserved.

Comment

Even if the state decided that deterrence, incapacitation, rehabilitation or any one of a number of other reasons would justify intervention by the state in an individual's life, the limiting principle requiring that retribution be appropriate would protect the individual, unless his conduct in a sense was blameworthy. This can be seen as a protection to the individual against the power of the state and a guarantee of security from punishment, including rehabilitation, for those who are not morally culpable.

(2) DEUTERONOMY 24:16 *

Fathers shall not be put to death for their children, nor children for their fathers; a man shall be put to death only for his own sin.

Comment

Certainly, we would increase deterrence by punishing a son for the sins of his father. Indeed, Soviet law until relatively recently provided serious punishment for the family of a Soviet citizen who unlawfully defected. In the United States, parents are sometimes civilly liable to

---

* The New English Bible.

pay for damage done by their children up to a given amount—often $300. Is it possible that in both these cases the point is not so much to deter the wrongdoer by threatening to punish his loved ones, but rather to make those close to an individual exercise proper supervision? If that is the case, it is an absolute liability offense in those cases where they exercise the best supervision they can be expected to exercise, but the forbidden event nonetheless occurs.

(3) SOME EREWHONIAN TRIALS **

In Erewhon as in other countries there are some courts of justice that deal with special subjects. Misfortune generally, as I have above explained, is considered more or less criminal, but it admits of classification, and a court is assigned to each of the main heads under which it can be supposed to fall. Not very long after I had reached the capital I strolled into the Personal Bereavement Court. . . .

[One] case was that of a youth barely arrived at man's estate, who was charged with having been swindled out of large property during his minority by his guardian, who was also one of his nearest relations. His father had been long dead, and it was for this reason that his offense came on for trial in the Personal Bereavement Court. The lad, who was undefended, pleaded that he was young, inexperienced, greatly in awe of his guardian, and without independent professional advice. "Young man," said the judge sternly, "do not talk nonsense. People have no right to be young, inexperienced, greatly in awe of their guardians, and without independent professional advice. If by such indiscretions they outrage the moral sense of their friends, they must expect to suffer accordingly." He then ordered the prisoner to apologize to his guardian, and to receive twelve strokes with a cat-of-nine-tails.

But I shall perhaps best convey to the reader an idea of the entire perversion of thought which exists among this extraordinary people, by describing the public trial of a man who was accused of pulmonary consumption—an offense which was punished with death until quite recently. He pleaded not guilty, and the case proceeded. The evidence for the prosecution was very strong; but I must do the court the justice to observe that the trial was absolutely impartial. Counsel for the prisoner was allowed to urge everything that could be said in his defense: the line taken was that the prisoner was simulating consumption in order to defraud an insurance company, from which he was about to buy an annuity, and that he hoped thus to obtain it on more advantageous terms. If this could have been shown to be the case he would have escaped a criminal prosecution, and been sent to a hospital as for a moral ailment. The view, however, was one which could not be reasonably sustained, in spite of all the ingenuity and eloquence of one of the most celebrated advocates of the country.

** Samuel Butler, *Erewhon* (Modern Library, New York).

The summing up of the judge was admirable. He dwelt upon every point that could be construed in favor of the prisoner, but as he proceeded it became clear that the evidence was too convincing to admit of doubt, and there was but one opinion in the court as to the impending verdict when the jury retired from the box. They were absent for about ten minutes, and on their return the foreman pronounced the prisoner guilty. There was a faint murmur of applause, but it was instantly repressed. The judge then proceeded to pronounce sentence in words which I can never forget, and which I copied out into a note-book the next day from the report that was published in the leading newspaper. I must condense it somewhat, and nothing which I could say would give more than a faint idea of the solemn, not to say majestic, severity with which it was delivered. [Upon conviction] the sentence was as follows:—

This is not your first offense: you were convicted of aggravated bronchitis last year: and I find that though you are now only twenty-three years old, you have been imprisoned on no less than fourteen occasions for illnesses of a more or less hateful character; in fact, it is not too much to say that you have spent the greater part of your life in a jail.

It is all very well for you to say that you came of unhealthy parents, and had a severe accident in your childhood which permanently undermined your constitution; excuses such as these are the ordinary refuge of the criminal; but they cannot for one moment be listened to by the ear of justice. Your presence in the society of respectable people would lead the less able-bodied to think more lightly of all forms of illness; you may say that it is not your fault. The answer is ready enough at hand, and it amounts to this—that if you had been born of healthy and well-to-do parents, and been well taken care of when you were a child, you would never have offended against the laws of your country, nor found yourself in your present disgraceful position. If you tell me that you had no hand in your parentage and education, and that it is therefore unjust to lay these things to your charge, I answer that whether your being in a consumption is your fault or no, it is a fault in you, and it is my duty to see that against such faults as this the commonwealth shall be protected. You may say that it is your misfortune to be criminal; I answer that it is your crime to be unfortunate.

Lastly, I should point out that even though the jury had acquitted you—a supposition that I cannot seriously entertain—I should have felt it my duty to inflict a sentence hardly less severe than that which I must pass at present; for the more you had been found guiltless of the crime imputed to you, the more you would have been found guilty of one hardly less heinous—I mean the crime of having been maligned unjustly.

I do not hesitate therefore to sentence you to imprisonment, with hard labor, for the rest of your miserable existence.

(4) PROPORTIONALITY **

"What sort of conduct may justifiably be punished?" and "How severely should we punish different offenses?" are distinct and independent questions. There are many reasons why we might wish the legal gradation of the seriousness of crimes, expressed in its scale of punishment, not to conflict with common estimates of their comparative wickedness. One reason is that such a conflict is undesirable on simple utilitarian grounds: it might either confuse moral judgments or bring the law into disrepute, or both. Another reason is that principles of justice or fairness between different offenders require morally distinguishable offenses to be treated differently and morally similar offenses to be treated alike—that we should attempt to adjust the severity of punishment to the moral gravity of offenses.

Questions

How would you feel about life imprisonment for overtime parking? It would probably take care of most violations and might even not have to be invoked very often. Would it be wrong?

To what extent does the idea that punishments should be in some way proportionate to the crime follow from the principle that we should not punish those who are morally guiltless? Do you agree with the principle of proportionality? What if deterrence or incapacitation demands more punishment?

6. NOTE ON THE SIGNIFICANCE OF THE REASONS FOR CRIMINAL PUNISHMENT

It is obvious that different reasons generally justify the use of the criminal law against tax evaders, child molesters, heroin pushers, and drunken drivers.

In law, we typically divide criminals according to the crimes they have committed. This is by no means the only such breakdown that could be made. We could classify them in other ways. For instance we could divide criminals into those who do and those who do not commit violent crimes, political crimes, acquisitive crimes, impulsive crimes, "white collar" crimes and all sorts of other kinds of crime. In fact for different purposes each of these latter (non-legal) classifications of crime may be quite helpful. It is, moreover, interesting to try to tell which purposes of criminal punishment apply to which crimes. Can you do this?

The criminal law in the U.S. today treats those who commit white collar crimes far more leniently than those who commit crimes of violence. What is the justification for this? Should the criminal law

** Hart, H.L.A., LAW, LIBERTY AND MORALITY, (Stanford University Press,   Stanford, CA 1963) pp. 36–37. Copyright 1963 (Reprinted with permission).

treat all crimes in the same way? Should it treat all crimes with the same legislatively imposed maximum sentence the same way?

As we have seen, members of the white middle class tend to commit most "white collar" crimes while the poor, the Black, the Spanish American and the Native American are far more likely to be involved in crimes of violence. Should not we worry about building a discrimination into our criminal law which works further to the disadvantage of those who are already most disadvantaged in our society? Do the purposes of the criminal law require this?

Is deterrence through threat of prison more necessary for those who have a steady job which they may lose and savings which could go toward a fine or toward restitution to the victim? Or is deterrence by threat of prison more necessary for one who has no job, no assets, and no "social standing" to lose. In other words is it not true that, in the words of the popular song, "Freedom's just another word for nothing left to lose?"

Does the embezzler, the tax evader or the anti-trust violator, need to be isolated in prison for the protection of the public—or does the armed robber or rapist have a prior claim on our limited prison space?

Who better needs what rehabilitation the criminal law can provide (assuming, for the sake of argument, that the criminal law can provide any) the heroin addict or the fraudulent securities dealer?

Even if your answers are as expected, is it fair? What shall we do about it?

C. DEFENSES TO CRIMINAL CHARGES

Introduction

There are a number of categories of cases where the accused has violated the criminal law with the intent legally sufficient to make his act a crime, but where we do not think he should be punished. He may, on some broader ground, not be blameworthy in his conduct, or else the conduct itself may not be the kind we wish to discourage. As a result, we provide in the law a number of defenses to criminal charges where we feel that the purposes of criminal punishment do not apply. Of course, regardless of whether the defendant feels justified in his conduct, whether to exempt him from criminal punishment is a decision which society must make through its legal institutions.

In this section, we will not consider the area of justification which has received the greatest attention in recent years—civil disobedience. The issues presented by "non-violence" are many and complex, and would take too much space for us to go into here. In this section, however, we will, beginning with self-defense, discuss some of the less complex issues which relate to the nature and scope of a justification defense to criminal charges.

1. SELF DEFENSE

(a) COMMONWEALTH v. SHAFFER

Supreme Judicial Court of Massachusetts, 1975.
367 Mass. 508, 326 N.E.2d 880.

TAURO, Chief Justice.

The defendant . . . was tried and convicted of manslaughter and appealed. . . .

From the evidence, the jury could have found the following: The defendant, who was separated from her husband and in the process of being divorced, resided with her two children in a one-story ranch house. . . . The victim, to whom the defendant was engaged, [also] lived in the house. . . . The defendant had received several severe beatings at the hands of the victim, and on at least one occasion he had threatened to kill her and the children. . . . Although the defendant loved the victim, she feared for herself and the children, and had persuaded him to seek psychiatric help.

On the morning of the homicide, the defendant was having breakfast with the victim when an argument ensued. At one point, the victim rose, saying, "Never mind. I'll take care of you right now." The defendant threw a cup of tea at him and ran downstairs to the basement playroom, where the children were having breakfast and watching television.

Shortly thereafter, the victim opened the door at the top of the basement stairs and said "If you don't come up these stairs, I'll come down and kill you and the kids." She started to telephone the police, but hung up the telephone when the victim said he would leave the house. Instead, he returned to the top of the stairs, at which time the defendant took a .22 caliber rifle from a rack on the wall and loaded it. She again started to telephone the police when the victim started down the stairs. She fired a fatal shot. More than five minutes elapsed from the time the defendant went to the basement until the shooting took place.

The defendant's principal argument for reversal is that the judge erred in his instructions to the jury regarding self-defense. She contends that the judge in effect instructed the jury that she had a duty to retreat from her home and that this was error. A review of the charge in its entirety discloses no error.

The defendant asks us in this case to adopt the majority rule that one assaulted in his own home need not retreat before resorting to the use of deadly force. . . . This has never been the law of the Commonwealth, and we see no reason to adopt it now. We prefer instead to follow our long-established rule that the right to use deadly force by way of self-defense is not available to one threatened until he has availed himself of all reasonable and proper means in the circumstance to avoid combat, . . . and hold that this rule has equal application to one assaulted in his own home.

This rule does not impose an absolute duty to retreat regardless of considerations of personal safety. The proper application of this doctrine does not require an innocent victim to increase his own peril out of regard for the safety of a murderous assailant, . . . because one need only retreat as far as necessary in the circumstances, until there is "no probable means of escape." . . . Our rule gives due recognition to the value of human life, and requires that all available means for escape be exhausted. . . .

To what extent one who is threatened may go in defending himself and whether he has availed himself of all proper means of escape ordinarily are questions of fact for the jury, to be decided in light of all the existing circumstances. . . . The jury must receive complete instructions from the trial judge, including an explanation of the proper factors to be considered in determining the issue of self-defense. The fact that one is threatened in his own home or in a place where he has exclusive right to be is one of the more important factors in making such determination, but this factor is not without limitations in its application.

. . .

In the instant case, the jury could have found that the defendant was not in imminent danger for her life or of serious injury at the hands of the victim. There was no evidence that he had a dangerous weapon at any time. He was only two or three steps from the top of the stairway when he was shot. The defendant had ample opportunity to call the police. She could have left the basement with her children. A period of five minutes had elapsed from the time the defendant first went down to the basement until the shooting occurred. The defendant did not warn the victim that she would shoot if he continued his descent down the stairway. There was evidence from the defendant's husband that she had considerable experience in the use of that rifle. One shot was sufficient to kill the victim.

In these circumstances, there was no error in the judge's instruction to the jury, on the question of reasonableness, that the jury could consider the "means of escape from the basement area." This is clearly a part of the totality of circumstances which must be considered in every case.

. . .

Judgment of Superior Court affirmed.

b. NOTE ON SELF DEFENSE *

.   .   .

What I have in mind as a feminist critique of criminal law includes (among many diverse elements) two particularly central ideas. The first is that the prevailing concept of normality in regard to force and aggression is one-sided ("male-sided"); it has been systematically blind to the pervasive intimidation that colors a woman's experience of the world. That concept of normality reflects and in turn perpetuates the pervasive and profound subordination of women. The second idea is that the prevailing concept of morality is also one-sided in its preoccupation with autonomy and rights and its blindness to the elements of caring and connection that assume relatively great importance in the moral thinking of women. These ideas, despite their undeniably debatable character, deserve to be taken quite seriously. Any useful rethinking of the criminal law must proceed from the premise that a woman's situation, in terms of her conception of morality and normality, may indeed be profoundly different from that of a man.

II. ORGANIZING ASSUMPTIONS OF CRIMINAL LAW

Before entering into the concrete controversies relating to the law of self-defense and rape, I want to remain at a general level just long enough to contrast the central ideas of feminism with several organizing principles of traditional criminal law. These principles need to be made explicit here, because they help locate what makes the feminist critique so hard for mainstream (male) scholars to assimilate.

To comment on these organizing principles, I will have to abstract from a good deal of detail; some qualifications and exceptions will be related to footnotes. In law, general principles are inevitably vulnerable to counterexample. Nonetheless, my claim is that these principles organize and dominate criminal law's doctrinal complexity and that they are so central that we usually just take them for granted (when we notice them at all).

The first principle is that criminal law is *judgmental.* It accuses. In the event of conviction, it does not (immediately, or perhaps ever) forgive. Rather, it condemns, it blames, and it punishes.

These accusatory, judgmental features of criminal law are a bit muted in the legal systems of continental Europe, where criminal law proceeds along the lines of a somewhat more community-oriented, "family," or helping model. (Interestingly, those societies are not noted for being less patriarchal or less misogynist than we are. Evidently, the connections between male domination of culture and social practice on the one hand and the importance of allegedly "male" concepts in legal doctrine on the other is more problematic than some legal feminists have allowed.) The judgmental features of the criminal law

* Stephen J. Schulhofer, "The Gender Question in Criminal Law," Social Philoso-   phy & Policy, Spring 1990, Vol. 7, Issue 2, pp. 111–115 (Reprinted with Permission).

are also considerably muted at the sentencing stage, or at least they used to be, under the regime of the rehabilitative ideal. Recently that approach has given way to the more rights-oriented punishment philosophy of "just deserts." (Again, we are struck by the problematic character of the connection between culture and legal constructs that legal feminists inspired by Carol Gilligan have posited. Just when women's voices have become more audible and more accepted in our culture and in our law, legal doctrine in sentencing and many other areas has become more individualistic, abstract, and rights-oriented than ever.) In any event, the traditional posture of our formal mechanisms for the adjudication of guilt remains heavily rights-oriented, accusatory, and judgmental.

The second principle is that criminal law is *demanding*. Criminal law prohibitions are not addressed solely, or even primarily, to people who can easily comply. Robbery prosecutions bear mainly on the very poor, those who face the strongest of temptations. Homicide prosecutions often concern those who have acted under the most substantial external or internal pressures. And the point I am making is not limited to statistical patterns in enforcement. It is deeply embedded in the structure of existing (traditional) criminal law doctrine. Social and economic circumstances that strongly predispose to crime ("rotten social background") do not afford a defense. Duress excuses only in very limited circumstances of extreme, overbearing compulsion; lesser pressures afford no excuse, even when they render the decision to comply very difficult.

Impaired mental capacity provides several clear illustrations of the principle. When a defendant suffers from an identifiable mental abnormality short of "mental disease" (severe neurosis or personality disorder, for example), such diminished mental capacity provides no affirmative defense. Many jurisdictions exclude evidence of such mental impairment even when it would be logically relevant to rebut a required element of an offense. The upshot: defendants with impaired capacity, for whom compliance may be very difficult, are held to precisely the same standard as defendants who enjoy normal powers of self-control. Indeed, impairment short of "mental disease" affords no excuse even when it *totally* deprives the defendant of the capacity for self-control.

My claim—that the law is unwilling to vary its standards for defendants with diminished capacities of self-control—requires some qualification to the extent that such defendants may gain mitigation of punishment at the sentencing stage. In principle, their reduced culpability should mean a reduced sentence. And often this principle wins out: for example, in those jurisdictions that allow diminished capacity as a partial defense, or in the rules that almost everywhere permit reducing murder to manslaughter when the defendant acts in response to serious provocation. Even here, note that the partial defense of provocation is available only if a *reasonable person* would have been likely to lose the power of self-control. The defense is situational rather than character-specific; in fact, it is crafted to insure that defendants with less than normal capacities for self-control do *not* gain mitigation of sentence. More generally, the problem is that reduced culpability also means *increased* dangerousness. Should the drug addict who commits a robbery or burglary receive a shorter sentence because the acute need to support his habit reduces his capacity to avoid criminal conduct? Or should he receive an increased sentence because he is harder to deter and more likely to offend again? In practice, sentencing judges respond primarily to the latter consideration, so that the term of confinement is, if anything, longer.

Similar conclusions can be drawn with respect to impairments that do rise to the level of "mental disease." Only a minority of jurisdictions now accept the Model Penal Code proposal that mental disease should excuse whenever it substantially impairs the capacity either to appreciate the wrongfulness of the conduct or to exercise self-control. On the contrary, severely impaired capacity for self-control generally is *not* sufficient to establish the defense. Even in those jurisdictions (probably a minority) that accept "irresistible impulse" as a basis for an insanity defense, a defendant who lacks substantial capacity for self-control, as a result of mental disease, is still held responsible; a successful defense requires the jury to conclude that the impairment be *complete*. And under the more prevalent *M'Naghten* test, even a *total* impairment of volitional controls is insufficient to establish the defense; only a cognitive impairment will do. In all these ways, traditional criminal law demands compliance (and punishes non-compliance) even in the case of those for whom compliance is demonstrably quite difficult.

A final illustration, from the law of intoxication, makes the point in perhaps its starkest form. Voluntary intoxication is a defense only under quite limited circumstances. But what if the defendant has been tricked into swallowing a mind-altering drug? Such involuntary intoxication can be a defense if it produces legal insanity (e.g., an inability to know right from wrong) or if it negates a required element of the offense (as when it triggers hallucinations that result in a decisive mistake of fact). In other cases, even *in*voluntary intoxication affords no defense. A defendant who becomes loud, emotional, and unruly and then commits an assault because of drugs secretly forced upon him has no defense. But for the drugs, he would not have committed the assault, and the drug consumption was wholly beyond his control. Nonetheless, he is held responsible. The premise is that even though circumstances beyond his control made compliance much harder for him than for the average citizen, he still retained some residual capacity for self-control and therefore can still be blamed for his improper choice. (Punishment of the impoverished ghetto dweller is justified on the same ground.)

The short of it is that in criminal law, empathy for the defendant is not the strong suit. One must add, of course, that the relatively uncompromising position of legal doctrine is substantially softened in practice by prosecutorial discretion, plea-bargaining, and the jury system. Nonetheless, in countless, deeply engrained ways, criminal law doctrine demands compliance even from those (and one could say *particularly* from those) for whom compliance is extremely difficult.

In terms of the feminist critique I previously described, these central elements of criminal law—its pervasively judgmental and demanding features—would be described as highly "male" characteristics. From the feminist perspective, criminal law doctrine seems gendered to its very core. The implications of the feminist critique are thus ultimately quite far-reaching. They lead to questions about whether criminal law's core commitments to an allegedly "male" conception of rights and responsibilities ought to be altered or abandoned.

A third feature of the criminal law is also relevant. Criminal law is *pacifist*. There is an irony here because the mode of the criminal law—its procedure and style—is abstract and aggressive. But substantive criminal law *doctrine* is pacifist. By that I mean that it rejects violence as a solution to interpersonal problems. Some important countercurrents qualify this generalization. The law-in-action tolerates violence much more than the law on the books. The law on the books sometimes departs from pacifist principles too, but we usually recognize such departures as compromises or imperfections deserving of criticism. (As another section of this paper shows, the departures are more pervasive—and the need for criticism more profound—in the law of rape.) The general theme still holds—the criminal law commands respect for the fundamental humanity of the other even when that other is an egregious wrongdoer. Force can be used only when necessary. Deadly force can be used *only* to prevent death or great bodily harm and, in many jurisdictions, only if there is no possibility of retreat. So, in principle, the law requires that the attacked party submit to a non-deadly beating rather than defend with deadly force. The laws prefers retreat and loss of honor to the unnecessary taking of life. And it generally construes the requirements of retreat and necessity very strictly.

One example will vividly illustrate these commitments. In a Nebraska case, two prisoners—Schroeder and a much bigger convict—were locked in a cell. The larger cellmate said that in the morning he was going to rape Schroeder, and then went to sleep. In this situation, a "snitch letter" to the guards does not offer much protection. If anything, it would expose Schroeder to even more serious reprisals. So, during the night, Schroeder stabbed the sleeping cellmate. The court held that there was no need to instruct the jury on self-defense here, because the threat of harm was not imminent: Schroeder could have waited till morning to see what his cellmate might do. This is quite an extreme result in terms of its insistence upon a truly imminent threat. On the facts of this case, the result is probably wrong. Nonetheless, the case reflects the law's heavy presumption against resort to deadly force. Criminal law requires sacrifice of property, honor, and pride as well as acceptance of non-serious personal injury before it will tolerate the sacrifice of human life.

Questions

1. Why should we allow self-defense as a defense to a charge of murder? Do the purposes of the criminal law require the punishment of one who has acted in self defense?

2. Should it make a difference whether the accused turns out to have been wrong about the need to defend him or herself? What if it had been shown at trial that the victim hadn't really intended to do the defendant any harm but that the defendant *had* reasonably thought his or her life was in danger?

3. Should one have to retreat "to the wall" before one can kill in self defense? Even if one should have to retreat, should this require-ment not apply in one's own home? (Most states which do require retreat (less than half of the 50) do not go so far as to require it in one's own home.)

4. Most of the states which require retreat tend to be the Eastern United States, while in the Western states there generally is no such requirement. Can you think of any explanation for this?

5. Should one be permitted to kill in order to escape a beating which does not threaten one's life?

6. Do you think that the criminal laws organizing principles (as described by Schulhofer) are "gendered?" If so, should we have two laws of self-defense, one for women and one for men?

2. NECESSITY

a. THE DILEMMA OF CHOICE *

The strongest utilitarian case for withholding punishment arises in the situation in which the actor's conduct results in a greater quantum of good (or a lesser quantum of bad) than would any other course of action open to him, including inaction. This utilitarian precept arises from the perception, intuitive but usually not articulated, that life is full of dilemmas, in which no matter what is done something undesir-able will result. If we cannot maximize gains, then the principle of utility tells us that we must minimize losses. The policeman kills the kidnapper to save his innocent victim. The lost alpinist breaks into a mountain cabin to take refuge from the storm. The fire-fighters destroy property in order to confine the forest fire. The ambulance driver runs through a red light in order to rush a critically ill person to the hospital. In each case, the actor is confronted with a dilemma, in the sense that whatever he does will result in a loss. In each case, the choice he makes involves the breach of some positive rule of the

* Herbert Packer, *The Limits of the Criminal Sanction*, Stanford, Stanford Uni- versity Press, Copyright 1968, pp. 114–117. Reprinted with permission.

criminal law. Yet we intuitively sense that it would be wrong to punish him for doing so.

. . . [If] one who is confronted with a choice of evils makes the "right" choice, and that choice involves conduct that would violate some criminal law, he is excused from that violation. It is of course crucial to this position that someone other than the actor determines that his choice was the "right" one. In a legal system, this decision is confided in the first instance to law enforcement officials: to police, who must decide whether an arrestable offense has been committed, and to prosecutors, who must decide whether to charge the accused with crime, thereby initiating the more formal phases of the process. Ultimately, however, the validity of the choice-of-evils excuse must be passed on by a competent adjudicator—a judge or jury. There has to be, in short, a series of post-audits, which involves the expenditure of resources and which, like all human activities, admits of the possibility of error.

b. MODEL PENAL CODE *

Section 3.02. Justification Generally: Choice of Evils.

(1) Conduct which the actor believes to be necessary to avoid a harm or evil to himself or to another is justifiable, provided that:

(a) the harm or evil sought to be avoided by such conduct is greater than that sought to be prevented by the law defining the offense charged; and

(b) neither the Code nor other law defining the offense provides exceptions or defenses dealing with the specific situation involved; and

(c) a legislative purpose to exclude the justification claimed does not otherwise plainly appear.

(2) When the actor was reckless or negligent in bringing about the situation requiring a choice of harms or evils or in appraising the necessity for his conduct, the justification afforded by this Section is unavailable in a prosecution for any offense for which recklessness or negligence, as the case may be, suffices to establish culpability.

c. NECESSITY AND CIVIL DISOBEDIENCE *

One of the high points of law school is the discussion of the "lifeboat" cases, in which sailors adrift at sea throw their companions overboard or, in desperation, eat them (*Regina v. Dudley and Stevens* (1884)). The discussion generally turns to the idea that some crimes may be justified in order to prevent greater wrongs. This old philosophical question is now coming before California courts in the most

* American Law Institute, Model Penal Code, Proposed Official Draft, Philadelphia: American Law Institute, 1962, pp. 45–46.

* California Lawyer, March 1984 p. 20. Reprinted with permission.

modern of contexts: prosecutions for civil disobedience protesting the design and manufacture of nuclear weapons.

At the trial of 267 of the more than 1,000 people arrested last June in a non-violent protest at the Lawrence Livermore National Laboratory, the defendants did not deny they had intentionally blocked the road. They offered to show, however, that they did so in order to prevent a greater harm—nuclear war—and that their illegal act, consequently, was justified by the defense of necessity. Oakland-Piedmont Municipal Court Judge Clifford B. Bach and ruled that the necessity defense did not apply to the facts of the case, and the defendants have appealed.

California's standards for the defense of necessity are best outlined in *People v. Lovercamp* ((1974) 43 C3d 823, 118 CR 208), a case in which two women escaped from prison camp to avoid sexual assault and immediately surrendered to authorities. The court ruled that the defense applied because: the defendants were reacting to an imminent threat of substantial bodily harm; complaints to controlling authorities had proved futile; the courts could not be utilized in a timely fashion; force or violence was not used; and the defendants turned themselves in immediately.

[In the nuclear protest case] the court ruled, among other things, that the "immediate threat" standard was not met. "The defendants had no information that the button was about to be pushed," says Alameda County Deputy District Attorney Joseph R. Hurley, the prosecutor in the trial. Even if one allowed an expansive definition of immediacy, Hurley says, the protest was not an effective way to prevent the alleged harm. "There was no necessity to block traffic that day. It didn't make fewer missiles; it didn't stop anything."

Defense attorney Alan Ramo of Oakland says it does not matter whether the defendants' beliefs were true. "The jury should have been allowed to consider whether the defendants were *reasonable* in believing the direction of the arms race constituted a grave threat to human life," Ramo argues. The effectiveness and the futility of other tactics to end the threat of nuclear war also are questions of fact, he says. "To decide that, the jury would have to look at how social change happens in this country," Ramo explains, noting that discriminatory laws were not changed overnight by sit-ins at lunch counters in the South.

Hurley says these questions are political and have no place in a criminal court. "The issue is, 'Did the defendant break the law?' We don't pick jurors to be society's conscience," he says. "To know how society feels, you count ballots."

Ramo and Oakland's Leonard Post, also an attorney with the Western States Legal Foundation representing the protestors, have used the necessity defense successfully in the past. In 1979, they defended anti-nuclear protestors who trespassed at the Rancho Seco nuclear power plant shortly after the Three Mile Island accident. Several federal trial courts have rejected the defense, however, in similar situations.

The defense attorneys say they look forward to an appellate court opinion that would clarify the rights of non-violent protestors to use the necessity defense, but Hurley worries that a decision in favor of the appellants would open a Pandora's box. "It seems to me that 'right-to-lifers' blocking an abortion clinic have a better case," Hurley says. "If they stop one person from going in to get an abortion, they have effectively prevented an immediate act that they think is wrong."

Hurley also bristles at the defendants' suggestion that they are political descendants of Martin Luther King Jr. "King practiced classic civil disobedience by accepting punishment for violating a bad law," says Hurley. "These people are trading their violation of a good law just to get publicity." But the defense attorneys suggest there should be a place in our courts to acquit a person like King at the time of his illegal act, instead of honoring him later. "The Livermore defendants knew the risk," says Ramo. "They are willing to accept punishment, but they are asserting that under principles of justice, they should not be punished."

d. NOTE ON JUSTIFICATION

These principles of justification may dispose of a number of cases which otherwise would not be easily handled by the criminal law. Thus, a car carrying a badly injured person to a hospital should be permitted to go through a red light or exceed the speed limit if it is otherwise safe to do so.

Examine the above section carefully. Does it permit a President of the United States to order burglary of the homes of American citizens where the President believes that the national security will be advanced by his action? If it does, should it? What if the statute does permit this—but the Constitution doesn't?

What about a case where an engineer at a dam is confronted with the situation whereby he can save the dam, and presumably the lives of several thousand people protected by it, only if he immediately opens the flood gates and releases enough water to drown several dozen people living immediately below the dam? If these very people would be drowned anyway, the case would be much easier. Assume, however, that these people, although nearest to the dam would be the first to receive warning of an impending flood, and therefore would be least likely to be killed should the dam later rupture.

Consider a case where a motorist, driving safely, rounds a curve and sees five pedestrians in his lane and only one in the opposing lane. Would he be justified, assuming there was no other way to avoid a fatality, in moving out of his lane even though he knew that this would kill one person, rather than continuing straight ahead and almost certainly killing the five people in his lane? Is there, in this circumstance, no measure of the value of lives but a quantitative one? In other words, should it matter that the five persons in the driver's lane were all elderly drunks while the one in the other lane was a brilliant medical researcher?

Next, how should the legal system handle a case where the defendant, accused of assassinating a United States Senator, seeks to defend himself on the ground that the Senator was blocking a health appropriation which would save the lives of many people? How does this case differ from the previous hypothetical? Is it possible that in a democracy which recognizes legislative supremacy there are certain issues of justification which the courts cannot be expected to litigate?

Finally, is taking life ever justified simply to save property? Consider the dam engineer faced with the decision whether to open the flood gates and save the dam, at the cost of a dozen lives, or to wait until everyone had reached high ground at the cost of a $120 million dam. Is it relevant that 25 workmen had been killed in the construction of the dam to begin with and that, considering the rules of thumb in the construction industry, another 20 would be killed in the rebuilding? Would it matter that if by tripling the cost of the dam (or of any heavy construction project) the death rate could be cut by three quarters?

Does it even matter that we know that spending a considerable amount more on our highways would save twenty-thousand of the fifty thousand lives a year now lost in automobile accidents?

Now, re-read *The Queen v. Dudley and Stephens* on pp. 49–53.

D. RECOMMENDED READING

Allen, Francis. *The Decline of the Rehabilitative Ideal: Penal Policy and Social Purpose.* Yale University Press, New Haven, 1981.

American Friends Service Committee. *Struggle for Justice: A Report on Crime and Punishment in America.* Hill and Wang, New York, 1971.

Cohen, Stanley. *Visions of Social Control.* Polity Press, Cambridge, 1985.

Ezorsky, Gertrude, ed. *Philosophical Perspectives on Punishment.* State Univ. of New York Press, Albany, N.Y., 1972.

Garland, David and Young, Peter, eds. *The Power to Punish: Contemporary Penalty and Social Analysis.* Hienemann, London, 1983.

Packer, Herbert. *The Limits of the Criminal Sanction.* Stanford Univ. Press, Stanford, Calif., 1968.

Van den Haag, Ernest. *Punishing Criminals: Concerning a Very Old and Painful Question.* Basic Books, New York, 1975.

von Hirsch, Andrew. *Doing Justice: The Choice of Punishments.* Hill and Wang, New York, 1976.

Chapter III

AN OVERVIEW OF THE CRIMINAL SYSTEM

A. HOW JUSTICE WORKS:

THE PEOPLE vs. DONALD PAYNE *

An 18–year-old named Donald Payne came handcuffed and sullen into the [courthouse] building last year—a tall, spidery, black dropout charged with the attempted armed robbery and attempted murder of a white liquor-store owner in a "changing" fringe neighborhood. The police report told it simply: ". . . At 2100 [9 p.m.] . . . Aug. 4, 1970 . . . victim stated that two male Negroes entered his store and the taller of the two came out with a gun and announced that this is a hold up, 'give me all of your money.' With this the victim . . . walked away from the area of the cash register. When he did this, the smaller offender shouted 'shoot him.' The taller offender aimed the pistol at him and pulled the trigger about two or three times. The weapon failed to fire. The offenders then fled . . .". It was a botched job—nobody was hurt and nothing stolen—and so Payne in one sense was only another integer in the numbing statistics of American crime.

Donald Payne's passage from stick-up to station house to jail to court and finally into the shadow world of prison says more than any law text or flow chart about the realities of crime and punishment in America. The quality of justice in Chicago is neither very much better nor very much worse than in any major American city. The agents of justice in Chicago are typically overworked, understaffed, disconnected, case-hardened and impossibly rushed. Payne protested his innocence to them every step of the way, even after he pleaded guilty. There is, given the evidence, no compelling reason to believe him, and no one did—least of all the lawyer who represented him. So the agents of justice handed him and his case file along toward a resolution that satisfied none of them wholly. "That we really have a criminal-justice system is a fallacy," remarked Hans Mattick, co-director of the Center for Studies in Criminal Justice at the University of Chicago Law School. "A system is artificially created out of no system. What we have is a case-disposition system." In the winter of 1970–71, the system disposed of People vs. Payne—and the sum of Donald Payne's

* Peter Goldman and Don Holt, "How Justice Works: The People vs. Donald Payne." *Newsweek,* 8 March 1971, pp. 20– 37. © Newsweek, Inc. 1971, reprinted with permission.

case and tens of thousands more just like it across the nation is the real story of justice in America.

The Defendant

They fought over Donald Payne, home against street, a war of the worlds recapitulated ten thousand times every day in the ghetto; only, when you live in a ghetto, you can never get far enough away from the street to be sure of the outcome.   Payne's mother tried.   Her first husband deserted her and their four kids when Donnie, the baby, was still little.   But she kept them together and, thirteen years ago, was married to Cleophilus Todd, a dark, rumbly-voiced man who preaches Sundays in the storefront Greater Mount Sinai M.B. (for Missionary Baptist) Church and works weekdays to keep his family and his ministry afloat.   She bore two more children and worked some of the time to supplement the family's income; and two years ago they were able to put enough together to escape the gang-infested section where Donald grew up and move into a little green-and-white frame house in a fringe working-class neighborhood called Roseland. . . .   But it may have come too late for Donald.   He had already begun sliding out of school: it bored him ("They'd be repeatin' the same things over and over again, goin' over the same thing, the same thing") so he started skipping, and when the school called about him, he would pick up the phone and put it back on the hook without saying anything.   *Maybe I thought it was too much happenin' out there in the streets to be goin' to school.*   Or church either.   "They have to go to church long as they live with us," says Cleophilus Todd.   For years, Donald did: he spent his Sunday mornings in the peeling, blue-curtained storefront, shouting gospel in the choir, listening to his stepfather demanding repentance of a little congregation of women and small children in the mismatched, second-hand pews and hardwood theater seats.   But it got claustrophobic on Mount Sinai.   "I just slowed down," Payne says.   "I started sayin' I'd go next Sunday, and then I wouldn't.   And then I just stopped."

The street was winning.   Payne showed a knack for electricity; he made a couple of lamps and a radio in the school shop before he stopped going and brought them home to his mother, and she would ask him why he didn't think about trade school.   "He could fix everything from a light to a television set," she says.   "He was all right as long as he was busy.   Only time you had to worry about him was when he had nothin' to do."   He did work sometimes, two jobs at once for a while, and once he talked to a man working on a house about how you get into electrical work.   The man told him about apprenticeships and gave him the address of his union.   "But I just hated to travel.   It bored me even when I was workin'—I just hated to take that trip.   So I kept puttin' it off and puttin' it off."   . . .

Nobody knows, really, why the street swallows up so many of them. Poverty in the midst of affluence is surely part of it, and color in the midst of whiteness; so are heroin and broken homes and the sheer get-it-now impulsiveness of life in so empty and so chancy a place as a ghetto. But no one can say which ones will go wrong—why a Donald Payne, for example, will get in trouble while three brothers and two sisters come up straight. "I told 'em all," says Todd. "I'm not going to be spending all my time and money on jail cases for you doing something you don't need to get into." Only Donald got into it. . . .

[H]e did get run in a few times for disorderly conduct, routine for kids in the ghetto street. And, in 1968, he was arrested for burglary.

It was a kid-stuff, filling-station job, two tires and a sign, and Payne was caught with the tires a few blocks away. He insisted he was only trying to help a friend sell them, but Todd says he confessed to the family ("Sometimes it makes no difference how good a kid is or how good he is brought up") and he wound up pleading guilty in a deal for a few days in jail and two years on probation. It came to little: probation in theory is a means to rehabilitation, but probation offices in fact, in Chicago and around the country, tend to have too many cases and too little time to do much active rehabilitating. Payne's papers were lost for several months until he finally got scared and came in to find out why no one had called him. After that, he reported once every month, riding two hours on buses to see his probation officer for ten minutes. "We talked about was I workin' and how was I doin' out on the street"—that was all. Once the probation officer referred him to a job counselor. Payne never went, and no one seems to have noticed.

And now, at 18, he is in big trouble . . . ..

The Victim

A voice said "I want that." Joe Castelli looked up from the till, and there across the counter stood this tall colored kid with an insolent grin and a small-caliber, blue-steel automatic not 4 feet from Castelli's face. . . .

And finally the tall one with the blue-steel .25 and the scornful half-smile—the one Castelli identified later as Donald Payne. He and another, smaller youth came in the out door that cool August evening, just as Castelli was stuffing $250 or $300 in receipts from cash register No. 2 into his pocket. "I want that," the tall one said. Castelli edged away. "Shoot him! Shoot him!" the small one yelled. The tall one started at Castelli and poked the gun across the counter at him. "Mother f___er," he said. He squeezed the trigger, maybe once, maybe two or three times.

The gun went *click*.

The two youths turned and ran. Castelli started after them, bumped against the end of the counter and went down. He got up and dashed outside, but the youths disappeared down a dark alley. An old white man emptying garbage saw them go by. The tall one pointed the pistol toward the sky and squeezed again. This time it went off.

A clerk from across the street came over and told Castelli that a woman had seen the boys earlier getting out of a black Ford. "People around here notice things like that," Castelli says. "They watch." Castelli found the car parked nearby and wrote down the license number. The driver—a third Negro youth—followed him back to the store. "What you taking my license for?" he demanded. "I was just waiting for my wife—I took her to the doctor." He stood there yelling for a while, but some of Castelli's white neighbors crowded into the store, and the black youth left. Castelli went back into the street, flagged down an unmarked police car he recognized and handed over the number, and the hunt was on.

The Cops

The evening was clear and mellow for August, a cool 67 and breezy. Patrolman Joe Higgins nosed his unmarked squad car through the night places of the Gresham police district, watching the alleys and storefronts slide past, half-listening to the low staccato of the radio, exchanging shorthand grunts with his partner, Tom Cullen, slouched low in the seat beside him. They had been riding for three humdrum hours when, shortly after 9 p.m., they picked up the call: gunfire in the street up in the north reaches of the district. The two cops glanced at one another. Cullen got the mike out of the glove compartment and radioed: "Six-sixty going in." Higgins hit the accelerator and snaked through the sluggish night traffic toward Shop-Rite Liquors—and the middle of his own neighborhood.

 . . . Higgins lives just a few blocks from Shop-Rite; he has traded there for twenty years, and when he saw Joe Castelli waving in the streets that August evening, he forgot about the shooting call and hit the brakes fast. Castelli blurted out the story and gave Higgins the license number of the black Ford. But it checked out to a fake address—a schoolyard—and Higgins and Cullen spent the next six hours cruising the dark, fighting drowsiness and looking.

It was near first light when they spotted the car, parked in a deserted industrial area with two Negro runaways, 13 and 17 years old, curled up asleep inside. The two patrolmen rousted the boys out, searched the car—and found the blue-steel .25 under a jacket in the front seat. One of the boys, thoroughly scared, led them to a 17-year-old named James Hamilton * who admitted having driven the car but not having gone into the store. Hamilton led them to his kid cousin, Frank, who admitted having gone into the store but not having handled the gun or clicked the trigger. And Frank Hamilton led them to Donald Payne.

And so, red-eyed and bone-weary, Higgins and Cullen, along with a district sergeant and two robbery detectives, went to the little green-

---

* The names of Hamilton and his cousin have been changed since both are juveniles.

and-white frame house in Roseland at 9 a.m. and rang the bell. Payne's sister let them in and pointed the way upstairs.

Payne was sleeping when the cops crowded into his little attic bedroom, and he came awake cool and mean. "Get moving," someone said. "You're under arrest." The police started rummaging around while Payne, jawing all the while, pulled on a pair of green pants and a red jacket. "You don't have no warrant," he said. As Payne told it later, one of the cops replied, "We got a lawyer on our hands." But Higgins insists he misunderstood—"What I said was we'd *get* him a lawyer."

They marched him out in handcuffs past his mother, took him to the district station and shackled him to a chair while one of the officers started tapping out an arrest report: "PAYNE DONALD M/N [for male Negro] 18 4–19–52 . . ." Higgins got Castelli on the phone. It's Joe, he said, come in—we think we've got the man. Castelli came in with DeAngelo. The cops put Payne into a little back room with a few stray blacks. Castelli picked him out—and that, for the cops, was enough. Payne was taken to the South Side branch police headquarters to be booked, then led before a magistrate who set bond at $10,000. The bounty is a paper figure: the Chicago courts require only 10 percent cash. But Payne didn't have it, and by midafternoon he was on his way by police van to the Cook County Jail.

Joe Higgins and Tom Cullen by then had worked twelve hours overtime; in four hours more, Tac Unit 660 was due on patrol again. They talked a little about Donald Payne. "He had a head on him," Cullen said in some wonder. "Maybe if he didn't have a chip on his shoulder. Maybe—"

The Jail

He clambered down out of the van with the rest of the day's catch and was marched through a tunnel into the white-tiled basement receiving area. He was questioned, lectured, classified, stripped, showered, photographed, fingerprinted, X-rayed for TB, bloodtested for VD and handed a mimeographed sheet of RULES OF THE COOK COUNTY JAIL. (". . . You will not escape from this institution . . . You will be safe while you are in this institution . . .") He says he was marked down as a Blackstone Ranger over his objections—"I told them I was a little old to be gang-bangin' "—and assigned to a teen-age tier, E–4. He was issued a wristband, an ID card and a ceiling ticket, led upstairs and checked into a tiny 4-by-8 cell with an open toilet, a double bunk, two sheets, a blanket and a roommate. The door slammed shut, and Donald Payne—charged with but still presumed innocent of attempted robbery and attempted murder—began nearly four and a half months behind bars waiting for his trial.

Jails have long been the scandal of American justice; nobody even knew how many there were until a recent Federal census counted them (there are 4,037)—and found many of their 160,000 inmates locked into what one official called "less than human conditions of overcrowding and filth." And few big-city jails have had histories more doleful than Cook County's. The chunky, gray fortress was thought rather a model of penology when Anton Cermak started it in 1927. But its first warden hanged himself, and its last but two, an amiable patronage princeling named Jack Johnson, was sacked when a series of investigations found the jail ridden with drugs, whisky and homosexual rape and run by inmate bully boys.

Johnson gave way to warden (and now director of corrections) Winston Moore, 41, a round black buddha with wounded eyes, short-shaven hair, a master's and a start on a doctorate in psychology and some iron-handed notions about managing jails and jail inmates. Moore's mostly black reform administration has tamed the inmate tier bosses, cleaned up the cells and the prisoners, repainted the place for the first time, hired more guards at better pay, started some pioneering work and work-training programs, opened an oil-painting studio in the basement room where the county electric chair used to be and begged free performances by B.B. King, Ramsey Lewis, Roberta Flack and even, minus the nude scene, the Chicago company of "Hair." But there has never been enough cash, and lately the John Howard Association, a citizens' watchdog group that gave Moore top marks for his first year, has turned on him with a series of reports charging a miscellany of cruelties within the walls. And worst of all is the desperate overcrowding. The rise in crime and the slowing processes of justice have flooded Moore's 1,300 claustrophobic cells with 2,000 prisoners, most of them doubled up at such close quarters that if one inmate wants to use the toilet, the other has to climb on the bunk to let him by.

Roughly 85 per cent of the inmates are Negro, and most, like Donald Payne, are stuck inside because they are too poor to make bail—not because they have been convicted of crimes. But the presumption of guilt infects a jail as it does so much of American justice, and Moore squanders little sympathy on his charges. He came up in black New Orleans, the son of a mailman struggling for decency, and when any of his inmates blames his troubles on hard times or bad conditions, Moore explodes: "Bulls___! Don't give me that—I was there too, I know what it's like and I made it. You got in trouble because you *wanted* to get in trouble."

[H]e has small pity for the Donald Paynes and enormous scorn for those white liberals who seem more concerned with explaining them than with punishing them. It is there that he sees the real racism of the system—"these bleeding liberals who have so much guilt that they can justify blacks killing blacks because we're immature. They're the ones who want to *keep* you immature. Quit justifying why I kill my buddies on Saturday night and try to stop me from doing it."

Moore has no such tender feelings; he lays on rock concerts and painting classes but he also maintains The Hole—a tier of isolation cells into which the hard cases are thrown with no beds, no day-room privileges, no cigarettes, no candy bars, no visitors, nothing to do but lie or sit or squat on a blanket on the floor and wait for the days to go by. "You will always have to have a place like The Hole," Moore says without a hint of apology. "Much of the problem of crime is immaturity, and the greatest reflection of immaturity is rage—blind rage. There is no other way to contain it." The Hole nevertheless is a degrading place for people on both sides of the bars. The men crouch like caged animals, eyes glinting in the half light. The guards in The Hole wear white because the men throw food at them and white is easier to launder.

It took Donald Payne less than 24 hours to get there.

He came onto tier E–4 angry at being put with the gang kids and shortly ran into a youth from his block who had been a member of the Gangsters. "He had me classified as a Gangster, too," Payne says. "He thought I was just scared to say so cause we were on a Blackstone tier. He ran up in my face and wanted to fight. We had a fight and I went to The Hole for 30 days and he got fifteen."

So they gave Payne a cage, and he sat it out. What do you do? "You sit on the toilet. You wait for the food to come around." What do you think about? "Gettin' out." How do you feel about The Hole leaving it? "It didn't matter much." Not enough, in any case, to keep him out: he went straight back in for four days for sassing a guard, emerged with a reputation as a troublemaker with a "quick attitude" and later did 30 more when Moore's men put down a noisy Blackstone hunger strike on E–4. After that, Payne was transferred to a men's tier and did a bit better. "Those Rangers," he says, "they keep talkin' about killin' up people. What they did when they was outside. What they gonna do when they get out." The older men by contrast idled away their time in the dayroom playing chess and cards and dominoes. They taught Payne chess and let him sit in. "People over here been playin' five and six years," he says, grinning a little. "They're pretty good, too. But I don't wanta be *that* good."

All the while, his case inched through the courts. Illinois requires that the state bring an accused man to trial within 120 days or turn him loose—a deadline that eases the worst of the courthouse delays and the jailhouse jam-ups that afflict other cities. But the average wait in jail still drags out to six or seven months, occasionally because the state asks for more time (it can get one 60–day extension for good cause), more often because delay can be the best defense strategy in an overloaded system. Evidence goes stale; witnesses disappear or lose interest; cases pile up; prosecutors are tempted to bargain. "You could get twenty years on this thing," Constantine Xinos, the assistant public defender who drew Donald Payne, told him when they met. "Don't be in a hurry to go to trial."

Waiting naturally comes easier to a man out on bail than to one behind bars, but Payne sat and waited. On Aug. 24, nineteen days after his arrest, he went from The Hole down through the basement tunnel to the courthouse, stripped naked for a search, then dressed and was led upstairs for a hearing in Room 402—Violence Court. Room 402 is a dismal, soot-streaked place, its business an unending bleak procession of men charged with armed robbery, rape and murder, its scarred old pews crowded with cops, witnesses, wives, mothers and girl friends jumbled uncomfortably together. Payne waited in the lockup until a clerk bellowed his name, then stood before Judge John Hechinger in a ragged semicircle with his mother, the cops, the victims, an assistant state's attorney and an assistant public defender and listened to the prosecution briefly rehearse the facts of the case.

Frank Hamilton—Payne's alleged accomplice—by then had been turned over to the juvenile authorities, and Hechinger dismissed the case against James, the driver of the car, for want of evidence that he had had anything to do with the holdup. But he ordered Payne held for the grand jury. The day in court lasted a matter of minutes; Payne was shuffled back through the lockup, the nude search, the basement tunnel and into The Hole again. On Sept. 18, word came over that the grand jury had indicted him for attempted armed robbery (gun) and attempted murder, and the case shortly thereafter was assigned to Circuit Judge Richard Fitzgerald for trial.

So Payne waited some more, and the rhythm and the regularity of the life inside crept into his blood. Connie Xinos, appalled by the surge in black crime, thinks it might help a little to put one of those tiny cells on display on a street corner in the middle of the ghetto as an object lesson. But, talking with Donald Payne, one begins to wonder about its power as a deterrent. Payne was irritated by the days he spent in court; nobody brings you lunch there. "I sort of got adjusted to jail life," he says. "It seem like home now."

The Defender

Connie Xinos disliked Donald Payne from the beginning. They met in October in the prisoners' lockup behind Judge Fitzgerald's courtroom, and all Xinos had to go on then was the police report and Payne's public-defender questionnaire ("All I know is I was arrested for attempt murder on Aug. 5") and that insinuating half smile. *He did it,* Xinos thought; all of them except the scared children and the street-wise old pros swear they are innocent, but you get a feeling. And that smile. *He's cocky,* Xinos thought. *A bad kid.* Xinos has been at it less than four years, but four years in the bullpens is a long time. He thinks Chicago is dying. And he thinks thousands of black street kids much like Donald Payne—his clients—are doing the killing.

Xinos is 30, the son of a Greek cafeteria owner bred in the white Chicago suburbs, a stumpy young bachelor with quizzical eyes, a shock of straight, dark hair and a Marine Reserve pin glinting gold in the lapel of his three-piece suit. He came to the building a year out of John Marshall Law School, hoping for a job as an assistant state's attorney ("It seemed to be glamorous—you don't get parking tickets and you carry a gun") but hungry enough for steady pay and trial experience to settle for what he could get.

The state's attorney had no openings, so he went upstairs to see public defender Gerald Getty. . . .

Ideals die young in a public defender's office, Chicago's is one of the oldest and best in the U.S.; it was organized in 1930, three decades before the Supreme Court asserted the right of the poor to counsel in any felony case, and its staff now numbers 68 mostly young and energetic lawyers. But they remain enormously overworked, partly because crime rates keep rising, partly because all the defendants' rights announced by the High Court in the 1960s have vastly increased and complicated their caseload. Xinos and his colleagues, squeezed in four desks to a cubicle, handle more than half of Cook County's yearly 3,700 criminal cases; their clients are 70 per cent black and typically too poor either to hire private lawyers or to make bail pending trial. At any given time, says Xinos, "I got a hundred guys sitting over there in County Jail wondering if Xinos is working on my case out there." And he knows the most he will be able to do for 90 per cent of them is "cop them out"—plead them guilty—"and look for the best deal you can get."

That they are all nominally innocent under the law is little more than a technicality: public and private defenders learn quickly to presume guilt in most cases and work from there. "I tell 'em I don't have to presume innocence," says one senior hand in the office. "That's a legal principle, but it doesn't have to operate in a lawyer's office." It stops operating when a rookie lawyer discovers that practically all his clients come in insisting that they didn't do it. "You can almost number the stories," says one of Xinos's colleagues, Ronald Himel. " 'I walked into the alley to urinate and I found the TV set.' 'Somebody gave me the tires.' Well, God forbid it should be true and I don't believe you. My first case out of law school, the guy told me he walked around the corner and found the TV set. So I put that on [in court]. The judge pushed his glasses down his nose, hunched up and said, 'Fifty-two years I have been walking the streets and alleys of Chicago and I have never, ever found a TV set.' Then he got me in his chambers and said, 'Are you f___ing *crazy?* ' I said, 'That's what he told me.' The judge said, 'And you *believed* that s___? You're goofier than he is!' "

Xinos learned fast. . . . "It's our court," Xinos says. "It's like a family. Me, the prosecutors, the judges, we're all friends. I drink with the prosecutors. I give the judge a Christmas present, he gives me a Christmas present." And you learn technique. The evidence game. The little touches: "The defendant should smile a lot." The big disparities: which judge gives eighteen months for a wife-killing and which one gives twenty to 40 years. How to make time and the caseload work for you. "The last thing you want to do is rush to trial. You let the case ride. Everybody gets friendly. A case is continued ten or fifteen times, and nobody cares any more. The victims don't care. Everybody just wants to get rid of the case." Then you can plead your man guilty and deal for reduced charges or probation or short time. You swing.

Xinos took an apartment in the distant suburbs.

And, like any commuter, he tries to leave it all at the office. The ones you can't are the few you plead guilty when you really believe they are innocent: "When you're scared of losing. When they've got a case and you believe your guy but you lose your faith in the jury system. You get scared, and he gets scared and you plead him." But the Donald Paynes—the great majority of his cases—are different. Xinos never liked Payne; Payne fought him, and Xinos much prefers the pros who tell you, "Hey, public defender, I killed the f___er, now get me off." Xinos thought Payne should plead guilty and go for short time. But Payne clung to Standard Alibi Number Umpty-one ("I was home at the time this was supposed to have broke out") and demanded a trial, so Xinos gave him the best shot he could. He had to lay aside his misgivings—his upset at crime in the streets and his suspicion that Payne was part of it. "Me letting ten or twenty guys out on the street isn't going to change that," he says. "This violence—it's like Niagara Falls. You can't stop it."

The Trial

Everybody kept trying to talk him out of his trial. "Plead guilty, jackass, you could get ten to twenty for this," Xinos whispered when they finally got to trial. *Ain't no need for that,* said Payne. "You really want a jury?" the assistant state's attorney, Walter Parrish, teased him. "Or you want to plead?" *I want my trial,* said Payne. Everything in the building says cop out, make a deal, take the short time. "They ought to carve it in stone over the door," an old court-house hand, then a prosecutor and now a judge, told a friend once. "NO CASE EVER GOES TO TRIAL HERE." The People vs. Donald Payne did get to trial, halfway at least. But then his case went sour, and the deal got sweeter, and in the end Donald Payne copped out, too.

Practically everybody does: urban justice in America would quite simply collapse if even a major fraction of the suspects who now plead guilty should suddenly start demanding jury trials. The Payne case was only one of 500 indictments on Judge Richard Fitzgerald's docket last year; it would have taken him four years to try them all. So 85 to 90 per cent of them ended in plea bargaining—that backstairs haggling process by which pleas of guilty are bartered for reduced charges or shorter sentences or probation. "Plea bargaining used to be a nasty word," says Fitzgerald; only lately have the bar and the courts begun to call it out of the closet and recognize it as not just a reality but a necessity of the system. "We're becoming a little more sophisticated about it. We're saying 'You're doing it, we know you're doing it and you have to do it; this is the way it has to be done.'"

The pressures to plead are sometimes cruel, the risks of going to trial high and well-advertised. There is, for waverers, the cautionary tale of one man who turned down one to three years on a deal—and got 40 to 80 as an object lesson when a jury convicted him. Still, Payne insisted, and Xinos painstakingly put a defense together. He opened with a pair of preliminary motions, one arguing that the pistol was inadmissible because the evidence tying it to Payne was hearsay, the other contending that the police should have offered Payne a lawyer at the line-up but didn't. The witnesses straggled in for a hearing on Dec. 1. Joe Castelli took the stand, and Patrolman Cullen, and, for a few monosyllabic moments, Payne himself. Had anyone advised him of his rights to a lawyer? "No." Or let him make a phone call? "No." But another of the arresting officers, Robert Krueger, said that Payne had been told his rights—and such swearing contests almost always are decided in favor of the police. Everybody admired Xinos's energy and craftsmanship. Nevertheless, Fitzgerald denied both of the defense motions and docketed the case for trial on Dec. 14.

And so they all gathered that wintry Monday in Fitzgerald's sixth-floor courtroom, a great dim cave with marbled and oak-paneled walls, pitted linoleum floors and judge, jury, lawyers, defendant and gallery so widely separated that nobody could hear anything without microphones. Choosing a jury took two hours that day, two the next morning. Parrish, an angular, Ivy-cut Negro of 41, worked without a shopping list. "I know some lawyers say fat people are jolly and Germans are strict," he says, "but none of that's true in my experience. If you get twelve people who say they'll listen, you're all right."

But Xinos is a hunch player. He got two blacks on the jury and was particularly pleased with one of them, a light-skinned Urban League member who looked as if she might be sympathetic. And he deliberately let one hard-hat sit on the panel. Xinos had a point to make about the pistol—you couldn't click it more than once without pulling back the slide to cock it—and the hard hat looked as if he knew guns.

That afternoon, slowly and methodically, Parrish began to put on his case. He opened with the victims, and Castelli laid the story on the record: "About ten after 9, the gentleman walked in . . .. He had a small-caliber pistol . . .. I edged away . . .. The other lad came up to me and he said, 'Shoot him, shoot him, shoot him' . . . [The first youth] pointed the gun at me and fired three times or four—at least I heard three clicks." And the gunman—Did Castelli see him in court?

"Yes, I do, sir."

"And would you point him out, please?"

Castelli gestured toward the single table shared by the prosecution and defense. "That," he said, "is Donald Payne."

But Xinos, in his opening argument, had promised to alibi Payne—his mother was prepared to testify for him—and now, on cross-examination, he picked skillfully at Parrish's case. Playing to his hard hat on the jury, he asked Castelli whether the stick-up man had one or two hands on the gun. "Only one, sir," said Castelli. "And was that trigger pulled in rapid succession—click-click-click?" Xinos pressed. "Yes, sir," said Castelli, and Xinos had his point: it takes two hands to keep pulling the slide and clicking the trigger. Next came Patrolman Joe Higgins, who remembered, under Xinos's pointed cross-examination, that Castelli had described the gunman as weighing 185 pounds— 30 more than Payne carries on his spindly 6-foot-1 frame. Payne had nearly blotched that point by wearing a billowy, cape-shaped jacket to court, but Xinos persuaded him to fold it up and sit on it so the jurors could see how bony he really was. The 30–pound misunderstanding undercut Castelli's identification of Payne—and suddenly the People and their lawyer, Walter Parrish, were in trouble.

Parrish didn't show it: he is a careful, phlegmatic man born to striving parents in the Chicago ghetto and bred to move smiling coolly through the system. He came into it with a Howard law diploma, a few years' haphazard practice and the right sort of connections as counsel to and precinct captain for the 24th Ward regular Democratic organization. He figured on the job only as an apprenticeship for private practice, but he has stayed six years and seems rather comfortable where he is. The black kids over in the County Jail call him "The Devil," and he likes that; he fancied that the edgy hostility he saw in Donald Payne's eyes was a tribute to his hard-guy reputation. He likes his public law firm, too. It pays him $18,000—he guesses he would have to gross $50,000 in private practice to match that—and it puts all the enormous resources of the state at his service. Investigators? The state's attorney has 93 to the public defender's six. Police, the sheriff, the FBI? "All you got to do is call them." Pathology? Microanalysis? "Just pick up the phone. You've got everything at your beck and call."

What he had in People vs. Payne was the Hamilton boys, the two cousins through whom the police had tracked Payne. Parrish had hoped he wouldn't have to put them on the stand. "It was a risk," he said later. "They could have hurt us. They could have got up there and suddenly said Donald wasn't there." But he was behind and knew it. He needed Frank Hamilton to place Payne inside the store, James to connect him with the car and the pistol. So, that afternoon, he ordered up subpoenas for the Hamiltons. "We know how to scramble," said his young assistant, Joe Poduska. "That's the name of the game."

The subpoenas were being typed when Connie Xinos happened into the state's attorney's office to socialize—*it's like a family*—and saw them in the typewriter. Xinos went cold. He had talked to the mother of one of the Hamiltons; he knew their testimony could hurt. So, next morning, he headed first thing for Parrish's austere second-floor cubicle—and found the Hamiltons there. "We're going to testify," they told Xinos, "and we're going to tell the truth."

Xinos took Parrish aside. "Let's get rid of this case," he said.

"It's Christmas," Parrish said amiably. "I'm a reasonable man."

"What do you want?" Xinos asked.

"I was thinking about three to eight."

"One to five," said Xinos.

"You got it."

It's an absolute gift, Xinos thought, and he took it to Payne in the lock-up. "I can get you one to five," he said. Payne said no. Xinos thought fast. It was a dead-bang case—the kind Clarence Darrow couldn't pull out—and it was good for a big rattle, maybe ten to twenty years. Xinos went back downstairs, got the Hamiltons and sat them down with Payne in Fitzgerald's library. "They rapped," he remembers, "and one of them said, 'Donald—you mean you told them you weren't *there?*' I told him again I could get him one to five. They said, 'Maybe you ought to take it, Donald.' I said, 'You may get ten to twenty going on with the trial.' And he said, 'Well, even if I take the one to five, I'm not guilty.' That's when I knew he would go."

But would Fitzgerald buy it? Xinos was worried. The judge is a handsome 57, with a pink Irish face rimmed with silver hair and creased to smile. "He looks like God would look and acts like God would act if God were a judge," says Xinos. "He doesn't take any s___." He was a suburban lawyer in Calumet City when Mayor Richard Daley's organization slated him for judge seven years ago, a reward for having backed a Daley man for governor once when it was tough to do so. He started in divorce court and hated it: "I think I'd rather have 150 lashes than go back down there. Jeez—it's a lot easier to give a guy the chair than it is to take five kids away from a mother." He is happier where he is, and he has made a considerable reputation in the building as a solid, early-rising, hardworking judge—no scholar but conscientious and good on the law. He can be stern as well: he isn't the hanging type, but he does think the pendulum has swung pretty far lately in the defendant's favor. "We've clothed 'em in swaddling clothes," he says, "and laid 'em in a manger of bliss." So Xinos fretted. "The judge is the judge," he told Payne while they waited for an audience with Fitzgerald. "He might give you three to eight. You better think about it."

But Fitzgerald agreed to talk, and the ritual began to unfold. Xinos led Payne to the bench and announced for the record that they wanted to discuss pleading—"Is that correct, Donald?" Payne mumbled, "Correct," and, while he went back to the lockup to wait, the lawyers followed the judge into chambers. A bailiff closed the door behind them. Fitzgerald sat at his desk and pulled a 4–by–6 index card out of a box; he likes to keep his own notes. Parrish dropped into a deep, leathery sofa, his knees coming up almost to his chin. Xinos sat in a green guest chair in a row along the wall. There were no outsiders, not even a court stenographer. The conference, not the courtroom, has become the real focus of big-city criminal justice, but its business is transacted off the record for maximum flexibility.

Fitzgerald scanned Parrish's prep sheet, outlining the state case. Xinos told him glumly about the Hamiltons. "We look beat," he conceded.

"Walter," asked the judge, "what do you want?"

"I don't want to hurt the kid," Parrish said. "I talked to Connie, and we thought one to five."

They talked about Payne's record—his jobs, his family, his old gas-station burglary rap. "Two years probation," Xinos put in hopefully. "That's nothing." Fitzgerald pondered it all. He had no probation report—there isn't time or manpower enough to do them except in major cases—and no psychological work-up; sentencing in most American courts comes down to a matter of instinct. Fitzgerald's instincts told him one to five was a long enough time for Payne to serve—and a wide enough spread to encourage him to reform and get out early. "Up to five years," he feels, "that's the area of rehabilitation. Beyond five, I think they get saturated". So he made up his mind.

"Will he take it?" the judge asked Xinos.

"I'll go back and see," Xinos replied. He ducked out to the lockup and put the offer to Payne.

"Let's do it," Payne said. "Right now."

A light snow was falling when they brought him back into court, grinning slightly, walking his diddybop walk. A bailiff led him to a table below Fitzgerald's high bench. His mother slipped into place beside him. He spread his fingers out on the tabletop and looked at them. The judge led him through the prescribed catechism establishing that he understood what he was doing and that no one had forced him to do it. Payne's "yeses" were barely audible in the cavernous room.

The choice now was his. Fitzgerald told him. He could go to the pen and cooperate and learn a trade and come out on parole in eleven months; or he could "go down there and do nothing at all and sit on your haunches . . . and you will probably be going [back] down there for twenty or 30 years." Payne brushed one hand across his eyes and studied the tabletop. "I'm giving you the first break you probably ever got in your life," the judge said. ". . . The rest of it, Donald, is up to you. Do you understand that?"

"Yes," said Payne.

And then it was over. Fitzgerald called the jurors in and dismissed them. They knew nothing of the events that had buried Donald; they sat there for a moment looking stunned. Xinos slipped back to the jury room to see them before they scattered. "But you were *ahead*," one told him.

Payne's mother walked out to a pay phone, eyes wet and flashing. "They just pressed Donnie," she insisted, "until he said he did it." Parrish packed up. "An hour, a day—even that's punishment," he said. "One to five is enough." Joe Higgins went back to Tac Unit 660.

"Donald," he said, "is a very lucky man." Winston Moore heard about it in his office at the jail. "One to five?" he snorted. "S_____. That's no sentence for armed robbery." Xinos went home to his apartment in the suburbs. "One to five," he said. "Fantastic. Payne *should* go to the penitentiary. He's a bad kid, he's better off there. He's dangerous. He'll be back."

And Payne was sulky sore. He shook hands with Xinos and grinned broadly when the deal went down, but when Xinos told him later what that juror had said—*you were ahead*—he felt cheated. A break? "The best break they could have given me was letting me go." But there was nothing for him to do just then but go brooding back down to the tunnel and to jail. "Everybody do something wrong," he told himself. "Maybe my time just caught up with me."

Prison and Beyond

You can write to your lawyer, your preacher and six other people, the sergeant was saying, only remember—your letters are censored so watch what you say. No. 69656, born Donald Payne, sat half listening in the front row in his gray prison coveralls, his eyes idling over the chapel wall from the flag to the sunny poster—GOOD MORNING WORLD. Nothing controversial about prison in your letters, the sergeant was saying. "Let's keep this personal, fellas, your parents get a lot of this on TV." No sex either—"Let's keep this down to personal matters, fellas, we're not in a Sunday school class but let's keep our hands above the table." No double talk, no jive talk, no hep talk, no profanity. And fellas—don't risk your mail privileges by breaking the rules. "The more mail you get, the easier it will be for you," the sergeant was saying. "It gets depressing in here."

Payne had been marched aboard a black sheriff's bus by early light only a few days before and had been shipped with sixteen other County Jail inmates to Joliet prison, a 112-year-old yellow-stone fortress on the Des Plaines River 40 miles southwest of Chicago. The transfer, typically, was accidental. Payne was to have been held in jail until this month, when he is due in court on charges of having violated his old probation for burglary, but the papers got mixed up and he was bused out early. He didn't really mind, since by then he hated the jail so badly that even the pen seemed preferable. And so, on Feb. 5, he checked into Joliet's diagnostic center, drew his number and his baggy coveralls, was stripped, showered and shorn and began four to six weeks of testing to see which prison he would fit into best and what if anything it could do for him. Coveralls aren't much, but Payne, sharp, flipped the collar rakishly up in back and left the front unbuttoned halfway down his chest. Cool. Good morning, world.

Except in this world, as the sergeant of the guard said, it gets depressing. Illinois's prisons, like most of America's, had fallen over the years into a sorry state of neglect until Richard B. Ogilvie made them a campaign issue at some hazard in his 1968 gubernatorial campaign and got elected. Ogilvie since has trusted the problem to a new director of corrections, Peter Bensinger, the 34-year-old heir to the Brunswick Corp. money and position, and Bensinger—an energetic beginner—has put Joliet and its neighbor, Stateville, under the management of reform-minded pros. The new team has begun upgrading the guard force, putting new emphasis on correction as against punishment and doing away with some of the pettiest dehumanizing practices; now, for example, they no longer shave a man's body hair off when he arrives, and prisoners are called to the visiting room by name, not by number. "We've taken everything else from the man," says Stateville's 33-year-old warden, John Twomey. "If we take his name, too, how can he feel he's a worthwhile human being?"

But money is short and reform painfully slow. "We've moved ahead about 50 years," says Joliet's black warden, Herbert Scott. "We're now up to about 1850." And 1850 dies hard. Donald Payne, a child of the city streets, is rousted from his bunk at 6 a.m., fed breakfast at 7, lunch at 10 and dinner at 3 and locked back in his cell before sundown. The language of the place confirms his devalued humanity: men are "tickets," meals are "feeds." The battery of IQ, personality and aptitude tests he is undergoing at Joliet are exhaustive but of uncertain value, since the prisons still lack programs enough to make use of what the tests tell them. So Payne is consigned to his bars and his bitterness. In Joliet at mealtime 900 men sit at long stone tables spooning food out of tin dishes and facing an enormous American flag—"to instill patriotism," a young staff psychologist explained wryly. A visitor asked how the men respond to this lesson. "I imagine," said the psychologist, "that they think, 'F_____ the flag'."

It is here that society has its last chance with the Donald Paynes—and here that the last chance is squandered at least as often as not. The lesson of People vs. Payne and countless cases like it is that the American "system" of justice is less a system than a patchwork of process and improvisation, of Sisyphean labor and protean inner motives. Payne was arrested on chance and the tenacity of two policemen; was jailed for want of money while better-off men charged with worse crimes went free on bail; was convicted out of court and sentenced in a few minutes' bargaining among overworked men who knew hardly anything about him. It cannot be said that justice miscarried in People vs. Payne, since the evidence powerfully suggests his guilt and the result was a penalty in some relation, however uneven, to the offense. But neither was justice wholly served—not if the end of justice is more than the rough one-to-one balancing of punishments with crimes.

The punishment most commonly available is prison, and prisons in America have done far better at postponing crime than at preventing or deterring it. Joliet is a way station for Payne. He may wind up at Pontiac, where most younger offenders do their time; he would prefer the company of older men at Stateville, a vintage 1925 maximum-security prison with cells ranged in enormous glassed-in circles around a central guard tower. He says that in either event he will stick to his cell and go for early parole. "When I get out," he told his mother once in jail "I'll be in church every day." Yet the odds do not necessarily favor this outcome: though the Illinois prisons have made progress toward cutting down on recidivism, a fifth to a third of their alumni get in trouble again before they have been out even a year. "Well," said Payne, smiling that half-smile at a visitor during his first days as No. 69656, "I'm startin' my time now and I'm on my way home." But his time will be a long and bleak one, and, unless luck and will and the last-chance processes of justice all work for him, Donald Payne may be home right now.

Comment

The treatment of Donald Payne is, in most respects, typical of the armed robbery defendant in our large urban areas.

The criminal process is very different, however, as applied to different kinds of cases. Nearly half of all of the criminal arrests in the nation are for drunkenness, and these cases are processed very differently from the case of Payne. Complicated commercial crimes such as securities fraud or tax evasion not only involve far wealthier defendants, who have access to retained counsel and other expert help, but also involve very different kinds of legal and factual issues. Moreover, some criminal prosecutions are especially notorious—because of the nature of the victim, as in the assassination of a political figure, because of the nature of the defendant, who may be a militant political leader, or because of something about the crime which has attracted nationwide attention. These may be processed very differently from the run-of-the-mill case described in the excerpt on Donald Payne.

We must also remember that the criminal process will appear very different when viewed from different vantage points. First, of course, there is the point of view of the criminal defendant himself and his family. Then, there is that of the victim. Then, that of the legal officers, the policeman, prosecutor, public defender or private attorney, judge, and probation officer, each of whom will have a unique perspective on the case. And, finally, there is the point of view of the detached impartial observer—whose very detachment and impartiality may cause him problems in understanding the view of the process held by those who are more intimately involved.

B. THE PROCESS

1. THE PROSECUTION OF FELONY ARRESTS *

Typical outcome of 100 felony arrests
brought by the police for prosecution

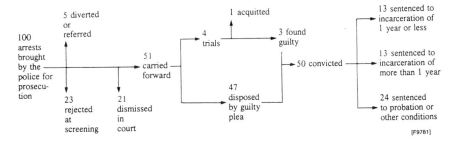

Comment and Questions

The chart above shows the path of the criminal process from citizen reports to sentencing of offenders. At each stage of this process, a sizeable proportion of cases are shunted out of the system, either because the evidence does not warrant further processing or someone has determined that in the interests of justice or for some other reason the matter is not worth pursuing further. So, for every person arrested on a felony charge only a small portion—on average around forty to sixty percent—are convicted of any charge, and only a small fraction—perhaps fifteen percent nationwide—are sentenced to felony time, that is longer than one year. Much of what follows in this book is an examination of the factors that account for the attrition of cases as they proceed along this path. Is anything served by this process of attrition? Is anything lost?

2. NIGHT COURT **

Judge Richard T. Andrias will take the bench in Manhattan Criminal Court at 1 a.m., and for him it will be the start of an eight-hour drizzle of punks, prostitutes, addicts and thieves in a legal forum that is not only the nation's busiest but also one of its most troubled.

"As a young, idealistic lawyer, I always thought I could do better than what I saw on the bench," Andrias recalled. "Being a judge was something I had always thought about."

But in cities like New York, being a criminal court judge is no longer such a sought-after position. "You can't retire to the bench now. Not in this city and not in most urban areas," said Andrias, one

* Barbara Boland, et al. The Prosecution of Felony Arrests, 1982, U.S. Department of Justice Bureau of Justice Statistics, May 1988 NCJ–106990.

** Jenkins, "The Lobster Shift", *American Bar Association Journal*, Nov. 1, 1986,

pp. 56–60 Copyright 1986 (Reprinted with permission of the ABA Journal, the lawyer's magazine.)

of two Vietnam veterans on the city's criminal court bench. "A judge can get worn down."

By Andrias' own candid admission, he presides over a court that is "intellectually bankrupt." As supervising judge, Andrias earns $82,000 a year and functions as something of a traffic cop in the court. Reporting to him in Manhattan are 21 other judges, each assigned by Andrias to one of three court "parts."

At age 42, after four years on the bench, the young judge is experiencing the frustrations of turnstile justice. Each city borough has its own branch of criminal court, and virtually every criminal case in the city passes through one of them—266,590 misdemeanors and felonies in 1985, as well as 619,157 administrative summonses.

This is where most of the work of the criminal justice system is done. Misdemeanors and summonses are disposed of in criminal court, and felonies are arraigned there before being sent on to the supreme court, the state's court of general jurisdiction.

HORROR SHOW

It is truly assembly line justice, "a horror show," in Andrias' words. Cases that need more attention are shunted to a "jury" part, but the appellation is a misnomer. Few cases are ever tried by a jury there.

Because the criminal court judges rarely preside over a trial, most of their work involves disposing of cases through guilty pleas or initiating them through arraignments. Because the caseload is much higher in Manhattan than anywhere else, the arraignment part operates 24 hours a day, 365 days a year—the only court in the nation to do so. Judges from all five boroughs rotate, a week at a time, on the "lobster shift" that runs from 1 a.m. until 9 a.m. Andrias takes his turn in the rotation, to fill in for a fellow judge as he is doing on this night, and to check on the system.

"This isn't like a life appointment in federal court, where you have two summa cum laude law assistants from Harvard and Yale," Andrias remarked. "We do a lot of the work ourselves. We don't have the support. We don't have life tenure. All we have is this *crush*."

It is ironic that this judge has chosen to establish his career in such a moribund system. Andrias is a Phi Beta Kappa graduate of Bowdoin College; he was selected by the mayor on the basis of merit instead of politics.

This is the story of how a principled judge survives with his court in collapse. His efforts to infuse reforms into this hidebound system have made only a marginal difference. "There's a limit to how much you can squeeze out of even the most motivated, determined group of judges," Andrias said. "I've seen the limit."

Despite what Andrias says about his court—"in many respects, it is the most troubled court in the country right now"—the system appears to be functioning smoothly tonight. "Brutally efficient," he calls it.

"People who were arrested in the last 15 hours are being arraigned and sent out the door in a constitutionally acceptable period of time."

On the bench, Andrias wears a dark blue Haspel suit instead of the traditional black robe. He chats easily with the others who've drawn the lobster shift: an assistant district attorney who will represent the state in all 79 cases Andrias will arraign during the next eight hours; three lawyers from the Legal Aid Society who will take turns representing every defendant; and a half-dozen armed court officers.

A sign is tacked up at the front of the room: "This is not information. Go to room 131 for any questions. This means you!! Have a nice day. Elsewhere." There is space in the courtroom's varnished walnut gallery for perhaps a hundred spectators but tonight there is nobody.

The night's first defendant is a 21-year-old charged with entering the subway without paying. A routine check for outstanding warrants revealed that the defendant has failed to appear in court to answer a prior charge of possessing an envelope of PCP. Thus to these two charges a third has been added: bail jumping.

Assistant D.A. Alejandro Schwed and Legal Aid lawyer Edwin Rollins walk toward the bench for the first of many off-the-record conferences that predictably produce a plea bargain.

"You try to give each case what it's worth," Andrias said a short time later. "If you squeeze all the crap out of the system, then the judges in the trial parts can spend their time where they're needed the most."

But in the criminal court, only the rare case gets to trial. City-wide, the likelihood of a case going to trial in the criminal court is .4 percent.

THE PLEA BARGAIN GAME

Critics claim plea bargaining means serious charges are punished by a slap on the wrist, and that the process encourages guilty pleas by those who might have a legitimate defense. In a 1983 report, a City Bar Association committee called the criminal court "legally dead. . . . There is no debating that a court system which tries even less than one percent [of its cases] is in its death throes."

As a judge on the front line, Andrias reluctantly accepts plea bargaining. Of necessity, he encourages it by assigning to the arraignment parts those judges who can bang out on-the-spot guilty pleas the fastest.

"Sharp lawyers know precisely what a case is worth, given the prior record and the strength of the People's case," Andrias said. "There's a market rate."

Andrias acknowledges that the power of his robe is largely theoretical; defendants know that if they ask for a trial, their case most likely will have to be dismissed for lack of a judge to hear it.

"The public cries out for stiffer penalties," Andrias said, "but the resources are never forthcoming. The public is getting more than it's paying for, but it doesn't see it that way. It sees this tide of criminality and says, 'Why can't you stop it?' And we in the lower court don't have adequate resources to resolve enough of our cases by trial.

"We're getting more work out of fewer people, compared with five years ago. Is that efficiency? There's a limit to what 'efficiencies' one should have in the criminal justice system. We're not building widgets here."

A plan recently sent to the state legislature by Gov. Mario Cuomo would ease the strain on the criminal court by adding 40 new judges to the city court system over the next two years.

By 1:50 a.m., only three other cases, all petty, have been arraigned, and Andrias offers an opinion on the night ahead: "Garbage cases." He would prefer some felonies to liven things up.

Instead, Jimmy Green, 27, appears on the charge of attempting to pick pockets on the subway [the names of the defendants in this article were changed to protect the confidentiality of off-the-record discussions]. The rap sheet shows that this is his second arrest, and that on the first one he was given a conditional discharge—in effect, a dismissal.

"The only offer is a B misdemeanor," Schwed said. This would reduce Green's maximum possible jail sentence to six months instead of one year.

"One year's probation," Andrias told the lawyers instead. Unlike the first "jostling" charge, this one will give Green a permanent criminal record. He also could be forced to serve the year if he gets into trouble while on probation.

Robert Jaffe walked back and whispered the offer to Green, then, having gained an assent, turned back to the bench and called to Andrias, "All right, judge."

"Listen carefully, sir," Andrias told Green as he prepared to pronounce the sentence. "This will be your first criminal conviction."

As each case comes before him, Andrias checks the elapsed time between arrest and arraignment. Last year, it had been averaging more than two full days in Manhattan—an interval so unacceptable that the court itself was sued by prisoners alleging unconstitutional confinement. The lawsuit was settled in April 1985, a week before Andrias was given his new job. Andrias knew he would have to enforce the settlement's requirement that arrest-to-arraignment time be limited to 24 hours.

Andrias understands well that to achieve such a dramatic reduction, he must be an agent of change among courthouse unions and bureaucratic fiefdoms that reflexively resist it.

An added nuisance is the aged granite courthouse. The city, which owns and maintains it, is spending an extra $3 million a year on maintenance and security. The city also committed $25 million for needed capital improvements, including more holding pens and lawyer-prisoner interview booths that will allow faster processing of prisoners. But because of the city's competitive bidding process it would be 18 months before construction could begin.

To survive, however, Andrias must compromise. An ingrained idealism attracted him to the court, but the reality of what he now sees also makes him brazenly cynical about the cases he handles. The judge insists that he hasn't become disillusioned, as others might have, because, "I didn't come into this job with any ideals or goals that weren't realistic.

"You care about every case: the victim, the defendant, even the participating lawyers. But there's a limit," Andrias said. "To some extent, you must intellectualize the job. You must know the law and apply the law. If you try to be a social worker, the burnout factor will be very high."

Former judge Frank Brenner may be one such victim. Appointed in 1983 to the criminal court at age 55, he resigned a year later and returned to private practice. "Everything is a problem there," he said of the criminal court. "There's a tremendous volume of work. It's repetitive. It's the trenches. Mass production. There are no exotic intervals. You've got night court [from 5 p.m. to 1 a.m.] and the lobster shift. Night court isn't too bad. It's like watching the late show—you go to bed at 1:30 and sleep late the next morning.

"But the lobster shift is the one that can kill you. After the second day you don't know if it's night or day. And it's all meaningless. It's all a charade. You know Citibank's motto: 'The Citi never sleeps.' The lobster shift is the same kind of public relations. Everybody's supposed to feel safe knowing the courts never sleep. So what good does it do to lock up another dozen hookers?"

Andrias, however, tries to infuse himself with the belief that what he does makes a difference. "To avoid becoming a cynic, you have to think what you're doing is important." Moreover, Andrias seems to derive an almost Calvinistic reassurance from seeking out other causes that he can champion off the bench.

He steered the Bronx Legal Services Corp. out of serious financial difficulty as its board chairman from 1980 to 1983, and he recently volunteered to become a board member of the Vietnam Veterans Leadership Program, which helps veterans find jobs.

At the court, though, the idealism Andrias holds onto is a defense mechanism, a way of beating the frustration that otherwise might overwhelm him.

"You have to see the importance of every case," Andrias said. "You have to guard against the human nature of having it become routine. You wouldn't want your heart surgeon looking at your operation in a routine fashion."

By 2:30 a.m., Andrias has gotten guilty pleas in 12 of the 20 cases that he has arraigned during his first 90 minutes on the bench—run-of-the-mill citations for prostitution, drug possession and assault. Charges against two sisters who quarreled and called the police are dropped because now neither wants to testify against the other. Bail is set for those who haven't pleaded.

During the first of several breaks he will take, Andrias retires to what passes for a robing room at the rear of the courtroom. Alone, he smokes a pipe as a solitary table fan clatters.

THE SECOND WAVE

During the break, police officers will bring up from the lock-up a new group of defendants. They will be signed over to the court officers and taken to three holding cells just off the courtroom, where each prisoner will be briefly interviewed by a Legal Aid lawyer in preparation for arraignment. When the next group of prisoners begins walking out, Andrias is summoned by a court officer and walks back to the bench.

"Hey, judge, somebody just got shot right outside the courthouse," one of the officers informs him with surprising dispassion. "He got shot in the neck."

As the prisoners enter the courtroom, they are seated on a long wooden bench against the wall to Andrias' left. One of them is noticeably ill. Hector Garcia, charged with attempted grand larceny, is still wearing a plastic hospital bracelet as he shuffles to a spot in front of the bench.

Andrias examines the paperwork on the case. In addition to the arresting officer's typewritten complaint the judge gets a rap sheet. Fingerprints of the accused are also transmitted by facsimile to Albany, where a check is made to see whether the same person might have been arrested or convicted under an alias.

According to the arrest record, the owner of a car caught Garcia trying to break into it, and then, with some of his friends, severely beat and kicked him. Garcia has been in Metropolitan Hospital for nearly a week.

Andrias looks at Garcia's Legal Aid lawyer Patrick Joyce, who is already at the bench: "A little street justice, eh?"

"He has three broken ribs and a bruised spleen, judge," Joyce explained.

"Wanna clear it up?" Andrias asked.

"I'm thinking 15 days," Joyce answered.

"More," Andrias responded. "He has a long record. I'm thinking 60 to 90 days."

Joyce wants some time to ponder the offer. Garcia shuffles back to the prisoner's bench.

Jerry Franklin, 36, is also charged with attempted grand larceny. It is alleged he distracted a shopkeeper while his 15-year-old half-sister tried to steal merchandise.

"Does he want to take a plea?" Andrias asked Joyce. "If he wants 90 days he can have it."

Joyce walks back to his client and whispers the offer, but Franklin instantly spits out a one-word expletive. "Not guilty, judge," Joyce translated. Bail is set at $500 and Franklin is taken to Riker's Island.

By now, Legal Aid lawyer Joyce has had enough time to converse with Garcia, his client who allegedly broke into the car and was beaten as a result. The issue for Andrias is whether the beating Garcia got on the street is a greater deterrent to future crime than jail would be, and it poses a dilemma for him.

"Certainly there's a strong deterrent factor [to the street beating]," Andrias told the prosecutor and defense lawyer as they huddled at the bench. "But you can't endorse that kind of justice. Thirty days."

"Would you consider 20 days?" Joyce asked. "He's so pathetic. He's gotten a lot of punishment for what's happened."

"He pointed mace at the guys," Schwed said. "Swung a screwdriver at them."

"He denies that," Joyce responded. "He may have done that in protection of himself. Does he look like he'd take on four guys?"

Andrias can think of no better alternative: "Twenty-five days. We'll split the difference." He looks at Schwed: "Attempted petty larceny?" The assistant D.A. nods his assent.

If Andrias remains a criminal court judge, he can look forward to this routine until the expiration of his term in 1988. He could get a 10-year reappointment, or if things break the way he hopes, the criminal court might be merged into the trial-level court under a merit selection plan being considered by the state legislature. Andrias would be brought in as a full-fledged supreme court justice and given the equal status he now lacks in criminal court.

The prestige would be appealing to him, but Andrias wouldn't want to be just another [Trial] court justice. Characteristically, he sees his present role as being more important than any he might assume on the higher court as presently structured. "I would consider it a demotion," he said firmly. "There are 43 people trying felonies over there and they're doing a good job. If I'm doing the job here, it's far more important to the overall process. This is a far more important job to me, and to the system."

3. PROCESSING MISDEMEANORS *

At 10 a.m. each day the bailiff calls the main courtroom into session. In one five-second breath his voice above the continuing din announces:

> Oyez, Oyez, Oyez! ThishonorableCourtofCommonPleasforthe SixthGeographicalAreaatNewHavenisnowopenandinsessionin thisplace/Allpersonshavin'causeofactionpendin'orhavin'been dulysummonedareboundtoappearhereinandtakeduenotice thereofandgivetheirattentionaccordin'tolaw/TheHonorable JudgeMancinipresidin'/Kindlybeseated/Notalkin'orwalkin' whilehisHonor'sonthebench.

This manner of speech and delivery capture well the court's preoccupation with speed and efficiency. With the arrival of the judge the court goes into formal session, but the intense sideline activity continues. Defense attorneys hold whispered conferences with their clients and prosecutors, badger the clerk for a preferred position on the day's calendar, or dart about trying to locate clients whose faces they can barely recognize. After they finish this business, they gravitate to the never-used juror's space, exchanging gossip as they wait for their cases to be called. The bondsman, in his customary seat next to the clerk of court, may be writing bonds for people arrested the night before. A secretary sits in the seldom-used witness box to the right of the judge taking applications for public defenders. Late arrivals continue to file in, and the gallery which often overflows into the hall is peppered with noisy children made restive by the strange scene and crowded conditions.

But after the judge enters the room, a new activity is added to the hubbub, a ritual before the bench, a ritual which might easily remain wholly unintelligible if not overlooked entirely amid all the other activity to a visitor watching from the gallery. A clerk mumbles out a name and a long series of numbers (identifying numbers for relevant sections of the criminal code) and someone (a defense attorney) springs forward. At the same time someone else (a prosecutor) peers up at the judge as he begins shuffling through a set of papers which has just been thrust into his hands by the clerk, and announces to the judge what he is going to do with the case—whether he will continue it for another week, nolle the charges, or urge the accused to plead guilty.

This preliminary business is completed at just about the same time the defendant has finished moving forward from the gallery and crossing the courtroom floor until he arrives in front of the bench between the prosecutor and his defense attorney. He might arrive just in time to hear the resolution of the case. If it is a continuance, either the prosecutor or the defense attorney instructs him to show up again at the same time and place a week later. If it is a nolle, they point to the

---

* Malcolm F. Feeley, *The Process is the Punishment*, Russell Sage Foundation,   New York, pp. 154–158 (Reprinted with Permission).

door and tell him he is free to go. If it is to be a plea of guilty, he makes the plea and the clerk then recites the charges anew, after which the prosecutor interjects his sentence recommendation to the judge, usually a fine of $10 or $25 or a suspended sentence. If it is a suspended sentence, the judge tells the defendant not to get in trouble again. If it is a fine, the prosecutor points out the bailiff who will instruct him as to how to pay the fine. If the defendant has any questions, it is unlikely that they will be answered because the prosecutor and defense attorney have already turned their attention to the next case.

Off to the side of the main courtroom—in the "backroom" as it is called—another drama is unfolding. Sitting at a table with a handful of case files spread out before him is a prosecutor. Seated across from him are several defense attorneys waiting to talk to him about their cases which, if all goes well, will be sent out to the open courtroom a few minutes later. After each attorney in turn takes up his cases with the prosecutor, he may carry the case file out to another prosecutor in open court for disposition. The following is a typical backroom exchange.

> The prosecutor holds out the arresting officer's report so that both he and the defense attorney can read it for the first time. The defendant is charged with receiving stolen goods and larceny (theft). The prosecutor argues that the case is cut and dried, but the defense attorney counters by claiming that the report is filled with ambiguities and that there are serious questions about the strength of the evidence. This, he suggests, is cause for leniency.

> The prosecutor refuses to acknowledge this line of reasoning, saying, "The defendant knew that they were stolen; two TV sets, stereos, and all that other stuff for fifty dollars!"

> The defense attorney protests, "Yea, but a black-and-white TV may not be worth very much."

> The prosecutor shrugs off this line of reasoning, but does concede, "I'll give the guy a suspended sentence because the goods were recovered—I'll give you a suspended on the larceny and nolle the other charge."

> The defense attorney pleads, "My client has no record and he's only nineteen years old. Give me a break."

> The prosecutor returns with, "This is a good deal. I'm giving you a break because of no prior and because the stuff was recovered."

> Whereupon the defense attorney asks, "How long is the suspended sentence?"

> The prosecutor replies, "Three months."

> And the defense attorney backs down: "OK, I'll take it."

After the attorneys reach this agreement, the case file is carried out to another prosecutor doing duty in "the pit," as the main courtroom is known, and placed in line to be called later in the day. In the interim the defense attorney scans the gallery looking for his client, then holds a brief conference with him in the corridor, explaining what the terms of the arrangement are and instructing him on what to do when his case is called.

Most cases are closed after one or two appearances, after a consideration about as detailed as the one described above. But in the event that a quick settlement cannot be reached, the prosecutor will readily agree to pass over or continue the case. The defense attorney may want to talk further with his client, try his luck with a different prosecutor, or simply stall, hoping for a better deal later. Because judges usually accept the prosecutor's recommendations, the continuance is rarely sought to avoid or obtain a particular judge. The prosecutors who periodically rotate in assignment to this courtroom are more than willing to postpone decisions, transferring work and responsibility to one of their colleagues and allowing them to finish their day's work earlier. If the case is especially serious or if there are substantial differences between the prosecutor and defense attorney, then the latter may have the case placed on the jury list, which means automatic removal to the other, less crowded courtroom. It does not mean, however, that the attorney has any serious intention of going to trial, nor is the move necessarily born of a desire to get the case before another prosecutor. Instead it allows for a protracted period of delay during which the defense attorney may expect to obtain additional information on the case, or "work on" the prosecutor or his client.

During this interim there is often little if any consideration of the case, and it resurfaces on the agenda of the prosecutor and defense attorney the morning of its appearance on the jury room's calendar. At this time the two adversaries move off again into the backroom of this courtroom and discuss the case under less hectic conditions. No matter where the issues are finally resolved, however, the decision process remains essentially the same, and this process is the main subject of this chapter.

4. PLEA CONTRACTS IN WEST GERMANY *

A West German penal order is a court order prepared by a prosecutor and signed by a judge. It describes the wrongful behavior of the defendant and the evidence gathered by the state and indicates the applicable provisions of the criminal code. It then specifies the punishment to be imposed upon the defendant. If the defendant does not object in writing or in person within one week, the order becomes effective and has the same status as a conviction after trial. If the defendant objects to the order, it is nullified and the case will go to

* William L.F. Felstiner, "Plea Contracts in West Germany," Law and Society Review, Vol. 13, 1979, pp. 310–316 (Reprinted with Permission).

trial. The prosecutor may not make a second attempt to dispose of a case by penal order. Since 1975, the penal order may not provide for imprisonment. The most common penalties are fines and suspensions of drivers' licenses.

Penal orders may be used only for crimes called *Vergehen*, the American equivalent of which is misdemeanors involving criminal intent or criminal negligence and felonies concerned with protecting property. *Vergehen* do not encompass petty traffic offenses or violations of business and health regulations. Nevertheless, a wide range of crimes from shoplifting and speeding to car theft, embezzlement, and grand larceny may be the subject of penal orders.

The penal order was designed to handle the routine, unproblematic case. It is a cursory procedure, and is not to be used if either the person or the behavior involved appears to require individualized treatment. The penal order is therefore inappropriate if the file shows any doubt about the guilt of the defendant, or a record of repeated violations, or behavior growing out of a disturbed interpersonal relationship.

Penal orders are numerically important in criminal case dispositions in West Germany. In the 1960s more cases were disposed of by penal order than by trial. Jescheck estimated that penal orders were used to process 70 percent of *all criminal matters* in which charges were filed. The importance of the penal order was unaffected by 1975 reforms which provided that such orders could no longer impose short prison sentences. But the number of penal orders was reduced by the 1969 decriminalization of many motor vehicle and administrative law violations. In 1976, after these revisions, the proportions of penal orders and trials in the lower criminal courts was roughly equal.

The relative frequency with which penal orders are used in seven common crimes is indicated in the following table derived from a study of prosecutor-police relations in nontraffic cases by Blankenburg, Sessar, and Steffen.

Table 1

Relative Frequency With Which Penal Orders Were Used in Seven Common Crimes Throughout West Germany in 1970

Crime	Percentage of cases disposed of by penal order
Simple theft	68
Sanitation law	65
Tax fraud	62
Embezzlement	41
Fraud	35
Serious theft	21
Auto theft	19

Although penal orders are used for many different crimes, Hans Kerner believes that in 1976 over half the orders concerned shoplifting, other minor theft (less than $100), or motor vehicle violations.

Investigations of *Vergehen* are usually opened and conducted by the police without prosecutorial supervision. The police will have decided on the charge—i.e., what it is they are investigating. They will write to the suspect asking him to come to the police office and give a statement. Most suspects do come, although their attendance cannot be compelled. The suspect will be told what he is alleged to have done and the legal consequences of such behavior.

When the investigation is as complete as the police believe appropriate, the file goes to the prosecutor. It contains the witnesses' statements, any experts' statements, the suspect's statement, and a case summary. It may include a record of prior convictions, but it is assumed that prosecutors routinely check a defendant's "legal history" after receipt of the police report. One should not be misled by the myth of the continental dossier. For these routine cases, the file amounts to no more than two or three pages; it resembles an American police report and rap sheet, not a presentence report.

The prosecutor must then decide whether to ask the police to investigate further, dismiss the case because the evidence is insufficient, issue a penal order, or go to trial. The decisions to issue a penal order or go to trial require a similar—and minimal—amount of effort: the prosecutor mechanically crosses out sections and fills in blanks, completing the form in a matter of minutes. In most cases, moreover, the punishment to be set by the penal order is standardized within a prosecutorial district: so much alcohol in the blood leads to suspension of a driver's license for a given period; theft of an article of a certain value will lead to a day fine of so many days.

Since penal orders generally impose fines, it is necessary to understand the day fine system that was adapted by the West Germans from Swedish practice. To equalize the deterrent effect of fines across income groups, fines are fixed in units of days rather than by amount. The daily rate varies with income, from as little as DM2 to as much as DM10,000 per day ($1 and $5,000, in August 1978). In routine penal order cases, no explicit investigation of income is actually made. The defendant may have stated his income when he was questioned by the police, or the prosecutor may simply estimate it from the defendant's occupation, residential area, the property involved in the case, and, in small communities, from local knowledge. It appears that income estimates are likely to be more accurate for wage earners than for businessmen, professionals, or those who live on unearned income. Although a defendant will not know what income the prosecutor has attributed to him, he can compare his fine with that of others whose income he knows; if he concludes that the fine is excessive, his only recourse is to reject the penal order and go to trial. Although no formal restrictions exist, the proceedings at such a trial may in fact be limited to establishing the defendant's income.

If the prosecutor has decided to use a penal order, he sends the file to the judge. Although the prosecutor's review may be perfunctory, the penal order is a prosecutorial instrument, and judicial review tends to be even more cursory. A judge in Hamburg told me that he could review 70 *routine* cases in fifteen minutes (shoplifting, for instance, or riding a subway without a ticket), an average of one case every 13 seconds; more attention is obviously paid to unusual cases. A judge will only deny a penal order if he finds something out of the ordinary— a psychologically disturbed defendant, a problem too complicated to be captured on paper, a difficult family situation, an offense with a history, or a defendant who appears to contest the facts. In 1976, the judical denial rate was less than 1 percent. Judges may discuss the content of penal orders with prosecutors, but neither can force the other to issue a specific order. If the judge signs the penal order, it is mailed to the defendant. If the defendant rejects it, the case is set for trial a few weeks later. The trial prosecutor is unlikely to be the one who prepared the penal order. Frequently he will be an *Amtsanwalt* rather than a *Staatsanwalt*—that is, a paraprofessional bureaucrat with a law degree from a *Fachhochschule* (training school for civil servants), while the prosecutor who issued the penal order is generally a university-trained lawyer. However, the judge who signed the penal order is likely to be the trial judge.

. . .

West German defendants are, I believe, not penalized for rejecting a penal order and insisting upon a trial.

If defendants are unlikely to be sentenced more harshly after a trial, why do approximately 75 percent (charged with any crime in any court) accept the penal order? No direct research on this question has been conducted in Germany, but the people I interviewed suggested that:

(a) Defendants seek to avoid publicity. A penal order is private. Trials are open to the public and may be reported in the press.

(b) The self-image of the accused is involved. A proper German citizen is not a defendant in a criminal proceeding. The recipient of a penal order can avoid becoming a defendant in court by accepting the penal order.

(c) The language of the penal order may sound imperative. The German word is *Strafbefehl* which literally means punishment *order.* Two informants suggested that *Strafbefehl* might sometimes be understood as an order rather than an offer. Hans Ziesel and John Langbein are skeptical. To the extent, however, that it *is* understood as an order, it may be coercive to a people who have a high respect for order.

(d) Acceptance of the penal order avoids the bother of a trial, the burden of court costs and, on occasion, a lawyer's fee.

(e) Some defendants are said to be intimidated by court proceedings and to accept a penal order to avoid the unfamiliar and troubling experience of a trial.

5. INSIDE A JUVENILE COURT *

A focal point of controversy since its inception in 1899, the juvenile justice system has been simultaneously heralded as a symbol of enlightenment and humanism as well as condemned as a bastion of discrimination and oppression. The court's most distinctive yet most controversial characteristics are its ideological emphasis on individualized justice and the unique organizational structure through which this philosophy is pursued.

Traditional juvenile justice philosophy depicts the court as nonpunitive and therapeutic, a legal institution whose espoused goals are the protection and guidance of children. It is praised as a socialized court offering individualized consideration and treatment on the basis of juvenile needs and characteristics. In order to implement the ideal of individualized justice, court personnel have been granted vast discretionary power. The nature and extent of that decision-making power as well as the procedures established to facilitiate it are paramount issues in the controversy that presently engulfs the juvenile court.

Although not without detractors, the juvenile court has enjoyed an extended period of widespread acceptance and support within American society. For over 80 years the prevailing interpretation of the court has depicted it as an expression of humanitarian sentiments in which children are not truly capable of criminal intent and the state, embodying the principle of *parens patriae,* is their benevolent protector.

Traditionally, court personnel have envisioned themselves as providing the protection necessitated by juveniles' inexperience and age: protection from adult exploitation and abuse and protection from their own youthful indiscretion. Not only has the juvenile court been portrayed as providing guidance and protection, but it has purported to do so in a manner tailored to the needs of each individual child. Few would deny that children need and have a right to be shielded from abuse and exploitation by adults and to receive reasoned counsel from mature, experienced advisors. Nevertheless, increasingly vocal critics have accused the court not only of failing to meet the needs of juveniles, but, equally damning, failing to protect society.

The juvenile justice system is an institution in crisis, one which can no longer rest on the rhetoric proclaiming individualized justice. Rather, it must face close scrutiny of the manner in which it has implemented that ideal. This book is about individualized justice, not the ideal,

* M.A. Bortner, *Inside a Juvenile Court,*
New York University Press, 1982 pp. 1–5;
(Reprinted with Permission).

but the embodiment of that ideal within the context of a contemporary metropolitan juvenile court.

The Emergence of an Experiment

Created at the end of the nineteenth century, the juvenile justice system may be viewed as the culmination of several major historical elements: an era of vast social change; positivistic explanations of delinquency; a belief in scientific social work as a vehicle for rehabilitation; and the proliferation of social reform movements (Mennel, 1973; Schlossman, 1977; Ryerson, 1978).

The historical era in which the juvenile court emerged was foremostly a time of widesweeping social change and unrest. Immigration, industrialization, and urbanization combined to create a society of turmoil, one in which former values and institutions seemed incapable of supporting a new developing social structure. The plethora of reform movements designed to quell social unrest and restore the status quo encompassed many activities viewed as "social problems," including youthful misbehavior.

There are divergent interpretations of the juvenile court origins. One portrays the juvenile justice system as a thinly disguised system of oppression, dedicated to controlling the indigent and powerless. The founders of the juvenile system are viewed as representatives of the entrenched interests within society, actors engaged in a power struggle between the status quo and emergent challenges to that order. But the most pervasive image of the system's beginnings portrays it as a benign and child-oriented institution. In this interpretation founders of the juvenile system were well-intentioned reformers who sought to create an institution permitting a unique status for juveniles and providing the nurturance and guidance necessitated by a changing society. In this image, the court was a symbol of society's concern for its young, an expression of humanitarian sentiment and enlightened legal philosophy. This is the image that has dominated within American society, an image that presently is being challenged severely.

Innocence and Individualized Justice

The concept of criminal responsibility is central to traditional Anglo–American criminal law. Inherent in this concept is the assumption that criminal behavior is voluntaristic, that is, that crime is a willful breach of legal codes. Accordingly, criminal behavior is portrayed as freely chosen by the individual; the perpetrator is resonsible and, most importantly, punishable for such behavior.

Despite this stance regarding free will and individual responsibility, the legal codes have traditionally acknowledged excusing conditions. Certain situations have been accepted as evidence demonstrating a lack of criminal intent, therefore absolving the individual of criminal responsibility. The conditions in which criminal behavior might be excused have included necessity (self-defense), insanity, and infancy.

The legal tradition of depicting "infancy" as a mitigating circumstance and as a basis for excusing a child from full culpability necessitates specification of criteria for defining infancy. Historically, divergent images of adolescence and childhood have emerged; even so, infancy as an excusing factor has been defined disparately. In the eighteenth and nineteenth centuries children were legally as responsible and punishable as adults, but, . . . the judiciary was reticent to execute the harsher sentences meted out to children. Nevertheless, concern regarding the lack of care and special treatment for children has been viewed as a contributing factor to the creation of the juvenile court.

Reformers asserted that children must be afforded a unique status, one in which criminal responsibility is mitigated and the state acts as benevolent protector rather than vengeful punisher. But even though children were not to be punished, their unlawful behavior was of great concern to the society. Under the principle of *parens patriae,* the state was to assume the position of a substitute parent and intervene in the lives of wayward children. Thus, although they were relieved of full criminal responsibility, juveniles were given a unique status that facilitated extensive state involvement in their activities and development.

. . . The theoretical distinctions between the juvenile court and the adult criminal court are many. The juvenile court is civil, not criminal; juveniles are "taken into custody," never arrested; a petition is filed "on behalf of" juveniles, not against them; allegations are made, but no criminal charges are filed; a hearing is held, but juveniles are not on trial; juveniles may be adjudicated "delinquent," but never convicted; juveniles may be found "in violation of the juvenile code," but they are never found guilty; and if allegations are ruled true, juveniles are supervised and treated, never punished.

All of the distinctions between the adult and juvenile system purportedly are made on behalf of juveniles and designed to provide a cloistered, confidential atmosphere in which juvenile life circumstances may be reviewed, problems diagnosed, and individualized treatment prescribed. Noting the theoretical distinctions, a major question becomes the extent to which they are reflected in present day realities. Numerous critics have charged that they are more rhetorical than real, and equally disparaging, that the advantages of such a structure are dubious.

6. UNDERSTANDING REVERSIBLE ERROR IN CRIMINAL APPEALS *

Where do criminal appeals come from in terms of the trial court proceeding being challenged, the offenses involved, and the issues raised? What are the outcomes of criminal appeals? Are successful

* Joy Chapper and Roger Hanson, "Understanding Reversible Error in Criminal Appeals," National Center for State Courts, 1990, pp. 3; 5–8 (Reprinted with Permission).

Table 1

Percentage Distribution of Alternatives Outcomes
Five–Court Pattern

Appeal Outcomes	Percent all Appeals	Percent Nonaffirmances
Affirmed	79.4	—
Reversed	20.6	100.0
Acquittal	1.9	9.4
New trial	6.6	31.9
Resentencing	7.3	35.3
Other	4.8	23.4

appeals associated with certain configurations of proceedings and is-sues? What kinds of errors are being made in the trial courts? Answers to these questions are essential to efforts to enhance the effectiveness of the trial process and to inform our understanding of cases on appeal. In response, the National Center for State Courts (NCSC) has undertaken a study of these questions with data collected from five state appellate courts hearing first-level criminal appeals.

The conventional wisdom is that with free appeals there is little incentive not to appeal, and, as a result, a large number of criminal appeals are meritless, if not frivolous. Given that perspective, one might not expect to find a great many successful appeals. In fact, the overall affirmance rate for the five courts is 79.4 percent. Four of the courts (all but Rhode Island) are within plus-or-minus two percentage points of that figure (78.6, 79.3, 79.3, and 81.7 percent); Rhode Island's affirmance rate was 70.8 percent.

As seen in Table 1, instances in which a conviction or judgment were overturned and the case either remanded for a new trial or the charges dismissed were quite infrequent. Acquittals constituted only 1.9 percent of all appeals and only 9.4 percent of all nonaffirmances or "winners." In no jurisdiction did acquittals occur in as many as 4 percent of all appeals. A remand with the possibility of retrial was more likely—6.6 percent of all appeals and 31.9 percent of all winners.

Defendants had the most success in obtaining a new sentencing hearing or a corrected sentence entered by the appellate court. These constitute 7.3 percent of all appeals and 35.3 percent of all winners. Defendants obtain some relief in an additional 4.8 percent of the appeals; many of these are appeals with multiple convictions where at least one conviction is affirmed.

Issues, Error, and Outcomes

. . . [C]losely related to outcomes is the nature of the issues raised on appeal. As seen in Table 2, the appeals courts identified 267 prejudicial errors affecting other than the sentencing hearing or the

Table 2

Reversible Error by Issue

Issue	Percentage of all Error Associated With Issue	Success Rate
Admission/exclusion of evidence	20.6%	7.7%
Instructions	13.5	9.7
Procedural or discretionary ruling	13.1	7.8
Sufficiency of the evidence	12.0	5.8
Merger of offenses	10.5	51.9
Suppression of evidence, statements, or identification	10.5	8.4
Ineffective assistance/waiver of counsel	6.0	12.9
Other constitutional claims (double jeopardy, speedy trial)	4.9	11.5
Jury selection or deliberation	3.4	8.8
Statutory interpretation or application	2.2	19.4
Plea	2.2	15.0
Prosecutorial misconduct	1.1	1.9
	100%	
	N=267	

sentence in jury trial cases. Quantitatively, just over 20 percent of the errors related to rulings on the admission or exclusion of evidence; instructions accounted for 13.5 percent, sufficiency of the evidence 12 percent. However, as Table 2 also indicates, some issues are more successful than others in resulting in reversible error.

The "success rate" among different issues can be estimated by dividing the number of times a particular type of error is found by the total number of times the issue is raised. According to Table 2, the success rate appears in large measure to be inversely related to the relative frequency with which an issue is raised. That is, the most frequently raised issues have lower error rates than less frequently raised ones.

Substantively, error seemed to fall into three broad categories, although specific case precedents differ from court to court. Those categories are:

- perennial problems arising from the context in which they are raised. Evidentiary questions raised during the examination of witnesses at trial are a classic example.

- issues that result from new areas of litigation. Trial judges have problems with new areas until law and procedure become settled. Where these problems will occur is hard to predict, but when they occur they exist across courts with each jurisdiction having wrinkles on the basic theme. This is seen in sex offenses involving child victims where every jurisdiction has reversals as a result of the trial judge's decisions permitting testimony on the veracity of the child victim. Another example involves questions regarding the admissibility of roadside sobriety tests in prosecutions for driving under the influence or driving while impaired.

- inattention or lack of deliberation. Error in many instances appeared less the result of the idiosyncratic nature of state law than of the trial judge's failure to follow established rules or procedures. These included the failure to afford allocution before sentencing and to provide notice before a revocation hearing.

An Emerging Issue—Sentencing Error

The research reveals a growing trend that warrants separate treatment. This is the emergence of sentencing issues as a problem, regardless of the jurisdiction's particular sentencing law. Sentencing issues were raised in one-quarter of the appeals, and it appears that sentencing issues are not simply "add-on" issues to appeals that would otherwise have been filed; a great number of appeals were filed raising only sentencing issues. In addition, sentencing issues have a high error rate. In fact, when sentencing is raised, the courts find error 25 percent of the time.

The appeals raised a wide range of issues relating to the sentence and the sentencing hearing, not simply disparity claims. Sentencing issues included enhancements (aggravating factors warranting a departure from the guidelines or the computation of the time enhancement); mitigating factors; the imposition of consecutive as opposed to concurrent terms; problems with the conduct of the sentencing hearing, including the denial of allocution; and the trial judge's illegal considerations (e.g., pleaded not guilty). Although the nature of the error differed across the five courts, even in Rhode Island, which has indeterminate sentencing, sentencing issues had a 38.5 percent error rate.

C. VALUES UNDERLYING TWO MODELS OF THE CRIMINAL PROCESS

1. THE CRIME CONTROL AND DUE PROCESS MODELS *

[I]t is possible to identify two competing systems of values, the tension between which accounts for the intense activity now observable in the development of the criminal process. . . . [T]he polarity of the two models is not absolute. Although it would be possible to construct models that exist in an institutional vacuum, it would not serve our purposes to do so. We are postulating, not a criminal process that operates in any kind of society at all, but rather one that operates within the framework of contemporary American society. . . .

Crime Control Values. The value system that underlies the Crime Control Model is based on the proposition that the repression of criminal conduct is by far the most important function to be performed by the criminal process. The failure of law enforcement to bring criminal conduct under tight control is viewed as leading to the breakdown of public order and thence to the disappearance of an important condition of human freedom. If the laws go unenforced—which is to say, if it is perceived that there is a high percentage of failure to apprehend and convict in the criminal process—a general disregard for legal controls tends to develop. The law-abiding citizen then becomes the victim of all sorts of unjustifiable invasions of his interests. His security of person and property is sharply diminished, and, therefore, so is his liberty to function as a member of society. The claim ultimately is that the criminal process is a positive guarantor of social freedom. In order to achieve this high purpose, the Crime Control Model requires that primary attention be paid to the efficiency with which the criminal process operates to screen suspects, determine guilt, and secure appropriate dispositions of persons convicted of crime.

. . .

The model, in order to operate successfully, must produce a high rate of apprehension and conviction, and must do so in a context where the magnitudes being dealt with are very large and the resources for dealing with them are very limited. There must then be a premium on speed and finality. Speed, in turn, depends on informality and on uniformity; finality depends on minimizing the occasions for challenge. The process must not be cluttered up with ceremonious rituals that do not advance the progress of a case. Facts can be established more quickly through interrogation in a police station than through the formal process of examination and cross-examination in a court. It follows that extra-judicial processes should be preferred to judicial processes, informal operations to formal ones. But informality is not enough; there must also be uniformity. Routine, stereotyped proce-

* Herbert Packer, *The Limits of the Criminal Sanction,* Stanford University   Press, 1968, pp. 154–173. Copyright 1968 (Reprinted with permission)

dures are essential if large numbers are being handled. The model that will operate successfully on these presuppositions must be an administrative, almost a managerial, model. The image that comes to mind is an assembly-line conveyor belt down which moves an endless stream of cases, never stopping, carrying the cases to workers who stand at fixed stations and who perform on each case as it comes by the same small but essential operation that brings it one step closer to being a finished product, or, to exchange the metaphor for the reality, a closed file. The criminal process, in this model, is seen as a screening process in which each successive stage—pre-arrest investigation, arrest, post-arrest investigation, preparation for trial, trial or entry of plea, conviction, disposition—involves a series of routinized operations whose success is gauged primarily by their tendency to pass the case along to a successful conclusion.

What is a successful conclusion? One that throws off at an early stage those cases in which it appears unlikely that the person apprehended is an offender and then secures, as expeditiously as possible, the conviction of the rest, with a minimum of occasions for challenge, let alone post-audit. By the application of administrative expertness, primarily that of the police and prosecutors, an early determination of probable innocence or guilt emerges. Those who are probably innocent are screened out. Those who are probably guilty are passed quickly through the remaining stages of the process.

· · ·

The presumption of guilt is what makes it possible for the system to deal efficiently with large numbers, as the Crime Control Model demands. The supposition is that the screening processes operated by police and prosecutors are reliable indicators of probable guilt.

· · ·

It would be a mistake to think of the presumption of guilt as the opposite of the presumption of innocence that we are so used to thinking of as the polestar of the criminal process and that, as we shall see, occupies an important position in the Due Process Model. The presumption of innocence is not its opposite; it is irrelevant to the presumption of guilt; the two concepts are different rather than opposite ideas. The difference can perhaps be epitomized by an example. A murderer, for reasons best known to himself, chooses to shoot his victim in plain view of a large number of people. When the police arrive, he hands them his gun and says, "I did it and I'm glad." His account of what happened is corroborated by several eyewitnesses. He is placed under arrest and led off to jail. Under these circumstances, which may seem extreme but which in fact characterize with rough accuracy the evidentiary situation in a large proportion of criminal cases, it would be plainly absurd to maintain that more probably than not the suspect did not commit the killing. But that is not what the presumption of innocence means. It means that until there has been adjudication of guilt by an authority legally competent to make such an adjudication, the suspect is to be treated, for reasons that have nothing whatever to do with the probable outcome of the case, as if his guilt is an open question.

The presumption of innocence is a direction to officials about how they are to proceed, not a prediction of outcome. The presumption of guilt, however, is purely and simply a prediction of outcome.

. . . In the presumption of guilt this model finds a factual predicate for the position that the dominant goal of repressing crime can be achieved through highly summary processes without any great loss of efficiency (as previously defined), because of the probability that, in the run of cases, the preliminary screening processes operated by the police and the prosecuting officials contain adequate guarantees of reliable fact-finding. Indeed, the model takes an even stronger position. It is that subsequent processes, particularly those of a formal adjudicatory nature, are unlikely to produce as reliable fact-finding as the expert administrative process that precedes them is capable of. The criminal process thus must put special weight on the quality of administrative fact-finding. It becomes important, then, to place as few restrictions as possible on the character of the administrative fact-finding processes and to limit restrictions to such as enhance reliability, excluding those designed for other purposes.

. . . The pure Crime Control Model has very little use for many conspicuous features of the adjudicative process, and in real life works out a number of ingenious compromises with them. Even in the pure model, however, there have to be devices for dealing with the suspect after the preliminary screening process has resulted in a determination of probable guilt. The focal device, as we shall see, is the plea of guilty; through its use, adjudicative fact-finding is reduced to a minimum. It might be said of the Crime Control Model that, when reduced to its barest essentials and operating at its most successful pitch, it offers two possibilities: an administrative fact-finding process leading (1) to exoneration of the suspect or (2) to the entry of a plea of guilty.

Due Process Values. If the Crime Control Model resembles an assembly line, the Due Process Model looks very much like an obstacle course. Each of its successive stages is designed to present formidable impediments to carrying the accused any further along in the process. Its ideology is not the converse of that underlying the Crime Control Model. It does not rest on the idea that it is not socially desirable to repress crime, although critics of its application have been known to claim so. Its ideology is composed of a complex of ideas, some of them based on judgments about the efficacy of crime control devices, others having to do with quite different considerations. The ideology of due process is far more deeply impressed on the formal structure of the law than is the ideology of crime control; yet an accurate tracing of the strands that make it up is strangely difficult. What follows is only an attempt at an approximation.

The Due Process Model encounters its rival on the Crime Control Model's own ground in respect to the reliability of fact-finding processes. The Crime Control Model, as we have suggested, places heavy reliance on the ability of investigative and prosecutorial officers, acting in an informal setting in which their distinctive skills are given full sway, to elicit and reconstruct a tolerably accurate account of what actually took place in an alleged criminal event. The Due Process Model rejects this premise and substitutes for it a view of informal, nonadjudicative fact-finding that stresses the possibility of error. People are notoriously poor observers of disturbing events—the more emotion-arousing the context the greater the possibility that recollection will be incorrect; confessions and admissions by persons in police custody may be induced by physical or psychological coercion so that the police end up hearing what the suspect thinks they want to hear rather than the truth; witnesses may be animated by a bias or interest that no one would trouble to discover except one specially charged with protecting the interests of the accused (as the police are not). Considerations of this kind all lead to a rejection of informal fact-finding processes as definitive of factual guilt and to an insistence on formal, adjudicative, adversary fact-finding processes in which the factual case against the accused is publicly heard by an impartial tribunal and is evaluated only after the accused has had a full opportunity to discredit the case against him. Even then, the distrust of fact-finding processes that animates the Due Process Model is not dissipated. The possibilities of human error being what they are, further scrutiny is necessary, or at least must be available, in case facts have been overlooked or suppressed in the heat of battle. How far this subsequent scrutiny must be available is a hotly controverted issue today. In the pure Due Process Model the answer would be: at least as long as there is an allegation of factual error that has not received an adjudicative hearing in a fact-finding context. The demand for finality is thus very low in the Due Process Model.

. . . Even if the discussion is confined, for the moment, to the question of reliability, it is apparent that more is at stake than simply an evaluation of what kinds of fact-finding processes, alone or in combination, are likely to produce the most nearly reliable results. It still remains to ask how much weight is to be given to the competing demands of reliability (a high degree of probability in each case that factual guilt has been accurately determined) and efficiency (expeditious handling of the large numbers of cases that the process ingests).

. . . The Due Process Model insists on the prevention and elimination of mistakes to the extent possible; the Crime Control Model accepts the probability of mistakes up to the level at which they interfere with the goal of repressing crime, either because too many guilty people are escaping or, more subtly, because general awareness of the unreliability of the process leads to a decrease in the deterrent efficacy of the criminal law. In this view, reliability and efficiency are not polar opposites but rather complementary characteristics. The system is reliable *because* efficient; reliability becomes a matter of independent concern only when it becomes so attenuated as to impair efficiency. All of this the Due Process Model rejects. If efficiency demands shortcuts around reliability, then absolute efficiency must be rejected. The aim of the process is at least as much to protect the factually innocent as it is to convict the factually guilty. It is a little like quality control in industrial technology: tolerable deviation from standard varies with the importance of conformity to standard in the destined uses of the product. The Due Process Model resembles a factory that has to devote a substantial part of its input to quality control. This necessarily cuts down on quantitative output.

All of this is only the beginning of the ideological difference between the two models. [In the Due Process model,] [t]he combination of stigma and loss of liberty that is embodied in the end result of the criminal process is viewed as being the heaviest deprivation that government can inflict on the individual. Furthermore, the processes that culminate in these highly afflictive sanctions are seen as in themselves coercive, restricting, and demeaning. Power is always subject to abuse—sometimes subtle, other times, as in the criminal process, open and ugly. Precisely because of its potency in subjecting the individual to the coercive power of the state, the criminal process must, in this model, be subjected to controls that prevent it from operating with maximal efficiency. According to this ideology, maximal efficiency means maximal tyranny. And, although no one would assert that minimal efficiency means minimal tyranny, the proponents of the Due Process Model would accept with considerable equanimity a substantial diminution in the efficiency with which the criminal process operates in the interest of preventing official oppression of the individual.

The most modest-seeming but potentially far-reaching mechanism by which the Due Process Model implements these anti-authoritarian values is the doctrine of legal guilt. According to this doctrine, a person is not to be held guilty of crime merely on a showing that in all probability, based upon reliable evidence, he did factually what he is said to have done. Instead, he is to be held guilty if and only if these factual determinations are made in procedurally regular fashion and by authorities acting within competences duly allocated to them. Furthermore, he is not to be held guilty, even though the factual determination is or might be adverse to him, if various rules designed to protect him and to safeguard the integrity of the process are not given effect: the tribunal that convicts him must have the power to deal with his kind of case ("jurisdiction") and must be geographically appropriate ("venue"); too long a time must not have elapsed since the offense was committed ("statute of limitations"); he must not have been previously convicted or acquitted of the same or a substantially similar offense ("double jeopardy"); he must not fall within a category of persons, such as children or the insane, who are legally immune to conviction ("criminal responsibility"); and so on. None of these requirements has anything to do with the factual question of whether the person did or did not engage in the conduct that is charged as the offense against him; yet favorable answers to any of them will mean that he is legally innocent. Wherever the competence to make adequate factual determinations lies, it is apparent that only a tribunal that is aware of these guilt-defeating doctrines and is willing to apply them can be viewed as competent to make determinations of legal guilt. The police and the prosecutors are ruled out by lack of competence, in the first instance, and by lack of assurance of willingness, in the second. Only an impartial tribunal can be trusted to make determinations of legal as opposed to factual guilt.

. . .

The possibility of legal innocence is expanded enormously when the criminal process is viewed as the appropriate forum for correcting its own abuses. This notion may well account for a greater amount of the distance between the two models than any other. In theory the Crime Control Model can tolerate rules that forbid illegal arrests, unreasonable searches, coercive interrogations, and the like. What it cannot tolerate is the vindication of those rules in the criminal process itself through the exclusion of evidence illegally obtained or through the reversal of convictions in cases where the criminal process has breached the rules laid down for its observance. And the Due Process Model, although it may in the first instance be addressed to the maintenance of reliable fact-finding techniques, comes eventually to incorporate prophylactic and deterrent rules that result in the release of the factually guilty even in cases in which blotting out the illegality would still leave an adjudicative fact-finder convinced of the accused person's guilt. Only by penalizing errant police and prosecutors within the criminal process itself can adequate pressure be maintained, so the argument runs, to induce conformity with the Due Process Model.

Another strand in the complex of attitudes underlying the Due Process Model is the idea—itself a shorthand statement for a complex of attitudes—of equality. This notion has only recently emerged as an explicit basis for pressing the demands of the Due Process Model, but it appears to represent, at least in its potential, a most powerful norm for influencing official conduct. Stated most starkly, the ideal of equality holds that "there can be no equal justice where the kind of trial a man gets depends on the amount of money he has." The factual predicate underlying this assertion is that there are gross inequalities in the financial means of criminal defendants as a class, that in an adversary system of criminal justice an effective defense is largely a function of the resources that can be mustered on behalf of the accused, and that the very large proportion of criminal defendants who are, operationally speaking, "indigent" will thus be denied an effective defense. This factual premise has been strongly reinforced by recent studies that in turn have been both a cause and an effect of an increasing emphasis upon norms for the criminal process based on the premise.

. . .

It should be observed that the impact of the equality norm will vary greatly depending upon the point in time at which it is introduced into a model of the criminal process. If one were starting from scratch to decide how the process ought to work, the norm of equality would have nothing very important to say on such questions as, for example, whether an accused should have an effective assistance of counsel in deciding whether to enter a plea of guilty. One could decide, on quite independent considerations, that it is or is not a good thing to afford that facility to the generality of persons accused of crime. But the impact of the equality norm becomes far greater when it is brought to bear on a process whose contours have already been shaped. If our model of the criminal process affords defendants who are in a financial position to do so the right to consult a lawyer before entering a plea, then the equality norm exerts powerful pressure to provide such an opportunity to all defendants and to regard the failure to do so as a malfunctioning of the process of whose consequences the accused is entitled to be relieved. In a sense, this has been the role of the equality norm in affecting the real-world criminal process. It has made its appearance on the scene comparatively late, and has therefore encountered a system in which the relative financial inability on most persons accused of crime results in treatment very different from that accorded the small minority of the financially capable. For this reason, its impact has already been substantial and may be expected to be even more so in the future.

There is a final strand of thought in the Due Process Model that is often ignored but that needs to be candidly faced if thought on the subject is not to be obscured. This is a mood of skepticism about the morality and utility of the criminal sanction, taken either as a whole or in some of its applications. The subject is a large and complicated one, comprehending as it does much of the intellectual history of our times.

. . .

This skepticism, which may be fairly said to be widespread among the most influential and articulate contemporary leaders of informed opinion, leads to an attitude toward the processes of the criminal law that . . . engenders "a peculiar receptivity toward claims of injustice which arise within the traditional structure of the system itself; fundamental disagreement and unease about the very bases of the criminal law has, inevitably, created acute pressure at least to expand and liberalize those of its processes and doctrines which serve to make more tentative its judgments or limit its power." In short, doubts about the ends for which power is being exercised create pressure to limit the discretion with which that power is exercised.

The point need not be pressed to the extreme of doubts about or rejection of the premises upon which the criminal sanction in general rests. Unease may be stirred simply by reflection on the variety of uses to which the criminal sanction is put and by a judgment that an increasingly large proportion of those uses may represent an unwise invocation of so extreme a sanction.

. . . Recognizing that our models are only models, what agencies of government have the power to pick and choose between their competing demands? Once again, the limiting features of the American context come into play. Ours is not a system of legislative supremacy. The distinctively American institution of judicial review exercises a limiting and ultimately a shaping influence on the criminal process. Because the Crime Control Model is basically an affirmative model, emphasizing at every turn the existence and exercise of official power, its validating authority is ultimately legislative (although proximately administrative). Because the Due Process Model is basically a negative model, asserting limits on the nature of official power and on the modes of its exercise, its validating authority is judicial and requires an appeal to supra-legislative law, to the law of the Constitution. To the extent that tensions between the two models are resolved by deference to the Due Process Model, the authoritative force at work is the judicial power, working in the distinctively judicial mode of invoking the sanction of nullity. That is at once the strength and the weakness of the Due Process Model: its strength because in our system the appeal to the Constitution provides the last and the overriding word; its weakness because saying no in specific cases is an exercise in futility unless there is a general willingness on the part of the officials who operate the process to apply negative prescriptions across the board. It is no accident that statements reinforcing the Due Process Model come from the courts, while at the same time facts denying it are established by the police and prosecutors.

2. A THIRD MODEL OF THE CRIMINAL PROCESS *

American thought about criminal procedure is confined within a prevailing ideology. By describing an alternative, I shall seek to illustrate that our present assumptions are not the inevitable truths they often seem to be. The alternative presented is not especially novel, nor is it one to which I necessarily subscribe. My purpose is merely to explore the problem of ideology in criminal procedure, and to that end the self-conscious posing of an alternative is justified by its heuristic value.

A single unifying conception underlies Packer's two Models, despite the fact that he presents them as diametrically opposed. He derives the two Models from the alternative responses he conceives to the problem of the relationship of the state to the individual in the criminal process; and the unarticulated major premise of his article is that the essential nature of that problem is such as to permit only two, polar responses.

* John Griffiths, "Ideology in Criminal Procedure or A Third 'Model' of the Criminal Process," *Yale Law Journal*, Vol. 79, 1970, pp. 359–360; 364; 367–371 (Reprinted with Permission).

The basic object of the criminal process is "to put a suspected criminal in jail," as he puts it at one point. In the service of this fundamental dogma, Packer consistently portrays the criminal process as a struggle—a stylized war—between two contending forces whose interests are implacably hostile: the Individual (particularly, the *accused* individual) and the State. His two Models are nothing more than alternative derivations from that conception of profound and irreconcilable disharmony of interest. Since the metaphor of battle roughly suits this silent premise about the nature of the relationship of state and individual reflected in the criminal process, I shall use it to characterize Packer's position: the Battle Model of the criminal process.

If Packer's article rests not upon two but upon a single, albeit unarticulated, basic conception of the nature of criminal process—that it is a battleground of fundamentally hostile forces, where the only relevant variable is the "balance of advantage"—we can expand the conceptual (and perhaps the practical) possibilities available to us if we create another fundamental conception to substitute for it. It may well be that there are many possibilities, but we can do a great deal even while confining ourselves to the simple opposite of Packer's ideological starting point. He assumes disharmony, fundamentally irreconcilable interests, a state of war. We can start from an assumption of reconcilable—even mutually supportive—interests, a state of love.

Of course, it is easy to react reflexively that such an ideological premise is utopian, or confused, or absurd. Like Packer, I make no claim of direct applicability for my alternative "model." I should nevertheless induce the doubter to suspend disbelief, at least temporarily, by making the proposed alternative ideology as plausible as possible. So I propose to gather some respectability by using an allusive name for it: a name, that is, that invokes a "real world" institution which occasionally inflicts punishments on offenders for their offenses but which is nonetheless built upon a fundamental assumption of harmony of interest and love—and as to which no one finds it odd, or even particularly noteworthy, that this is the case. I will, then (following Packer in using the word "model" only for convenience' sake, and preferring to think of it as an ideological metaphor), offer a "Family Model" of the criminal process. I wish to emphasize, however, that this allusive reference is to our family *ideology* as I take it to be, not to the facts of all or particular families.

In what follows, it should be emphasized that I am talking about "punishment" in the strict sense which requires that it be exacted from an offender for his offense—not about things done for the good of the person concerned, nor about things done prophylactically for the good of society, and certainly not about things called "punishment" metaphorically because they share the element of unpleasantness. That "punishment" in this strict sense goes on in a family is plain. I spank my child for tearing my books, not because to tear them is bad for him, nor because he "needs to learn" about books, but because I and the rest of the members of the family don't want our books destroyed and want to accomplish that objective by appealing to our children's capacity for self-control rather than by taking preventive measures.

"Punishing" thus does go on in a family. One could impose a conceptual "process" of adjudication and exaction upon the facts of family life if it seemed worthwhile. Although punishments are expected to and do come out of the family's adjudication process, it is not a bitter "struggle from start to finish." A parent and child have far more to do with each other than obedience, deterrence, and punishment, and *any* process between them will reflect the full range of their relationship and the concerns growing out of it. Everyone expects and believes that whatever is done, it will be consistent with what the parent recognizes as the basic well-being of his child.

What, then, would be the general thrust of a Family Model?

The Changed Conception of Crime and of the Criminal. A thoroughgoing Family Model of the criminal process would be accompanied by a basic change of attitude toward "anti-social" behavior; the very vocabulary with which the subject is discussed would necessarily be affected. People operating within a process built upon the assumption of an ultimate reconcilability of interest between the state and the accused (and the convicted as well, of course), could not lose sight, while concerned with the criminal process, of the range and variety of relationships between the state and its citizens. Seeing "criminal" conduct in its essential variousness and its inseparability from other social events, they would reflect this perception through their attitudes and behavior in the criminal process. They would be unlikely, that is, to think about or try to deal with "crime" or "criminals" in the isolated way which is characteristic of our criminal process because they would regard these categories as of very limited and specialized usefulness.

Under a Family Model, the entire concept of a "crime" would also be quite different. One could be expected to recognize quite explicitly the role of society in perceiving an occurrence as criminal deviance, and reacting to it accordingly, as of joint importance with the actual uncharacterized conduct of the "criminal" in producing "a crime." This approach now prevails only among sociologists, who impose detachment on themselves by special discipline. For the rest of us, it is very hard to adopt so balanced an attitude toward an enemy in a battle. What now derives from sociological discipline could equally well, it seems to me, derive from a genuine acceptance of the idea that criminals are just people who are deemed to have offended—that we are all of us both actual and potential criminals—that "criminals" are not a special kind and class of people with a unique relation to the state. So adherents to the Family Model would not talk (or think) about "offenders," or "criminals," or "people who commit crimes," as if these words referred to people in any other aspect than their exposure to the criminal process.

Comment

We will, throughout the remainder of this book, be discussing one legal rule or aspect of the criminal process after another. At each point, the student is urged to reflect upon whether the rule or aspect embodies crime control or due process values, or some combination of them. And, does the "family model" ever emerge? If so, where?

D. RECOMMENDED READING

Bortner, M.A. *Inside a Juvenile Court.* New York University Press, New York, 1982.

Cole, George F. *Criminal Justice: Law and Politics.* Duxbury Press, North Scituate, Mass., 4 ed., 1984.

Eisenstein, James and Jacob, Herbert, *Felony Justice.* Little Brown, Boston, 1977.

Eisenstein, James, Flemming, Roy, and Novdulli, Peter, *The Contours of Justice.* Little Brown, Boston, 1988.

Feeley, Malcolm M. *The Process is the Punishment.* Russell Sage Foundation, New York, 1979.

Gottfredson, Michael R. and Gottfredson, Don M. *Decisionmaking in Criminal Justice: Toward the Rational Exercise of Discretion.* Ballinger Publishing, Cambridge, Mass., 1980.

Radzinowicz, Leon and Wolfgang, Marvin, eds. *Crime and Justice,* 3 volumes. Basic Books, Inc., New York, 2d ed. 1977.

Chapter IV

THE POLICE

A. INTRODUCTION: THE HISTORY OF THE PO-
   ## LICE *

"Every constitution must first *gain* authority, and then *use* authority," Walter Bagehot observed. "It must first win the loyalty and homage of mankind, and then employ that homage in the work of government." In societies with representative governments, the police must obtain and then utilize voluntary compliance with their authority. Effective law enforcement requires general agreement that the power of the police is legitimate. As Edwin Chadwick said, "A police force . . . must owe its real efficiency to the sympathies and concurrent action of the great body of the people." The experience of the Royal Irish Constabulary, a semimilitary police established in 1822 to bolster English rule in Ireland, proved that police officers were helpless if local citizens did not give them aid and information. The "great body" of Irishmen never accepted the force's legitimacy. Public sympathy and support is by no means automatic; the police must work to achieve and maintain legitimacy. Certainly, as is clear in the case of the Irish constabulary, people's view of the police reflects their general attitude toward the government which policemen represent. Nevertheless, the police have an active role in creating their own public image, and in fact many people's perception of the government derives from their contact with its lowest level of authority, the policeman. Chief William Parker of the Los Angeles police bluntly rephrased Bagehot's idea: "The vital elements of civilized life, including our most sacred institutions, at one time or another have been laboriously *sold* to the people."

The laws which established modern patrol forces in London in 1829 and in New York City in 1845 outlined their basic structure but did not provide a formula for "selling" or legitimating the police. In both cities conscious decisions and historical circumstances shaped the police image. The commanders of the forces were influenced by the ideological, political, and economic contexts of two different societies as reflected in their greatest cities.

Establishment of the New Police

London's Metropolitan Police Act, which Sir Robert Peel finally steered through Parliament in 1829, created a full-time day and night

* Wilbur R. Miller, *Cops and Bobbies: Police Authority in New York and London, 1830–1870* (Chicago: University of Chicago Press, 1977) pp. 1–5. Copyright 1977 (Reprinted with permission).

141

patrol force for a police district. The new police, commanded by two commissioners appointed by the home secretary as permanent heads of the force, supplanted most of the old police apparatus. Although the police were an arm of the national government divorced from local control, the parishes, or units of London's local government, had to support them from their tax revenues. The new police were the first force in the world organized to prevent crime by constant patrolling instead of merely apprehending offenders after the fact.

Sir Robert Peel's main contributions to the new institution were synthesizing decades of thought about police reorganization, using his political skill to secure passage of the Metropolitan Police Act and his insistence that political patronage be excluded from appointments and promotions. . . . The two commissioners whom he appointed established the police's military organization and discipline, the system of patrolling fixed beats, the distinctive blue uniform, and numerous important details of structure and practice which added up to the London bobby, or peeler. The New York City's Municipal Police Act was put into effect in 1845 after several years of political wrangling. The measure spelled out more details of the new institution than did its London forebear. It established a semimilitary day and night patrol force to replace the old system and also specified the qualifications for appointment, fixed the men's terms of office, and established the pay of various ranks. With the mayor's approval, each alderman appointed the police of the ward he represented. Unlike the London police, which remained largely unchanged after the commissioners established its structure and policy, the New York force was altered in various major and minor ways throughout the mid-nineteenth century. The 1853 reorganization put the force under the command of a commission of three elected officials, the mayor and two judges. The most drastic change, in 1857, shifted control from city to state authorities, entrusting direction to commissioners appointed by the governor. In 1870 control was returned to the city with a commission appointed by the mayor. In contrast to the London police, the New York force was an evolving and changing institution.

In neither London nor New York could daily police work be codified by statutes. The commanders of the forces responded both to common fears of excessive police power and to common demands for order in two heterogeneous, expanding cities. However, they developed structures and practices which reflected the different qualities of London's and New York's political and social conflicts and different public expectations of the police.

The initial task of the police commanders in winning legitimacy for their institutions was alleviation of mid-nineteenth-century Londoners' and New Yorkers' suspicion of expanded governmental power. The old police system which the two cities shared had been casual and sporadic. During the day there was no regular patrol force covering the whole city. Detective officers attached to the criminal courts and elected or appointed constables drawn from the local citizenry served warrants and apprehended offenders for a fee. After dark the night watch, ancient in the sense of both the institution's long history and the age of many of its members, patrolled the streets. However, the watch was not centrally coordinated and in most districts was undermanned and inefficient, the butt of standing jokes like the New Yorkers' quip, "While the city sleeps, the watchmen do too." There was little sense of a police presence: the law was most visible in the public punishment of petty and major offenders.

In contrast, the modern preventive police established in London and New York represented an unprecedented, highly visible increase of the state's power over the lives of ordinary citizens. The new forces patrolled the streets round the clock and could subject citizens to constant surveillance if necessary. To many people the cop on the beat was an ominous intrusion upon civil liberty. Englishmen feared an importation of despotic France's secret political police—"the Continental spy system"—or the creation of a more formidable variety of England's own network of informers and agents provocateurs which had harassed radicals during the Napoleonic Wars. Americans believed that adoption of such an institution was too authoritarian for their democratic society. Citizens of both nations, each with a long tradition of rejection of a professional army in favor of volunteer forces, saw preventive police as a standing army susceptible to the political manipulations of an ambitious despot.

To overcome public suspicion and fear, the police had to address themselves to different elements of a heterogeneous public. The social and economic position and ideology of various individuals and groups influenced their views of the political order and consequently of the policemen who upheld that order. Because of unequal wealth and power, some people regarded the law and its enforcers as protective while others saw the system as oppressive. Even if "the great body of the people" accepted the police, there were many degrees of acceptance and a substantial minority may have only yielded to superior power without acknowledging any rightfulness of police authority. The police upheld the society which created them; in heterogeneous communities, with unequal distribution of wealth and power, they could not expect a uniform response to their definition of the balance between liberty and authority.

1. The Strategy of Minimal Force *

With characteristic forthrightness, Sir Robert Mark once articulated the crowd control strategy of the Metropolitan Police thus: 'The real art of policing a free society or a democracy is to win by appearing to lose.' Their secret weapon was not water cannon, tear gas or rubber bullets, but public sympathy. To this end, he claimed the Metropolitan Police had trained an especially comely horse—the 'Brigitte Bardot' of

* Robert Reiner, *The Politics of The Police* (Brighton: Wheatsheaf Books, 1985) p. 54 (Reprinted with permission.).

police horses—to collapse, feigning death, at a word of command. This was guaranteed to win the support of the animal-loving British public. The British 'police advantage' of public support rather than lethal hardware as a means of crowd control was a deliberately chosen strategy. It was a calculated response to the fears of an oppressive *gendarmerie* which motivated so much resistance to the force.

Comment

The police in the United States are perhaps even more complicated, both historically and ideologically, than the police in England. America is geographically far larger, with greater regional and urban differentiation. Besides, no police department in America has been so carefully thought through and organized as was the London Metropolitan Police. As Roger Lane comments in his history of the Boston police, "The employment of police in municipal administration was governed not by theory but by convenience." In early nineteenth-century Boston, for example, the major problem was not crime but public order. Boston established its first full-time police in 1837 after roving bands of Protestants destroyed nearly every Irish home on Broad Street. The police also performed what we think of today as nonpolice functions—enforcing laws governing refuse and sewage. When the sewer, health, street, and building departments were created, the role of the police diminished considerably.

American cities have seen a progressive exchange of functions between the citizenry and the police. At first, the citizenry were primarily responsible for guarding themselves against criminals through a watch system. As other agencies took over other areas of municipal administration, the police began to be increasingly concerned with crime. All this, however, was not dictated by a governing plan or idea but came as a response to historical circumstances. Today many people regard the public police as inadequate to control crime. As a result, we see the development of private police, particularly in business and commercial establishments, and a sizable investment in residential burglar alarms and measures of defense for the citizen.

Certain issues seem characteristically to have affected American police, however, and these issues, in turn, reflect historical problems of American society.

The themes of brutality against blacks, of discrimination against immigrants, of immigrant hostility toward blacks—all set against a turbulent background of social and class conflict—appear time and again. Richardson, in his book *The New York Police*, describes an American riot of the year 1900 in New York City that grew out of the competition between Irish and blacks for jobs and living space.

"After the classical precipitating incident of a fatal fight between a black civilian and a white policeman, rampaging crowds moved up and down Eighth and Ninth avenues beating

Negroes. Policemen swarmed over the area, cracking the heads of Negroes and doing nothing to restrain the Irish mob."

The legislative tendency to enforce morality through the criminal law has also affected police conduct and community relations. For example, the attempt of the New York Police of the Seventeenth Ward to enforce the Sunday closing laws in 1855 led to three days of rioting between the police and the predominantly German residents of the ward. The Germans accused the police of being unduly harsh, of using their clubs indiscriminately, and of shooting to death an innocent man who was walking with his wife. The problem of the police use of deadly force is still with us.

Moralistic laws are related to another classic problem in American police history of official corruption. Corruption operates at a number of levels ranging from systematic complicity with organized crime to the acceptance of small bribes and gifts for favors and service. Although it is often claimed that police corruption may be traced to a few "rotten apples" who wear the uniform, many observers have charged that police corruption can occur only with the knowledge and often the complicity of high police and government officials. The argument is that since a "numbers" racket, for instance, depends on thousands of small daily bets and scores of "runners," the police and city officials must be either extraordinarily naive or complicitous to allow this sort of widespread organized gambling to occur.

In a free society, the police institution continually poses problems. Broadly and ultimately, the questions are how to ensure that police use their powers wisely, how to define the limits of police authority, and how to curb those who abuse their authority. The materials in this chapter will address a number of these issues, including the ambiguity of the police role, the limits and temptations of discretion, the police subculture, the role of police unions, use and abuse of force, and corruption.

B. WHAT THE POLICE DO

1. ORGANIZATION

Table of Organization

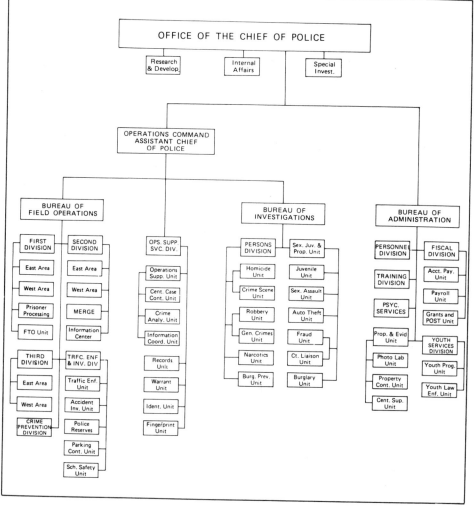

[C4354]

2. THE POLICE ROLE

a. THREE NIGHTS IN A SQUAD CAR *

Friday

[The patrol district is a white, residential area in Minneapolis comprised of apartment buildings and moderately priced, single family dwellings.]

9:10 We pulled alongside a car that had been involved in a drag race. One of the officers said, "Don't play games. I'll take that car away from you."

10:02 Lyndale and Lake, DK (drunk) *on the bus bench.* We located a 19 year old girl who appeared to have passed out on the bench. It was immediately evident, however, that she was not drunk, although she was giving a good performance of drunkenness. At first, she refused to talk to the officers except to say that she wanted to go to jail. Eventually, it was learned that she wanted to escape her drunken, assaultive husband. "I just want a good night's sleep," she said. The officers advised her that if she went to jail she would not be able to sleep because of the noise coming from the drunk tank. They suggested that she go rent a hotel room. She said that she couldn't afford that. One of the officers then said that if she couldn't afford a hotel room, she surely could not afford a $25 fine for being drunk. Some helpful bystanders offered to let her sleep in their homes for the night, but she turned those offers down.

10:27 In front of the Silver Dollar Bar, PD (property damage automobile accident). A squad car had been hit by another car. An accident report was prepared.

11:13 25—Dupont, loud party. We were advised by the owner of the home next door that the boys who rented the house were always having parties that lasted long into the night and prevented residents from sleeping. By the time we arrived, however, the boys were gone and the house was empty. We listened, at first sympathetically and then not so sympathetically, to a long harangue from the woman who lived next door, saying that the boys were bad boys, that they urinated out the window, that they threw garbage on her lawn and that they did other bad things. The woman was advised to call the police the next time such things happened.

11:13 33—Humboldt, loud radio. Although we received this call at the same time as the call on Dupont, it was 11:40 before we were able to answer it. By that time, we could hear no loud radio in the neighborhood.

11:52 We were stopped at Blaisdell and Lake by a man who informed us that a bystander had left the license number of a hit-and-

---

* Joseph M. Livermore, "Policing," *Minnesota Law Review*, 55 (1971) 660–62, 672– 77. Copyright 1971 (Reprinted with permission).

run car that had run into his car. We obtained the name of the person to whom that license had been issued and gave it to the man.

12:30   34—Grand, suspicious car. We located the car in question and determined that the occupant was only waiting for the owner of the nearby house to return from work.

12:33   29—Bryant, sick person. We learned from the woman who answered the door that her husband was having serious ulcer difficulty. An ambulance was called, but the officers did not wait for its arrival.

12:42 As we were passing a house, we heard a very loud party. The participants were warned to reduce the volume.

12:50   30—Finley, DK at door. When we arrived, the drunk was gone.

12:50   21—Grand, loud party. The yard of the house was a mess, with cans and bottles strewn everywhere. The officers told the occupants of the house that they were pigs and a discredit to the neighborhood. Nothing more was done since the party was in the process of breaking up.

1:02   24th and Lyndale, H-and-R (Hit-and-Run). Since the victim of the hit-and-run accident had moved his car and had been struck on private property, no report was made.

1:10 A car was given a speeding tag.

1:14   32nd and 1st, DK in the street. When we arrived, the drunk was gone.

1:20 A car was given a tag for running a red light.

1:30   Magoo's Bar, take a stolen (stolen auto report). When we arrived, no one was there from whom to take a stolen auto report.

1:50 We provided transportation to jail for a prisoner booked for traffic offenses by the sergeant on duty.

2:55   Blaisdell and Lake, PD. We were told by the driver who had been rear-ended that the other driver had refused to give his name. In addition, the man's date had taken his place in the driver's seat. We talked to the man who had been driving, obtained his name and then checked by radio to see if he had a driver's license. His license had been revoked. Since the officers had not seen this man driving, it was necessary, in order to arrest him for driving without a license and driving while intoxicated, to obtain a citizen's arrest from the person who had been the victim of his driving, which we were able to do. While we were on the scene, another police officer came up and said that the man we proposed to book had on prior occasions assaulted police officers and that, consequently, we should be very careful. We booked the man, but he refused to take an intoxication test.

5:10 As we were returning to the precinct station, we saw a car run a red light. We stopped it, discovered that the driver had no driver's license in his possession and radioed to see if he had a driver's license. We were told by radio that there was no record that he had a license. We were also told by a passing police officer that this had happened before and that the driver did indeed have a license but that the state agency could never locate it. We allowed the driver to go with that police officer to his home and obtain his license. He was, however, given a tag for running a red light.

Saturday

[The patrol district is in the heart of downtown Minneapolis and includes shopping and business areas, warehouses, office buildings, bars, night clubs and movie theaters.]

6:45 We saw some derelicts drinking wine, and the officers forced them to pour the wine out.[1]

7:00 9—West Franklin, Apt. —, unwanted guest. The caretakers of the apartment building advised us that the ex-husband of one of their tenants was threatening harm to the tenant and abduction of the tenant's child. He had also threatened the babysitter. We determined the kind of car that the ex-husband was driving. The tenant then returned with a friend and asked us to keep out of the area so that her husband would not be afraid to find her. She then hoped to tell him that the divorce was final and that he ought not to bother her any more.

7:50 Cassius Bar, fight. It had been settled by the time we arrived.

7:58 —Cafe, domestic. A 20 year old girl and her sister-in-law met us and advised us that the girl's stepfather, the proprietor of the cafe, had let the air out of the tires of the girl's car. He had also pulled loose some wires under the hood and then had blocked their car with his. All of this had occurred in the cafe's parking lot. She also claimed that he had hit her. We talked to the stepfather and mother of the girl, and they said that they had taken this action in order to prevent the girl from driving to Wisconsin until she had cooled down. They claimed that she had had a fight with her husband, that she wanted to get away by driving to see her grandmother in Wisconsin, and that she was too emotionally upset to drive. This was apparently evidenced by the fact that she was willing to take her baby with her in only a short sleeved shirt. The mother also told us that the girl was a bad driver with many arrests and that the car wasn't safe. The officers advised the girl that she could call a tow truck and that, if she wished, she could sign a complaint against her parents in the morning. We then left.

8:28 —Cafe, "settle it this time." The sister-in-law claimed that she had been verbally abused by the stepfather. The officers decided to wait until the tow truck arrived. The stepfather moved the car that was blocking. The parents of the girl began to criticize the officer in

1. Under [a local ordinance], it is illegal to consume alcoholic beverages "in any place frequented by the public."

sarcastic terms, saying such things as, "Isn't it a shame that the police have nothing better to do than to spend hours helping to start a car." They also threatened not to give half price food to police officers any more. The tow truck arrived and reinflated the tires of the car. However, the tow truck driver was unable to start the car. The stepfather, although advised by one of the officers not to do so, tried to move his car in a position to block his daughter's car. The officer at that point booked him for reckless driving and failure to obey a lawful police order.[2] The officer had the stepfather's car towed away. Another squad car came to sit on the situation until the tow truck had moved the girl's car to a service station. We took the stepfather to jail, where he immediately arranged to bail himself. The stepfather said that he was going right back. The officer replied, "We can book you more than you've got money." As soon as we left the police station, we went back to the parking lot and found that the girl's car had been started and that she had left town.

9:55 —Spruce, Apt. —, unwanted guest. The tenant told us that she had been ill and that she had not opened the door when her landlady knocked. The landlady then had opened the door and walked in. The girl tenant was upset. The officers went to talk to the landlady and told her, "You can't just walk in. You are invading her privacy." The landlady replied, "The hell I can't, you damned hippie-lover. I'm going to call the mayor." "Go ahead," the officer said. He then added, "The next time this happens, we will advise the tenant to use a citizen's arrest on you."

10:35 We saw a woman crying outside a downtown bar and a man with his hands on her. We stopped but were told by both that this was merely a domestic situation.

10:50 The officers saw a drunk in an alley, awakened him and sent him on his way.

10:55 We saw a door open in a downtown automobile dealership. When we checked, we learned that all the employees were there to carry out an inventory.

11:15 As we drove by an area near the University which was known as a gathering place for the disaffected young, we noticed an elderly man in a car talking to a number of rather rough looking motorcycle types. We stopped and learned from the motorcyclists that the man was very intoxicated. They offered to drive the car for him to a parking spot, and the officers allowed them to do this. The man was told by the officers to sleep off his drunk condition, and the officers took the keys from the car and threw them into the trunk so that he would be unable to drive further that evening.[3]

---

2. Since all this occurred on property owned by the "offender," it is difficult to see what crime had occurred or what right the police had to give orders.

3. The officers knew that the man would have to obtain another set of keys or have a new set made, each option involving some cost, but viewed this administrative punishment as substantially less harsh than its criminal counterpart.

11:45   15th and Hawthorne, gang fight. When we arrived, the officers from two other squad cars were busy booking some young men. The officers believed that occupants of the top floor of the building adjoining this corner had been throwing things at them. When the landlord refused admittance to that building, the officers broke the door down. The apartment from which the objects had been thrown was locked, and the tenants refused admittance. Again, the officers broke down the door and booked the occupants.[4]

12:25   Nicollet Hotel, blocked alley. By the time we arrived, the car which had blocked the alley had been driven away.

12:55   11th and LaSalle, take a stolen. We made a report of a stolen automobile.

1:22 As we were driving through a lower class apartment neighborhood, we saw one woman and two men standing outside an apartment building. The men appeared to be fighting. One man and the woman said that the other man was bothering them. We sent him away. The couple then went into an apartment building. As we drove away, we saw the man who had been sent returning and trying to obtain entrance to the apartment building. We returned and booked him as a public drunk.

1:45   Continental Hotel, see a robbery victim. We took a report from a young man who had been robbed at knife point. We drove around the neighborhood looking, without success, for his assailant.

Sunday

[The patrol district is a primarily black, residential area of Minneapolis with low and middle income housing.]

Car 447 serves as a back-up car for the same district covered by Car 441. This district is approximately a mile and a half square and lies about one mile north and a mile and a half west of downtown Minneapolis. This district includes some public housing projects, a large area of lower priced, mainly Black housing and at its northern edge some lower middle class White housing. Car 447 also answers calls in the district adjoining on the east. This district is characterized by lower class and lower middle class housing and has a large number of Indians residing within it.

8:37 A car was tagged for speeding and for jumping a red light.

9:15 The officers saw a man believed to have committed a number of burglaries. They kept him in view while they checked by radio to see if any warrants were outstanding on him. None were.

9:34   6—Oliver, domestic. When we arrived, no one was there.

---

4. One common difficulty for policemen, present in this case, is that officers arriving at a call after other officers are present are forced to follow the lead of the initial officers. If those officers have made a mistake, later arrivals will compound it since they will not have the means of learning what happened earlier.

11:00 The officers stopped a bedraggled car for no apparent reason, other than that the occupants of such cars often are either presently engaged in criminal activity or have arrest warrants outstanding against them. These weren't and didn't.

11:02 The officers went to Morgan and Plymouth, the heart of the Black area, in order to back up another squad car that was waiting for a tow truck to tow the car of a person who was being arrested. The back-up was thought necessary because a crowd might gather and thus endanger the officers.

11:12 6—15th Avenue, unwanted guest. A woman greeted us at the door, led us into a flat where a young man was drinking beer at the kitchen table and proceeded to tell [of domestic complaints accumulated in 18 years of marriage]. The husband and wife then began yelling at each other. The officers advised them that if they had to return, someone would be going to jail.[5]

11:26 7—16th Avenue, juvenile trouble. We received information from a resident of the neighborhood about kids shooting off firecrackers.

11:30 27th and 4th, in the park, rape. We drove quickly to the scene and were met by two men, one of whom said that he had stumbled over a nude girl while he was walking his dog. One of the officers approached the girl, took her pulse and found that she was dead. The ambulance crew which arrived shortly thereafter confirmed the officer's impression. A call was placed for the sergeant on duty and for the homicide car. The officers guarded the scene, got the names of witnesses and then listed the cars parked nearby. The officers then went to City Hall to dictate a report of what had happened.

1:35 A bedraggled car was stopped and the occupants were asked to give their names, addresses and birthdates so that a check could be made to see if any arrest warrants were outstanding. None were.

1:50 As we were driving by Plymouth and Morgan, we saw a car which apparently had gone out of control and over the curb onto the sidewalk. We approached and discovered that the occupant had been brutally beaten. An ambulance was called, as was the homicide car. It became apparent that the victim had been beaten across the street in the lot of a closed gasoline service station. We could find no witnesses willing to speak. The remains of the assault were inventoried for the detective.

Questions

The police, whether legally empowered or not, seem to settle a number of situations simply by giving orders. How important is it that

---

5. Officers often say that should they have to return, an arrest will be made. This is done even in circumstances where a basis for arrest is unlikely and where there is no real intent to make an arrest. It is enough for the officers that the hollow threat seems to work. If their bluff is called, they would probably rely on a convenient Minnesota statute making it a crime to be drunk even in private.

they have this power? How do we protect the rights of citizens when the police exercise such a power?

b. A GENERAL VIEW–DISTRIBUTION OF SITUATIONALLY JUSTIFIED FORCE *

Many puzzling aspects of police work fall into place when one ceases to look at it as principally concerned with law enforcement and crime control, and only incidentally and often incongruously concerned with an infinite variety of other matters. It makes much more sense to say that the police are nothing else than a mechanism for the distribution of situationally justified force in society. The latter conception is preferable to the former on three grounds. First, it accords better with the actual expectations and demands made of the police (even though it probably conflicts with what most people would say, or expect to hear, in answer to the question about the proper police function); second, it gives a better accounting of the actual allocation of police manpower and other resources; and, third, it lends unity to all kinds of police activity. These three justifications will be discussed in some detail in the following.

The American city dweller's repertoire of methods for handling problems includes one known as "calling the cops." The practice to which the idiom refers is enormously widespread. Though it is more frequent in some segments of society than in others, there are very few people who do not or would not resort to it under suitable circumstances. . . .

Two patrolmen were directed to report to an address located in a fashionable district of a large city. On the scene they were greeted by the lady of the house who complained that the maid had been stealing and receiving male visitors in her quarters. She wanted the maid's belongings searched and the man removed. The patrolmen refused the first request, promising to forward the complaint to the bureau of detectives, but agreed to see what they could do about the man. After gaining entrance to the maid's room they compelled a male visitor to leave, drove him several blocks away from the house, and released him with the warning never to return.

In a tenement, patrolmen were met by a public health nurse who took them through an abysmally deteriorated apartment inhabited by four young children in the care of an elderly woman. The babysitter resisted the nurse's earlier attempts to remove the children. The patrolmen packed the children in the squad car and took them to Juvenile Hall, over the continuing protests of the elderly woman.

While cruising through the streets a team of detectives recognized a man named in a teletype received from the sheriff of an adjoining county [and arrested him].

* Egon Bittner, *The Functions of the Police in a Modern Society,* Public Health Service Publication No. 2059 (Chevy Chase, Md.: National Institute of Mental Health, 1970) pp. 38–44. Copyright 1970 (Reprinted with permission).

In a downtown residential hotel, patrolmen found two ambulance attendants trying to persuade a man, who according to all accounts was desperately ill, to go to the hospital. After some talk, they helped the attendants in carrying the protesting patient to the ambulance and sent them off.

In a middle-class neighborhood, patrolmen found a partly disassembled car, tools, a loudly blaring radio, and five beer-drinking youths at the curb in front of a single-family home. The home-owner complained that this had been going on for several days and the men had refused to take their activities elsewhere. The patrolmen ordered the youths to pack up and leave. When one sassed them they threw him into the squad car, drove him to the precinct station, from where he was released after receiving a severe tongue lashing from the desk sergeant.

In the apartment of a quarreling couple, patrolmen were told by the wife, whose nose was bleeding, that the husband stole her purse containing money she earned. The patrolmen told the man they would "take him in," whereupon he returned the purse and they left.

What all these vignettes are meant to illustrate is that whatever the substance of the task at hand, whether it involves protection against an undesired imposition, caring for those who cannot care for themselves, attempting to solve a crime, helping to save a life, abating a nuisance, or settling an explosive dispute, police intervention means above all making use of the capacity and authority to overpower resistance to an attempted solution in the native habitat of the problem. There can be no doubt that this feature of police work is uppermost in the minds of people who solicit police aid or direct the attention of the police to problems, that persons against whom the police proceed have this feature in mind and conduct themselves accordingly, and that every conceivable police intervention projects the message that force may be, and may have to be, used to achieve a desired objective. It does not matter whether the persons who seek police help are private citizens or other government officials, nor does it matter whether the problem at hand involves some aspect of law enforcement or is totally unconnected with it.

It must be emphasized, however, that the conception of the centrality of the capacity to use force in the police role does not entail the conclusion that the ordinary occupational routines consist of the actual exercise of this capacity. It is very likely, though we lack information on this point, that the actual use of physical coercion and restraint is rare for all policemen and that many policemen are virtually never in the position of having to resort to it. What matters is that police procedure is defined by the feature that it may not be opposed in its course, and that force can be used if it is opposed. This is what the existence of the police makes available to society. Accordingly, the question, "What are policemen supposed to do?" is almost completely identical with the question, "What kinds of situations require remedies that are non-negotiably coercible?" [1]

Because the idea that the police are basically a crimefighting agency has never been challenged in the past, no one has troubled to sort out the remaining priorities. Instead, the police have always been forced to justify activities that did not involve law enforcement in the direct sense by either linking them constructively to law enforcement or by defining them as nuisance demands for service. The dominance of this view, especially in the minds of policemen, has two pernicious consequences. First, it leads to a tendency to view all sorts of problems as if they involved culpable offenses and to an excessive reliance on quasi-legal methods for handling them. The widespread use of arrests without intent to prosecute exemplifies this state of affairs. These cases do not involve errors in judgment about the applicability of a penal norm but deliberate pretense resorted to because more appropriate methods of handling problems have not been developed. Second, the view that crime control is the only serious, important, and necessary part of police work has deleterious effects on the morale of those police officers in the uniformed patrol who spend most of their time with other matters. No one, especially he who takes a positive interest in his work, likes being obliged to do things day-in and day-out that are disparaged by his colleagues. Moreover, the low evaluation of these duties leads to neglecting the development of skill and knowledge that are required to discharge them properly and efficiently.

While everybody agrees that the police actually engage in an enormous variety of activities, only a part of which involves law enforcement, many argue that this state of affairs does not require explanation but change. Smith, for example, argued that the imposition of duties and demands that are not related to crime control dilutes the effectiveness of the police and that the growing trend in this direction should be curtailed and even reversed.

Unfortunately, this view overlooks a centrally important factor. While it is true that policemen often aid sick and troubled people because physicians and social workers are unable or unwilling to take their services where they are needed, this is not the only or even the main reason for police involvement. In fact, physicians and social workers themselves quite often "call the cops." For not unlike the case of the administration of justice, on the periphery of the rationally ordered procedures of medical and social work practice lurk exigencies that call for the exercise of coercion. Since neither physicians nor social workers are authorized or equipped to use force to attain desirable objectives, the total disengagement of the police would mean al-

---

1. By "non-negotiably coercible" we mean that when a deputized police officer decides that force is necessary, then, within the boundaries of this situation, he is not accountable to anyone, nor is he required to brook the arguments or opposi- tion of anyone who might object to it. We set this forth not as a legal but as a practi- cal rule. The legal question whether citi- zens may oppose policemen is complicated. . . .

lowing many a problem to move unhampered in the direction of disaster. But the non-law-enforcement activities of the police are by no means confined to matters that are wholly or even mainly within the purview of some other institutionalized remedial specialty. Many, perhaps most, consist of addressing situations in which people simply do not seem to be able to manage their own lives adequately. Nor is it to be taken for granted that these situations invariably call for the use, or the threat of the use, of force. It is enough if there is need for immediate and unquestioned intervention that must not be allowed to be defeated by possible resistance. And where there is a possibility of great harm, the intervention would appear to be justified even if the risk is, in statistical terms, quite remote. Take, for instance the presence of mentally ill persons in the community. Though it is well known that most live quiet and unobtrusive lives, they are perceived as occasionally constituting a serious hazard to themselves and others. Thus, it is not surprising that the police are always prepared to deal with these persons at the slightest indication of a possible emergency. Similarly, though very few family quarrels lead to serious consequences, the fact that most homicides occur among quarreling kin leads to the preparedness to intervene at the incipient stages of problems.

In sum, the role of the police is to address all sorts of human problems when and insofar as their solutions do or may possibly require the use of force at the point of their occurrence. This lends homogeneity to such diverse procedures as catching a criminal, driving the mayor to the airport, evicting a drunken person from a bar, directing traffic, crowd control, taking care of lost children, administering medical first aid, and separating fighting relatives.

Questions and Comment

1. Does Professor Bittner's view of what the police really do square with the report of Professor Livermore?

2. If Professor Bittner is correct, is it not obvious that since the police have to be around for all of the tasks he mentions, their presence will thrust upon them a great many other tasks. Even though such tasks could, in theory, be performed by others, this could be done only at the much greater cost of making their presence as easily available as that of the police. The administration of first aid, either physical or psychiatric, and similar functions normally performed by psychiatrists, physicians and social workers fall in this category of service. It is likely that, because of the enormous number of things police may have to specialize in, they cannot do any of them as well as professionals involved in that area. We may thus have to sacrifice performance for the cost savings when we turn over various tasks to the police.

c. THE POLICE AND CRIME PREVENTION *

An extraordinary concordance of new ideas about policing has arisen during the past few years, amounting almost to a new conception of the role of the police in democratic societies.

At first thought, this is quite surprising. Why should police executives in places as different as London, Oslo, and Santa Ana, California, be advocating similar reforms? Why should such notions as police-community reciprocity, decentralisation of command, reorientation of patrols, generalised rather than specialised policing, even civilianisation of the force, seem so applicable to all these places with their different locales, different cultures, different economies, different traditions and systems of government? London is perhaps the world's most cosmopolitan metropolis, Oslo is the relatively small (750,000) capital of a homogeneous Scandinavian welfare state, while Santa Ana has a population about the size of a London borough and it sits 30 miles south east of Los Angeles.

The answer has to be this: with respect to crime—and, perhaps more importantly, to perceptions and fear of crime—there is almost an international language, a virtually predictable set of public responses to rises in crime and fear of crime. One part of the response is to seek to punish criminals more heavily, to fill the prisons to capacity and overcapacity. Another part is to look to the police to prevent crime from occurring in the first place. The question then becomes: is it possible for police to prevent crime? The answer is a firm "maybe."

Police managers generally understand the limits of police activity in fighting crime. In particular, they comprehend how unsuccessful crime prevention strategies have been over the past 20 years. They have learned—that increasing the numbers of police does not necessarily reduce crime rates, nor raise the proportions of crimes solved. Neither does simply boosting police budgets. Certainly, there would be more crime if there were no police. But once a certain threshold has been reached, neither more police nor more money helps very much.

The managers have also learned that randomised motor patrolling neither reduces crime nor improves the chances of catching suspects. Police who ride in cars become self-contained and remote, neither reassuring citizens enough to affect their fear of crime, nor engendering trust. In fact, there is really no need for two-person cars; studies have shown that police are no more likely to be injured in one-person patrol cars. And two-person patrol cars are no more effective in catching criminals or reducing crime.

In Santa Ana and other Californian cities, even those very dangerous to the police, such as Oakland with its machine-gun armed drug dealers, that lesson has been learned. But in Europe, even in relatively peaceful Scandinavia, rank-and-file police regard the two-man car as a

* Skolnick, "Police: The New Professionals," *New Society,* Sept 5, 1986, pp 9–11— Copyright 1986 (Reprinted with permission)

necessity. Although they acknowledge that—with an ever-present radio—there is little added danger to the one-person car, they still insist
that the two-man car is an unassailable prerequisite of the job.

It used also to be thought that saturating an area with patrol cars
would prevent crime. That strategy does reduce crime, but only
temporarily—largely by displacing it to other areas. Moreover, even
when an area is saturated, police rarely see a serious crime in progress.
Only "Dirty Harry" has his lunch disturbed by a nearby bank robbery.

During the 1970s, response time was seen as the hallmark of police
efficiency. In a sense it was, in that it provided a hard measure of
whether police were working. But follow-up studies were to show little
relation between improving response time to emergency calls and the
likelihood of arresting criminals, or even in satisfying citizens involved.
One recent and very large study showed that the chances of making an
arrest on the spot drops below 10 per cent if even a minute elapses from
the time the crime is committed.

These findings are nothing short of devastating to earlier police
assumptions. To the thoughtful police administrator the findings suggest that traditional strategies are neither reducing crime nor reassuring its potential victims. In effect, thinking police professionals have
had to come up with some new ideas. Perhaps most intriguing is the
concordance of these themes despite the thousands of miles and cultural barriers separating Oslo from Santa Ana.

What are the themes? The first is police-community reciprocity.
The Norwegian report *The Role of The Police in the Society* says that its
main concept "is that the police are able to carry out their tasks
satisfactorily only through constructive cooperation with the public."

Police-community reciprocity means that police must feel, and
genuinely communicate a feeling, that the public they are serving has
something to contribute to the policing enterprise. One of the most
interesting conceptual distinctions was made by a Santa Ana business-
man who distinguished between the "old" and the "new" professionalism that had been introduced by Chief Raymond Davis. The old
professional was not especially interested in hearing from citizens, even
from businessmen, to say nothing of representatives of minority groups.
The old legalistic professional of the 1960s saw himself as a policeman
adequately trained in the penal code, arrest law, interrogation tactics
and the fine points of when and how to apply a truncheon. His
training, he felt, overcame the need for additional input from the lay
public.

Still, the idea of police-community reciprocity poses at least two
sorts of problem. A reciprocal or cooperative conception of policing
ordinarily suggests some sort of decentralisation of command. The
Norwegian report talks about "small, local stations" as an "essential
condition for the police to be able to carry out their functions." But
when Hans Klette and I studied the Oslo police this summer [1986] we
were able to find only one such station.

The latest annual report, as well as the strategy report on the Broadwater Farm Estate riots, of Sir Kenneth Newman, speaks bravely of the need for police-community relations, but that aspiration is sorely impeded by the very centralised structure of the metropolitan police. Can London be regarded as a "community?" A huge bureaucracy like Scotland Yard, located in a metropolitan city like London, must be frustrated in carrying out a community-reciprocity mandate. The formal requirement to report to the Home Secretary further undermines Scotland Yard's flexibility in relating to local communities. It is difficult to reconcile the admirable aspirations for "consent policing" of Scotland Yard's chief officer with the reality of centralised government control over the policing of London.

In the US, [there are] some scattered success stories across the breadth of the country—fixed substations in Santa Ana, directed response teams in Houston, Texas, mini-stations in Detroit, Michigan, storefront stations in Newark, New Jersey.

Even where decentralisation does occur, the idea of police-community reciprocity remains unclear. Community is an inherently ambiguous, almost elusive, idea. It implies a commonalty of interest, values, identities, demands, expectations. When one considers how fragile a two-person relationship can be, it requires little imagination to comprehend the difficulties of expanding the notion of mutuality of interest to a larger group of discrete human beings. Nevertheless, the quest for community seems an almost universal aspiration. Community is the apple pie and motherhood of social organisation. As Raymond Williams has observed, unlike other such similar terms as state, nation and society, *community* "seems never to be used unfavourably, and never to be given any positive opposing or distinguishing meaning."

Police-community reciprocity can be achieved only where there is an actual commonalty of interests between the police and the served citizenry. That is possible but increasingly difficult in demographically complex urban areas. Assuming that London is not properly to be regarded as a "community," conflicting neighbourhood interests may occur even in an area as small as a London borough.

Are we therefore to conclude that the idea of police-community reciprocity is without substance? I do not think so. The idea is central to policing in a democracy, but it isn't enough to employ it as a slogan. It needs to be considered carefully, studied in actual practice, and its limitations candidly discussed. Clearly, its alternative, an aloof and socially distant police, will not work well at all.

Reorientation of patrol is another related theme in the cities we recently studied. Wherever surveys of ordinary people are conducted—of all races—it turns out that the average citizen (not the average criminal, of course) prefers a police presence—an idea that is catching on with the political Left. Rather than despising the sight of police, people feel safer when police are clearly in evidence; the foot patrolman is the most approachable policeman of all.

So why is there less foot patrol in every city than citizens and many police executives would like to see? The answer is, inevitably, that foot patrol ranks low as a priority. If, as in London, hundreds of police are assigned every day to area cars, ten men to a car, the number of police available for foot patrol must surely decline. Similarly, if two men are routinely assigned to a patrol car, as they are in relatively peaceful Scandinavia, fewer officers will be available for either foot patrol or neighbourhood assignment.

Two other sources of police manpower might possibly free officers for civilian-orientated policing. The police specialist, particularly the detective, could be out patrolling the streets. Many police departments are top heavy with detectives and bureaucrats who would serve the public more effectively if assigned to patrol functions. The idea of the policeman as "generalist" tends, however, to be more popular with management than with the rank-and-file police.

If reassignment isn't possible, civilianisation might be. A move towards this implies reconsidering the fit between the job and the badge. When are high-paid sworn officers needed and when would lower paid civilians do as well? Fully fledged cops used to serve as secretaries to high-ranking managers. In most police departments, chiefs will now employ civilian secretaries. Departments vary as to whether civilians or sworn police are used in the radio rooms: Scandinavian police departments and New Scotland Yard assign uniformed police to the radio room; most police departments in California use civilians, with a sergeant in charge to take over when a genuine emergency occurs, and in Santa Ana, civilians handle traffic accident reports where no crime is involved.

Crime prevention is the ultimate goal of all these strategies. Police haven't come to believe in the need for reciprocity with citizens just because it is pleasant to chat with ordinary people. Rather, they have learned that communication is essential to catching criminals and reducing crime. If the rape or burglary victim fears or dislikes the police, the rate of unreported crime will rise. That is one reason crime statistics—and clear-up rates—are so difficult to interpret. When a department achieves better relations with the public, crime may even appear to rise because reported crime does go up. When the substantially large illegal immigrant population in Santa Ana, California, became convinced that the police were interested primarily in solving local crimes, not in reporting victims to the Immigration and Naturalisation Service for deportation, reported crime rose.

To sum up, the need for the innovations we have discussed seems to be widely agreed upon by police executives around the world. But it is often easier to develop an ideology of innovation than an implementation of its component parts. However, the more difficult it becomes to introduce these ideas into practice, the harder it will be to offer much more than lip service to the goal of crime prevention.

d. NEW YORK'S COMMUNITY POLICING PLAN *

New York City Mayor David N. Dinkins has released a massive set of proposals to change the city's approach to crime control. The plan, which would cost $1.8 billion over the next four years, includes an increase in the level of patrol officers, an acceleration of the shift toward community-based, problem-oriented policing, and a new emphasis on crime prevention initiatives, such as efforts to keep youths from dropping out of school.

"If we have learned any lesson from the rising tide of violence that has flooded our cities for the past 30 years, it is this: the police cannot stop the criminals alone," the mayor said in announcing his "Safe Streets, Safe City" program. "The plan we unveil today maps out a strategy for weaving community policing into the fabric of our neighborhoods."

The plan calls for the hiring of more than 3,400 new patrol officers. Combined with another 3,000 officers to be hired under current budget plans, and efforts to hire civilians to handle desk jobs currently done by police officers, the plan would raise the average daily patrol strength from 6,640 to more than 10,000 by 1993.

Many of the new officers would be assigned to the Community Officer Patrol Program, in which foot patrol officers are given flexibility to develop contacts with residents and community groups in order to solve local problems that result in crime, instead of merely responding to calls for service. The community policing program currently has one 10–officer unit in each of the city's 75 precincts; under the Dinkins plan, each precinct would receive at least three community policing units, and some high-crime precincts would receive as many as seven units.

As new officers are hired, Police Commissioner Lee P. Brown plans to intensify programs aimed at recruiting from minority groups, so the community patrol officers will more closely reflect the racial makeup of the community. He also is expected to seek legislation requiring newly hired officers to live in New York City.

The biggest share of the plan's $1.8 billion in planned spending would go to the Police Department, but the budget also reflects the mayor's interest in attacking what he has called the "root causes" of crime. More than one-fourth of the funds would go to education, employment and related programs, such as beefing up security in schools, creating more summer jobs for youths, and opening up community recreation facilities.

Question

Should more than one-fourth of the funds go to education, summer jobs and so forth? Or is that percentage about right?

* Criminal Justice Newsletter, Vol. 21, No. 20, October 15, 1990.

3. THE POLICE DISCRETION

a. LAW AND THE POLICE MANDATE *

More than any other agency, as the police are so acutely aware, they are available and required to deal with citizen claims for assistance.   The police were designed to respond to citizen demands and requirements for service as much because this represented prevention or deterrence of the sources of crime as because the police were intended to act symbolically as one citizen would to another in time of need.   The symbolic centrality of police action as standing for the collective concern of people, one for another, cannot and should not be underestimated.   Law has grown up as a means of formalizing the conditions under which the police *must* act and *cannot* act but does not provide the basis on which they do or should act.   The almost random accretion of skills, tools, technology, and intelligence (information and communication) systems associated with urban policing must be seen in the context of the police's virtual inability to exclude human difficulties from their stated purview.   The law should be seen as one important source of the coercive right, but one only.

Agencies entrusted with provision of services with a high potential for violence, noncompliance, and conflict, view and claim the law as the fount of legitimacy.   The view that the law is the sole legitimator of official violence has become conventional wisdom in mass societies and thus suffuses the ideology of everyday law and order conceptions.   The relationship between the law and the police can be stated in a more forceful manner: *the law serves as a mystification device or canopy to cover selectively, legitimate, and rationalize police conduct.*   It does not prospectively guide police action, nor does it provide the principal constraint upon police practices.

Comment

Professor Manning argues that law offers little, if any, guidance to police in the performance of their duties, and in the exercise of their discretion on whether to act, and on what to do, in particular situations.   When you read the next three selections, consider whether Manning's assertion is or is not borne out.   Although books have been written listing cases where policemen have abused their discretion, could not the same be done with respect to business executives, bureaucrats, social workers, physicians, lawyers, and any other large group in our society?   Concern with police abuse of discretion cannot then be limited to any recitation of "horror" stories.

On the other hand, this is not a complete answer.   The fact is we are worried more about the police misuse of authority than about certain other kinds.   First, police abuse of authority tends to be more

* Peter K. Manning, *Police Work: The Social Organization of Policing,* (Cambridge, MA: The MIT Press, 1977), pp. 100–101.   Copyright 1977 (Reprinted with permission).

often physical and hence a threat to perhaps the most basic human right, security of the person. Second, police wield governmental power and are charged with an enormous number of extremely difficult tasks. As a result, we worry more when they do not live up to the standards we have set for them. Finally, so far as we can tell, misconduct by the police with respect to citizens is not randomly distributed across the population. Though research on this issue points in various directions, (see excerpt below), insofar as police misconduct is directed against poor members of minority groups, it tends to exacerbate one of the most basic and important American problems, race relations.

b. POLITICAL POWER AND THE POLICE *

When the cop approached my car I explained that I was waiting for a passenger. "Obstructing the pier entrance," he said. "You can't stay here. My orders are to keep it open. Besides, passengers won't be off for another hour."

A block away, the middle of the street under the West Side Highway was painted with about twenty parking spaces. Two large signs dangled from a rope fence: CUSTOMS OFFICIALS ONLY and TOW–AWAY ZONE. The cop motioned toward the customs lot. "Pull over there," he said. "For an hour I won't bother you and if the tow truck comes I'll tell them you're waiting."

I thanked him for being helpful. As I turned to look, I noticed a closer area—also on the street, painted and roped-off. It was only about half-filled with cars. A sign said: LONGSHOREMEN ONLY. "How about there?" I asked. "It's closer."

The officer scowled. "Mister," he said, "you gotta be kidding. If you parked there, there wouldn't be enough left to tow away. Maybe the car gets set on fire—or the windows are smashed, your motor's busted and the tires gone. *They* gotta have a place to park," he added, by way of explanation. "It's their *job!*"

Meeting that passenger could also have been my job. But the cop was protecting my property, I had to admit. For I was getting from him an incredibly frank disclosure to the effect that he, in fact the whole police force, turned their backs on whatever gangsterism happened on a portion of public land that had been informally ceded to longshoremen. That particular turf was left entirely to the workings of private law. The understanding that gave longshoremen sovereignty over these approximately 1,000–square-yards was so overt that the necessity of maintaining an illusion of official enforcement there—from ticketing or towing to preventing the destruction of property, and possibly more—had been abandoned.

Still, police at the pier had a definite task in helping to sustain this sovereignty. They were paid from city funds to warn the general

* Joseph S. Lobenthal, *Power & Put-On*   1970), p. 20 et seq. © 1970. (Reprinted
(New York: Outerbridge & Dienstfrey,   with permission).

public that a private government was enforcing its own law on the premises. This aspect of their job served to minimize the costs a union might spend for parmilitary, strong-arm services: if a "free" watchman did his job, the number of "necessary" crimes that would have to be committed in order to protect their turf could be minimized and, if he were vivid enough, words alone might suffice. In that sense, police were deterring and preventing crime. They maintained order by acknowledging and assisting a power group to which public authority had become subordinate.

A watchman's position, with overtones of public relations, was a very demanding role for the cop at the pier. The judgments that he had to make, according to his own sense of priorities, frequently called for an instantaneous assessment of conflicts that might potentially explode the established balance between various forces and interests. None of the rules by which a cop could be guided in resolving these conflicts was official; on the other hand, none of the official rules that ostensibly govern a policeman's conduct had much relevance. Should misjudgments occur, his own neck would be in a noose because full disclosure of what was actually at play—even if he really understood and could formulate what was going on—would have to be disowned by the authorities.

The job required fast wits and fancy footwork, which the working conditions made feasible: the cop had professional elbow-room. As the only representative of official authority on the scene, his decisions were likely to be respected as final, if only because the stakes were so very low and any appeal to the next highest authority required a tremendous expenditure of time and energy by an aggrieved party. The cop was a small-claims court unto himself. And more, as we shall see. . . . Aside from serving as a symbol—just being there—and keeping the longshoremen's space cleared, he was primarily concerned with supervising lawbreaking and permitting offenders to function under "color of the law." His job, in essence, was the orderly enforcement of illegality.

From among a sparse handful of illegal alternatives that were available, he made balanced choices according to what seemed to him to be demanded in a situation geared toward one single priority: expediting the flow of people and cars—impediments of official law to the contrary notwithstanding. Under the circumstances that he faced, enforcing the literal law would have meant human and economic chaos. But it was not an alternative that seemed to have occurred to him.

Throughout, he appeared guided by a sense of traffic justice that transcended law, one that was based, instead, on a combination of common sense, first-come-first-served fundamentalism, snap judgments about who looked more important—or less argumentative—than whom, necessity (a particular car-and-trailer combination, for example, could fit into only one spot and was directed there), and fast decisions about "hardship" cases involving, variously, a man who said he was meeting a lady with three infants ("okay, stay here"), a driver whose passenger was on crutches (ditto), and a young traveller with an unusual amount of luggage to be unloaded ("sorry mac, that's the law; you'll have to move out").

The status and authority of that cop at the pier derived from the convergence of various interests and sources of power. Their relationships with each other are fairly typical of what goes on in many different kinds of situations when law is enforced.

In the situation on the piers, the law obviously could not be enforced literally unless the steamship companies—and their associated economy, including the union—were to be closed down. Such a radical and disruptive decision certainly would not be initiated by a low-level operative like the officer on the beat. Instead, he naturally assumed that his superiors' and the public's expectations were that he would continue the precedent, or safe practice, routinized over decades, of protecting commerce by speeding an "illegal" traffic flow. It is unlikely that any thought would cross the enforcer's mind suggesting that his duty included volunteering for the part of St. George against the powerful twin dragons of an international union and the international shipping industry in the nation's major port. The power, real or imagined, of either labor or industry to destroy him professionally or obliterate him physically would discourage any such idea from germinating, even if its seed existed. His job was to enforce priorities determining the permissible private use of public land that had long ago been resolved in anonymous councils.

So the cop was *interpreting and applying the law,* in this situation, according to the interests of private commerce. This interest was so entrenched that to the unaided eye it was invisible. Despite the domineering physical presence of business—the giant pier apparatus and operations—enforcement created the impression of being only a matter between individual citizens and the policeman on the scene. There was no visible link to the shipping companies or the union—. .. Business protection was simply an inherent police priority, the birthright of power.

But another interest had to be accommodated as a part of the established order: that of ordinary citizens who briefly shared a common concern for getting themselves, their cars, and their cargos safely through the vehicular stampede that took place before and after docking. So long as their ends could be accomplished, these citizens would remain uninterested, or at least uninvolved, in who ran the piers and how the law was interpreted there. Although too transiently constituted to be a "group" in any strict sense of the word, if stymied they could and probably would—bring to bear all the resources and influence that were available to individual members of the upper and middle classes.

. . . The interests of the dock visitors had to be accommodated efficiently and with a minimum of discomfort.

In this case, the interests of the travelling public and of shippers and the union actually converged. Both could be satisfied by similar police actions. It is necessary, however, to keep in mind an important difference between the two—their relative power.

As a class, travellers had only a fleeting concern for how things were done at the pier. They can be labeled *ostensible* consumers of police legal services. Most were one- or two-time ship's visitors and, therefore, unfamiliar with details of "normal" operation and actual procedures. Their expectations were not well defined. In the event of unusual occurrences or delays they would tend to be slow to recognize or react when their concerns did not receive priority attention.

By contrast, shipping and union interests were permanent. [W]e may fairly regard them as *controlling* consumers of police legal services.

Their investment in operations at the pier were, of course, far greater than any single traveller's. Their joint resources for controlling the operation were concentrated and far-reaching, in fact, and overwhelmingly so compared to the scattered and diffuse potential of individuals who picked up or delivered passengers and then went about their unrelated businesses. Labor and industry alike, because of a continuing and vital association with the waterfront, were highly motivated to use their power to protect the existing system and defend their prerogative to implement whatever changes they decided comprised their interests.

That, in this situation, the interests of *ostensible* and *controlling* consumers largely coincided—that travellers were more or less served—constituted a sort of inferential fiction that the police, in serving labor and industry, were also serving the "general" public. Actually, however, this tenuous harmony of interests was artificially controlled. Competing interests of the public were simply not represented in the cauldron of forces in which decisions about the piers were compounded.

But what about the law—the official, written law—and those activities that constituted its enforcement?

In a sense, both signs and the police served the same purpose: *to warn and inform the public.* But in this case, as in many others, the warning and information were contradictory. Signs declared in words what conduct was illegal. They were the written law. A police uniform was another kind of sign—nonverbal, a symbol conveying the message that a particular enforcement mechanism, the cop, was then and there representing official society. Thus, what he and not the signs said became effective law at the time. He was the law's spokesman. What he endorsed, tolerated, or directed amounted to functional legality. Those who accepted his interpretations received the protection of authority: immunity from harassment and prosecution.

Fairly obviously, the posted law was a tool of control that actually facilitated, not prevented, parking. It was intended and used for a purpose exactly opposite to the one stated in words. Changeable and changing conditions at the pier required a means by which one individual would have authority to make decisions on the spot. Signs, then, were a device for conferring this authority in order to regulate parking, to *restrict* not prevent it. Any cop would know that he was expected to use the law only against those who failed to obey orders. Signs were necessary to make these orders lawful because, without them, anyone could park anywhere, any time. The area could not then be reserved for shipping customers unless leased by the companies. Like the cop himself, the signs were a free offering that excluded the "wrong" people. They were intended to be disobeyed—but selectively and under the "safe" supervision of the police. Once put up, they legitimated the cop's role and it then became his job, in turn, to supersede them.

Questions

Is the policeman described in the above excerpt acting the way we, as a society, would wish him to act?

This excerpt reveals in a dramatic way the fact that the role of the policeman is often severely constrained by the realities of power in the society about him. Considering these realities, could the policeman in the excerpt have done a better job? If he could have, could you draft the kind of rules that would tell him with some particularity how to do better?

c. RACE AND THE POLICE *

Since in modern America so many more blacks than whites are poor, race is a crude measure of wealth. It is also a crude measure of ethnicity: Most black Americans are members of a cultural minority that to some degree has its own way of life. They are more likely than whites to have certain other social characteristics as well, such as a low level of education, unemployment, and a criminal record. It should be remembered, moreover, that most police are white—nearly 90% of those observed during the present study. All of these conditions increase the legal vulnerability of blacks, and they also decrease their capacity to mobilize law against others. Hence, when they have disputes such as those in the present sample, it might be expected that blacks will receive less help from the police. This is, in fact, what the evidence indicates: Blacks often call upon the police to settle their disputes—they do so proportionately more than whites—but they are less likely to get what they request, and the police expend less time and energy on their problems. At the same time, they are as likely as whites to be punished.

It is relevant to note that blacks and whites call upon the police to handle a comparable array of problems. Twice as many of the calls from blacks involve women complaining about the violence of men, however, while only half as many pertain to property disputes or noise

* Donald Black, *The Manners and Customs of the Police* (New York: Academic Press, 1980), pp. 134–141, 152–155. Copyright 1985 (Reprinted with permission)

and other miscellaneous disturbances. These differences by themselves do not demonstrate that black women are beaten or threatened by men more often than white women, that blacks have fewer disputes about property, or that blacks have quieter neighborhoods, since the propensity of each race to report such matters to the police may differ substantially. The actual patterns of conduct could even be the opposite of what the calls might first suggest. In any event, the larger similarity in calls from blacks and whites makes it possible to compare how the police respond to people of each race.

Although in many cases involving blacks the police do little beyond knocking at the door, when they choose to exercise authority it appears that it is more likely to be coercive in character than in comparable cases involving whites. In one case, for instance, the police were called by a black woman whose estranged common-law husband had broken into her apartment in order to repossess furniture that he claimed was his. The woman insisted that the property was jointly owned, not his alone. The officers advised the man to bring a lawsuit against the woman, but he did not seem to take the suggestion seriously, and proceeded to carry a television set toward the door. The woman shoved him, and he fell to the floor, at which time the police intervened and placed him under arrest for being "drunk and disorderly." The observer reported that the officers used "quite a bit of force" to handcuff him and move him to the patrol car, and that he struggled against them, striking his head on the cement landing of the stairs in the process.

In a number of cases the arrest and injury of a person might have been avoided if the police had made a greater effort to work out a solution with the people involved. Moreover, black policemen might well have handled these cases in a different manner. Thus, in another case (not included in the sample of disputes) two black officers were dispatched to pick up a black man who had been arrested by a white officer on foot patrol, and they were openly unhappy with how the man had been handled. After they heard the details of what had happened—largely a display of disrespect by the black man—they remarked to the observer that if they had handled the situation there surely would not have been an arrest. Consistent with this, another investigator found that "Negro officers were less reticent, more flexible, and hence more effective than white officers in handling Negro disputes." It should be added, however, that there is also evidence that black officers show more concern than white officers about black victims, a pattern that may result in a higher likelihood of arrest when black officers handle blacks who victimize other blacks.

Though in some cases white officers may be especially coercive toward blacks, this does not mean that they hold blacks to a higher standard of conduct in their dealings with other blacks. On the contrary, they appear to be relatively unconcerned about how blacks treat each other, and less likely to invoke the law when a black complains against a black than when a white complains against a white (see Black, 1976:17).[1] In one case, a white woman complained that a man (apparently her estranged husband) had broken into her apartment and threatened her children. She directed the police to a nearby tavern where the man was drinking. Doing what the woman asked, the police walked into the tavern and immediately placed the man under arrest for "disorderly conduct." It is difficult to imagine the same response to a complaint by a black woman under the same circumstances. Instead, it is more likely that the complainant would have been told that there was nothing the police could do. White policemen are less likely to make a judgment of any kind when a black complains about another black.

d. AGE AND POLICE CONDUCT *

The social inferiority of juveniles is so extreme in modern society that their experiences with the police deserve special comment. . . . While a bit less likely than an adult to be arrested and considerably less likely to be threatened with arrest, the juvenile is correspondingly more likely to be scolded or admonished. It is in this sense that the police are comparatively moralistic toward juveniles, while treating adults—if they handle them in the penal style at all—in a more legalistic fashion. The police give very few lectures to adults about how they should behave. They are unlikely to invoke standards of right and wrong at all, even when making an arrest or threatening to do so. If they exercise their authority, then, they usually do so in an impersonal and bureaucratic manner, without explicit reference to their own values. This does not apply to juveniles, however. In these cases the police readily give lectures and exhortations about the proper way for a young person to behave, particularly toward his or her elders. Typically the elders in question are parents.

In one case, for example, a worried white woman called the police because her 15–year-old son had left the house in the afternoon, saying that he would be back in "a little while," and hours later he had yet to return. While the police were in the house, the boy arrived and explained that he had been on a bicycle trip with a friend. His mother

---

1. There is also evidence that white citizens themselves hold each other to higher standards of conduct. Thus, they seem more likely to mobilize the police concerning matters that lower-class blacks presumably ignore or handle themselves, such as "noisiness," juveniles defined as "rowdy" or "disorderly," and intoxicated persons. In fact, lower-class blacks are relatively unlikely to call the police unless violence occurs or is threatened (which may be precipitated by what seem to an outsider to be trivial matters), whereas whites routinely call when physical danger is not involved in any way. It appears, then, that for many lower-class blacks an absence of violence is "public order" enough, while many whites demand what they view as quiet and seemliness as well (see page 135). At the same time, whites may be less likely than lower-class blacks to call the police about violence that occurs within their families (see pages 124–128). In any event, all generalizations about the conditions under which people call the police must be understood as highly speculative until a great deal more information is available about how each group behaves and handles its grievances in everyday life.

* Donald Black, *The Manners and Customs of the Police,* Academic Press, New York, 1980, pp. 153–155. Copyright 1980 (Reprinted with permission).

raised her voice and said, "Do you know how much worry you put us to? How could you do a thing like this?" The boy "snarled" at her in a loud voice, "Oh, get off my back. Why do you have to make such a big thing out of it?" At this, one of the officers got up from his chair and said, "Just a minute, buddy. You tell me where you learned to act like that to your mother. Don't you know how to behave when your mother talks to you?" The boy replied, "Well, she doesn't have to get so excited about nothin', does she?" This prompted the officer to continue: "Listen here, your mother can say what she pleases, how she wants to, to her son. You know that? My mother never would have allowed me to act the way you do. She would've smacked me in the face. One thing you better get straight—you only have one mother in your life, and you better remember that. You better start respecting her right now. At least you're going to show respect when *I'm* here. You got that?" The boy said, "Yes, sir," and immediately everything quieted down. The woman thanked the police warmly. Afterward, one of the officers remarked that "the trouble" was that "there's no man in the house."

In another case involving a white family, a woman called to complain that her teenaged daughter was staying out too late—violating the city's curfew law—and creating other unspecified "problems" as well. The daughter was sitting outside in a car with her boyfriend when the police arrived, and both were asked to come into the mother's apartment. According to the observer, the officers "tried very hard to convince the girl that she was hurting herself and her poor working mother's well-being by such recurring trouble." The girl was "openly nasty" to the police and told them, "Too bad. I don't like curfews." Before leaving, the police gave her a ticket for curfew violation and warned her that future violations could mean that she would be sent away to an institution . . .

. . . In sum, the police readily use their authority against a juvenile who is criticized by a parent, but when the situation is reversed—with a juvenile complaining against an adult—they show no sympathy at all, and usually treat the complaint itself as an offense. Patterns of this kind should be expected wherever one person or group is far below another in social status, as is true of slaves and women in many societies. . . . In modern America, however, hardly anyone is lower than juveniles. . . .

Questions

Police are called upon to deal with people differing in wealth, ethnicity, social class, age, and so forth. Do the descriptions of police encounters in this chapter show that police respond differently to such social differences? When is it proper that they should, and when is it improper? Is it ever proper?

C. CONTROLLING THE POLICE

1. INTRODUCTION

a. CONTROL IN THE WESTERN WORLD *

Patterns of control of the police vary considerably in Western Europe and North America. In Britain, control is in the hands of the "Police Authority" in each force area except London. The "Police Authority" is an appointed body two-thirds of which is composed of elected members of local government councils and one-third of magistrates. Control in Britain can be characterized, therefore, as being situated at local levels of government and exercised largely by political persons. In France, on the other hand, supervision is national and bureaucratic. Any local control is exercised only by delegation from the central government. Moreover, it is carried out primarily by permanent civil servants, such as prefects. Such national and bureaucratic control is the dominant continental pattern, being found also in Italy, Spain, Norway, Sweden, Denmark, and the Netherlands. In Germany, control is bureaucratic as well, but it emanates from the states, an intermediate level of government. Sweden and Denmark are unique in having established advisory boards of elected persons at national and local levels, but their advice is not binding.

Control of the police in the United States is local and political. Considering that there are several layers of police in the United States, it is perhaps better to say that control is exercised wherever police command is exercised, which means primarily locally, and most often by elected persons. Some may argue that contact between a chief of police and politicians is not always direct, being mediated by a manager of public safety, a professional city manager, or occasionally a police board. The judgment is a relative one. Politicians are in much closer contact with command personnel in the United States than anywhere on the European continent.

Granting that systems of control over the police in Western Europe and North America are varied, several generalizations can be made:

1. Although all the countries of the sample are democracies, some with longer and more respectable pedigrees than others, there is no single pattern of supervision. It is not possible to say that democratic government requires a particular mode of control. Put more generally, the structure of supervision of the police does not appear to be tied to the character of government.

2. It does not appear that repressiveness of a police system is a function of the place at which political supervision is exercised. A centralized political regime may not necessarily be more repressive in police policy than a decentralized one.

* David H. Bayley, "Police Function, Structure, and Control in Western Europe and North America: Comparative and Historical Studies," in Morris and Tonry, eds., *Crime and Justice*, Vol. 1, 1979, pp. 130–135. Copyright 1979 (Reprinted with permission)

3. Patterns of supervision over the police are relatively unchanging over time. Americans have insisted throughout their history on local control. Canadians, too, have eschewed national control, though they have stressed intermediate supervision by the provinces more than Americans have state control. Germany, apart from the Hitler interlude, has had supervision of the police by the states of its federal system since 1871. France's system of central supervision by appointed civil servants is to be found before the Revolution. The Italian system, quite similar to the French, began at unification over a hundred years ago, building on Piedmontese precedents that were even older.

This is not to suggest that there have been no changes in patterns of supervision. There have been and they can be labeled significant in the sense that they involved intense struggles over considerable periods of time. However, though momentous by local standards of opposition, they have not represented a change in character by international standards. This is an excellent example of how comparison provides perspective. A genuine revolution in control was certainly accomplished in the United States between 1890 and 1960. Control in all aspects had been exercised by political machines, negating even centralized command within cities. During the twentieth century political control became attenuated, sometimes absent altogether, in hiring, promotion, discipline, and operational command. Indeed, some observers now argue that the police have become too autonomous and insufficiently responsive to public opinion, especially within ethnically distinct neighborhoods. So change has certainly been real, even though it has not challenged two characteristics of American control of the police, namely, close contact by elected officials with the command hierarchy and extreme decentralization.

4. Throughout Western Europe and North America control of the police is seen as requiring a balance between impartiality under law and responsiveness to community direction. The police are a peculiar executive agency of government. Like all administrative departments, they are accountable to the community that has authorized them to act. Unlike other executive agencies, however, they do not simply carry out particular policies stated in law; they are responsible for enforcing law generally. Political responsibility and the rule of law intersect at the police.

Recognition of this dual responsibility has grown slowly in Western Europe and North America with different countries starting from different places. In Europe the notion of state responsibility to the common interest, rather than to representative opinion, emerged very early. Popular control of the police was, therefore, anathema. The British shared this view, making policemen crown officers, like magistrates and justices of the peace, and insulating them from partisan politics. In the United States, however, the police were considered instruments of representative government. And government was politics for Americans, not administration under law as was the case in Europe.

During the past century and a half there has been a convergence in the philosophies of police control of Europe and North America. In Europe fairness was gradually seen to be enhanced by making government responsive to public opinion. As a result, the franchise has been steadily widened. Across the Atlantic, where political participation had always been very open, impartiality was understood to be enhanced by lessening direct political control. Police were urged to develop a sense of professional responsibility to law transcending local interests. Throughout North America and Western Europe the ideal is now very nearly the same, though mechanisms for achieving balanced control vary considerably as befits national traditions.

Control of the police has been discussed thus far in terms of formal structures. Anyone familiar with administration knows that what really goes on may be very different. Some scholars have suggested, for instance, that in Britain and the United States the police are much more autonomous than they appear. There has been almost no research, however, into the interaction between police and erstwhile supervising agencies. How often do such authorities inquire into departmental affairs? How often do they meet and who sets the agenda? Do the police seek out their advice? On what sort of issues? What do members discuss when they meet? Are policies formulated explicitly or are they submerged in ad hoc discussion?

While it is clearly important to determine the nature of control over the police, paying particular attention to the role of politicians, it is no less important to examine the role of the police in politics. Police and politics have a reciprocal relationship. Space does not permit a full discussion of this meaty topic, so three comments must suffice. First, since police activities in politics are one indication of the character of political life, writing about them tends to be emotional. Some of the most superficial, careless, and tendentious studies of the police have been done on this subject. Second, the police affect political life in many ways besides spying, intelligence gathering and crowd control. Attention needs to be given, in addition, to police supervision of elections, granting of licenses for parades and meetings, use of the criminal law to harass dissidents, actions that antagonize public opinion and undermine the legitimacy of regimes, and lobbying and voting en bloc. Equally destructive of discriminating analysis is the easy identification of any police activity as politics, which is the argument from the radical left. It thereby becomes impossible to discover differences in the impact of the police on political life in different times and places. Third, I suggest the following negative hypothesis about the relation between the police and politics that contradicts accepted beliefs: the salience of the police in a country's political life is not related either to the extent of penetration by politicians into policing or to the degree that external control of the police is centralized. Bureaucratic control of the police may impel police intrusion into politics as much as political control. Politicians are not the only politically interested persons. French experience would be to the point. Decentralized supervision, too, may produce as much partisan intrusion as centralized control. Certainly American experience suggests this.

The relation between the police and politics is much more complex than is commonly assumed. Careful nonpolemical comparative research, sensitive to conceptual problems in separating "police" from "politics," is sadly lacking.

Questions

To what extent are the police becoming political activists? To the extent that they have, do you regard this development as desirable or undesirable? To what extent does the police potential for political activism change the degree of control other organs of society may exercise?

b. THE POLICE IN THE UNITED STATES AND JAPAN *

American policemen fulfill their responsibilities when they bring people into compliance with law; Japanese policemen seek more than compliance, they seek acceptance of the community's moral values. They are not merely the law's enforcers; they are teachers in the virtue of the law. The Japanese police have been given a moral mandate, based on recognition of their importance in shaping the polity; American policemen have been given legal instructions, and have been enjoined from straying beyond the law.

The fundamental argument of this book is that police institutions are shaped by social context. Policemen do not stand in isolation; they reflect the society.

[P]olice reform cannot be directed exclusively at policemen. Take the case of police brutality. Excessive and unjustified use of force is related to such factors as the presence in a population of categories of people considered marginal to customary morality; to low levels of public respect for policemen which impel them to defend their self-esteem in physical ways; and to popular attachment to firearms that raises the intensity of apprehension in any police-citizen contact and makes experimentation by the police with nonlethal force more dangerous. Or consider the difficulties of changing the way policemen act on the street. How they move, stand, and talk is affected by popular resentment of police in personal affairs, by the unwillingness of the public to share policing tasks, by the tradition of thinking of policemen as legal instruments rather than agents of moral authority, and by the belief that justice is obtained by assertion rather than submission.

Police institutions are complex; activities must be disaggregated if they are to be studied intelligently. Rather than talking generally about reforming the police, discussion should focus on deployment, anonymity of personnel, nonenforcement contacts, use of weapons,

---

* Bayley, *Forces of Order—Police Behavior in Japan and The U.S.* (Berkeley, U. of Cal.Press, 1975) pp. 186, 195–198. ©1975   Reprinted with the permission of the Regents of the University of California.

complaint procedures, individuation of treatment, counselling, and so forth. There is not a single problem of respect for the police; there are a host of them.

Having specified in practical terms what is to be changed, the second step in analysis is to discover whether the crucial constraints exist within the police organization or outside it. There are three possibilities, not just two as one might think. First, the police may have total control, lacking only the will or imagination to do differently. For example, few people would care very much if the police wanted to recruit at two rank levels in order to provide a higher proportion of officers with educational skills appropriate for staffing senior executive positions. Similarly, the police are free to experiment with nonlethal uses of force if they wish; the public cannot compel them to use firearms. Second, the police may not have effective control over what they do and changes in practice will require community support. For example, if the police want to increase the amount of formal training required of recruits, additional funds would have to be appropriated. Again, if police patrolling is deemed inadequate for preventing crime, then the public must consider shouldering more of the burden of policing or allowing penetration by the police in novel ways. Third, changes in police practice may require cooperation from the community but the police can be instrumental in generating that response. Policemen need not always stand helpless before social constraints. They have demonstrated effective political capabilities already that need not be confined to defensive trade-unionism. For instance, the police could make a major contribution to transforming the public's view of the utility of firearms for private protection. Or they could encourage the growth of community spirit in residential neighborhoods by helping to develop an expanded role for private citizens in crime prevention.

Only after determining what specific aspects of police activity must change and where the impediments to change lie can an assessment be made of the difficulties of bringing it about.

Perhaps the greatest impediment to change in the American police is perspective. Americans have a narrow vision of the police. They are unaccustomed to seeing the police as social actors; they see them only as enforcement technicians. Because Americans are anxious about the creation of governmental authority, the great injunction they lay on the police is to fight crime within the letter of the law. They do not demand that they fight crime within the law in particular ways that reinforce the values that undergird democratic life. Legality and efficiency in enforcement do not exhaust the contributions police make to society. Can American perspectives on the police be broadened? It is doubtful. Political tradition as well as contemporary scandals combine to make the police protectively self-denying and the public loath to trust them further. The dilemma of the police in the United States can be posed in a single question: how can esteem be kindled for a role most people accept only as an unpleasant necessity?

Question

How much police reform is actually under the control of the police? To what extent does the existence of police unionism change the degree of control the police may exercise? To what extent does police unionism change the degree of control which other organs of society may exercise?

2. THE POLICE HIERARCHY

a. CONTROL THROUGH SELECTION

(1) The Social Characteristics of Police *

INDIVIDUAL EXPLANATIONS

Police reformers since Theodore Roosevelt have assumed that who a police officer is makes a difference in how the officer acts (Fogelson, 1977). Recent research has tested that proposition with at least eight specific characteristics of the individuals performing police roles: age, length of service, sex, height, race, education, job satisfaction, and racial attitudes. Some of these characteristics are ascribed; others are actively achieved or passively developed, either before or after entering police work. All of them are assumed to influence behavior regardless of the influences of other variables. Most have substantial policy implications, since the decision about who will become a police officer is a more "tractable" variable (Scott and Shore, 1974; Davis, 1975) than are most of the other factors thought to influence police behavior.

Officer Age

Conventional police wisdom holds that younger officers are more aggressive, and also more likely to make mistakes, than older officers. Yet it is difficult to test that proposition in a way that separates biological age from length of service in policing, since most police departments only hire officers between the ages of twenty-one and thirty. The limited evidence from one archival study shows that when controlling for length of service there is no difference among officers of different ages in their likelihood to gather sufficient evidence (or do whatever is necessary) for the arrests they make to lead to a conviction (a detection measure) or in their overall quantity of arrests (Forst, Lucianovic, and Cox, 1977:50). Another archival study did, however, find that officers in a single cohort who were oldest at time of appointment were less likely than average to have civilian complaints filed against them for such offenses as discourtesy, racial slurs, or excessive use of force—best treated as a measure of service (Cohen and Chaiken, 1972:15). Younger officers were also assaulted more often in the thirteen Southwestern cities investigated in one archival study, but this

* Lawrence W. Sherman, "Causes of Police Behavior: The Current State of Quantitative Research," *Journal of Research in* *Crime and Delinquency,* Vol. 17, No. 1, January 1980, pp. 71–76. Copyright 1980 (Reprinted with permission).

may be a spurious result of their more frequent assignment to patrol duties in high-crime areas (Hale and Wilson, 1974:8).

Length of Service

Both archival and observation research supports the proposition that more experienced officers do less police work, but the work they do is often "better" than that of their less experienced colleagues. Friedrich's (1977:278–284) reanalysis of the Black-Reiss data (1967) found that less experienced officers do more to detect crime: They initiate more citizen contacts, do more active preventive patrolling, and record crime reports from citizens more often than do officers with more experience, particularly than those with more than eight years of service. Yet Forst, Lucianovic, and Cox (1977:48–49) found that more experienced officers, when they made arrests, were more likely to have the arrest result in conviction. Both Forst et al. and Friedrich found that less experienced officers made more arrests. The Friedrich finding was more significant since it examined only patrol officers; Forst and his colleagues did not control for assignment, and more experienced officers are more likely to get desk jobs.

This pattern is more complicated in the area of service, however. Friedrich (1977:278) found that more experienced officers were more likely than their juniors to be friendlier to nonoffenders and "tougher" with offenders. But an observation study in Miami found more senior officers to be more sympathetic and less threatening with citizens generally (Cruse and Rubin, n.d.:157).

Generational differences might well be the underlying cause of these apparent effects of differences in the length of service. Differences in the nature of early socialization into police work, specific events that transpired over the years in which the older cohort served, or other factors unique to those years rather than the simple passage of time might cause the observed differences. The agreement between the Forst et al. analysis of Washington, D.C. officers in 1974 and Friedrich's (1977:467) analysis of the same city (along with Boston and Chicago) in 1966, however, shows the relationships holding up across generations in one city and therefore tends to refute this rival hypothesis.

Officer Sex

Although interpretations of the findings may differ, the evaluations of women newly assigned to patrol duties in recent years show that they do generally differ from men in both their detection and arrest behaviors. An observation study in Washington, D.C. of the first eighty-six women assigned to patrol after recruit training (with eighty-six comparison male recruits) found that the female officers initiated fewer citizen encounters (detection) and made fewer felony and misdemeanor arrests than the male officers (Bloch and Anderson, 1974:5, 14). An observation study of sixteen females and sixteen males on patrol in St. Louis County (Sherman, 1975) confirmed both the patrol style and arrest findings of the Washington study. Archival research in the

Philadelphia Police Department (Bartell Associates, n.d.) and the New York City Police Department (Sichel et al., 1977) also found that women made fewer arrests, in the latter study by a difference of four to one. One exception to the "less arrest" pattern is an earlier study of a much smaller sample in New York, where no difference in arrest frequency was found (reported in Melchionne, 1974:356). One exception to the different detection pattern is the Washington, D.C. finding that arrests made by "new women" and comparison men were equally likely to result in conviction (Bloch and Anderson, 1974:25–26), a finding confirmed by a later archival study of all officers in that city that controlled for length of service (Forst, Lucianovic, and Cox, 1977:52).

These studies do not show many differences in the kind of service female officers provide, nor do they offer enough data to test the hypothesis that women have more of a calming effect on violent or emotionally upset citizens than male officers do (Sherman, 1973), since so few incidents in this category were observed (but see Bloch and Anderson, 1974:18–19). All the studies are limited by the lack of experienced females to compare with experienced males, as well as by the possibility that male officers are intentionally limiting the detection and arrest activity of their female partners.

Officer Height

The closely related proposition that shorter officers (including most females) do police work differently (or less well, in policy terms) is generally unsupported by recent research on male patrol officers, most of which has been conducted by police departments themselves. No evidence is available on the issue of detection, but a study of San Diego officers found that there was no relationship between height and frequency of arrest (Hoobler and McQueeny, 1973). A review and reanalysis of research in several other police departments (White and Bloch, 1975) found either no differences or inadequately controlled data on citizen complaints (a service measure) and assaults on the police officer (which usually means the officer has used force as well). The latter finding received further support from an archival study of thirteen Southwestern police departments (Swanson and Hale, 1975). So despite the biological and psychological arguments about the influence of officer height on police conduct, the evidence suggests height actually has little influence.

Officer Race

Theorists of many persuasions have argued that black police officers behave differently from white officers. The recent research supports the general argument, although some of the findings are unexpected. Black officers in three large cities in 1966 patrolled more aggressively, initiated more citizen contacts, and recorded crime reports more often than white officers. They also made more arrests than white officers regardless of citizen race (although the black officers in only one of the three cities, Chicago, were responsible for all of this difference in the aggregated data; it is not clear whether they faced more serious offenses). But when faced with black suspects, black officers were more likely to make an arrest than when they were faced with white suspects. This disparity in favor of the opposite race was shown by white officers as well (Friedrich, 1977:300–319, 453).

The same study found black officers to be slightly more neutral (less frequently friendly or unfriendly) in their manner toward citizens than white officers were (Friedrich, 1977:314), but an observation study in Miami in 1970–71 found that the two older black officers in the sample the study observed for six months were less "threatening" in their behavior toward blacks than older white officers were (Cruse and Rubin, n.d.:157). Black officers hired in New York in 1957 received the same number of citizen complaints as white officers, on average, throughout their careers (Cohen and Chaiken, 1972:14). Most unexpected was the finding that black officers in 1966 used unjustified force more often than white officers, both in general and especially against black citizens (Reiss, 1972:303). An archival study of police use of deadly force in New York City (1971–75) also found that black officers used force more often than whites, but concluded that the relationship was a spurious result of overrepresentation of black officers' assignment and residence in high-crime neighborhoods (Fyfe, 1978:ix).

Officer Education

The theory that college-educated officers behave differently from less educated officers (see Sherman, 1979) has generally been unsupported by studies of indirect performance indicators such as attitudes and supervisory evaluations (Smith, 1978). The four studies that directly measured (through archival research) those aspects of police work considered in this discussion, however, all show college-educated officers to behave differently. McGreevy (1964) found college-educated officers in the St. Louis Police Department to be more active in such detection practices as stopping vehicles and checking businesses. Bozza (1973) found that better educated officers (in a sample of 24) in a California police department made more arrests. Cohen and Chaiken (1972) found that officers who had some college education when they joined the New York City Police in 1957 were the subjects of fewer citizen complaints than were those who had no college upon joining. Cascio (1977) replicated that finding in a study of 940 officers in Dade County, Florida, and also found that more educated officers suffered fewer injuries from assaults and were the subjects of fewer allegations of having used excessive force. A study of thirteen southwestern police agencies, however, found that more educated officers ($n = 1,745$) were more likely to be assaulted than were those with less education (Hale and Wilson, 1974:20).

All of these studies, unfortunately, suffer from a number of flaws. Most important is the failure to control for other factors, such as motivation or I.Q., that might be the true cause of both educational achievement and job performance. Additional considerations, even though they do not affect the interpretation of the findings, are the failure to examine the kind of education officers receive; the erroneous assumption that a year of education is a fungible property at an interval level of measurement; and an absence of sufficient variance in levels of education so that if an interval level of measurement is assumed it may be used with its full potential. While we may be fairly confident that education is at least a correlate of these aspects of police behavior, we are much less certain whether and to what degree it is a cause.

Job Satisfaction

Police morale is a prime concern of both police union leaders and police administrators, but only one study of its effect on aspects of police behavior could be found. Friedrich (1977:292–299) found support in the Black-Reiss data for the assumption that job satisfaction influences performance. More satisfied officers initiated more citizen contacts, patrolled more aggressively, and took crime reports more often. They also made arrests more often than their less satisfied colleagues, but their manner toward citizens was no different.

Racial Attitudes

Black and Reiss's (1967:138) original conclusion that racial attitudes are generally unrelated to police behavior was based on separate analyses of attitudes, which were generally prejudiced, and behavior, which they concluded was not discriminatory. An analysis of their data linking the attitudes and behavior of specific officers, however, found that the more white officers disliked blacks, the more likely they were to arrest black suspects (Friedrich, 1977:321). Yet the analysis also found that racial attitudes were unrelated to white officers' decisions to take crime reports from black complainants. The relationship reappears in the area of service quality, with negative behavior toward black citizens more frequent among white officers whose dislike of blacks is more pronounced (Friedrich, 1977:329). Yet all of these relationships are weak (percentage differences no greater than 15 percent; gammas no greater than .2), as they are for many of the correlations of police behavior and individual officers' characteristics.

Questions

Does Dr. Sherman's systematic review of the research findings correlating job performance with key variables lead to any relatively clear policy judgments? How should we advise police departments to shape their recruitment policies on the basis of these findings? For example, would it not be fair to conclude that police departments should do away with height requirements when recruiting? Are there other policies we might suggest?

(2) Affinity for Police Work *

Of eight candidates interviewed in my presence, three passed the examination. The other five were rejected for the following reasons, as stated by the members of the Selection Board. The first appeared for the interview dressed in a high school athletic jacket, dirty dungarees, and a T-shirt. On entering the room, he made no eye-to-eye contact with the board members but instead fixed his eyes on the chair he was to be seated in. Furthermore, the interview revealed that he had applied for the position on a whim. Finally, the applicant was face-tious, stating to the board members that he should be hired because he would either be a thief or a police officer. The interview was terminated at this point.

The second applicant was visibly shaken by the interview and began to perspire and fidget with his hands as soon as seated. When asked why he wanted to become a police officer, he stated that he had a strong sense of morality and he wanted to be in a position where he could make sure people did what was "right."

The third candidate proved the most interesting. He made an excellent presentation of self both in his appearance and bearing on entering the room. His reactions to the questions posed by the board were calm and deliberate, and his answers reflected some prior thinking on the role of the police. His answers were slow, however, and there seemed an interminable silence between question and answer. His voice was soft and laconic. The turning point in the interview came when the following question was posed:

> "Suppose you are in uniform and you've been asked to check a bar and a man 6'4" and 230 pounds is blocking your way and refuses you entrance to the bar, what would you do?"

> The candidate said he would ask the man to move.

> The members of the board asked: "What would you do if the man refused?"

> "I would go," he said, "to the back door of the bar."

> "But suppose," the candidate was asked, "the man stopped you from entering?"

> The candidate replied: "I would physically remove the man if he wasn't too big."

The board rejected this applicant on grounds that he lacked the verbal skills and aggressiveness to become what they considered a "good cop."

The fourth candidate lied to the board members concerning a past arrest record. He had failed to report an arrest for assault which took place some five years prior to the interview. When asked about the

* Thomas C. Gray, "Selecting for a Police Subculture," from *Police in America*, edited by Jerome Skolnick and Thomas C. Gray (Boston: Little, Brown and Co., 1975), pp. 50–52. Copyright 1975 (Reprinted with permission).

arrest the candidate said he hadn't thought it important and therefore didn't report it. The board rejected him for failing to report his past arrest record.

The fifth candidate was rejected because he told the board that he did not want a permanent position. His real interest was in law, and he said that he would leave the force as soon as he was admitted to law school. The board rejected him because they felt that a permanent employee would be preferable.

Rejection Versus Acceptance

If the criteria for rejection are held up against the value system of the police subculture, they fit neatly. To one degree or another, all of the rejected candidates displayed a potential for violating the value system of the police subculture. The first displayed a lack of potential loyalty to the group, the second displayed a moral squeamishness, the third a strong internalization of prohibitions against the use of violence, the fourth a lack of trustworthiness, and the fifth a potential lack of commitment. Any one of these factors would offer a threat to the police subculture and hence (if the explanation is valid) would render an applicant unfit for employment.

Acceptable candidates were all conservatively dressed in suits and ties, made eye contact with the members of the board, walked directly to the board and shook the hands of the board members. These candidates answered the questions in a calm, straightforward manner looking the board members in the eye. None displayed reservations concerning the use of violence, violation of privacy, deception or the denigration of an individual's character, and all conveyed a high sense of loyalty to their present group of acquaintances.

The Mark of Affinity

On the basis of these interviews, what concrete factors seem to suggest an affinity for police work? One such factor is an individual's personal history from which is inferred a predisposition to engage in certain types of conduct. It is experience with some elements of police subculture, such as engaging in contact sports, that suggests an affinity for police work. For example, playing football provides an individual with an experience that contains some elements of the police subculture: (1) controlled use of violence, (2) teamwork and group loyalty, (3) memorization of codes, (4) uniform behavior, (5) experience with personal pain, (6) a willingness to inflict pain on others, (7) dirty tricks, and (8) authoritarianism (leading or being led).

Possessing a predisposition for police work appears to be a necessary but not a sufficient requirement for employment as a police officer. This is illustrated by the fact that certain individuals possess all of the necessary technical skills and the necessary predispositions but still are not seen as potential members of either the formal police organization or the police subculture. Women fall into this latter category. This observation reinforces the earlier contention of masculine identification as part of the basis upon which the police subculture is built. Women in their presentation of self are hard-pressed to overcome the impact of their physical makeup regardless of their capacity to do the job. In short, women would, if hired for patrol, potentially undercut the basis of male solidarity.

Questions

How do the criteria Dr. Gray found to be employed by oral boards relate to the research findings on the characteristics of the police as reported in the previous excerpt? If there is conflict, why do you think it occurs?

b. CONTROL THROUGH INTERNAL GOVERNANCE

(1) CONTROL THROUGH "SETTING A STYLE" *

Wilson asserts that "[t]he patrolman's role is defined more by his responsibility for *maintaining order* than by his responsibility for enforcing the law." He hypothesizes three styles of police conduct, which he describes and exemplifies in three successive chapters. He calls them the watchman style, the legalistic style, and the service style. This threefold typology is the heart of Wilson's book, for it prescribes a conceptual framework for understanding how police behavior is shaped.

Wilson characterizes the watchman style as viewing order maintenance rather than law enforcement as the principal function of the police. He sees the patrolman's responses as heavily influenced by the identity of the potential offender and by the standards of the social group with which the patrolman identifies him. If the offender is a community notable who has committed a minor crime, the patrolman is likely to excuse him. If he is a juvenile, the patrolman probably applies informal sanctions (calls his parents) or dismisses him with a warning. Blacks are either ignored or arrested, depending on the patrolman's view of the seriousness of their conduct. Prostitution and gambling are typically ignored under the watchman style because they are viewed as "minor offenses" typically committed by blacks. "Under-enforcement" is very common in communities having the watchman style; so is corruption. These communities produce few traffic tickets, relatively few misdemeanor arrests, and tolerance of discreet immorality. . . .

Wilson found that the watchman style predominated in Albany, Amsterdam, and Newburgh—the first a large city and the others small cities in New York state. In each of the three communities the economy was in a declining state and the population was socially

* Herbert L. Packer, "The Police and the Community," *Stanford Law Review,* 22 (1969), 1314–1317. © 1969. Reprinted with permission of the Board of Trustees of the Leland Stanford Junior University.

heterogeneous. In all three, the political culture was dominated by politicians who appeal mainly to a working-class and lower middle-class constituency through such factors as party loyalty, ethnic identification, the exchange of favors, personal acquaintance, and maintaining a low tax rate. The police in all three are poorly paid, lack professionalization, have few staff personnel or civilian employees, lack written rules, and offer little or no specialization.

The legalistic style was found to predominate in Oakland and Highland Park and, to a growing extent, in Syracuse. In these communities, "the police administrator uses such control as he has over the patrolmen's behavior to induce them to handle commonplace situations as if they were matters of law enforcement rather than order maintenance."

The patrolman in these communities tends to issue traffic tickets at a high rate, arrest a high proportion of juvenile offenders, act vigorously against illegal enterprises, and make a large number of misdemeanor arrests, even when public order has not been breached. The patrolman acts, on the whole, as if there were a single standard of community behavior rather than (as in the watchman style) different standards for "juveniles, Negroes, drunks and the like." Because such persons may be more likely than most to be arrested, Wilson concludes that "the law will fall heavily on them and be experienced as 'harassment.'"

Police administrators in these communities want high arrest and ticketing records both because they see such records as "right" and also to reduce the probability of corruption. As Wilson says, "the best way to stifle rumors of corruption or favoritism is to make sure that everybody gets a traffic ticket, every bookie is put out of business, and every glue-sniffing teenager is hauled in for questioning."

Wilson generalizes that in the three cities with a legalistic style

[T]he principal effect of the political culture on police behavior . . . has been to make possible the appointment of chiefs strongly committed to the doctrines of "police professionalism," to permit them to acquire control over the department free of the lateral interventions of politicians or special-interest groups, and to insulate the department from community pressures seeking changes in police policies.

The growth of promotion opportunities and specialization under a "reform" chief has the effect of making the patrol force a reservoir from which the burgeoning "elite" units draw manpower. True efficiency in police work is almost impossible to define, Wilson opines, but the legalistic style puts a premium on "technical" efficiency.

Professionalism and the requirement of higher educational standards probably appeal "to both the middle-class consumer of police services and to the middle-class police recruit"; however, they may have the unfortunate tendency of creating an "up-tight" image, which hardly appeals to ghetto inhabitants. The legalistic style has the paradoxical consequence that, while it encourages lip service to the ideal that "all men are equal before the law," it breeds perceived if not actual inequality toward blacks. The legalistic style seems to create many complaints of police brutality and harassment.

. . .

In the service style, "the police take seriously all requests for either law enforcement or order maintenance (unlike police with a watchman style) but are less likely to respond by making an arrest or otherwise imposing formal sanctions (unlike police with a legalistic style). The police intervene frequently but not formally." They differ from the watchman style in that they ignore no group's complaints. They apply informal sanctions to all minor peccadilloes by juveniles, motorists, gamblers, and similar people. They differ from the legalistic style in that they do not issue large numbers of traffic tickets, they do not make many juvenile arrests, nor do they arrest routinely for misdemeanors like gambling.

Interestingly enough, population figures appear to have little to do with the existence of this style. Wilson found the service style in Nassau, a department with over 3200 members serving a community of over one million inhabitants and in Brighton, a town with about 27,000 inhabitants and a police force of 30. Nassau County and Brighton are both primarily residential communities with relatively high family incomes and very low proportions of blacks. The indicia of the legalistic style that they share include professionalization and specialization plus the absence of corruption. Where they differ radically from the legalistic style is in their emphasis on "public education" and "community relations," and in their devotion to the older ideal of patrolmen walking a beat, as opposed to the much greater use of motorized patrols, which are thought to represent the acme of "professionalization" in such cities as Oakland. They differ also in the relative absence of complaints from blacks about police practices.

The service style shares an attribute of the watchman style in that it takes a relaxed attitude and does not use the arrest power so extensively. However, it is less sloppy and less discriminatory than the watchman style. As Wilson points out:

> The political leaders of Brighton and Nassau County believe that their citizens want something more from law enforcement than they would get in Amsterdam and something different from what they would get in Albany and Newburgh. Politics in general is regarded, at least by the politicians, as providing services and amenities to persons clearly able to afford them. Though taxes are an issue, the politicians believe that people are willing to pay for programs that improve the quality of community life beyond what is minimally necessary. Government, besides keeping the streets clean and putting fires out, is also expected to sustain a prosperous business life, provide excellent public schools, hire courteous and obliging

public officials, and maintain the "character of the community." The political consumer—the voter—is thought to have
high standards and thus would be impatient with a caretaker
government and outraged by a corrupt one. If the politicians
are to make money out of their public life, it had better not be
obvious or clearly at the public's expense.

Comment and Questions

The above excerpt is important because it relates the police exercise of discretion to two very important variables—first, the style of the
police department, and second, the nature of the community the police
serve.

Is it not clear that different styles are appropriate in different
communities? A style may have serious disadvantages as applied to a
given community—but one must then consider whether a different
style might raise even greater problems?

It is likely that, in any given area in the United States, a student
can find each of the police styles represented—though probably not in
pure form. Students may find interesting an attempt to classify nearby
communities according to police style, according to the apparent desires
of the community, and according to the advantages and disadvantages
of that style in operation. Do you know of a minority community
where the "service style" is practiced? Do you know of a wealthy
community where it is not?

Can you conceive of any style not mentioned in the above excerpt
which might prove practical in a given type of community?

Who determines the style of policing that a community receives?
How?

As noted above, the use of—or failure to use—police discretion
often brings the police into conflict with various sections of the community they are to serve. This is one aspect of a much broader problem—
and one of the most urgent in our society today—that of improving
police [accountability to] the community. This is the subject of the next
section.

3. THE PUBLIC

a. CONTROL THROUGH EXTERNAL REVIEW

(1) NOTE ON CIVILIAN REVIEW BOARDS

There are only a few ways, other than through the courts and
internal procedures, in which attempts have been made to control
police misconduct. Prominent among them—and most controversial—
has been the civilian review board. Impetus for its creation came from
a general feeling on the part of many members of the public, particularly the members of minority groups or inner-city residents, that they
had no opportunities to have their complaints heard. Written docu-

mentation of police illegality as well as the visual documentation on television of the brutal treatment of civil rights demonstrators, brought to the surface problems which most Americans had never known existed.

The independent police review board, which seemed to many to provide a potential means of handling grievances and clearing the air of tensions between the police and the public, giving the public greater confidence in its police and the police a certain amount of protection from malicious and unfounded complaints, never was able to achieve its purpose.

Although the police themselves played a major role in defeating civilian review boards in many cities, inherent defects in the idea of the review board also contributed to its lack of success. Primary among these was the fact that the review board focused solely on the misdeeds of policemen while ignoring the potential for abuse of discretion and impact on minority groups of other administrative agencies: the welfare department, the board of education, the Immigration Service, among others. Secondly, the procedures for determining the truth of any complaint in order to protect the rights of both parties require many procedural safeguards. Informal settlements, used in Philadelphia, avoid these problems (a typical settlement procedure might be a meeting of the complainant and the immediate superior of the officer involved, followed by an apology by the department or a withdrawal of the complaint by the citizen) and often result in an adjustment of the dispute which is quite satisfactory to the complainant. Yet many members of the community are not satisfied without a formal finding of guilt or innocence. Finally, the creation of civilian review boards tended to make police administrators defensive and often caused the administrator and his department to close ranks against the outside instead of taking aggressive action against obvious individual or pervasive abuses.

The American Bar Foundation recently commissioned several experts to study police complaint procedures in the United States and to comment upon them. We reprint below two excerpts, one by Wayne Kerstetter, a Professor of Criminal Justice in Chicago, and former Assistant First Deputy Commissioner of the New York City Police Department; and Amitai Schwartz, a San Francisco attorney who served formerly as staff counsel to the Northern California American Civil Liberties Union.*

(a) Kerstetter's View **

Why should the police department be given the authority to be the primary mechanism for complaint review? The departmental adminis-

---

* William A. Geller, ed., *Police Leadership in America: Crisis and Opportunity.* American Bar Foundation, Praeger, New York, Copyright 1985 (Reprinted with permission).

** Wayne A. Kerstetter, *Who Disciplines The Police?* id. pp. 178–180.

trative structure has by far the greatest potential for efficient, effective action to prevent, to investigate, to adjudicate, or to punish police misconduct. Ultimately, the major purpose of any system should be to prevent inappropriate conduct by police officers. The department has great capacities to contribute to this goal by the actions it takes in hiring, training, and supervising employees and by the care it exercises in adopting policies and procedures that minimize the likelihood of misconduct. The first-line supervisor is the person who can contribute the most—in informal but extremely effective ways—in discouraging inappropriate conduct.

The actions that the department and its managerial and supervisory personnel must take in discharging this function are sometimes costly and often unpleasant. The effect of removing the responsibility for dealing with instances of misconduct from the department is to reduce substantially its motivation to address problem areas and individuals before they get out of control. It allows the administrative structure to evade responsibility by pointing to some other agency. It also allows them to be "good guys" and implicitly or explicitly side with their nominal charges. It encourages a "we-they" mentality and a conspiracy of silence to impede misconduct investigations.

Placing primary misconduct review responsibility outside the department also fragments an administrative authority in significant ways. With the police this authority is inevitably fragmented already by several factors: the agency's position as a subordinate part of a larger administrative structure that itself is situated in a governmental system involving explicit legislative review authority; the department's role as part of a criminal charge processing system in which important activities on its part are subject to prosecutorial and judicial review; and, increasingly, aggressive community, media, and union challenges to its claims of expertise and managerial prerogatives.

It might be argued that this decentralization of authority is a desirable trend that should be encouraged. Historically, the American experience with municipal police in the nineteenth century does not support the notion that decentralization enhances the likelihood of controlled police conduct. Indeed, a principal strategy of police reformers for the first half of the twentieth century was the centralization of administrative authority as a way of establishing greater accountability. Even the most radical proposals for restructuring police organizations, which have been criticized by some for overly optimistic assumptions about behavior control mechanisms, retain in their new organizational structures a centralized misconduct review unit.

The police department is better situated to assume the primary review responsibility because it is a repository of the administrative and investigative expertise necessary to conduct thorough investigations and make sound decisions about the appropriateness of particular conduct. The fact that the investigators are experienced police officers will aid the investigation in at least two ways. They will be less susceptible to being confused by misleading statements or lack of understanding of police procedures. Further, the ability to think oneself into a situation and understand the dynamics of it is of crucial importance in ferreting out evidence. Their prior experience as police officers will enhance the capacity of internal investigators for this task.

This same base of experience will provide a foundation for making sound decisions on the appropriateness of challenged officer conduct. I have argued that a central difficulty in the review of police use of coercive power lies in the fact that the use of coercion is essential to their function, that the legal limitations on its use are imprecise, and that the realities of the police role create further ambiguities by virtue of the tension between judicial and legislative accountabilities and by virtue of being existentially situated between custom and law (as control mechanisms) and needing to respond effectively on both levels. Sorting out this tangle is best done by those who have been there, provided that the discretion they must exercise is not open-ended.

Administrative processes also have an advantage by virtue of their superior flexibility, capacity for subtle responses, procedural freedom, and ability to pursue and modify quickly when necessary a course of action. These advantages allow responses to problems to be tailored to the needs of specific situations.

A final consideration is governmental efficiency. To create an external agency, particularly in a sizable city, that has the capacity to accept and process numerous complaints is to establish yet another large bureaucracy that inevitably will experience various institutional problems, including a tendency to become focused on the needs of its staff rather than its clients. The bittersweet benefits of civil service and public employee unionization undoubtedly will be bestowed on it as well. And over time it will face the substantial danger, encountered by all regulatory bodies, of being co-opted by those that it ostensibly regulates.

But what is to prevent those who operate this internal review mechanism from succumbing to the temptation to protect fellow officers and the department's reputation by covering up instances of misconduct? The answer, of course, is meaningful external review, premised not so much on the actuality of cover-ups as on the inherent lack of credibility of any internal review system that is not open to outside scrutiny. That lack of credibility cuts deeply into the police legitimacy in the community. Paradoxically, the review of misconduct allegations is so important that it should use police expertise, but it is also too important to be left solely to police administrative discretion.

What principles should govern the structure and operation of this external review? The central principle is that external review should be focused on the adequacy and integrity of the police department's response to complaints—that is, on the system rather than on individual cases. Individual cases should be addressed (in fact, a sample, varying in size depending on the perceived need, should routinely be reinvestigated to ensure the integrity of the police investigations), but they should be examined primarily in order to make judgments about the police department's discharge of its responsibility to provide a fair, objective, and credible review of allegations of police misconduct. The external review should be sensitive to overzealous "head-hunting" tendencies on the part of the internal affairs unit and, indeed, should accept complaints from police officers on these matters.

Preferably, the external review should include allegations involving any of the administrative agencies in the jurisdiction, not just the police. This broad scope makes sense both because other agencies provide important services and in order to avoid the implication that only the police engage in misconduct. There is justification for singling out the police because of their extraordinary authority, but it is poor judgment to do so.

(b) Schwartz's View *

In my experience working as an ACLU attorney in connection with police misconduct issues in the San Francisco Bay area, I have found that police self-investigation has rarely worked to protect constitutional rights. While some enlightened police administrators will impose self-discipline by promulgating police policies that limit police discretion on the streets and will enforce those policies through command supervision, most police departments fail to make a fair evaluation of alleged misconduct and rarely sustain a serious complaint of wrongdoing.

Ironically, most self-investigative units, like the IAB in San Francisco, are called internal affairs bureaus or similar names, denoting internal concerns that do not involve the public. But police misconduct is not an internal affair; it is the public's business.

Since police officers on street patrol are not routinely supervised as they work alone or in pairs, a primary source of information about the officers' street conduct must come from the public, often in the form of complaints. Unless the police are prepared to accept the feedback that comes from the complaint process and fairly evaluate the information given to them, they will deprive themselves of an important means of assuring self-discipline and management. Self-investigation, however, frequently yields distorted findings and deprives police management of important information because the police investigations are biased and inadequate. Several factors produce these results.

First, there is a constant tension between the observance of constitutional rules and the necessity to catch criminals and keep order. When the courts suppress evidence or award citizens damages because of illegal search and seizure, illegal entry and restraint, or mishandling of evidence, it is rare for police departments to discipline the responsible officers. Police internal investigations are unlikely to put as much emphasis on constitutional rules of behavior as on the exigencies facing

---

* Amitai Schwartz, *Reaching Systemic Police Abuses*, id. at 187–190.

an officer who had been attempting to fight crime and generated a complaint of misconduct in the process. In fact, police departments rarely impose discipline for conduct that courts have found to be illegal.

Second, many police administrators and street officers fail to recognize various sorts of constitutional violations as abusive. As was the case with warrantless (but probable cause) entries of suspects' homes, for example, the police frequently will engage in questionable practices until such time as the courts call them to task and declare the practices unconstitutional. As a practical matter the police have little incentive to impose restraints on themselves.

Third, it is difficult to discipline a hero. In my experience the most abusive officers frequently tend to be the most aggressive. Their ability to generate complaints is matched by their ability to make arrests. Interorganizational pressures and the maintenance of morale make the thorough investigation of these officers a difficult and unlikely prospect. Their aggressiveness is usually condoned by higher ranking officials, and police investigators have a tendency to forgive their behavior or look the other way. Of course there are occasions where constitutional violations will not be excused; but in my experience this is usually due to external political pressure that requires that some action be taken to root out blatant examples of misconduct, such as abuses by a highly visible SWAT team.

I do not suggest that outside civilian review boards are the only answer to the age-old question of "Who shall watch the watchmen?" However, I do believe that civilian investigation of complaints is essential so that police management can make supervisory and disciplinary decisions on the basis of facts that have been fairly gathered and evaluated. There are simply too many ways in which the fact-finding process can be distorted to trust this function solely to police investigators. . . .

Part of the value of civilian investigation is that civilians may find abusive and unnecessary certain types of conduct to which a police administration has become insensitive because "that's the way it's done." Tight handcuffing, which can leave welts and bruises on suspect's wrists, is an example. Police investigators may not think such injuries are important—or they may attempt to cover up the offending officers' uncaring or punitive behavior by routinely accepting the claim that the marks and wounds resulted from the suspects' attempts to wriggle free of the restraints. I have not heard of a case in the San Francisco Bay area in which an investigating police officer found excessive force solely in the misuse of handcuffs.

[The] assumption that police can be depended on "to make sound decisions about the appropriateness of particular conduct" is illusory because the criterion police are most likely to use to determine the propriety of behavior is habitual operating practice. Although a new police chief with fresh ideas might have progressive opinions about "appropriate conduct" that differ from the habits of the rank and file, the complaint process is not likely to provide many new recommendations for changes in policy so long as veteran officers are in charge of investigating complaints and spotting troublesome departmental practices in need of review and change. The ombudsman . . . is not likely to be in any better position to comment on ongoing styles of police behavior. The ombudsman would be concerned with the procedural fairness of the complaint process itself, rather than underlying police practices generating those complaints. He would also, as I understand it, provide a mechanism for conciliation for disputes between police and citizens. But the ombudsman would leave the assessment of underlying police conduct to the police. This process is then ultimately devoid of civilian restraint.

Even [the] idea that spotchecking a handful of investigations would put controls on the investigators is not likely to have much of an impact because the spot checks could not comprehensively evaluate the ongoing investigative judgments and biases of the police investigators. It is easy enough for a spot check to point out that a police investigation missed a useful witness; it is quite another matter for the ombudsman to second-guess the police evaluation of the witness or the police assessment of the evidence gathered by the investigators.

As most trial lawyers know, the identity of the fact finder or judge can make an enormous difference in the way evidence is treated and interpreted and ultimately in the final outcome of a factual dispute. In San Francisco, the police would not seriously investigate a complaint unless there were "independent" witnesses or other evidence. Although the term "independent" was not defined explicitly in police rules, in common practice it meant that a complainant's word was never good enough to find wrongdoing on the part of an officer and that some uninvolved bystander, neither a friend nor a relative of the complainant, had to be present to refute an accused officer's version of events. In contrast, the police officers present at the scene were considered reliable because they were under a departmentally imposed obligation to tell the truth to the police investigators.

Another reason complaints are rarely sustained by police investigators is that they require the complainant to meet an enormous burden of proof. While the standard of proof in an ordinary civil lawsuit is proof by a preponderance of evidence (that is, the claim is more likely true than false), the police in the California jurisdictions that I have seen require uncontradicted or overwhelming proof of misconduct; otherwise, the departments fail to sustain the complaints. This is one of the reasons one frequently encounters jury awards of money damages in situations where a police self-investigation previously found no wrongdoing at all.

In the long run, the police would be far better off to lower the burden of proof they require to something more akin to that used by the courts. Then they would find misconduct in their ranks, impose discipline or other corrective remedies, and hopefully avoid future civil liability. Under the present system, the police are simply hiding their heads in sand.

Comment and Questions

Note that Kerstetter is not opposed to civilian review. He distinguishes instead between offering the police department the *primary* responsibility for complaint review, rather than some outside authority. Many police chiefs would disagree with Kerstetter and would argue that complaint review should rest entirely with the police, mainly on grounds that the police, as trained and experienced professionals, are the only group in society capable of understanding and appreciating the realities of police work. For this reason, they would argue, civilians are as unqualified to investigate police as they are to investigate lawyers or doctors. What do you think of that argument? Are police akin to doctors and lawyers? In what ways would you suggest they are different?

Suppose you have decided that civilian review of police is a pretty good idea. The next question is, what form should it take? The Berkeley, California Civilian Review Board is composed of nine persons, each of whom is appointed by a member of the City Council. As a result, the police review board necessarily reflects the political coloring and conflicts of the City Council. Some observers have argued that since a civilian review board is supposed to judge police who have been accused of misconduct, the members should be selected less for their political allegiances, than for their competence in judging. Assume that you had the power to organize a civilian review board for your community, what criteria would you employ in selecting its members? To what extent would you feel that members should represent the community? Or would you think that representativeness was secondary? Put another way, do you want on the board members who are qualified primarily by being members of the community team; or do you want people who, like umpires, are impartial?

When a police officer is accused of misconduct by a complaining citizen, the officer is, in effect, a "defendant." Do you think the officer ought to be "presumed to be innocent?" Should the officer be exonerated unless guilt is proved "beyond a reasonable doubt?"

(2) NOTE ON INVESTIGATION BY AD HOC GROUPS

In the absence of an institutionalized system of civilian review, some communities have authorized investigative commissions on an ad hoc basis to respond to a particular incident of police-community tension or to charges of inefficiency, corruption, and illegality in the police department.* In some cases these are groups specially constitut-

---

* One example of this approach was the formation of the Commission to Investigate Alleged Police Corruption (the Knapp Commission) in April 1970 by Mayor John Lindsay in New York City. This commission was formed following the publication of charges in the New York Times of widespread police corruption and charges that high officials in the Lindsay Administration and the police department had not

ed for the investigation; in other instances, an existing group or a committee of the city council handles the study. In a few cases, as in the famous study of criminal justice in Cleveland,* outside experts are utilized. The disadvantages of such an approach to the continuing supervision of community policing policies are obvious. The investigation, in response to a large-scale controversy, must be carried on in an atmosphere of recrimination and defensiveness. It is necessarily focused on one primary cause of concern to the exclusion of other potential problems. Generally there is no follow-up on the recommendations over any period of time—in fact, the recommendations are usually forgotten, once the purpose of the study, which is to divert responsibility for the resolution of the conflict from those who do not wish to assume it, is achieved.

(3) NOTE ON THE FAILURE OF EXISTING METHODS

Existing methods of review of and control over police conduct are inadequate. The reasons are numerous. Failure on the part of the courts and the public to understand the actual nature of police work or to acknowledge the amount of discretion exercised at the lowest levels of the department; failure to recognize the factors which influence change in any organization; failure to appreciate the opportunities for abuse in the vagueness of the criminal statutes, so that what appears to be the legal nondiscretional enforcement of the law can be a tool for selective discrimination and harassment, are only a few of the obstacles in the past to an effective system of review and control.

b. CONTROL THROUGH LAW

(1) REGULATING POLICE PRACTICES **

I think I should emphasize that I am not a specialist about the police. I have been trying to study discretion in government agencies in general and that has included the police. I have a little book entitled *Police Discretion* that was prepared on the basis of interviews of the Chicago police during the summer of 1974. I had five law students between their second and third years who worked full time interviewing about 300 officers of the Chicago police at all levels. What I know about the police is based on that interviewing and on very little more. Whether or not what we found in the Chicago police is representative of police in large cities of the country, I do not know, but I have impressions that it may be. My main point is: policy is made primarily at the bottom of the organization, not at the top. Now, that's a rather surprising fact. I know of no other organization, governmen-

acted when informed of specific acts of corruption. Burnham, *City Opens Study of Policing Police*, The New York Times, April 24, 1970, p. 1, col. 1. Reprinted with permission.

* In 1922.

** Testimony of Kenneth Culp Davis: U.S. Commission on Civil Rights, Police Practices and the Preservation of Civil Rights. (Washington, D.C.; U.S. Government Printing Office, 1978), pp. 57–62. Reprinted with permission.

tal or nongovernmental, in which policy is made primarily at the bottom.

Let me give examples. A 19-year-old standing in the street fired three shots at a woman standing in a doorway. All three shots missed. Neighbors witnessed the second and third shots. The police apprehended the young man. The woman requested that they let him go. They did let him go. I was startled at those facts and suggested to my research assistants, "Let's find out what the general policy is," and we interviewed on that question. The question was: if the victim of the crime refuses to sign a complaint, is an arrest still made or is the offender released? What we found was, with our sampling at the patrolman level, nearly all patrolmen agreed if the victim does not sign a complaint, you have to let the person go. At the sergeant level, it was a little different. There were a few more that would make the arrest. At the top level, the superintendent and the five deputy superintendents, the division on the question was four to two in favor of making the arrest.

After it was pointed out to the top six officers that most of the patrolmen or nearly all of the patrolmen would not make the arrest, they did nothing about it. They were rather amused about the fact that they were divided, and their view was one way and the view of the men was the other way.

One patrolman answered our question by saying, "Why, I was standing in a dark doorway, and I witnessed an armed robbery. I stepped out and I got the robber all right. The victim asked me to release him, and, of course, I had to." Now, that's a sample of the way the law is enforced in Chicago.

Who makes the policy? I would say the policy is made almost entirely at the bottom level. A part of the terms on which I could make my study of the Chicago police was that I could not inquire into corruption, brutality, or racial discrimination. I inquired into selective enforcement, which inevitably got over into the area to some extent of discrimination of all kinds, including racial.

My research assistants would come back with stories. "Do you know that there are two kinds of people? We just learned this from the people we've been interviewing," they would tell me. "There are the kinky ones and then the law-abiding people." I hadn't heard the word kinky. I had to have that explained to me, what that meant. You can tell a kinky person by his appearance usually, by his dress, by the way he wears his hair. If you can't do it that way, you look him in the eye and you can tell.

The answer to the question of what the policy is, about arresting or not, depends upon which of these two kinds of people you're dealing with. The policy is made by the officers on the basis of ignorance, on the basis of their own backgrounds. They have a group spirit about this. The top people, when I would ask them about this, wouldn't even know about what the men are doing in this respect, and they didn't care.

I think I can summarize this way, that there are five major deficiencies in the manner in which selective enforcement policy is made. First, the top officers fail to make most of the policy, so that patrolmen become the prime makers of the policy. Secondly, no one in the department makes special studies for the purpose of formulating policy. The policy choices are based on nothing better than the patrolmen's offhand judgments. Three, the department does not employ professional staffs who have the requisite training in various fields. The department does not even have a staff of legal advisors. Four, the department has no administrative procedure for ascertaining preferences of the community about enforcement policy or for allowing members of the public to know and to criticize the department's enforcement policy. Five, the department makes no effort to coordinate its enforcement policy with the policy of prosecutors and of judges, and some of its enforcement policy is based on misimpressions of the policy of prosecutors and judges. An example of the misimpression is what I spoke about the 19-year-old firing the three shots.

The usual reason that patrolmen give for not making the arrest is, "You can't get a conviction if the victim will not testify willingly against the offender." Well, I thought I knew that wasn't so, but I had my boys check with the State's attorney's office to see what they would say, and they all said, "Well, if you have a witness to the crime, that surely does suffice. You can be pretty sure of getting a conviction whether or not the victim is there."

Questions

To what extent can and should policy guidelines cover the range of situations police encounter? What sanctions should we impose on police if they violate guidelines? How would we find out how the police behaved?

(2) OCCUPATIONAL ENVIRONMENT AND THE RULE OF LAW *

Five features of the policeman's occupational environment weaken the conception of the rule of law as a primary objective of police conduct. One is the social psychology of police work, that is, the relation between occupational environment, working personality, and the rule of law. Second is the policeman's stake in maintaining his position of authority, especially his interest in bolstering accepted patterns of enforcement. Third is police socialization, especially as it influences the policeman's administrative bias. A related factor is the pressure put upon individual policemen to "produce"—to be efficient rather than legal when the two norms are in conflict. Finally, there is

* Jerome H. Skolnick, *Justice Without Trial: Law Enforcement in Democratic Society* (New York: John Wiley & Sons, Inc., 1966) pp. 203–245. © 1966 (Reprinted with permission of the publishers).

the policeman's opportunity to behave inconsistently with the rule of law as a result of the low visibility of much of his conduct.

Although it is difficult to weigh the relative import of these factors, they all seem analytically to be joined to the conception of policeman as *craftsman* rather than as *legal actor,* as a skilled worker rather than as a civil servant obliged to subscribe to the rule of law.

. . .

The police are increasingly articulating a conception of professionalism based on a narrow view of managerial efficiency and organizational interest. A sociologist is not surprised at such a development. Under the rule of law it is not up to the agency of enforcement to generate the limitations governing its actions, and bureaucrats typically and understandably try to conceal the knowledge of their operations so that they may regulate themselves unless they are forced to make disclosures. But the police in a democracy are not merely bureaucrats. They are also, or can be conceived of as, legal officials, that is, men belonging to an institution charged with strengthening the rule of law in society. If professionalism is ever to resolve some of the strains between order and legality, it must be a professionalism based upon a deeper set of values than currently prevails in police literature and the "professional" police department studied, whose operations are ordered on this literature.

The needed philosophy of professionalism must rest on a set of values conveying the idea that the police are as much an institution dedicated to the achievement of legality in society as they are an official social organization designed to control misconduct through the invocation of punitive sanctions. The problem of police in a democratic society is not merely a matter of obtaining newer police cars, higher order technical equipment or of recruiting men who have to their credit more years of education. What must occur is a significant alteration in the ideology of police, so that police "professionalization" rests on the values of a democratic legal order, rather than on technological proficiency. . . .

The Community and Police Conduct

If the police are ever to develop a conception of *legal* as opposed to *managerial* professionalism, they will do so only if the surrounding community demands compliance with the rule of law by rewarding police for such compliance, instead of looking to the police as an institution solely responsible for controlling criminality. In practice, however, the reverse has been true. The police function in a milieu tending to support, normatively and substantively, the idea of administrative efficiency that has become the hallmark of police professionalism. Legality, as expressed by both the criminal courts community with which the police have direct contact, and the political community responsible for the working conditions and prerogatives of police, is a weak ideal. . . .

Under these circumstances of mass administration of criminal justice, presumptions necessarily run to regularity and administrative efficiency. The negation of the presumption of innocence permeates the entire system of justice without trial. All involved in the system, the defense attorneys and judges, as well as the prosecutors and policemen, operate according to a working presumption of the guilt of persons accused of crime. As accused after accused is processed through the system, participants are prone to develop a routinized callousness, akin to the absence of emotional involvement characterizing the physician's attitude toward illness and disease.

The overwhelming presence of the "official" system of justice without trial provides normative support for the policeman's own attachment to principles of administrative regularity in opposition to due process of law. Under such circumstances, it should not be surprising to find the policeman adopting the "official" perspective too, since his role is to make the initial decision as to whether a charge has been warranted. Having made the charge, he of all people can hardly be expected to presume the innocence of the defendant. He has, in practice, listened to the defendant's story and assured himself of the latter's culpability. In his own mind, there are numerous guilty parties whom he has not arrested because he does not feel their cases will hold up in court, even though he is personally convinced of their guilt to a moral certainty. Police may feel most strongly about the "irrationality" of due process, but in fact other role players in the system of criminal justice may also be observed to be more concerned with efficiency than legality. If the policeman is the strongest advocate of a "rational bureaucratic" system emphasizing factual over legal guilt, he may well be simply because it is the definition of his ability as a worker that is most affected by the application of the rule of law. . . . An "order" perspective based upon managerial efficiency also tends to be supported by the civic community. The so-called power structure of the community, for example, often stresses to the police the importance of "keeping the streets clear of crime." Indeed, when a newspaper runs an editorial, or a political figure emphasizes the importance of "making the streets safe for decent people," the statements are rarely qualified to warn law enforcement officials that they should proceed according to the rule of law. On the contrary, such injunctions are typically phrased as calls for zealous law enforcement or strict law enforcement.

The emphasis on the maintenance of order is also typically expressed by the political community controlling the significant rewards for the police—money, promotions, vacations. Mayors, city councilmen, city managers draw up police budgets, hire and fire chiefs of police, and call for "shake-ups" within the department. Even the so-called "liberal" politician is inclined to urge police to disregard the rule of law when he perceives circumstances as exceedingly threatening. . . .

In contrast to that of political authority, the power of appellate courts over the police is limited. In practice, the greatest authority of judges is to deny the merit of the prosecution. Thus, by comparison to the direct sanctions held by political authority, the judiciary has highly restricted *power* to modify police behavior. Not only do appellate courts lack direct sanctions over the police but there are also powerful political forces that, by their open opposition to the judiciary, suggest an alternative frame of reference to the police. By this time, however, the police have themselves become so much a part of this same frame of reference that it is often difficult to determine whether it is the political figure who urges "stricter law enforcement" on the policeman, or the law enforcement spokesman who urges the press and the politician to support his demands against laws "coddling criminals," by which he typically means rulings of appellate courts upholding constitutional guarantees, usually under the Fourth, Fifth, Sixth, and Fourteenth Amendments. . . . As workers in a democratic society, the police seek the opportunity to introduce the means necessary to carry out "production demands." The means used to achieve these ends, however, may frequently conflict with the conduct required of them as legal actors. In response to this dilemma, police "experts" have increasingly adopted a philosophy of professionalism based upon managerial efficiency, with the implied hope that advancing technology will somehow resolve their dilemma. As indicated, it has not, and by its very assumptions cannot. First of all, in those areas where violations of the rule of law occur, advanced technology often results in greater violation. Technological advances in the form of wiretaps, polygraphs, stronger binoculars, and so forth only make the police more competent to interfere with individual liberty. Secondly, the model of efficiency based on bureaucracy simply does not work out in practice. . . .

The working policeman is well aware of the limitations of "scientific" advances in police work and organization. He realizes that his work consists mostly of dealing with human beings, and that these skills are his main achievement. The strictures of the rule of law often clash with the policeman's ability to carry out this sort of work, but he is satisfied to have the argument presented in terms of technological achievement rather than human interaction, since he rightly fears that the public "will not understand" the human devices he uses, such as paying off informers, allowing "fences" to operate, and reducing charges, to achieve the enforcement ends demanded of him.

Police are generally under no illusions about the capacity of elected officials and the general public to make contradictory demands upon them. A certain amount of lip-service may be paid to the need for lawful enforcement of substantive criminal law, but the police are rarely, if ever, rewarded for complying with or expanding the area of due process of law. On the contrary, they are rewarded primarily for apprehension of so-called "notorious" criminals, for breaking "dope-rings," and the like. As a matter of fact, police are often much more sophisticated about their practices than the politicians who reward them. . . .

If this analysis is correct in placing ultimate responsibility for the quality of "law and order" in American society upon the citizenry, then the prospects for the infusion of the rule of law into the police institution may be bleak indeed. As an institution dependent on rewards from the civic community, police can hardly be expected to be much better or worse than the political context in which they operate. When the political community is itself corrupt, the police will also be corrupt. If the popular notion of justice reaches no greater sophistication than that "the guilty should not go free," then the police will respond to this conception of justice. When prominent members of the community become far more aroused over an apparent rise in criminality than over the fact that Negroes are frequently subjected to unwarranted police interrogation, detention, and invasions of privacy, the police will continue to engage in such practices. Without widespread support for the rule of law, it is hardly to be expected that the courts will be able to continue advancing individual rights, or that the police will themselves develop a professional orientation as *legal* actors, rather than as efficient administrators of criminal law.

Questions and Comment

Professor Skolnick points out that the crime control or "administrative" model is far closer to the view that the police take of themselves than is the due process model. Is this, in part, explained by the fact that the police do so much more than catch criminals?

Professor Skolnick's view that a police officer is a craftsman, rather than a legal officer,—or a professional or bureaucrat for that matter— implies that, in the words of James Q. Wilson:

> "As with most crafts, his has no body of generalized, written knowledge nor a set of detailed prescriptions as to how to behave—it has, in short, neither theory nor rules. Learning in the craft is by apprenticeship, but on the job and not in the academy. The principal group from which the apprentice wins (or fails to win) respect are his colleagues on the job, not fellow members of a discipline or attentive supervisors. And the members of the craft, conscious of having a special skill or task, think of themselves as set apart from society, possessors of an art that can be learned only by experience, and in need of restrictions on entry into their occupation. But unlike other members of a craft—carpenters, for example, or newspapermen—the police work in an apprehensive or hostile environment producing a service the value of which is not easily judged." . . .

If this is the case, would it be true that binding the policeman closely to carefully drawn rules of conduct would be every bit as difficult as binding a physician, psychotherapist, or architect to closely drawn rules of behavior?

Is not another major problem that we wish our police to be legal officers and to obey precise legal direction, and yet at the same time, we demand that they produce the kind of results which, at least in the short run, can be produced only be disregarding the legal restraints upon their powers?

4. CONTROL BY THE POLICE THEMSELVES

POLICE UNIONS *

Collective bargaining can be divided into two general categories— the public sector and the private sector. The police are, of course, in the public sector. The nation employs some 375,000 police officers at a cost of nearly seven billion dollars annually. Therefore, one can see the significance and importance placed on collective bargaining in just this one segment of public employment. The police are the largest group of local public employees, second only to public school teachers. Many of the issues associated with police collective bargaining disputes can also be found with schoolteachers, social workers, garbage collectors, public transportation employees, fire fighters, public works employees, and numerous other groups.

The history of police collective bargaining has been one of much turmoil, misunderstanding, confusion, and mistrust. It is commonplace today to read about police strikes, "blue flu," picketing, work slowdowns, ticket blitzes, and even police rioting. Recently, the New York City Police Benevolent Association was accused of riotous behavior because of a "raw deal" over scheduling that the police alleged they were receiving from the city administration. Also, the police of Phoenix, Arizona, recently resigned en masse as a form of protest; and during the past decade we have witnessed outright strikes in Montreal, Baltimore, Phoenix, San Francisco, Oklahoma City, and in numerous other parts of the country. . . .

. . . Like most unions, the police struggle to participate in formal collective bargaining processes has not been an easy one. Starting with the 1919 Boston police strike, police unions have grown in size, power, and impact. Today, 60% or better of the American police are covered by some form of collective bargaining agreement, contract, memorandum of understanding, or formal recognition in the form of a local ordinance. In the decade ahead, we probably will see almost all of the American police covered by some form of collective bargaining agreements. The reason for this is not complex, but rather quite simple. Cities just do not approach public employee unions once a year, or for that matter every other year, and offer voluntarily a pay hike, improved fringes, and plans to enhance working conditions. This is Alice-in-Wonderland and wishful thinking. Nor for that matter can the public employee expect its chief of police, superintendent, or commissioner to work hard on his behalf in these areas. Politics and the political facts of life inhibit this administrative behavior. Therefore, the struggle for a written contract, formal recognition, increased bene-

* William H. Hewitt, Sr., "Current Issues in Police Collective Bargaining," in *The Future of Policing*, Alvin M. Cohn, Sage Publications, Beverly Hills, 1978, pp. 207–209, 211, 214, 217. Copyright 1978 (Reprinted with permission)

fits, and a better way of life has been exceedingly difficult. This difficulty has been produced by three major identifiable factors: (1) public apathy, (2) apathetic, inefficient and unenlightened public officials, and (3) the complexity of the contemporary police role.

One of the major critical issues in police collective bargaining is recognition. By recognition is meant the employer's formal agreement that the police union *exists* and they have sound employee relations to bargain collectively with that union concerning wages, fringe benefits, and working conditions. Whether the police group is called a fraternal group, an association, a guild, a benevolent association, or a patrolman's association, it is still in the final analysis a *union*.

The police union is in business to enhance its lot. It does this either with or without the aid of collective bargaining legislation. The union also exists as the official voice of the department's patrolmen—the work force—and the unofficial voice of the supervisors and command officers. It succeeds or accomplishes its task in the latter category of employees under the "me-tooism" concept, wherein cities today automatically grant to the upper ranks, including the chief, any and all benefits earned by the patrolmen. In some cases, as under Pennsylvania's Act III, *all* policemen can bargain under one contract with their employer. In all the remaining states, they *may* bargain under one contract with their employer. Therefore, it is the patrolmen who carry on the fight, pay all the bills, and truly represent the police employees. To say that the chief of police, city manager, or the mayor truly speak for the police department is one of the greatest myths in contemporary police administration. Police unions have much to say about policy, safety, working conditions, discipline, and other issues of police administration.

Although in most cities the union is not an agency shop, it is nonetheless comprised of all patrolmen working in that job classification. Historically and traditionally, although not always, the more outspoken person tends to emerge as the police union leader. The reasons for this are quite simple: for the union to survive and produce for its members the group's expectations, it must be vocal and it must be argumentative when necessary. It must be prepared to shout, scream, and bang the table in fighting for its demands. And last, in all cases if the leaders are to be reelected, it must reflect the views, opinions, attitudes, and values of the working class it represents. Is this not true of any labor union?

In a related issue, and a serious one I might add, the police unions in every major city and in some states are embroiled in a controversy over the employment—and, in many cases, promotion—of the black police officer, female officers, and the Chicano officer. In quite a few cities, the black officer has created his own organization. . . .

. . . An example of what one minority police officer organization has done is the case of the Afro-American Police League (AAPL) of Chicago. A recent lawsuit by the AAPL charged the Chicago Police

Department with bias in the hiring and job assignments of minority officers. This resulted in the impoundment of 133 million dollars in federal revenue sharing funds for the city by a federal court. Litigation over the resolution of this matter is still pending. The judge in this matter, Prentice Marshall, has imposed a strict quota system on Chicago.

. . . It goes without saying that police unions have had an enormous impact and influence on policy and as an instrument of police reform. In fact, for all intents and purposes, where police unions are strong, we will probably find civil service weak and on its way out. It has been suggested that perhaps the only future for civil service will be in the testing of recruits and those seeking promotion. Unions now speak to all of their salary areas, that is, wages, shift differential, short-shift changeover, time and a half, pyramiding, vacation, holiday, and other pay issues. The unions have also made large gains in the fringe benefit areas, including Blue Cross-Blue Shield and other health plans (major medical, dental, drug, optical), bereavement leave, sick leave, pension, disability, educational incentive, and numerous others. Last, the unions have vastly improved working conditions, that is a bill of rights, free speech, labor-management committees, the elimination of polygraph tests, the elimination of press releases for arrested officers, establishing evaluation criteria, personnel files policy, job bidding procedures, layoffs, the eight-hour day, the 40-hour week, the 16-hour break between shifts, disciplinary hearings, suspension provisions, and numerous other improvements. . . .

The future impact of police collective bargaining will undoubtedly be found in its impact on management. That is, the chief's ability to administer his department free of any union constraints. The major impact of the union is without a doubt a creation of an entirely new system of governance in the police department, a new model to which management, specifically the chief, will have to adapt. . . .

Questions

Is it possible to strengthen the police administrator's control over police conduct, given the impact of police unions on management? Is it really desirable to do so, or is it more desirable to have patrolmen and management share authority? How do you think that impact will be felt? To what extent is the development of police unions compatible with police goals of professionalism? Are police really like other government workers, or are they more like the judiciary, interpreting and imposing laws upon the population? If not, why not?

In 1969, a researcher for the National Commission on the Causes and Prevention of Violence lamented that "as the affluence of the country has risen, in general, the relative rewards of police work have lagged badly." In 1990, the salary range for Oakland police officers was $35,868–$43,248 and for police captains was $70,020. Does not this change in the relative affluence of the police demonstrate the desirability of police unions?

5.　TWO PROBLEMS IN POLICE CONTROL

a.　POLICE CORRUPTION

(1) DEFINING THE PROBLEM *

There is considerable disagreement about what constitutes police corruption.　On the one hand, there is a tendency to define the term so broadly as to include all forms of police wrongdoing, from police brutality to the pettiest forms of questionable behavior.　On the other hand, police corruption is sometimes defined so narrowly that patterns of behavior with all the characteristics and consequences of corrupt acts are excluded.

For purposes of this inquiry, police corruption means acts involving the misuse of authority by a police officer in a manner designed to produce personal gain for himself or for others.　Excluded from consideration are the various forms of police misconduct where authority may have been abused, but where there is no indication that the abuse was motivated by a desire for personal gain.　Police administrators devote substantial time to investigating complaints about officers' misuse of authority when, for example, they stop and question people, seize contraband, make arrests, or conduct searches.　Many would argue that such actions should be seen as part of the corruption problem, involving a corruption of power.　But unless an officer's action in such encounters was motivated by a desire for personal gain, the problems raised differ significantly from those raised where personal gain is a primary objective.

Admittedly, the line is not a clear one.　Corruption and physical abuse are sometimes inseparable.　Police have, for example, been known to use force or the threat of force to obtain payoffs.　But most of the complaints alleging improper use of force do not include charges of corruption for personal gain.

Drawing a line that excludes police wrongdoing with no personal gain is not intended to minimize the gravity of other forms of police misconduct.　On the contrary, it is essential to emphasize that a significant body of police wrongdoing exists apart from that analyzed here.

The term bribery is commonly used to describe all forms of police corruption, but this is technically incorrect.　All police bribery is corruption, but not all police corruption is bribery.　In the criminal offense of bribery the officer must usually have solicited, received, retained, or agreed to accept something of value or personal advantage

---

* Herman Goldstein, *Police Corruption: A Perspective on its Nature and Control* (Washington, D.C.: Police Foundation, 1975), pp. 3–5.　Copyright 1975 (Reprinted with permission)

which he or she was not authorized to accept. The officer must also have known the bribe was offered with the intention of influencing official actions. Many patterns of police corruption lack these elements. This is not to say these other forms of corruption are legal. Officers guilty of corrupt acts may be charged with a number of other offenses, such as official misconduct, perjury, extortion, or theft.

Since most forms of corruption are criminal, it is important to view police corruption in criminal terms. But should all forms of crime involving police officers be viewed as part of the corruption problem? What about those occasional incidents where police commit crimes such as petty theft, burglary, or robbery—behavior referred to as police criminality? In most communities such incidents are commonly regarded as the ultimate form of corruption, as blatant violations by those entrusted with preventing criminal activity and enforcing the law. This view is reinforced because such activities usually occur in agencies known to have a high tolerance for corruption. This relationship is understandable, since many of the conditions contributing to the commission of these offenses by police also allow corruption to thrive. The officer who uses his authority, along with the camouflage, information, and access to premises that it provides, in order to steal or rob, is very much a part of the corruption problem.

This does not mean, however, that all police criminality falls into this category. The officer who commits a burglary without making use of his authority is no more a part of the corruption problem than the officer who murders his wife. In the police community, as in the larger community, one can expect a certain percentage of the population to engage in deviant conduct. Obviously, every effort should be made to prevent these crimes, but to ignore the possibility that they will occur reflects more faith in the ability to identify persons likely to commit crimes than is justified by current knowledge. Crimes committed by police will probably continue to be seen as a form of corruption. But without the misuse of authority, which is the defining element of corruption, crime by police presents a problem which differs little from the problem of crime in the larger community.

(2) POLICE CORRUPTION IN NEW YORK

(a) The Knapp Commission *

We found corruption to be widespread. It took various forms depending upon the activity involved, appearing at its most sophisticated among plainclothesmen assigned to enforcing gambling laws. In the five plainclothes divisions where our investigations were concentrated we found a strikingly standardized pattern of corruption. Plainclothesmen, participating in what is known in police parlance as a "pad,"

* From a report by the Commission to Investigate Allegations of Police Corruption in New York City, Whitman Knapp, Chairman (August 3, 1972). Reprinted with permission.

collected regular biweekly or monthly payments amounting to as much as $3,500 from each of the gambling establishments in the area under their jurisdiction and divided the take in equal shares. The monthly share per man (called the "nut") ranged from $300 and $400 in midtown Manhattan to $1,500 in Harlem. When supervisors were involved they received a share and a half. A newly assigned plainclothesman was not entitled to his share for about two months, while he was checked out for reliability, but the earnings lost by the delay were made up to him in the form of two months' severance pay when he left the division.

Evidence before us led us to the conclusion that the same pattern existed in the remaining divisions which we did not investigate in depth. This conclusion was confirmed by events occurring before and after the period of our investigation. Prior to the Commission's existence, exposures by former plainclothesman Frank Serpico had led to indictments or departmental charges against nineteen plainclothesmen in a Bronx division for involvement in a pad where the nut was $800. After our public hearings had been completed, an investigation conducted by the Kings County District Attorney and the Department's Internal Affairs Division—which investigation neither the Commission nor its staff had even known about—resulted in indictments and charges against 37 Brooklyn plainclothesmen who had participated in a pad with a nut of $1,200. The manner of operation of the pad involved in each of these situations was in every detail identical to that described at the Commission hearings, and in each almost every plainclothesman in the division, including supervisory lieutenants, was implicated.

Corruption in narcotics enforcement lacked the organization of the gambling pads, but individual payments—known as "scores"—were commonly received and could be staggering in amount. Our investigation, a concurrent probe by the State Investigation Commission, and prosecutions by federal and local authorities all revealed a pattern whereby corrupt officers customarily collected scores in substantial amounts from narcotics violators. These scores were either kept by the individual officer or shared with a partner and, perhaps, a superior officer. They ranged from minor shakedowns to payments of many thousands of dollars, the largest narcotics payoff uncovered in our investigation having been $80,000. According to information developed by the SIC and in recent federal investigations, the size of this score was by no means unique.

Corruption among detectives assigned to general investigative duties also took the form of shakedowns of individual targets of opportunity. Although these scores were not in the huge amounts found in narcotics, they not infrequently came to several thousand dollars.

Uniformed patrolmen assigned to street duties were not found to receive money on nearly so grand or organized a scale, but the large number of small payments they received present an equally serious if less dramatic problem. Uniformed patrolmen, particularly those assigned to radio patrol cars, participated in gambling pads more modest in size than those received by plainclothes units and received regular payments from construction sites, bars, grocery stores, and other business establishments. These payments were usually made on a regular basis to sector car patrolmen and on a haphazard basis to others. While individual payments to uniformed men were small, mostly under $20, they were often so numerous as to add substantially to a patrolman's income. Other less regular payments to uniformed patrolmen included those made by after-hours bars, bottle clubs, tow trucks, motorists, cab drivers, parking lots, prostitutes, and defendants wanting to fix their cases in court. Another practice found to be widespread was the payment of gratuities by policemen to other policemen to expedite normal police procedures or to gain favorable assignments.

Sergeants and lieutenants who were so inclined participated in the same kind of corruption as the men they supervised. In addition, some sergeants had their own pads from which patrolmen were excluded.

Although the Commission was unable to develop hard evidence establishing that officers above the rank of lieutenant received pay-offs, considerable circumstantial evidence and some testimony so indicated. Most often when a superior officer is corrupt, he uses a patrolman as his "bagman" who collects for him and keeps a percentage of the take. Because the bagman may keep the money for himself, although he claims to be collecting for his superior, it is extremely difficult to determine with any accuracy when the superior actually is involved.

Of course, not all policemen are corrupt. If we are to exclude such petty infractions as free meals, an appreciable number do not engage in any corrupt activities. Yet, with extremely rare exceptions, even those who themselves engage in no corrupt activities are involved in corruption in the sense that they take no steps to prevent what they know or suspect to be going on about them.

It must be made clear that—in a little over a year with a staff having as few as two and never more than twelve field investigators—we did not examine every precinct in the department. Our conclusion that corruption is widespread throughout the department is based on the fact that information supplied to us by hundreds of sources within and without the department was consistently borne out by specific observations made in areas we were able to investigate in detail.

The Nature and Significance of Police Corruption

Corruption, although widespread, is by no means uniform in degree. Corrupt policemen have been described as falling into two basic categories: "meat-eaters" and "grass-eaters." As the names might suggest, the meat-eaters are those policemen who, like Patrolman William Phillips who testified at our hearings, aggressively misuse their police powers for personal gain. The grass-eaters simply accept the payoffs that the happenstances of police work throw their way.

Although the meat-eaters get the huge payoffs that make the headlines, they represent a small percentage of all corrupt policemen. The truth is, the vast majority of policemen on the take don't deal in huge amounts of graft.

And yet, grass-eaters are the heart of the problem. Their great numbers tend to make corruption "respectable." They also tend to encourage the code of silence that brands anyone who exposes corruption a traitor. At the time our investigation began, any policeman violating the code did so at his peril. The result was described in our interim report: "The rookie who comes into the department is faced with the situation where it is easier for him to become corrupt than to remain honest."

More importantly, although meat-eaters can and have been individually induced to make their peace with society, the grass-eaters may be more easily reformed. We believe that, given proper leadership and support, many police who have slipped into corruption would exchange their illicit income for the satisfaction of belonging to a corruption-free department in which they could take genuine pride.

The problem of corruption is neither new nor confined to the police. Reports of prior investigations into police corruption, testimony taken by the Commission, and opinions of informed persons both within and without the department make it abundantly clear that police corruption has been a problem for many years. Investigations have occurred on the average of once in twenty years since before the turn of the century, and yet conditions exposed by one investigation seem substantially unchanged when the next one makes its report. This doesn't mean that the police have a monopoly on corruption. On the contrary, in every area where police corruption exists it is paralleled by corruption in other agencies of government, in industry and labor, and in the professions.

Our own mandate was limited solely to the police. There are sound reasons for such a special concern with police corruption. The police have a unique place in our society. The policeman is expected to "uphold the law" and "keep the peace." He is charged with everything from traffic control to riot control. He is expected to protect our lives and our property. As a result, society gives him special powers and prerogatives, which include the right and obligation to bear arms, along with the authority to take away our liberty by arresting us.

Symbolically, his role is even greater. For most people, the policeman is the law. To them, the law is administered by the patrolman on the beat and the captain in the station house. Little wonder that the public becomes aroused and alarmed when the police are charged with corruption or are shown to be corrupt.

(b) In 1986 *

It has been 18 years since two frustrated New York City police officers, David Durk and Frank Serpico, went to newspapers with allegations of widespread police corruption after being all but ignored by their superior officers.

The result was the last major scandal to hit the department—one in which corruption was found to be endemic and widespread.

Since then, the country's largest police department has undergone an era of upheaval and overhauls. In a peculiar way, several analysts said yesterday, those sweeping changes were reflected in the suspension Tuesday of 13 police officers in Brooklyn who were accused of extorting money and drugs from narcotics dealers.

Unlike the situation in 1968, when the two policemen took their grievances to the press to get justice, the analysts said, this time the Police Department took seriously allegations of misconduct—even though they came from known street criminals.

(3) POLICE CORRUPTION IN PHILADELPHIA**

RECOMMENDATIONS TO CONTROL POLICE CORRUPTION

Although corruption is not ordinarily a subject for extended comment in a management study of a police department, its scope in the Philadelphia Police Department, as evidenced by recent and ongoing investigations, establishes it as an obstacle to the effective management of the Department. An ongoing grand jury investigation into alleged corruption within the Philadelphia Police Department, conducted by the United States Attorney's Office for the Eastern District of Pennsylvania and staffed by the Philadelphia Office of the Federal Bureau of Investigation, has resulted in the indictment and (in the vast majority of cases) convictions of sworn Philadelphia police officers and high-ranking officials. Thirty-six policemen have so far been indicted. Thirty-one have been convicted. Among those convicted are a deputy commissioner, two chief inspectors, two inspectors, one captain, six lieutenants, and one sergeant. The investigations are continuing and more indictments are likely.

The federal indictments and trial testimony, offered by the United States Attorney's Office, describe a pattern of systemic corruption in vice enforcement. In exchange for money, police officers have provided "protection" or relief from enforcement. These leads are also being pursued in local investigations by the Philadelphia District Attorney's Office and by the Philadelphia Police Department itself.

* "13 Police Suspensions—Lessons of '68" Martin Gottlieb, New York Times, Sept. 25, 1986, p. 18. Reprinted with permission.

** Philadelphia and its Police: Towards a New Partnership, A Report by the Philadelphia Policy Study Task Force, March 1987, pp. 140–144 (Reprinted with Permission).

These investigations, arrests, indictments and convictions have confirmed for many what had been a lingering suspicion. In 1974 the Pennsylvania Crime Commission in its highly publicized report on the Philadelphia Police stated, ". . . corruption and political influence . . . have plagued the force since its inception . . . [Corruption has been] ongoing, wide-spread, systematic, and occurring at all levels of the police department." The Task Force's survey showed that a majority of residents believe that Philadelphia police officers engage in some form of illegal or unprofessional behavior, such as accepting free meals or gifts, taking or asking for bribes, sleeping or drinking on duty, or asking for sexual favors (See Appendix A).

Officials within the Department tend to understate the scope and seriousness of the problem. In our discussion, some said they thought the problem was exaggerated or largely confined to vice inforcement (gambling, liquor, narcotics and prostitution). Others said the police were being unfairly singled out, while other municipal employees were left alone. Yet, they did not deny its existence. This is a marked change from a decade ago, when police officials believed that to acknowledge that corruption was a major problem in the Department would be destructive of police morale.

Many former and present command officials, however, do not think that the existence of corruption interferes with the sound management of the Department. They think the commissioner can implement whatever organizational changes or experiments he feels are necessary without concern that patterns of corruption will interfere.

We do not share this view. When police officers are influenced or controlled through payoffs from outside parties, they are not only committing crimes, but the formal administrative machinery of the force—the rules and regulations that govern behavior—are taken less seriously and become ineffective. As one commentator said, "You can't expect cops on the take to take orders." A captain who takes or solicits bribes cannot easily control his subordinates. If officers learn about the captain's activities (and in the closed society of a police force one must assume officers will), they may feel immune from discipline for their own derelictions. The captain's authority is compromised. His misconduct, in effect, confers a license for the officers to operate without regard to department regulations. Without effective supervision, police officers typically respond more slowly to calls for assistance, avoid assigned duties, sleep on the job, and perform poorly in situations requiring discipline and organization.

In a profession dedicated to respect for the law, ethical considerations constitute the backbone of management decisions. The presence of corruption undermines the ethical health of a department. Morale suffers as well. All police officers, even honest ones, pay a price for corruption through the loss of reputation. Every policeman knows there are many people in the city who think of him as "just a crook in uniform." When he buys a new car, his neighbors may look at him suspiciously, wondering where he got the money. Poor people who see gamblers, pushers, and hookers in their neighborhoods think every cop is on the take, although such is far from the truth.

Because corruption is a first cousin to favoritism and nepotism, it is no surprise that in a department where corruption has existed over time, officers will also feel that the department is not fairly run. In this atmosphere, it is hard for officers to take pride in their everyday achievements in preventing crime, apprehending criminals, and assisting persons in distress. They may be more difficult to motivate or supervise.

It is, therefore, essential to police management that certain basic anticorruption measures be installed:

- Ethical standards must be clearly defined and communicated to the force.

- Managers at all levels within the Department must be required to monitor the integrity of their subordinates as part of their responsibilities.

- Managers at lower levels must be equipped with the resources, responsibility and authority to deal with corruption problems in their divisions.

If detecting corruption in the Philadelphia Police Department is seen as the exclusive concern of the Internal Affairs Unit, little progress to combat it will be made. The job is too big for a single unit. Indeed, at this point the resources of the Federal Bureau of Investigation, Internal Revenue Service, U.S. Attorney and District Attorney are needed as well.

Few cities have been successful in moving from a milieu of corruption into one relatively free of corruption, but success stories do exist. Leadership in this process must come from the commissioner. Only through his active, continuous involvement will the climate in the Department change. Presently, the only written guidance for Philadelphia police officers is the Disciplinary Code, which prohibits "bribes or gratuities for permitting illegal acts."

The Task Force therefore recommends:

1. The commissioner should issue a clear, detailed statement spelling out acceptable ethical behavior for police officers. The statement should make clear through specific illustrations that no police officer shall accept any gift of money, goods or services for which others would be expected to pay, or which is offered because the intended recipient is a police officer. Once the Department adopts a policy, a comprehensive communications effort must be implemented to notify, explain and reinforce it. The commissioner should also provide strong incentives to Police Department management to detect corrupt police officers and take appropriate corrective action. He should hold all managers accountable for corruption among their subordinates.

Hopefully, these measures will contribute to a change in attitude among the officers. What is often called "the blue wall of silence" or "the blue curtain" must be penetrated. This "blue wall" is an exaggerated sense of loyalty among police officers to their fellow officers. Although the Department does attempt to install a sense of moral and ethical responsibility in the new recruits in the Police Academy, as officers continue in their careers and socialize with other officers, some feel their overriding obligation is to their colleagues. They ignore their duty to report criminal conduct.

The spirit of brotherly solidarity that binds members of the police also segregates them from the rest of society. The late Chief William H. Parker, whose leadership made Los Angeles one of the nation's most honest and efficient police departments, considered this "false sense of fraternal obligation" to be a major obstacle to police reform and did everything in his power to eliminate it. Once police officers understand that to go against their "own kind" is better than tolerating the worse behavior in their midst, progress against the grosser forms of corruption and brutality will come quickly. At present, too often the most serious aspersion that one officer can cast upon another is that the latter breached the code of silent fraternity and provided information to the Internal Affairs Unit.

We realize there is some harshness in disciplining an officer who himself did nothing wrong but only failed to come forward with information. We also realize that officers who are suspected of providing the Internal Affairs Unit with information will be shunned by many and risk having their property vandalized, or even suffering physical injury. Nonetheless, we feel that if an officer discovers information that he knows is reliable and concerns serious criminal conduct by a fellow officer, he is as duty bound to take action as he is when the suspect is an ordinary citizen.

The Task Force recommends:

2. The commissioner should discipline officers who knowingly withhold valuable information concerning serious criminal conduct of other officers.

At the Police Academy more could be done to introduce the recruits to the dangers of corruption. Training should emphasize more than the legal obligations of a police officer not to accept or solicit benefits. It should prepare recruits for the temptations they will be exposed to and identify how to avoid and resist them. There are obvious dangers in such an approach, and for this reason many training academies avoid it. We believe that recruits should clearly understand the risks—that they will be selling their integrity for what often amounts to no more than a few dollars a week. Once they understand this, they will be better prepared to resist the constant breaks, free meals, tips or discounts they will be offered, and they will be more reluctant to solicit gratuities on their own. At present, too many rookies start work in the districts innocent of the world they are entering. Once there, their corruption happens so quicky and unobtrusively that they are involved—and thus silenced—before they know it.

For this reason the Task Force recommends:

3. The Training Academy should develop a realistic training program that frankly explains the corruption "opportunities" or risks that a recruit might confront and shows how to respond to them.

Corruption needs to be understood as not merely a police problem, but one that affects all who live and work in Philadelphia. Private citizens, who downplay the consequences of corruption or feel it is a price they are willing to pay as long as the police keep the streets reasonably safe, fail to recognize that corrupt officers may do little policing not related to graft. For these officers, a network of favoritism and personal accommodation takes precedence over official duties.

Each citizen can play a role, however modest, in combating corruption. A decision by Philadelphia's businesses, both small and large, to stop giving gifts to police officers would be a start. If citizens would refuse to patronize businesses that make payoffs, this too would make a difference. Beyond this, city officials—the judges, members of the city council, the mayor himself—must set an example. They should not take gifts, accept discounts, or dine at fancy restaurants "on the house." When police officers realize that the leaders of the city pay their parking and buy their admission tickets to sporting and entertainment events, the necessary climate will at last have been created for curbing corruption.

The Task Force therefore recommends:

4. The mayor of Philadelphia together with the managing director and the various department heads take steps to set an example of high ethical conduct to help curb corruption in city government.

(4) CORRUPTION AND DISCRETION *

The most troublesome rules in any police agency are rules against accepting gifts or gratuities. Even in American police departments enjoying a reputation for being incorruptible and "legalistic," such as Los Angeles's, the taking of commodities is acceptable and a fine line is drawn between commodities and cash. Joseph Wambaugh had years of service as a Los Angeles policeman and detective. In his novel, *The Choirboys,* one of Wambaugh's characters, an ordinary L.A. policeman, "had accepted a thousand packs of cigarettes and as many free meals in his time. And though he had bought enough clothing at wholesale prices to dress a dozen movie stars, he had never even considered taking a five dollar bill nor was one ever offered except once when he stopped a Chicago grocer in Los Angeles on vacation."

* Jerome H. Skolnick, *House of Cards: Legalization and Control of Casino Gambling* (Boston: Little, Brown and Co., 1978), pp. 259–261. © 1978 by Jerome H. Skolnick. Reprinted with permission of Little, Brown and Company.

Wambaugh explains his character's behavior by pointing out that "[t]he police department and its members made an exact distinction between gratuities and cash offerings, which were considered money bribes no matter how slight and would result in a merciless dismissal as well as citizen prosecution."

Corruption is a harsh word and few, if any, officials care to think of themselves as corrupt. So although a bribe can be given directly, the offerer is usually more cunning. Discussing the "moral blunders" of employees involved in the Equity Funding Fraud, Seidler, Andrews, and Epstein described the overtures, the sly subtleties, the invitations to rationalize that were suggested to a key auditor. "Bribes," they write, "don't come with labels; they aren't subject to truth in packaging. It takes moral courage, a willingness to step up to the plate, to stamp a bribe for what it is."

Questions

How is a policeman supposed to maintain friendly relations with those being policed if he refuses small gifts? Can you see anything wrong with a policeman accepting small gifts from businessmen and others in the community? Do you think that the recommendations of the Philadelphia Task Force will work?

(5) COMMUNITY POLICING AND CORRUPTION *

There is no evidence of corruption where community policing has been tried. It could be argued, however, that since community policing brings the police closer to the people, and that since decentralized policing may signify less departmental control over the daily activities of community police officers, the opportunities for corruption are enhanced. Moreover, since corruption is an essentially covert activity, its actual prevalence must surely be underreported.

Further, it could be asserted, under a regime of community policing, police organizations will be less accountable because police officers will enjoy greater freedom of action. Subordinate commanders can claim they know what particular communities need and will enjoy the political clout to implement their priorities. Officers in charge of neighborhood police stations speak proudly of their ability to mobilize resources, such as funds for crime-prevention programs, appearances of political VIP's at community functions, coverage by radio and television, and supportive services by area businesses. They also quietly mention that their support networks free them from accountability to the command hierarchy. Some might interpret this as a desirable loosening from command hierarchy, while others might interpret it as a dangerous independence from command policy and supervision.

* Jerome H. Skolnick and David H. Bayley, Community Policing: Issues and Practices Around the World, U.S. Department of Justice National Institute of Justice, May 1988, pp. 77–78.

When the conduct of community police officers is exemplary, their independent power base should not be a cause for concern. But if they should mismanage funds, take bribes, abuse authority, or wink at violations of the law, they may be better positioned to defy disciplinary action. Indeed, command centralization in American cities occurred early in the 20th century in direct reaction to the corruption and lack of discipline engendered by all too cozy relations between precinct commanders and local power structures.

So how should we think about the connection between community policing and corruption? Everything we know about police corruption suggests that where it has occurred, it was already institutionalized irrespective of community policing. Corruption seems to be attributable to a different vision of the role of police in the community from that proposed by advocates of community policing. Traditional precincts were tied to politics—police would have connections with "hooks" or "rabbis" in the local political machines, who could influence assignment or promotion within the police department. Police corruption was part of a larger pattern of corrupt practices that pervaded municipal government. Under those conditions, it was customary for police to accept small gifts or gratuities or payoffs from bookmakers or traffic offenders; or to tolerate criminal activities by local politicians in the belief that this would lead to a promotion. Thus, when we discuss police corruption, we often speak of a "climate" of corruption.

Community policing, by contrast, has been initiated by police executives who are reputedly among the most intelligent, progressive, and professional in the police management business. They are known to be people who will not tolerate corruption and will, if possible, root it out of their departments. They are characteristically opposed to the sort of climate in which corruption thrives. From this perspective, there is little or no relationship between community policing and corruption. Indeed, we would expect that police who are motivated by and genuinely subscribe to a philosophy of community policing must condemn corruption since it undermines a constructive notion of community.

At the same time, there is a danger that community policing will be introduced by a reform chief into a department that already has a climate and expectation of corruption. If that should happen, the decentralization associated with community policing could facilitate already existing corrupt practices. That result, however, would not properly be considered community policing, nor should it be attributed to the introduction of community policing. It would simply be another instance of the abuse of police authority conferred by the gun and the badge. Crooked cops, like other crooks, are capable of using any instrumentality—including the philosophy of community policing—to achieve unlawful and self-interested goals.

D. RECOMMENDED READING

Bayley, David H., *Forces of Order: Police Behavior in Japan and the United States.* Univ. of California Press, Berkeley, 1976.

Bittner, Egon. *The Functions of the Police in Modern Society.* National Institute of Mental Health, Public Health Service Publication No. 2059, November 1970.

Black, Donald. *The Manners and Customs of the Police.* Academic Press, New York, 1980.

Goldstein, Herman. *Policing in a Free Society.* Ballinger Publishing Co., Cambridge, Mass., 1977.

Miller, Wilbur E. *Cops and Bobbies: Police Authority in New York and London, 1830–1870.* The Univ. of Chicago Press, Chicago, London, 1977.

Muir, William K., Jr. *Police: Street Corner Politician.* The Univ. of Chicago Press, Chicago and London, 1977.

Reiner, Robert. *The Politics of the Police.* Wheatsheaf Books, Harvester Press, Sussex, 1985.

Rubinstein, Jonathan. *City Police.* Farrar, Straus and Giroux, Inc., New York, 1973.

Skolnick, Jerome H. *Justice Without Trial: Law Enforcement in Democratic Society.* Wiley, New York, 1975.

Skolnick, Jerome H. and Bayley, David H. *The New Blue Line: Police Innovation in Six American Cities.* Free Press, New York, 1986.

Wilson, James Q. *Varieties of Police Behavior.* Atheneum, New York 1973.

Chapter V

CONSTITUTIONAL RIGHTS AND THE EXCLUSIONARY RULE

A. INTRODUCTION

A MAN FOR ALL SEASONS *

[a play by Robert Bolt based on the life, trial and execution of Sir Thomas More, English humanist, statesman and author (1478–1535); More was canonized by the Catholic Church in 1935.]

from Act I: . . . . (Rich exits)

Roper: Arrest him!

Alice: Yes!

More: For What?

Alice: He's dangerous!

Roper: For libel; he's a spy.

Alice: He is! Arrest him!

Margaret: Father, that man's bad.

More: There is no law against that.

Roper: There is! God's law!

More: Then God can arrest him.

Roper: Sophistication upon sophistication!

More: No, sheer simplicity. The law, Roper, the law. I know what's legal, not what's right. And I'll stick to what's legal.

Roper: Then you set man's law above God's!

More: No, far below; but let *me* draw your attention to a fact— I'm *not* God. The currents and eddies of right and wrong, which you find such plain sailing, I can't navigate. I'm no voyager. But in the thickets of the law, there I'm a forester. I doubt if there's a man alive who could follow me there, thank God . . . (He says this last to himself)

Alice: (exasperated, pointing after Rich): While you talk, he's gone!

* Robert Bolt, *A Man for All Seasons,* (New York: Vintage Paperbacks, Random House, 1962) pp. 37–38. © 1960, 1962 by Robert Bolt. Reprinted by permission of Random House, Inc.

More: And go he should, if he was the Devil himself, until he broke the law!

Roper: So now you'd give the Devil benefit of law!

More: Yes. What would you do? Cut a great swath through the law to get at the Devil?

Roper: I'd cut down every law in England to do that!

More: (roused and excited): Oh, and when the last law law was down and the Devil turned round on you—where would you hide, Roper, all the laws being flat?

This country's planted thick with laws from coast to coast—man's laws, not God's—and if you cut them down— and you're just the man to do it—d'you really think you could stand upright in the winds that would blow then? (quietly) Yes, I'd give the Devil benefit of law, for my own safety's sake.

. . .

Comment

In this chapter, we will discuss two extremely inconvenient doctrines, the Fifth Amendment's privilege against self-incrimination and the Fourth Amendment's right to be free from unreasonable searches and seizures. Both these Constitutional provisions restrict the police and make it more difficult to convict guilty people. As in the above excerpt, they protect the criminal (the devil). Is it possible that one reason why we may regard these constitutional provisions as so inconvenient is that we do not see them as protecting ourselves should the devil turn?

B. THE PRIVILEGE AGAINST SELF–INCRIMINA-TION

1. THE CONSTITUTIONAL PRIVILEGE

A. AMENDMENT V, U.S. CONSTITUTION:

No person . . . shall be compelled in any criminal case to be a witness against himself.

b. THE HISTORY AND SCOPE OF THE PRIVILEGE

(1) In General *

One of the most significant, and yet at times the most controversial, of the provisions in the Bill of Rights is the privilege against self-incrimination. This privilege assures that no defendant need take the stand and thereby subject himself to cross-examination. It also assures

* *The Bill of Rights, A Source Book for Teachers,* California State Department of   Education (1967, pp. 79–81). Copyright 1967. (Reprinted with permission).

that no one can be compelled to answer any question if his answer can itself be used to implicate him or convict him of a criminal offense; if it may be the "link in the chain" of evidence used to convict him; or if it may lead to information which may, in turn, be used to convict him of a criminal offense. As a product of seventeenth century English experience, the privilege against self-incrimination has remained firmly established in our Constitutional order although it has been viewed differently over the years. On the one hand are those who view "taking the Fifth" or "pleading the Fifth" derisively or as an admission of guilt. On the other hand are those who consider the concept of forcing a man to contribute to his own conviction repugnant to decency and human dignity and who conceive the privilege as one of the most important values of the Bill of Rights. The controversy has been sharpest in recent years with respect to claims of the privilege by witnesses before congressional investigating committees. But the primary impact of the privilege is probably in the daily operation of federal and state criminal justice.

(2) THE DEVELOPMENT OF THE PRIVILEGE *

The privilege against self-incrimination can only be understood against the background of English history which produced it. In very brief and simplified form, this is what happened:

Early in the reign of Henry VIII, about 450 years ago, England was a Roman Catholic state. Protestants were vigorously persecuted. Then, when Henry broke with the Roman Catholic Church and Parliament established the Church of England, the Protestants reversed the situation and began to persecute the Catholics. This continued until the reign of Bloody Mary when once again the Catholics persecuted the Protestants. This situation was reversed yet again after the death of Mary, when Elizabeth took the throne. From the 1560's, moveover, Elizabeth's Church began persecuting (in addition to the Catholics) dissident Protestants called Puritans. This continued under James I and Charles I and helped provoke the Revolution in which Puritans and their allies were victorious.

After the Puritan victory, the authorities continued to persecute Catholics, while also persecuting both the Anglican clergy less reform-minded than themselves, and the "left wing" dissenters, who broke away from the main body of Puritans. Then, after the accession to power of Oliver Cromwell, the center of the Puritan establishment moved left and began its own campaigns against the "ungodly," persecuting the Catholics, the High Anglicans and the right-wing Puritans. By the time of the Restoration of the monarchy under Charles II, all England was sick of religious persecution and for the most part it ceased.

* Cohen and Kaplan, *The Bill of Rights* (Mineola, N.Y., Foundation Press, 1976) pp. 540–542. Copyright 1976 (Reprinted with permission).

This history is quite remarkable. In the course of about 150 years, members of every major religious group in England had been both the initiators and the victims of persecution—and the roles had changed with bewildering rapidity.

A major method of these persecutions was the oath. During the persecution of the Puritans by the Church of England under Elizabeth and James, for example, Puritan ministers were called before the High Commission and asked questions under oath about their beliefs. Being men of God, they could not lie—and, if they admitted to their deviant and nonconformist views, they could be very seriously punished. As a result, increasingly, they claimed the right not to answer and the existence or non-existence of such a right gradually became a major issue in 17th century England. One of the most celebrated cases involving the right was that of John Lilburne: *

"In 1637, Lilburne, a Puritan dissenter, was brought before the Star Chamber. Having just returned from Holland, he was charged with sending 'factitious and scandalous books' from there to England. Lilburne repeatedly contended that he could not be compelled to testify against himself.

"For refusing to respond to the questions, Lilburne was fined, was tied to a cart and, his body bared, was whipped through the streets of London. At Westminster he was placed in a pillory—his body bent down, his neck in a hole, and his lacerated back bared to the midday sun; there he stood for two hours and exhorted all who would listen to resist the tyranny of the bishops. Refusing to be quiet, he was gagged so cruelly that his mouth bled. . . . After Lilburne's release, his cruel treatment and bold resistance had two consequences. The first was the vote of the Long Parliament that his sentence was illegal and that he be paid reparations. The second was the abolition of both the Star Chamber and the Court of the High Commission by the same Parliament. [After the abolition of the Courts of the Star Chamber and of the High Commission,] [q]uestioning of the accused at his trial [in the regular criminal courts] continued unaltered for nearly two decades; the examination of the prisoner by the committing magistrate continued for as long as two centuries. Nevertheless, a gradual repugnance to compulsory self-incrimination developed. By the end of the reign of Charles II, the privilege was recognized in all courts when claimed by defendant or witness.

The privilege against self-incrimination in American law dates from the Massachusetts Body of Liberties of 1641 and the Connecticut Code of 1650. Practices of the courts of governor and council in the Colonies paralleled those used in England during this period; and their use solidified opinion against compulsory self-incrimination. Conse-

* *The Bill of Rights, A Source Book for Teachers,* California State Department of Education. (1967, pp. 79–81, 83). Copyright 1967. Reprinted with permission.

quently, the Virginia Bill of Rights of 1776, which was copied by Pennsylvania, Vermont, and North Carolina, provided that no one "can . . . be compelled to give evidence against himself." This provision also became the model for its inclusion in the Fifth Amendment.

(3) NOTE ON THE SCOPE OF THE PRIVILEGE

Although the Fifth Amendment states that no person shall be "compelled in any criminal case to be a witness against himself", the clause has long been interpreted to apply not only to a defendant in a criminal case but also to any witness in a civil or criminal case. In addition, the privilege has been held to apply to one testifying before any body which is authorized to compel testimony under oath, such as an administrative agency, a congressional committee, or a grand jury. As a result, any such witness may "plead the privilege" and refuse to answer any question when the answer might provide a "link in a chain of evidence" that might lead to criminal charges against himself. The privilege also grants an extra protection to the defendant in a criminal case by enabling him to refrain from taking the stand at all. The privilege against self-incrimination does not, however, protect a suspect from being required to furnish blood samples, handwriting exemplars and other things that are not "testimony."

In theory, a witness cannot refuse to answer questions whenever he chooses merely by claiming the privilege against self-incrimination. However, although there must be some basis for the claim, in practice the courts interpret this basis quite broadly and the fact that the witness is himself innocent is no reason for denial of the privilege.

As a result, immunity statutes are of considerable importance. The Supreme Court over a hundred years ago held that a witness may be compelled to answer incriminating questions if he is granted immunity from prosecution. Moreover, the Supreme Court has recently (1972) held that the immunity need not be from prosecution for any crime concerning which his answers may implicate him. All that is necessary is a "use" immunity which guarantees that neither the compelled testimony, nor any evidence developed from leads given by the compelled testimony, can be used against the witness.

The privilege does not protect a person from giving testimony merely because the testimony may embarrass him or implicate his friends. The protection applies only if the testimony would implicate him or lead to his implication in a criminal offense. Hence, valid immunity will negate the privilege and the witness can be required to testify. The theory behind this doctrine is that the immunity protects the witness to the same extent as does the privilege against self-incrimination. Therefore, a witness forced to testify has, in effect, lost nothing granted by the privilege.

. . .

Questions

1. Is it not clear that the privilege against self-incrimination is a serious impediment to convicting criminals?

2. Would it be desirable to have some or all members of society submit to a test on a machine which, if invented, could determine his guilt and the details of any crime he had ever committed? Would the use of such a machine eliminate crime? If crime could thus be eliminated, what kind of a society would we have?

3. Can the privilege against self-incrimination be defended as a method of making it harder for the legislature to enforce its laws? One can support such a view on the theory that the only thing that restrains those with political power from interfering with the rights of those without, is that when laws meet with too much opposition, they become unenforceable? Certainly, if the decrees of the legislature could have been enforced in previous times, might we still have Prohibition? All male suffrage? Is it even arguable that we might still have a Fugitive Slave law?

4. Can the privilege also be defended as a method of protecting the dignity of the individual in his dealings with the state? After all, we do not force a condemned man to dig his own grave, do we?

5. Is it possible that the privilege does not go far enough? Is it fair that a person may be called before a governmental body, stripped of the privilege through a grant of immunity from criminal prosecution, and then made to give statements that may humiliate or degrade him in public—or incriminate his friends?

c. THE PRIVILEGE AND THE ACCUSATORIAL SYSTEM *

The privilege against self-incrimination is at the cornerstone of the accusatorial system of justice as applied in English-speaking countries, as opposed to the continental European "inquisitorial" system. Apart from any other procedural rule, the privilege against self-incrimination theoretically prohibits the most obvious means of starting an investigation of an unsolved crime—calling in the prime suspect and asking him questions. By prohibiting this type of procedure, the privilege against self-incrimination tends to force the process into one where the state has to gather its evidence and then accuse the suspect. It is arguable that in some ways this is not a very rational method of procedure and that the most logical way to begin an investigation of a criminal case is to ask the person you think knows most about the crime—that is, the person you think committed it? One commentator has written **:

* Cohen and Kaplan, *The Bill of Rights,* Mineola, N.Y., Foundation Press, 1976, pp. 547–550. Copyright 1976 (Reprinted with permission).

** Abraham S. Goldstein, Reflections on Two Models: Inquisitorial Themes in American Criminal Procedures, 26 Stanford Law Review 1009, 1017–1020, Copyright, 1974 by the Board of Trustees of the Leland Stanford Junior University. Reprinted with permission.

. . . An accusatorial system assumes a social equilibrium which is not lightly to be disturbed, and assigns great social value to keeping the state out of disputes, especially when stigma and sanction may follow. As a result, the person who charges another with crime cannot rely on his assertion alone to shift to the accused the obligation of proving his innocence. The accuser must, in the first instance, present reasonably persuasive evidence of guilt. It is in this sense that the presumption of innocence is at the heart of an accusatorial system. Until certain procedures and proofs are satisfied, the accused is to be treated by the legal system *as if* he is innocent and need lend no aid to those who would convict him.

An accusatorial system is basically reactive, reflecting its origins in a setting in which enforcement of criminal laws was largely confined to courts. Police and prosecutors had hardly developed; the initiative was left to the complaining party to invoke criminal sanctions by gathering his proofs and presenting them at trial. Before trial, the state played a relatively passive role, doing only what was minimally required to enable the complainant to present his case. . . . In sum, the accusatorial model [is] reminiscent of a civil case, where the court leaves matters largely to the parties.

Comparativists generally assume that inquisitorial [as distinguished from accusatorial] systems are primarily concerned with enforcing criminal laws and are only incidentally concerned with the manner in which it is done. They point especially to the use of the accused as the primary source of evidence, both during the investigation and at trial. He is ordinarily called as a first witness and is questioned closely by the presiding judge about the facts of his life and his knowledge of the crime. Few rules of evidence inhibit the judge and the state has no explicit burden of proof or persuasion. The judge dominates the proceeding and often appears to move relentlessly toward a predetermined result of conviction. . . .

. . .

These portraits of accusatorial and inquisitorial systems are, of course, idealized. European criminal procedures are no more purely inquisitorial than ours are purely accusatorial. Europeans too have accusatorial elements and mixed systems; they may tolerate more discretion than their literature concedes and may, in many instances, be moving toward a greater role for counsel and more explicit protection for the accused.

Similarly, our central tendency has been toward an accusatorial system, but it would blink law and reality to ignore the strong inquisitorial elements in our procedure. Though our magistrates are no longer investigating officials, their contemporary analogues [include] the expanded role of special and regular grand juries. They take their place alongside other inquisitorial devices which have played an important part in the reality of American law: the use of the accused for interrogation and search [and] the practice of persuading him, directly or indirectly, to waive his rights and immunities by pleading guilty; . . .

Questions

Is the issue of whether it is a good thing to have the privilege against self-incrimination a very important one today? Since it is a part of the Bill of Rights, written into the Constitution, is it arguable that a simple adherence to the American System will take the existence of the privilege for granted and that all subsequent discussions should merely attempt to discover the scope of the Constitutional guarantee?

2. A COMPARATIVE LOOK

a. INTERROGATION IN JAPAN *

In Japan, written statements (*kyōjutsu chōsho*) prepared by interrogators in the name of suspects constitute important evidence in criminal trials. These statements are formally regarded as records of the suspect's confession, as taken down by the interrogator. However, the written statement is by no means a verbatim record of the suspects' statements or replies to questions. In actual practice, it is fair to regard it as "the interrogator's essay," reflecting his interpretation of the suspect's statements, his choice of words and his arrangement of the material.

The suspect is not permitted to read the completed statement to confirm its content. It is read to him and he is made to sign it and affix his fingerprint to it. In many instances, defendants claim in court that the content of these written statements differs from what had been read to them. In fact, there is no way of determining after the fact whether any or all of the pages of the statement beyond the one page bearing the suspect's signature and fingerprint have been switched.

In principle, Japan's code of criminal justice does not admit hearsay evidence, but if the court accepts a written statement as a voluntary confession by a suspect, the statement acquires the same value as testimony given in court. Japanese judges usually believe assertions by interrogators that the suspect's confession was not forced and accordingly rule that the confession is voluntary.

Since the present Code of Criminal Procedure (which conforms to the principles of English and American criminal law and is regarded as strongly oriented to the protection of human rights) was established in

* *Torture and Unlawful or Unjust Treatment of Detainees in Daiyo-Kangoku (Substitute Prisons) in Japan*, The Joint Committee of the Three Tokyo Bar Associations for the Study of the Daiyo-Kangoku (Substitute Prison) system, August 1989.

1948 following World War II, there have been only a very small number of cases in which written statements were ruled involuntary. Even in cases when suspects claimed to have been tortured and their bodies bore physical traces to back their claims, courts have still accepted their confessions.

In Japan, the vast majority of suspects who claim innocence in a court that has already admitted confessions drawn up in [this manner] are fated to be found guilty.

Questions

What value is the privilege against self-incrimination if judges almost always admit confessions that defendants claim were coerced?

Or is the problem that the police can keep someone in custody until he makes the statement they want him to make?

b. JUSTICE IN THE U.S.S.R.*

Soviet law cannot be understood unless it is recognized that the whole Soviet society is itself conceived to be a single great family. . . . As the state, it acts officially through the legal system, but its purpose in so acting is to make its citizens into obedient children, good students, ardent believers, hard workers, successful managers.

This, indeed, is the essential characteristic of the law of a total state.

We have seen that legal consequences follow from this conception of the role of law. Court procedure is informal and speedy; the judge protects the litigants against the consequences of their ignorance, and clarifies to them the nature of their rights and duties; there is elaborate pre-trial procedure directed toward uncovering the whole history of the situation.

Comment and Questions

Perhaps the basic difference between a constitutional democracy and a totalitarian state is to be located in their different conceptions of the relation between the state and the citizens. Why should not the government treat a citizen with the solicitude and authority of a parent? Did you ever have the right to remain silent when your parent(s) asked whether you had done something wrong? Should you have had the right? If not, why should a citizen have such a right against her own government?

How do you think justice in the U.S.S.R. will change in the 1990's?

* Harold J. Berman, *Justice in the U.S.S.R.*, New York: Random House (Vintage edition), 1963, p. 366. © 1963 (Reprinted with permission).

3. THE PRIVILEGE AND POLICE INTERROGATION

a. BROWN v. MISSISSIPPI

Supreme Court of the United States, 1936.
297 U.S. 278, 56 S.Ct. 461, 80 L.Ed. 682.

Mr. Chief Justice HUGHES delivered the opinion of the Court.

The question in this case is whether convictions, which rest solely upon confessions shown to have been extorted by officers of the State by brutality and violence, are consistent with the due process of law required by the Fourteenth Amendment of the Constitution of the United States.

Petitioners were indicted for the murder of one Raymond Stewart, whose death occurred on March 30, 1934. They were indicted on April 4, 1934, and were then arraigned and pleaded not guilty. Counsel were appointed by the court to defend them. Trial was begun the next morning and was concluded on the following day, when they were found guilty and sentenced to death.

Aside from the confessions, there was no evidence sufficient to warrant the submission of the case to the jury. After a preliminary inquiry, testimony as to the confessions was received over the objection of defendants' counsel. Defendants then testified that the confessions were false and had been procured by physical torture. The case went to the jury with instructions, upon the request of defendants' counsel, that if the jury had reasonable doubt as to the confessions having resulted from coercion, and that they were not true, they were not to be considered as evidence. On their appeal to the Supreme Court of the State, defendants assigned as error the inadmissibility of the confessions. The judgment was affirmed. . . .

The opinion of the state court did not set forth the evidence as to the circumstances in which the confessions were procured. That the evidence established that they were procured by coercion was not questioned. . . . There is no dispute as to the facts upon this point and as they are clearly and adequately stated in the dissenting opinion of Judge Griffith (with whom Judge Anderson concurred)—showing both the extreme brutality of the measures to extort the confessions and the participation of the state authorities—we quote this part of his opinion in full, as follows . . .:

"The crime with which these defendants, all ignorant negroes, are charged, was discovered about one o'clock p.m. on Friday, March 30, 1934. On that night one Dial, a deputy sheriff, accompanied by others, came to the home of Ellington, one of the defendants, and requested him to accompany them to the house of the deceased, and there a number of white men were gathered, who began to accuse the defendant of the crime. Upon his denial they seized him, and with the participation of the deputy they hanged him by a rope to the limb of a tree, and having let him down, they hung him again, and when he was let down the second time, and he still protested his innocence, he was tied to a tree and whipped, and still declining to accede to the demands that he confess, he was finally released and he returned with some difficulty to his home, suffering intense pain and agony. The record of the testimony shows that the signs of the rope on his neck were plainly visible during the so-called trial. A day or two thereafter the said deputy, accompanied by another, returned to the home of the said defendant and arrested him, and departed with the prisoner towards the jail in an adjoining county, but went by a route which led into the State of Alabama; and while on the way, in that State, the deputy stopped and again severely whipped the defendant, declaring that he would continue the whipping until he confessed, and the defendant then agreed to confess to such a statement as the deputy would dictate, and he did so, after which he was delivered to jail.

"The other two defendants, Ed Brown and Henry Shields, were also arrested and taken to the same jail. On Sunday night, April 1, 1934, the same deputy, accompanied by a number of white men, one of whom was also an officer, and by the jailer, came to the jail, and the two last named defendants were made to strip and they were laid over chairs and their backs were cut to pieces with a leather strap with buckles on it, and they were likewise made by the said deputy definitely to understand that the whipping would be continued unless and until they confessed, and not only confessed, but confessed in every matter of detail as demanded by those present; and in this manner the defendants confessed the crime, and as the whippings progressed and were repeated, they changed or adjusted their confession in all particulars of detail so as to conform to the demands of their torturers. When the confessions had been obtained in the exact form and contents as desired by the mob, they left with the parting admonition and warning that, if the defendants changed their story at any time in any respect from that last stated, the perpetrators of the outrage would administer the same or equally effective treatment.

"Further details of the brutal treatment to which these helpless prisoners were subjected need not be pursued. It is sufficient to say that in pertinent respects the transcript reads more like pages torn from some medieval account, than a record made within the confines of a modern civilization which aspires to an enlightened constitutional government.

"All this having been accomplished, on the next day, that is, on Monday, April 2, when the defendants had been given time to recuperate somewhat from the tortures to which they had been subjected, the two sheriffs, one of the county where the crime was committed, and the other of the county of the jail in which the prisoners were confined, came to the jail, accompanied by eight other persons, some of them deputies, there to hear the free and voluntary confession of these miserable and abject defendants. The sheriff of the county of the crime admitted that he had heard of the whipping, but averred that he had no personal knowledge of it. He admitted that one of the defendants, when brought before him to confess, was limping and did not sit down, and that this particular defendant then and there stated that he had been strapped so severely that he could not sit down, and as already stated, the signs of the rope on the neck of another of the defendants were plainly visible to all. Nevertheless the solemn farce of hearing the free and voluntary confessions was gone through with, and these two sheriffs and one other person then present were the three witnesses used in court to establish the so-called confessions, which were received by the court and admitted in evidence over the objections of the defendants duly entered of record as each of the said three witnesses delivered their alleged testimony. There was thus enough before the court when these confessions were first offered to make known to the court that they were not, beyond all reasonable doubt, free and voluntary; and the failure of the court then to exclude the confessions is sufficient to reverse the judgment, under every rule of procedure that has heretofore been prescribed. . . .

"The spurious confessions having been obtained—and the farce last mentioned having been gone through with on Monday, April 2d—the court, then in session, on the following day, Tuesday, April 3, 1934, ordered the grand jury to reassemble on the succeeding day, April 4, 1934, at nine o'clock, and on the morning of the day last mentioned the grand jury returned an indictment against the defendants for murder. Late that afternoon the defendants were brought from the jail in the adjoining county and arraigned, when one or more of them offered to plead guilty, which the court declined to accept, and, upon inquiry whether they had or desired counsel, they stated that they had none, and did not suppose that counsel could be of any assistance to them. The court thereupon appointed counsel, and set the case for trial for the following morning at nine o'clock, and the defendants were returned to the jail in the adjoining county about thirty miles away.

"The defendants were brought to the courthouse of the county on the following morning, April 5th, and the so-called trial was opened, and was concluded on the next day, April 6, 1934, and resulted in a pretended conviction with death sentences. The evidence upon which the conviction was obtained was the so-called confessions. Without this evidence a peremptory instruction to find for the defendants would have been inescapable. The defendants were put on the stand, and by their testimony the facts and the details thereof as to the manner by which the confessions were extorted from them were fully developed, and it is further disclosed by the record that the same deputy, Dial, under whose guiding hand and active participation the tortures to coerce the confessions were administered, was actively in the performance of the supposed duties of a court deputy in the courthouse and in the presence of the prisoners during what is denominated, in complimentary terms, the trial of these defendants. This deputy was put on the stand by the state in rebuttal, and admitted the whippings. It is interesting to note that in his testimony with reference to the whipping of the defendant Ellington, and in response to the inquiry as to how severely he was whipped, the deputy stated, 'Not too much for a negro; not as much as I would have done if it were left to me.' Two others who had participated in these whippings were introduced and admitted it—not a single witness was introduced who denied it. The facts are not only undisputed, they are admitted, and admitted to have been done by officers of the state, in conjunction with other participants, and all this was definitely well known to everybody connected with the trial, and during the trial, including the state's prosecuting attorney and the trial judge presiding." . . .

[T]he freedom of the State in establishing its policy is the freedom of constitutional government and is limited by the requirement of due process of law. Because a State may dispense with a jury trial, it does not follow that it may substitute trial by ordeal. The rack and torture chamber may not be substituted for the witness stand. The State may not permit an accused to be hurried to conviction under mob domination—where the whole proceeding is but a mask—without supplying corrective process. . . . It would be difficult to conceive of methods more revolting to the sense of justice than those taken to procure the confessions of these petitioners, and the use of the confessions thus obtained as the basis for conviction and sentence was a clear denial of due process. . . .

In the instant case, the trial court was fully advised by the undisputed evidence of the way in which the confessions had been procured. The trial court knew that there was no other evidence upon which conviction and sentence could be based. Yet it proceeded to permit conviction and to pronounce sentence. The conviction and sentence were void for want of the essential elements of due process. . . .

Reversed.

Questions and Comment

Is not the most surprising thing about Brown v. Mississippi that the events actually occurred in the United States about 60 years ago?

Or is it more surprising that, with full knowledge that these events occurred, the Supreme Court of Mississippi affirmed the conviction and death sentence of the petitioners in this case?

Is it likely that the deputy sheriff who whipped a confession out of his prisoner was disciplined for this in any way?

The focus in the confession area gradually changed over time. Brown v. Mississippi involved three factors. First, the prosecution had asked the courts to use an irrational method of determining guilt, in that confessions tortured out of suspects are extremely unreliable. Second, the decision in *Brown* was an attempt to control the police. Since the misconduct of the police in whipping their prisoner was obviously not going to be otherwise punished, the least the courts could do to discourage such activities was to prevent the police from gaining their objective—a confession admissible in court. Third, the values protected by the privilege against self-incrimination and perhaps even the very words of the 5th Amendment required that a court be prepared to exclude evidence where the accused was "compelled to testify against himself."

One more issue obviously had begun to disturb the Supreme Court—the glaring inequality in treatment between the wealthy, sophisticated defendant who knew his rights and had the services of a retained attorney and the poorer, more ignorant defendant without a lawyer who, in fact, was the subject of most of the cases involving allegedly improper confessions.

Note how the court grappled with all these problems in the *Miranda* case, the next excerpt.

b.   MIRANDA v. ARIZONA
Supreme Court of the United States, 1966.
384 U.S. 436, 86 S.Ct. 1602, 16 L.Ed.2d 694.

Mr. Chief Justice WARREN delivered the opinion of the Court.

The cases before us raise questions which go to the roots of our concepts of American criminal jurisprudence: the restraints society must observe consistent with the Federal Constitution in prosecuting individuals for crime. More specifically, we deal with the admissibility of statements obtained from an individual who is subjected to custodial police interrogation and the necessity for procedures which assure that the individual is accorded his privilege under the Fifth Amendment to the Constitution not to be compelled to incriminate himself.

. . .

Our holding will be spelled out with some specificity in the pages which follow but briefly stated it is this: the prosecution may not use statements, whether exculpatory or inculpatory, stemming from custodial interrogation of the defendant unless it demonstrates the use of procedural safeguards effective to secure the privilege against self-incrimination. By custodial interrogation, we mean questioning initiated by law enforcement officers after a person has been taken into custody or otherwise deprived of his freedom of action in any significant way. As for the procedural safeguards to be employed, unless other fully effective means are devised to inform accused persons of their right of silence and to assure a continuous opportunity to exercise it, the following measures are required. Prior to any questioning, the person must be warned that he has a right to remain silent, that any statement he does make may be used as evidence against him, and that he has a right to the presence of an attorney, either retained or appointed. The defendant may waive effectuation of these rights, provided the waiver is made voluntarily, knowingly and intelligently. If, however, he indicates in any manner and at any stage of the process that he wishes to consult with an attorney before speaking there can be no questioning. Likewise, if the individual is alone and indicates in any manner that he does not wish to be interrogated, the police may not question him. The mere fact that he may have answered some questions or volunteered some statements on his own does not deprive him of the right to refrain from answering any further inquiries until he has consulted with an attorney and thereafter consents to be questioned.

I.

The constitutional issue we decide in each of these cases is the admissibility of statements obtained from a defendant questioned while in custody or otherwise deprived of his freedom of action in any significant way. In each, the defendant was questioned by police officers, detectives, or a prosecuting attorney in a room in which he was cut off from the outside world. In none of these cases was the defendant given a full and effective warning of his rights at the outset of the interrogation process. In all the cases, the questioning elicited oral admissions, and in three of them, signed statements as well which were admitted at their trials. They all thus share salient features— incommunicado interrogation of individuals in a police-dominated atmosphere, resulting in self-incriminating statements without full warnings of constitutional rights.

An understanding of the nature and setting of this in-custody interrogation is essential to our decisions today. The difficulty in depicting what transpires at such interrogations stems from the fact that in this country they have largely taken place incommunicado. From extensive factual studies undertaken in the early 1930's, including the famous Wickersham Report to Congress by a Presidential Commission, it is clear that police violence and the "third degree" flourished at that time. In a series of cases decided by this Court long after these studies, the police resorted to physical brutality—beatings, hanging, whipping—and to sustained and protracted questioning incommunicado in order to extort confessions. The Commission on Civil Rights in 1961 found much evidence to indicate that "some policemen still resort to physical force to obtain confessions," 1961 Comm'n on Civil Rights Rep., Justice, pt. 5, 17.

.   .   .

Again we stress that the modern practice of in-custody interrogation is psychologically rather than physically oriented. As we have stated before, "Since Chambers v. State of Florida, 309 U.S. 227, 60 S.Ct. 472, 84 L.Ed. 716, this Court has recognized that coercion can be mental as well as physical, and that the blood of the accused is not the only hallmark of an unconstitutional inquisition." Blackburn v. State of Alabama, 361 U.S. 199, 206, 80 S.Ct. 274, 279, 4 L.Ed.2d 242 (1960). Interrogation still takes place in privacy. Privacy results in secrecy and this in turn results in a gap in our knowledge as to what in fact goes on in the interrogation rooms. A valuable source of information about present police practices, however, may be found in various police manuals and texts which document procedures employed with success in the past, and which recommend various other effective tactics. These texts are used by law enforcement agencies themselves as guides. It should be noted that these texts professedly present the most enlightened and effective means presently used to obtain statements through custodial interrogation. By considering these texts and other data, it is possible to describe procedures observed and noted around the country.

The officers are told by the manuals that the "principal psychological factor contributing to a successful interrogation is privacy—being alone with the person under interrogation." The efficacy of this tactic has been explained as follows:

> "If at all practicable, the interrogation should take place in the investigator's office or at least in a room of his own choice. The subject should be deprived of every psychological advantage. In his own home he may be confident, indignant, or recalcitrant. He is more keenly aware of his rights and more reluctant to tell of his indiscretions or criminal behavior within the walls of his home. Moreover his family and other friends are nearby, their presence lending moral support. In his office, the investigator possesses all the advantages. The atmosphere suggests the invincibility of the forces of the law."

To highlight the isolation and unfamiliar surroundings, the manuals instruct the police to display an air of confidence in the suspect's guilt and from outward appearance to maintain only an interest in confirming certain details. The guilt of the subject is to be posited as a fact. The interrogator should direct his comments toward the reasons why the subject committed the act, rather than court failure by asking the subject whether he did it. Like other men, perhaps the subject has had a bad family life, had an unhappy childhood, had too much to drink, had an unrequited desire for women. The officers are instructed to minimize the moral seriousness of the offense, to cast blame on the victim or on society. These tactics are designed to put the subject in a psychological state where his story is but an elaboration of what the police purport to know already—that he is guilty. Explanations to the contrary are dismissed and discouraged.

The texts thus stress that the major qualities an interrogator should possess are patience and perseverance. One writer describes the efficacy of these characteristics in this manner:

> "In the preceding paragraphs emphasis has been placed on kindness and stratagems. The investigator will, however, encounter many situations where the sheer weight of his personality will be the deciding factor. Where emotional appeals and tricks are employed to no avail, he must rely on an oppressive atmosphere of dogged persistence. He must interrogate steadily and without relent, leaving the subject no prospect of surcease. He must dominate his subject and overwhelm him with his inexorable will to obtain the truth. He should interrogate for a spell of several hours pausing only for the subject's

necessities in acknowledgment of the need to avoid a charge of duress that can be technically substantiated. In a serious case, the interrogation may continue for days, with the required intervals for food and sleep, but with no respite from the atmosphere of domination. It is possible in this way to induce the subject to talk without resorting to duress or coercion. The method should be used only when the guilt of the subject appears highly probable."

The manuals suggest that the suspect be offered legal excuses for his actions in order to obtain an initial admission of guilt. Where there is a suspected revenge-killing, for example, the interrogator may say:

"Joe, you probably didn't go out looking for this fellow with the purpose of shooting him. My guess is, however, that you expected something from him and that's why you carried a gun—for your own protection. You knew him for what he was, no good. Then when you met him he probably started using foul, abusive language and he gave some indication that he was about to pull a gun on you, and that's when you had to act to save your own life. That's about it, isn't it, Joe?"

Having then obtained the admission of shooting, the interrogator is advised to refer to circumstantial evidence which negates the self-defense explanation. This should enable him to secure the entire story. One text notes that "Even if he fails to do so, the inconsistency between the subject's original denial of the shooting and his present admission of at least doing the shooting will serve to deprive him of a self-defense 'out' at the time of trial."

When the techniques described above prove unavailing, the texts recommend they be alternated with a show of some hostility. One ploy often used has been termed the "friendly-unfriendly" or the "Mutt and Jeff" act:

". . . In this technique, two agents are employed. Mutt, the relentless investigator, who knows the subject is guilty and is not going to waste any time. He's sent a dozen men away for this crime and he's going to send the subject away for the full term. Jeff, on the other hand, is obviously a kindhearted man. He has a family himself. He has a brother who was involved in a little scrape like this. He disapproves of Mutt and his tactics and will arrange to get him off the case if the subject will cooperate. He can't hold Mutt off for very long. The subject would be wise to make a quick decision. The technique is applied by having both investigators present while Mutt acts out his role. Jeff may stand by quietly and demur at some of Mutt's tactics. When Jeff makes his plea for cooperation, Mutt is not present in the room."

The interrogators sometimes are instructed to induce a confession out of trickery. The technique here is quite effective in crimes which require identification or which run in series. In the identification situation, the interrogator may take a break in his questioning to place the subject among a group of men in a line-up. "The witness or complainant (previously coached, if necessary) studies the line-up and confidently points out the subject as the guilty party." Then the questioning resumes "as though there were now no doubt about the guilt of the subject." A variation on this technique is called the "reverse line-up":

> "The accused is placed in a line-up, but this time he is identified by several fictitious witnesses or victims who associated him with different offenses. It is expected that the subject will become desperate and confess to the offense under investigation in order to escape from the false accusations."

The manuals also contain instructions for police on how to handle the individual who refuses to discuss the matter entirely, or who asks for an attorney or relatives. The examiner is to concede him the right to remain silent. "This usually has a very undermining effect. First of all, he is disappointed in his expectation of an unfavorable reaction on the part of the interrogator. Secondly, a concession of this right to remain silent impresses the subject with the apparent fairness of his interrogator." After this psychological conditioning, however, the officer is told to point out the incriminating significance of the suspect's refusal to talk:

> "Joe, you have a right to remain silent. That's your privilege and I'm the last person in the world who'll try to take it way from you. If that's the way you want to leave this, O.K. But let me ask you this. Suppose you were in my shoes and I were in yours and you called me in to ask me about this and I told you, 'I don't want to answer any of your questions.' You'd think I had something to hide, and you'd probably be right in thinking that. That's exactly what I'll have to think about you, and so will everybody else. So let's sit here and talk this whole thing over."

Few will persist in their initial refusal to talk, it is said, if this monologue is employed correctly.

In the event that the subject wishes to speak to a relative or an attorney, the following advice is tendered:

> "[T]he interrogator should respond by suggesting that the subject first tell the truth to the interrogator himself rather than get anyone else involved in the matter. If the request is for an attorney, the interrogator may suggest that the subject save himself or his family the expense of any such professional service, particularly if he is innocent of the offense under investigation. The interrogator may also add, 'Joe, I'm only looking for the truth, and if you're telling the truth, that's it. You can handle this by yourself.'"

[The dissenting opinions of Justices HARLAN, CLARK, STEWART, and WHITE are omitted.]

c. POST–MIRANDA INTERROGATION *

MIRANDA, TWENTY YEARS LATER *

This Friday marks the 20th anniversary of the United States Supreme Court's decision in Miranda v. Arizona, perhaps the most highly publicized—and most misunderstood and severely maligned—criminal procedure in American history. The occasion provides a timely opportunity to explain what Miranda was and was not.

The Miranda ruling applied the Fifth Amendment privilege against compelled self-incrimination to the informal compulsion exerted by the police in the interrogation room and in other kinds of "in-custody questioning." Previously, the privilege had applied only to judicial or other formal proceedings.

The Court concluded that in the "interrogation environment," the suspect typically assumed, or was led by the police to believe, that he had to answer questions or that it would be so much the worse for him. Thus, unless "adequate protective devices" were used to dispel the coercion inherent in custodial police interrogation, no statement obtained from the suspect could truly be the product of his free choice. The "adequate protective devices" deemed necessary were, of course, the now-familiar warnings—for example: "You have the right to remain silent," and, "Anything you say can be used against you."

To many, Miranda was the high water mark of the Warren Court's due-process revolution. Indeed, not a few viewed it as the red flag of Warren Court liberalism. In fact, the case reflects considerable moderation and compromise.

Although most people think that a suspect must be given the warnings immediately upon arrest or before being questioned, this is not so: Neither custody *alone,* nor questioning *alone* if one is not under arrest, requires the warnings. It is the impact on the suspect of the *combination* of interrogation *and* custody—each reinforcing the pressures and anxieties produced by the other—that, as the Court correctly discerned, makes "custodial police interrogation" so intimidating that the neutralizing warnings are required.

Thus, Miranda leaves the police free to hear and act upon "volunteered" statements even though the so-called volunteer is handcuffed and in the back seat of a police car or at the station house, and neither knows or is informed of his rights. It also allows the police to conduct "general on-the-scene questioning" or other general questioning of citizens even though those citizens are not informed of their rights.

On the eve of the decision, many bar leaders warned that law enforcement could not survive if the Court projected defense counsel into the police station. As it turned out, however, Miranda did so only in a very limited way. The Court did not require that an arrested

* Kamisar, "Miranda Twenty Years Later," New York Times, June 11, 1986, p   A.35. © 1986. Reprinted with permission of the New York Times.

person first consult with a lawyer, or actually have a lawyer present, in order for his waiver of rights to be effective. The principle weakness of Miranda (or its saving grace, depending on one's viewpoint) is that it does allow someone subjected to the pressures of arrest and detention to waive his rights without actually obtaining a lawyer's advice.

Whether suspects do not fully grasp the significance of the warnings, or whether conscience (and the desire to get the matter over with) override the impact of the warnings, it is plain that for the past 20 years suspects have continued to confess with great frequency. It is equally plain that this would not have been the case if Miranda really had projected counsel into the police station.

Although there are exceptions (Attorney General Edwin Meese 3d comes to mind), most law-enforcement officials admit that, as a practical matter, Miranda has not hurt them very much, if at all. Their main complaint seems to be that the decision constituted a "symbolic slap in the face" to the police.

Clearly, the case is an important symbol. But what follows from that? The police should never forget that they do not establish their own interrogation rules and do not police themselves. As Liva Baker, author of "Miranda: Crime, Law and Politics," has pointed out, the warnings "serve a civilizing purpose"—they remind the police officer that however lowly the suspect before him, he is still a human being possessing certain rights.

Comment and Questions

Note how the Court was troubled by the fact that the police often do not merely take the voluntary statement of a suspect in custody. Rather, if they obey their manuals, they engage in an elaborate cat and mouse game with the suspect in which the police have an enormous advantage.

Obviously, one solution was to merely make a confession inadmissible if it were the result of psychological coercion and hence not voluntary. That was the law before *Miranda*. The problem was that lower court judges, listening to the defendants and the police's stories as to what happened, almost invariably believed the police. The same situation even occurred where allegations were made that physical brutality had produced the defendant's confession. Although we know that psychological coercion is quite common and physical brutality is not unknown in the station house, the complete absence of any witnesses other than the police and the defendant make investigation into the facts of a confession impossible.

Notice that Brown v. Mississippi might have been decided differently if the deputy sheriffs had bothered to deny any mistreatment of their prisoner.

The problem is—what good does the *Miranda* ruling do in the cases where the police are willing to lie about their methods? Can't they just as easily make up warnings and waivers of a defendant's rights? In fact, would not a simple requirement that the police record all conversations with an accused, on sound, or better yet TV, tape, be much more productive of civilized law enforcement than is the *Miranda* decision?

Is the only issue whether the confession was reliable? If so, would Brown v. Mississippi have to be decided differently if the petitioners under torture had confessed not only to the crime but to certain details that only the murderer could know?

If a policeman poses as a priest to take the confession of a suspect and elicits incriminating statements, should these statements be admitted as evidence against the accused? Does it matter whether the suspect is accused of an especially atrocious crime? Or should we say that regardless of the crime we will demand that the police not engage in such behavior? Are we willing to pay the price for such a rule? Should the decisions we reach on all of these difficult issues be affected by the fact that the privilege against self-incrimination is granted in the Constitution?

Should *Miranda* warnings be required before police are allowed to question someone who is not in custody, but whom the police suspect of a crime? The Supreme Court has held that the warnings are not then required. Is this in keeping with the privilege against self-incrimination?

What should the limits be on the opportunity of the police to outsmart a suspect? After the police have given him warnings, should they be permitted to mislead him as to the evidence they have against him in order to secure a confession?

If an accused legally waives his *Miranda* rights, does he in effect flash a green light—allowing the police to engage in deceptive interrogatory practices which the Supreme Court found so abhorrent in *Miranda*? That seems to be the case. One legal scholar, Welsh S. White, has proposed that a deceptive practice should be forbidden whenever it creates an "unacceptable risk" that the accused's constitutional rights have been infringed, or where there is a reasonable doubt that the resulting confession was not voluntary.

What do you think? Should the police be allowed to use tactics like "Mutt and Jeff" interrogation after a subject has voluntarily waived *Miranda* rights?

Should a waiver of *Miranda* rights by an accused be permitted if, despite the warnings, the accused was too drunk or too young to understand the meaning of these rights? Even if his statements are reliable?

Is it true that no person who is in fact guilty (if he is not guilty, it may sometimes be a very different story) should waive his *Miranda* rights, at least until he has talked to an attorney? If so, is it right to take advantage of his mistake in judgment?

Miranda holds that a person may waive his rights provided that the waiver "is made voluntarily, knowingly and intelligently." Is it ever intelligent to waive your *Miranda* rights?

d. NOTE ON THE POST–MIRANDA DECISIONS

The *Miranda* majority opinion may prove to be the high water mark for the rights of criminal suspects during interrogation. Subsequent decisions, though not abandoning the precise holding of the case, have eroded some of the sweeping protections which *Miranda* seemed to provide.

Six years after *Miranda,* the Court ruled that police violation of a suspect's Miranda rights does not preclude all uses of the suspect's testimony. In *Harris v. New York*, 401 U.S. 222, 91 S.Ct. 643, 28 L.Ed. 2d 1 (1971), a suspect under interrogation made certain admissions which were concededly inadmissible under Miranda because he had not first been informed of his right to an attorney. At his trial, after he testified to his innocence, the prosecution was permitted to introduce his admissions to impeach his credibility as a witness. A majority of the Supreme Court held that this did not violate *Miranda.*

In *Michigan v. Tucker*, 417 U.S. 433, 94 S.Ct. 2357, 41 L.Ed.2d 182 (1974), a defendant in a rape case had been questioned, again without first being advised of right to counsel. During the interrogation, he mentioned the name of a witness who later provided damaging testimony. The Court refused to exclude the witness' testimony even though it was obtained because of a violation of the Miranda rule.

In *Michigan v. Mosely*, 423 U.S. 96, 96 S.Ct. 321, 46 L.Ed.2d 313 (1975) the suspect exercised his right to remain silent after receiving his Miranda warnings from a detective in the Robbery Bureau. Two hours later, another detective, this time from the Homicide Bureau, gave him another set of Miranda warnings and began another interrogation. This time, not only did the suspect not claim any right to silence but he made several damaging admissions. The Supreme Court in a 7–2 decision held that, despite the defendant's initial refusal to talk, his admissions were admissible in evidence against him.

In *Oregon v. Bradshaw*, 462 U.S. 1039, 103 S.Ct. 2830, 77 L.Ed.2d 405 (1983), the suspect in a murder case made certain admissions after being advised of his Miranda rights. During further interrogation he invoked his right to counsel and the questioning ceased as required by *Miranda.* As he was being transferred from the police station to jail later that day, the suspect asked a police officer, "Well, what is going to happen to me now?" The officers talked to the suspect, who subsequently confessed. In a plurality opinion, the Court held in effect that this question renewed the authority of the police to interrogate the suspect and led to a valid waiver of his rights to silence and counsel. Therefore, his confession in the absence of counsel was held admissible in evidence against him.

In *New York v. Quarles,* 467 U.S. 649, 104 S.Ct. 2626, 81 L.Ed.2d 550 (1984), the suspect was apprehended in a deserted supermarket. After frisking revealed an empty gun holster, the suspect was handcuffed, surrounded by four police officers, one of whom asked him where the gun was. The Court held the suspect's answer admissible, ruling that officers need not comply with *Miranda* requirements when "exigent circumstances" pose a threat to public safety. This rule is intended to simplify the decisionmaking of police officers: if they need information to avert danger to themselves or the public, they need no longer be concerned about whether the suspect's incriminating statements will be admissible.

The Supreme Court continued to narrow *Miranda's* scope in *Oregon v. Elstad,* 470 U.S. 298, 105 S.Ct. 1285, 84 L.Ed.2d 222 (1985). In this case, two police officers obtained a confession from a burglary suspect without advising him of his *Miranda* rights. About one hour later they administered the *Miranda* warnings and obtained another confession. The Court rejected its prior rule that the prosecution has the burden of proving that when a suspect makes an initial confession without being told his rights, the second confession after the *Miranda* warnings have been given is still "voluntary." Instead, the Court placed the burden on the defendant to prove that the confession was involuntary.

Questions

1. A number of studies have been undertaken to measure the crime control costs of Miranda. On one issue they seem to agree. Suspects seem about as likely to confess if they are given Miranda warning, as they are if not warned at all. What could account for this?

Perhaps *Miranda's* most important impact has been felt through television portrayals of law enforcement. Most people in the United States learned of their rights to remain silent and to have counsel from fictional accounts of the police and criminal courts. Even if most Americans do not comprehend the significance of their rights, what do you think the public's reaction would be if the U.S. Supreme Court directly overturned the *Miranda* decision?

2. Do you think that a person who confesses once—without warnings—is more likely to confess a second time, even though the warnings have been given? Should the initial confessions be considered to have been extracted by "psychological coercion?"

3. How do the recent decisions regarding the privilege against self-incrimination affect the exercise of governmental power over the citizens? Do they strike a fair balance between the state and the individual?

4. One consequence of the decisions is to sanction some police interrogations carried out prior to the administration of *Miranda* warnings. Does this merely provide law enforcement officers with the discretion they need to carry out their duties efficiently? Or, does it invite officers to coerce suspects into making incriminating statements?

How closely should the courts monitor police practices in the area of confessions?

The Court's reasoning in these decisions follows a balancing approach to the privilege against self-incrimination, weighing the protection of the individual's Fifth Amendment rights against society's interest in the use of police interrogation and self-incrimination as means for the enforcement of the criminal law. Prior decisions took a different approach, holding that the interest in individual liberty requires limits on interrogation to safeguard Fifth Amendment rights, even though these "bright line" requirements might lead to less efficient law enforcement. Which is the better approach? Should the permissibility of police practices depend on a cost-benefit analysis of the value of a constitutional right?

As previously noted, the *Miranda* decision was intended, among other things, to cure problems arising from admitting confessions on the basis of case-by-case inquiry into their voluntariness. Do the recent Supreme Court decisions suggest a return to such a case-by-case analysis?

Numerous state supreme courts have reached conclusions contrary to the United States Supreme Court regarding the state privilege against self-incrimination. Under the authority of their state constitutional provisions, they have retained the broader scope of constitutional protection along lines developed by the Warren Court.

In addition, many commentators believe that recent United States Supreme Court decisions in this area have led it to overemphasize the goal of convicting the factually guilty while failing to sufficiently protect individuals' constitutional rights. The following editorial is an example of this point of view.

e. JUSTICE DENIED *

Six justices of the U.S. Supreme Court have come to an outrageous and indefensible conclusion about the rights of criminal suspects, a conclusion that undermines the principles that the court says it supports. The justices say they believe that an accused person has a right to have a lawyer while being questioned by the police. But they have let stand a murder conviction even though the police denied that right to the accused man, interrogating him while keeping his lawyer out.

Twenty years ago the court laid down the law: A suspect must be told that he has a right to remain silent and that he has a right to have a lawyer. As a result, police throughout the country now routinely read suspects their Miranda rights—named for the case in which the issue was decided, *Miranda v. Arizona*, 384 U.S. 436 (1966). Before that, third-degree interrogations and forced confessions were routine. What that court sought to do was lessen the inherent imbalance

* Los Angeles Times, Editorial, March 12, 1986.

between the vast power of the state and the near-powerlessness of an individual accused of a crime. The current court seems not to care.

In the case decided last week, *Moran v. Burbine*, 84–1485, a 20-year-old man, Brian K. Burbine, was arrested by the police in Cranston, R.I., in 1977 on a charge of breaking and entering. He was read his Miranda rights, but he did not ask for a lawyer. While he was in custody, the police linked him to the murder of a 35-year-old woman who had been severely beaten with a metal pipe.

In the meantime, Burbine's sister had retained a public defender to represent him on the breaking-and-entering charge. The lawyer, unaware that a murder charge was also in the making, called the police station at 8:15 p.m. and was told by a detective that Burbine would not be questioned on the burglary charge that night. A short time later, questioning began. Burbine, who was not told that a lawyer had tried to reach him, confessed to the murder and was subsequently convicted.

Justice Sandra Day O'Connor, writing for six justices, upheld the conviction. The justices were not pleased by the "misleading" police actions, she said, but as long as Burbine had been told his rights and waived them, his confession stood. What message does this unbelievable opinion send to the police? As long as you follow the letter of the law, chicanery is all right even if it violates the fairness demanded by the Miranda rule.

Only three justices—John Paul Stevens, William J. Brennan Jr., and Thurgood Marshall—recognized that the decision flies in the face of the essence of *Miranda*. "Today, incommunicado questioning is embraced as a societal goal of the highest order that justifies police deception of the shabbiest kind," Stevens wrote for the three dissenters. "The court has trampled on well-established legal principles and flouted the spirit of our accusatorial system of justice." At least three of them had their heads screwed on right.

The police should be required to bend over backward to ensure that suspects—certainly murder suspects—are treated fairly. If an accused person tells a judge that he doesn't want a lawyer, the judge will usually assign one to him anyway. While the police don't have to do that, they should be prevented from keeping out a lawyer who has been retained to represent a suspect and from deceiving the lawyer in the bargain. The way to prevent police abuse is to throw out the conviction.

f. THE MIRANDA CONTROVERSY CONTINUES

(1) THE SELF–INCRIMINATION DEBATE *

The period surrounding the twentieth anniversary of the Supreme Court decision in *Miranda v. Arizona*, 384 US 436 (1966), brought with

* Mark Berger, "The Self–Incrimination Debate," Criminal Justice, Vol. 5, No. 2, Summer 1990, pp. 7–8 (Reprinted with Permission).

it a renewed debate focusing on the role of the self-incrimination privilege in American criminal law. A flurry of articles appeared in legal journals that raised questions concerning the constitutional legitimacy of *Miranda* and challenged the wisdom of its requirement that custodial interrogations be preceded by a warning and waiver of the right to remain silent and the right to consult with an attorney. A major participant in the debate was the U.S. Department of Justice, which issued a report recommending that the Supreme Court be urged to reverse the *Miranda* ruling.

Miranda has had its supporters as well as its detractors. The recent exchanges serve to remind us of the controversial character of the privilege against self-incrimination. Critics continue to object to the requirement that suspects be warned prior to custodial police questioning, and they challenge the principle that prohibits drawing an adverse inference from the suspect's silence after the police warning has been administered. Beyond that, some commentators disagree with the Supreme Court's interpretation of the self-incrimination privilege, which allows a defendant to remain silent at trial without being exposed to adverse comment (*Griffin v. California,* 380 US 609 (1965).)

The language of the self-incrimination privilege offers only limited guidance in determining the reach of the right to remain silent. The Fifth Amendment commands that no one may be "compelled in any criminal case to be a witness against himself." While the language can be easily read to prohibit the use of force—legal, physical, or psychological—to secure incriminating statements, it can also be interpreted to permit adverse inferences when the suspect refuses to answer official questions. If the individual is not misled by a *Miranda* warning to believe that silence will not be used against him (as was the case in *Doyle v. Ohio,* 426 US 610 (1976)), a jury instruction that permits an inference of guilt to be drawn from the suspect's silence at trial or at the police station might be considered to fall short of the compulsion barred by the Fifth Amendment.

While these issues are being argued in the United States, Great Britain has been actively engaged in the process of reforming its law governing confessions by drastically curtailing the right to silence for suspects facing police interrogation as well as for defendants at trial. At the request of the Home Secretary, a Working Group was established in the Home Office with directions to formulate proposals for limiting the right to silence in English and Welsh prosecutions. This followed the implementation of right-to-silence restrictions in Northern Ireland prosecutions and the passage of general legislation that altered the standards for the admissibility of confessions.

The British proposals do not create a legal duty to provide information to the police, nor do they require the defendant to testify at trial. As a result, there are no criminal penalties to which suspects and defendants who remain silent are subject, and thus, arguably, no compulsion to provide self-incriminatory information in the sense of the

American Fifth Amendment. But whether or not the British proposals are consistent with American constitutional law, their relevence to the American debate over self-incrimination is a separate question.

If British legal history, practice, and policy are leading to a devaluation of the right to silence in Great Britain, does that indicate that a comparable shift would be appropriate for the United States?

(2) Post Miranda Interrogation Tactics *

As treated in the leading text on interrogation tactics, Inbau, Reid, and Buckley (1986), the process of eliciting a confession is a *tour de force* of social influence. According to these writers, a guilty suspect must be "persuaded" to confess. The idealized guilty suspect is conceived to be a rational actor who can be controlled by manipulating his expected outcomes for different decisions. The keys to persuasion are:

1. Convincing the suspect that his situation is hopeless because the evidence against him is sufficient to produce a successful prosecution. To this end, trickery, invention of evidence, and gross distortion of the significance of the evidence pointing to the suspect may be used to manipulate expectations.

2. Manipulating the suspect's emotional state by attempting to make the stress of continuing to deny responsibility greater than the suspect's anxiety about admitting guilt. To accomplish this, tactics designed to manipulate the suspect's emotions are brought into play to induce feelings of guilt and distress. It is hoped that these aversive emotional experiences will drive the suspect to seek forgiveness through confession.

3. Manipulating the suspect's expectations about the level of punishment that will follow from immediately confessing as opposed to continuing to hold to a denial of guilt. The supposed advantage to be gained through cooperation and immediate confession is represented as the ability to demonstrate remorse and demonstrate the suspect's good character. The implication of all of this is that the suspect will be less severely punished if he confesses.

Inbau, Reid, and Buckley suggest that it is permissible to deceive a suspect in order to create the belief that he has entered into a deal in which lenient treatment is to be exchanged for a confession. These authors caution, however, that this is legally permissible only as long as the deal is not real.

Inbau, Reid and Buckley repeatedly warn their readers that the interrogation techniques they teach (as well as certain other techniques whose use is well known) can elicit false confessions from innocent suspects. They do not, however, provide interrogators with either an

* Richard Ofshe, "Coerced Confessions: Cultic Studies Journal, Vol. 6, No. 1, 1989, The Logic of Seemingly Irrational Action,"   pp. 2–3 (Reprinted with Permission).

understanding of why this can occur or sufficient insight into the phenomenon to identify when it may be happening in front of them.

Question

Do you think that the police practices described above are justified by the serious crime problem we face in this country?

(3) AN INTERROGATION *

The one great advantage to the police in their investigation was Peter's willingness to be kept in custody and to answer questions without a lawyer present. If he was the killer, then getting a confession out of him was vital before anyone could interfere. . . .

Peter was told to relax by Sergeant Schneider when he was left alone in the polygraph room. He was unaware that his voice was being recorded or that Lieutenant Shay and the other officers were watching him through a one-way glass. Shay . . . gave Sergeant Kelly thorough briefing on the Gibbons murder and the reasons for suspecting Peter. Kelly, like Shay, was in civilian clothes—a uniformed interrogator has more difficulty earning the confidence of a suspect. . . .

On the tape, Peter can be heard clearing his throat, but otherwise sits quietly, waiting for Kelly to appear and the polygraph test to begin. The door squeaks open and closes with a bang. "Peter, how are ya?" says Kelly. He speaks slowly. His deep voice is warm and friendly. . . . He talks about Peter's constitutional rights, saying, "You can leave here any time you want. You just say, hey, Tim, I want to go home, let me take the equipment off, and you can go home. Fair enough?"

Peter agrees that it is fair. Kelly explains the questions for the test will be reviewed beforehand because "I'm not here trying to trick you or anything like that." Peter comments that "Even if you are, it's for the better" because it will help get out the truth. "Well," says Kelly, "I'm not, in no way, trying to trick you."

Before beginning the test, Kelly and Peter talk about the events of the previous day. Kelly reveals that Peter's mother, according to the autopsy, had two broken legs. Peter expresses surprise and he is encouraged to speculate about how they could have been broken. . . . Kelly asks whether he has told the truth in his earlier statements to the police. Peter says he has. Now they will all know for sure, Kelly says, because the polygraph "reads your brain for me."

"Does it actually read my brain?" Peter asks.

"Oh, definitely, definitely. And if you've told me the truth this is what your brain is going to tell me."

"Will this stand up and protect me?"

* Donald S. Connery, *Guilty Until Proven Innocent,* (New York: G.P. Putnam's Sons, 1977) pp. 53–54, 59–61. Copyright © 1977   by Donald S. Connery. Reprinted by permission of G.P. Putnam's Sons.

"Right, right."

"Good. That's the reason I came up to take it, you know."

Peter is so eager that he says, "Let's go!" when he thinks the test is about to begin. Kelly says they don't want to rush things: "We take our time, all right?"

When Kelly, still asking preliminary questions, asks Peter if he has ever done anything that he is really ashamed of in his life, Peter doesn't want to answer unless he is promised his words will not leave the room. Kelly assures him that the answer will stay "right here," just between the two of them. Peter reveals that he is ashamed because a homosexual once made an advance to him. Although "nothing really happened," the incident has stuck in his mind. He mentions, too, that he lied to his mother about smoking marijuana, but that seems to be the extent of his shameful memories. He agrees with Kelly that murdering his mother would be "a damned shameful thing," but he says, "It would be ridiculous for me to come down and volunteer for this test" if he wasn't confident that he was innocent.

This may seem logical to Peter, but, Kelly observes, "I've had people actually come in here and take this test because they knew they were guilty but they didn't know how to tell somebody." He says to Peter: "Maybe you're looking for somebody to help you, I don't know. . . . A lot of time people come here and take this test, then let the test say they need help."

The test questions are discussed. . . .

Peter has a question of his own when the test is over: "How'd I do?" Kelly gives a cautious answer: "You're very cooperative, let me put it that way." The reaction is not what Peter expected. Disappointment and confusion cloud his voice when he asks, "What do you mean?"

Kelly explains that the first test was just a warm-up and that to give the results from the polygraph chart wouldn't be fair because "You're nervous. . . . Definitely nervous this first time." Kelly reassures Peter that he is not lying to him about how the test is conducted: "We run it once to show you there's no electric shock or tricks. I'm not going to lie to you one iota. . . . I don't make it a habit to lie to people."

Kelly asks whether any of the questions bothered Peter. If so, he might have to change the wording.

"Well, one thing I noticed is that, like, the question whether I harmed my mother or not."

"Why?" Kelly asks.

"Well, that question—like they told me up at the barracks yesterday that—how some people don't realize—all of a sudden fly off the handle for a split second and it leaves a blank spot in their memory."

This is an important observation by Peter. . . . It reveals that someone at the barracks had already put into Peter's mind the thought that he might have killed his mother in a sudden rage and then blanked it from his mind. "Well, I thought about that last night," Peter says, "and I thought and I thought and I thought, and I said no, I couldn't have done it. . . . And now, when you ask me the question, that's what I think of."

Kelly comments, "If you did it, this is probably how it could have happened."

"What do you mean?"

"Bango, just like this . . . if you did it, it was a split-second thing that you did. You lost your head." Kelly goes on to suggest that Peter might have been high on narcotics when he did the killing or maybe there was an argument or maybe his mother attacked him. "If anything like that happened, I'll know it over here on these charts."

. . . Peter is told that in the next exercise he will be asked to deliberately lie so that they can be sure that they are getting proper recordings from him. Kelly says that 8 percent of the people tested cannot be usefully recorded on the machine because "they're just blah."

. . .

When the test is over, . . . Peter [is complimented] on being a "textbook reactor. You give me such responses in here that you must be so honest that I don't think the sun would come up. . . . Peter, you're about the best reactor I've had in here for a long time. . . . You know the difference between right and wrong . . . when you tell a lie you go right to the top of the chart. . . . In other words, this is great for us because we'll have no trouble here today."

Peter thinks it is good news too. "I'm perfect," he says. . . .

Kelly tightens the arm cuff. . . .

"Do you have a clear recollection of what happened last night?" Kelly asks.

"Yes," Peter answers. . . .

"Well, I think we got a little problem here, Pete."

"What do you mean?"

"About hurting your mother last night."

"I didn't do it."

Expecting the machine to confirm his truthfulness, Peter is stunned when he is told that the machine indicates that he is lying. From then on, he is no longer the confident volunteer, but an accused person struggling to demonstrate his innocence. . . .

Kelly tells Peter that "You're giving me a reaction, that's why I put in these questions towards the end there. I'm just wondering, do you have any doubt in your mind?" Peter explains his confusion by referring back to the dialogue in the barracks: "About hurting my mother. Because the thing is, like, when we went over, and over, and over it. . . . When he told me I could have flown off the handle I gave it a lot of consideration."

"All right," Kelly says.

"But, I don't think I did."

"But, you're not sure, are you?"

"That's right. Well, I could have."

"Okay," says Kelly. "Now I think you possibly did from what I'm seeing here, okay?"

Peter explains that "I'm sure what I did," but says he is not sure what happened in the house. Kelly speculates that he might have hit his mother with the car outside the house and then "set it up to look like something really violent happened in the house."

Peter protests that "it wouldn't have been like me . . . honestly, if I had hit my mom the first thing I would have done was call the ambulance." Kelly says that "I think you got doubts as to what happened there last night. Don't you?"

"I've got doubts because I don't understand what happened and —"

"What do you mean you don't understand?"

"—well, I mean, I'm afraid to uh—"

"Are you afraid that you did this thing?"

"Well, yeah, of course I am. That's natural."

A little later, when Peter says that not being sure "scares me a little bit." Kelly says, "I don't think you're *crazy* or anything like this, but I think you need a little help."

"With a psychiatrist?" Peter asks.

"Yes," says Kelly.

The exchange is the beginning of a constant refrain: that Peter has a mental problem and that is why he cannot remember murdering his mother. Peter feels, however, that the bad reaction on the polygraph must be due to nervousness—"I mean my mother did die"—and says that "I'd like to come in and take another test. I mean rather than go by this one."

Kelly puts him off, saying that "what I'm interested in here, Pete, is that you said you're not sure if you hurt your mother or not last night."

Peter's response is that "what I say I did, I'm absolutely sure of. But if I had a lapse of memory, that's what I'm not sure of." Kelly asks whether he thinks he had a lapse of memory and Peter says flatly, "No." He is just as firm in denying that he is covering up for somebody else.

No longer able to rely on the lie detector to get him out of this fix, Peter turns to another hope. He says, "If I did it and I didn't realize it, there's got to be some clue there in the house anyway that's gonna connect with it . . . there *has* to be something in that house, some-place. If I did it. Or whoever did it. There's got to be something, somehow, somewhere."

The dialogue goes on. Peter is asked whether he has any doubt about hurting his mother and says that "this test is giving me doubt right now." He speaks of having been "drilled and drilled" and then he tries to recall what he had been told back in the Canaan Barracks. He remembers the proposition that he might have killed his mother and "the fact that I could have forgotten . . . that really shook me because I never heard of anything like that before." . . .

[A sergeant now enters with the news that other evidence confirms the fact that Peter was at home when his mother was killed.]

Kelly says . . . "Pete, I think you got a problem. I really do. . . . And Jack feels the same way when he looked at these charts. . . . These charts say you hurt your mother last night."

When Peter says that he cannot remember, Kelly suggests that "what happened here was a mercy thing"—perhaps Peter's mother had a fatal disease and he was doing her a favor by ending her life. On the other hand, Kelly says, Peter might have hit her with his car and then panicked. If so, "this is only an accident." But Peter insists that he did not even hit her with the car.

"Then if you didn't," Kelly says, "then you killed your mother deliberately."

"I didn't though," Peter responds. "I don't remember it." . . .

The interrogation is a contest of wills: Peter versus the polygraph as interpreted by Kelly. Peter is still attached to the machine, two hours after the session began. Kelly removes the last of the connections, but the interrogation continues in the polygraph room. Kelly speculates that "something happened between you and your mother last night and one thing led to another and some way you accidently hurt her seriously."

Peter says, "but how? It's not like me." He adds: "I wouldn't mind so much if they could *prove* I did it. . . . I'm positive to myself that I didn't. Consciously. But subconsciously, you know, who knows?"

By this time his confidence is gone. "Now I'm afraid," he says, "because I was so sure, you know, that I didn't do something. . . . And I still want to stay in school. I don't have any place to go. . . . I don't want to go into—like Newtown or something."

By "Newtown" Peter means Fairfield Hills Hospital in Newtown, Connecticut, a mental-health institution. Peter seems persuaded that he has a mental problem. Kelly encourages this belief, saying that "This isn't the end of the world. I've talked to a lot of people who have been involved in a lot of serious things and they're normal individuals today. Once they got it straightened out upstairs."

When Kelly insists that Peter "did it" even though Peter cannot remember doing it, Peter asks if there is any way "they can kind of pound it out of me, if I did it?" Kelly seems to be shocked. He exclaims, "Peter!"

Soon Peter admits that "now there's doubt in my mind. Maybe I did do it." He says, "we got to keep drilling at it" to get the answer.

The search begins in earnest, with Peter as an active participant, to figure out how he could have carried out the terrible deed. Once again, Peter relates the story of his homecoming. But now he says that when he entered the house and looked up at the top bunk in the bedroom "I thought I saw her" lying in the bed. "See?" Sergeant Kelly says. "I think this is probably where you flipped over a little bit. You probably *did* see your mother standing there." But Peter says, "No, laying in bed." He explains about his mother's habit of lying in bed reading with all her clothes on when it is too cold to read outdoors.

Kelly seems to feel that he is getting closer to a confession. When Peter says that "I wish I could go out and have that cigarette now," Kelly leaves the room briefly to get an ashtray and cigarettes. As they light up, Peter muses that "the thing that's messing me up" is not whether or not he killed his mother, but "the fact that *if* I did do it, why don't I remember it?"

Kelly says that Peter is so ashamed of what he did that he is afraid to admit it and says that he thinks Peter is deliberately lying to him. Denying that he is lying, Peter once again asks about clues: "Are my footprints going into the bedroom there?" Kelly says that such things take time to check out. He continues with the line that Peter is too ashamed to admit his guilt. "Once we get this out in the open and we get you the proper help it will be over with. . . . No one's going to lock you up and throw the keys away."

Peter says that "I *want* to tell you I did it, now, but I'm still not sure I did do it." Kelly is virtually telling him that the only penalty will be a short spell of psychiatric treatment: "As I said, Peter, three months out of your life—that's not a very long time." Peter accepts that he has a serious mental problem. "I think I've been sliding for a long time, to something. . . . I've *always* had a question in my mind if I was mentally right." He had worried about his family's history of mental problems and alcoholism.

Kelly and Peter speculate together about why Peter "went off the handle." Or what he did when his mother "flew off the handle and went at you or something and you had to protect yourself." Peter is being offered an opportunity to claim that he acted only in self-defense, but he does not accept it because "self-defense goes just so far."

After they both agree that Peter is not a cold-blooded killer but just "a guy sitting here with a problem," Kelly asks again what happened and Peter says, "I'm still in a fog. I don't know."

When Sergeant Kelly returns to the polygraph room he tells Peter that he has been on the telephone with the investigators in Canaan. "I think I have a reason why it happened." He says that the police have learned from Peter's friends that "your mother was always on your back. Constantly." She was always telephoning around for him. "She'd been bugging you so f_____ long that last night you came in the house and she started bugging you again and you snapped. Am I right?"

"I would say you're right," Peter replies, "but I don't remember doing the things that happened. That's just it. I believe I did it now."

His words are the beginning of the confession. Peter has snapped at the bait. He is hooked. Now it is just a matter of reeling him in and getting his signature on a formal confession.

Comment and Questions

Peter Reilly confessed to murdering his mother, and was found guilty on April 12, 1974. His case later became a *cause célèbre*; a retrial was ordered; and the charges were eventually dropped on November 24, 1976. A Grand Jury investigation into the conduct of the case concluded:

> The great reliance on the polygraph tests seemed to impede the investigation. The use of polygraph tests in this probe confirms the wisdom of our rules of evidence in prohibiting the admissibility of the polygraph results as evidence. In one instance Michael Parmalee and Sandra Ashner made contradictory statements about the whereabouts of Parmalee on the evening of September 28, 1973. Both persons consented to take the polygraph test administered by the State Police and both were found to be truthful. As a result of these tests and tests given to other suspects the police curtailed their investigations of those persons in the early stages of the investigation. The failure to investigate other reasonable suspects with the same intensity and vigor as applied to Peter A. Reilly is hard to understand.

(4) A DISHONEST TOOL WON'T TELL LIES *

The polygraph is an instrument that measures changes in blood pressure, pulse, respiration and perspiration. Presumably, the measurable changes tell us whether a person is lying. But the theory behind lie-detection is flawed. It holds that: (1) The conscious act of lying produces emotional conflict; (2) conflict induces fear and anxiety; (3) these emotions are accompanied by measurable and interpretable physiological changes.

* Jerome Skolnick, "A Dishonest Tool Won't Tell Lies," Los Angeles Times, Sunday, March 20, 1983/Part IV (Reprinted with Permission).

In fact, the act of lying does not always bring about these effects. Some people believe their own false stories. Sophisticated liars may experience little fear. Truth-tellers may experience fear and anxiety just by being asked threatening questions.

When people do experience fear and anxiety, these emotions do not necessarily register as changes in bodily response. If physiological reactions rose and fell precisely according to changes in emotional states, they would correlate exactly with one another. But that doesn't happen. Bodily responses do not follow such patterns. If they did, only a unigraph, not a polygraph, would be required; four imprecise measures are not more accurate than one precise measure.

Since the cause-and-effect relationships of lying, conflict, emotion and physiological response are so fuzzy, the lie-detector's accuracy is not comparable to the accuracy of, say, blood tests or X-rays. The outcome of a lie-detector examination is not determined by the squiggles produced by the machine. Ultimately, the result is determined by the personal interpretation of the examiner.

Although the public may be unfamiliar with the polygraph's deficiencies—and television programs that hype its accuracy don't exactly help dispel the myths—I suspect that high-ranking federal investigators understand its scientific inadequacies.

So why is the polygraph used in Central Intelligence Agency investigations, and why is it now being authorized for large segments of the federal bureaucracy? For practical reasons that have nothing to do with scientific merit. An unreliable technique can sometimes produce results by heightening the interrogator's coercive powers. A suspect strapped to a machine may be frightened into a confession or into making incriminating statements.

By endorsing the polygraph, the government is sanctioning a blatant invasion of privacy. Consider some typical questions: Is your name Jane Jones? Do you reside in Washington? Have you ever done anything you're ashamed of? Have you ever engaged in homosexual acts? Stolen anything? Leaked information? And so forth.

The polygraph is not effective because of its accuracy, but because it is cloaked in a scientific mantle and therefore appears to justify intrusive questioning that otherwise would be considered outrageous.

g.　MIRANDA AND MODELS OF THE CRIMINAL PROCESS *

Detention and Interrogation After a "Lawful" Arrest

The Crime Control Model. The police cannot be expected to solve crimes by independent investigation alone. The best source of information is usually the suspect himself. Without the cooperation of sus-

* Herbert Packer, *The Limits of the Criminal Sanction*, Stanford, Stanford University Press, 1968, pp. 186–203. © 1968 (Reprinted with permission).

pects, many crimes could not be solved at all. The police must have a reasonable opportunity to interrogate the suspect in private before he has a chance to fabricate a story or to decide that he will not cooperate. The psychologically optimal time for getting this kind of cooperation from the suspect is immediately after his arrest, before he has had a chance to rally his forces. Any kind of outside interference is likely to diminish the prospect that the suspect will cooperate in the interrogation; therefore he should not be entitled to summon his family or friends, and most particularly, he should not be entitled to consult a lawyer. The first thing that a lawyer will tell him is to say nothing to the police. Once he gets that kind of reinforcement, the chances of getting any useful information out of him sink to zero.

Of course the police should not be entitled to hold the suspect for interrogation indefinitely, nor would they want to do so. The point of diminishing returns in interrogation is reached fairly soon, and anyway, the police don't have extensive enough resources to allow them to go on interrogating indefinitely. But no hard and fast rule can be laid down about how long the police should be permitted to interrogate the suspect before bringing him before a magistrate. The gravity of the crime, its complexity, the amount of criminal sophistication that the suspect appears to have—all of these are relevant factors in determining how long he should be held. The standard ought to be the length of time, given all the circumstances, during which it is reasonable to suppose that legitimate techniques of interrogation may be expected to produce useful information or that extrinsic investigation may be expected to produce convincing proof either of the suspect's innocence or of his guilt.

The suspect should not be held incommunicado under normal circumstances. His family is entitled to know where he is; but they should not be entitled to talk with him, because that may impair the effectiveness of the interrogation. Occasionally it may be justifiable not to notify them at all, as when a confederate is still at large and does not know that his partner in crime has been apprehended.

The point of all these illustrations, however, is that hard and fast rules cannot be laid down if police efficiency is not to be impaired. It follows that the rules must be flexible and that good-faith mistakes about their applicability in any given case should not be penalized. If the police err by holding a suspect too long, he has no complaint, because they would not be holding him unless they had some good basis for their belief that he had committed a crime. The public has a complaint to the extent that police resources are thereby shown to have been used inefficiently; but the redress for that is intradepartmental discipline in flagrant cases and a general program of administrative management that keeps such occasions to a minimum.

Any trustworthy statement obtained from a suspect during a period of police interrogation should of course be admissible into evidence against him. Criminal investigation is a search for truth, and anything that aids the search should be encouraged. There is, to be sure, a danger that occasionally police will not live up to professional standards, and will use coercive measures to elicit a confession from a suspect. That is not to be condoned, but at the same time we should keep in mind that the evil of a coerced confession is that it may result in the conviction of an innocent man. There is no way of laying down hard and fast rules about what kinds of police conduct are coercive. It is a factual question in each case whether the accused's confession is unreliable. A defendant against whom a confession is introduced into evidence should have to convince the jury that the circumstances under which it was elicited were so coercive that more probably than not the confession was untrue. In reaching a determination on that issue, the trier of fact should of course be entitled to consider the other evidence in the case, and if it points toward guilt and tends to corroborate the confession, should be entitled to take that into account in determining whether, more likely than not, the confession was untrue.

To say this is not to say that the unlawful use of force by the police on an accused is ever to be condoned. The point is simply that the use of force is not in itself determinative of the reliability of a confession and should therefore not be conclusive against the admissibility of a confession. The sanctions available for mistreating a person in custody are ample, if vigorously pursued, to ensure that this kind of conduct will be rare. It is by raising professional standards through internal administrative methods rather than by altering the outcome of randomly selected criminal prosecutions that improper police conduct is being eliminated. It follows from what has been said that practices less likely than the use of force to be coercive, such as an overlong period of detention unaccompanied by physical abuse, should not count conclusively against the admissibility of a confession.

The Due Process Model. The decision to arrest in order to be valid must be based on probable cause to believe that the suspect has committed a crime. To put it another way, the police should not arrest unless information in their hands at that time seems likely, subject to the vicissitudes of the litigation process, to provide a case that will result in a conviction. It follows that if proper arrest standards have been employed, there is no necessity to get additional evidence out of the mouth of the defendant. He is to be arrested so that he may be held to answer the case against him, not so that a case against him that does not exist at the time of his arrest can be developed.

Once a suspect has been arrested, he should be brought before a magistrate without unnecessary delay, which is to say as soon as it is physically possible to do so, once the preliminary formalities of recording his arrest have been completed. Anyone who is held in arrest has the right to test the legality of his arrest, i.e., whether there is probable cause to hold him, in a judicial proceeding. As a practical matter, that right is diluted through delay unless the accused is promptly brought before a magistrate. Since a suspect is entitled to be at liberty pending the judicial determination of his guilt or innocence, there must be as promptly as possible after arrest a proceeding in which the conditions of his release—for example release on bail—are determined. This right too is diluted by delay unless the suspect is promptly brought before a magistrate. And the suspect is entitled to the assistance of counsel, assistance that he needs most acutely as soon as he is arrested. As a practical matter, he is unlikely to receive that right unless he is promptly advised of it. Once again, his prompt production before an impartial judicial officer is necessary if his right is not to be diluted by delay.

It is never proper for the police to hold a suspect for the purpose of interrogation or investigation. Of course, some interval of time must always elapse between his arrest and his production before a magistrate, and it would be unrealistic to expect the police to maintain complete silence toward him during that period. However, there is all the difference in the world between an interrogation conducted during the relatively brief span of time necessary to get the suspect before a magistrate and an interrogation whose length is measured by the time necessary to get him to confess. Any such interrogation should, by that fact alone, be held illegal.

As soon as a suspect is arrested, he should be told by the police that he is under no obligation to answer questions, that he will suffer no detriment by refusing to answer questions, that he may answer questions in his own interest to clear himself of suspicion (but that anything he says may be used in evidence), and, above all, that he is entitled to see a lawyer if he wants to do so.

If the suspect does make self-incriminating statements while under arrest and before he is brought before a magistrate, their admissibility into evidence against him should be barred under any of the following conditions: (1) if the police failed to warn him of his rights, including his right to the assistance of a lawyer; (2) if he was questioned after the required warnings were given, unless he expressly waived his right to be silent and to see a lawyer; (3) if the confession was made during a period of detention that exceeded what was necessary to get him promptly before a magistrate; or (4) if the confession was made by other coercive means, such as the use of force. Any confession made under these circumstances should be regarded as "involuntary," and should be excluded at the trial in order to deprive the police of any incentive to obtain such a confession.

The rationale of exclusion is not that the confession is untrustworthy, but that it is at odds with the postulates of an accusatory system of criminal justice in which it is up to the state to make its case against a defendant without forcing him to cooperate in the process, and without capitalizing on his ignorance of his legal rights. It follows, then, that the existence of other evidence of guilt has no bearing on the admissibility of the confession or on the necessity for reversing a conviction based in part on such a confession. It also follows that the procedure for determining the admissibility of a confession must be such as to avoid any possibility of prejudice to the defendant through the process of determining admissibility. Specifically, in a jury trial the issue of the admissibility of a confession should be litigated on a record made before the judge and out of the hearing of the jury, so that the trial judge has the clear and undivided responsibility for deciding whether the jury should hear the confession and so that a reviewing court can have an unambiguous basis for deciding whether the trial judge reached the proper conclusion.

. . .

Access to Counsel

Running through most of the issues that arise during this preliminary phase of the criminal process is the pervasive theme of access to counsel. . . . It seems worthwhile, then, to reexamine briefly the question of access to counsel at this stage of the process, as an independent feature of the process.

The Crime Control Model. The period from the time that a suspect is arrested until he is brought before a magistrate is likely to be the crucial phase in the investigation of a crime. This phase is investigative, not judicial. There is nothing going on at this point that requires or can tolerate the intervention of a lawyer. The defendant's rights are sufficiently protected by the offer to see that his lawyer, if he has one, is notified that he is being held. If there is anything illegal about his detention, that can be remedied by his applying for habeas corpus. Otherwise, all issues that could conceivably arise from the police conduct during this phase are open to scrutiny at later stages of the proceeding. Particularly if the sanction of excluding evidence is to be applied, there is no reason at all for the accused to be given a chance to consult with his lawyer during this period. And, it should be noted, it is absolutely necessary for the police to question the suspect at this point without undue interference. This is their only chance to enlist the cooperation of the one person most likely to know the truth. Because the police do not arrest without probable cause, there is a high degree of probability that useful information can be learned from the suspect. If he is given an opportunity to consult a lawyer at this stage of the proceeding, he will invariably be told to say nothing. The most expeditious way of clearing a case will then be foreclosed, and the police will have to take the more laborious route of developing evidence unaided by leads supplied by the suspect. This foreclosure will also redound to the disadvantage of the innocent suspect, because he will be deterred from making statements that would otherwise lead to his early release. The only person benefiting from this procedure will be the guilty suspect, who is accordingly enabled to make it difficult, if not impossible, for a conviction to be obtained. If the police must conduct a full investigation without the suspect's aid in every case, trivial as well as serious, the number of cases that can be processed at a given level of police resources will sharply diminish. To put it more directly, the protection that the community enjoys against criminal activity will decline. A lawyer's place is in court. He should not enter a criminal case until it is in court.

The Due Process Model. A hardened and sophisticated criminal knows enough to keep silent in the face of police interrogation. He knows that self-exculpatory statements are often incriminating. He knows that he does not have to talk, and that he is not likely to realize any advantage by talking. An inexperienced person in the toils of the law knows none of this. Unless the operative rules forbid it, the situations of these two categories of suspects are bound to be unequal.

Likewise, there is no moment in the criminal process when the disparity in resources between the state and the accused is greater than at the moment of arrest. There is every opportunity for overreaching and abuse on the part of the police. There is no limit to the extent to which these opportunities are taken advantage of except in the police's own sense of self-restraint. Later correctives palliate but do not suffice. What actually takes place in the police station is known only to the suspect and to the police. It is not hard to predict whose word will be taken if a contradiction arises.

The only way to ensure that these two equally obnoxious forms of inequality do not have a decisively malign impact on the criminal process is to require at the time of arrest (1) that the suspect be immediately apprised of his right to remain silent and to have a lawyer; (2) that he promptly be given access to a lawyer, either his own or one appointed for him; or (3) that failing the presence of a lawyer to protect the suspect's interest, he not be subjected to police interrogation.

Questions

Granted that the wealthy criminal probably already knows his constitutional rights, and can get his lawyer to advise him, is this a reason to extend the same rights to the poor criminal?

Is it possible that we worry more about just the kinds of crimes that tend to be committed by the poor? On the other hand, is it arguable that a felt unfairness of our society toward the poor produces more crime and anti-police behavior than would be prevented by the overruling of Miranda?

C. THE RIGHT TO BE FREE FROM UNREASON-ABLE SEARCH AND SEIZURE

1. AMENDMENT IV, U.S. CONSTITUTION

The right of the people to be secure in their persons, houses, papers, and effects, against unreasonable searches and seizures, shall not be violated, and no Warrants shall issue, but upon probable cause, supported by Oath or affirmation, and particularly describing the place to be searched, and the persons or things to be seized.

Questions

Read this amendment over carefully. What does it mean? What is the relation between the existence of a warrant and the reasonableness of the search? Is this clear from the words of the amendment?

2. THE NATURE OF THE RIGHT *

a. HISTORICAL DEVELOPMENT

The Fourth Amendment guarantees that the privacy of individuals in their persons and in their homes and offices can be breached by the police only when a search warrant has been issued by an appropriate judicial officer or when certain unusual circumstances occur, such as the search of a moving vehicle or the "search of the person" of someone who is being lawfully arrested. The enforcement of this protection against "unreasonable searches and seizures" has been met by strongly voiced opposition, primarily on the grounds that the restrictions unduly hamper efficient law enforcement. The opposition reached a peak in 1961 when the Supreme Court of the United States decided that evidence which had been obtained as a result of an unlawful search and seizure was inadmissible in state criminal trials just as, in 1914, it had been declared inadmissible in federal criminal trials.

A. *History.* Although English common law prohibited search warrants and arrest warrants that did not describe in detail the places to be searched and the things or persons to be seized, Parliament authorized exceptions to this rule in the American Colonies. Antagonism toward these exceptions had an important influence on the development of American rights.

In the eighteenth century, Parliament enacted legislation which authorized general searches, called *writs of assistance,* in the enforcement of the Trade Acts. Under the authority of the writs of assistance, royal customs officers conducted random and general searches for contraband; the writs enabled royal officers to search any house or ship, break down doors, open trunks and boxes, and seize goods at will.

The writs of assistance were to have expired after the death of George II in 1760, but the law which authorized their use was renewed. This renewal furnished the occasion for the famous argument of James Otis in 1761 when he urged that the Boston court should refuse to issue writs of assistance. He said, in part:

> This writ is the worst instrument of arbitrary power, the most destructive of English liberty, and the fundamental principles of laws, that ever was found in an English law book . . . [because it places] the liberty of every man in the hands of every petty officer. A man is as secure in his house as a prince in his castle. This is the Privilege of the House, and it obtains

* William Cohen, Murray Schwartz and Dee Ann Sobul, The Bill of Rights: A Sourcebook for Teachers, California State Dept. of Education pp. 160–166. Reprinted with permission.

if a man be deeply in debt or if civil process be served against him. Only for felonies may an officer break and enter—and then by special, not general warrant. For general warrants there is only the precedent of the Star Chamber under the Stuarts . . ..

. . .

The principle enunciated by Otis was given constitutional embodiment in the Virginia Bill of Rights, adopted in 1776. . . .

A similar provision was included in the constitutions of most of the states by the close of the Revolutionary War. Its inclusion in the Bill of Rights, adopted in 1791, was regarded as imperative. Today, the constitution of every state in the Union has a similar clause.

B. *Lawful Searches.* The language of the Fourth Amendment clearly permits searches under the authority of a properly issued warrant. Although the amendment might have been interpreted to prohibit other types of searches, searches without warrants in certain types of circumstances—particularly the search of a moving vehicle and of a person incident to a lawful arrest—have been permitted.

The language of the Fourth Amendment could have been interpreted to imply that for a search or seizure to be "reasonable," the first essential condition to be satisfied is that it take place under the authority of a properly issued warrant. If that had been the interpretation, the only searches which the police could execute would be those under authority of a search warrant issued by a judicial officer.

The theory of the search warrant is that an independent judicial officer should review the reasons—"probable cause"—which led the police to believe that materials subject to seizure are in the place they wish to search; thus, the objectives advanced for requiring a search warrant include the following:

a. Searches should be conducted only upon "probable cause" to believe that certain material is located in a specific place.

b. The scope of the search should be limited to specific objects in a well-defined location.

c. The independent judgment of a judicial officer regarding the objectives in *a* and *b* should be obtained. Before a search warrant may be issued, a police officer must persuade a magistrate that he has reason to believe that particular objects are located in a particular place.

b. LIMITING ZEALOUS OFFICERS *

The point of the Fourth Amendment, which often is not grasped by zealous officers, is not that it denies law enforcement the support of the

* Johnson v. United States, 333 U.S. 10, 68 S.Ct. 367, 92 L.Ed. 436 (1948) (Justice Jackson).

usual inferences which reasonable men draw from evidence. Its protection consists in requiring that those inferences be drawn by a neutral and detached magistrate instead of being judged by the officer engaged in the often competitive enterprise of ferreting out crime. Any assumption that evidence sufficient to support a magistrate's disinterested determination to issue a search warrant will justify the officers in making a search without a warrant would reduce the Amendment to a nullity and leave the people's homes secure only in the discretion of police officers. Crime, even in the privacy of one's own quarters, is, of course, of grave concern to society, and the law allows such crime to be reached on proper showing. The right of officers to thrust themselves into a home is also a grave concern, not only to the individual but to a society which chooses to dwell in reasonable security and freedom from surveillance. When the right of privacy must reasonably yield to the right of search is, as a rule, to be decided by a judicial officer, not by a policeman or government enforcement agent.

3. EXCEPTIONS TO THE SEARCH WARRANT REQUIREMENT

a. OPEN FIELDS **

The most pressing issue in the pot wars concerns the "open fields" doctrine, which government lawyers say permits law enforcement officers to fly over or enter onto private land without warrants to search for illegal substances, notably marijuana plants. The doctrine was first stated by Justice Oliver Wendell Holmes more than 60 years ago: "[T]he special protection accorded by the Fourth Amendment to the people in their 'persons, houses, papers and effects,' is not extended to the open fields. The distinction between the latter and the house is as old as the common law." *Hester v. U.S.* (1924) 265 U.S. 57, 59.

The Supreme Court reaffirmed *Hester* last year in a case involving the warrantless search of a Kentucky farm for marijuana plants, stating, "There is no societal interest in protecting the privacy of those activities, such as the cultivation of crops, that occur in open fields." *Oliver v. U.S.* (1984) 104 S.Ct. 1735, 1741.

The problem in many Northern Californian counties, however, does not hang on a fine point of law. Marijuana growing is so pervasive that hundreds if not thousands of rural people have been affected by low-flying helicopter surveillance, leaving many non-pot-growing residents up in arms. Law enforcement may call it an "open fields" doctrine, they say, but all too often government sweeps amount to an "open season" on law-abiding citizens.

Helicopters are the key. All last year, from the sprouting of seedlings in early April through the September harvest, CAMP squads

** California Lawyer, Aug. 1985, pp. 46, 47. Copyright 1985 (Reprinted with permission).

buzzed up and down the hollows and over the mountain crests of Humboldt and Mendocino counties. Helicopter surveillance is necessary, CAMP officials say, because growers scatter their marijuana plants in small gardens all over the hills rather than place them in single large plots. Gardens of a dozen plants would be virtually impossible to find in any number without low-flying helicopters.

Residents claim such flights, occurring almost daily in the prime growing areas for three or four months at a time, terrorize children, cause cows to stop giving milk and in general wreak havoc on the countryside. Numerous other complaints contend that government agents were "out of control," regularly buzzed private homes as close as 50 to 150 feet above ground and turned the countryside into a "war zone."

Comment

Much of the law that has developed around the Fourth Amendment goes to the issue of defining basic terms. What, for example, is a search? What is a seizure? What is unreasonable? Even a term like "house" which seems familiar enough can generate considerable legal controversy. What is the boundary line for a house? When does the yard become an "open field"? What reasonable expectations of privacy should people have with respect to fields that they have cultivated? As the preceding excerpt suggests, this issue is especially relevant in the drug enforcement context.

b. OTHER COMMON EXCEPTIONS *

Because of the urgent nature of many law enforcement situations, most arrests and searches occur without warrants, and a number of Constitutionally acceptable exceptions to the warrant requirement have been recognized.

a. While the police are not permitted to search a house without a search warrant merely because they have "probable cause" to believe that there are seizable objects in it, they may search an automobile without a warrant when there is probable cause to believe it contains articles that offend against the law. This exception developed because of the mobility of automobiles and the problems of obtaining a search warrant in time to make an effective search before the car in question has been moved. . . .

b. The *search incident to a lawful arrest* is the most significant exception to the rule that searches must be made on warrant. In fact, the great majority of searches are incident to an arrest rather than under a warrant.

(1) The law permits an arresting officer to search the arrested person for concealed weapons, to deprive him of the means of escaping,

* William Cohen, Murray Schwartz and Dee Ann Sobul, *The Bill of Rights: A Sourcebook for Teachers,* California State Dept. of Education. Reprinted with permission.

and to prevent the destruction of evidence he may possess. Initially this exception to the requirement of a warrant for a search was probably justified as an emergency measure. However, serious differences of opinion and judgment have arisen as to whether a search of more than the immediate person of the one being arrested is really justified. . . .

The Search Warrant Controversy. Under the law a police officer may not simply search a home or a person whenever he wishes; he may not search even if he has "probable cause" to believe that the place he wishes to search contains contraband. He can search only if he has a warrant or if one of the exceptions to the search warrant requirement is present. This limitation on law enforcement activity has created a good deal of controversy.

a. Some persons would abolish the requirement of a search warrant altogether and permit the law enforcement officials to search on "probable cause" alone. They argue that the search warrant is an anachronism—a needless technicality which provides no protection to the individual.

(1) In practice, the warrant is signed as a matter of course by an uninterested, as opposed to a disinterested, judge. Practically, therefore, the independent judicial judgment that there is "probable cause," which the system presumes, is not assured.

(2) The urgency basis of the moving-car and arrest exceptions is also constantly present in modern life. Modern law enforcement requires that policemen be permitted to make on-the-spot search decisions without having to delay by referring to a magistrate for confirmation.

b. Other persons would rigidly enforce the search warrant requirement. They urge that in a democracy it is abhorrent to empower a police officer to decide by himself when an individual's privacy should be violated, when his home should be searched, or when his possessions should be seized.

(1) There should be vigorous enforcement of the principle that only the judiciary should be empowered to authorize these invasions of individual rights.

(2) The exceptions to the rule should be kept as narrow as possible, confined in scope, and limited to their peculiar circumstances. The power of law enforcement to invade individual rights should not be increased. . .

Comment

The question with which we will concern ourselves throughout the rest of the chapter is how to enforce the rights discussed in the previous excerpt. In a sense, these rights are a restriction on the police and could have been discussed in the previous chapter under "The Police and the Community." It has been the courts, however, which have taken up the burden of enforcing these rights and, as we will see, this has caused unique problems worthy of separate discussion.

D. THE EXCLUSIONARY RULE

1. PEOPLE v. DeFORE
Court of Appeals of New York, 1926.
242 N.Y. 13, 150 N.E. 585.

CARDOZO, J. A police officer arrested the defendant on a charge that he had stolen an overcoat. The crime, if committed, was petit larceny, a misdemeanor, for the value of the coat was not over $50. The defendant, when taken into custody, was in the hall of his boarding house. The officer, after making the arrest, entered the defendant's room and searched it. The search produced a bag, and in the bag was a blackjack. The defendant, after trial at Special Sessions, was acquitted of the larceny. In the meantime he had been indicted as a second offender for the possession of the weapon. He made a motion before trial to suppress the evidence obtained through search without a warrant. The motion was denied. He made objection again upon the trial when the bag and the contents, i.e., the blackjack and a hat, were offered in evidence by the people. The objection was overruled. He contends that through these rulings he has suffered a denial of his rights under the statute against unreasonable search and seizure.

.   .   .

The people stress the fact that the weapon was contraband, a nuisance subject to destruction. This might have justified the seizure, the abatement of the nuisance, if the weapon had been exposed to view. It might even have justified the refusal to return the weapon, though discovered by unlawful means. It did not justify the search. There is no rule that homes may be ransacked without process to discover the fruits or the implements of crime. To make such inquisitions lawful, there must be the support of a search warrant issued upon probable cause. .   .   .   Means unlawful in their inception do not become lawful by relation when suspicion ripens into discovery. .   .   .   We must determine whether evidence of criminality, procured by an act of trespass, is to be rejected as incompetent for the misconduct of the trespasser. .   .   .   For the high intruder and the low, the consequences become the same. Evidence is not excluded because the private litigant who offers it has gathered it by lawless force. By the same token, the state, when prosecuting an offender against the peace and order of society, incurs no heavier liability.

The federal rule as it stands is either too strict or too lax. A federal prosecutor may take no benefit from evidence collected through the trespass of a federal officer. The thought is that, in appropriating the results, he ratifies the means. .   .   .   The criminal is to go free because the constable has blundered.

.   .   .

We are confirmed in this conclusion when we reflect how far-reaching in its effect upon society the new consequences would be. The pettiest peace officer would have it in his power, through overzeal or indiscretion, to confer immunity upon an offender for crimes the most flagitious. A room is searched against the law, and the body of a murdered man is found. If the place of discovery may not be proved, the other circumstances may be insufficient to connect the defendant with the crime. The privacy of the home has been infringed, and the murderer goes free. Another search, once more against the law, discloses counterfeit money or the implements of forgery. The absence of a warrant means the freedom of the forger. Like instances can be multiplied. We may not subject society to these dangers until the Legislature has spoken with a clearer voice. In so holding, we are not unmindful of the argument that, unless the evidence is excluded, the statute becomes a form and its protection an illusion. . . . No doubt the protection of the statute would be greater from the point of view of the individual whose privacy had been invaded if the government were required to ignore what it had learned through the invasion. The question is whether protection for the individual would not be gained at a disproportionate loss of protection for society. On the one side is the social need that crime shall be repressed. On the other, the social need that law shall not be flouted by the insolence of office. There are dangers in any choice. . . .

Questions and Comment

Justice Cardozo's criticism of the exclusionary rule has become famous. Is it the case under the exclusionary rule that "the criminal is to go free because the constable has blundered?" What if, but for the blunder of the constable, the police would not have learned of the incriminating evidence in the first place? Moreover, what if the constable did not blunder but deliberately violated the Fourth Amendment? Do you think the police officer "blundered," or did he follow the normal practice of not obtaining a warrant?

The classic statement of the view contrary to Cardozo's is that of another great jurist, Justice Oliver Wendell Holmes, in his dissent in a wiretapping case: Olmstead v. United States, 277 U.S. 438, 469, 48 S.Ct. 564, 72 L.Ed. 944 (1928):

> We must consider the two objects of desire, both of which we cannot have, and make up our minds which to choose. It is desirable that criminals should be detected, and to that end that all available evidence should be used. It also is desirable that the Government should not itself foster and pay for other crimes, when they are the means by which the evidence is to be obtained. . . . I can attach no importance to protestations of disapproval if it knowingly accepts and pays [the offending police officer] and announces that in future it will pay for the fruits. We have to choose, and for my part I think

it a less evil that some criminals should escape than that the Government should play an ignoble part. . . .

Do any organs of society other than the courts have an interest in lowering the number of "blunders" by the police? If such blunders tended to violate the rights of the rich and powerful, it might be that the political processes would take a sufficient interest in the matter to better train, supervise and discipline the police. Studies, however, indicate strongly that it is more likely the poor, the ethnic minority, the juvenile or others of little political power whose Fourth Amendment rights are violated by police. In that case, can one argue that the exclusionary rule is the means by which the judiciary exerts pressure on politically powerful groups to see that the Fourth Amendment rights of *all* are protected?

Can you think of alternative methods (other than the exclusionary rule) for policing the police? Would any of these methods actually work?

2. MAPP v. OHIO

Supreme Court of the United States, 1961.
367 U.S. 643, 81 S.Ct. 1684, 6 L.Ed.2d 1081.

Mr. Justice CLARK delivered the opinion of the Court. . . .

On May 23, 1957, three Cleveland police officers arrived at appellant's residence in that city pursuant to information that "a person [was] hiding out in the home, who was wanted for questioning in connection with a recent bombing, and that there was a large amount of police paraphernalia being hidden in the home." . . . Upon their arrival at that house, the officers knocked on the door and demanded entrance but appellant, after telephoning her attorney, refused to admit them without a search warrant. They advised their headquarters of the situation and undertook a surveillance of the house.

The officers again sought entrance some three hours later when four or more additional officers arrived on the scene. When Miss Mapp did not come to the door immediately, at least one of the several doors to the house was forcibly opened and the policemen gained admittance. Meanwhile Miss Mapp's attorney arrived, but the officers, having secured their own entry, and continuing in their defiance of the law, would permit him neither to see Miss Mapp nor to enter the house. It appears that Miss Mapp was halfway down the stairs from the upper floor to the front door when the officers, in this high-handed manner, broke into the hall. She demanded to see the search warrant. A paper, claimed to be a warrant, was held up by one of the officers. She grabbed the "warrant" and placed it in her bosom. A struggle ensued in which the officers recovered the piece of paper and as a result of which they handcuffed appellant because she had been "belligerent" in resisting their official rescue of the "warrant" from her person. Running roughshod over appellant, a policeman "grabbed" her, "twisted [her] hand," and she "yelled [and] pleaded with him" because "it was hurting." Appellant, in handcuffs, was then forcibly taken upstairs to her bedroom where the officers searched a dresser, a chest of drawers, a closet and some suitcases. They also looked into a photo album and through personal papers belonging to the appellant. The search spread to the rest of the second floor including the child's bedroom, the living room, the kitchen and a dinette. The basement of the building and a trunk found therein were also searched. The obscene materials for possession of which she was ultimately convicted were discovered in the course of that widespread search.

At the trial no search warrant was produced by the prosecution, nor was the failure to produce one explained or accounted for. At best, "There is, in the record, considerable doubt as to whether there ever was any warrant for the search of defendant's home." . . .

. . . [T]his Court in Weeks v. United States, 232 U.S. 383, 34 S.Ct. 341, 58 L.Ed. 652 (1914), stated that

"the Fourth Amendment . . . put the courts of the United States and Federal officials, in the exercise of their power and authority, under limitations and restraints [and] . . . forever secure[d] the people, their persons, houses, papers and effects against all unreasonable searches and seizures under the guise of law . . . and the duty of giving to it force and effect is obligatory upon all entrusted under our Federal system with the enforcement of the laws." At pp. 391–392.

Specifically dealing with the use of the evidence unconstitutionally seized, the Court concluded:

"If letters and private documents can thus be seized and held and used in evidence against a citizen accused of an offense, the protection of the Fourth Amendment declaring his right to be secure against such searches and seizures is of no value, and, so far as those thus placed are concerned, might as well be stricken from the Constitution. The efforts of the courts and their officials to bring the guilty to punishment, praiseworthy as they are, are not to be aided by the sacrifice of those great principles established by years of endeavor and suffering which have resulted in their embodiment in the fundamental law of the land." At p. 393.

"The striking outcome of the *Weeks* case and those which followed it was the sweeping declaration that the Fourth Amendment, although not referring to or limiting the use of evidence in courts, really forbade its introduction if obtained by government officers through a violation of the Amendment." . . .

In 1949, 35 years after *Weeks* was announced, this Court, in

. . .

Wolf v. Colorado, ..., again for the first time, discussed the effect of the Fourth Amendment upon the States through the operation of the Due Process Clause of the Fourteenth Amendment. It said:

"[W]e have no hesitation in saying that were a State affirmatively to sanction such police incursion into privacy it would run counter to the guaranty of the Fourteenth Amendment."

. . .

Nevertheless, . . . the Court decided that the *Weeks* exclusionary rule would not then be imposed upon the States as "an essential ingredient of the right." . . . While in 1949, prior to the *Wolf* case, almost two-thirds of the States were opposed to the use of the exclusionary rule, now, despite the *Wolf* case, more than half of those since passing upon it, by their own legislative or judicial decision, have wholly or partly adopted or adhered to the *Weeks* rule. . . . Significantly, among those now following the rule is California, which, according to its highest court, was "compelled to reach that conclusion because other remedies have completely failed to secure compliance with the constitutional provisions . . .."

. . .

Today we once again examine *Wolf's* constitutional documentation of the right to privacy free from unreasonable state intrusion, and, after its dozen years on our books, are led by it to close the only courtroom door remaining open to evidence secured by official lawlessness in flagrant abuse of that basic right, reserved to all persons as a specific guarantee against that very same unlawful conduct. We hold that all evidence obtained by searches and seizures in violation of the Constitution is, by that same authority, inadmissible in a state court.

Since the Fourth Amendment's right of privacy has been declared enforceable against the States through the Due Process Clause of the Fourteenth, it is enforceable against them by the same sanction of exclusion as is used against the Federal Government. Were it otherwise, then just as without the *Weeks* rule the assurance against unreasonable federal searches and seizures would be "a form of words," valueless and undeserving of mention in a perpetual charter of inestimable human liberties, so too, without that rule the freedom from state invasions of privacy would be so ephemeral and so neatly severed from its conceptual nexus with the freedom from all brutish means of coercing evidence as not to merit this Court's high regard as a freedom "implicit in the concept of ordered liberty." . . . In short, the admission of the new constitutional right by *Wolf* could not consistently tolerate denial of its most important constitutional privilege, namely, the exclusion of the evidence which an accused had been forced to give by reason of the unlawful seizure. To hold otherwise is to grant the right but in reality to withhold its privilege and enjoyment. Only last year the Court itself recognized that the purpose of the exclusionary rule "is to deter—to compel respect for the constitutional guaranty in the only effectively available way—by removing the incentive to disregard it."

. . .

There are those who say, as did Justice (then Judge) Cardozo, that under our constitutional exclusionary doctrine "[t]he criminal is to go free because the constable has blundered." People v. Defore, 242 N.Y., at 21, 150 N.E., at 587. In some cases this will undoubtedly be the result. But, as was said in *Elkins,* "there is another consideration—the imperative of judicial integrity." 364 U.S., at 222. The criminal goes free, if he must, but it is the law that sets him free. Nothing can destroy a government more quickly than its failure to observe its own laws, or worse, its disregard of the charter of its own existence. As Mr. Justice Brandeis, dissenting, said in Olmstead v. United States, 277 U.S. 438, 485, 48 S.Ct. 564, 72 L.Ed. 944 (1928): "Our Government is the potent, the omnipresent teacher. For good or for ill, it teaches the whole people by its example. . . . If the Government becomes a lawbreaker, it breeds contempt for law; it invites every man to become a law unto himself; it invites anarchy." Nor can it lightly be assumed that, as a practical matter, adoption of the exclusionary rule fetters law enforcement. . . .

The ignoble shortcut to conviction left open to the State tends to destroy the entire system of constitutional restraints on which the liberties of the people rest. Having once recognized that the right to privacy embodied in the Fourth Amendment is enforceable against the States, and that the right to be secure against rude invasions of privacy by state officers is, therefore, constitutional in origin, we can no longer permit that right to remain an empty promise. Because it is enforceable in the same manner and to like effect as other basic rights secured by the Due Process Clause, we can no longer permit it to be revocable at the whim of any police officer who, in the name of law enforcement itself, chooses to suspend its enjoyment. Our decision, founded on reason and truth, gives to the individual no more than that which the Constitution guarantees him, to the police officer no less than that to which honest law enforcement is entitled, and, to the courts, that judicial integrity so necessary in the true administration of justice.

The judgment of the Supreme Court of Ohio is reversed and the cause remanded for further proceedings not inconsistent with this opinion.

Reversed and remanded.

Questions and Comment

The exclusionary rule as laid down by Mapp v. Ohio raises a host of sub-issues. First, if evidence is illegally seized from one person, can it be used against another person? Second, is evidence illegally seized by a private person, not in any way acting for the government, properly admissible in a criminal proceeding? Third, should evidence illegally seized by Government officials be usable in non-criminal litigation such as an attempt to take a battered child from the custody of allegedly unfit parents? Fourth, should such evidence be usable in a divorce suit between two private parties?

The decisions as to what are the consequences of illegally seized evidence are troublesome enough. Even more complex is the issue of just what kind of seizures of evidence are illegal. There is an enormous volume of litigation on this, and the rules—to the consternation of the police—are so complicated that they are constantly the subject of dispute among judges and learned commentators. Although the complexity of the rules forbids further discussion here, a safe statement as to these rules can probably be made: No person other than a lawyer can be sure, in a vast range of situations, whether a given search is legal or not. And even where the rules are clear it is likely that the legality of the search and seizure will depend on information not known to the subject of the search at the time. Certainly, the simple rule of thumb that searches always require warrants is far from accurate.

If this is so, does it cast any implications on the issue of whether the citizen should have a right forcibly to resist an illegal search or arrest by someone he knows to be a police officer? The states split on this issue.

3. ILLEGALLY SECURED EVIDENCE AND TWO MODELS OF THE CRIMINAL PROCESS *

The Crime Control Model. The police are bound to make mistakes, and it is of course desirable that these mistakes be minimized. Here, as elsewhere, the way to deal with mistakes is to afford a remedy for actual damages suffered by people whose privacy has been improperly invaded and to correct, by discipline and education, the future conduct of the officers who make the mistakes. It is unwise and unnecessary to provide the allegedly injured party with a windfall in the form of freedom from criminal conviction when his guilt is demonstrable.

There is no need for any special aid to private legal actions initiated for redress of illegal searches. The ordinary tort action that is available to law-abiding people when their interests have been invaded ought to be good enough for the criminal. Let him hire a lawyer, sue the police, and persuade a jury, if he can, that he has been actually damaged in a way that entitles him to monetary compensation. The discipline and education of the police is a matter, like any other problem of maintaining morale and standards in this large bureaucratic organization, for the police department itself. The "victim" is entitled to have his complaint considered; but he has no further interest, once the facts have been drawn to the attention of the proper departmental authorities.

In any event, there is no reason why evidence should not be used in the criminal process without regard to the manner in which it has been obtained. Here, unlike the problem of the confession, there is no question of trustworthiness or reliability. Physical evidence is physical evidence, regardless of how it is obtained. If one suspected of illegally

* Herbert Packer, *The Limits of the Criminal Sanction,* Stanford, Stanford University Press, 1968, pp. 198–201. © 1968 (Reprinted with permission).

possessing heroin is found to have heroin on the kitchen shelf, this supply of narcotics is reliable evidence of his guilt, whether the search that turned it up is later found by some judge to be legal or illegal.

The Due Process Model. The ordinary remedies for trespass upon one's property are totally deficient as a means for securing police compliance with rules regarding illegal searches and seizures. The victim usually is in no position to sue; even if he is, juries are notoriously unlikely to provide a remedy; and even if they do, police officers are often judgment-proof. Likewise, departmental discipline is an ineffective deterrent. The police are expected to get evidence upon which convictions may be obtained; if they do so, it is unlikely that their superiors will regard their illegal conduct as inefficient. The problem is that legality may mean inefficiency from the police stand-point, and efficiency is a value they tend to place above adherence to the finer points of constitutional law.

The only practical way to control illegal searches is to take the profit out of them. This means that any evidence illegally obtained cannot be permitted as evidence. It should be suppressed before or during trial; if it is not, convictions obtained in whole or in part on its basis should be reversed. Beyond that, any evidence obtained by leads provided by the result of an illegal search should also be banned so that there may be no easy evasion of the mandate. In doubtful cases, where it is unclear whether there is a connection or how strong it is, the standard should be one that resolves doubts most strongly against the proffered evidence whenever its discovery has been preceded by illegal searches. It may also be useful to enact a prophylactic rule that requires dismissal of the prosecution, not merely exclusion of the evidence, whenever an illegal search for evidence is shown to have taken place.

. . .

Comment and Questions

The exclusionary rule as to illegally seized evidence has generated an enormous amount of controversy. From a public relations point of view, it is the worst possible kind of rule because it only works at the behest of a person, usually someone who is clearly guilty, who is attempting to prevent the use against himself of evidence of his own crimes. As a result, in almost every case in which the rule is invoked, the behavior of the person invoking the rule was much more reprehensible than that of the police. Moreover, even if the newspapers do not make this clear, the policeman himself knows this and it offends his sense of justice.

On the other hand, the argument that the exclusionary rule prevents conviction of guilty people by no means settles the question. Any rule which actually enforced the demands of the Fourth Amendment (whatever they may be) would prevent the conviction of those who would be caught through evidence obtained in violation of the Fourth

Amendment. The problem with the exclusionary rule is that it works after the fact, so that by then we know who the criminal is, the evidence against him, and the other circumstances of the case. If there were some way to make the police obey, in advance, the commands of the Fourth Amendment, we would lose at least as many criminal convictions as we do today, but we would not know of the evidence which the police could discover only through a violation of the Fourth Amendment. Perhaps the real problem with the exclusionary rule is that it flaunts before us the price we pay for the Fourth Amendment.

By the way, is it true that the only people protected by the exclusionary rule are criminals with something to hide from the police? Is anyone else protected? How?

4. THE EFFECT OF THE EXCLUSIONARY RULE

a. THE LIMITED POWER OF THE SUPREME COURT *

According to Pär Lagerkvist, the role of the Pythia or priestess of the Oracle at Delphi was of incomparable grandeur and futility. This young maiden was periodically lashed to a tripod above a noisome abyss, where her god dwelt and from which nauseating odors rose and assaulted her. There, the god entered her body and soul, so that she thrashed madly and uttered inspired, incomprehensible cries. The cries were interpreted by the corps of professional priests of the Oracle, and their interpretations were, of course, for mere mortals the words of the god. The Pythia experienced incalculable ecstasy and degradation; she was viewed with utmost reverence and abhorrence; to her every utterance, enormous importance attached; but, from the practical point of view, what she said did not matter much.

On its tripod atop the system of American criminal justice, the Supreme Court of the United States performs in remarkably Pythian fashion. Occasional ill-smelling cases are wafted up to it by the fortuities of litigation, evoking its inspired and spasmodic reaction. Neither the records nor the issues presented by these cases give the Court a comprehensive view—or even a reliably representative view— of the doings in the dark pit in which criminal suspects, police and the functionaries of the criminal courts wrestle with each other in the sightless ooze. It is not surprising, then, that in these cases the Court should be incapable of announcing judgments which respond coherently to the real problems of the pit. No matter. The significance of the Court's pronouncements—their power to shake the assembled faithful with awful tremors of exultation and loathing—does not depend upon their correspondence with reality. Once uttered, these pronouncements will be interpreted by arrays of lower appellate courts, trial judges, magistrates, commissioners and police officials. *Their* interpre-

* Amsterdam, Anthony G., The Supreme Court and the Rights of Suspects in Criminal Cases, *45 N.Y.U.Law Rev.* 785 (1970). From *The Rights of Americans: What They Are—What They Should Be,* edited by Norman Dorsen. Copyright © 1970, 1971 by Random House, Reprinted by Permission of the Publisher.

tation of the Pythia, for all practical purposes, will become the word of god.

To some extent this Pythian metaphor describes the Supreme Court's functioning in all the fields of law with which the Court deals. But the metaphor has special cogency with regard to the field of criminal procedure and particularly procedure that regulates the rights of suspects in their dealings with police prior to the time of the suspect's first court appearance. . . .

First, the Supreme Court, like any other court, lacks the sort of supervisory power over the practices of the police that is possessed by the chief of police or the district attorney. The Court can only review those practices, and thus can only define the rights of suspects subject to those practices, when the practices become an issue in a lawsuit. There are several ways in which police practices may become the subject of a lawsuit. An individual who thinks that he has been mistreated by the police may file a civil action for damages or, in limited circumstances, for an injunction, complaining of false arrest or false imprisonment or assault or the violation of his constitutional rights. But such lawsuits are very rare, and until recently were so rare as to be insignificant, because the obstacles to their maintenance are formidable. Most persons mistreated by the police are marginal types who are quite happy, once out of police clutches, to let well enough alone. Few have the knowledge or resources to obtain the services of a lawyer. Many lawyers who might otherwise be available to them cannot afford to tangle with the police because these lawyers depend upon the good will of the police in other cases (e.g., to protect a divorce client who is being badgered by her estranged husband or to reduce charges against a criminal client) or upon police testimony in other cases (e.g., motor vehicle accident cases) or upon more dubious police services (e.g., referrals).

Juries are not sympathetic to suits against the police; policemen are seldom sufficiently solvent to make verdicts against them worth the trouble to obtain; even fairly solid citizens who sue policemen may have to fear reprisals in the form of traffic tickets, refusals to give needed aid and similar harassments. As a result, civil suits seldom bring police practices under judicial scrutiny. And for reasons too obvious to detail, criminal charges against policemen for mistreatment of citizens are even rarer than civil suits.

So, to date the Supreme Court has had occasion to review the conduct of police almost exclusively in criminal cases where the defendant is the asserted victim of police misconduct. The way in which the issue of police misconduct is presented in such cases almost invariably involves the application of the "exclusionary rule"—that is, an evidentiary rule which disallows the admission against a criminal defendant, at his trial, of certain kinds of evidence obtained in violation of his rights. This exclusionary rule, whose scope and utility in enforcing various constitutional guarantees has been considerably expanded by the Supreme Court in the past decade, is today the principal instrument of judicial control of the police and the principal vehicle for announcement by the courts of the rights of suspects in their dealings with the police.

This last point, in itself, has important implications. Certain police practices (for example, the "booking" and "mugging" of suspects and the assorted minor or major indignities that attend stationhouse detention of suspects, ranging from the taking of a suspect's belt and shoelaces to vicious beatings) will virtually never become the subjects of judicial scrutiny because they virtually never produce evidence against the suspect. Since there can arise no exclusionary rule challenges to these practices, there have been no significant judicial decisions concerning them; and since . . . judicial decisions are almost the only source of legal rights of suspects, suspects do not now have legal rights against or in connection with such practices.

Second, the Supreme Court of the United States is uniquely unable to take a comprehensive view of the subject of suspects' rights. In part its inability is simply a function of the Court's workload. Saddled with a back-breaking docket and properly occupied with other matters of grave national importance, the Court can only hear three or four cases a year involving the treatment of criminal suspects by the police.

Workload is not the Court's only problem.

Additional selective factors prevent many of the cases that are tried from being appealed or from being carried all the way to the Supreme Court. Factual findings by the trial judge concerning contested police conduct frequently obscure or entirely obstruct the presentation to appellate courts of issues relating to that conduct. A convicted defendant cannot challenge on appeal any treatment by the police that the trial court, crediting incredible police denials, finds did not occur. (For example, suspects invariably "trip" and strike their heads while entering their cells; they are never shoved against the bars by police.) Also, the trial court may admit the police conduct but credit incredible explanations of it. (For example, the humiliating anal examinations to which some suspects are subjected in police stations are justified as "weapons searches" on police testimony that such suspects are known to conceal razor blades between their buttocks.) Finally, the trial court may admit and resolve against the defendant an issue relating to the legality of police conduct, then sentence him so lightly that an appeal is not worthwhile.

Third, the Court is further disabled by the fact that almost the only law relating to police practices or to suspects' rights is the law that the Court itself makes by its judicial decisions. Statutes and administrative regulations governing these matters are virtually nonexistent. The ubiquitous lack of legislative and executive attention to the problems of police treatment of suspects both forces the Court into the role of lawmaker in this area and makes it virtually impossible for the Court effectively to play that role.

This point has been largely ignored by the Court's conservative critics. The judicial "activism" that they deplore, usually citing the Court's "handcuffing" of the police, has been the almost inevitable consequence of the failure of other agencies of law to assume responsibility for regulating police practices. In most areas of constitutional law the Supreme Court of the United States plays a backstopping role, reviewing the ultimate permissibility of dispositions and policies guided in the first instance by legislative enactments, administrative rules or local common-law traditions. In the area of controls upon the police, a vast abnegation of responsibility at the level of each of these ordinary sources of legal rulemaking has forced the Court to construct *all* the law regulating the everyday functioning of the police. Of course, the Court has responded by being "activist"; it has had to. Its decisions have seemed wildly "liberal" because the only other body of principles operating in the field, against which the Court's principles may be measured, are the principles under which individual policemen act in the absence of any legal restraint.

This same subconstitutional lawlessness which forces the Court to act also prevents it from acting informedly. . . . [W]hen the Court reviews conduct, such as police conduct, that is essentially ruleless, it is seriously impeded in understanding the nature, purposes and effects of what it is reviewing. Its view of the questioned conduct is limited to the appearance of the conduct on a particular trial record or records—records which may not even isolate or focus precisely upon that conduct. The Court cannot know whether the conduct before it is typical or atypical, unconnected or connected with a set of other practices or—if there is some connection—what is the comprehensive shape of the set of practices involved, what are their relations, their justifications, their consequences.

Operating thus darkly, the Court is obviously deprived of the ability to make any coherent response to, or to develop any organized regulation of, police conduct. Nor can the Court predict or understand the implications of any rule of constitutional law that it may itself project into this well of shadows. If the Court announces a decision striking down or modifying, for example, some rule of criminal trial practice, it can reasonably foresee how a trial will be conducted following its decision since its decision will operate within a system governed by other visible and predictable rules. But if the Court strikes down a police practice, announces a "right" of a criminal suspect in his dealings with the police, God only knows what the result will be. Out there in the formless void, some adjustment will undoubtedly be made to accommodate the new "right," but what the product of this whole exercise will be remains unfathomable. So, again, the Court is effectively disarmed.

Fourth, when and if the Supreme Court ventures to announce some constitutional right of a suspect, that "right" filters down to the level of flesh and blood suspects only through the refracting layers of lower courts, trial judges, magistrates and police officials. All pronouncements of the Supreme Court undergo this filtering process, but in few other areas of law are the filters as opaque as in the area of suspects' rights.

Let there be no mistake about it. To a mind-staggering extent—to an extent that conservatives and liberals alike who are not criminal trial lawyers simply cannot conceive—the entire system of criminal justice below the level of the Supreme Court of the United States is solidly massed against the criminal suspect. Only a few appellate judges can throw off the fetters of their middle-class backgrounds—the dimly remembered, friendly face of the school crossing guard, their fear of a crowd of "toughs," their attitudes engendered as lawyers before their elevation to the bench, by years of service as prosecutors or as private lawyers for honest, respectable business clients—and identify with the criminal suspect instead of with the policeman or with the putative victim of the suspect's theft, mugging, rape or murder. Trial judges still more, and magistrates beyond belief, are functionally and psychologically allied with the police, their coworkers in the unending and scarifying work of bringing criminals to book.

These trial judges and magistrates are the human beings that must find the "facts" when cases involving suspects' rights go into court (that is, when police treatment of a suspect is not conclusively masked behind a guilty plea or ignored by a defense lawyer too overworked or undercompensated to develop the issues adequately). Their factual findings resolve the inevitable conflict between the testimony of the police and the testimony of the suspect—usually a down-and-outer or a bad type, and often a man with a record. The result is about what one would expect. Even when the cases go to court, a suspect's rights as announced by the Supreme Court are something he has, not something he gets.

But, of course, for the reasons mentioned previously, most cases do not go to court. In these cases, the "rights" of the suspect are defined by how the police are willing to treat him. With regard to matters of treatment that have no evidentiary consequences and hence will not be judicially reviewable in exclusionary rule proceedings, the police have no particular reason to obey the law, even if the Supreme Court has had occasion to announce it. With regard to police practices that may have evidentiary consequences, the police are motivated to obey the law only to the extent that (1) they are more concerned with securing a conviction than with some other police purpose which is served by disobeying the law (in this connection, it is worth noting that police departments almost invariably measure their own efficiency in terms of "clearances by arrest," not by conviction), and (2) they think that they can secure the evidence necessary for conviction within the law.

Police work is hard work; it is righteous work; it is combative work, and competitive. Policemen are undereducated, they are scandalously underpaid, and their personal advancement lies in producing results according to the standards of the police ethic. When they go to the commander's office or to court, their conformity to this ethic is almost always vindicated. Neither their superiors nor the judges whom they know nor the public find it necessary to impede the performance of their duties with fettering rules respecting rights of suspects. If the Supreme Court finds this necessary, it must be that the Court is out of step. So its decisions—which are difficult to understand anyway—cannot really be taken seriously.

By what I have said so far, I do not mean to suggest that Supreme Court decisions respecting suspects' and defendants' rights are unimportant. Like the Pythia's cries, they have vast mystical significance. They state our aspirations. They give a few good priests something to work with. They give some of the faithful the courage to carry on and reason to improve the priesthood instead of tearing down the temple.

Also, they have *some* practical significance. With the Pythia shrieking underground, the priests may pervert the word of god, but they cannot ignore it entirely, nor entirely silence those who offer interpretations of it different from their own. Indeed, fear lest these alternative explanations gain popular support may cause the priests to bend a little in their direction.

Questions

Is it likely that if the courts stopped attempting to use the exclusionary rule to control police behavior, some other organ of society would take over the job? Or is it more likely that if the courts—and particularly the U.S. Supreme Court—stop that no effort at all will be made to control unconstitutional police behavior? Do any of the other organs of our society seem at all interested in the problem?

b. THE EXCLUSIONARY RULE'S IMPACT ON THE POLICE *

Twenty-five years ago, when Jerome Skolnick was collecting observations of the Oakland police department for his book *Justice Without Trial*, California had adopted the exclusionary rule seven years earlier. The department he studied, however, was still engaged in systematic violations of the Fourth Amendment. This important fact can be explained in several different ways. It may have been that not enough time had elapsed to achieve changes in organizational structure or motivation. It may have been that the Supreme Court had not yet reviewed enough cases to have provided detailed, working rules. It is also possible that other exogenous factors accounted for the failure to comply with the exclusionary rule. We tend to subscribe to this third explanation. Below we show that the social conditions generating pressure for bureaucratic rationalization of the police did not appear

* Jonathan Simon and Jerome H. Skolnick, "Federalism, The Exclusionary Rule, And The Police," in Power Divided: Essays on the Theory and Practice of Federalism, Harry N. Scheiber & Malcolm M. Feeley, Eds., Institute of Governmental Studies, University of California at Berkeley, 1989, pp. 79–81; 83–84 (Reprinted with Permission).

until the mid–1960s, and once they appeared, a higher rate of compliance with the exclusionary rule was one of the results.

During the 1950s and 1960s, in Oakland as in most urban police forces, the primary measure of compliance with organizational imperatives was arrest figures and clearance rates. As Skolnick showed, both were poor measures of competence. Police officers enjoy discretionary control over arrests. At the time field sergeants decided whether arrests were made for the right reasons, or whether arrests would hold up as cases moved through the criminal process. Similarly, detectives controlled clearance rates. Thus, the very agents supposedly evaluated by the device of arrest and clearance figures were in the best position to manipulate the results.

So long as police commanders focus on these statistics they cannot tell if the organization is accomplishing its aims. Furthermore, reliance on such measures sends a message about the organization's goals—"we care more about arrest and clearance than about conviction." But, as we shall see, the introduction of the exclusionary rule and a greater concern with conviction has helped to clarify police goals and to strengthen the management capabilities of police chiefs.

Observations of Oakland conducted by Skolnick and Simon between 1984 and 1988 suggest that adherence to the Fourt Amendment has improved significantly. This is, of course, a claim difficult to verify. We have not collected statistics, nor could a statistical test of legal compliance be fashioned. Our assertion that improvement is real stems in major part from two observed patterns.

First, we saw procedures designed to enforce the Fourth Amendment integrated into almost every sector of the policing enterprise. In an earlier version of this paper we call this a "legal archipelago" because it seemed as if a set of islands of legal values had been distributed throughout the broad experience of policing. We have come to see this as central to maintaining control over the police in a democratic society.

Second, we observed changes in the discourse and behavior of police officers. The idea of enforcing the Fourth Amendment has become normalized. Although police continue to disparage the exclusionary rule and lawyers in general, nevertheless at all levels police now routinely demonstrate a higher awareness and appreciation of procedure. Concern with proper procedures and legality is now as much a part of the job as using the radio. This change is both structural and ideological. There are four important aspects of this change.

1. *Training in legal and departmental rules.* In the early 1960s police received very little training in the law. Today it is a major part of police training. New cadets must pass tests, and veterans are resubjected to legal training on police procedures. Furthermore, training may be conducted alongside minorities and women who tend to infuse police recruits with more positive notions of legal and community responsibility.

2. *The role of the prosecutor.* Once distant and mistrusted, the prosecutor now is intimately involved with the police. His office produces legal update materials for the police, conducts training sessions, and works with the police during pretrial motions, the production of warrants, and the evaluation of cases. Indeed, the police now have their own legal specialists who transmit the norms of legality and an appreciation of procedures into the department.

3. *Visibility of police practices.* Police practices become more visible to higher managers and to prosecutors when evaluations are made on *convictions* rather than *arrests.* Convictions imply procedural knowledge. Police actions in the field are observable and subject to criticism from others when they deviate from procedural requirements. This internal law enforcement review process has facilitated the rise of a more rationalized form of managerial control over the police organization.

4. *Suppression motions.* Hearings to consider motions to suppress illegally seized evidence are now a normative ritual that powerfully links police and prosecution and reinforces police appreciation for legal procedures. As Harold Garfinkel speaks of the criminal trial as a "degradation ceremony," it is possible to view the suppression motion as a ceremony reinforcing the legal identity of the police officer. That dense wall of values that we often call "the police subculture" has not disappeared, but it has been modified by legal process norms—not only norms of procedure but also norms of fairness.

. . .

It is difficult to remember now how bitterly the exclusionary rule and court decisions expanding Fourth Amendment rights were greeted during the 1960s. In interviews we conducted with big city police chiefs at the 1985 meeting of the Police Executive Research Forum, the overwhelming message was that the exclusionary rule has become routinized. These chiefs—among the most thoughtful and progressive in the U.S.—acknowledge not only the importance of preserving evidence, but the importance of respecting the privacy of citizens. Besides, as compared with new challenges like civil lawsuits and police civilian review commissions, the exclusionary sanction has dimmed in significance.

c. EXCLUSIONARY RULE RUINS FEW FEDERAL CASES *

The Fourth Amendment exclusionary rule does not have a statistically large effect on federal prosecutions, the Comptroller General of the United States reports. A small percentage of cases considered for federal prosecution are lost or damaged by the operation of the rule. And only a small fraction of judicial and prosecutorial resources devoted to federal prosecutions is expended on dealing with motions to

* Vol. 25, *Criminal Law Reporter,* 2185–2186, May 23, 1979. Reprinted by special permission from *The Criminal Law Reporter,* © 1979 by The Bureau of National Affairs, Inc., Washington, D.C.

suppress. However, once a motion to suppress is granted, the government's chance of obtaining a conviction plunges dramatically.

The GAO study focused on 2,804 "defendant cases" handled by 38 U.S. Attorneys' offices from July 1 through August 31, 1978. Also covered by the study were 9,400 potential felony violations screened by these offices during the two-month study period.

Less than eleven percent of the defendants whose cases were closed during this period filed suppression motions based on the Fourth Amendment, the GAO found, although about one-third of the defendants who actually went to trial moved for suppression on Fourth Amendment grounds. As a group, these defendants did not appear to enjoy a high rate of success. The GAO studied the suppression rate in cases handled by U.S. Attorneys' offices that fit the "very large" and "large" categories. Eighty percent of these motions were denied in cases handled by the very large offices and 90 percent were denied in cases handled by large offices.

"Overall," the report states, "in only 1.3 percent of the 2,804 defendant cases was evidence excluded as a result of filing a Fourth Amendment motion." However, a successful motion to suppress was followed by a conviction rate of 50 percent or less, while convictions were obtained against more than 84 percent of the defendants whose motions to suppress were unsuccessful.

The study also found that the rule had little direct impact on the case-screening process. "About 15 percent of the defendants' cases screened involved search and seizure," the report says, and in only about 6.3 percent of the cases declined were there search and seizure issues. "But for those involving search and seizure that were declined, the U.S. attorneys indicated that search and seizure problems were the primary reason for declining only 6.3 percent of the cases. Thus, search and seizure problems are indicated as the primary declination reason in only about 0.4 percent of the total declined cases."

d. DOES THE EXCLUSIONARY RULE RUIN MANY STATE CASES? *

Into the current debate about the exclusionary rule, the staff of the National Institute of Justice (NIJ) has released a study of the rule's "practical effects" on state criminal justice operations. In its report, NIJ—the research arm of the U.S. Department of Justice—presents data concerning California cases in which prosecutions were rejected or dismissals obtained because of apparently violative searches and seizures.

NIJ first sought to describe the effects of the exclusionary rule upon police screening of arrests made by officers. Statewide data for such an analysis were not available, but the researchers found and

---

* James J. Fyfe, "Enforcement Workshop," 19 *Crim.Law Bulletin* 253–260, May-June 1983 © 1983 (Reprinted with permission).

were given access to records of all San Diego Police Department felony arrests during October 1981, in which the police department itself declined to forward cases to the prosecutor, but instead released arrestees without charges. Here, [it concluded that, in 1981, 130 cases were "lost" because of the exclusionary rule].

Both quantitatively and qualitatively, therefore, it is evident that the effects of the exclusionary rule on police screening of San Diego felony arrestees is minuscule in comparison to the effects of problems with victims and witnesses or evidence sufficiency. If 130 people, most of whom were arrested for drug offenses, were released by San Diego police because of search and seizure problems during 1981, it must be that more than 1,300 people, a far greater percentage of whom were arrested for crimes against people or property, were released for reasons other than the exclusionary rule. The major implication of that finding appears to be that eliminating problems with victims and witnesses and seeking means of developing evidence sufficient for successful prosecution would have far greater effect on the operations of San Diego's police arrest screening process than would any alteration of the exclusionary rule.

The NIJ study also examined the degree to which the exclusionary rule affected prosecutors' decisions to proceed against the arrestees brought to them by police. Statewide, the researchers report that 4.8 percent of the felony cases rejected for prosecution during 1976–1979 were rejected primarily because of search and seizure problems. Thus, more than twenty-four of every twenty-five cases rejected for prosecution were rejected for reasons other than the exclusionary rule. Further, as a percentage of *all* felony cases brought by police to California prosecutors, search and seizure rejections are infinitesimal. During 1976–1979, the study reports, California prosecutors were presented by police with 520,993 felony cases. Of these, they rejected 86,033 (16.5 percent), 4,130, of which (0.8 percent of total cases) were rejected for search and seizure reasons. In San Diego during 1980, the study reports, prosecutors were presented with 14,478 felony cases. Of these, they declined to proceed in 3,840 cases (26.5 percent), citing search and seizure problems in 327 cases (8.5 percent of total rejections; 2.3 percent of all felony cases). In the Los Angeles County District Attorney's Pomona office in 1981, prosecutors declined to proceed in 493 felony cases, fifty-eight (11.8 percent) of which involved search and seizure problems. NIJ researchers also selected a random sample of 432 felony cases rejected by the Los Angeles County District Attorney's Central Operations office in 1981, and found that sixty-three (14.6 percent) were rejected because of search and seizure problems.

What do these numbers show? They show that, in California as a whole, and in the San Diego and Los Angeles offices studied, the great majority of rejected cases involve prosecutory problems other than search and seizure. As both a percentage of cases rejected and as a percentage of all cases handled by prosecutors (where those data are available), therefore, search and seizure rejections are quite small.

Equally interesting is what the numbers do *not* show. Like the police screening figures presented in the study, the prosecutory rejection figures provide no information concerning the numbers of people who are searched under circumstances violative of the exclusionary rule, and who are released on the street without being arrested because they are found to be in possession of no contraband.

Conclusion

NIJ's study is certain to draw considerable attention and, as NIJ notes, to serve as a basis for arguments on both sides of the debate over the justification and need for alteration of the exclusionary rule. Even though the study does not address the *major* question in this debate— the effects of the rule on police misconduct—it is a valuable piece. It suggests that the rule affects very few of the felony cases that enter the California system, and that most of those it does affect involve drug offenses rather than crimes against persons or property. If the outcome of those cases is unsatisfactory, it may be best to alter police techniques of enforcing drug laws, rather than to consider alteration of a rule that is the best approach to deterrence of police misconduct the courts have been able to devise over the last 200 years. Similarly, if we are to earnestly seek means of assuring that those who have committed criminal acts do not escape liability for their misconduct, we should first explore means of reducing the relatively great number of cases in which prosecutions are dropped because of problems with witnesses, victims, and the sufficiency of evidence. Alongside those police and prosecutory problems, the exclusionary rule shrinks to insignificance from even the toughest law enforcement perspective.

Questions

Is it possible to argue that the police can be deterred by sanctions even though criminals cannot? On the other hand, is the exclusionary rule a sanction against the police—or rather is it against society as a whole?

If we do away with the exclusionary rule completely how else can we, as a practical matter, enforce the Fourth Amendment?

Given the findings of the Federal and State cases, do you think the Exclusionary Rule is defeating justice?

5. THE FUTURE OF THE EXCLUSIONARY RULE

a. DO AWAY WITH IT

CALIFORNIA v. MINJARES *

Mr. Justice REHNQUIST, with whom The Chief Justice joins, dissenting from denial of stay. I believe, that this case, [is] the

---

* Cert. denied, 443 U.S. 916, 100 S.Ct. 9,
61 L.Ed.2d 892 (1979).

culmination of a sport of fox and hound which was begun by this Court's decision in United States v. Weeks, 232 U.S. 383 (1914), 65 years ago. So many factors material to that decision, and to Mapp v. Ohio, 367 U.S. 643 (1961), which applied it to the States, have occurred after the rendition of these decisions that I think a re-evaluation of the so-called "exclusionary rule" enunciated by Weeks is overdue. . . .

The anomalous consequences of the exclusionary rule are readily apparent from an examination of the police conduct in this case. The officers who conducted the search were responding to a report of a robbery that had recently been committed. The robbery took place around 8:30 p.m., on December 19, 1975, at a Safeway Store in Fremont, California. It was committed in the presence of several witnesses by two individuals armed with handguns. One of the witnesses followed the two men, observed them get into a car, and trailed the car for several miles until he was able to identify it as a 1968 or 1969 Ford Fairlane and to write down the license number. The witness then went directly to the police station and reported what he had seen. At approximately 9:00 p.m., the police department broadcast a description of the getaway vehicle and its license number. Shortly thereafter, a Fremont police officer spotted a vehicle matching the description, called for backup units, and stopped the vehicle. The driver, respondent, was ordered out of the car, searched, and advised he was under arrest for robbery. He was the only person in the vehicle and fit the description of one of the suspects. The officers also searched the passenger compartment of the car, but neither that search nor the search of respondent revealed any evidence of the crime or the whereabouts of the second robber. After an unavailing attempt to locate the key to the car's trunk, the officers had the car towed to the city corporation yard. Upon its arrival, the officers picked the lock to the trunk and discovered it contained a red tote bag. They opened the tote bag, which contained clothing similar to that described by witnesses to the robbery, three guns, and a roll of pennies in a wrapper from the bank used by Safeway.

When the officer who initially stopped the vehicle was asked why he did not obtain a warrant while "making the decision to search the car and the trunk," he stated. "Basically, I think, time. In other words, by searching without the search warrant, we would save a matter of hours." He was then asked why time was a factor at this stage, and responded, "Well, we were still looking for a second suspect." The trial court denied respondent's motion to suppress the evidence discovered in the tote bag. Respondent was convicted of two counts of first-degree robbery and was found to have been armed at the time of his arrest. The Supreme Court of California, however, reversed the conviction. It concluded that although a warrantless search of an automobile, if based on probable cause to believe that the auto contains contraband or evidence of a crime, is permissible when it takes place after the auto has been towed to a police station, a search of a container in the automobile is invalid unless the officers first obtain a warrant.

The foregoing discussion reveals that respondent was apprehended as a result of conscientious police work, and that the subsequent search of the trunk of his auto occurred in the course of an ongoing investigation, while the second suspect was still on the loose. The case is thus not one in which the officers lacked probable cause to arrest respondent and to search the trunk of his auto and tote bag; it appears rather that "the criminal is to go free" solely because of a good-faith error in judgment on the part of the arresting officers, who were not sufficiently prescient to realize that while it was constitutionally permissible for them to search the trunk of an automobile at the city corporation yard under the exigency exception to the warrant requirement, courts would later draw a distinction between searching the trunk and a tote bag in the trunk. This distinction would obtain even though it was equally likely that the tote bag contained the evidence they were looking for and they had no reason, prior to opening the trunk, to anticipate that such evidence might be hidden from their view because it was in the tote bag.

I do not claim to be an expert in comparative law, but I feel morally certain that the United States is the only nation in the world in which the most relevant, most competent evidence as to the guilt or innocence of the accused is mechanically excluded because of the manner in which it may have been obtained.   . . .

Of course, the "primary" justification for the exclusionary rule is the need for deterrence of illegal police conduct. But since Mapp, various changes in circumstances make redress more easily obtainable by a defendant whose constitutional rights have been violated.

Four months prior to the decision in Mapp, this Court resurrected a long-dormant statute, § 1 of the Ku Klux Act, 42 U.S.C. § 1983, which gave a private cause of action for redress of constitutional violations by state officials. The subsequent developments in this area have, to say the least, expanded the reach of that statute. Monell v. Department of Social Services, 436 U.S. 658 (1978), made not only the individual police officer who may have committed the wrong, and who may have been inpecunious, but the municipal corporation which employed him equally liable under many circumstances. Bivens v. Six Unknown Agents, 403 U.S. 388 (1971), made individual agents of the Federal Bureau of Investigation suable for damages resulting from violations of Fourth Amendment guarantees. In addition, many States have set up courts of claims or other procedures so that an individual can as a matter of state law obtain redress for a wrongful violation of a constitutional right through the state mechanism.

In his dissent in Wolf v. Colorado, Mr. Justice Murphy disparaged civil actions as a remedy for illegal searches and seizures. Some of his objections have been vitiated by Monroe's provision of a federal forum for the dispute or by Monell's provision of a deep state pocket. As for other concerns voiced by Mr. Justice Murphy, I believe that modern juries can be trusted to return fair awards in favor of injured plaintiffs who allege constitutional deprivations. If, juries are capable of awarding damages as between injured railroad employees and railroads, they surely are capable of awarding damages as between one whose constitutional rights have been violated and either the agent or the government agency who violated those rights. Thus, most of the arguments advanced as to why the exclusionary rule was the only practicable means for enforcing the Fourth Amendment, whether or not they were true in 1949 or 1961, are no longer correct.

Comment and Questions

Is the real problem here not the issue of whether the exclusionary rule is an appropriate remedy for an unconstitutional search, but whether the search in Minjares should be held to be unconstitutional?

If it were unconstitutional, do you think a jury would have awarded damages to Mr. Minjares for the unlawful search of his tote bag containing the three guns used in robbing the Safeway store? Does Mr. Justice Rehnquist think so?

Another, less radical change in the exclusionary rule was suggested by Justice Byron White. He was prepared to hold * that the exclusionary rule:

> "should be substantially modified 'so as to prevent its application in those many circumstances where the evidence at issue was seized by an officer acting in the good-faith belief that his conduct comported with existing law and having reasonable grounds for this belief.' "

What are the advantages of such a rule? Would it have caused the suppression of the evidence in Minjares? What are the problems with such a rule?

It has also been suggested that to lower political costs of the exclusionary rule in terms of dissatisfaction with the judiciary and the whole criminal justice system, "The rule [should] not apply in the most serious cases—treason, espionage, murder and armed robbery or kidnapping by organized groups."

Such a rule would have the advantage of preventing such a gross disproportion between the magnitude of the policeman's constitutional violation and that of the crime where the exclusionary rule would otherwise work to free the criminal. What are the disadvantages of such a change in the rule?

b. LOOSEN THE STANDARDS FOR LEGALITY

Note on *Illinois v. Gates*

The police, in *Illinois v. Gates*, 462 U.S. 213, 103 S.Ct. 2317, 76 L.Ed.2d 527 (1983), had received a letter from an anonymous informant

---
* Stone v. Powell, 428 U.S. at 501, 96 S.Ct. at 3056.

that Lance and Sue Gates had "over $100,000.00 worth of drugs in their basement." The letter also contained information about the Gates' travel plans which, on the whole, checked out under police surveillance.

Under the prevailing rule, the so-called *Aguilar-Spinelli* test, judges who were issuing search warrants were required to make sure the police application for a warrant answered two questions. One was, "How does your informant know what he is talking about?"; the other was, "How do you know that your informant is a truthful person?" The warrant, therefore, should not have been issued because the police could not say whether or not the informant was truthful, or how the informant came to know.

Justice Rehnquist, writing for the majority, laid down a new rule regarding what constitutes "probable cause" for the issuance of a search warrant when an informant is relied upon to establish that elusive concept.

The new rule directs judges to weigh only the "totality of the circumstances" before issuing the warrant. The informant's reputation for "veracity" and her "basis of knowledge" could be considered as part of the circumstances, he said, but strict reliance on these factors was held to be hyper-technical.

Critics of this new rule have argued that, under it, the police are given very little direction as to what they should think about when presenting the judge with a warrant. Can you figure out the meaning of "totality of the circumstances?" Does it seem to offer too much discretion to judges who issue warrants?

c. ADOPT A "GOOD FAITH" EXCEPTION

Note on *U.S. v. Leon*

The *Leon* investigation began when an informant—of unproven reliability—told a police officer that two people were selling large quantities of narcotics from their residence. How did the informant know? He said he had seen a narcotics sale there five months earlier. The police responded to the tip by watching that residence plus a couple of others. They observed suspicious activities that they, "as experienced and well-trained narcotics investigators", felt indicated trafficking in drugs. Based on their observations, and the informant's information, the officers prepared a warrant application to search three residences. A search warrant was issued and the ensuing searches produced large quantities of narcotics.

The case came before a Federal District Court judge who ruled that the police had acted in good faith by obtaining a warrant, but that the facts did not establish "probable cause." The judge reasoned that "probable cause" was not established for two reasons: First, the police did not know beforehand whether the informant was a truthful person; and second, since the informant had allegedly seen the narcotics sale five months earlier, the tip was stale. If the "totality of the circumstances" in *Illinois v. Gates* rule had been operative, perhaps the court would have ruled that "probable cause" had been established, but at the time the *Aguilar-Spinelli* rule was still in effect.

In any event, in *U.S. v. Leon*, 468 U.S. 897, 104 S.Ct. 3405, 82 L.Ed. 2d 677 (1984), the government argued for a different kind of a rule—if, in good faith, the police succeed in obtaining a search warrant from a judge, evidence seized in the search should be admitted at trial. The U.S. Supreme Court sided with the government in *Leon*. It said that the purpose of the exclusionary rule is to deter police misconduct. But because officers who act in good-faith reliance on a warrant don't intentionally violate the fourth amendment, the exclusionary rule cannot deter them.

Justice Brennan, in his dissent, argued that the purpose of the exclusionary rule is not to deter the *individual* police officer, but to establish standards of conduct for training police officers and to incorporate Fourth Amendment values into their investigative practices.

> "If the overall educational effect of the exclusionary rule is considered, application of the rule to even those situations in which individual police officers have acted on the basis of a reasonable but mistaken belief that their conduct was authorized can still be expected to have a considerable long-term deterrent effect."

With whom do you agree? Do you think that the exclusionary rule should primarily be construed as a deterrent to the individual officer? Or should it be seen as a means of educating the police, generally, through exclusion of illegally seized evidence? If police obeyed the law by conforming to the requirements of the Fourth Amendment, would evidence ever need to be excluded?

A serious problem with the *Leon* decision is suggested by the seven city study of the search warrant process conducted by the National Center for State Courts. Writing in the *Yale Law Journal*, Professor Steven Duke summarizes the findings of that study as follows:

> The warrant practices described in the NCSC study are a litany of perversions of the Fourth Amendment. Many of the magistrates regarded themselves as adjuncts to law enforcement. In 43% of the cases, magistrates reviewing warrant applications failed to ask even a single question. When a question was asked, it was often answered by referring to something in the application, which implies that the magistrate asked the question as a substitute for reading the application. A median time of 2.2 minutes was spent in the application process. Shopping for rubber stamp magistrates was commonplace. The applications almost always contained boilerplate. Police sometimes sought and magistrates granted warrants that all knew were illegal, in order to get contraband "off the street" or to harass somebody. It is inconceivable that 95%, or even 80%, of these warrants were lawful.

Recall Justice Brennan's justification for the exclusionary rule—that it is intended to educate police regarding the Fourth Amendment rights of citizens. Recall that Simon and Skolnick (pp. 275–277) found that the exclusionary rule offered police a powerful incentive to develop Constitutional values. Will the good faith exception undermine this incentive? If the judges have so much difficulty absorbing the lessons of the Fourth Amendment, what can we really expect from the police? Does the National Center for State Court Study show how hard it is even for trial judges not to be swayed by factual guilt? Might the same pressures be operating on appellate courts?

E. RECOMMENDED READING

Baker, Liva. *Miranda: Crime, Law and Politics.* Atheneum, New York, © 1983. Reprinted with permission.

Berger, Mark. *Taking the Fifth: The Supreme Court and the Privilege Against Self-Incrimination.* Lexington Books, Lexington, Mass., 1980.

Kamisar, Yale. *Police Interrogation and Confessions: Essays in Law and Policy.* Univ. of Michigan Press, Ann Arbor, 1980.

Levy, Leonard. *Origins of the Fifth Amendment.* Oxford Univ. Press, New York, 1968.

Lykken, David T. *A Tremor in the Blood: Use and Abuse of the Lie Detector.* McGraw-Hill Book Co., New York, 1981.

Matte, James Allen. *The Art and Science of the Polygraph Technique.* Charles C. Thomas, Springfield, Ill., 1980.

Way, Frank H. *Criminal Justice and the American Constitution.* Duxbury Press, North Scituate, Mass., 1980.

Chapter VI

THE ROLE OF THE ATTORNEY

A. THE ADVERSARY SYSTEM AND THE ROLE OF THE LAWYERS AND JUDGE *

The theory of the adversary system of adjudication is perhaps most clearly distinguished by its sharply defined roles for litigants and judge. Normally the system of judicial decision-making in an adversarial proceeding envisions two contestants—or, more precisely, their representatives—arguing their cases before a neutral and largely passive judge. The adversary process proceeds by pitting the two partisan advocates against each other and having their differences resolved by the judge, who bases his or her decision upon legal principles and the evidence presented by the adversaries. The judge has no staff or resources to make an extended, independent investigation, and the norms associated with the adversary system require that the judge's decision be based upon the evidence presented by the contesting parties. What they do not present the judge cannot consider, and what they stipulate the judge cannot easily question. This same passive role extends to juries as well. Because of this the adversary system has often been likened to a battle or sporting event in which the litigants are the players and the judge and jury are the umpires.

Correlative to this, it is the task of the advocates to present their clients in the best possible light. Extending the analogy of the sporting event, the goal of the advocate is focused and limited. In the adversary system the goal of the advocate is not to determine truth but to win, to maximize the interests of his or her side within the confines of the norms governing the proceedings. This is not to imply that the theory of the adversary process has no concern with truth. Rather, the underlying assumption of the adversary process is that truth is most likely to emerge as a by-product of vigorous conflict between intensely partisan advocates, each of whose goal is to win. Thus, the duty of the advocate in the adversary system is to present his or her side's position in the very best possible light and to challenge the other side's position as vigorously as possible.

Although often criticized for elevating partisan interests above the search for truth and justice, the adversary process is also defended as the most effective means of getting at the truth and rendering justice. Defenders argue that the clash of limited and partisan interests—

* Malcolm Feeley, "The Adversary System", in Robert J. Janosik (ed.) *Encyclopedia of the American Judicial System,* Scribners, New York, 1987, pp. 753–755 (Reprinted with permission of the author).

through the making of claims and counterclaims, challenges and counterchallenges, examinations and cross-examinations—is most likely to yield the maximum of relevant information and subject it to careful scrutiny and, in so doing, be most likely to expose falsehood and reveal truth. The sharply defined and antagonistic roles, it is felt, foster thoroughness and vigor that might be absent in a more cooperatively organized process.

In his defense of the adversary system, Richard Posner likens the adversary system to competition in the market. Just as customers, he argues, are most likely to make the best choices if they have the benefit of fiercely competitive salesmen, each of whom extols the virtues of his or her own product and raises questions about the other's, so too a judge is most likely to gain the most and best information for making the fairest decision after listening to the arguments of two vigorous and fiercely partisan advocates.

The distinctive features of the theory of the adversary system are perhaps best appreciated when contrasted to other styles of adjudication. In general, the norms that govern inquisitorial systems more directly assign truth-seeking roles to each of the central actors in the process. Rather than being a by-product of the activities of fierce partisans whose conflict is umpired by a passive judge, inquisitorial systems envision a more active role for the judge and, correspondingly, a less active role for the advocates, at least in courtroom proceedings. In theory, the judge dominates the formal proceeding by actively questioning witnesses, requesting information, and in some systems— for example, the French judge d'instruction—actually supervising the pretrial investigation and marshaling the evidence. If the judge in an adversarial system can be likened to a consumer assessing the positions of competitive salesmen, the judge in an inquisitorial system might be likened to a leader of a seminar, the collective goal of which is to get at the truth and each of whose members is expected to volunteer what they know. In the criminal process, where practices in adversarial and inquisitorial systems are distinguished most sharply, this difference is underscored by the fact that in inquisitorial systems there are fewer safeguards of a defendant's interests and the judge assumes a more active role in questioning witnesses. . . .

Defenders of the adversary system claim that in an inquisitorial system an advocate's dual role as representative of client interests and coseeker of truth conflict with one another. If one is to be a zealous advocate, they maintain, he or she cannot simultaneously be an active participant in the cooperative and joint venture of discovering the whole truth. Zealous advocacy, they insist, requires that an advocate refrain from doing anything that hurts a client and requires that the advocate emphasize only those things that advance a client's interests. Perhaps the classic expression of this limited and highly focused role of the advocate in an adversary system is found in Lord Brougham's well-known observation made in the course of defending Queen Caroline:

An advocate, in the discharge of his duty, knows but one person in all the world, and that person is his client. To save that client by all means and expedients, and at all hazards and costs to other persons, and, amongst them, to himself, is his first and only duty; and in performing this duty he must not regard the alarm, the torments, the destruction which he may bring upon others. Separating the duty of a patriot from that of an advocate, he must go on reckless of the consequences, though it should be his unhappy fate to involve his country in confusion.

Comment

As you read through the balance of the material in this chapter, ask yourself to what extent the reports of criminal lawyers in action in fact reflect the theory of the adversary system described above.

B. THE PROSECUTING ATTORNEY

1. INTRODUCTION

THE OFFICE OF THE PROSECUTOR *

In the American system of criminal justice the prosecutor differs markedly from his counterpart in the systems from which our legal institutions spring—the Roman Law and the English Common Law. In continental Europe the prosecutor is an appointed permanent or career official and has a different and closer relationship to the court, giving him in some respects certain advantages and in other respects less autonomy than the American prosecutor. He is generally not considered as part of the practicing bar nor does he participate in lawyers' associations. While he is like his American counterpart in being a key figure in the administration of criminal justice, his authority stems from being part of a central rather than a local government.

In England, prosecution is administered by a Director of Public Prosecutions, who is a career official and a subordinate of a cabinet minister. The actual trial of cases, however, is assigned to barristers in private practice designated as Crown Counsel. A British barrister may prosecute for the Crown in one case and act for the defense in others. The Crown Counsel has no part in preliminary decisions as to whether to prosecute or what particular crimes are to be charged; in court he functions as a professional advocate.

The American prosecutor, representing the executive branch under a system of divided powers defined in a written constitution, is an officer of the court only in the same sense as any other lawyer. He is not a career official or civil servant; relatively few American prosecu-

* American Bar Association Standards for the Administration of Criminal Justice, *Standards Relating to the Prosecution Function and the Defense Function* (Chica-go, 1970), pp. 17–20, 51–52. Available from American Bar Center, 1155 East 60th St., Chicago, Illinois 60637.

tors have devoted their entire professional lives to this work. At the state level, he is usually an elected local official, largely autonomous and generally having no ties with the chief officer of the executive branch of which he is a part, nor even with the Attorney General of the state.

The political process has played a significant part in the shaping of the role of the American prosecutor. Experience as a prosecutor is a familiar stepping stone to higher political office. The "D.A." has long been glamorized in fiction, films, radio, television and other media. Many of our political leaders had their first exposure to public notice and political life in this office. A substantial number of executive and legislative officials as well as judges have served as prosecuting attorneys at some point in their careers. The political involvement of a prosecutor varies. In most jurisdictions he is required to run with a party designation. In some places prosecutors are elected on a nonpartisan basis. The powers of a prosecutor are formidable and he is an important personage in his community. If he is not truly independent and professional, his powers can be misused for political or other improper purposes. Perhaps even more than other American public officials, the prosecutor's activity is in large part open to public gaze—as it should be—and spotlighted by the press. The importance of his function is such that his least mistake is likely to be magnified, as are many of his successful exploits.

Traditionally, the American prosecutor is a local official whose area of responsibility is limited to a particular district, county or city. Division of prosecutorial responsibility on this basis serves to emphasize the need for the prosecutor to be responsive to local conditions. His familiarity with the community aids him in gathering evidence, in allocating his resources to the various activities of his office, and in appraising the disposition appropriate to particular offenses and offenders.

The emphasis on a locally functioning prosecutor and a large, if not unlimited, autonomy for such official stemmed from early American experience with distant Crown officials not responsive to local attitudes and traditions. What began as a valid opposition to non-representation and non-responsive officialdom took root and became a parochialism which persists today in spite of vastly changed conditions and manifests itself in an unreasoning opposition to statewide coordination of the prosecution function designed to promote reasonable uniformity of policies and practices.

There are two major problems with the present system of prosecutorial offices which require attention. The first is the lack of coordination among prosecution offices resulting from their autonomy.

The other major source of difficulty is the existence of offices based on small territorial areas. Many territorial units are too small in terms of population to support more than a part-time office. In at least

32 states a majority of the prosecutors devote half or less of their time to the prosecutorial duties of their office.

Questions and Comment

In most Western nations, the prosecutor is a career civil servant. Does the fact that the prosecutor's office in the United States is often seen as a stepping stone to higher political office have any influence on the criminal justice system in this country?

In your area, is the prosecutor's a partisan political office? Is it an office for which contested elections are, in fact, held?

In many jurisdictions, the local prosecutor, after being initially appointed, has run successfully for re-election on many occasions. Often he retires between elections so that his successor can be re-appointed and run for re-election as an incumbent. Does this solve some of the problems of the elected prosecutor? Does it raise others?

2. THE PROSECUTORIAL DISCRETION

a. INTRODUCTORY NOTE

Just as we worried, in Chapter IV, about police discretion and its possible abuses, we must also worry about the discretion of the prosecutor. In certain other countries, the institution of private prosecution is maintained, whereby a private citizen can cause the initiation of a criminal prosecution. In the United States, however, the prosecutor is given final authority for this decision—subject only to being voted out of office if the citizenry is sufficiently outraged over his failure to prosecute, or, in some states, to the power of the State Attorney General to remove him for misfeasance in office.

This problem, of course, would not be very serious if it were practical to direct the prosecutor to prosecute all violations of the law discovered by the police. In fact, just as the police cannot possibly have sufficient resources to apprehend all those committing crimes, the prosecutor lacks sufficient resources to try all whom the police apprehend. As a result, he will have to make choices, and it is the choices he makes and the ways he goes about making them that account for the importance and interest of the prosecutorial discretion.

b. HOW IT WORKS

(1) IN A FEDERAL PROSECUTOR'S OFFICE *

. . . . Faced with the problem of making the most effective use of their limited time and energies, and with that of staying out of trouble with each other, the United States Attorney, the judges, the press and

* John Kaplan, "The Prosecutorial Discretion—A Comment," *Northwestern Law Review,* 60 (1965), 174, 178–193. ©1965 (Reprinted with permission).

K., S. & F. Crim.Justice 5th Ed. FP—11

the bar, the assistants ** over the years had evolved a largely tacit but nonetheless real set of standards for making the prosecutorial decision.

The first and most basic standard was the assistant's view of the accused's guilt of the crime to be charged. It was generally agreed that, regardless of the strength of the case, if the prosecutor did not actually believe in the guilt of the accused, he had no business prosecuting. This was more than a mere question of prosecutorial policy. The great majority, if not all, of the assistants felt that it was morally wrong to prosecute a man unless one was personally convinced of his guilt. Of course, to reach this decision, the assistant might rely on much more than the evidence he could introduce at trial. He might consider the statements of informers whose identity could not be disclosed, illegally seized materials, hearsay, rumor, and many other more or less reliable bits of information.

. . .

In two types of cases, however, the ethic regarding belief in guilt appeared to be somewhat relaxed. First, where the physical facts were clear, prosecution might be undertaken even though the prosecutor had an honest doubt as to whether the act charged was committed with the necessary willfulness [i.e. mens rea] or whether the defendant was somehow unaware of what any reasonable man would know. In this situation the assistant would often say, "Who knows how stupid a man can be?" and leave this question to the jury. A second category of cases existed where prosecution was much harder to justify. Commonly, in tax evasion cases where husband and wife had signed a fraudulent return, both might be prosecuted even though the assistant felt that only the husband was guilty. Otherwise the prosecutor might be faced at trial by the wife's testifying for her husband that she kept all the family's private records and that she alone was responsible for the fraud. Such testimony is often effective and difficult to refute since only the husband and wife know exactly what happened.

. . . Occasionally, in conspiracy cases, for similar reasons, those on the fringes might be prosecuted despite genuine doubt as to whether their involvement was sufficiently great. Otherwise they might either take the entire blame themselves or, more likely, testify as to the complete innocence of the central figures. In the latter case, their testimony might be especially damaging where they were not themselves accused and had no apparent motive to falsify. Thus, as a general principle, a far lower degree of belief in guilt (or perhaps even none at all) seemed to be required when the question was whether the subject under consideration should be joined as a co-defendant with one whom the prosecutor did believe to be guilty.

Assuming, then, as was generally assumed in the office, that the prosecutor believed the prospective defendant to be guilty, the next

** The informal name used for assistant United States Attorneys. The United States Attorney, the local federal prosecutor, is appointed at the pleasure of the President and serves under the general direction of the Attorney General. The assistants serve under the U.S. Attorneys.

fundamental question to be asked was whether, in light of the habits of judges and juries in the area, the case could be expected to result in a conviction. Though the assistant might regard differing probabilities of conviction as sufficiently high in different types of cases, prosecution would almost never be commenced unless the chances of success seemed better than fair. Not only was the staff generally hard pressed to accommodate all of the cases which should have been brought to trial, but the assistants regarded the time and money spent on an unsuccessful prosecution as completely wasted. Assistants would often phrase this: "There are enough cases that we can win without bringing any of the other kind." Moreover, retaining a high rate of conviction was important in encouraging guilty pleas, one of the principal means of hoarding the scarce resources of prosecutorial time and effort.

In addition to these "governmental" factors, there were many personal ones which tended to influence an assistant toward declining prosecution in doubtful cases. If the assistant making the decision expected to try the case himself, his previous record—often a matter of status within the office—would be at stake. And if he both authorized and tried a losing case, it would be hard for him to contend that he did not make an error in one action or the other. Moreover, since the criticism or, more usually, unwelcome sympathy, produced by the loss of a case was generally far in excess of the congratulations produced by a winning one, the assistant did not wish to authorize his own prosecution of a dubious case or saddle one of his cohorts with the trial of a "turkey." Finally, most assistants felt that it was not right to use the prosecutorial system just to harass an individual, however guilty he might be and hence, unless the case could be won, it was morally wrong to prosecute it.*

There were also some very personal reasons for the assistant to exercise caution in authorizing prosecution. Although he was under relatively little supervision in his daily activities, he had to be careful to stay in the good graces of the United States Attorney, who, holding an essentially political position, was very sensitive to the criticism of the press, the judges, and the defense bar, all of whom were quick to note a rising number of acquittals and ascribe this to either incompetence in the staff or to overzealousness in the choice of targets for prosecution. The feeling that it was important to make certain that the office came under no undue criticism applied with additional force where the defendant was prominent in the community. Though such prosecutions, of course, were not always successful, it was generally felt that where the public eye would be on the prosecution, the criticism would be all the more severe if the case were lost. As a result, it was

---

* The whole problem of the moral restraints upon the government attorney is a very complicated one. In essence the prosecutor is both attorney and client. While the ordinary private attorney may have a duty to point out to his client the moral aspects of a case he will often assist his client to the full benefit the law allows. The government attorney being an official as well as an attorney may have the duty to make sure that he does not allow unconscionable conduct on the part of his "client," regardless of the particular law.

often stated that "if you go after a big one, you must be pretty sure you can get him."

On the other hand, in some types of cases, prosecution was undertaken even though the chances of conviction appeared somewhat less than was usually demanded. Although it would seem that a case lost through suppression of essential government evidence is just as thoroughly lost as one where a jury has acquitted, assistants generally prosecuted on a smaller likelihood of conviction where the decisive question was one of search and seizure. This type of issue could generally be disposed of far more easily and quickly than a jury trial, and hence much less effort was wasted by a wrong decision to prosecute. Moreover, the loss of a motion to suppress was generally not considered as part of the assistant's batting average and thus not regarded as nearly so damaging to his prestige as an acquittal by a jury.

. . .

Prosecution was undertaken in certain other situations where the chances of conviction fell somewhat below the norm. In the case of the more serious crimes, it was often felt that the accused should be put on trial even though prosecution might routinely be declined for a lesser crime where conviction was equally uncertain. In fact, in a few cases where the defendant was believed to be guilty of previous offenses and likely to commit future ones unless prevented, the assistant concluded that he was justified in taking a considerably greater chance of losing the case in order to attempt a conviction—a conclusion which was fortified where the case under consideration appeared to be as good a one as the investigatory agency could obtain. On the other hand, the weaker the case, the more difficult it became to justify the prosecution and the greater the weight the assistant gave to the view that an unsuccessful prosecution would only both embolden the defendant and make later prosecution, perhaps on a stronger case, more difficult. And where it appeared that even on conviction the accused would be unlikely to receive what the assistant felt was a severe enough sentence, the assistant tended to conclude that the possible gains were not worth the effort and decline prosecution until either a stronger case or one more likely to result in sufficient punishment came along.

[Most] interesting are those cases where the government's case looked strong on paper, but for some reason lacked jury-appeal. Fortunately, the problem faced by many local prosecutors of juries refusing to convict one Negro for a crime against another was not common. One reason was that the majority of crimes where this effect was most noticeable—knifings, beatings and theft—were state not federal offenses. However, assistants would decline prosecution in a host of cases where experience indicated that juries were loathe to convict. These included . . . where for one reason or another crucial witnesses are reluctant to testify, for in many cases reluctant witnesses are bad witnesses; cases where the credibility of the government witnesses was open to attack because they were convicted felons; and cases where the government's case was built upon the testimony of an admitted accomplice who either was not being prosecuted or who expected to receive a lighter sentence for his testimony. In the latter type of case, the prosecution would have had to overcome not only the jury's scepticism as to the quality of the testimony, but also its sense of unfairness at the unequal treatment given to two wrongdoers.

The assistant in deciding to prosecute had to consider not only the worth of the prosecution's testimony but also the likelihood of its availability. Thus in one case where a crucial link in the prosecution case would have had to be the evidence of an aged and infirm woman, the assistant felt she was so unlikely to be available at the time of trial that he could not justify a decision to incur all the cost and difficulties of prosecution. . . .

In calculating the likelihood that he would be able to prove the facts at issue, the assistant had to realize that certain crimes, by their nature, seemed to demand a higher quantum of proof than did others. Thus, assistants hesitated before authorizing prosecutions for receipt of stolen goods. The witnesses for the prosecution tended to be admitted thieves, and circumstances refuting the usual defense, a good faith purchase without knowledge of theft, were difficult to come by. Commonly, the defendant was from the middle class with no previous record, and the assistant realized that in such a case the jury would not only find it easy to identify with him, but would also regard his conviction as a more serious matter, requiring a higher standard of proof. . . .

On the other hand, just as certain crimes seemed to require more than normal proof, others seemed to require less. In a narcotics case, if the prosecution could survive a motion to suppress and a motion for a directed verdict of acquittal, the odds would be heavily in its favor. Jury acquittals in narcotics cases were extremely rare, even in cases where the evidence was not strong.

The calculation of the chances of conviction often included factors other than the intrinsic strength of the government case. The assistant would consider the competence of the agent who had done the investigation, and where he regarded the agent as unreliable, . . . the assistant would probably agree to prosecution only if he was satisfied that, even discounting for any unforeseen difficulties which might arise and for the inability of the agency to throw in emergency manpower to straighten things out, the case still was sufficiently likely to produce a conviction. Thus, the proportion of close cases where prosecution was declined varied not only among agents but among agencies as well.

Similarly, the schedule for assignment of judges, where this could be determined, exerted an influence on the pattern of authorizations and declinations of prosecution. When a judge who was known to be a light sentencer was in a position to receive the pleas of guilty, the number of such pleas would rise, and the assistant would therefore raise his estimate of the chances of successfully terminating the prosecution he was asked to authorize. He would not raise his estimate by a great deal, however, as he had to allow a margin of safety in case for some reason the defendant chose to go to trial. For various administrative reasons it was far easier to decline prosecution in the first instance than to *nolle prosse* a case after indictment. The latter course required the approval of the Department of Justice where many of the attorneys, not trying cases themselves, seemed perennially sanguine about the chances of persuading juries and hence were extremely reluctant to allow dismissal of cases within their areas of authority.

The assistant also had to gauge the likelihood that the case might come up before a judge who for one reason or another would be unsympathetic to the prosecution. An extreme but well known example of this type of problem existed in a nearby district. There, one of the judges, whose nomination was confirmed by the Senate only after discussion of some unfavorable material uncovered by the F.B.I., had been notoriously hostile to prosecutions in which that agency had played a part.

.   .   .

Conceptually distinct from the cases which were declined because the likelihood of conviction was felt to be too low, were those where the assistant felt that even an obviously successful prosecution should not be undertaken.

The most striking case where this occurred—though by no means the most common situation—was where the prosecution used an accomplice to a crime as a witness instead of prosecuting him. Actually this did not happen very often. Many times a lesser participant in a conspiracy—against whom the government had a strong case—could be induced to plead guilty and testify against the more serious offenders, hoping only that the court, in passing sentence upon him, would consider his cooperation. On other occasions, the accomplice would not testify for the prosecution unless he were offered more of an inducement than the mere contingent benefit of favorable consideration by the sentencing judge. In this case, a plea of guilty to a lesser offense might be worked out. Occasionally, however, even this inducement might not be enough and the assistant had to decide whether he was willing to let a known offender off with no prosecution at all, in order to convict a more serious criminal.

In an entirely different type of situation, the assistant would decline prosecution despite a provable case. Often the same equitable or emotional factors which would have lessened the chances of conviction by a jury influenced the assistant, and to this extent, he might have been able to claim two reasons for his action. That in a large class of cases the chance of failure was not determinative, however, is shown by the fact that prosecution was sometimes declined even where a guilty plea was certain or where, due to a complete confession, the government's case was strong enough to prevail despite its unsympathetic nature. In this situation the equities bore upon the assistant either directly, because of his personal feelings in the matter, or indirectly, because he was not willing to expose himself and the United States Attorney's office to the charge of being heartless and of overburdening the courts.

The types of cases where prosecution was declined despite a provable violation of federal law included those where the only sanctions available were too severe, considering the magnitude of the offense. While the United States Attorney's Office, in dealing with federal crimes, was not required to pass on the trivial squabbles between neighbors, marital quarrels, drunken brawls, and collection cases that form such a large part of the jurisdiction of the local prosecutor, this type of matter could and did occasionally arise in the context of the federal criminal law. For the assistant, the problem was complicated by the fact that the federal law was not nearly as well supplied as local law with lesser included offenses of varying degrees of seriousness, to which a guilty plea might be negotiated. Hence the choice often had to be made between prosecuting a minor violator for an unduly serious offense or not prosecuting him at all. . . .

Even when the federal law did provide a relatively light punishment for a trivial offense, prosecution would often be declined. It is hard to conceive of an assistant authorizing prosecution of a first offender for the misdemeanor of making commercial use of "the character Smokey Bear." Moreover, prosecution would be declined for somewhat less trivial offenses where the accused enjoyed such stature in the community that the prosecution would receive far more publicity and attention than it would otherwise merit. The assistant tended to feel that in this type of case the publicity given to the prosecution, even apart from conviction, would impose too severe a punishment. Thus, though these particular situations did not occur, it would have been the rare assistant who would not use every possible means to avoid prosecuting a senator or the governor of the state for shooting from a baited duck blind, unless, of course, the offense were repeated after warning or somehow aggravated by additional circumstances. Similarly, there were occasional cases in which the assistant concluded that the ill will generated toward the government by a prosecution for a relatively trivial offense might outweigh the advantages of conviction. For example, in one case where the accused was a former war hero, the assistant, foreseeing the inevitable charges of governmental ingratitude, declined to press the government's case. And, commonly, where the defendant was aged and sickly, his pitiable condition induced the assistant to decline prosecution. Where, in addition, the condition of the accused was such that he would not be able to commit another offense, the declination was almost routine except in the case of serious crimes or where, as in tax evasion, the prosecution would be undertaken primarily as a deterrent to others.

A conceptually distinct category of offenses were those in which prosecution would be declined because, in a sense, the prosecutorial arm of the government was second guessing the courts or the Congress. Even where the action of the accused was through judicial construction or obvious legislative intent, technically within the proscription of federal statute, prosecution might be declined because the case was not an appropriate one for criminal sanctions. . . .

The problem in this category which proved most troublesome was the typical airplane bomb hoax case. There, the passenger aloft might say jocularly to the stewardess, "Be careful with my coat, there's a bomb in the pocket." The stewardess would then immediately run to the pilot who, despite the jokester's pleas and explanations would turn the airplane around and land so that the entire airplane could be thoroughly searched. Though most assistants would not on their own have prosecuted a defendant who so obviously lacked any evil intent, a Department of Justice policy required that the passenger be prosecuted for giving a false report of a bomb aboard an airplane. Finally, a case arose where the jokester turned out to be a Roman Catholic priest. This was too much of course, and not only was no prosecution instituted, but the entire rigid policy soon was modified leaving much more room for case by case consideration.

Another category of cases in which prosecution was often declined consisted of those where the assistant, often under an informal office policy, attempted to lighten the work load of his office by turning the matter over to other agencies of government. In many cases the agency which assumed jurisdiction had means at its disposal which were more efficacious than criminal prosecution. Thus, juveniles were generally turned over to the state authorities partly on the theory that the conduct of its youth was primarily a state responsibility and partly because California was generally conceded to have better facilities for juvenile correction than the federal government. And where the accused was mentally ill, commitment proceedings under state law were generally instituted.

In another area "prosecution" might be left to other federal authorities—but not out of any wish to deal leniently with the offender. Where the accused was subject to revocation of parole or probation and "owed time" approximately equal to the sentence he would probably receive, the assistant generally declined prosecution in favor of action by the probation or parole authorities.

I have concentrated thus far on the reasons for declining prosecution rather than on those for authorizing it on the ground that the psychological make-up and role definition of the assistant were usually such that he would prosecute in the absence of any reason not to do so. Nonetheless, after weighing all the factors previously mentioned, the assistant would have to consider one more broad and almost all-encompassing category—whether the prosecution in the long run would do more harm than good. Although the number of possible circumstances that could fall in this category is quite large and incredibly varied, cases where they actually occurred were extremely rare. Probably the clearest example of this principle was a case which arose out of a raid made jointly by officers of two different federal agencies.

Though the guilt of the defendant could easily have been proved, two serious problems required the assistant to decline prosecution. First, as to a relatively peripheral but nonetheless admissible matter, the stories of the two groups of agents were diametrically opposed. The assistant felt that there was some rational explanation for this, but since he could discover none, he looked ahead to the newspaper stories that federal agents of differing agencies were contradicting each other under oath. The harm that this type of publicity could have done to the many prosecutions in which the government relies almost completely on the word of its agents was incalculable. Moreover, it soon turned out that one of the groups of agents had violated its agency's instructions by participating in the raid without first securing permission. Had this fact achieved publicity, not only would the agents involved have been severely disciplined, but the assistant who had caused this by going forward with the prosecution would have engendered ill will among a large group of government agents whose cooperation was essential to his continued functioning. It is, of course, possible to conceive of a prosecution so important that these two severe disadvantages might have to be accepted. In the case of most crimes, however, this would be far too great a price to pay. As a result, everyone agreed that the assistant had made the correct decision in declining prosecution, as he put it "in the interests of Justice."

Questions and Comment

The above excerpt describes in some detail how the prosecutor goes about the job of exercising his prosecutorial discretion. Note that he seems very interested in minimizing pressures upon him from various external sources. Does he seem very concerned with fairness?

Note also that he does not discuss any "political" cases. Would you expect that these cases if they existed, would be handled on a higher level? Note also that the Assistant United States Attorney in question was himself neither a career prosecutor nor politically ambitious (in fact, he went on to become a Professor of Law). Would the factors entering his decisions have been any different, had he been a locally elected District Attorney?

In the excerpt, it is mentioned that in some areas juries are notoriously reluctant to convict one black person of an assault upon another. In the South, at least until quite recently, juries were even more reluctant to convict anyone regardless of race (but typically white) of an assault upon a civil rights worker. In such a case, the prosecutor is caught in a dilemma: on the one hand, he may seriously believe that he has no business prosecuting someone whom he cannot expect to convict, and that doing so would be an abuse of his office. On the other hand, he must also recognize that the reason he cannot convict is, in some sense, an unworthy one and that his efforts to gain a conviction will give the matter publicity which, in the long run, may change public attitudes.

Until the late 1950's it looked very much as if prosecutors in the South were failing to prosecute cases of attacks upon civil rights workers or blacks arising out of racial feeling. Then although, at first, no convictions resulted, they began to prosecute. Within about ten years, perhaps because of the feeling generated by the unsuccessful prosecutions of clearly guilty men, though certainly for other reasons as well, the resistance of juries lessened and convictions became considerably easier to obtain.

(2) WHITE COLLAR CRIME *

The prosecutor often has not had the opportunity to review a case of common crime intimately before it enters the system formally through an arrest. When the prosecutor drafts a complaint for an agent at the initial appearance, the circumstances often severely limit his or her ability to evaluate the case. The arresting agent, having acted in haste, may be confused as to basic facts; time constraints often preclude further inquiry. As a result the prosecutor, in drafting the complaint, will be less interested in giving a full account of what he regards as the charge or charges worth prosecuting than in paring down the agent's assertions to a minimum so that they will not come back to haunt him by contradicting evidence subsequently developed. The prosecutor's later dismissal or reduction of charges will often reflect how the charge would have been handled initially had he controlled the entrance of the case into the system.

In many cases neither the prosecutor nor the agent will wish to carry the matter beyond the initial charge. Police frequently make arrests in response to situational pressures, for example to break up a domestic or barroom fight, with little or no thought to treatment by later stages of the criminal enforcement process. Even when agents specifically set out to construct cases that can be prosecuted, they frequently make ill-considered arrests under emergency conditions. A drug sale may be "going down" in an apartment that contains numerous people with varying degrees of involvement in the transaction, such as the girlfriend, child, or neighbor of the principals. If someone identifies an undercover agent inside or detects surveillance outside and "all hell breaks loose," everyone who can be fitted into the agents' cars may be arrested.

By the time the case reaches the prosecutor, no one in the criminal justice system may want to devote further time or resources to pursuing it. Prosecutors routinely find matters to be less serious than the initial charges—invoked under time pressures or to justify emergency intervention—make them appear. Even in many cases charged as felonies, prosecutor and police will see the process as the proper

---

* Jack Katz, "Legality and Equality: Plea Bargaining in the Prosecution of White Collar and Common Crimes" 13 *Law* *and Society Review*, Winter 1979, pp. 443–447. © 1979 (Reprinted with permission).

punishment and be content with a nolo contendere plea to a misdemeanor or a dismissal accompanied by a warning.

Although the prosecutor is relatively passive, "exercising discretion" whether to prosecute cases already defined as ripe by police or federal enforcement agents, specialized works on white-collar crime show prosecutors actively "making" cases through lengthy investigations. Prosecutors in the Antitrust Division of the Justice Department characterize an investigation completed in ten months as "quick". Two alumni of the U.S. Attorney's Office for the Southern District of New York have described how prosecutors investigate securities fraud, tax evasion, and currency crimes by examining permanent files that cross-index people, companies, and foreign banks . . ..

Resource allocation policies in prosecutors' offices indicate the investigative investment necessary for making white-collar cases. Offices that put substantial resources into white-collar prosecution do so by placing assistants in specialized sections in order to keep their trial caseloads light. In the U.S. Attorney's office in Brooklyn, about one-third of the assistants are assigned to either the Fraud or the Corruption section. Within the office, assignment from General Crimes to one of these sections is taken as a mark of prestige, but also means that opportunity for trial experience will be severely limited. Assistants in the Fraud and Corruption sections complain that their specialized caseloads may produce only one trial in a year, or even none, while those in the General Crimes and Narcotics sections can expect half a dozen or more. The staff member with the highest court caseload is a law student-paraprofessional who annually processes scores of postal theft and check forgery cases to misdemeanor guilty pleas.

Each of three features of white-collar crime, . . . contributes to the creation of an investigative role for the prosecutor in the enforcement process. Because the crime is not discrete and bounded, but rather designed into ongoing occupational routines, it will be necessary to investigate a series of events or transactions in order to make out a prima facie case. This itself does not require the prosecutor's involvement. And with all but the most sensitive charges, such as political corruption, there usually will have been an agency investigation before the case reaches the prosecutor's office. But the agency is often stymied for lack of an effective means to obtain business records. After interviewing numerous, related consumer fraud complainants, postal inspectors come to the U.S. Attorney's office to get direct access to the company's books. The U.S. Attorney may receive a complaint of bankruptcy fraud from a district court referee and ask the FBI to investigate; but the latter may quickly return to the prosecutor if banks refuse to reveal the records of the target's commercial transactions on the grounds that "voluntary" disclosure might violate the privacy of their depositors. Grand jury subpoena powers, under the exclusive control of the prosecutor, will usually be necessary to document the crime. In contrast to the prosecutor's role in obtaining search warrants for agents who have been investigating common crimes, the prosecutor's initial use of grand jury subpoena powers will generally occur long before the case is prepared for formal charging.

Because white-collar crimes leave no telltale signs on victims and produce no concrete artifacts, that embody the crime, the search for documentary proof will not start with precise directives. Even if "smoking guns," busted locks, caches of drugs and injured victims do not tell agents whom to look for, they usually define the crime being investigated. In white-collar crime investigations, . . . even the existence of the crime will often be unclear. "Specific questions which are quite common in representative white-collar criminal cases," [include] issues of criminal intent, such as whether stock promoters "were in a position to have had access to the kind of information which would have been disclosed in the course of registration"; whether a homeowner borrowing money guaranteed by the FHA initially or subsequently formed the intent to use the money for a purpose other than that stated in his application; whether a road contractor's failure to supply all the truckloads of fill for which he was paid expressed his intent, that of his employees, or mismanagement; whether a corporate officer responsible for a deliberately misleading promotional blurb was "only 'puffing' " to increase sales or was attempting to affect the price of the corporation's shares. The determination that "sufficient" proof has been accumulated to resolve such questions calls for a lawyer's expertise in applying substantive theory and evidentiary rules and in planning trial strategy.

The third feature . . . defining white-collar crime is concerted ignorance. Because participants will be able to profess ignorance of the overall criminal scheme, it will be necessary to choose a "target" and then "turn" one or more insiders in order to generate evidence of inculpating understandings. Often a prosecutor will not understand what the crime was (how it occurred, who made money how) without the guidance of an insider. A preliminary effort may be necessary to build pressure sufficient to turn an insider, perhaps even by inducing perjury or investigating an unrelated set of transactions in order to create the "exposure" that will give the prosecutor effective "leverage." Grants of immunity, formally within the exclusive authority of the prosecutor, typically will be necessary to obtain essential cooperation. . . .

(3) THE DECISION NOT TO CHARGE *

Common Practices

(a) In a particular community the local attitude toward state liquor laws was such that the prosecutor would charge offenders for liquor violations only when they became extensive or notorious or were combined with other vice crimes. He said that though the state

* Remington, Newman, Kimball, Melli, Goldstein, *Criminal Justice Administration, Materials and Cases,* (Indianapolis, Bobbs-Merrill Co., Inc., 1969), pp. 429–430. ©1969 (Reprinted with permission of Bobbs-Merrill).

legislation was strict the laws were unpopular in his county and it was almost impossible to get a jury that would convict.

(b) A warrant had been issued for passing bad checks and the offender arrested in a distant state. The prosecutor, noting that it would cost about $500 to extradite him and that the checks amounted only to $60, decided against requesting extradition. The prosecutor stated that if the checks had totaled $100 or more he would probably have gone ahead with extradition.

(c) In a case of burglary where the evidence was somewhat weak, the prosecutor agreed with the one of two offenders whom he considered only a follower not to charge him with burglary if he would agree to testify against the other. The fellow said he would, and the prosecutor pointed out that the charge could always be filed later on if he backed down.

. . .

(d) A seventeen-year-old defendant in Michigan was charged with sale of narcotics based upon the sale of some marihuana cigarettes to a friend. While the state's evidence was clearly sufficient to establish the crime of "sale," the prosecutor's office reduced the charge to "possession," a lesser offense. A prosecutor explained, "We can't take these kinds of cases to trial. In the first place the law isn't intended to cover this type of situation. In the second place, when juries find out that the mandatory penalty is twenty years to life they just won't convict. Who is going to send a seventeen-year-old to prison for twenty years? And the judges don't like the law either, because they are caught in the same bind." The defendant pleaded guilty to the "possession" charge.

Question

Do any of the prosecutor's decisions in the above excerpt seem wrong?

(4) THE DECISION TO CHARGE WHERE REFUSAL TO CHARGE IS NORMAL *

(a) A 78–year-old man was arrested for indecent exposure upon complaint of the father of a young girl who had seen him. The old man had no record and explained that he was merely urinating in the alley and offered to get a statement from his doctor to the effect that he had a kidney ailment. The prosecutor asked the father what he wanted done and the father said, "I think the man should be punished for what he did." The prosecutor said, "Well, he's pretty old and has never committed any offense before. Don't you think jail is the wrong place for him?" The father replied, "He committed a crime and I think he

* Remington, Newman, Kimball, Melli, Goldstein, *Criminal Justice Administration, Materials and Cases,* Indianapolis, Bobbs-Merrill Co., Inc., 1969, pp. 440–442. © 1969 (Reprinted with permission).

ought to be punished." The prosecutor eventually shrugged his shoulders and approved the warrant recommendation.

(b) Police stopped a known criminal for a traffic offense and searched his car, finding a loaded pistol in the glove compartment. The police arrested him for carrying a concealed weapon and the prosecutor approved the charge even though he knew the case would be lost as soon as a motion was made to suppress the only evidence of guilt.

(c) Several inmates of the House of Corrections had escaped and were apprehended. In recent months there had been a large number of escapes. Though escapees from the House of Corrections (in contrast to the prison) were usually charged under a misdemeanor statute, an assistant prosecutor approved warrants charging each of this latest group with a felony.

. . .

(d) A 66–year-old man had been plaguing the prosecutor's office and courts with his frequent misconduct as a beggar. He was arrested for begging and $199 in cash was found on him. He also had in his possession two bank books showing deposits of $5,700. He had been arrested some thirty-five times and convicted twenty times of begging or some related offense. It was felt by the prosecuting attorney's office that it was time to teach the old man a lesson. The charge was that of being a third offender, with substantially higher maximum penalty.

(e) A young lady complained to the police that a dentist slapped her across the face when she told him he was hurting her while extracting a tooth. He failed to respond to the letter routinely sent to professional men about complaints of that nature. In a phone conversation as a follow-up to the letter, he told the police sergeant to go to hell. He failed to appear at the police felony detail at the requested time for a discussion of the matter. His firm had been repeatedly complained against for fraud but there was never enough evidence to support charges. Despite the practice not to charge doctors and dentists with minor offenses alleged by their patients, a warrant was issued charging this dentist with assault and battery.

Questions

The above excerpt contains difficult decisions for the prosecutor.

Did the prosecutor fail to show sufficient courage in case (a)?

Did he violate his legal duty in (b)?

Was it right for him to raise the charge in (c) just because the public was becoming concerned with the problem?

Was it proper for the prosecutor in (d) to consider the wealth of the prospective defendant and his previous record, in deciding with what crime to charge him?

In (e) was it proper, first of all, to have a practice not to charge doctors and dentists with minor offenses alleged by their patients? Second, was it proper to consider, in departing from this policy, the fact that the dentist had failed to show the proper courtesy to law enforcement officials, or that he had previously been repeatedly charged with an entirely different type of crime for which there was insufficient evidence to prosecute?

c.   NOTE ON ALTERNATIVES TO PROSECUTION

Several alternatives to prosecution are available to add flexibility to the prosecutor's decision as to whether or not to prosecute:

(1) *Commitment of the Mentally Ill.*   For minor crimes committed by otherwise respectable defendants, the prosecutor may drop charges on the assurance of the defendant's family that he will receive treatment and supervision.   In the case of defendants who have serious mental illness, most states provide for commitment proceedings, nominally non-criminal or "civil," which allow the prosecutor or relatives of the mentally ill person to force him to live in, and receive treatment at, special institutions for the mentally ill.   Where the criminal charges are serious, the prosecutor may petition the court to determine whether a defendant is mentally competent to stand trial.   If not, based on the examinations of a panel of medical experts, the defendant will be sent to a mental hospital until he is certified to be well enough to stand trial.

(2) *Nuisance Proceedings.*   For crimes requiring a particular place, such as prostitution or gambling, the prosecutor can institute proceedings to have the building, store, office, hotel, etc., closed as a public nuisance.   Ordinarily, the proprietor or lease holder must be convicted on criminal charges first, but afterwards nuisance proceedings allow the prosecutor to shut the whole operation down without bothering to prosecute every person involved.

(3) *Warning.*   In many misdemeanor cases, especially assaults between spouses or neighbors, the prosecutor often resorts to mediation. Through a variety of informal and semi-formal procedures, including investigation of facts, circumstances and the parties' backgrounds and meetings in a detective's or prosecutor's office, the matter may be settled without a formal charge.   The most common method of settlement is to place the one or both possible defendants under a stern warning that if the same similar misconduct occurs in the future, the police will have a record of the previous events and severe punishments will ensue.

(4) *Restitution.*   For crimes involving larceny or property damage, especially "white collar" crimes where proof of the necessary criminal intent is difficult, the prosecutor may insist that the defendant pay for the victim's loss.

Questions

Under what circumstances should the prosecutor use the above alternatives?   Consider how each reflects on the purposes of the criminal law discussed in the second chapter.

d. CONTROLS ON THE PROSECUTORIAL DISCRETION

(1) THE PROBLEM OF STANDARDS *

It has been observed that if the criminal law were followed to its strict letter the results would be intolerable, in part because of the anarchic and archaic state of our substantive criminal law. But even if our criminal proscriptions were framed with exquisite discrimination, it would still be necessary for the human beings who operate the criminal process to exercise judgment about whether or not to arrest, release, prosecute, dismiss, or accept a plea of guilty in a given case. The criminal law is neither a slot machine nor a computer. But to admit the need for discretion is not to make a virtue of it. And it is far from being a virtue in the enforcement of the criminal sanction.

The basic trouble with discretion is simply that it is lawless, in the literal sense of that term. If police or prosecutors find themselves free (or compelled) to pick and choose among known or knowable instances of criminal conduct, they are making a judgment which in a society based on law should be made only by those to whom the making of law is entrusted. For the rough approximation of community values that emerges from the legislative process there is substituted the personal and often idiosyncratic values of the law enforcer. When victims of discriminatory enforcement see what is happening, secondary effects subversive of respect for law . . . are produced.

The worst abuses of discretion in enforcement occur in connection with those offenses that are just barely taken seriously, like most consensual sex offenses. Here, especially in the case of fornication and adultery, enforcement is so sporadic as to be just one step short of complete cessation. And it is here that the greatest danger exists of using enforcement discretion in an abusive way: to pay off a score, to provide a basis for extortion, to stigmatize an otherwise deviant or unpopular figure.

. . .

The enforcement authorities, most often the public prosecutors, will sometimes mitigate the harsh effects of statutes that they believe to be overly broad. Social gambling is usually ignored, except on occasion when ulterior motives prompt a raid on a friendly poker game. But even this informal exemption is not uniformly applied. The lower-class counterpart to an evening of bridge at a tenth of a cent a point may be the back-alley crap game, which is far from being immune to arrests. Abortion provides another example of differential treatment. Reputable doctors performing illegal but "therapeutic" abortions in reputable hospitals are virtually immune from prosecution, although the availability of hospital records to prosecutorial inspection would appear to make this kind of illegal abortion uniquely easy to detect.

* Herbert Packer, *The Limits of the Criminal Sanction*, Stanford, Stanford University Press, 1968, pp. 290–291. © 1968 (Reprinted with permission).

Perhaps prosecutors are right to prefer bridge to craps and "therapeutic" to hole-in-the-corner abortions. But these are not choices that they should be free to make. It would not be so bad if this kind of differential enforcement were the harbinger of law reform. More often it is simply the substitute.

Comment

The above excerpt points out that prosecutorial discretion is often used as a substitute for more tightly drafted laws. Interestingly enough, prosecutors usually oppose tightly drafted laws on the grounds that they can be trusted to prosecute those cases which should be prosecuted and not to prosecute the others. They typically feel that the more tightly drafted the law, the more difficult it will be to prove the case against someone who should be covered by the law.

Thus, a general statute prohibiting all gambling allows much easier conviction of the professional gambler than does a statute which proscribes professional gambling. Of course, our understanding is that prosecutors will use the statute only on professional gamblers and that they will exercise discretion not to prosecute social gamblers. The price paid for vesting prosecutors, rather than the courts, with the decision-making power as to who is, and who is not, a professional gambler is that we will have legally authorized the prosecutor to prosecute, and the courts to convict, social gamblers.

(2) PROSECUTORIAL MOTIVE

(a) *The Restrictive View* *

. . . . [T]here can be no area of professional ethics more in need of analysis than that of the prosecuting attorney, since there are a substantial number of ethical problems that are unique to his high and difficult calling.

First, Cases where the Primary Motive for the Prosecution Relates to Matters Other Than Commission of the Particular Crime for which the Defendant Is Being Prosecuted. An instance often suggested to justify this kind of conduct is the prosecution of Al Capone for tax evasion. If the government cannot successfully prosecute a notorious criminal for the numerous serious offenses he is suspected of having committed, some prosecutors consider it to be proper to subject him to prosecutions for a variety of other crimes, ranging from traffic offenses to tax evasion, for which he would not be investigated and charged were it not for his notoriety. In support of such practices, it is argued that if the individual is in fact guilty of the crime with which he is charged, the motive of the prosecutor is immaterial. This contention overlooks the fact that there are few of us who have led such unblemished lives as to

* Monroe H. Freedman, "The Professional Responsibility of the Prosecuting Attorney", 55 *Georgetown Law Journal*, (1967), 1034–1045. © 1967 (Reprinted with permission).

prevent a determined prosecutor from finding some basis for an indictment or an information. Thus, to say that the prosecutor's motive is immaterial, is to justify making virtually every citizen the potential victim of arbitrary discretion. . . .

[A] recent conviction for income tax evasion was reversed when it was shown that the prosecution had been motivated by the defendant's political views and activities.** Prosecutions have even been motivated by personal grudges of public officials. From the day that James Hoffa told Robert Kennedy that he was nothing but a rich man's kid who never had to earn a nickel in his life, Hoffa was a marked man. When Kennedy became Attorney General, satisfying this grudge became the public policy of the United States, and Hoffa, along with Roy Cohn and perhaps other enemies from Kennedy's past, was singled out for special attention by United States Attorneys. This is, of course, the very antithesis of a rule of law, and serves to bring into sharp focus the ethical obligation of the prosecutor to refrain from abusing his power by prosecutions that are directed at individuals rather than at crimes.

(b) The Prosecutor's View *

The essence of Professor Freedman's point seems to be that prosecution of a person for one crime is improper when the prosecutor's real motive is to "get" the defendant because of some other type of wrongful activity. It may be that prosecutors should not develop grudges; when, *solely* because of ill will or dislike by the prosecutor, the defendant is singled out for persecution, I would agree that the prosecutor is abusing his power. It is also probably correct to say that a person who has committed some *minor* infraction for which he would not normally be prosecuted should not be prosecuted simply because he has committed other wrongs. The examples cited by Mr. Freedman, however, do not fall into these categories. One of them, the *Lenske* case, does present an example of prosecutorial excesses, but these excesses were clearly recognized by the appellate court which reversed the conviction. The charges against Hoffa and Capone were not minor. They involved serious felonies for which many other individuals have been prosecuted.

The assertion that a person should not be prosecuted for one crime because he has committed other more serious crimes for which prosecution is not feasible is unsound. Such a theory would tend to protect the most powerful gangsters and racketeers in the land, who could always complain that they had committed a more serious offense than that with which they were charged. One might also question whether, under this theory, many defendants in civil rights cases could success-

---

** Lenske v. U. S., 383 F.2d 20 (9th Cir. 1967). The case was reversed for other reasons. One judge concurring in the reversal based his decision also on the fact that the Internal Revenue agent recommended prosecution in a report which emphasized that the defendant, a lawyer who represented "left wing causes", was thought to be a communist.

* Richard L. Braun, "Ethics in a Criminal Case: A Response," 55 *Georgetown Law Journal*, (1967), 1049, 1056–1057. © 1967 (Reprinted with permission).

fully claim that the failure to prosecute them for more serious offenses (e.g., murder) would preclude their indictment on civil rights charges.

Many offenses are not prosecuted for a variety of reasons, including the good record and character of the defendant. Professor Freedman seems to criticize the practice of prosecuting some defendants in part because of the defendants' records of other criminal activities or their well-established reputations for bad character. Surely he would not remove the prosecutor's discretion to *decline* cases. Yet the discretion to decline must carry with it the discretion to prosecute. Of course, this discretion should not be abused, but the consideration of a person's character or prior record in deciding whether or not to prosecute is neither improper nor unethical. On the contrary, it is fundamental to the proper exercise of the prosecutor's function.

Comment

The two above excerpts discuss the situation where the defendant is felt to be provably guilty of a crime but would not ordinarily be prosecuted for that crime. Does not the existence of a prosecutorial discretion imply that the prosecutor will bring charges against some, but not all, of those he might convict?

Another problem, more serious but fortunately less common, occurs where the prosecutor brings charges against one he or she cannot convict. Except in the situations discussed at p. 300 this is highly improper, since the expense and embarrassment of even a successful defense place an enormous power to do injury in the hands of the prosecutor. Fortunately, the political checks upon an unfounded "grudge" prosecution are strong since, when it is revealed that the prosecutor has no case, he or she will generally suffer severe criticism for harassing a defendant and for wasting the taxpayer's money.

In both of these situations, the courts are sometimes asked to take a hand. Usually they refuse.

e.　CONTROL THROUGH RULES *

Why should a prosecutor—say, a county prosecutor—have discretionary power to decide not to prosecute even when the evidence of guilt is clear, perhaps partly on the basis of political influence, without ever having to state to anyone what evidence was brought to light by his investigation and without having to explain to anyone why he interprets a statute as he does or why he chooses a particular position on a difficult question of policy? Why should the discretionary power be so unconfined that, of half a dozen potential defendants he can prove guilty, he can select any one for prosecution and let the other five go, making his decision, if he chooses, on the basis of considerations extraneous to justice? . . . Why should the vital decisions he makes be immune to review by other officials and immune to review by the

* Kenneth Culp Davis, *Discretionary Justice* (Baton Rouge, Louisiana State University Press, 1969) pp. 189–190, 224. © 1969 (Reprinted with permission).

courts, even though our legal and governmental system elsewhere generally assumes the need for checking human frailties? Why should he have a complete power to decide that one statute duly enacted by the people's representatives shall not be enforced at all, that another statute will be fully enforced, and that a third will be enforced only if, as, and when he thinks that it should be enforced in a particular case? Even if we assume that a prosecutor has to have a power of selective enforcement, why do we not require him to state publicly his general policies and require him to follow those policies in individual cases in order to protect evenhanded justice? Why not subject prosecutors' decisions to a simple and general requirement of open findings, open reasons, and open precedents, except when special reason for confidentiality exists? Why not strive to protect prosecutors' decisions from political or other ulterior influence in the same way we strive to protect judges' decisions?   . . .

The seeming unanimity of American prosecutors that their discretionary power must be completely uncontrolled is conclusively contradicted by the experience of West Germany, where the discretionary power of prosecutors is so slight as to be almost nonexistent, and where almost all they do is closely supervised.**

Hence the German prosecutor never has discretionary power to engage in plea bargaining.

"The German and American systems also differ when the evidence or the law or both seem to the prosecutor to be doubtful. When a doubt seems to require a discretionary choice, the German prosecutor does not resolve the doubt; he almost always presents a doubtful case to the judge, who determines the sufficiency of the evidence and the proper interpretation of the law.

"Even when the prosecutor finds prosecution of a suspect clearly inappropriate, the German system, unlike the American system, provides protection against abuse of power. When a crime is reported by the police or by a private party, a file is opened and registered; the file can be traced at any time. A German prosecutor can never simply forget about the case as his American counterpart may do. The file cannot be closed without a statement of written reasons, which in important cases must be approved by the prosecutor's superior, and which must be reported to any victim of the crime and to any suspect who was interrogated. Every prosecutor is supervised by a superior in a hierarchical system headed by the Minister of Justice, who is himself responsible to the cabinet. The supervision is real, not merely a threat;

** At pp. 194–195, Professor Davis contrasts the German and American systems:

"The most important difference between the German system and the American system is this: *Whenever the evidence that the defendant has committed a serious crime is reasonably clear and the law is not in doubt, the German prosecutor, unlike the American prosecutor, is without discretionary power to withhold prosecution. This means that selective enforcement, a major feature of the American system, is almost wholly absent from the German system. . . .*

files are in fact often reviewed. Availability to victims of crimes of procedure to compel prosecution constitutes still another check."

I think we Americans should learn from other nations that the huge discretionary power of prosecutors need not be unconfined, unstructured, and unchecked. We should reexamine the assumptions to which our drifting has led us.

Prosecutors, in my opinion, should be required to make and to announce rules that will guide their choices, stating, as far as practicable, what will and what will not be prosecuted, and they should be required otherwise to structure their discretion.

Question

Are there any differences between the proper methods of controlling police and prosecutorial discretion? Which is easier?

3. THE PROSECUTOR AS AN ADVOCATE

a. THE PROSECUTOR'S DUTY OF FAIRNESS

BERGER v. UNITED STATES

Supreme Court of the United States, 1935.
295 U.S. 78, 55 S.Ct. 629, 79 L.Ed. 1314.

Mr. Justice SUTHERLAND.

The United States Attorney is the representative not of an ordinary party to a controversy, but of a sovereignty whose obligation to govern impartially is as compelling as its obligation to govern at all; and whose interest, therefore, in a criminal prosecution is not that it shall win a case, but that justice shall be done. As such, he is in a peculiar and very definite sense the servant of the law, the twofold aim of which is that guilt shall not escape or innocence suffer. He may prosecute with earnestness and vigor—indeed, he should do so. But, while he may strike hard blows, he is not at liberty to strike foul ones. It is as much his duty to refrain from improper methods calculated to produce a wrongful conviction as it is to use every legitimate means to bring about a just one.

.   .   .

Judgment reversed.

Comment

Our interest in the prosecutorial discretion should not obscure the fact that prosecutors have another important function. They are the trial lawyers for the government in criminal cases. As the above excerpt indicates, in this task the prosecutor is more than just a trial lawyer whose duty is to do the best for his or her client, within the limits of the rules. The prosecutor is also a representative of the government upon whom the courts, and society, impose a standard of ethics which may transcend any particular rule. Of course, this is not to say that prosecutors never do anything which violates the ethical or legal standards imposed upon them. If in fact prosecutors always obeyed the norms and rules of their calling, they would be the only occupational group we know of that did this unfailingly. On the other hand, the above excerpt represents a commitment to a standard of prosecutorial behavior and, as the next excerpt indicates, this is a standard which the courts will enforce.

b. NAPUE v. ILLINOIS
Supreme Court of the United States, 1959.
360 U.S. 264, 79 S.Ct. 1173, 3 L.Ed.2d 1217.

Mr. Chief Justice WARREN.

At the murder trial of petitioner the principal state witness, then serving a 199–year sentence for the same murder, testified in response to a question by the Assistant State's Attorney that he had received no promise of consideration in return for his testimony. The Assistant State's Attorney had in fact promised him consideration, but did nothing to correct the witness' false testimony. The jury was apprised, however, that a public defender had promised "to do what he could" for the witness. The question presented is whether on these facts the failure of the prosecutor to correct the testimony of the witness which he knew to be false denied petitioner due process of law in violation of the Fourteenth Amendment to the Constitution of the United States.

The record in this Court contains testimony from which the following facts could have been found. The murder in question occurred early in the morning of August 21, 1938, in a Chicago, Illinois, cocktail lounge. Petitioner Henry Napue, the witness George Hamer, one Poe and one Townsend entered the dimly lighted lounge and announced their intention to rob those present. An off-duty policeman, present in the lounge, drew his service revolver and began firing at the four men. In the melee that followed Townsend was killed, the officer was fatally wounded, and the witness Hamer was seriously wounded. Napue and Poe carried Hamer to the car where a fifth man, one Webb, was waiting. In due course Hamer was apprehended, tried for the murder of the policeman, convicted on his plea of guilty and sentenced to 199 years. Subsequently, Poe was apprehended, tried, convicted, sentenced to death and executed. Hamer was not used as a witness.

Thereafter, petitioner Napue was apprehended. He was put on trial with Hamer being the principal witness for the State. Hamer's testimony was extremely important because the passage of time and the dim light in the cocktail lounge made eyewitness identification very difficult and uncertain, and because some pertinent witnesses had left the state. On the basis of the evidence presented, which consisted largely of Hamer's testimony, the jury returned a guilty verdict and petitioner was sentenced to 199 years.

Finally, the driver of the car, Webb, was apprehended. Hamer also testified against him. He was convicted of murder and sentenced to 199 years.

Following the conviction of Webb, the lawyer who, as former Assistant State's Attorney, had prosecuted the Hamer, Poe and Napue cases filed a petition in the nature of a writ of error *coram nobis* on behalf of Hamer. In the petition he alleged that as prosecuting attorney he had promised Hamer that if he would testify against Napue, "a recommendation for a reduction of his [Hamer's] sentence would be made and, if possible, effectuated." The attorney prayed that the court would effect "consummation of the compact entered into between the duly authorized representatives of the State of Illinois and George Hamer."

This *coram nobis* proceeding came to the attention of Napue, who thereafter filed a post-conviction petition, in which he alleged that Hamer had falsely testified that he had been promised no consideration for his testimony, and that the Assistant State's Attorney handling the case had known this to be false. A hearing was ultimately held at which the former Assistant State's Attorney testified that he had only promised to help Hamer if Hamer's story "about being a reluctant participant" in the robbery was borne out, and not merely if Hamer would testify at petitioner's trial. He testified that in his *coram nobis* petition on Hamer's behalf he "probably used some language that [he] should not have used" in his "zeal to do something for Hamer" to whom he "felt a moral obligation." . . .

[i]t is established that a conviction obtained through use of false evidence, known to be such by representatives of the State, must fall under the Fourteenth Amendment . . . The same result obtains when the State, although not soliciting false evidence, allows it to go uncorrected when it appears. . . .

The principle that a State may not knowingly use false evidence, including false testimony, to obtain a tainted conviction, implicit in any concept of ordered liberty, does not cease to apply merely because the false testimony goes only to the credibility of the witness. The jury's estimate of the truthfulness and reliability of a given witness may well be determinative of guilt or innocence, and it is upon such subtle factors as the possible interest of the witness in testifying falsely that a defendant's life or liberty may depend. As stated by the New York Court of Appeals in a case very similar to this one, People v. Savvides.
. . .

> "It is of no consequence that the falsehood bore upon the witness' credibility rather than directly upon defendant's guilt. A lie is a lie, no matter what its subject, and, if it is in any way relevant to the case, the district attorney has the responsibility and duty to correct what he knows to be false and elicit the truth. . . . That the district attorney's silence was not the result of guile or a desire to prejudice matters little, for its

impact was the same, preventing, as it did, a trial that could in any real sense be termed fair."

. . .

Reversed.

Questions

In a great many criminal trials, witnesses for the prosecution— often in order to protect themselves from charges of complicity in the defendant's crime—will testify falsely as to one detail or another. So far as the defendant is concerned, why should it make any difference whether the prosecutor knew or did not know of the falsity at the time?

If prosecutors know of witnesses who can help defendants, are they ethically obliged to tell defense attorneys? Does it matter whether they believe that witnesses are lying or mistaken?

Does it matter whether prosecutors believe that, although witnesses can help defendants and are telling the truth, defendants are nonetheless guilty? Entirely apart from any ethical standards as to their behavior in court, do prosecutors have an ethical duty not to prosecute anyone unless they believe that person to be guilty? If so, is not excusing prosecutors from any duty of disclosure, on the ground that they believe defendants are guilty, the same thing as saying there is no such duty?

c. THE CONVICT'S VIEW OF THE PROSECUTOR *

The defendants consistently believe that the prosecutor is the central figure in the operation of the criminal justice system. His is the power to determine their fate. Although many decisions by the prosecutor are formally within the power of the judge to alter, this is thought to occur infrequently. The prosecutor is the man to see; bargaining with him (and with the defendant's attorney) is the key to determining how well one emerges from his encounter with the legal system. What is the prosecutor up to? What is he after?

He might very well be seen as the enemy, as a villain whose intentions are to harm the defendant. This view of the prosecutor emerged occasionally ("he was out to get me") but was not the predominant mode of looking at the prosecutor. Rather, like the police officer, the prosecutor is seen as a worker, and he tries to do his job as efficiently as possible. The defendants are aware of the burdensome caseloads with which most prosecutors must deal. Thus, to get his job done, he must make deals. He cannot (or else does not much care to) spend much time on any given case. Rather, he must get it over with so that he can get on to the next:

* Jonathan D. Casper, *American Criminal Justice: The Defendant Perspective*, Prentice-Hall Inc., Englewood Cliffs, N.J., 1972, pp. 128–130. © 1972 (Reprinted with permission).

Let me ask you a few questions about the prosecutor in your case. How do you think he saw his job? Think he was interested in giving you a fair shake, punishing you, getting rid of the case?

He wanted a conviction.

Why? Cause it makes him look good?

No, not really. No, it don't make him look good. Like nobody knows about it, you know. Who really cares if I'm guilty or not?

It's just like it might help him a little bit more in getting a better job; but, you know, with all the convictions he got, little convictions like mine don't really mean nothing. Cause any prosecutor can get that. But he might of thought that I was guilty, I don't know. I think the prosecutor goes along with most of what the police does or said. I don't think a prosecutor will, say, sit down and read the case over and he'll say, Police was wrong—because they only got one side of it. Like if I get arrested for anything—like anybody get arrested for any-thing—they can't prove themselves until they get into court. You know, like the police got, they shoot all their evidence to the prosecutor, like he got all the one side, what he did. I think he see most people come in front of him—maybe every-body that comes in front of him—is guilty. All he see is them being guilty because he got the evidence that show the guilt, if any. That they're arrested—he figures, It's my job to see that they stay in jail.

Why do you think he sees his job that way, rather than sort of looking at it independently and saying, he's innocent: we'll let him go. He's guilty: we ought to prosecute him?

I don't think that. I think that's all like this loose busi-ness, television shit where you see people, you know, fair play and what not. Everybody's thinking, when you're in that courtroom, everybody's thinking for theirselves, man. They thinking that's their job, man. Anything they see in there get them a better position, they get it, do it. So small cases, like I said before, don't help his position too much, but it helps some. But I don't think he'll be looking at where it's going to be fair or not; I think he's looking at it whereas he can get a conviction, you know.

Is it the kind of man who becomes a prosecutor or what the job does to him?

No, I don't think it's so much what the job does to him or what it takes to be a prosecutor. It's just like anything—like when you get a job, you start working on it. You start working on it, and it's a job, that's all. It's not nothing else, just your paycheck every week. When he go home, I don't think he be, you know, thinking about, saying, Man, I sent a man to prison for seven years; seven years, man, he got to be there for seven years. I don't think he be saying that if he gotta do life. I don't think he's going to cheer; he don't think on that. He see you—your face is just like this [other] man's face. Like every day, you walking down the street, you see somebody, you don't think of their face next week. He don't think about faces next week.

Comment and Question

Remember again that the sample questioned here consisted primarily of those in prison, almost all of whom admitted their guilt. (Indeed most had committed many crimes).

Note that the convicts' views are colored by the prosecutor's role in plea bargaining, a matter which we take up in a subsequent chapter. Is there anything in the above excerpt inconsistent, however, with any of the other materials on the prosecutor?

C. THE DEFENSE ATTORNEY

1. THE DEFENSE OF THE UNPOPULAR

THE DEFENSE OF THE "GUILTY"

a. PRO *

Sir (said Dr. Johnson), a lawyer has no business with the justice or injustice of the cause which he undertakes, unless his client asks his opinion, and then he is bound to give it honestly. The justice or injustice of the cause is to be decided by the judge. Consider, sir, what is the purpose of courts of justice? It is, that every man may have his cause fairly tried, by men appointed to try causes. A lawyer is not to tell what he knows to be a lie: he is not to produce what he knows to be a false deed; but he is not to usurp the province of the jury and of the judge, and determine what shall be the effect of evidence—what shall be the result of legal argument. As it rarely happens that a man is fit to plead his own cause, lawyers are a class of the community who, by study and experience, have acquired the art and power of arranging evidence, and of applying to the points at issue what the law has settled. A lawyer is to do for his client all that his client might fairly do for himself, if he could. If, by a superiority of attention, of knowledge, of skill, and a better method of communication, he has the advantage of his adversary, it is an advantage to which he is entitled. There must always be some advantage on one side or other; and it is better that advantage should be had by talents, than by chance. If lawyers were to undertake no causes till they were sure they were just,

* James Boswell, *The Journal of a Tour,* (Temple Classics), pp. 13–14. (Reprinted with permission).

a man might be precluded altogether from a trial of his claim, though were it judicially examined, it might be found a very just claim.

b.   CON **

When employed to defend those charged with crimes of the deepest dye, and the evidence against them, whether legal, or moral, be such as to leave no just doubt of their guilt, I shall not hold myself privileged, much less obliged, to use my endeavours to arrest, or to impede the course of justice, by special resorts to ingenuity—to the artifices of eloquence—to appeals to the morbid and fleeting sympathies of weak juries, or of temporarizing courts—to my own personal weight of character—nor finally, to any of the overweening influences I may possess, from popular manners, eminent talents, exalted learning, etc. Persons of atrocious character, who have violated the laws of God and man, are entitled to no such special exertions from any member of our pure and honourable profession; and, indeed, to no intervention beyond securing to them a fair and dispassionate investigation of the *facts* of their cause, and the due application of the law: all that goes beyond this, either in manner or substance, is unprofessional, and proceeds, either from a mistaken view of the relation of client and counsel, or from some unworthy and selfish motive, which sets a higher value on professional display and success, than on truth and justice, and the substantial interests of the community.

c.   JUSTIFICATIONS *

Which of the following arguments justifying the representation of the "guilty" is most persuasive?

a. Lawyers are advocates, and not judge and jury. If lawyers begin to judge their clients, the adversary system of justice will be destroyed.

b. The fact that a client appears to be guilty, indeed, has confessed to the commission of a crime, does not mean that he committed it. For every notorious crime, a number of people who could not possibly have committed it take credit for it. Frequently, men and women confess to crimes they did not commit in order to protect their families and friends. In no case, therefore, should a lawyer assume that because his client told him he committed the crime he actually is guilty.

c. The term, "guilty" has neither a moral nor a factual connotation in the law. It is strictly a legal term which refers to a formal adjudication after a prescribed process has been followed. The commis-

** David Hoffman, *A Course of Legal Study* (Baltimore: J. Neal, 1836), II, 755–57.

* Murray L. Schwartz, Cases and Materials on Professional Responsibility and the Administration of Criminal Justice (New York, Council on Legal Education for Professional Responsibility, 1961), pp. 113–115. © 1961 (Reprinted with permission).

sion of an *act* merely sets the process in operation; it does not mean *legal* guilt.

d. Under our system the prosecution has the burden of proving the defendant's guilt beyond a reasonable doubt. The fact that one human being, an attorney, may be persuaded of his client's guilt does not mean that twelve other human beings, the jury, will be.

e. Juries are rough instruments of justice, who may and do, take into consideration "non-legal" factors in deciding whether to convict, just as a prosecutor may take these factors into consideration in deciding whether to prosecute. Each defendant is entitled to this kind of consideration—which he cannot receive unless he pleads not guilty.

f. Criminal law is so complex that no defendant really knows whether he is guilty of any particular crime or not. To say that a lawyer is persuaded of his client's guilt may imply that the lawyer knows which form of theft or which degree of homicide, or which kind of burglary the defendant has committed. This is a determination which is properly for the court and jury, and can be obtained only after a plea of not guilty.

g. If lawyers refuse to represent defendants who they believe are guilty, the right of a defendant to be represented by counsel is eliminated and with it the entire traditional criminal trial.

Questions and Comment

Does anyone seriously deny the propriety of an attorney's representing somebody who is guilty, if that person pleads guilty and leaves the attorney to make the best case he or she can for a lenient sentence?

The issue, of course, is more difficult where the attorney representing someone who is guilty pleads not guilty and puts the state to its burden of proving guilt. If one believes that a person is innocent until proven guilty, does one then have to admit that both the defendant and the defense attorney have the right to put the state to its proof?

Where the accused is indigent and is provided with a lawyer at public expense, there seems to be no stigma attached to the public defender or the court-appointed counsel for doing his job. In the main, it is the private attorney who can, but does not, refuse the case who may suffer from a community reaction against one who defends the guilty.

How different is this from the case of a physician who cures someone of a disease knowing that, when cured, his patient will do harm to others? Presumably we would say that the patient's future conduct—or, even more clearly, his or her past conduct—is simply none of the physician's business. Why do we not simply say the same thing about the guilty client and the defense attorney? Is it possible that the reason for the difference in the way we look at the two roles is that we can think of ourselves as needing a physician but not as needing a defense attorney?

In any event the important issue is not whether a defense attorney can defend a particular unpopular client, but rather what the defense attorney can legally and ethically do for his or her client.

2.　THE ETHICS OF DEFENDING CRIMINALS

a.　NEW ANSWERS TO OLD QUESTIONS *

Most people in our society do not respect the mandate of the law just because it is the law. Most refrain from beating or mugging others because of some internal sense that it is wrong to treat people that way rather than from a fear of the law. The values that our criminal law teaches to those poor, minority defendants who confront it, however, lead to different conclusions. If human beings are worthy of so little respect, if having money is everything, if power itself is the justification for fulfilling one's desire at the expense of the powerless, and if law is merely one tool of such power, then the only reason not to commit any type of crime is fear of the law's power.

Abstaining from even a violent crime thus ceases to be the product of a moral decision, but becomes one based on expediency. As the costs decrease (or the risk of the cost becomes more remote) while the benefits remain clear and immediate, no compunction stands between the would-be offender and his criminal object. Moreover, if the costs are raised, the result may not be less crime, but rather more desperate and skillful criminals.

Our criminal courts must teach better lessons. It is to this end that I defend the guilty, for they, above all, must be taught the right lesson. It is not that I naively believe that most convicted defendants would thank a judge for being "fair" while sending them to prison. From my experience, however, the prevalent injustice in the current process does do harm by further lessening respect for the law, not just in the criminal defendants, but also in friends, family, witnesses, and spectators. The lessons are communicated to all of those who are touched by the process.

The defense of the guilty teaches new lessons. The act of defense itself teaches that the indigent defendant is not alone and worthless without money. The slow process of a rigorous defense may anger the judge by delaying the court's schedule, but it also forces the court to view the defendant as a person rather than a file. On some deeper level, the attorney's ardent defense itself communicates to the judge a sense of the defendant's human worth, and to the extent that a sincere, competent advocate earns the grudging respect of the court, some of that respect transfers to the defendant. As a result of this respect— and the knowledge that every ruling adverse to the defense will be contested—the judge rules more favorably for the defendant in order to

* John B. Mitchell, "The Ethics of the Criminal Defense Attorney," vol. 32 *Stanford Law Review* January 1980, pp. 325, 326, 327. Copyright 1980. Reprinted by permission of the Board of Trustees of the Leland Stanford Junior University.

avoid complications. Finally, police and prosecutors, aware that a defense attorney is carefully questioning and reviewing all their actions, begin to hesitate to engage with such broad abandon in illegality and misconduct for fear of getting caught.[1] Power will thus begin to conform more to law than the other way around.

b. FURTHER REASONS FOR DEFENDING THE GUILTY *

By providing a rigorous defense for the factually guilty, an attorney fulfills two significant functions. First, the attorney insures that the guilty defendant (to whom our society has promised the absolute right to the full benefit of our legal process, regardless of guilt or innocence) will be treated with fairness, equanimity and human decency while in that legal process. . . . The second function is one which protects every one of us in this society. I will call this function making the "screens" work.

Our criminal justice system should be more appropriately defined as a screening system, rather than a truth-seeking one. The principal function of the criminal justice system is to actively engage in a screening process throughout our entire society. (The system also deters crime through use and threat of its sanction and teaches lessons in justice). This screening process is directed at accurately sorting out those members of the society whose deviancy has gone beyond what is considered tolerable and has passed into the area which substantive law labels as criminal. . . . The ultimate objective of this screening is to determine who is a proper subject of the criminal sanction. This screening process goes on continually at every level of the society. We all make constant judgments about, e.g., someone's unusual behavior, a window that looks pried open, a suspicious looking stranger. Neighbor talks to neighbor and information is filtered to the police. The police in turn comb the streets night and day gathering information to help them determine whose behavior warrants being selected out from the rest. Finally, prosecutors, courts and juries are constantly sifting through those the police have selected to make final determinations regarding the most serious question of who is to be subject to the criminal sanction, including decisions regarding who is to be forcibly removed from our society or even executed.

In carrying out this screening process, however, the criminal justice system does not operate as a truth-seeking process in the scientific

1. Especially great strides can be made in curbing police perjury by pointing out inconsistencies between police testimony at trial and prior testimony at pretrial hearings or materials in police reports. When the conflicting statements are obviously helpful to the prosecution, the inference of perjury is clear. Defense attorneys are further aided in that police, who for years had been spoiled at suppression hearings by judges' refusal to question the most outrageous testimony, and at trials by pre-
Watergate juries who implicitly trusted the government and its agents, tend to be very poor liars.

* John B. Mitchell, "The Ethics of Defending the Guilty and Dangerous—New Answers to Old Questions 3–5;" unpublished manuscript delivered to University of California School of Law, Berkeley, California, March, 1978. © 1978 (Reprinted with permission).

sense. It is weighted at trial in favor of protecting the innocent at the cost of acquitting the guilty. It is weighted on the streets in favor of protecting the individual from intrusion by the state at the cost of the more efficient method of crime control which would result if police could stop, question and search anyone they desired. In so doing, our process protects two interrelated and overlapping values (or perhaps, more accurately, two aspects of the same value, i.e., human freedom)— dignity and autonomy.

The "weighting" of the system to avoid conviction of the innocent reflects the paramount value this society places upon the dignity of the individual, as well as our concern for the value of human autonomy, a concern which makes us reluctant to allow government to enter our daily lives, either to restrict our freedom or to intrude into our privacy. The "weighting" against police intrusion similarly reflects these two interrelated values.

Despite the screening system discussed [above] most defendants never get near a trial court.

It is common wisdom that in most instances (at least in the metropolitan-urban areas of state court systems) our legal system operates as an administrative system, processing 90% of its dispositions through an "assembly-line" like plea bargaining system. The prosecutor assumes the position of the central figure in the system, while the judge assumes more of a figure-head role, rubber-stamping consummated plea bargains through the hollow incantation of the "cop out" litany. Of most significance, I believe, is that, for the most part, there are no true advocates for the defendant. In short, for most criminal defendants, our legal system has ceased in practice to be the traditional accusatorial-adversarial-judicial.

. . .

Those who are brought into the process . . . arrive there as the result of the probable cause determination of the arresting police officer and the prosecutor's discretionary decision to file charges, both of these determinations falling well below "beyond a reasonable doubt." Thus if the tendency of the institution to deny trials to all who enter it is left unchecked, many whose guilt has not been established beyond a reasonable doubt will be coerced by the institution into pleading guilty. Among these will be innocent people.

In theory, several different sources could serve as a check on this tendency and insure that the innocent are still protected. The legal system is a political institution. The general public thus could serve as a check on hasty convictions. . . . But fear of violent crime has made the public far more concerned about the conviction of the guilty than the protection of the innocent and has thus, if anything, encouraged rather than checked the tendency of the legal institution to coerce guilty pleas. . . .

. . .

The last possible restraint on the court could come from an independent advocate who would insure that the innocent were protected by reasonable doubt and jury trials if necessary. . . .

The relationship between the defense of the guilty and the protection of the innocent in our plea bargaining system thus becomes a complex one . . . . No doubt, regardless of the dedication of the defense attorney, most defendants will still plead guilty due to strong evidence of guilt and good "deals." Yet in order to convince innocent defendants that if they refuse such "deals," there are competent attorneys who are willing to fight their cases at trial, attorneys must go to trial as much as possible. This means representing guilty as well as innocent defendants. . . .

[The author goes on to make the point that the only time the screening system is realistically tested is when the accused, who is probably himself guilty, goes to trial. As a result, the lawyer who defends the guilty at trial is also making sure the screening system works on behalf of the great majority of defendants who are taken into the system and induced into pleading guilty.]

c. PROSECUTORIAL ETHICS VERSUS DEFENSE COUNSEL ETHICS *

Defense counsel and prosecutor have significantly different roles and functions, and . . . their ethical difficulties vary accordingly. Defense counsel has obligations deriving from the importance, to the adversary system, of confidentiality between attorney and client, the presumption of innocence and burden of proof, the constitutional right to counsel, and the constitutional privilege against self-incrimination. The prosecutor, who does not represent a private client, is not affected by these considerations in the same way. For example, the defense attorney is privileged to withhold evidence: there is nothing unethical in keeping a guilty defendant off the stand, and putting the government to its proof. The Constitution guarantees nothing less than this. Obviously, however, it does not follow that the prosecutor is also privileged to withhold or suppress material evidence, or that there is something essentially unfair in this double standard.

Similarly, it is ethical for defense counsel to cross-examine a prosecution witness to make him appear to be inaccurate or untruthful, even when the defense attorney knows that the witness is testifying accurately and truthfully. Although it appears to be inconsistent with their general position that counsel should never mislead the court in any way, . . . [Chief Justice] Judge Warren E. Burger agrees with this conclusion. He reach[es] this result on the reasoning that the defense is entitled to "put the government to its proof" and to "test the truth of the prosecution's case," whereas I base the same conclusion on the necessities of the obligation of confidentiality. However, neither of

* Monroe H. Freedman, "The Professional Responsibility of the Prosecuting Attorney," 55 *Georgetown Law Journal*, 1967, p. 1030. © 1967 (Reprinted with permission).

these rationales would justify a prosecutor in obtaining a conviction by making a defense witness appear to be lying when the prosecutor knows that the witness is testifying truthfully. The defendant, who is presumed innocent, does not have a burden of proof to be tested, nor does the prosecutor function under the burden of an obligation of confidentiality in conducting himself at trial.

Also bearing upon the different obligations of defense counsel and prosecutor are the relevant and important distinctions between the government and the individual citizen who is prosecuted. One such distinction is the paramountcy of the individual and the sanctity of his personality in our society. Another is the awesome power of the government, a power that the Founding Fathers had good reason to circumscribe in the Bill of Rights and elsewhere in the Constitution. A third difference is the majesty and dignity of our government. Conduct that may be tolerable in individuals may be reprehensible when done "under color of law" on behalf of the nation or a state. These considerations must be given due regard in setting the standards of ethical conduct to be expected of the prosecutor as attorney for the government. In addition, the prosecutor has enormous and unique discretion in defining the particular crime, affecting the punishment, and even in deciding whether to prosecute at all. Thus, to say that the prosecutor has special responsibilities in exercising his discretion is simply to recognize that he is the attorney who has discretion to exercise.

Comment

One major difference between the prosecutorial ethics and the defense counsel's ethics, as a practical matter, is related to the fact that the prosecution cannot appeal an acquittal. As a result, if unethical conduct by a defense attorney has resulted in his client's acquittal, the matter typically receives little further attention. If, however, the prosecutor has misbehaved, that matter can be reviewed by an appellate court or, even after the defense has exhausted its appeals, by a writ of habeas corpus. The continuing interest we have in the derelictions of prosecutors allows us to hold them to a higher standard than we do defense attorneys.

d. LAWYERS' DUTIES TO CLIENTS VERSUS THEIR DUTIES TO THE COURT

(1) THE DUTY OF THE ADVOCATE IN OTHER LEGAL SYSTEMS

(a) *Note on the Kostov Case:*

In 1949, Traicho Kostov, Former Vice Premier of Bulgaria was tried in that country for espionage and treason. His lawyer, Lueben Diukmejiev, began his defense by drawing a distinction between the role of the defense lawyer in a socialist country as opposed to his role in a Western "bourgeois" state. In a socialist state, he said, a lawyer could not defend a criminal whom he knew was guilty, "merely by scoring technical points" against the prosecution. As he stated "In a Socialist state there is no division of duty between the judge, prosecutor and defense counsel . . . the defense must assist the prosecution to find the objective truth in a case." There were several other defense counsel all of whom agreed with Mr. Kostov and joined in what seemed to be his apology for defending the case at all. They pointed out that under the Bulgarian Constitution, every accused was entitled to a defense.

The charges apparently involved a treasonous conspiracy with Marshall Tito and what was considered to be the renegade Yugoslavian Communist Party. Mr. Diukmejiev stated that his client, Mr. Kostov, had asked him to show, in refutation of the charges, first, that he (Kostov) had presented an anti-Tito report at the Communist Party conclave that expelled the Yugoslav party, and second, that Tito himself had said that he had always believed that Kostov was the agent of a foreign power. The defense lawyer did not bother waiting for the court's refutation of these remarks and said that the first was "hardly a serious argument as Mr. Kostov was presenting a report only in behalf of the central committee of the Bulgarian Communist Party." The second point, Diukmejiev said, was invalid because Marshall Tito was only "covering up his tracks for the day when Mr. Kostov would be arrested so he could prove Mr. Kostov had not been his agent."

In conclusion, Kostov's lawyer stated "If Traicho Kostov finds words to show he recognizes his crimes, then I beg this may be taken in his favor." Kostov was convicted and executed.

About six years later, a re-examination of the trial cleared Kostov's name.*

Comment

It is possible, of course, that even a vigorous defense would not have saved Mr. Kostov. It is clear, however, that the kind of defense he received from his attorneys—who conformed to the norms of their profession—had three consequences. First, it made Kostov's erroneous conviction that much more likely. Second, the fact that the officials in charge of the prosecutorial apparatus could count on such an apologetic defense allowed them to prosecute cases of, at best, dubious strength. And finally, the failure of the defense to reveal the weakness of the prosecution's case, prevented the publicity which might have acted as a check upon such prosecutions in the future.

(b) Cuban Defense Lawyers **

Cuban justice is not an adversary system. As the law professors at the University of Havana explained, "the first job of a revolutionary

---

* The trial of Kostov and its aftermath were reported in the New York Times of December 14, 1949, pp. 1 and 9, and April 4, 1956, p. 1. (Reprinted with permission).

** Jesse Berman, "The Cuban Popular Tribunals," *Columbia Law Review,* 60 (1969), 1341. © 1969 (Reprinted with permission).

lawyer is not to argue that his client is innocent, but rather to determine if his client is guilty and, if so, to seek the sanction which will best rehabilitate him."

Questions

If this is the duty of the revolutionary defense lawyer, what does the revolutionary prosecutor do? Under this view of the defense lawyer's role, is he or she not simply a spy on the defendant?

(2) WHAT DOES THE LAWYER KNOW? †

If there is a reason why a lawyer should not behave differently where she knows her client is guilty, it is not because she never knows, or because her role prevents her from knowing, but rather because her role requires her to act as if she did not know—a very different matter. Certainly, there is nothing incorrect in applying our common sense and concluding that a lawyer may know the guilt of her client in the same way that all of us know anything: the lawyer may examine the evidence available on the proposition and make her decision.

The real issue is what follows from the lawyer's examining all of the evidence, and concluding that she has no reasonable, or even unreasonable, doubt about her client's guilt. Do we wish her to behave differently in handling the defense? Even without considering what differences in behavior we would require where we were prepared to conclude that the lawyer did know her client's guilt, we can see that in some situations the source of the lawyer's knowledge should require no change at all in her behavior. Take the case where the lawyer concludes that her client is guilty, based on evidence that will be presented to the fact-finder. Here, there is no reason to assume that the strength of the case against her client, which has influenced the lawyer, will be lost upon the judge and jury. If the lawyer for the defendant is required to make important decisions based on her own finding as to the innocence or guilt of her client, one may ask, "Why have the judge or jury?". Of course, the lawyer's advice and tactics may vary with the strength of the evidence against her client, but this is not because of her view of the client's guilt.

What about the case where the lawyer concludes her client is guilty based upon hearsay or character evidence which is inadmissible and, hence, would not be heard by the jury? As a first approximation, the answer is relatively simple. To a considerable extent, the reason why these types of evidence are inadmissible is that they are not sufficiently probative to be relied on by the fact finder. Presumably, we would not wish to have less stringent rules of proof for the lawyer as fact finder than we have for the ultimate fact finder.

† John Kaplan, Defending the Guilty,—
Bridgeport Law Review—(1987) © 1987
(Reprinted with permission).

There are a whole series of more difficult cases, however, where our analysis is somewhat more complex. The problem is particularly difficult in two other situations. The first is where the lawyer's knowledge of her client's guilt is based on probative, but illegally seized, evidence. Again, we generally hold that this makes no difference. Perhaps here we can argue that the deterrent effect of the exclusionary rule would be compromised and police would still have an incentive to violate the Constitution if, even though the evidence were inadmissible, the defense lawyer would be influenced by it to her client's detriment. The second situation occurs where the defense attorney, in the course of her investigation, discovers probative testimony which convinces her of her client's guilt. Here we must argue that the same requirements of the adversary system which prevent her from revealing this information to the prosecution or the court also prevent her from relying on that evidence to the detriment of her client.

In both of these situations the law, as if unhappy with one extreme or the other, has attempted some kind of a compromise. In the case of the illegally seized evidence, the lawyer's conduct may not be influenced but the client takes the stand to deny the crime only at his own risk; the suppressed evidence may become admissible against him "as impeachment." In the second situation, though the lawyer need not reveal witnesses or testimony against her client, she does in many jurisdictions have the duty to turn over physical evidence that may help the prosecution. Presumably, in this case she makes no representation nor does she change tactics based on a belief her client is guilty, but rather merely turns over material that may or may not be probative evidence against her client.

In any event, these rules are relatively narrow and do not negate the basic principle that a lawyer's conduct in her client's case should not be influenced by whether, based on the strength of the admissible or unadmissible evidence against her client, she actually believes that her client is guilty. This result may be regarded as a refusal to require a lawyer to disbelieve her own client. Of course, it does not really matter whether the lawyer disbelieves her client; she is not to change what would otherwise be her behavior based on her personal belief that her client is lying.

The one important situation, however, where the lawyer is required to judge the guilt of her client seems to be a consequence of this phrasing of the rule. If the lawyer reaches a conclusion as to her client's guilt, relying on her client's own statements, she cannot be said to be disbelieving her own client. Quite the contrary; the problem for the client is that the lawyer does believe him.

There are still reasons why we might not wish to have a lawyer, relying on the client's inculpatory statements, act to a defendant's detriment. In part, these stem from the symbolic role of the lawyer as the defendant's only friend. If the lawyer uses a client's confidential admissions to the detriment of her client, to some extent she is more a spy for the prosecution than a loyal friend to the accused.

More important, we must also consider the practical effect of our rules in this area. If we hold that a lawyer must act to her client's detriment based on her client's admissions, lawyers will probably attempt to avoid hearing such statements. Certainly, this is the most obvious way to balance the demands of loyalty to one's client with any rule forcing a lawyer to act against the client's interests should her client confess to her. Lawyers then would have to give their clients almost the equivalent of Miranda warnings, explaining that a client who expects certain behavior from his lawyer (the precise content of which we will go into later) cannot afford to make inculpatory statements. To insure that the client understands which statements are inculpatory, the lawyer would have to rely on "the lecture," initially doing all the talking herself, laying out the law in the area and what she knows of the prosecution's evidence, and making it clear what the client can and cannot admit.

(3) The Lecture *

I paused and lit a cigar. I took my time. I had reached a point where a few wrong answers to a few right questions would leave me with a client—if I took his case—whose cause was legally defenseless. Either I stopped now and begged off and let some other lawyer worry over it or I asked him the few fatal questions and let him hang himself. Or else, like any smart lawyer, I went into the Lecture. I studied my man, who sat as inscrutable as an Arab, delicately fingering his Ming holder, daintily sipping his dark mustache. He apparently did not realize how close I had him to admitting that he was guilty of first degree murder, that is, that he "feloniously, wilfully and of his malice aforethought did kill and murder one Barney Quill." The man was a sitting duck. . . .

And what is the Lecture?

The Lecture is an ancient device that lawyers use to coach their clients so that the client won't quite know he has been coached and his lawyer can still preserve the face-saving illusion that he hasn't done any coaching. For coaching clients, like robbing them, is not only frowned upon, it is downright unethical and bad, very bad. Hence the Lecture, an artful device as old as the law itself, and one used constantly by some of the nicest and most ethical lawyers in the land. "Who, me? I didn't tell him what to say," the lawyer can later comfort himself. "I merely explained the law, see." It is a good practice to scowl and shrug here and add virtuously: "That's my duty, isn't it?"

Verily, the question, like expert lecturing, is unchallengeable.

* Voelker, John Donaldson (R. Travers, pseudonym), *Anatomy of a Murder*, (New York: St. Martin's Press, 1958), pp. 32–49. © 1958 (Reprinted with permission).

I was ready to do my duty by my client and he sat regarding me quietly, watchfully as I lit a new cigar.

"As I told you," I began, "I've been thinking about your case during the noon hour."

"Yes," he replied. "You mentioned that."

"So I did, so I did," I said. "Now I realize there are many questions still to be asked, facts to be discussed," I went on. "And I am not prejudging your case." I paused to discharge the opening salvo of the Lecture. "But as things presently stand I must advise you that in my opinion you have not yet disclosed to me a *legal* defense to this charge of murder."

I again paused to let this sink in. It is a necessary condition to the successful lecture. . . .

"Yes, but how about that bastard Quill raping my wife?" my man said quietly. "How about the 'unwritten law'?"

I had been waiting for that one. "There is no such thing as the 'unwritten law' in Anglo-American jurisprudence," I said, a little pontifically. "It is merely another one of those dearly hugged folk-myths that people regularly die for, like the notion that raw rhubarb is good for the clap or that all chorus girls lay or that night air is bad. In fact many a man who has depended on the myth of the 'unwritten law' has instead descended from a rope." I paused, rather relishing the phrase, and resolved to remember it.

"Have we disposed of the 'unwritten law'?" I said.

"Perhaps," he said. "But unwritten law or no, doesn't a man have a legal right to kill a man who has raped his wife? Isn't that the *written* law then?"

"No, only to prevent it, or if he has caught him at it, or, finally, to prevent his escape." We were treading dangerous ground again and I spoke rapidly to prevent any interruption. "In fact, Lieutenant, for all the elaborate hemorrhage of words in the law books about the legal defenses to murder there are only about three basic defenses: one, that it didn't happen but was instead a suicide or accident or what not; two, that whether it happened or not you didn't do it, such as alibi, mistaken identity and so forth; and three, that even if it happened and you did it, your action was legally justified or excusable." I paused to see how my student was doing.

The Lieutenant grew thoughtful. "Where do I fit in that rosy picture?" he responded nicely.

"I can tell you better where you don't fit," I went on. "Since a whole barroom full of people saw you shoot down Barney Quill in apparent cold blood, you scarcely fit in the first two classes of defenses. I'm afraid we needn't waste time on those." I paused. "If you fit anywhere it's got to be in the third. So we'd better bear down on that."

"You mean," Lieutenant Manion said, "that my only possible defense in this case is to find some justification or excuse?"

My lecture was proceeding nicely according to schedule. "You're learning rapidly," I said, nodding approvingly. "Merely add *legal* justification or excuse and I'll mark you an A."

"And you say that a man is not justified in killing a man who has just raped and beat up his wife?"

"Morally, perhaps, but not legally. Not after it's all over, as it was here." I paused, wondering why I didn't go to Detroit and lecture in night school. That way, too, I would be close enough to go see all my old school's home football games. "Hail to the victors valiant. . . ." "You see, Lieutenant," I went on, "it's not the *act* of killing a man that makes it murder; it is the circumstances, the time, and the state of mind or purpose which induced the act." I paused, and could almost hear my old Crimes professor, J.B. "Jabby" White, droning this out in law school nearly twenty years before. It was amazing how the old stuff stuck.

The Lieutenant's eyes narrowed and flickered ever so little. "Maybe," he began, and cleared his throat. "On second thought, maybe I did catch Quill in the act. I've never precisely told the police one way or the other." His eyes regarded me quietly, steadily. This man, I saw, was not only an apt student of the Lecture; like most people (including lawyers) he indubitably possessed a heart full of larceny. He was also, perhaps instinctively, trying to turn the Lecture on his lawyer. "I've never really told them," he concluded.

A lawyer in the midst of his Lecture is apt to cling to the slenderest reed to bolster his wavering virtue. "But you've told *me*," I said, pausing complacently, swollen with rectitude, grateful for the swift surge of virtue he'd afforded me. "And anyway," I went on, "you would have had to dispatch him then, not, as you've already admitted, an hour or so later. The catching and killing must combine. And that's true even if you'd actually caught him at it—which you didn't. I've just now told you that *time* is one of the factors in determining whether a homicide is a murder or not. Here it's a big one. Don't you see?—in your case *time* is the rub; it's the elapsed *time* between the rape and the killing that permits the People to bear down and argue that your shooting of Barney Quill was a deliberate malicious and premeditated act. And that, my friend, is no more than they've charged you with."

Stoically: "Are you telling me to plead guilty?"

"Look, we've been over that. When I'm ready to advise you to cop out you'll know it. Right now I want you to realize what you're up against, man."

The Lieutenant blinked his eyes thoughtfully. "I'm busy realizing," he said.

"As things now stand in your case, all the *law* would be against you. The judge would be virtually forced to instruct the jury to convict you. Don't you see? A jury would find it tough to let you go; they'd have to really work at it. Legally your situation presents a classic one of premeditated murder."

Quietly: "You don't want to take my case, then?"

"Not quite so fast. I'm not ready to make that decision. Look, in a murder case the jury has only a few narrow choices. Among them, it *might* let you go. It *might* also up and convict you. A judge trying you without a jury would surely have to, as I have said. Now do you want to go into court with the dice loaded? With all the law and instructions stacked against you?" I paused to deliver my clincher. "Well, whether you're willing to do so, I'm not. I will either find a sound and plausible legal defense in your case or else advise you to cop out." I paused thoughtfully. . . . "I'm a lawyer, not a juggler or a hypnotist nor even a magician or boy orator. When I undertake to defend a man before a jury I want to have a fighting *legal* chance to acquit him. That includes having a decent chance to move for a new trial or successfully appeal. Maybe you were morally entitled to plug Barney Quill. I'll even concede it. But in court I prefer to leave the moral judgments to the angels. I doubtless possess my fair share of ham, like most lawyers, but I do not want to go into court and depend simply upon the charity or stupidity or state of the liver of twelve jurors." I paused. . . . "What's more, I don't intend to," I said. "Have I made myself clear?"

"I'm afraid you have, Counselor." . . .

"That brings me to my sixty-four-dollar point. Even jurors have to save face. Get this now. The jury in your case might simply be dying to let you go on your own story, or because they have fallen for your wife, or have learned to hate Barney Quill's guts, or all of these things and more. But if the judge—who's got a nice big legal face to save, too—must under the law virtually tell the jurors to convict you, as I think he must now surely do, then the only way they can possibly let you go is by flying in the face of the judge's instructions—that is, by losing, not saving face. Don't you see? You and I would be in there asking twelve citizens, twelve total strangers, to publicly lose their precious face to save yours. It's asking a lot and I hope you don't have to risk it."

Lieutenant Manion produced the Ming holder and studied it carefully, as though for the first time. "What do you recommend then?" he said.

It was a good question. "I don't know yet. So far I've been trying to impress you with the importance, the naked necessity, of our finding a valid legal defense, if one exists, in addition to the 'unwritten law' you so dearly want to cling to. Put it this way: what Barney Quill might have done to your wife before you killed him may present a favorable condition, an equitable climate, to a possible jury acquittal. But alone it simply isn't enough." I paused. "Not enough for Paul Biegler, anyway."

"You mean you want to find a way to give the jurors some decently plausible legal peg to hang their verdict on so that they might let me go—and still save face?"

My man was responding beautifully to the lecture. "Precisely," I said, adding hastily: "Whether you have such a defense of course remains to be seen. But I hope, Lieutenant, I have shown you how vital it is to find one if it exists."

"I think you have, Counselor," he said slowly. "I rather think now you really have." He paused. "Tell me, tell me more about this justification or excuse business. Excuse me," he added, smiling faintly, "I mean *legal* justification or excuse."

"First I've got to go phone my office," I said arising. "That'll also give me a chance for some solitary skull practice. It's been quite a while since I've had to brush up on my murder." . . .

I was back with my man and ready to go. The signs were good: for the first time he was smoking *without* the Ming holder. "We will now explore the absorbing subject of legal justification or excuse," I said.

"You may fire when ready, Gridley," the Lieutenant said.

I looked hopefully at the man. Was it barely possible that he possessed a rudimentary sense of humor? "Well, take self-defense," I began. "That's the classic example of justifiable homicide. On the basis of what I've so far heard and read about your case I do not think we need pause too long over that. Do you?"

"Perhaps not," Lieutenant Manion conceded. "We'll pass it for now."

"Let's," I said dryly. "Then there's the defense of habitation, defense of property, and the defense of relatives or friends. Now there are more ramifications to these defenses than a dog has fleas, but we won't explore them now. I've already told you at length why I don't think you can invoke the possible defense of your wife. When you shot Quill her need for defense had passed. It's as simple as that."

"Go on," Lieutenant Manion said, frowning.

"Then there's the defense of a homicide committed to prevent a felony—say you're being robbed—; to prevent the escape of the felon— suppose he's getting away with your wallet—; or to arrest a felon— you've caught up with him and he's either trying to get away or has actually escaped."

At this point I paused and blinked thoughtfully. An idea no bigger than a pea rattled faintly at the back door of my mind. Let's see. . . . Wouldn't it be true that if Barney Quill actually raped Laura Manion *he* would be a felon at large at the time he was shot? The pea kept faintly rattling. But so what, so what? "Hm. . . ." I said. It would bear pondering.

The Lieutenant's eyes gleamed and bored into mine. "Who—what do you see?" he said. It was becoming increasingly clear that this soldier was no dummy.

"Nothing," I lied glibly. "Not a thing." The student was getting ahead of the lecturer and that would never do. And wherever my idea might drop into the ultimate defense picture, I sensed that now was not the time to try to fit it. "I was just thinking," I concluded.

"Yes," Lieutenant Manion said. "You were just thinking." He smiled faintly. "Go on, then; what are some of the other legal justifications or excuses?"

"Then there's the tricky and dubious defense of intoxication. Personally I've never seen it succeed. But since you were not drunk when you shot Quill we shall mercifully not dwell on that. Or were you?"

"I was cold sober. Please go on."

"Then finally there's the defense of insanity." I paused and spoke abruptly, airily: "Well, that just about winds it up." I arose as though making ready to leave.

"Tell me more."

"There is no more." I slowly paced up and down the room.

"I mean about this insanity."

"Oh, insanity," I said, elaborately surprised. It was like luring a trained seal with a herring. "Well, insanity, where proved, is a complete defense to murder. It does not legally justify the killing, like self-defense, say, but rather excuses it." The lecturer was hitting his stride. He was also on the home stretch. "Our law requires that a punishable killing—in fact, any crime—must be committed by a sapient human being, one capable, as the law insists, of distinguishing between right and wrong. If a man is insane, legally insane, the act of homicide may still be murder but the law excuses the perpetrator."

Lieutenant Manion was sitting erect now, very still and erect. "I see—and this—this perpetrator, what happens to him if he should—should be excused?"

"Under Michigan law—like that of many other states—if he is acquitted of murder on the grounds of insanity it is provided that he must be sent to a hospital for the criminally insane until he is pronounced sane." I drummed my fingers on the Sheriff's desk and glanced at my watch, the picture of a man eager to be gone.

My man was baying along the scent now. "How long does it take to get him out of there?"

"Out of where?" I asked innocently.

"Out of this insane hospital!"

"Oh, you mean where a man claims he was insane at the time of the offense but is sane at the time of the trial and his possible acquittal?"

"Exactly."

"I don't know," I said, stroking my chin. "Months, maybe a year. It really takes a bit of doing. Being D.A. so long I've never really had to study that phase of it. I got them in there; it was somebody else's problem to spring them. And I didn't dream this defense might come up in your case."

My naïveté was somewhat excessive; it had been obvious to me from merely reading the newspaper the night before that insanity was the best, if not the only, legal defense the man had. And here I'd just slammed shut every other escape hatch and told him this was the last. Only a cretin could have missed it, and I was rapidly learning that Lieutenant Manion was no cretin.

"Tell me more," Lieutenant Manion said quietly.

"I may add that the law that requires persons acquitted on the grounds of insanity to be sent away is designed to discourage phony pleas of insanity in criminal cases."

"Yes?"

"So the man who successfully invokes the defense of insanity is taking a calculated risk, ..."

I paused and knocked out my pipe. The Lecture was about over. The rest was up to the student. The Lieutenant looked out the window. He studied his Ming holder. I sat very still. Then he looked at me. "Maybe," he said, "maybe I was insane."

Very casually: "Maybe you were insane when?" I said. "When you shot the German lieutenant?"

"You know what I mean. When I shot Barney Quill."

Thoughtfully: "Hm. . . . Why do you say that?"

"Well, I can't really say," he went on slowly. "I—I guess I blacked out. I can't remember a thing after I saw him standing behind the bar that night until I got back to my trailer."

"You mean—you mean you don't remember shooting him?" I shook my head in wonderment.

"Yes, that's what I mean."

"You don't even remember driving home?"

"No."

"You don't even remember threatening Barney's bartender when he followed you outside after the shooting—as the newspaper says you did?" I paused and held my breath. "You don't remember telling him, 'Do you want some, too, Buster?'?"

The smoldering dark eyes flickered ever so little. "No, not a thing."

"My, my," I said, blinking my eyes, contemplating the wonder of it all. "Maybe you've got something there."

The Lecture was over; I had told my man the law; and now he had told me things that might possibly invoke the defense of insanity. It had all been done with mirrors. Or rather with padded hammers. There remained only the loose ends to gather in. I'd try to make it short.

I turned and looked out the sooty window. "Let me think a minute," I said. Then I turned and studied the impaled cockroach. All right, I thought—maybe my man was insane when he shot Barney Quill. Maybe he was nuttier than a fruit cake and maybe he had blacked out and didn't remember a thing. So far so good. But there was one flaw, one small thorn in this insanity business, and one that had to be faced, and fast. And wasn't it far better to face it now, before I got committed in the case, than later on in the harsh glow of the courtroom? I turned back to my man.

"Look, Lieutenant. Hold your hat. I'm about to pitch you a fast ball. . . . Maybe you were insane. Maybe you didn't remember a thing. But you and the newspaper agree on one thing. Both of you tell me that right after you returned to the trailer park, after shooting Barney Quill, you woke up the deputized caretaker and told him: 'I just shot Barney Quill.' Now is that correct?" Again I held my breath.

I rather think he saw what was coming, but he replied steadily enough. "That is right," he answered because he had to, there was no other answer, no escape; he was already committed on that one far past the point of no return.

Slowly, easily: "All right, then, Lieutenant. Now tell me, how come you could tell the caretaker you had just shot Barney Quill if you had really blacked out and didn't remember a thing? *Who told you?*"

"Well," he began. Then he stopped cold and closed his eyes. He was stalled. It was the first time I'd seen him really grope. The silence continued. Was I, I wondered, developing into one of those incurable ex-D.A.'s, the unreconstructed kind who can always find more reasons for convicting their clients than acquitting them?

"Come, come, Lieutenant," I said. "Think!"

Impatiently, the lower lip still projected: "I *am* thinking! I'm trying to remember, damn it."

I was thankful a jury wasn't watching him during the process. It also occurred to me that he must have been a charming child. "Come now man," I pressed, "what could possibly have led you to tell the caretaker you'd just shot Barney if it is true that you didn't remember it?"

He spoke rapidly, jerkily. "All right. . . . It's coming back. . . . Barney Quill was the last man I saw before I blacked out. . . . In fact his was the only face I saw in the whole damned place. . . . My gun. . . . I knew when I entered the barroom the clip of my lüger was loaded. When I got back to my trailer I saw it was empty. There's a thing that pops up. . . ." He threw out his hands. "Don't you see? I figured I *must* have shot him, that's all. So I went and told the caretaker I had." He paused and looked up at me like a child who'd just recited his Christmas poem. Had he done all right?

It was the only plausible explanation he could have made. "I see," I said thoughtfully. "So that's the way it is?" But, old fire horse that I was, I yearned to be D.A. and be faced with such an answer. It would have been a pleasure to rip and dig at this man. "I see," I repeated. So far, I felt, this was the biggest flaw, the highest hurdle, to a successful plea of insanity. It, too, would take some pondering.

I glanced at my watch and arose. After all I hadn't fished for two whole days. "That's enough for today," I said. "Class is dismissed. I'll see you again tomorrow."

Questions

Is there anything wrong with lawyers telling their clients what the law is before their clients give their side of the story? If there is something wrong, what can we do about it, since all defendants would have to do is to go to one lawyer to ask what the law is and then, knowing this, go to another and tell their stories?

One commentator has written:

"[T]he lawyer [in the *Anatomy of a Murder* case] is giving the client more than just 'information about the law,' but is actively participating in—indeed, initiating—a factual defense that is obviously perjurious. To suggest that the less well-educated defendant is entitled to that extent of participation by the attorney in manufacturing perjury carries the 'equalizer' concept of the lawyer's role too far. Moreover, even though the client has initially been truthful in telling his story to the attorney in confidence, it does not follow that there is any breach of confidentiality if the lawyer simply declines to create a false story for the client." *

How can one draw the line between giving legal advice to clients and helping them make up stories?

(4) WHAT SHOULD THE LAWYER DO? **

In almost any area of legal counseling and advocacy, the lawyer may be faced with the dilemma of either betraying the confidential communications of his client or participating to some extent in the purposeful deception of the court. This problem is nowhere more acute than in the practice of criminal law, particularly in the representation

---

* Monroe Freedman, *Lawyer's Ethics in an Adversary System,* Bobbs-Merrill Co., Indianapolis 1975, pp. 71, 73. © 1975 (Reprinted with permission).

** Monroe H. Freedman, "Professional Responsibility of the Criminal Defense Lawyer: The Three Hardest Questions," 64 *Michigan Law Review,* (1966), 1469. © 1966 (Reprinted with permission).

of the indigent accused. The purpose of this article is to analyze and attempt to resolve some of the most difficult issues in this general area:

Is it proper to put a witness on the stand when you know he will commit perjury? . . .

The attorney functions in an adversary system based upon the presupposition that the most effective means of determining truth is to present to a judge and jury a clash between proponents of conflicting views. It is essential to the effective functioning of this system that each adversary have, in the words of Canon 15, "entire devotion to the interest of the client, warm zeal in the maintenance and defense of his rights and the exertion of his utmost learning and ability." It is also essential to maintain the fullest uninhibited communication between the client and his attorney, so that the attorney can most effectively counsel his client and advocate the latter's cause.

. . . Assume, for example, that the witness in question is the accused himself, and that he has admitted to you, in response to your assurances of confidentiality, that he is guilty. However, he insists upon taking the stand to protest his innocence. There is a clear consensus among prosecutors and defense attorneys that the likelihood of conviction is increased enormously when the defendant does not take the stand. Consequently, the attorney who prevents his client from testifying only because the client has confided his guilt to him is violating that confidence by acting upon the information in a way that will seriously prejudice his client's interests.

Perhaps the most common method for avoiding the ethical problem just posed is for the lawyer to withdraw from the case, at least if there is sufficient time before trial for the client to retain another attorney. The client will then go to the nearest law office, realizing that the obligation of confidentiality is not what it has been represented to be, and withhold incriminating information or the fact of his guilt from his new attorney. On ethical grounds, the practice of withdrawing from a case under such circumstances is indefensible, since the identical perjured testimony will ultimately be presented. More important, perhaps, is the practical consideration that the new attorney will be ignorant of the perjury and therefore will be in no position to attempt to discourage the client from presenting it. Only the original attorney, who knows the truth, has that opportunity, but he loses it in the very act of evading the ethical problem.

The problem is all the more difficult when the client is indigent. He cannot retain other counsel, and in many jurisdictions, including the District of Columbia, it is impossible for appointed counsel to withdraw from a case except for extraordinary reasons. Thus, appointed counsel, unless he lies to the judge, can successfully withdraw only by revealing to the judge that the attorney has received knowledge of his client's guilt. Such a revelation in itself would seem to be a sufficiently serious violation of the obligation of confidentiality to merit severe condemnation. In fact, however, the situation is far worse, since it is entirely possible that the same judge who permits the attorney to withdraw will subsequently hear the case and sentence the defendant. When he does so, of course, he will have had personal knowledge of the defendant's guilt before the trial began. Moreover, this will be knowledge of which the newly appointed counsel for the defendant will probably be ignorant.

. . .

If a lawyer has discovered his client's intent to perjure himself, one possible solution to this problem is for the lawyer to approach the bench, explain his ethical difficulty to the judge, and ask to be relieved, thereby causing a mistrial. This request is certain to be denied, if only because it would empower the defendant to cause a series of mistrials in the same fashion. At this point, some feel that the lawyer has avoided the ethical problem and can put the defendant on the stand. However, one objection to this solution, apart from the violation of confidentiality, is that the lawyer's ethical problem has not been solved, but has only been transferred to the judge. Moreover, the client in such a case might well have grounds for appeal on the basis of deprivation of due process and denial of the right to counsel, since he will have been tried before, and sentenced by, a judge who has been informed of the client's guilt by his own attorney.

A solution even less satisfactory than informing the judge of the defendant's guilt would be to let the client take the stand without the attorney's participation and to omit reference to the client's testimony in closing argument. The latter solution, of course, would be as damaging as to fail entirely to argue the case to the jury, and failing to argue the case is "as improper as though the attorney had told the jury that his client had uttered a falsehood in making the statement."

Of course, before the client testifies perjuriously, the lawyer has a duty to attempt to dissuade him on grounds of both law and morality. In addition, the client should be impressed with the fact that his untruthful alibi is tactically dangerous. There is always a strong possibility that the prosecutor will expose the perjury on cross-examination. However, for the reasons already given, the final decision must necessarily be the client's. The lawyer's best course thereafter would be to avoid any further professional relationship with a client whom he knew to have perjured himself.

Comment

Professor Freedman's views on the ethical responsibilities of the defense attorney have aroused a stormy controversy. Not only was considerable space in law reviews and in the American Bar Association Journal devoted to attacking his arguments, but he was, at the instance of a local judge, brought up on charges before the local bar association. The matter, however, went no further than that.

As often happens in law, we have here two important principles which simply collide head on. We want to encourage defendants to confide in their attorneys and in order to do this, we wish to avoid using defendants' confidences against them in any way. On the other hand, we regard defense attorneys as officers of the court who have no right to help foist perjurious testimony on the court. The problem is that, in the real world, one cannot maintain both of these principles at the same time with respect to defendants who wish to lie. If attorneys take no part in the questioning or ask to withdraw, will not they betray their clients' confidence? If they treat their clients like truthful witnesses, will they not be helping foist perjurious testimony upon the courts?

Most of those disagreeing with Professor Freedman's views have assumed that he was accurately describing the view (and practice) of many criminal lawyers. Some have argued, however, that the dilemma of attorneys whose clients wish to commit perjury can be avoided if the attorneys insist upon their right to control the case and to keep their clients off the witness stand. Should attorneys have such a right?

(5) In Re Ryder
United States District Court, Eastern District of Virginia, 1967.
263 F.Supp. 360.

.   .   .

On August 24, 1966 a man armed with a sawed-off shotgun robbed the Varina Branch of the Bank of Virginia of $7,583. Included in the currency taken were $10 bills known as "bait money," the serial numbers of which had been recorded.

On August 26, 1966 Charles Richard Cook rented safety deposit box 14 at a branch of the Richmond National Bank. Later in the day Cook was interviewed at his home by agents of the Federal Bureau of Investigation, who obtained $348 from him. Cook telephoned Ryder, who had represented him in civil litigation. Ryder came to the house and advised the agents that he represented Cook. He said that if Cook were not to be placed under arrest, he intended to take him to his office for an interview. The agents left. Cook insisted to Ryder that he had not robbed the bank. He told Ryder that he had won the money, which the agents had taken from him, in a crap game. At this time Ryder believed Cook.

Later that afternoon Ryder telephoned one of the agents and asked whether any of the bills obtained from Cook had been identified as a part of the money taken in the bank robbery. The agent told him that some bills had been identified. Ryder made inquiries about the number of bills taken and their denominations. The agent declined to give him specific information but indicated that several of the bills were recorded as bait money.

The next morning, Saturday, August 27, 1966, Ryder conferred with Cook again. He urged Cook to tell the truth, and Cook answered that a man, whose name he would not divulge, offered him $500 on the day of the robbery to put a package in a bank lockbox. Ryder did not believe this story. Ryder told Cook that if the government could trace the money in the box to him, it would be almost conclusive evidence of his guilt. He knew that Cook was under surveillance and he suspected that Cook might try to dispose of the money.

That afternoon Ryder telephoned a former officer of the Richmond Bar Association to discuss his course of action. He had known this attorney for many years and respected his judgment. The lawyer was at home and had no library available to him when Ryder telephoned. In their casual conversation Ryder told what he knew about the case, omitting names. He explained that he thought he would take the money from Cook's safety deposit box and place it in a box in his own name. This, he believed, would prevent Cook from attempting to dispose of the money. The lawyers thought that eventually F.B.I. agents would locate the money and that since it was in Ryder's possession, he could claim a privilege and thus effectively exclude it from evidence. This would prevent the government from linking Ryder's client with the bait money and would also destroy any presumption of guilt that might exist arising out of the client's exclusive possession of the evidence.

Ryder testified: . . .

"[T]he idea was that I assumed that if anybody tried to go into a safety deposit box in my name, the bank officials would notify me and that I would get an opportunity to come in this court and argue a question of whether or not they could use that money as evidence."

The lawyers discussed and rejected alternatives, including having a third party get the money. At the conclusion of the conversation Ryder was advised, "Don't do it surreptitiously and to be sure that you let your client know that it is going back to the rightful owners."

On Monday morning Ryder asked Cook to come by his office. He prepared a power of attorney, which Cook signed.

Ryder took the power of attorney which Cook had signed to the Richmond National Bank. He rented box 13 in his name with his office address, presented the power of attorney, entered Cook's box, took both boxes into a booth, where he found a bag of money and a sawed-off shotgun in Cook's box. The box also contained miscellaneous items which are not pertinent to this proceeding. He transferred the contents of Cook's box to his own and returned the boxes to the vault. He left the bank, and neither he nor Cook returned.

Ryder testified that he had some slight hesitation about the propriety of what he was doing. Within a half-hour after he left the bank, he talked to a retired judge and distinguished professor of law. He told this person that he wanted to discuss something in confidence. Ryder then stated that he represented a man suspected of bank robbery. The judge recalled the main part of the conversation. [concerning Ryder's actions]

. . . The judge also testified that Ryder certainly would not have been under the impression that he—the judge—thought that he was guilty of unethical conduct.

The same day Ryder also talked with other prominent persons in Richmond—a judge of a court of record and an attorney for the Commonwealth. Again, he stated that what he intended to say was confidential. He related the circumstances and was advised that a lawyer could not receive the property and if he had received it he could not retain possession of it.

On September 7, 1966 Cook was indicted for robbing the Varina Branch of the Bank of Virginia. A bench warrant was issued and the next day Ryder represented Cook at a bond hearing. Cook was identified as the robber by employees of the bank. He was released on bond. Cook was arraigned on a plea of not guilty on September 9, 1966.

On September 12, 1966 F.B.I. agents procured search warrants for Cook's and Ryder's safety deposit boxes in the Richmond National Bank. They found Cook's box empty. In Ryder's box they discovered $5,920 of the $7,583 taken in the bank robbery and the sawed-off shotgun used in the robbery.

On October 14, 1966 the three judges of this court removed Ryder as an attorney for Cook; suspended him from practice before the court until further order; referred the matter to the United States Attorney, who was requested to file charges within five days . . .. We reject the argument that Ryder's conduct was no more than the exercise of the attorney-client privilege.

It was Ryder, not his client, who took the initiative in transferring the incriminating possession of the stolen money and the shotgun from Cook. Ryder's conduct went far beyond the receipt and retention of a confidential communication from his client. Counsel for Ryder conceded, at the time of argument, that the acts of Ryder were not within the attorney-client privilege. . . .

Ryder violated Canon 32. He rendered Cook a service involving deception and disloyalty to the law. He intended that his actions should remove from Cook exclusive possession of stolen money, and thus destroy an evidentiary presumption. His service in taking possession of the shotgun and money, with the intention of retaining them until after the trial, unless discovered by the government, merits the "stern and just condemnation" the canon prescribes. . . .

Ryder's action is not justified because he thought he was acting in the best interests of his client. To allow the individual lawyer's belief to determine the standards of professional conduct will in time reduce the ethics of the profession to the practices of the most unscrupulous. Moreover, Ryder knew that the law against concealing stolen property and the law forbidding receipt and possession of a sawed-off shotgun contain no exemptions for a lawyer who takes possession with the intent of protecting a criminal from the consequences of his crime.

[Ryder] will be suspended from practice in this court for eighteen months effective October 14, 1966.

Questions and Comment

Did Mr. Ryder try to do the right thing?

If Mr. Ryder committed a crime, why was he not prosecuted for it?

What should he have done when his client told him about the money? Would it have violated his client's confidence to have done nothing? Is that perhaps the distinction between what Ryder did and the case of the lawyer who allows his client to tell a false story on the witness stand, without disassociating himself from it some way?

Is not the issue just where to draw the line in the services lawyers can perform for their clients? In the communist countries lawyers can do relatively little for their clients except perhaps to plead for mercy and, to help convict their clients if in fact they are guilty. In the American system lawyers have a duty to do as much as possible for their clients, within the rules, and to avoid using clients' confidences and appeals for help to make their convictions more likely.

(6) NOTE: CONFIDENTIALITY AND THE BEREAVED FATHER

After his arrest for murdering a male camper, defendant Robert Garrow told his court-appointed lawyers that he had slain two other persons—and his confessions led his lawyers to the discovery of their bodies (Susan Petz and Alicia Hauck). However, the lawyers did not report what they knew about the additional slayings, even after the bodies were accidentally discovered several months later. Nor did the lawyers feel they could tell the father of one of the slain women anything about whether his daughter was still alive. (The father had called on the lawyers because their client was being prosecuted for a murder that had taken place at about the same time and in the same area as his daughter's disappearance).

For nine months the lawyers kept quiet about what they had found—until their client, on the witness stand at his trial for the murder of the male camper, blurted out the information that he had also slain the Petz and Hauck women. Once their client spoke, the lawyers considered themselves relieved of their obligation to keep their information confidential.

The lawyers maintained that since what their client had told them was "a privileged communication" they could not reveal any of the information given to them in confidence until their client did.

Questions

Is there any difference in the duty of the attorney where the interests of a worried and bereaved father are also at stake? Were Garrow's lawyers guilty of "obstructing justice"? What is the difference between this case and In re Ryder? Was the problem that

Garrow's lawyers seemed to be under two conflicting obligations: the commitment to keeping their client's confession of a completed crime confidential and their obligation not to hide physical evidence from the prosecution?

Before the bodies were discovered, could Garrow's lawyers have resolved this conflict by, as the father of one of the slain women suggested, "making an anonymous phone call to the police"?

Once Garrow's lawyers undertook to corroborate their client's information through their own investigation, were they still bound by confidentiality?

(7) Does a Lawyer's Character Matter? *

In the proficient performance of the duties of the role, the lawyer cannot altogether avoid doing unsavory acts, acquiring unattractive traits, and developing dubious aspirations. Effective adversarial advocacy on behalf of a criminal defendant demands measures that are unacceptable from a moral point of view. For example, it may not be enough to show that the defendant has some worthy aims or that the prosecutor has not met the burden of proof: the lawyer may have to deliberately convey the impression that the client is completely innocent of wrongdoing; the lawyer may conclude that it is crucial to discredit an opposing witness whose testimony is known to be truthful, or to be less than forthright about information damaging to the client's case. Protracted engagement in these and similar practices must leave its trace on a person. And since the practices are undertaken as part of an accepted and socially rewarded professional calling, there is little to encourage the lawyer either to retain character traits contrary to these actions or to resist the cultivation of traits corresponding to them. A firm and settled disposition to truthfulness, fairness, goodwill, and the like would thwart the lawyer's capacity to do his tasks well. To excel as a lawyer, combative character traits such as cunning are most beneficial. In this way, the conduct required of an adversarial lawyer gradually produces undesirable features on his character.

The moral damage to character that lawyers in time tend to sustain in executing their important professional tasks can vary in degree and kind. Persons of good character who resort to the shady means of their trade while managing to maintain a lively picture of the justified, ultimate aims of their vocation will no doubt regret their infidelity to truth and justice as well as their unfairness to particular individuals. Remaining attached both to the ultimate aspirations of their office and to their good character, they cannot serenely undertake the everyday tasks that seem to go against their own personal and social ideals. Such persons would suffer the strain born of the knowledge that living fully and well the kind of life that they have chosen

* Andreas Eshete, "Does a Lawyer's Character Matter?" in David Luban (ed.), The Good Lawyer, Rowman & Allanheld, 1983, pp. 274–275 (Reprinted with Permission).

cannot yield a life that is of a piece: their moral integrity is constantly imperiled. Others who have less self-mastery and a less firm attachment to ideals are more likely to lose sight of the more distant justifying aims of the profession. Instead, they shift their attachments to more immediate goods such as the wealth and status with which society rewards the successful exercise of their combative skills. Still different lawyers may acquire unworthy aspirations: they prize the acts of cunning, manipulation, and humiliation for their own sake. For them, the satisfactions of the profession consist in the enjoyment of the spectacle of others being subject to their power.

I do not, of course, mean to suggest that adversarial lawyers can be neatly classified into the three groups. What is outlined is a rough and crude classification of types of character that could be acquired upon entering the adversarial role. Accordingly, it is possible that a lawyer in his professional life would progress through the different types or oscillate between types at different stages of life. It is clear, for example, that the first type of character is unstable. Nagging feelings of regret and self-contempt may inhibit these lawyers' adversarial instincts. And since succumbing to these feelings might be entirely incapacitating, they may react by retreating from the ideals that engender them. Such lawyers may decide to throw themselves into the adversarial role, switching their allegiance to its social rewards. Nor are inner collision and instability excluded by the other types of character. For instance, self-deception could arise in the second type of character as a result of what might be called the "halo effect." The halo effect is produced when a person makes himself believe that worldly success in a profession or a way of life is a sure sign of success in other dimensions that are less accessible to public appreciation and appraisal.

(8) THE LAWYERS KNOW TOO MUCH *

Why is there always a secret singing

When a lawyer cashes in?

Why does a hearse horse snicker

Hauling a lawyer away?

3. THE DEFENSE OF THE POOR

a. ARGERSINGER v. HAMLIN

Supreme Court of the United States, 1972.
407 U.S. 25, 92 S.Ct. 2006, 32 L.Ed.2d 530.

Mr. Justice DOUGLAS delivered the opinion of the Court.

Petitioner, an indigent, was charged in Florida with carrying a concealed weapon, an offense punishable by imprisonment up to six

---

* *The Complete Poems of Carl Sandburg* 189 (1969, 1970), Harcourt Brace Jova- novich Inc., New York. © 1969 (Reprinted with permission).

months and a $1,000 fine. The trial was to a judge and petitioner was unrepresented by counsel. He was sentenced to serve 90 days in jail and brought this habeas corpus action in the Florida Supreme Court, alleging that, being deprived of his right to counsel, he was unable as an indigent layman properly to raise and present to the trial court good and sufficient defenses to the charges for which he stands convicted. The Florida Supreme Court by a four-to-three decision, in ruling on the right to counsel, held that the right to court-appointed counsel extends only to trials "for non-petty offenses punishable by more than six months imprisonment." 236 So.2d 442, 443.[1]

The assistance of counsel is often a requisite to the very existence of a fair trial. The Court in Powell v. Alabama, supra, 287 U.S. 68–69, 53 S.Ct. 64—a capital case—said:

> "The right to be heard would be, in many cases, of little avail if it did not comprehend the right to be heard by counsel. Even the intelligent and educated layman has small and sometimes no skill in the science of law. If charged with a crime, he is incapable, generally, of determining for himself whether the indictment is good or bad. He is unfamiliar with the rules of evidence. Left without the aid of counsel he may be put on trial without a proper charge, and convicted upon incompetent evidence, or evidence irrelevant to the issue or otherwise inadmissible. He lacks both the skill and knowledge adequately to prepare his defense, even though he may have a perfect one. He requires the guiding hand of counsel at every step in the proceedings against him. Without it, though he be not guilty, he faces the danger of conviction because he does not know how to establish his innocence. If that be true of men of intelligence, how much more true is it of the ignorant and illiterate, or those of feeble intellect."

In Gideon v. Wainwright, we dealt with a felony trial. But we did not so limit the need of the accused for a lawyer. We said:

> ". . . in our adversary system of criminal justice, any person haled into court, who is too poor to hire a lawyer, cannot be assured a fair trial unless counsel is provided for him. This seems to us to be an obvious truth. Governments, both state and federal, quite properly spend vast sums of money to

---

1. Twelve States provide counsel for indigents accused of "serious crime" in the misdemeanor category. Id., pp. 119–124.

Nineteen States provide for the appointment of counsel in most misdemeanor cases. Id., pp. 124–133. One of these is Oregon whose Supreme Court said in Application of Stevenson, 254 Or. 94, 458 P.2d 414, 418. "If our objective is to insure a fair trial in every criminal prosecution, the need for counsel is not determined by the seriousness of the crime. The assistance of counsel will best avoid conviction of the innocent—an objective as important in the municipal court as in a court of general jurisdiction."

California's requirement extends to traffic violations. Blake v. Municipal Court, 242 Cal.App.2d 731, 51 Cal.Rptr. 771.

Overall, 31 States have now extended the right to defendants charged with crimes less serious than felonies. Comment, Right to Counsel, supra, at 134.

establish machinery to try defendants accused of crime. Lawyers to prosecute are everywhere deemed essential to protect the public's interest in an orderly society. Similarly, there are few defendants charged with crime, few indeed, who fail to hire the best lawyers they can get to prepare and present their defenses. That government hires lawyers to prosecute and defendants who have the money hire lawyers to defend are the strongest indications of the widespread belief that lawyers in criminal courts are necessities, not luxuries. The right of one charged with crime to counsel may not be deemed fundamental and essential to fair trials in some countries, but it is in ours. From the very beginning, our state and national constitutions and laws have laid great emphasis on procedural and substantive safeguards designed to assure fair trials before impartial tribunals in which every defendant stands equal before the law. This noble ideal cannot be realized if the poor man charged with crime has to face his accusers without a lawyer to assist him." 372 U.S., at 344, 83 S.Ct., at 796.[2]

Both *Powell* and *Gideon* involved felonies. But their rationale has relevance to any criminal trial, where an accused is deprived of his liberty.

The requirement of counsel may well be necessary for a fair trial even in a petty offense prosecution. We are by no means convinced that legal and constitutional questions involved in a case that actually leads to imprisonment even for a brief period are any less complex than when a person can be sent off for six months or more.

. . .

We must conclude, therefore, that the problems associated with misdemeanor and petty offenses often require the presence of counsel to insure the accused a fair trial. Mr. Justice Powell suggests that these problems are raised even in situations where there is no prospect of imprisonment. . . . We need not consider the requirements of the Sixth Amendment as regards the right to counsel where loss of liberty is not involved, however, for here, petitioner was in fact sentenced to jail. And, as we said in Baldwin v. New York, 399 U.S., at 73, 90 S.Ct., at 1890: "[T]he prospect of imprisonment for however short a time will seldom be viewed by the accused as a trivial or 'petty' matter and may well result in quite serious repercussions affecting his career and his reputation."

2. See also Johnson v. Zerbst, 304 U.S. 458, 462–463, 58 S.Ct. 1019, 1022, 82 L.Ed. 1461:

"[The Sixth Amendment] embodies a realistic recognition of the obvious truth that the average defendant does not have the professional legal skill to protect himself when brought before a tribunal with power to take his life or liberty, wherein the prosecution is represented by experienced and learned counsel. That which is simple, orderly and necessary to the lawyer—to the untrained layman—may appear intricate, complex, and mysterious."

We hold, therefore, that absent a knowing and intelligent waiver, no person may be imprisoned for any offense, whether classified as petty, misdemeanor, or felony, unless he was represented by counsel at his trial.

Under the rule we announce today, every judge will know when the trial of a misdemeanor starts that no imprisonment may be imposed, even though local law permits it, unless the accused is represented by counsel. He will have a measure of the seriousness and gravity of the offense and therefore know when to name a lawyer to represent the accused before the trial starts.

The run of misdemeanors will not be affected by today's ruling. But in those that end up in the actual deprivation of a person's liberty, the accused will receive the benefit of "the guiding hand of counsel" so necessary when one's liberty is in jeopardy.

Reversed.

. . .

b. DRAWING THE LINE: SCOTT v. ILLINOIS
Supreme Court of the United States, 1979.
440 U.S. 367, 99 S.Ct. 1158, 59 L.Ed.2d 383.

Petitioner Scott was charged with shoplifting merchandise valued at less than $150.00, a misdemeanor punishable under Illinois law by a fine of up to $500 or one year in jail, or both. He was not represented by counsel at his bench trial, where he was convicted and fined $50. Scott appealed his conviction, claiming that his constitutional rights had been violated because Illinois had not provided him with counsel at public expense. The Illinois Supreme Court rejected his contention, and the United States Supreme Court agreed to accept his petition for a writ of certiorari.

Mr. Justice REHNQUIST delivered the opinion of the Court.

. . .

In *Argersinger* the Court rejected arguments that social cost or a lack of available lawyers militated against its holding, in some part because it thought these arguments were factually incorrect. . . . But they were rejected in much larger part because of the Court's conclusion that incarceration was so severe a sanction that it should not be imposed as a result of a criminal trial unless an indigent defendant had been offered appointed counsel to assist in his defense, regardless of the cost to the States implicit in such a rule. The Court in its opinion repeatedly referred to trials "where an accused is deprived of his liberty," . . . and to "a case that actually leads to imprisonment even for a brief period." . . . The Chief Justice in his opinion concurring in the result also observed that "any deprivation of liberty is a serious matter." . . .

Although the intentions of the *Argersinger* Court are not unmistakably clear from its opinion, we conclude today that *Argersinger* did indeed delimit the constitutional right to appointed counsel in state criminal proceedings. Even were the matter *res nova,* we believe that the central premise of *Argersinger*—that actual imprisonment is a penalty different in kind from fines or the mere threat of imprisonment—is eminently sound and warrants adoption of actual imprisonment as the line defining the constitutional right to appointment of counsel. *Argersinger* has proved reasonably workable, whereas any extension would create confusion and impose unpredictable, but necessarily substantial, costs on 50 quite diverse States. We therefore hold that the Sixth and Fourteenth Amendments to the United States Constitution require only that no indigent criminal defendant be sentenced to a term of imprisonment unless the State has afforded him the right to assistance of appointed counsel in his defense. The judgment of the Supreme Court of Illinois is accordingly

Affirmed.

Mr. Justice BRENNAN, with whom Mr. Justice MARSHALL and Mr. Justice STEVENS join, dissenting.

The Court, in an opinion that at best ignores the basic principles of prior decisions, affirms Scott's conviction without counsel because he was sentenced only to pay a fine. In my view, the plain wording of the Sixth Amendment and the Court's precedents compel the conclusion that Scott's uncounseled conviction violated the Sixth and Fourteenth Amendments and should be reversed.

.   .   .

In my view petitioner could prevail in this case without extending the right to counsel beyond what was assumed to exist in *Argersinger*. Neither party in that case questioned the existence of the right to counsel in trials involving "non-petty" offenses punishable by more than six months in jail. The question the Court addressed was whether the right applied to some "petty" offenses to which the right to jury trial did not extend. The Court's reasoning in applying the right to counsel in the case before it— that the right to counsel is more fundamental to a fair proceeding than the right to jury trial and that the historical limitations on the jury trial right are irrelevant to the right to counsel—certainly cannot support a standard for the right to counsel that is more restrictive than the standard for granting a right to jury trial.

.   .   .

The offense of "theft" with which Scott was charged is certainly not a "petty" one. It is punishable by a sentence of up to one year in jail. Unlike many traffic or other "regulatory" offenses, it carries the moral stigma associated with common-law crimes traditionally recognized as indicative of moral depravity. The State indicated at oral argument that the services of a professional prosecutor were considered essential to the prosecution of this offense. . . . Likewise, nonindigent defendants charged with this offense would be well advised to hire the "best lawyers they can get." Scott's right to the assistance of appointed counsel is thus plainly mandated by the logic of the Court's prior cases, including *Argersinger* itself.

But rather than decide consonant with the assumption in regard to non-petty offenses that was both implicit and explicit in *Argersinger,* the Court today retreats to the indefensible position that the *Argersinger* "actual imprisonment" standard is the *only* test for determining the boundary of the Sixth Amendment right to appointed counsel in state misdemeanor cases, thus necessarily deciding that in many cases (such as this one) a defendant will have no right to appointed counsel even when he has a constitutional right to a jury trial. This is simply an intolerable result. Not only is the "actual imprisonment" standard unprecedented as the exclusive test, but the problems inherent in its application demonstrate the superiority of an "authorized imprisonment" standard that would require the appointment of counsel for indigents accused of any offense for which imprisonment for any time is authorized.

Questions and Comment

If the only issue in a criminal case were whether or not the defendant had done something, it might be argued that he or she could proceed without a lawyer. In a legal system which uses the exclusionary rule and follows, in part, the due process model, is it not clear that only an attorney can be familiar enough with the defendant's legal rights to give him or her an adequate defense?

If lawyers are that important to defendants' rights, is there any excuse for trying them for a serious crime without one? Should it matter that they cannot afford one?

In *Scott,* the Court interprets *Argersinger* as advocating an "actual imprisonment" criterion for the constitutional requirement of right to counsel. The minority urges an "authorized imprisonment" standard. Which do you think is fairer? Which would be easier to administer? Which do you think would be more costly? Is justice rationed?

Even before *Argersinger*, the Supreme Court held that the indigent accused should have a right to appointed counsel on appeal as well as at trial.

Should the accused who has already lost at his trial and appeal have appointed counsel for an application for parole? To defend against a revocation of parole? What about to prosecute a civil suit to redress an alleged wrong done by the government? Done by a private person?

What about other aids for indigent defendants at trial? May they not need expert help in addition to that of an attorney? In appropriate cases a well-financed defendant may hire an investigator, an accountant, a handwriting expert or a psychiatrist. Should the indigent defendant have to do without such help?

c. THE CONVICT'S VIEW OF THE PUBLIC DEFENDER *

Did you have a lawyer when you went to court the next day?

No. I had a public defender. *A defendant, 1971 . . .*

Nearly 70 percent of the men interviewed were represented by the public defender. They had little choice in the matter: they did not have the money to hire a lawyer, and the judge appointed the public defender to represent them. A defendant typically encountered his lawyer in the hallway or bullpen (lock-up) of the courthouse, or else he found himself before the judge with a man beside him who turned out to be his attorney. The typical defendant reported that he spent a total of five to ten minutes conferring with his attorney, usually in rapid, hushed conversations in the courthouse. Thus, a man who may receive five or ten years in prison spends five or ten minutes with the man who is supposed to supply the "guiding hand of counsel," to ensure that his rights are exercised and protected, to make certain that the "noble ideal" of a fair trial is protected.

What can a defendant talk about in five to ten minutes with "his" attorney? His social and psychological background? His motives for committing the crime, if he did indeed do it? The nature of police investigation and interrogation and possible legal defenses dealing with search and seizure and entrapment? His goals and treatment needs? Hardly. What he can talk about is the deal. Most of the men reported that among the first words uttered by their public defender were: "I can get you _____ if you plead guilty." Perhaps they do not remember other words that came before, but certainly these were the most salient words the public defender uttered.

> You know, his name in superior court is known as "cop-out Kujawski." This what everybody in prison calls him cause that's the first thing as soon as he comes in your cell in superior court, that's the first thing he says—cop out, cop out, cop out. Through the past years everybody's known him as cop-out Kujawski. He's earned a name for himself.

Thus, the public defender is not "their" lawyer, but an agent of the state. He is the surrogate of the prosecutor—a member of "their little syndicate"—rather than the defendant's representative.

> He seemed like he didn't care one way or the other. He just cop out, you know. Like, you see a police walking on the street writing a ticket out, you know. He puts a ticket on the car. He don't care whose car it is. [The public defender] say, just, you know, You cop out to this, and you say no, and he says, I see if I can get a better deal. Then he brings another

* Jonathan D. Casper, *American Criminal Justice: The Defendant's Perspective*, Prentice-Hall, Inc., Englewood Cliffs, N.J., 1972, pp. 101, 106–108, 124–5. © 1972 (Reprinted with permission).

offer: You cop out to this. Just like that, you know. Just checking on the cop-outs.

. . .

A public defender is just like the prosecutor's assistant. Anything you tell this man, he's not gonna do anything but relay it back to the public defender [*sic;* he means the prosecutor]; they'll come to some sort of agreement, and that's the best you're gonna get. You know, whatever they come to and he brings you back the first time, well, you better accept it because you may get more.

. . .

He just playing a middle game. You know, you're the public defender, now, you don't care what happens to me, really. You don't know me, and I don't know you; this is your job, that's all; so you're gonna go up there and say a little bit, make it look like you're trying to help me, but actually you don't give a damn.

. . .

[I]f we are truly concerned with a defendant's perspective, with his sense that his encounter with the criminal justice system has been equitable, something must be done to remove the feeling that the defendant stands alone. We have detailed the activities of the system that lead the defendant to feel that he is an object being processed by people who don't have very sound notions of what they are up to, except to keep the assembly line operating. If the system of criminal justice is to teach defendants lessons about different modes of living, if it is to make them less likely to engage in "antisocial" conduct, it must not only treat them fairly but also give them the feeling that they have been treated fairly. We have attempted to point out here how the public defender system—in one jurisdiction—simply does not perform this function. If, as the Supreme Court so nobly stated in the *Gideon* opinion, "the right of one charged with crime to counsel" is deemed "fundamental and essential to fair trials" in our country, this right must have some real meaning—meaning not only from the viewpoint of legal standards about what constitutes adequate representation, but also in the eyes of defendants themselves. Currently our system does not appear to offer meaningful defense to indigents. It must if we are to convince defendants that they are being treated not as "files" to be closed but as human beings.

Questions

How can one square the view of convicts in the above excerpt with the research indicating that, when factors such as previous record, employment record etc., are controlled for, clients of the public defender do about as well as those of private attorneys?

Does this show merely that public defenders do not have time for public relations activities with their clients? Or is it merely that convicts are so suspicious and cynical that they cannot believe anyone not paid by them could be sincerely devoted to their interests? Or is it possible that the convicts are correct in their assessment of the superiority of the private attorney over the public defender and the research is somehow wrong?

In any event, should we take account of the convicts' views in deciding how to afford representation to the indigent defendant?

d. CRIMINAL DEFENSE FOR THE POOR *

The predominant level of government responsible for providing indigent criminal defense was the county. In 24 States, county governments were solely responsible for providing criminal defense for the poor. In 17 States the State government was responsible (up from 13 in 1982). Three States reported a district- or circuit-organized system, compared to four in 1982. Six States combined more than one of these systems.

There are three basic program types used throughout the country to provide defense services to the poor:

Assigned counsel programs—In these programs there is a case-by-case appointment of counsel who are local members of the private bar.

Contract attorney programs—In these programs the funding source contracts with individual private attorneys, private law firms, or local bar associations to provide representation to indigent defendants for a given period of time.

Public defender programs—In these programs a salaried staff of full-time or part-time attorneys is organized to provide defense services to indigent defendants. The organization may be a public agency, that is, part of a State or local government, or a private, non-profit corporation that contracts with State or local governments to provide indigent defense services.

The service delivery system in a given State or county may consist of more than one type of program. Within each jurisdiction, however, there is one primary type of program. Assigned counsel systems were the most common type of program; however, during the 1982–86 period there was a decrease in the number of counties using this type of system and an increase in the use of public defender and contract programs. Between 1982 and 1986 the number of counties primarily using assigned counsel programs decreased from 1,833 to 1,609, or from almost 60% to 52% of all counties. Among the States, only Maine continued to rely exclusively on an assigned counsel system. Public defender programs increased from 34% to 37% of all counties. Con-

* Criminal Defense for the Poor, 1986, U.S. Department of Justice, Bureau of Justice Statistics Bulletin, September 1988.

tract defense programs grew by nearly two-thirds, from almost 7% to 11% of all counties.

The Midwest experienced a number of changes in the types of primary defense programs used by the individual counties. The number of counties using primarily assigned counsel programs declined 21%, while public defender programs increased by almost 34%, and contract programs nearly doubled, growing by 84% (table 3).

The overall reduction in assigned counsel programs and increase in public defender programs in the Midwest region resulted largely from changes in Missouri (which shifted to a statewide public defender program) and, to a lesser extent, in Minnesota and Wisconsin.

The West also experienced changes in primary program types between 1982 and 1986. In that region the number of counties using assigned counsel programs declined by almost 45%, while the number of counties using contract programs increased by nearly 75%. Changes in New Mexico, Oregon, and Washington accounted in large measure for these shifts. In 1982 New Mexico reported an equal number of counties (16) using public defender programs and assigned counsel programs (table 2). In 1986, eight counties used public defenders, and the remaining counties had contract programs. Oregon reported similar program changes: In 1986, 14 counties had contract programs as their primary source of indigent criminal defense, compared to 3 contract counties in 1982. Two of Washington's 39 counties had contract programs in 1982; 20 Washington counties reported using contract systems for primary defense services in 1986.

In the South, 79 of Kentucky's 120 counties reported using a contract system in 1986, compared to 37 in 1982.

The two primary financial sources for providing legal counsel to poor persons charged with a criminal offense were State and county governments. Twenty States funded their indigent defense system with State dollars; programs in 10 States were county funded; and the remaining States funded programs through a combination of State and county funding.

. . .

In 1986 approximately $991 million was spent nationwide on defense services for the poor. This figure was 60% higher than the estimated $625 million expended in 1982. County governments accounted for 61% of the overall funding in 1986; States, for 38%; and other sources, for about 1%. State expenditures showed a greater overall increase (80%) than county expenditures (52%) between 1982 and 1986. Expenditures from other sources increased by 14% during the 4-year period.

. . .

The total caseload reported nationwide for 1986 was about 4.4 million cases, an increase of approximately 40% between 1982 and 1986. Indigent defense cases per 1,000 persons in the population rose from an average of 14 in 1982 to 19 in 1986.

The nationwide average cost per case in 1986 was $223, or 14% higher than the $196 cost per case in 1982. Among the States, average cost per case ranged from a low of $63 in Arkansas to a high of $540 in New Jersey. The New Jersey figure increased by almost 50%; the Arkansas figure, in contrast, decreased 45% during this period.

Six of the 10 States with the lowest average costs per case in 1986 were found in the South, 2 in the Northeast, and 2 in the Midwest. Most of the States with lower case costs used assigned counsel systems to provide indigent criminal defense. Fee schedules and maximum rates for court-appointed counsel were among the lowest in the country for many of these States.

.   .   .

Per case costs in any jurisdiction are affected by the type of indigent defense program and the related budget process. In most public defender programs, the county or State negotiates an annual appropriation for the program. The figure may be determined by negotiations between the funding source and the public defender or, increasingly, may be based upon caseload or workload standards agreed to by both parties. In either case, the appropriation is intended to support a full-time or part-time salaried staff and other necessary expenses.

The costs for assigned counsel programs are affected by other factors. For example, most assigned counsel programs establish a set of hourly rates for appointed counsel, usually based upon a lower rate for out-of-court work than in-court work. In addition, the local jurisdiction may establish a set of maximum allowable fees for each case or each set of case types. For example, one jurisdiction may establish an hourly rate of $25 per hour for out-of-court work and $35 per hour for in-court work, with a maximum allowance per case of $750 for a misdemeanor and $1,500 for a felony. Typically, waivers of the maximum fee may be requested in extraordinary cases. However, a few jurisdictions do not permit a waiver of the maximum fee level.

The hourly rates and maximum fees per case may be established by legislation or court rule for uniform application throughout the State. In many jurisdictions, however, the fee levels are left to the discretion of the individual trial court judge. Substantial variation is found both among States and between jurisdictions within States (and even among judges in the same local court in some instances). Maximum fees per case can substantially affect the cost per case among the assigned counsel jurisdictions. In some States there are no established maximum levels, and the local trial judge determines whether the total fee requested is reasonable. In comparing the cost per case for assigned counsel programs, an understanding of what the local fee levels are and the maximum fee levels permitted is required.

In contract programs there are a variety of payment mechanisms. One of the most common is to establish a cost level for each type of case. For example, a county may contract with a private lawyer or law firm to handle a given number of felony cases at $1,000 per case. In other jurisdictions, the funding source may offer to pay a total annual amount for the handling of all cases requiring appointment of counsel in a given jurisdiction. This contract method has recently been under attack in several States and was held unconstitutional by the Arizona Supreme Court in Smith v. State, 140 Arizona 355 (1984). In the Smith case, the Arizona Supreme Court found that the Mohave County contract system, which by design assigned the indigent defense system representation to the lowest bidder, violated the fifth and sixth amendments to the U.S. Constitution for four reasons:

1) The system did not take into account the time the attorney is expected to spend in representing his share of indigent defendants.

2) The system did not provide for support costs for the attorney, such as investigators, paralegals, and law clerks.

3) The system failed to take into account the competence of the attorney. An attorney, especially one newly admitted to the bar, for example, could bid low in order to obtain a contract but would not be able to represent adequately all of the clients assigned according to the standards.

4) The system did not take into account the complexity of the case.

Question

Is this good enough, or must we try harder?

D. RECOMMENDED READING

Auerbach, Jerold S. *Unequal Justice: Lawyers and Social Change in Modern America.* Oxford Univ. Press, New York, 1976.

Carlin, Jerome E. *Lawyer's Ethics.* Russell Sage, New York, 1966.

Hermann, Robert, Single, Eric, and Boston, John. *Counsel for the Poor: Criminal Defense in Urban America.* Lexington Books, Lexington, Mass., 1977.

Jacoby, Joan E., *The American Prosecutor: A Search for Identity.* Lexington Books, Lexington, Mass., 1980.

Krantz, Sheldon, et al. *Right to Counsel in Criminal Cases.* Ballinger Publishing Co., Cambridge, Mass., 1966.

Lewis, Anthony. *Gideon's Trumpet.* Random House, New York, 1964.

Luban, David. (ed.), *The Good Lawyer.* Rowman & Allanheld, Tutowa, N.J., 1983.

Mann, Kenneth. *Defending White Collar Criminals.* Yale University Press, New Haven, 1986.

McIntyre, Lisa. *The Public Defender.* University of Chicago Press, Chicago, 1987.

Miller, Frank W. *Prosecution: The Decision to Charge a Suspect with a Crime.* Little, Brown & Co., Boston, Toronto, 1969.

Chapter VII

PRETRIAL RELEASE AND DETENTION

A. INTRODUCTION

1. BAIL: THE HORNS OF THE DILEMMA *

Bail is the law's pragmatic method of compromise between the principle that a man is innocent until proven guilty and the obvious fact that a large portion of the defendants in criminal proceedings are well on the way to being convicted. Although bail has obvious uses in preventing an accused criminal who cannot provide bail from repeating his presumed transgression, in theory the only purpose of bail is to guarantee the appearance of the accused at the proceedings against him. The thought is that having posted the amount of cash or collateral named in the bail bond, he will appear in court rather than forfeit his money or property. As applied to a defendant threatened with the death penalty, there is an obvious fallacy in this reasoning. It is difficult to envision a bail so large as to guarantee a man's returning for a trial which he has reason to believe will result in his death or lengthy imprisonment. The horns of the dilemma are that (a) if a man has enough money to put up bail, the chances are that his bond will not guarantee his appearance at trial; and (b) if he does not have the money, the setting of bail will be irrelevant to his appearance since he will not be able to make bail at all.

To complicate things further, in the vast majority of cases the prisoner himself does not provide his own bail. The bail system has produced the phenomenon of the professional bail bondsman. The bail bondsman puts up the designated collateral on receipt of a percentage—usually 10 per cent—of the total from the prisoner. If the prisoner appears for trial, the bail bondsman gets back his collateral and retains the accused's payment as his profit. If the accused does not show up for trial, the unhappy bail bondsman risks forfeiture of the entire bail. Until fairly recently it was thought that the failure of the defendant to appear almost always resulted in the forfeiture of his bail. Recent studies have shown that in many areas a high (and often suspicious) rate of forgiveness was extended to bail bondsmen. In any event, the risk of loss, if any, caused by nonappearance is borne by the bail bondsman, not the defendant. On first glance one might think that reliance on a device as quixotic and self-contradictory as bail could only result in large numbers of accused criminals disappearing before

* John Kaplan and Jon R. Waltz, *The Trial of Jack Ruby,* (New York: Macmillan and Company, 1965), pp. 36–80. © 1965 (Reprinted with permission).

trial. The fact is that the great majority of defendants freed on bail do appear for trial, although their bail usually has little to do with it. The average defendant shows up in court for three principal reasons. First, he knows that the chances are overwhelming that he will be caught if he attempts to run. Second, he realizes that any attempt to flee will weaken his chances at his trial since the prosecution can be counted on to argue with vehemence to the jury that "the wicked flee when no man pursueth, but the righteous are bold as a lion." And, lastly, almost every defendant going to trial nurtures in his heart the hope, however faint, that he will somehow either be acquitted or given a suspended sentence and this very optimism helps to assure his appearance.

In many criminal cases an attorney for the defense will fight vigorously to have his client released on bail for reasons going far beyond the accused's desire for temporary freedom. The defendant out on bail is often able to aid substantially in the preparation of his own defense by locating and interviewing witnesses. Moreover, by showing that he can be trusted "on the street", he makes his eventual imprisonment less likely even if he should be convicted. This is especially so if he can show a favorable change in his pattern of living, making it less likely that he would again "turn to crime." Religious conversions, marital reconciliations and, most important the securing of honest, steady employment occur far more readily when the defendant is at large.

An unpublicized but potent reason for an attorney's advocacy of release on bail is that freedom may be prerequisite to an accused's ability to earn his lawyer's fee. (Unfortunately, in many instances the accused attempts to earn his attorney's fee for defending one crime by committing another. In Chicago, for example, an accused burglar grew more and more desperate in attempting to meet his pyramiding legal expenses and less and less discriminating in his selection of places to burglarize. He was arrested and released on bail a total of fourteen times before being tried for his first offense.)

Comment

As the above excerpt indicates, there are several basic problems with the institution of bail. It is that part of the criminal process which most obviously and blatantly discriminates on the basis of wealth. Moreover, it is not really very effective. The great majority of those who are now forced to put up bail would appear anyway in the absence of a bail system, and those who cannot make bail are often, in fact, perfectly good risks to appear in court.

A second concern in pretrial release policy is dangerousness, the likelihood that the defendant will commit crime while released and awaiting trial. Historically judges have responded to this concern by setting bail so high that the defendant could not afford it, and hypocritically justifying the amount on the basis of fear of flight. Recently, however, courts and legislatures have been more forthright. In 1984 the Congress enacted a Bail Reform Act, which provided for pretrial detention of those whom the court, after a hearing, declared dangerous.

Since then many states have adopted preventive detention statutes, although many courts still prefer to detain defendants by setting bail beyond the accused's means rather than by conducting an elaborate and time-consuming "dangerousness hearing" which requires a "clear and convincing" standard for proving dangerousness.

2. THE ORIGINS OF MONEY BAIL *

A bail system like the one in use in the United States today developed during the first thousand years A.D. in England. Judges traveled on circuits, and their visits to an area might be several years apart. Until the judges arrived, prisoners were held in the custody of the local sheriffs.

Prison conditions, however, were atrocious. Prisons were also insecure, and inmates frequently escaped. Maintaining the prisons was a financial burden. Thus, the sheriffs were happy to have someone else assume the responsibility of maintaining custody of defendants. They frequently relinquished defendants into the custody of sureties, usually friends or relatives of the accused. [Originally, if the accused did not appear for trial, his sureties, who had promised his return, would themselves be tried. As time passed if] . . . the defendant failed to appear for his trial, the custodian was no longer seized bodily, but was required to pay over a sum of money. This liability of the surety for the appearance of the defendant, and the ability to discharge the liability by the payment of a sum of money remain the basis of our present system of bail.

The Eighth Amendment to the United States Constitution provides that "excessive bail shall not be required." The historical antecedents of the amendment go back to the efforts of the English to implement the promise of the 39th chapter of the Magna Carta that "no free man shall be arrested, or detained in prison . . . unless . . . by the law of the land."

Professor Caleb Foote, who has done extensive historical research into the origins of bail, has concluded that the particular words in which the subject of bail is dealt with in the Eighth Amendment to the Constitution are the result of historical accident, and that the most plausible interpretation of the words, "excessive bail shall not be required," is that they were intended to grant a constitutional right to bail.

Professor Foote's research would seem to indicate that all defendants have the absolute right to bail. This view has generally been adopted by the courts except for capital offenses. Thus, the Federal Rules of Criminal Procedure provide:

> A person arrested for an offense not punishable by death
> shall be admitted to bail. A person arrested for an offense

---

* *Law and Order Reconsidered,* Report of the Task Force on Law and Law Enforcement to the National Commission on the Causes and Prevention of Violence (Washington, D.C.: GPO, 1968) pp. 427–430. © 1968 (Reprinted with permission).

punishable by death may be admitted to bail by any court or judge authorized by law to do so in the exercise of discretion, giving due weight to the evidence and to the nature and circumstances of the offense.

State constitutions contain similar provisions under which an exception is made to the general guarantee of bail: only when he is charged with a noncapital offense does a defendant have the right to be released on bail.

3. THE CONSTITUTIONAL RIGHT TO BAIL

STACK v. BOYLE

Supreme Court of the United States, 1951.
342 U.S. 1, 72 S.Ct. 1, 96 L.Ed. 3.

Mr. Chief Justice VINSON delivered the opinion of the Court.

Indictments have been returned in the Southern District of California charging the twelve petitioners with conspiring to violate the Smith Act, 18 U.S.C.A.* Upon their arrest, bail was fixed for each petitioner in the widely varying amounts of $2,500, $7,500, $75,000 and $100,000. On motion of petitioner Schneiderman following arrest in the Southern District of New York, his bail was reduced to $50,000 before his removal to California. On motion of the Government to increase bail in the case of other petitioners, and after several intermediate procedural steps not material to the issues presented here, bail was fixed in the District Court for the Southern District of California in the uniform amount of $50,000 for each petitioner.

Petitioners moved to reduce bail on the ground that bail as fixed was excessive under the Eighth Amendment.[1] In support of their motion, petitioners submitted statements as to their financial resources, family relationships, health, prior criminal records, and other information. The only evidence offered by the Government was a certified record showing that four persons previously convicted under the Smith Act in the Southern District of New York had forfeited bail. No evidence was produced relating those four persons to the petitioners in this case. At a hearing on the motion, petitioners were examined by the District Judge and cross-examined by an attorney for the Government. Petitioners' factual statements stand uncontroverted.

After their motion to reduce bail was denied, petitioners filed applications for habeas corpus in the same District Court. Upon consideration of the record on the motion to reduce bail, the writs were denied. The Court of Appeals for the Ninth Circuit affirmed. 192 F.2d

---

* The Smith Act provided that ". . . it shall be unlawful for any person . . . to knowingly or willfully advocate, abet, advise, or teach the duty, necessity, desirability, or propriety of overthrowing or destroying any government in the United States by force or violence . . . .."

1. "Excessive bail shall not be required, nor excessive fines imposed, nor cruel and unusual punishments inflicted." U.S. Const. Amend. VIII.

56. Prior to filing their petition for certiorari in this Court, petitioners filed with Mr. Justice Douglas an application for bail and an alternative application for habeas corpus seeking interim relief. Both applications were referred to the Court and the matter was set down for argument on specific questions covering the issues raised by this case.
. . .

First. From the passage of the Judiciary Act of 1789, 1 Stat. 73, 91, to the present Federal Rules of Criminal Procedure, Rule 46(a)(1), 18 U.S.C.A., federal law has unequivocally provided that a person arrested for a non-capital offense *shall* be admitted to bail. This traditional right to freedom before conviction permits the unhampered preparation of a defense, and serves to prevent the infliction of punishment prior to conviction. Unless this right to bail before trial is preserved, the presumption of innocence, secured only after centuries of struggle, would lose its meaning.

The right to release before trial is conditioned upon the accused's giving adequate assurance that he will stand trial and submit to sentence if found guilty. Like the ancient practice of securing the oaths of responsible persons to stand as sureties for the accused, the modern practice of requiring a bail bond or the deposit of a sum of money subject to forfeiture serves as additional assurance of the presence of an accused. Bail set at a figure higher than an amount reasonably calculated to fulfill this purpose is "excessive" under the Eighth Amendment.

Since the function of bail is limited, the fixing of bail for any individual defendant must be based upon standards relevant to the purpose of assuring the presence of that defendant. . . . In this case petitioners are charged with offenses under the Smith Act and, if found guilty, their convictions are subject to review with the scrupulous care demanded by our Constitution. Upon final judgment of conviction, petitioners face imprisonment of not more than five years and a fine of not more than $10,000. It is not denied that bail for each petitioner has been fixed in a sum much higher than that usually imposed for offenses with like penalties and yet there has been no factual showing to justify such action in this case. The Government asks the courts to depart from the norm by assuming, without the introduction of evidence, that each petitioner is a pawn in a conspiracy and will, in obedience to a superior, flee the jurisdiction. To infer from the fact of indictment alone a need for bail in an unusually high amount is an arbitrary act. Such conduct would inject into our own system of government the very principles of totalitarianism which Congress was seeking to guard against in passing the statute under which petitioners have been indicted.

Questions and Comment

What is the meaning of "excessive" in the Constitutional provision, "excessive bail shall not be required"? Is any bail that the accused lacks the financial means to post therefore excessive? If so, the bail system can no longer apply to the indigent defendant.

Alternatively, perhaps the issue is not how much the accused can afford, but rather whether any bail over a particular dollar amount is "excessive." If so, what is the magic number?

Finally, of course, the prohibition of excessive bail might simply mean that the bail cannot be required in any amount more than necessary to guarantee the appearance of the accused at his trial. That is, in fact, the way most courts have interpreted the provision. If this is correct, how is the judge supposed to decide what is the minimum amount that will guarantee the defendant's appearance? Moreover, what if the defendant simply does not have that much?

B. BAIL REFORM

1. THE O. R. RELEASE

a. BAIL REFORM: THE PROMISE AND THE COUNTER MOVEMENT *

The decade of the 1960s saw the emergence of a significant bail reform effort in the United States. The effort drew upon the empirical studies of Caleb Foote and earlier critics of the money bail system which showed that:

> Vast numbers of defendants spent months, even years, in jails before trial because they could not raise bail money;

> The amount of bail set was generally based solely on the nature of the charge with little individual attention given to factors in the individual defendant's life that related to the likelihood he would flee;

> The defendants who stayed in jail before trial for want of bail pled guilt or were convicted after trial more often and received prison sentences more often than those on bail and in virtually all cases lost their jobs and self-respect. Their families were often broken up and deprived of economic support;

> The conditions in pretrial detention jails were usually worse than in the reformatories housing convicted prisoners;

> Commercial bail bondsmen charged fees of 10 percent or more of the bond set by the court for doing virtually nothing;

> Only a very small number of defendants (a few percent) actually fled to avoid trial.

Aroused by the insidious discrimination in the existing money bail system, reform efforts took two main routes; (1) investigative projects aimed at persuading judges to release more defendants on their own

* Patricia Wald, "The Right to Bail Revisited: A Decade of Promise Without Fulfillment," in *The Rights of the Accused,* ed. Stuart S. Nagel, Sage Publications, 1972, pp. 180–185. © 1972 (Reprinted with permission).

recognizance, and (2) legislation to require pretrial release when defendants met certain criteria. The Vera Foundation, sponsored by a civic-minded industrialist, Louis Schweitzer, mounted the Manhattan Bail Project in 1961, which sent law student investigators into the detention pens of New York City's teeming criminal courts to check out the residences, families, jobs, past records and other indicia of stability of defendants awaiting bail setting, and to make recommendations to the judges for the release without money bail of those with solid roots in the community. In the first year, the judges to whom the Vera investigators submitted their recommendations for release without money bail, based upon a point system for rating the accused's community ties, agreed to ROR (release on their own recognizance or promise to appear) prisoners in 59 percent of the cases. (4) That batting average later soared to a much higher percent. The project operated three years under Vera's auspices and released 3,500 defendants; the return rate of ROR'd defendants was 98.4 percent; there was no significant rate of rearrest while on release, and the released group fared far more successfully in acquittals, suspended sentences and probation than detained accuseds. At the end of the three years in 1964, Vera turned over the operation of the release project to the New York City Probation Department.

In the early sixties, too, Senator Sam Ervin of North Carolina of the Senate Subcommittee on Constitutional Rights of the Judiciary Committee began looking toward a legislative solution to the injustice of bail practices. An Attorney General's Committee on Poverty and the Administration of Federal Criminal Justice, appointed by Attorney General Robert Kennedy, reported in 1963 on the appalling rates of pretrial detention due to indigency in 4 federal districts. (In one district 78 percent of the defendants could not raise $500 bail.) The study resulted in an Order to U.S. Attorneys to recommend release without money bail in federal courts whenever no substantial likelihood of flight existed.

The President's Commission on Law Enforcement and the Administration of Criminal Justice in 1967 seconded the plea that bail projects be started to investigate defendants and recommend release without money bail whenever possible. It also suggested that legislation create a presumption in favor of such release. In the mid-sixties over 100 bail projects patterned after the Vera model were begun throughout the nation. In addition, several communities copied New York City's summons program which permitted the police themselves to release misdemeanants at the precinct if they had sufficient community ties. In 1970, New York City police released 27,000 arrestees at the stationhouse, thereby saving an estimated eight to ten hours of police time per case and a total of $2 million.

Legislative efforts at reform culminated on the federal level with the passage of the Bail Reform Act of 1966. Applicable only to the federal courts and the District of Columbia, it (a) created a presumption in favor of release on recognizance without money before trial; (b) authorized a scale of "conditions of release" which the judge might impose during the pretrial period beginning with release on personal recognizance and an unsecured appearance bond and proceeding through third party custody, limitation of travel, residence or association, cash deposit of 10 percent of the amount of a bond into the court, returnable upon appearance, a surety bond, release into the community by day with return to custody at night, and finally any "other condition" thought appropriate to ensure that the defendant reappeared at trial. The judge was to make his decision on the proper conditions of release taking into account all "available information" about the nature and circumstances of the offense charged, the weight of the evidence, family ties, employment, financial resources, length of residence in the community, character and mental condition, record of convictions and appearances in prior cases. Regular rules of evidence did not apply to bail hearings.

Imposition of release conditions that resulted in the arrestee's incarceration or daytime release could be reviewed first by the judge who laid them down, anytime after 24 hours, then by the court with jurisdiction to try the case and finally by an appellate court. If the conditions were not changed to permit release, the judge had to state the reasons why in writing. The teeth of the Act were to lie in the severe criminal penalties for failure to appear at trial: $5,000 fine and/or five years in prison in a felony case; $1,000 and/or one year prison in misdemeanor cases. Defendants charged with capital crimes or already convicted and awaiting sentence or appeal could be detained only if the judge found that they posed a danger of flight or danger to the community. Defendants detained before trial were to be given full credit for any time in custody on any prison sentence subsequently rendered. It was hoped and optimistically expected in 1966 that states would quickly follow suit with little Bail Reform Acts.

The federal Bail Reform Act came under attack almost immediately, principally by law enforcement officials and trial judges in the District of Columbia who complained that it required the release of dangerous defendants accused of street crimes. Elsewhere, the Act was and continues to be generally conceded as a workable and worthwhile improvement on former bail practices. In 1969, the United States Court of Appeals for the District declared:

> The life of the Bail Reform Act has been marked by woefully inadequate awareness of its requirements by the lay public, resulting in often savage and invariably unfair criticism of judges for simply abiding by their sworn oaths to administer the laws of the United States.

This same appellate court had unswervingly insisted that the spirit and the letter of the new law be carried out and that trial judges could not continue to set high money bail in order to prevent future crime. It had also required judges to explore fully the alternatives to money bail before allowing detention of any accused for failure to make a money bond.

Despite such herculean efforts, the Bail Reform Act failed to prevent a substantial percentage of defendants from continuing to be detained before trial. In the District of Columbia, 1968–1969 studies showed between 35 percent and 40 percent of defendants still being detained. In 1971, over 1,000 men were being held in a pretrial detention status in the D.C. Jail, a greater number than before bail reform efforts began. Throughout the country, the number of man-days in detention for federal offenses increased from 1.2 million in 1965 to 1.4 million in 1969. The cost to federal taxpayers for pretrial detention [rose] 58 percent from 4.5 million in 1965 to 9.5 million in 1971 . . . In the large cities, even those with bail projects, a sizable pretrial detention population [persisted] as well . . . Ten years after the Manhattan Bail Project began the New York City Council Subcommittee [reported]:

> Our present bail system constitutes a *de facto* system of preventive detention of the poor; the process by which a person is detained bears less relationship to considerations of justice or correction than to economic status. The bail hearing typically consumes about one or two minutes. A release on recognizance report if present at all under the limited existing program will mention family ties, local residence, employment, and criminal record. But if the prosecutor recommends a bail amount, it will probably be based solely on the charge and the past record. Defense counsel will just have met his client and will very likely do little more than acquiesce or ask for a lower amount. Evidence will rarely be taken on whether the defendant can afford the proposed amount. . . . As a result, over 40 percent of all defendants in New York City are remanded by the courts to detention, not because they are likely to commit a crime or jump bail, but because they lack sufficient resources either to post bond or to justify the risk of the bail bondsman.

Comment

During the 1960s and 1970s, bail reform projects were begun in a variety of places throughout the United States with mixed results. The materials that follow describe some of these attempts, and the reasons for the results. As you read them, consider whether the reasons given actually explain why bail reform was limited.

b. BAIL REFORM IN PHILADELPHIA *

. . . . As a result of the publication of Professor Caleb Foote's study of bail and detention in Philadelphia in 1954, Philadelphia became a

* Goldkamp, John S. "Philadelphia Revisited: An Examination of Bail and Detention Two Decades after Foote," *Crime and Delinquency,* Vol. 26, No. 2, April

symbol of all that was "wrong" with the American bail system. Although Foote was certainly not the first to criticize the American way of bail, he was the first to undertake a comprehensive examination of bail practices, pretrial detention, and their implications for criminally charged defendants. The Philadelphia Bail Study, as his study was called, was significant not only because it documented many inequities and raised questions concerning the constitutionality of bail and detention practices, but also because it served as a major catalyst for bail reform efforts that began in New York in the early 1960s. Many years after publication of the study—and partly as a result of it—Philadelphia came to be viewed as an entirely different kind of bellwether: as a model of bail reform and exemplary pretrial services that other cities sought eagerly to emulate. From the point of view of bail practices, Philadelphia had been transformed from a "traditional" to a "reform" jurisdiction.   . . .

THE PHILADELPHIA BAIL STUDY

It is difficult to discover an issue that was addressed by the bail reform movement of the 1960s that was not first discussed by Foote in his 1954 study. Because of the comprehensive treatment of bail and detention in that study, it may be helpful to organize the issues raised by Foote (as follows):   . . .

> . . . the unstructured exercise of discretion in bail matters, the procedural impediments to the fair administration of bail, the presumption of guilt and pretrial punishment, the inequitable treatment of defendants at bail, and questions about the effectiveness of bail practices.

As part of a broader investigation of bail decision making and the role of pretrial detention in American criminal justice, bail practices in Philadelphia were again studied in 1977. Cases of a large number of defendants who had bail decided in the fall of 1975 were studied after their final resolutions by 1977.

Perhaps the most striking departure from the Philadelphia of 1954 in present bail matters is the fact that the bail function is transacted in a centrally organized fashion. All defendants (except homicide defendants) have bail decided no more than twelve hours after their arrest, at a court held in one location and then only after they have been thoroughly interviewed for information on community ties, employment, income, health problems, and prior record.

The Foote of more than two decades ago would be further astonished to discover that, according to the more recent study, the use of cash bail as a decision option has considerably diminished. Nearly half of all defendants in the 1977 study were granted release on personal recognizance. Compared with the 75 percent detention rate reported by Foote in 1954, only 25 percent of Philadelphia defendants exper-

1980, pp. 179–192.   © 1980 (Reprinted with permission).

ienced pretrial detention beyond a twenty-four-hour period in 1975; half of these—only 12 percent of all defendants—remained confined during the entire preadjudicatory interval. In addition, defendants in 1975 who were not released immediately after first appearance still had a further recourse: They were considered for conditional release, a form of release that is conditioned by participation in certain programs or supervision. There is evidence also that defendants who were detained in Philadelphia in 1975 were confined for considerably shorter periods than previously. Where possible, they were given an accelerated court calendar. Moreover, special sessions of court were held at the jail to expedite the processing of minor cases (usually misdemeanors) that might otherwise have been unnecessarily delayed.

In addition to centrally organized bail and pretrial release functions and the appearance of "individualized" bail decision making, a further major alteration in the Philadelphia way of bail can now be observed: the disappearance of the bondsman. In a major reform, Philadelphia's courts have replaced bondsmen with a Ten Percent program which allows defendants to deposit 10 percent of the amount of their cash bail with the court. The deposit is refundable (minus a service charge) as soon as it has been ascertained that the defendant has appeared in court. In the event that defendants cannot afford the 10 percent amount themselves, the use of third-party bail is strongly favored as a way of inducing relatives or friends to have a stake in assuring that a defendant will not face the necessity of resorting to a bondsman. Apparently, many of Foote's criticisms concerning the use of cash bail in Philadelphia were addressed by the time of the 1977 study.

HAVE THE MAJOR ISSUES BEEN RESOLVED?

Clearly, major reforms have been implemented in Philadelphia since the time of Foote's study. Philadelphia has been transformed from a jurisdiction symbolizing the disorder and abuses characteristic of the American bail system in the 1950s to a model bail reform jurisdiction. But have the major issues raised by Foote in 1954 been fully resolved? Perhaps not. The five critical dimensions used to summarize Foote's study in the beginning of this discussion will again be briefly considered to permit an issue-by-issue assessment of this question.

Discretion

On the surface, at least, it would appear that the discretion which under the former system was so vulnerable to abuse has now been solidly structured. Judges are presently instructed in the *Pennsylvania Rules of Court* to weigh as many as sixteen items of information about defendants in deciding bail. (Among these are not only the nature of the charge and the prior record, but also a variety of other kinds of data, such as defendants' community ties, employment, and financial resources.) The Pretrial Services Division was created to make possible this information-gathering and digesting function. Although implementation of this reform appears to be the very embodiment of the "individualization" ideal, it is interesting to note that the 1977 study found that the nature of the criminal charge still played the dominant role in bail determinations. The "standard," criminal charge, that was so criticized by Foote appears to survive undaunted—despite the existence of newer decision-making guidelines and an ROR (personal recognizance release) program to help operationalize them.

The fact that the alternative kinds of defendant data (e.g., community ties) diligently collected by the ROR program staff in Philadelphia did not play an influential role in either bail determinations or the determination of release or detention in the recent study suggests two hypotheses: (1) Either judges remain convinced that criminal charge is the most reliable predictor of risk of flight, or (2) they remain steadfast in adhering to a flexible, all-purpose standard that, as Foote explained, has the "practical effect of holding" any defendants who for various reasons may have impressed bail judges unfavorably.

Presumptions of Guilt and Pretrial Punishment

In the 1977 study, interviews with Philadelphia bail judges were conducted to learn the judges' views about bail decision making and pretrial detention. It was clear in those interviews that presumption of guilt is an unavoidable concomitant of the reliance on the criminal charge criterion and that both are features of preventive detention related to dangerousness concerns in bail. That is, when defendants are charged with serious crimes, judges may conservatively assume their guilt and further assume that they would be dangerous (or at least more dangerous than nonseriously charged defendants) if freely released before trial. In spite of the inexactness and the controversial nature of this sort of predictive "science," it is clear that this branch of bail ideology is and will remain a powerful force in Philadelphia, as elsewhere.

Inequitable Treatment of Defendants in Bail Practices

The inequities inherent in procedural delay and in the role of bondsmen in the former Philadelphia practices have been virtually eliminated, as noted above, but the problem of disparity in bail decisions has not. The 1977 study did not address the issue of judge-to-judge inconsistency, but there is no reason to assume that such variation has been noticeably affected by bail reform practices. . . .

In response to the issue of economic discrimination inherent in a system of cash bail raised by Foote in 1954, it must be said that reforms in Philadelphia have made substantial inroads. To begin with, ROR in 1975 was used in nearly half of all cases—compared with a negligible percentage of cases in 1954. For that half of defendants, then, economic discrimination is no longer a relevant concern. For the other half, it is certain that the economic impact of cash bail has been lessened through the Ten Percent program. If it cannot be stated for certain that the "price" of cash bail has gone down under the program (and some have suggested that judges have simply adjusted the amount of bail upward to compensate), it can at least be stated that defendants now regain the amounts that previously would have been lost to the bondsman's fee. Nevertheless, because even low bail may be unaffordable to poor defendants, any bail system relying on cash bail will always be discriminatory to a certain extent, by definition.

The third equity issue raised by Foote concerning the possible disadvantage suffered by detained defendants in the subsequent processing of their cases was specifically examined in the 1977 study. The question here was whether pretrial custody in itself had an influence on later outcomes of defendants' cases . . . detained defendants whose cases later progressed through the criminal process all the way to sentencing were substantially more likely to receive sentences to incarceration than their counterparts who had been released before the adjudication of their cases. [Pre-trial detention] still presents a serious equal protection dilemma.

Questions

Do you think Professor Foote would regard the Philadelphia story as a success? Might he think that the constitutional right to bail of the twelve percent of defendants still being preventively detained was being violated? Do you think so? If not, why not? If so, do you think the Philadelphia judges were systematically engaging in acts of civil disobedience? Should judges ever find themselves in the position of violating constitutional rights?

2. THE BONDSMAN

a. AS A PUBLIC SERVANT *

Despite a host of bail reform legislation during the past decade, Connecticut law continues to preserve the interests of bondsmen. During the late 1960s, when the state assembly was considering bail reform legislation, several bondsmen in the state organized a lobbying effort and pooled their resources to retain a lobbyist. While it is impossible to assess the precise impact of this effort, bondsmen were not adversely affected by the resulting legislation which promoted release on recognizance (OR) for those arrestees who previously had been released on low bonds. Some of the bondsmen even professed to applaud this expansion of OR, claiming that there is too little profit in small bonds to make them worthwhile. But a 1976 proposal in the state legislature to introduce more substantial bail reform and to institutionalize a court-administered 10 percent bond program similar to those in several other states was actively opposed by many of the state's bondsmen and was killed in committee. If it had been adopted, this proposal would have

* Malcolm Feeley, *The Process is the Punishment,* Russell Sage Foundation, 1979, pp. 97–100, 107–108. © 1979 by Russell Sage Foundation. Reprinted with permission of Russell Sage Foundation.

replaced the surety system with a 10-percent cash deposit system, whereby the accused could post a returnable deposit with the court rather than pay the same amount to a bondsman. Had this proposal passed, it could have put bondsmen out of business.

. . .

A bondsman needs little else besides initial capital to go into business. Most operate out of their homes or from small offices, or in some cases share office space with attorneys. While attorneys cannot advertise, bondsmen can, and the arrangement between them is mutually convenient. But the bondsman's real workplace is the courthouse. Bondsmen often appropriate space in a prosecutor's, a public defender's, or even a judge's office, and at times transact business from the clerk's table in the courtroom while court is in session.

Connecticut statutes restrict the fee or commission which a professional bondsman may charge; . . .

Although it is impossible for a bondsman to predict how long his money will be tied up in any particular bond, one study estimates that bond money is tied up for an average of ninety-five days, and the data I collected show it to be much less for the lower courts. . . .

The bond business is relatively risk-free, can operate on a low overhead, and can be pursued on a part-time basis. The theory of suretyship holds that the bondsman has a direct financial incentive to see that the defendant appears in court, and that if he fails to appear the bondsman must assume liability for him. . . .

. . .

The practice of reducing liability . . . is a complicated system of exchange among the bondsmen and the judges, prosecutors, defense attorneys, and various auxiliary court personnel, rooted in self-interest and sealed in friendship, small favors, and flattery. Bondsmen find it advantageous to remain on the good side of the police who can direct business their way, and to ingratiate themselves with judges and prosecutors who can pass cases, grant continuances, stay bond forfeitures, and facilitate reductions through compromises. Defense attorneys do not object because these practices benefit their clients.

Why do all these people help the bondsmen? Why, despite the theory of bail, can bondsmen run a low-risk business, largely by getting other people to help them? The answer is that bondsmen provide desired services for these people. In New Haven I found the two busiest bondsmen to be gregarious and friendly, always ready with a friendly word and a pleasant smile. They frequently took court personnel to lunch, occasionally threw parties for the court staff and prosecutors, and regularly picked up the tab at a local bar on Friday afternoons. They also dispensed holiday presents and tickets to local sporting events to court personnel, prosecutors, some judges, and defense attorneys. One judge, when he sat in New Haven, was often driven to court by one of them.

These two bondsmen also contributed to the efficient operation of the court. Indeed, but for them the rapid-paced processes in the courtroom might have ground to a halt, an unpleasant thought for court officials who were anxious to get through the day as early as possible. Prosecutors, judges, and defense attorneys turned to these bondsmen for answers as to the whereabouts of other attorneys and defendants, which they knew because they were constantly moving about the courthouse during the day. A bondsman sometimes asked a prosecutor to delay calling a case because the defense attorney was still arguing a motion in another case across the street, or informed the court that an attorney or his client was home in bed with the flu. At least one defense attorney regularly relied on the bondsmen to keep tabs on his clients who were out on bail, to remind them of their court appearance dates, and to give them instructions as to which courtroom they should appear in. The two bondsmen also apparently extended favors to the police by bailing out risky persons whom the police were using as informants, and by refusing to write bonds for others whom the prosecutor or police wanted to summarily punish.

They also served as sources of information and at times as agents for arrestees without attorneys. As one prosecutor noted, "Bondsmen will frequently approach us and ask us to nolle a case or to 'take care of this guy.' Often these are their clients, but sometimes they are not. He's just around and listens to the guy's story and comes over to talk to us." Another prosecutor commenting on one of the bondsmen noted that "_____'s good. He frequently comes back here and plea bargains for his clients. He does it a lot for defendants without attorneys and sometimes even for cases where PDs are appointed. He is pretty successful, and does a good job for his clients."

In contrast to the popular image of the bondsman as a pariah, a social outcast who sits stonefaced raking in money through a window gate, exploiting the human misery all around him, the two major bondsmen in New Haven were both naturally ebullient and gregarious men who obviously enjoyed their work and their association with the courtroom personnel, and in turn received friendship and respect from court personnel and criminal defendants, clients and nonclients alike. Their personalities served them well, for the bondsman's business involves a good deal of public relations and goodwill gestures. It is no small wonder that many spectators sitting in the gallery had the impression that these two busy men dressed in expensive suits, actively and authoritatively moving about the front of the courtroom, were important public officials. Unofficially, they were.

Questions

The above excerpt demonstrates the importance of field research in describing the realities of the criminal court. What was observed concerning bondsmen might be interpreted either as (1) a scandal or (2) a functional necessity or (3) both of the above. Which do you think it is? If you think it is (3), do you think the legal system ought to be permitted to engage in scandalous functional necessities? If you think not, how would you go about reforming the system?

b. AS A SOURCE OF CORRUPTION *

Bondsmen do not function in a vacuum. Their interrelationships with officials and agencies involved in the administration of justice are essential to their livelihood. These relationships, however, have often led to alarmed cries of collusion and have been used as another example of the bondsman's illegal activities. It is impossible to arrive at an impartial and factual estimation of the amount of collusion actually taking place.

The most frequently named group to be accused of engaging in collusive activities with bondsmen are defense attorneys. In many of the cities included in the study, lawyers were alleged to have paid a 10-percent kickback to bondsmen who recommended them. In St. Louis one attorney went so far as to state that bondsmen have made several lawyers wealthy by referring cases to them. At least part of the blame can be placed upon the local bar associations that fail to control their members and permit these types of activities to continue.

A second group charged with conspiring with bondsmen are judges. An investigation in Philadelphia in 1964 revealed that certain judges were receiving money from bondsmen to set bail in all cases regardless of their seriousness, so they would have more potential clients. According to a defense attorney interviewed, this practice still persists, although to a lesser degree. He commented that a few judges will allow bondsmen to tell them how much they believe the defendant can afford. The bondsman may attempt to improve a working relationship with a judge by contributing to his campaign fund. The bondsmen of Detroit and St. Louis seem to be the most politically active in this respect. One bondsman in St. Louis is party chairman of a congressional district.

A third group accused of illegal dealings with bondsmen are the police. This illicit relationship supposedly begins with the arresting officer or someone in the stationhouse recommending a particular bondsman to the defendant. At the end of the month, the policeman can expect to receive a kickback from that bondsman, based upon the number of clients referred. It has been learned through interviews and many hours of observations in stationhouses, lockups and jails that this practice has sharply declined in the past five years, although it still continues sporadically. Two reasons are given for the abatement of a seemingly lucrative practice for both parties: the increasing supervision over the operations of bail-bonding companies by state and city agencies and the decreasing profit margin of bonding companies that have been forced to curtail expenditures such as kickback payments. These financial pressures have reduced their clientele and forced bondsmen to be more selective in whom they choose to represent.

* Paul B. Wice, "Purveyors of Freedom; the Professional Bondsmen". Published by permission of Transaction, Inc. from Socie-ty, Vol. 11, No. 5, Copyright ©July/August 1974 by Transaction, Inc.

The contemporary bondsman may still exert a great deal of influence over a defendant's pretrial freedom but he is a member of a dying profession. As bail-reform projects expand, operating expenses rise and state and local regulation increases, the bonding industry continues its steady decline. The bondsmen are neither glamorous nor sinister—they are simply fighting to survive. Many of them are not sympathetic characters and several engage in clearly unlawful practices, but until the traditional bail system is radically reformed, they will continue to be the one group offering an opportunity for pretrial freedom for most of the unfortunate individuals enmeshed in our nation's criminal justice system.

C. PREVENTIVE DETENTION

1. INTRODUCTION

a. NOTE ON PREVENTIVE DETENTION AND BAIL REFORM

As we begin to face up to the bail issue and do something to reduce the large numbers of people incarcerated prior to trial because they cannot post bail to guarantee their later appearance at trial, another problem becomes of paramount importance. The fact is that the bail system had a major function all along, other than merely to assure the presence of the accused at his trial. The bail system has also acted as a means of preventive detention—of keeping incarcerated those who might be too dangerous to be released.

So long as we permitted bail to be set high enough to make sure that many defendants were detained anyway, this problem was not serious. Judges would simply set a bail higher than defendants could meet, ostensibly to guarantee appearance at trial. Usually this bail did not have to be extraordinarily high, since many of those whom we would consider to be most dangerous are poor as well.

However, now that preventive detention has been embraced in many jurisdictions, presumably we must face up to the old hypocracy in the bail system. In fact, however, we have not had to despite court rulings upholding preventive detention. We continue to prefer the simplicity of high bail. However, as we shall see when it is used, preventive detention does force us to determine how accurately we can predict future danger.

b. FIRST THE PUNISHMENT, THEN THE CRIME *

"For instance, now (the Queen states to Alice) . . . there's the King's Messenger. He's in prison now, being punished; and the trial doesn't even begin till next Wednesday; and of course the crime comes last of all." Alice replies: "Suppose he

---

* Lewis Carroll, *Through the Looking Glass* (New York: The Modern Library) pp. 226–27.

never commits the crime?"   "That would be all the better, wouldn't it?" the Queen responds.

c. U.S. v. SALERNO

Supreme Court of the United States, 1987.
481 U.S. 739, 107 S.Ct. 2095, 95 L.Ed.2d 697.

Chief Justice REHNQUIST delivered the opinion of the Court.

. . .

Responding to "the alarming problem of crimes committed by persons on release," Congress formulated the Bail Reform Act of 1984, as the solution to a bail crisis in the federal courts.   The Act represents the National Legislature's considered response to numerous perceived deficiencies in the federal bail process.   By providing for sweeping changes in both the way federal courts consider bail applications and the circumstances under which bail is granted, Congress hoped to "give the courts adequate authority to make release decisions that give appropriate recognition to the danger a person may pose to others if released."

To this end, § 3141(a) of the Act requires a judicial officer to determine whether an arrestee shall be detained.   Section 3142(e) provides that "[i]f, after a hearing pursuant to the provisions of subsection (f), the judicial officer finds that no condition or combination of conditions will reasonably assure the appearance of the person as required and the safety of any other person and the community, he shall order the detention of the person prior to trial."   Section 3142(f) provides the arrestee with a number of procedural safeguards.   He may request the presence of counsel at the detention hearing, he may testify and present witnesses in his behalf, as well as proffer evidence, and he may cross-examine other witnesses appearing at the hearing.   If the judicial officer finds that no conditions of pretrial release can reasonably assure the safety of other persons and the community, he must state his findings of fact in writing, § 3142(i), and support his conclusion with "clear and convincing evidence," § 3142(f).

The judicial officer is not given unbridled discretion in making the detention determination.   Congress has specified the considerations relevant to that decision.   These factors include the nature and seriousness of the charges, the substantiality of the government's evidence against the arrestee, the arrestee's background and characteristics, and the nature and seriousness of the danger posed by the suspect's release. § 3142(g).   Should a judicial officer order detention, the detainee is entitled to expedited appellate review of the detention order §§ 3145(b), (c).

Respondents Anthony Salerno and Vincent Cafaro were arrested on March 21, 1986, after being charged in a 29-count indictment alleging various Racketeer Influenced and Corrupt Organizations Act (RICO) violations, mail and wire fraud offenses, extortion, and various criminal gambling violations.   The RICO counts alleged 35 acts of racketeering activity, including fraud, extortion, gambling, and conspiracy to commit murder. At respondents' arraignment, the Government moved to have Salerno and Cafaro detained pursuant to § 3142(e), on the ground that no condition of release would assure the safety of the community or any person. The District Court held a hearing at which the Government made a detailed proffer of evidence. The Government's case showed that Salerno was the "boss" of the Genovese Crime Family of La Cosa Nostra and that Cafaro was a "captain" in the Genovese Family. According to the Government's proffer, based in large part on conversations intercepted by a court-ordered wiretap, the two respondents had participated in wide-ranging conspiracies to aid their illegitimate enterprises through violent means. The Government also offered the testimony of two of its trial witnesses, who would assert that Salerno personally participated in two murder conspiracies. Salerno opposed the motion for detention, challenging the credibility of the Government's witnesses. He offered the testimony of several character witnesses as well as a letter from his doctor stating that he was suffering from a serious medical condition. Cafaro presented no evidence at the hearing, but instead characterized the wiretap conversations as merely "tough talk."

The District Court granted the Government's detention motion, concluding that the Government had established by clear and convincing evidence that no condition or combination of conditions of release would ensure the safety of the community or any person.

.　.　.

Respondents present two grounds for invalidating the Bail Reform Act's provisions permitting pretrial detention on the basis of future dangerousness. First, they rely upon the Court of Appeals' conclusion that the Act exceeds the limitations placed upon the Federal Government by the Due Process Clause of the Fifth Amendment. Second, they contend that the Act contravenes the Eighth Amendment's proscription against excessive bail. We treat these contentions in turn.

.　.　.

Respondents first argue that the Act violates substantive due process because the pretrial detention it authorizes constitutes impermissible punishment before trial. The Government, however, has never argued that pretrial detention could be upheld if it were "punishment." The Court of Appeals assumed that pretrial detention under the Bail Reform Act is regulatory, not penal, and we agree that it is.

As an initial matter, the mere fact that a person is detained does not inexorably lead to the conclusion that the government has imposed punishment. . . .

We conclude that the detention imposed by the Act falls on the regulatory side of the dichotomy. The legislative history of the Bail Reform Act clearly indicates that Congress did not formulate the pretrial detention provisions as punishment for dangerous individuals. Congress instead perceived pretrial detention as a potential solution to a pressing societal problem. There is no doubt that preventing danger to the community is a legitimate regulatory goal.

. . .

Under the Bail Reform Act, the procedures by which a judicial officer evaluates the likelihood of future dangerousness are specifically designed to further the accuracy of that determination. Detainees have a right to counsel at the detention hearing. They may testify in their own behalf, present information by proffer or otherwise, and cross-examine witnesses who appear at the hearing. *Ibid.* The judicial officer charged with the responsibility of determining the appropriateness of detention is guided by statutorily enumerated factors, which include the nature and the circumstances of the charges, the weight of the evidence, the history and characteristics of the putative offender, and the danger to the community. The government must prove its case by clear and convincing evidence. Finally, the judicial officer must include written findings of fact and a written statement of reasons for a decision to detain. The Act's review provisions provide for immediate appellate review of the detention decision.

We think these extensive safeguards suffice to repel a facial challenge. . . . Given the legitimate and compelling regulatory purpose of the Act and the procedural protections it offers, we conclude that the Act is not facially invalid under the Due Process Clause of the Fifth Amendment.

B

Respondents also contend that the Bail Reform Act violates the Excessive Bail Clause of the Eighth Amendment. . . . We think that the Act survives a challenge founded upon the Eighth Amendment.

The Eighth Amendment addresses pretrial release by providing merely that "Excessive bail shall not be required." This Clause, of course, says nothing about whether bail shall be available at all. Respondents nevertheless contend that this Clause grants them a right to bail calculated solely upon considerations of flight. They rely on *Stack v. Boyle.* . . .

While we agree that a primary function of bail is to safeguard the courts' role in adjudicating the guilt or innocence of defendants, we reject the proposition that the Eighth Amendment categorically prohibits the government from pursuing other admittedly compelling interests through regulation of pretrial release. . . . *[D]icta in Stack v. Boyle* is far too slender a reed on which to rest this argument. The Court in *Stack* had no occasion to consider whether the Excessive Bail Clause requires courts to admit all defendants to bail, because the statute before the Court in that case in fact allowed the defendants to be bailed. Thus, the Court had to determine only whether bail, admittedly available in that case, was excessive if set at a sum greater than that necessary to ensure the arrestees' presence at trial.

. . .

In our society liberty is the norm, and detention prior to trial or without trial is the carefully limited exception. We hold that the provisions for pretrial detention in the Bail Reform Act of 1984 fall within that carefully limited exception. The Act authorizes the detention prior to trial of arrestees charged with serious felonies who are found after an adversary hearing to pose a threat to the safety of individuals or to the community which no condition of release can dispel. The numerous procedural safeguards detailed above must attend this adversary hearing. We are unwilling to say that this congressional determination, based as it is upon that primary concern of every government—a concern for the safety and indeed the lives of its citizens—on its face violates either the Due Process Clause of the Fifth Amendment or the Excessive Bail Clause of the Eighth Amendment.

The judgment of the Court of Appeals is therefore

Reversed.

Justice MARSHALL, with whom Justice BRENNAN joins, dissenting.

This case brings before the Court for the first time a statute in which Congress declares that a person innocent of any crime may be jailed indefinitely, pending the trial of allegations which are legally presumed to be untrue, if the Government shows to the satisfaction of a judge that the accused is likely to commit crimes, unrelated to the pending charges, at any time in the future. Such statutes, consistent with the usages of tyranny and the excesses of what bitter experience teaches us to call the police state, have long been thought incompatible with the fundamental human rights protected by our Constitution. Today a majority of this Court holds otherwise. Its decision disregards basic principles of justice established centuries ago and enshrined beyond the reach of governmental interference in the Bill of Rights.

. . .

A few preliminary words are necessary with respect to the majority's treatment of the facts in this case. The two paragraphs which the majority devotes to the procedural posture are essentially correct, but they omit certain matters which are of substantial legal relevance.

. . .

The situation with respect to respondent Cafaro is disturbing. In early October 1986, before the Solicitor General's petition for certiorari was granted, respondent Cafaro became a cooperating witness, assisting the Government's investigation "by working in a covert capacity." The information that Cafaro was cooperating with the Government was not revealed to his co-defendants, including respondent Salerno. On October 9, 1986, respondent Cafaro was released, ostensibly "temporarily for medical care and treatment," with the Government's consent. This release was conditioned upon execution of a personal recognizance bond in the sum of $1,000,000, under the general pretrial release provisions of 18 U.S.C. § 3141. In short, respondent Cafaro became an informant and the Government agreed to his release on bail in order that he might better serve the Government's purposes. As to Cafaro, this case was no longer justiciable even before certiorari was granted, but the information bearing upon the essential issue of the Court's jurisdiction was not made available to us.

The Government thus invites the Court to address the facial constitutionality of the pretrial detention statute in a case involving two respondents, one of whom [Salerno] has been sentenced to a century of jail time in another case and released pending appeal with the Government's consent, while the other was released on bail *in this case*, with the Government's consent, because he had become an informant. These facts raise, at the very least, a substantial question as to the Court's jurisdiction, for it is far from clear that there is now an actual controversy between these parties. . . .

. . .

The majority approaches respondents' challenge to the Act by dividing the discussion into two sections, one concerned with the substantive guarantees implicit in the Due Process Clause, and the other concerned with the protection afforded by the Excessive Bail Clause of the Eighth Amendment. This is a sterile formalism, which divides a unitary argument into two independent parts and then professes to demonstrate that the parts are individually inadequate.

On the due process side of this false dichotomy appears an argument concerning the distinction between regulatory and punitive legislation. The majority concludes that the Act is a regulatory rather than a punitive measure. The ease with which the conclusion is reached suggests the worthlessness of the achievement. The major premise is that "[u]nless Congress expressly intended to impose punitive restrictions, the punitive/regulatory distinction turns on ' "whether an alternative purpose to which [the restriction] may rationally be connected is assignable for it, and whether it appears excessive in relation to the alternative purpose assigned [to it]." ' " The majority finds that "Congress did not formulate the pretrial detention provisions as punishment for dangerous individuals," but instead was pursuing the "legitimate regulatory goal" of "preventing danger to the community." Concluding that pretrial detention is not an excessive solution to the problem of preventing danger to the community, the majority thus finds that no substantive element of the guarantee of due process invalidates the statute.

This argument does not demonstrate the conclusion it purports to justify. Let us apply the majority's reasoning to a similar, hypothetical case. After investigation, Congress determines (not unrealistically) that a large proportion of violent crime is perpetrated by persons who are unemployed. It also determines, equally reasonably, that much violent crime is committed at night. From amongst the panoply of "potential solutions," Congress chooses a statute which permits, after judicial proceedings, the imposition of a dusk-to-dawn curfew on anyone who is unemployed. Since this is not a measure enacted for the purpose of punishing the unemployed, and since the majority finds that preventing danger to the community is a legitimate regulatory goal, the curfew statute would, according to the majority's analysis, be a mere "regulatory" detention statute, entirely compatible with the substantive components of the Due Process Clause.

The absurdity of this conclusion arises, of course, from the majority's cramped concept of substantive due process. The majority proceeds as though the only substantive right protected by the Due Process Clause is a right to be free from punishment before conviction. The majority's technique for infringing this right is simple: merely redefine any measure which is claimed to be punishment as "regulation," and, magically, the Constitution no longer prohibits its imposition. . . .

The logic of the majority's Eighth Amendment analysis is equally unsatisfactory. The Eighth Amendment, as the majority notes, states that "[e]xcessive bail shall not be required." The majority then declares, as if it were undeniable, that: "[t]his Clause, of course, says nothing about whether bail shall be available at all." If excessive bail is imposed the defendant stays in jail. The same result is achieved if bail is denied altogether. Whether the magistrate sets bail at $1 billion or refuses to set bail at all, the consequences are indistinguishable. It would be mere sophistry to suggest that the Eighth Amendment protects against the former decision, and not the latter. Indeed, such a result would lead to the conclusion that there was no need for Congress to pass a preventive detention measure of any kind; every federal magistrate and district judge could simply refuse, despite the absence of any evidence of risk of flight or danger to the community, to set bail. This would be entirely constitutional, since, according to the majority, the Eighth Amendment "says nothing about whether bail shall be available at all."

. . .

The essence of this case may be found, ironically enough, in a provision of the Act to which the majority does not refer. Title 18 U.S.C. § 3142(j) provides that "[n]othing in this section shall be construed as modifying or limiting the presumption of innocence." But the very pith and purpose of this statute is an abhorrent limitation of the presumption of innocence. The majority's untenable conclusion that the present Act is constitutional arises from a specious denial of the role of the Bail Clause and the Due Process Clause in protecting the invaluable guarantee afforded by the presumption of innocence.

"The principle that there is a presumption of innocence in favor of the accused is the undoubted law, axiomatic and elementary, and its enforcement lies at the foundation of the administration of our criminal law." Our society's belief, reinforced over the centuries, that all are innocent until the state has proved them to be guilty, like the companion principle that guilt must be proved beyond a reasonable doubt, is "implicit in the concept of ordered liberty."

. . .

There is a connection between the peculiar facts of this case and the evident constitutional defects in the statute which the Court upholds today. Respondent Cafaro was originally incarcerated for an indeterminate period at the request of the Government, which believed (or professed to believe) that his release imminently threatened the safety of the community. That threat apparently vanished, from the Government's point of view, when Cafaro agreed to act as a covert agent of the Government. There could be no more eloquent demonstration of the coercive power of authority to imprison upon prediction, or of the dangers which the almost inevitable abuses pose to the cherished liberties of a free society.

"It is a fair summary of history to say that the safeguards of liberty have frequently been forged in controversies involving not very nice people." Honoring the presumption of innocence is often difficult; sometimes we must pay substantial social costs as a result of our commitment to the values we espouse. But at the end of the day the presumption of innocence protects the innocent; the shortcuts we take with those whom we believe to be guilty injure only those wrongfully accused and, ultimately, ourselves.

Throughout the world today there are men, women, and children interned indefinitely, awaiting trials which may never come or which may be a mockery of the word, because their governments believe them to be "dangerous." Our Constitution, whose construction began two centuries ago, can shelter us forever from the evils of such unchecked power. Over two hundred years it has slowly, through our efforts, grown more durable, more expansive, and more just. But it cannot protect us if we lack the courage, and the self-restraint, to protect ourselves. Today a majority of the Court applies itself to an ominous exercise in demolition. Theirs is truly a decision which will go forth without authority, and come back without respect.

I dissent.

2. IS PREVENTIVE DETENTION FAIR? *

a. PREVENTIVE DETENTION IN ACTION

Ricardo M. Armstrong of Columbus, Ohio, learned sooner than most about "preventive detention" and the new federal bail provisions of the Comprehensive Crime Control Act of 1984. But he learned the hard way.

In October 1984, the same month the bill was passed, Mr. Armstrong was arrested and charged with committing two armed bank robberies in Springfield, Ohio. Under the old bail law, he would have had a good chance for release pending trial. He had a stable address, a decent work history and only one prior conviction—a 1977 state charge of breaking into an occupied dwelling.

* John Riley, "Preventive Detention Use Grows—But is it Fair?" National Law Journal, March 24, 1986, pp. 1, 32. © 1986 (Reprinted with permission).

But the new law had changed things. It allowed magistrates and judges to consider "danger to the community" as well as risk of flight in setting bail conditions. And for certain defendants charged with major drug offenses or armed crimes, like Mr. Armstrong, it authorized a "rebuttable presumption" of dangerousness and allowed jailing without bail before trial.

Over the past 17 months that detention authority has been used in thousands of cases—far more widely than many expected—and the about-face in traditional procedure has received surprisingly quick acceptance by the courts. Cases like Mr. Armstrong's, however, reflect the serious questions of fairness, interpretation and effectiveness that also have accompanied the new era.

From the start, the 29–year-old defendant insisted he was innocent. He told his court-appointed lawyer, Thomas A. Schaffer of Dayton, Ohio's Sutton, Overholser & Schaffer, that he had alibi witnesses for the dates of the two robberies.

Mr. Schaffer, however, had only four days after interviewing his client to prepare for the detention hearing. He couldn't track down the alibi witnesses, and under the new law the government didn't have to present firsthand testimony. Instead, an FBI agent testified that seven witnesses had picked Mr. Armstrong's picture out of a photo array, and the government also presented a surveillance picture taken at one of the banks.

"If it's not the same person, it's his twin brother," said U.S. Magistrate Robert A. Steinberg of Cincinnati, "and it's a picture of him in a bank with a gun in his hand, and that's enough to convince me he's a danger to the community."

The magistrate found probable cause to believe Mr. Armstrong was guilty, ruled that he hadn't rebutted the presumption of dangerousness, and ordered him held pending trial. Mr. Schaffer's appeal finally was denied by the federal judge hearing the case in early January 1985— two days before the start of trial.

There was only one problem: The jury didn't agree.

The picture used in the photo array turned out to be 7 years old, and showed a younger and thinner man than Mr. Armstrong was at the time of trial. The alibi witnesses were persuasive. And jurors apparently didn't see the surveillance photo the same way the magistrate did. Following two months in jail, Mr. Armstrong was acquitted after a 30–minute deliberation.

"It was a travesty of justice," contends Mr. Schaffer. "They held an innocent man from late October until the beginning of January. It was a classic case of punishment before conviction. If ever there were a case that speaks of the dangers of that law, this was it."

Long a hobby horse of conservatives and the law-enforcement community, pretrial detention proposals were stalled in Congress for more than a decade before 1984. The key obstacle: opposition from liberals and defense advocates who contended that predictions of guilt and dangerousness are impossible and would flip the pretrial presumption of innocence on its head.

In the time since Congress finally acted, cases like Mr. Armstrong's have not been the rule. But experience has reduced the controversy surrounding detention only slightly, if at all.

The Reagan Justice Department, which pushed hard for the new bail law, is pleased with the results. Its own data-gathering efforts, despite significant underreporting, indicate that at least 2,853 detention hearings were held in the first 16 months after the bill was passed.

And despite the sudden impact and hotly debated legal issues involving detention, prosecutors have had a success rate of about 80 percent—with 1,114 detentions on risk-of-flight grounds, 381 on dangerousness grounds, and 705 on both.

That record, says Deputy Asst. Attorney General James Knapp of the Justice Department's Criminal Division, suggests that federal prosecutors are using their new detention powers with "restraint."

"We expected some resistance from judges and magistrates, but that has not been the case," he notes. "It's working, it's being used, the appellate decisions have been favorable, the constitutionality has been upheld so far and we're getting detention in appropriate cases."

Despite that sunny view, however, there are also abundant critics, skeptics and unanswered questions.

• Some object that the new law is being overused. U.S. magistrates reported to the Administrative Office of the U.S. Courts 4,178 detention hearings, or 835 per month, during a five-month period last year—figures far higher than the Justice Department's, suggesting an annual rate equivalent to nearly 25 percent of all federal felony defendants. The U.S. Marshal's Service says the new bail law was primarily responsible for a 32 percent increase in prisoner population and an 11 percent increase in total jail days during the first year after its passage.

• Others contend it is being misused—pushed by some prosecutors beyond Congress' central focus on major drug traffickers and violent felons. Defense attorneys in different parts of the country complain that detention on grounds of "dangerousness" has been sought in pornography cases, cases of economic crime ranging from money laundering to credit-card fraud and auto theft, and in cases involving relatively low-level drug busts.

"It's essentially a standardless statute," complains Richard A. Reeve, a federal public defender in New Haven, Conn.

"Prosecutors use it for their own purposes when a defendant won't cooperate and they want something to hold over his head," notes sole practitioner Joseph F. Sklarosky of Kingston, Pa., who represented a preventively detained client charged with using the mails to transmit child pornography.

• Still others say it is being underused. One key purpose of the statute, they argue, was to replace "sub rosa" detentions through impossibly high bails with up-front standards and procedures for detention. But there is widespread feeling that many defendants continue to be detained on high bail.

Even Mr. Knapp says that as many as 7 percent to 8 percent of all federal felony defendants may still be detained on high bails—compared with his personal estimate that 5 percent to 10 percent are being held after detention orders—and that resistance to using the new detention procedures in places, like the Southern District of Florida, has led to disagreements between U.S. attorneys and the Justice Department in Washington.

• The effectiveness of the new law in two other key areas—reducing non-appearances and crime on bail—is still in doubt. Mr. Knapp notes that crime rates in general are going down, and believes the new bail law is a contributing factor. But the Marshal's Service reported that in the first year after passage of the law, the number of bond-default warrants received went up by 13 percent—not down.

• Several major constitutional issues also remain unsettled. Some courts have interpreted the rebuttable presumptions of dangerousness narrowly to preserve their constitutionality. No federal appeals court has yet ruled on the broad issue of detention based on a prediction of dangerousness. And although the Supreme Court in 1984 approved a 17–day pretrial detention of a juvenile under a state law, the propriety of longer detentions in complex cases is unclear.

In early March, for example, a major Connecticut case concerning the prospect of lengthy detentions for nine Puerto Rican nationalists charged with involvement in the robbery of a Wells Fargo truck came before the 2d U.S. Circuit Court of Appeals. "You don't think there's a quantum leap from 17 days to two or three years?" Circuit Chief Judge Wilfred Feinberg asked the Justice Department lawyer. *U.S. v. Melendez-Carrion*, 85–1431.

• Some suggest that implementation of the new bail law so far is a "checkerboard," and that one key variable is the extent to which pretrial services officers are used to interview defendants and develop release or detention proposals prior to the initial appearance before a magistrate—a procedure required by the new bail law and the Pretrial Services Act of 1982.

A study released last fall by the General Accounting Office, however, reported that nationally the federal courts were doing a poor job in implementing pretrial services programs, with only 21,158 of 43,851 eligible defendants interviewed before their bail hearings in 1984.

"We reduced non-appearances 65 to 70 percent and crime on bail by 62 percent even before the new law," notes John A. Schoenberger, head of a model pretrial services program operating in the Southern District of New York since the mid–1970's. "But since the new bail law, the percentages haven't changed."

For researchers tracking the new law, the cross-currents are titillating but inconclusive. "The patterns have by no means stabilized," says Prof. Daniel J. Freed of Yale University Law School. "It's just too early to tell whether the new law is a strong success or a terrible failure."

b. PRETRIAL DETENTION UNDER THE BAIL REFORM ACT OF 1984: AN EMPIRICAL ANALYSIS *

In October 1987, the General Accounting Office ("GAO"), at the request of the Chairman, Subcommittee on Courts, Civil Liberties, and the Administration of Justice, Committee on the Judiciary, submitted a report entitled *Criminal Bail: How Bail Reform Is Working in Selected District Courts* ("GAO Study"). The study was conducted in four judicial districts representing both large and small caseloads: Northern Indiana, Arizona, Southern Florida and Eastern New York. Arizona, Southern Florida and Eastern New York were selected because Administrative Office records revealed that these districts had higher rates of defendants failing to appear and committing new crimes while on bail. Indiana was selected because of its small caseload.

Two samples of cases were selected for study. One sample selected felony defendants charged from January to June 1984 under the old Act and a second sample selected felony defendants charged from January to June 1986 under the new Act. Sample cases were randomly selected from a universe of defendants (not cases) taken from the records of the Administrative Office. Additionally, an attempt was made to identify old defendants who had committed new crimes while under pretrial release or failed to appear for at least one scheduled court appearance. Since not all documents in the latter two categories could be obtained, projections were based solely on those documents which actually were obtained. Ultimately, the *GAO Study* analyzed 639 defendants—605 from the random sample and thirty-four manually selected—whose cases commenced under the old Act. The study then projected these 639 cases to an adjusted universe of 2,086 defendants in the four districts. Under the new Act, the GAO Study analyzed 747 defendants—613 from the random sample and 134 manually selected. These results were then projected to an adjusted universe of 2,200 defendants in the four districts.

An audit was conducted from December 1985 to April 1987. To obtain the views of participants in the system, interviews were conducted with judicial officers and representatives of the prosecution, defense, and probation and pretrial services. Furthermore, to obtain information about the new Act in districts other than the four under study, the GAO analyzed information from six other United States Attorneys' Offices on all motions to detain defendants based on flight and/or

* Thomas E. Scott, "Pretrial Detention Under the Bail Reform Act of 1984," American Criminal Law Review, Vol. 27, No. 1, Summer 1989, pp. 19–24 (Reprinted with Permission).

danger between January and June 1986. Released in October 1987, the study revealed the following:

- More defendants were detained under the new Act than under the old Act.

- Fewer defendants were detained because of their inability to make surety or cash bonds, and the use of surety or cash bonds was less frequent under the new Act (but this varied significantly by district).

- Use of the statutory rebuttable presumption varied by district.

- Rates of failure to appear and crime on pretrial release, already low under the old Act, were even lower under the new Act.

The result of the *GAO Study,* like the earlier data examined, confirms that the new Act is being implemented on a much larger scale than was initially anticipated and that court personnel have quickly put it into practice.

GAO analysis in the four districts showed, overall, that more defendants remained incarcerated under the new Act. Thirty-one percent of defendants remained under detention during the pretrial period compared to 26 percent under the old Act. Likewise, all defendants under the old Act remained under detention because of their inability to meet bonds set by the court. However, the new Act's statistics showed that 51 percent were detained because they failed to meet bonds, but 49 percent were detained because they were found to be flight and/or danger risks. Of the 49 percent of those who were detained, 26 percent of the detentions were based on flight, 8 percent on flight and danger and 4 percent solely on danger. The basis of detention could not be determined for the remaining 11 percent of defendants.

Under the new Act, use of surety or cash bonds as a condition of release declined by 18 percent overall. In three of the four districts surveyed, the decrease was significant. For example, in Indiana and Eastern New York almost no defendants were detained because they could not meet bond. On the other hand, in the Southern District of Florida, detention for failure to make bail decreased only from 100 percent to 84 percent, a relatively small degree in comparison to other districts.

Four Districts

	Old Law	New Law
Released/Non-financial conditions	30%	35%
Released/Cash Bond	32%	23%
Detained/Did not pay bond	26%	16%
Fugitive and others	12%	11%
Detained/Flight and/or Danger Risk	N/A	15%

[Reasons for Detention, by District]

	Old Law		New Law	
	Failure to Pay Bond	Flight, Danger or Both	Failure to Pay Bond	Flight, Danger or Both
N.Ind.	100%	0%	0%	100%
Ariz.	100%	0%	34%	66%
S.D.Fla.	100%	0%	84%	16%
E.D.N.Y.	100%	0%	2%	98%
Total	100%	0%	51%	49%

Another concern of the *GAO Study* was the government's use of a provision in the 1984 Act which presumes that certain categories of defendants are flight and/or danger risks and shifts the "burden of production" to the defendant to produce evidence to show otherwise—the so-called "rebuttable presumption." The prosecution can invoke the rebuttable presumption only if the judicial officer finds that probable cause exists to believe that the defendant committed certain categories of crime. The most important category involves drug offenses, which carries a penalty of ten years or greater. Not surprisingly, the *GAO Study* found that most of the defendants who qualified for the presumption had been indicted for drug offenses. Indeed, 49 percent of all defendants surveyed under the new Act were charged with drug offenses. In three of the four districts, drug violations were the single largest type of offense: 41 percent in Arizona, 51 percent in Southern Florida and 58 percent in Eastern New York.

The government did not seek pretrial detention of all defendants who qualified for the rebuttable presumption. Detention was sought for only 39 percent of those who qualified. The government was successful in 61 percent of the cases; in the other cases, the court set conditions of release. Moreover, use of the rebuttable presumption by the government varied widely by district. For example, in the Southern District of Florida, pretrial detention was sought for only 13 percent of those eligible defendants.

Of final and perhaps most significant interest to the *GAO Study* was the rate of failure to appear and crime by arrestees during pretrial release before and after the new law. The rate of failure to appear in the four districts was 2.1 percent under the old bail Act and 1.8 percent under the new bail Act. However, two of the four districts had higher failure to appear rates under the new Act.

Failure to Appear Rates

District	Old Law	New Law
N.Ind.	0%	1.5%
Ariz.	3.8%	1.6%
S.D.Fla.	2.2%	2.1%
E.D.N.Y.	0.3%	1.3%

The overall rate of rearrested defendants who committed a new crime while released on bail in the four districts was 1.8 percent under the old Act and 0.8 percent under the new Act. One rearrest (not conviction) was used as the measure of crime on bail. Interestingly, two of the four districts had lower rearrest rates under the new Act, while the other two had higher rearrest rates. The offenses for which the defendants were arrested while on bail were mostly of a less serious nature, consisting of misdemeanors in more than half of the cases. The most frequent charges were driving offenses, either while intoxicated or with a suspended license.

Rearrest Rates

District	Old Law	New Law
N.Ind.	0%	0.8%
Ariz.	1.9%	0.8%
S.D.Fla.	2.4%	0.8%
E.D.N.Y.	0.6%	1.0%

In cases of both failure to appear and rearrest rates, the actual number of defendants involved was relatively small. Under both Acts, a total of 55 defendants failed to appear and 37 were rearrested while on bail in all four districts.

Finally, of a less statistical nature, the predominant view of participants in the system was that the new Bail Reform Act was an improvement over the old Act. Magistrates who set bail under both Acts opined that the new law was better because the new, more honest, bail process eliminated the need for *sub rosa* detention in order to hold dangerous defendants in pretrial custody. In addition to expressing this view, government lawyers also stated that the new Act gives them specific criteria to use in defining dangerous offenders.

3.　ALTERNATIVES TO PREVENTIVE DETENTION *

An additional reason for rejecting preventive detention is that its likely effect may be accomplished by alternative measures, whose costs may be smaller, and likely benefits greater. Assuring expedited trials, albeit more expensive than other alternatives, is doubtless the most effective response to bail crime. Other alternatives proposed by different authorities include restrictive conditions on pretrial release, revocation of the right to bail for serious misconduct while released, and stricter sentencing for recidivists.

1. Expedited Trials. Delay in the time required to bring cases to trial is one grave failing of the judicial system. Those not released on bail are often incarcerated under intolerable conditions, while those who are freed become more likely to commit crime as the length of

* Preventive Detention: An Empirical Analysis, Reprinted with permission from *Harvard Civil Rights—Civil Liberties Law* *Review* VI (1971), No. 2 (Cambridge, 1971), pp. 294–297. © 1971 by the Harvard Civil Rights—Civil Liberties Law Review.

pretrial release increases. Expedited trials have been suggested as an effective response to bail crime and the costs of preventive detention. The District of Columbia act itself encourages speedier trials by limiting the period of authorized detention to sixty days.

Data on the temporal incidence of bail crime from this and other studies suggest that expedited trials would stop a substantial amount of bail crime. In Boston, for example, 43% of those bailed were tried within 60 days, yet 29 of the 41 detected bail crimes and 15 of the 19 serious crimes occurred after the sixtieth day. Similarly, 29 of the 47 rearrests reported by the National Bureau of Standards occurred after two months of pretrial release. Other studies confirm this pattern. On the basis of these findings the National Bureau of Standards concluded: "Persons classified as dangerous appear to exhibit a greater propensity to be re-arrested the longer they are on release."

Providing for expedited trials within 60 days would not seem to impede the preparation of an adequate defense. The defendant would be free to aid in the preparation and investigation of his defense. Few cases could not be ready for trial within 60 days.

While the courtroom facilities and personnel, judges, district attorneys, defense lawyers and their staffs necessary to furnish expedited trials will require substantial additional expenditures, it is arguable that these monetary costs compare favorably with the overall costs of preventive detention. Significantly, the District of Columbia act itself requires that those detained be tried within 60 days after arraignment.

How much the expedited trial alternative will cost compared to expedited trials under preventive detention depends on the number of individuals detained. . . . There is a point beyond which the economic costs of preventive detention—hearings, appeals, incarceration, and expedited trial—will exceed the cost of expedited trials for all defendants charged with serious crimes.

It must of course be conceded that where the criminal courts are already overburdened, as in New York and Washington, any expedition, alone or in combination with preventive detention, will be quite costly. Measured by the practical burdens on the judiciary, at least in Massachusetts where the criminal trial backlog is not great, the overall costs, tangible and intangible, of providing expedited trials for all appear to be less than those for preventive detention. More recidivism would be prevented and the interests of the accused would be better protected. In sum, both existing and impending costs make expedited trials a less onerous alternative to preventive detention.

2. *Restrictive Conditions of Release.* The documented costs of incarceration make pretrial detention exceptionally undesirable. But even with expedition, a period (possibly as long as sixty days) during which an individual might commit a bail crime, will remain. An alternative to unconditioned release is the imposition of restrictive conditions based on alleged "dangerousness."

Restrictions on travel, association, and place of abode appear to be a comparatively ineffective way to protect the community, though these restrictions may have some cautionary effect.

Part-time jail custody is the most easily supervised mechanism provided in the Bail Reform Act. In conjunction with an effective program of job-placement and supervision, it could ameliorate some of the harsh effects of incarceration—inability to prepare for trial, loss of employment, and disruption of the family. With the defendant employed, the cost of family welfare would be reduced. But part-time custody is also the most restrictive release condition. The constitutional defects of preventive detention would not seem to be answered by ameliorated incarceration, which should be used seldom and only as a last resort.

Though of less consequence than incarceration, restrictive conditions of release are, nonetheless, significant deprivations of civil liberties which are often aggravated by administrative abuse. Even mild restrictions can only be justified by substantial fear of serious misconduct.

3. Forfeiture of the Right to Bail for Pretrial Crime. Another alternative to preventive detention is the proposal that defendants found to be responsible for crimes committed during pretrial release be denied the right to further bail. The theory is that the defendant, who has been informed of this forfeiture proviso, waives his constitutional right to bail by virtue of his subsequent criminal misconduct. The denial of bail under these circumstances would eliminate extreme repetitive criminal behavior and, to an extent, the need to predict "dangerousness." It may also deter bail crime to some extent. . . .

The plan also obviates the need to predict recidivist behavior. Although its justification rests in part on prevention of criminal conduct, and is therefore implicitly concerned with future behavior, forfeiture might be considered punishment for past behavior based upon self-selection, thus adhering to traditional notions of the function of criminal sanctions.

4. Stricter Sentences for Pretrial Offenses. Defendants arrested for bail crimes are often tried for the initial offense and the bail offense simultaneously. Defendants convicted of both often receive concurrent sentences or sentences no harsher than those received by defendants convicted of only one of the offenses. These practices, where they occur, are alleged to make bail crimes "free offenses," and weaken deterrence to commit them. It has been suggested that mandatory consecutive sentences and heavier penalties for the bail crime itself, eliminating a part of the judge's traditional discretion in sentencing, could be used to strengthen the deterrence.

The effects of consecutive or bonus sentencing on the incidence of bail crime have not been documented. The proposal assumes that a severe penalty is a significant deterrent to criminal conduct, but the uncertain and relative distinction between single sentences and consecutive or bonus sentences suggests that the effectiveness of the deterrent is uncertain. Furthermore, mandatory penalties may be unjustly harsh, ignoring mitigating circumstances. The American Bar Association has recommended that the judiciary retain its traditional discretion, [as to sentence] and most states leave sentencing to the judge. Stricter sentencing is unlikely to be the answer to the problem of bail crime.

Comment and Questions

A recent study in Charlotte, North Carolina, documented the strong effect of trial delay on the need for preventive detention. It showed that:

> Court disposition time was the variable of greatest importance to successful pre-trial release. The likelihood of avoiding either nonappearance or rearrest dropped five percentage points for each additional two weeks the defendant remained free on bail.

> Criminal history, measured by the number of prior arrests, had the next most important relationship to bail risk. Extended court disposition time has a much worse effect on defendants with two or more prior arrests than on those with zero or one prior arrest. Thus, at 12 weeks' disposition time, only 56% of the former avoided nonappearance and rearrest as compared with 79% of the latter.

Does it make sense to lump rearrest and non-appearance? Aren't these two different problems?

Studies of the impact of preventive detention, such as the one summarized by Judge Scott (see pp. 382–385) indicate that at best the new law has had marginal impact on the pretrial process. In light of this, we might ask whether it is worth taking the risk of undermining the presumption of innocence, as some say preventive detention does, if it does not offer some clear corresponding benefit? But, perhaps one reason the new preventive detention law has had such limited impact is that under the old (as well as the new) bail law judges could emphasize only "risk of flight," but in fact detain for "dangerousness" simply by setting bail so high the defendant could not possibly pay it. Isn't this hypocritical, and isn't there some virtue in the candor of the new law? Or is there virtue in maintaining our ideals regarding the presumption of innocence, recognizing that they will be violated from time to time? More generally, consider still another alternative. Wouldn't speedier trials go a long way towards minimizing the problems of preventive detention and high bail?

D. RECOMMENDED READING

Feeley, Malcolm M. *Court Reform on Trial.* Basic Books, New York, 1983.

Flemming, Roy B. *Punishment Before Trial.* Longman, New York, 1982.

Goldkamp, John. *Two Classes of Accused: A Study of Bail and Detention of American Justice.* Ballinger Publishing Co., Cambridge, Mass., 1979.

Murphy, John J. *Arrest by Police Computer: The Controversy Over Bail and Extradition.* Lexington Books, Lexington, Mass., 1975.

Thomas, Wayne H., Jr. *Bail Reform in America.* University of California Press, Berkeley, 1976.

Chapter VIII

THE TRIAL

A. INTRODUCTION

NOTE ON THE CRIMINAL TRIAL

The criminal trial is the phase of the criminal process that attracts the most public attention. Some trials in this country, and indeed most trials in certain other countries, are ritual dramas of good or evil—though it often depends on one's perspective which side is good and which is evil.

The criminal trial, however, has an importance beyond the public spectacle. It is in essence a fact-finding process, though a somewhat peculiar one. Not only do we want to reach the right result in terms of the guilt or innocence of the accused but we also want to do so fairly to all concerned. Indeed, the desire to be fair and the desire to reach the right result conflict in a host of ways—the exclusionary rules discussed in Chapter V provide an example of this.

Fairness, as we will see, is a very complicated concept. One thing it may mean is that we may favor one kind of error over another. We may thus prefer to acquit defendants if there is any reasonable doubt of their guilt, even though this practice acquits guilty persons far more often than it saves the innocent from conviction.

The criminal trial has an enormous importance in the operation of the whole criminal system. In some sense, it is the balance wheel of the entire process. Although, as we shall see, relatively few cases are disposed of after full trial, it is the threat of exclusion of evidence at trial that is the basis of the exclusionary rule's effort to control the police; it is the projected result of a trial which influences the exercise of prosecutorial discretion and it is the chance of success at trial which determines the bargaining positions of the lawyers attempting to dispose of the case through negotiations for a guilty plea. See Chapter IX.

In this chapter we will concentrate on several areas involving the trial: first, the use of evidence in an attempt to prove a conclusion beyond a reasonable doubt; second, two rules peculiar to Anglo-American law that are seen as being primarily in the service of the defendant—(1) the right to confrontation involved in the hearsay rule; (2) the exclusion of evidence used to show that the defendant is a bad person and hence is more likely to be guilty. Finally, we devote some attention to the problem of securing a fair finding of fact.

B.　THE TRIAL DECISION

1.　PEOPLE v. RINCON–PINEDA

Supreme Court of California, 1975.
14 Cal.3d 864, 123 Cal.Rptr. 119, 538 P.2d 247.

WRIGHT, C.J.　The judgment here under review arose from the wanton and brutal rape of a young woman who lived alone near defendant's temporary residence.　As is often typical of such a crime, it was witnessed by no one other than the victim and the rapist.　. . .

The trial judge was of the opinion that a once unimpeachable rule of law could not appropriately be applied to circumstances such as those present herein.　Because he considered it to be demeaning of the victim in the instant case, the judge refused to deliver to the jury a cautionary instruction which originated in the 17th century and which reflects adversely on the credibility of the complaining witness in a prosecution for sexual assault.　The judge's failure to so instruct the jury is the sole objection before us on this appeal.　We have previously held the instruction in issue to be mandatory. . . . However, . . . we are of the opinion that as presently worded the instruction is inappropriate regardless of the particular evidence which might be adduced at trial.　. . .

I

The victim testified that on the night of July 9, 1973, she retired at her customary hour of 11 p.m.　At approximately 3 a.m. the following morning, she awakened to find a person lying beside her in her bed.　As she screamed "Who is it?" she turned on a 100–watt bedside lamp and recognized defendant as the intruder.

. . . Although she had never spoken to him previously, the victim recognized defendant as one who had been living behind her cottage for the past few weeks.

Defendant had apparently gained ingress through the window the victim always left open for the use of her pet cats.　Drawing a robe around her partially nude body, the victim, . . . ordered defendant to leave.　When he did not respond, she began to scream.　Defendant grabbed her, tried to cover her mouth, and indicated his intention to have intercourse with her.　The victim ran screaming from the bedroom into the kitchen, where the open window was located.　Defendant, however, caught the victim, jammed a hand in her mouth, beat her about the face until she stopped screaming, and then began to choke her.　Having hitherto scratched and clawed at defendant's face, the victim realized her life was in great danger, and ceased resisting lest defendant discover the knives hanging directly above her head.　. . .

[At dawn defendant left and the victim thereafter made complaint to the police]

. . .

The arresting officer testified that after having spoken with the victim he approached defendant's bungalow and apprehended defendant in the act of leaving it. Defendant was wearing two pairs of trousers and had two sets of underwear rolled up in his jacket. The victim identified defendant as her assailant and he was formally arrested. At this time, defendant appeared to the arresting officer to be sober.

Shortly before noon on the day of the rape, the victim was examined by a doctor who testified at trial that "she had multiple bruises all over her body, especially over the face, nose, lips, the front side of her neck, over the left pelvic region, over the right frontal scalp region, and one tooth in the left upper front side of the jaw was loosened." . . . Because no internal ejaculation had taken place and because the victim had taken a shower since the assault, no attempt was made to gain medical evidence of her having been sexually assaulted.

At the time of his arrest defendant had a prominent scratch or abrasion on his forehead of clearly recent origin. . . . There was also evidence of a possible admission by defendant. While in custody at the police station on the day after his arrest, defendant was notified through an interpreter of his rights, and after waiver thereof was asked some questions concerning his conduct on the previous night. The interpreter testified that defendant could not explain how he had gotten the bump or scratch on his head. Defendant kept saying that he had been drunk. The interpreter testified: "I asked the defendant if he had done this thing that he was being charged with, he said if he did, he was very drunk when he did it."

. . .

There was no apparent official effort to obtain other evidence corroborating the victim's accusation of defendant, however. No evidence was presented by the prosecution or defense as to there having been any attempt to gather scientific evidence from either the scene of the crime, such as fingerprints, or from defendant's person and clothing, such as tissue or fiber traces.

Defendant [denying any knowledge of the crime] testified in his own defense that he was 24 years of age and . . . had spent the day before his arrest drinking with his companions in a neighborhood bar. He had no personal recollection of making his way back from the bar, but had been told by his friends the following morning that he had been helped home between 1 a.m. and 2 a.m. and had hit his head on a door or gate to the bungalow. . . . When he heard the police arriving, . . . he knew he would surely be arrested as an illegal alien, so he grabbed his extra clothes. Defendant denied that he was trying to flee when arrested. Defendant was able to produce none of his ostensible drinking companions as all allegedly had fled to avoid arrest as illegal aliens. . . .

. . .

On this evidence, the jury found defendant guilty of rape . . . [and defendant] was sentenced to state prison for the three-years-to-life [term] prescribed for rape.

II

There were in fact two trials of defendant. The first trial, which ended in a hung jury, had involved substantially the same evidence as the second. There were important differences in the evidence at the two trials, however. The victim was more specific at the second trial on the strength of the illumination which allowed her to identify her assailant, and the defendant's admissions to the police interpreter were described at the first trial as extending only to the facts that defendant had been drinking on the night in question and had little recollection of what had transpired—there was no "if I did it I was drunk" admission in evidence at the first trial. The first trial also differed in that defense counsel inquired in some detail into the victim's past sexual life, and the court accordingly instructed the jury at the first trial:

> "Evidence was received for the purpose of showing that the female person named in the information was a woman of unchaste character.

> "A woman of unchaste character can be the victim of a forcible rape but it may be inferred that a woman who has previously consented to sexual intercourse would be more likely to consent again.

> "Such evidence may be considered by you only for such bearing as it may have on the question of whether or not she gave her consent to the alleged sexual act and in judging her credibility."

The first trial court also read to the jury the text of the cautionary instruction which [is at issue in this appeal]:

> "A charge such as that made against the defendant in this case is one which is easily made and, once made, difficult to defend against, even if the person accused is innocent.

> "Therefore, the law requires that you examine the testimony of the female person named in the information with caution."

Given the overall context of the first trial, there was as much truth as irony in a slip of the tongue by the arresting officer during his testimony at that trial. When asked to identify several photographs of the victim showing the injuries inflicted by her assailant, the officer replied: "In these photographs is a picture of the defendant in different positions." The victim too seemed to feel that it was she who had been the defendant in the first trial. At the second trial, the victim was herself represented by counsel and refused to answer questions as to her past sexual conduct.

Defense counsel did not seek a ruling by the court at the second trial to force the victim to answer inquiries about her chastity, but did attempt to play on the point during closing argument by styling the victim's concern for her privacy as "arrogant" and "insulting" and indicative of "emotional instability," such that her testimony against the defendant was "just acting a fantasy role."

. . . The court refused over defense objection to give the cautionary instruction. The court acknowledged that the instruction was mandatory in sex cases, but noted that its compulsory use had not been authoritatively reexamined for decades.

. . .

III

. . . [W]e have decided that the time is ripe for review of the cautionary instruction . . . to the end of determining whether it should continue to be mandated in the trial of every case involving a charge of a sex offense. . . .

The instruction has its origin in the writings of Sir Matthew Hale, Lord Chief Justice of the Court of King's Bench from 1671 to 1676, which were published posthumously in 1736. Hale dealt at length with rape . . ., reciting the legislative and decisional evolution of the law to his day. After a technical discussion of what constituted rape and who might perpetrate it, Hale turned to the evidence competent to prove a charge of rape. This passage consisted of two parts. First, Hale stated the proposition that "[t]he party ravished may give evidence upon oath, and is in law a competent witness; but the credibility of her testimony, and how far forth she is to be believed, must be left to the jury, and is more or less credible according to the circumstances of fact that concur in that testimony."

. . .

[Hale added, however,] "It is true rape is a most detestable crime, and therefore ought severely and impartially to be punished with death; but it must be remembered, that it is an accusation easily to be made and hard to be proved, and harder to be defended by the party accused, tho never so innocent."

. . .

Hale's musings were introduced somewhat obliquely into the law of California by People v. Benson, 6 Cal. 221, involving a 13-year-old prosecutrix with a circumstantially improbable claim of rape and apparent malice against the defendant. In the course of ruling that evidence of specific instances of prior lewd conduct by the prosecutrix should have been admitted at trial—the apparent basis for the reversal of the judgment below—the court declaimed that:

"There is no class of prosecutions attended with so much danger, or which afford so ample an opportunity for the free play of malice and private vengeance. In such cases the accused is almost defenceless, and

Courts, in view of the facility with which charges of this character may be invented and maintained, have been strict in laying down the rule which should govern the jury in their finding.

"From the days of Lord Hale to the present time, no case has ever gone to the jury, upon the sole testimony of the prosecutrix, unsustained by facts and circumstances corroborating it, without the Court warning them of the danger of a conviction on such testimony."

In the wake of *Benson*, it became the rule in California that . . . the cautionary instructions [were] applicable to virtually all criminal prosecutions involving illicit sexual conduct.

IV

In light of our foregoing examination of the evolution of the cautionary instruction, and with the benefit of contemporary empirical and theoretical analyses of the prosecution of sex offenses in general and rape in particular, we are of the opinion that the instruction omitted below has outworn its usefulness and in modern circumstances is no longer to be given mandatory application.

  .   .   .

Even if the [cautionary] instruction here in issue did square with Hale's analysis, the changes in criminal procedure wrought in the intervening 300 years would suffice of themselves to sap the instruction of contemporary validity. It has been suggested that Hale's concern over fabricated rape prosecutions was a product of the accused's incompetence to testify in his own defense. But the accused's incompetency was one of form only; he was allowed, and indeed was expected to address the jury in an unsworn statement responsive to the evidence against him.

There are other, more dramatic differences in the position of the criminally accused in the United States today from one so accused in 17th century England. The fundamental precepts of due process, that an accused is presumed innocent and is to be acquitted unless proven guilty beyond a reasonable doubt . . ., were recognized as desiderata in Hale's era but had yet to crystallize into rights. . . . . The rights of an accused to present witnesses in his defense and to compel their attendance, subsequently enshrined in the Sixth Amendment, were barely nascent in the 17th century. Most importantly of all, in the context of a rape case, one accused of a felony in Hale's day had no right whatsoever to the assistance of counsel, while today he is constitutionally entitled to such assistance regardless of his personal means . . . .. Considering that under the Anglo-Saxon adversarial system of justice "[W]hen a prisoner is undefended his position is often pitiable, even if he has a good case", we recognize that there may well have been merit to Hale's assertion that a prosecution for rape was an ideal instrument of malice, since it forced an accused, on trial for his life, to stand alone before a jury inflamed by passion and to attempt to answer a carefully contrived story without benefit of counsel, witnesses, or even a presumption of innocence. But the spectre of wrongful conviction, whether for rape or for any other crime, has led our society to arm modern defendants with the potent accouterments of due process which render the additional constraint of Hale's caution superfluous and capricious.

. . .

We next examine whether such a charge is so difficult to defend against as to warrant a . . . cautionary instruction in the light of available empirical data. . . . Of the FBI's four "violent crime" offenses of murder, forcible rape, robbery, and aggravated assault, forcible rape has the highest rate of acquittal or dismissal. . . . Equally striking is the ranking of forcible rape at the bottom of the FBI's list of major crimes according to percentage of successful prosecutions for the offense charged. "Sixty-nine percent of those persons prosecuted for the offense of larceny were found guilty of that offense in 1973. This was followed by burglary with 49 percent found guilty of the original charge, 46 percent for robbery, 45 percent for murder, 43 percent for auto theft, 39 percent for aggravated assault, and 36 percent for forcible rape." . . . A similar situation is indicated by California crime statistics, which show forcible rape to have an acquittal rate second only to bookmaking, with prosecutions for other sex offenses resulting in acquittal or dismissal more frequently than the average for all felonies. . . .

These findings are consistent with the leading study of jury behavior, which found that "the jury chooses to redefine the crime of rape in terms of its notions of assumption of risk," such that juries will frequently acquit a rapist or convict him of a lesser offense, notwithstanding clear evidence of guilt. . . . This tendency is especially dramatic in the situation supposedly most conducive to fabricated accusations: where the prosecutrix and the accused are acquainted, and there is no "evidence of extrinsic violence" to the prosecutrix. The jury "closely, and often harshly, scrutinizes the female complainant and is moved to be lenient with the defendant whenever there are suggestions of contributory behavior on her part," sometimes carrying "to a cruel extreme," in cases "clearly aggravated by extrinsic violence," its tendency towards leniency for accused rapists. The same study found that the jury was also prone to seize upon mitigating factors in other sex offense cases so as to be lenient with defendants, as with indecent exposure to an adult, or the statutory rape of a previously unchaste minor.

The low rate of conviction of those accused of rape and other sexual offenses does not appear to be attributable to a high incidence of unwarranted accusations. Rape in particular has been shown by repeated studies to be grossly under-reported. . . . The initial emotional trauma of submitting to official investigatory processes, the fear of subsequent humiliation through attendant publicity and embarrassment at trial through defense tactics which are often demeaning, and a disinclination to encounter the discretion of the police in deciding whether to pursue charges of rape, especially with regard to what may appear to the police to be "victim-precipitated" rapes, are among the powerful yet common disincentives to the reporting of rape. . . . Those victims with the pluck to disregard such disincentives discover the utter fallaciousness of the conventional wisdom that rape is a charge easily made. A large number of reports of rape are deemed "unfounded" by the police and are pursued no further: the percentage has been set variously at 15 percent, 20 percent . . ., 25 percent, and 29 percent.

Even when an arrest is made, the charge may well proceed no further. In 1972 in California 28 percent of those arrested for rape were released outright by the police. . . .

Once a rape case does wend its way into the courts, there are factors besides jury leniency to account for the inconsistency between the high acquittal rate and the myth of rape charges being not only easy to bring, but also hard to defend against. Kalven and Zeisel found, in the course of their nationwide jury studies, that eyewitness evidence was presented by the defense in rape prosecutions more frequently than in burglary, narcotics, or drunk driving prosecutions. . . . [And] the victim testified in 97 percent of rape prosecutions [while] the defendant did so in only 85 percent. . . .

It is a significant measure of the difficulty of proving rape that in not a single one of the 72 rape cases studied by Kalven and Zeisel did the prosecution rely exclusively on the testimony of the complaining witness. Indeed, the prosecution turned to expert evidence in rape cases more frequently than in burglary, drunk driving and assault cases. Scientific evidence has for decades been a recognized if under-utilized resource for the proof of rape. . . .

Since it does not in fact appear that the accused perpetrators of sex offenses in general and rape in particular are subject to capricious conviction by inflamed tribunals of justice, we conclude that the requirement of a cautionary instruction in all such cases is a rule without a reason. . . .

V

. . . [W]e think the instruction as it has customarily been worded is inappropriate in any context, and the further use of such language is hereby disapproved.[1] . . .

We deem it appropriate instead to reaffirm and reinforce the existing instructions as to the credibility of witnesses which must presently be given—at least in part by the trial court in every criminal case. Thus the substance of the instruction set forth [2] should hence-

1. Nothing we say in this opinion should be construed as precluding the development of new instructions designed to enhance juries' consideration of particular types of evidence, such as the testimony of a child of tender years.

2. "Credibility of Witness" "Every person who testifies under oath is a witness.

forth always be given, while those paragraphs thereof inapplicable under the evidence may be omitted. . . .

The judgment is affirmed.

Questions and Comment

How likely is it that the defendant in the above case was actually guilty? Is it absolutely certain? The testimony of the victim constituted almost the whole case against the defendant, and it is *conceivable* that the victim might lie for some reason that we do not know. In civil cases the jury is asked to return a verdict based "on the preponderance of the evidence." In other words, the plaintiff will prevail if it is more likely than not, under the evidence, that he is so entitled. In a criminal case, the jury must find guilt "beyond a reasonable doubt." Why should there be a difference between the two standards? Alternatively, why not demand absolute certainty?

How could you convince somebody that there was no reasonable doubt in the above case? When is a doubt *reasonable* doubt? How can you convince somebody that there is no reasonable doubt in any case, however strong the evidence?

Is it remarkable that the jury convicted the defendant under the evidence in this case? Is it more remarkable that the jury failed to convict the defendant the first time? Note the first jury did not acquit him (or else the Double Jeopardy provision of the Constitution would have prevented a second trial), but rather the jury "hung", in that it could not reach a unanimous verdict.

Do you think the fact that the victim answered questions on her previous sex experience made the difference between the two trials? What relevance could that have had in this case where the defendant essentially denied the act, and did not in any way rely on consent as a defence? Interestingly, about half of American states have in the past five years restricted the admissibility of evidence of the sex history and reputation of the victim in rape cases. As you learned earlier (pp. 22–

You are the sole and exclusive judges of the credibility of the witnesses who have testified in this case.

"In determining the credibility of a witness you may consider any matter that has a tendency in reason to prove or disprove the truthfulness of his testimony, including but not limited to the following:

"His demeanor while testifying and the manner in which he testifies;

"The character of his testimony;

"The extent of his capacity to perceive, to recollect, or to communicate any matter about which he testifies;

"The extent of his opportunity to perceive any matter about which he testifies;

"His character for honesty or veracity or their opposites;

"The existence or nonexistence of a bias, interest, or other motive;

"A statement previously made by him that is consistent with his testimony;

"A statement made by him that is inconsistent with any part of his testimony;

"The existence or nonexistence of any fact testified to by him;

"His attitude toward the action in which he testifies or toward the giving of testimony;

"His admission of untruthfulness;

"His prior conviction of a felony."

31) in *People v. Barnes,* California also eliminated the "resistance requirement."

In *People v. Rincon-Pineda* is it possible that the instruction which was at issue on this appeal and which was given at the first, but not the second, trial made the difference? Is there any guarantee that the jury pays attention to the instructions anyway? And if the jury wishes to scrutinize testimony in a particular rape case especially carefully, what is to prevent them?

Is it possible that the court simply had a feeling that convictions in rape cases were too difficult and hence wished to make them easier? Under what conditions would this be right?

There is one other major variable in the trial of cases, which often escapes discussion. It is illustrated in the next excerpt.

2. THE INFLUENCE OF THE ATTORNEYS *

Q: ** You [Dr. Manfred Guttmacher, a distinguished psychiatrist and major witness for the defendant] examined Jack Ruby extensively, did you not, in your own particular specialty?

A: I have, sir.

Q: And you can answer this "yes" or "no." Do you have an opinion as to whether he knew the nature and consequences of his act, the difference between right and wrong, and knew what he was doing at the time he shot Lee Harvey Oswald?

A: Yes, I have an opinion.

Q: What is your opinion?

A: I don't think that he was capable of distinguishing right from wrong and realizing the nature and consequences of his act at the time of the alleged homicide.

[The witness then went on to explain the basis of his diagnosis.]

Henry Wade,* knowing that the witness was fully qualified to render an expert opinion on Ruby's sanity, had made no objection to Belli's failure to bring out his witness's education and experience. Furthermore, Wade knew that Belli could not risk leaving the matter there. The famous New York criminal lawyer Richard Howe around the turn of the century had tried this once with disastrous results. He placed his expert psychiatrist on the stand and drew from him merely the fact that he had examined the defendant and had found him insane within the meaning of the law. Then Howe rested his direct examination, confident that the greater the assaults on the witness's ability by the prosecution, the more his preeminent qualifications would appear—

* John Kaplan and Jon R. Waltz, *The Trial of Jack Ruby,* New York: MacMillan and Company, 1965, pp. 222–223. © 1965 (Reprinted by permission).

** By Melvin Belli, attorney for the defendant Jack Ruby, accused of murdering one Lee Harvey Oswald, who was thought to be the assassin of President John F. Kennedy.

* The chief prosecutor in the Ruby case.

and make a greater impression on the jury, to boot. To his astonish-
ment, however, the prosecutor in an inspired stroke merely rose and
said, "No cross-examination." And when Howe tried to begin a redirect examination to place the qualifications of his witness before the
jury, objections were sustained on the ground that redirect examination
was improper, there having been no cross-examination. Most laymen
perhaps might feel that the point of the story is that a clever trick by
an attorney can mean the difference between life or death for a
defendant. Lawyers, however, merely derive from it the injunction
that one must never rely on cross-examination to develop the information which one needs on direct.

Comment and Questions

Obviously, one fact of great importance in the outcome of criminal
trials is the relative skill of the lawyers. How could we prevent this?
How important would you think the skill of the lawyers is, compared to
the strength of the evidence? Who would you expect to be more
skillful, the prosecutor or the defense attorney? Why?

C. THE RIGHT TO CONFRONTATION

1. TRIAL OF SIR WALTER RALEIGH, KNIGHT, FOR HIGH TREASON, BY A SPECIAL COMMISSION OF OYER AND TERMINER, AT WINCHESTER, 17TH NOVEMBER, 1603, 2 JAMES 1 **

The general points of treason laid in the Indictment were these;—
that Sir W. Raleigh, with other persons, had conspired to kill the
King,—to raise a rebellion, with intent to change religion and subvert
the government,—and, for that purpose, to encourage and incite the
King's enemies to invade the realm. The overt acts charged were, that,
on the 9th of June, Sir Walter Raleigh had conferred with Lord
Cobham about advancing Arabella Stuart to the Crown of England, and
dispossessing the King; [The principal evidence against Sir Walter
Raleigh was a sworn statement made before trial by Lord Cobham, an
alleged co-conspirator, who also allegedly retracted the statement and
then retracted the retraction. Cobham himself was in prison and was
never produced at the trial.]

Sir W. Raleigh. But it is strange to see how you press me still with
my Lord Cobham, and yet will not produce him; it is not for gaining of
time or prolonging my life that I urge this; he is in the house hard by
and may soon be brought hither; let him be produced, and if he will yet
accuse me or avow this Confession of his, it shall convict me and ease
you of further proof.

Lord Cecil. Sir Walter Raleigh presseth often that my Lord
Cobham should be brought face to face; if he ask a thing of grace and

** David   Jardine,   *Criminal   Trials*   Walter Raleigh at Winchester, 17th No-
(London: C. Knight 1832–35) Trial of Sir   vember, 1603, 2 James 1.

favour, they must come from him only who can give them; but if he ask a matter of law, then, in order that we, who sit here as commissioners, may be satisfied, I desire to hear the opinions of my Lords, the Judges, whether it may be done by law. The Judges all answered, that in respect it might be a mean to cover many with treasons, and might be prejudicial to the King, therefore by the law it was not sufferable.

Sir W. Raleigh. Good my Lords, let my accuser come face to face and be deposed. Were the case but for a small copyhold,* you would have witnesses or good proof to lead the jury to a verdict; and I am here for my life!

Popham, C.J. There must not such a gap be opened for the destruction of the King as would be if we should grant this; you plead hard for yourself, but the laws plead as hard for the King. Where no circumstances do concur to make a matter probable, then an accuser may be heard; but so many circumstances agreeing and confirming the accusation in this case, the accuser is not to be produced; for having first confessed against himself voluntarily, and so charged another person, if we shall now hear him again in person, he may for favour or fear retract what formerly he hath said, and the jury may, by that means, be inveigled. . . .

Lord Cecil. Sir W. Raleigh, if my Lord Cobham will now affirm that you were acquainted with his dealings with Count Aremberg, that you knew of the letter he received, that you were the chief instigator of him, will you then be concluded by it?

Sir W. Raleigh. Let my Lord Cobham speak before God and the King, and deny God and the King if he speak not truly, and will then say that ever I knew of Arabella's matter, or the money out of Spain, or the surprising Treason, I will put myself upon it. God's will and the King's be done with me!

Lord Cecil. Then, Sir Walter, call upon God to help you, for I do verily believe my Lords will prove this.

Lord Henry Howard. But what if my Lord Cobham affirm anything equivalent to this, what then?

Sir W. Raleigh. My Lord, I put myself upon it.

Attorney-General. I shall now produce a witness *viva voce.***

He then produced one Dyer, a pilot, who being sworn, said, Being at Lisbon, there came to me a Portugese gentleman who asked me how the King of England did, and whether he was crowned? I answered him that I hoped our noble King was well and crowned by this, but the time was not come when I came from the coast for Spain. "Nay," said he, "your King shall never be crowned, for Don Cobham and Don Raleigh will cut his throat before he come to be crowned." And this in time was found to be spoken in mid July.

---

* A piece of land.

** In a live voice, as distinguished from a written statement.

Sir W. Raleigh. This is the saying of some wild Jesuit or beggarly Priest; but what proof is it against me?

Attorney-General. It must per force arise out of some preceding intelligence, and shows that your treason had wings.

.   .   .

Sir Walter Raleigh. But, my Lords, I claim to have my accuser brought here face to face to speak: . . . let Cobham be sent for; let him be charged upon his soul, upon his allegiance to the King, and if he will then maintain his accusation to my face, I will confess myself guilty.

Comment

The trial of Sir Walter Raleigh is often cited as one of the foundations of the right to confrontation. We must remember, however, that Raleigh's inability to confront either Lord Cobham or the "Portugese gentlemen" was by no means the only defect which modern observers might find in the case. First, the confession from Lord Cobham was extracted by torture. Second, Cobham had repudiated his confession by the time of trial. Third, the defendant, despite his request, was not permitted counsel. Fourth, he had no right to testify or to call witnesses. Fifth, the most inflammatory appeals to prejudice were made by the prosecutor, Lord Coke. And finally, Raleigh's punishment was not only hanging, but drawing and quartering as well.

2. SUSANNA AND THE ELDERS *

(C. 130 B.C.).

Then the two elders stood up in the midst of the people, and laid their hands upon her head. And she weeping looked up toward heaven: for her heart trusted in the Lord. And the elders said, "As we walked in the garden alone, this woman came in with two maids, and shut the garden doors, and sent the maids away. Then a young man, who there was hid, came unto her, and lay with her. Then we that stood in a corner of the garden, seeing this wickedness, ran unto them. And when he saw them together, the man we could not hold: for he was stronger than we, and opened the door, and leaped out. But having taken this woman, we asked who the young man was, but she would not tell us: these things so we testify."

Then the assembly believed them, as those that were the elders and judges of the people: so they condemned her to death.

Then Susanna cried out with a loud voice, and said, "O everlasting God, that knowest the secrets, and knowest all things before they be: thou knowest that they have borne false witness against me, and

* "Susanna and the Elders," The Bible, from The Books Called Apocrypha according to The Authorized Version. Oxford. Printed at the University Press. London: Oxford University Clarendon Text. Cum Privilegio. The History of Susanna, verses 34–63. Press Amen House, E.C. 4 Brevier 16mo.

behold, I must die; whereas I never did such things as these men have maliciously invented against me."

The Lord heard her voice.

Therefore when she was led to be put to death, the Lord raised up the holy spirit of a young youth, whose name was Daniel: who cried with a loud voice, "I am clear from the blood of this woman."

Then all the people turned them toward him, and said, "What mean these words that thou hast spoken?"

So he standing in the midst of them said, "Are ye such fools, ye sons of Israel, that without examination or knowledge of the truth ye have condemned a daughter of Israel? Return again to the place of judgment: for they have borne false witness against her."

Wherefore all the people turned again in haste, and the elders said unto him, "Come, sit down among us, and show it us, seeing God hath given thee the honour of an elder."

Then said Daniel unto them, "Put these two aside one far from another, and I will examine them."

So when they were put asunder one from another, he called one of them, and said unto him, "O thou that art waxed old in wickedness, now thy sins which thou has committed aforetime are come to light: for thou hast pronounced false judgment, and hast condemned the innocent, and hast let the guilty go free; albeit the Lord saith, 'The innocent and righteous shalt thou not slay.' Now then, if thou has seen her, tell me under what tree sawest thou them companying together?"

Who answered, "Under the mastic tree."

And Daniel said, "Very well; thou hast lied against thine own head; for even now the angel of God hath received the sentence of God to cut thee in two."

So he put him aside, and commanded to bring the other, and said unto him, "O thou seed of Chanaan, and not of Juda, beauty hath deceived thee, and lust hath perverted thine heart. Thus have ye dealt with the daughters of Israel, and they for fear companied with you: but the daughter of Juda would not abide your wickedness. Now therefore tell me under what tree didst thou take them companying together?"

Who answered, "Under a holm tree."

Then said Daniel unto him, "Well; thou hast also lied against thine own head: for the angel of God waiteth with the sword to cut thee in two, that he may destroy you."

With that all the assembly cried out with a loud voice, and praised God, who saveth them that trust in him. And they arose against the two elders, for Daniel had convicted them of false witness by their own mouth: and according to the law of Moses they did unto them in such sort as they maliciously intended to do their neighbour: and they put them to death. Thus the innocent blood was saved the same day.

Questions

What if a holm and a mastic tree look almost identical? Or if the two words are synonyms for the same kind of tree? Or if the witnesses, as most do, merely differed in unimportant details but remembered the crucial matters perfectly? Whom do you believe, Susanna or the Elders? How would you defend the Elders?

Does this excerpt illustrate the importance of cross examination?

3. NOTE ON THE HEARSAY RULE

The Sixth Amendment to the Constitution provides that ". . . the accused shall enjoy the right . . . to be confronted with the witnesses against him . . ." The right to confrontation (i.e., cross-examination) is, in most cases, also, protected by the hearsay rule—though there still is a lively dispute as to how much of the hearsay rule is compelled by the Sixth Amendment. For instance, the California Evidence Code makes hearsay inadmissible and defines it as "evidence of a statement that was made other than by a witness while testifying at the hearing and that is offered to prove the truth of the matter stated."

The rule, though quite rigid, has a large number of highly technical and almost equally rigid exceptions, each one justified on some apparently quite sensible ground. Though any exception, in itself, may be defensible, the result is that the actual administration of the hearsay rule is extremely complicated.

Some of the exceptions and their justifications are interesting enough to receive a little more discussion. For instance, it is held that one party can call a witness to testify to anything said by the other party to the case. For instance, the prosecution can call someone to repeat the admissions of the defendant in a criminal case. Admittedly, the statement by the witness ("Defendant said 'I shot the victim'") is hearsay because the defendant being quoted was not on the witness stand and available for cross-examination at the time the statement was made. It is an exception to the hearsay rule because the defendant cannot really ask that he cross-examine himself.

Similarly, a statement made by one dying, as to who had killed him, is admissible on the theory that one about to meet his Maker will be more inclined to be accurate and sincere.

In addition, the records of a business are generally admissible as an exception to the hearsay rule on two theories: first that business records tend to be the product of many people working together and it would be impossible to bring them all into court, each to testify about the small operation he or she performed; and second, that business records are, in general, reasonably accurate, if only because they are used in ventures that have an independent interest in being able to rely on their records.

Needless to say, merely because something is admissible as an exception to the hearsay rule does not mean that the jury must accord it great weight. The jurors may decide that, even though it is admissible, it is not very probative.

Conversely, one can think of a great deal of hearsay which might be extremely probative, in the sense that we would be prepared to act upon it in important affairs of our lives—but which would be inadmissible in court.

Most legal systems other than the Anglo-American do not regard the concept of hearsay as very important. They tend to accept hearsay and non-hearsay equally, looking mainly to see how probative the evidence is.

D. THE CHARACTER OF THE DEFENDANT

1. PEOPLE v. ZACKOWITZ
Court of Appeals of New York, 1930.
254 N.Y. 192, 172 N.E. 466.

(Joseph Zackowitz was convicted of murder in the first degree, and he appeals from Kings County Court.)

CARDOZO, Chief Justice. On November 10, 1929, shortly after midnight, the defendant in Kings County shot Frank Coppola and killed him without justification or excuse. A crime is admitted. What is doubtful is the degree only.

Four young men, of whom Coppola was one, were at work repairing an automobile in a Brooklyn street. A woman, the defendant's wife, walked by on the opposite side. One of the men spoke to her insultingly, or so at least she understood him. The defendant, who had dropped behind to buy a newspaper, came up to find his wife in tears. He was told she had been insulted, though she did not then repeat the words. Enraged, he stepped across the street and upbraided the offenders with words of coarse profanity. He informed them, so the survivors testify, that "if they did not get out of there in five minutes, he would come back and bump them all off." Rejoining his wife, he walked with her to their apartment house located close at hand. He was heated with liquor which he had been drinking at a dance. Within the apartment he induced her to tell him what the insulting words had been. A youth had asked her to lie with him, and had offered her $2. With rage aroused again, the defendant went back to the scene of the insult and found the four young men still working at the car. In a statement to the police, he said that he had armed himself at the apartment with a .25–caliber automatic pistol. In his testimony at the trial he said that this pistol had been in his pocket all the evening. Words and blows followed, and then a shot. The defendant kicked Coppola in the stomach. There is evidence that Coppola went for him with a wrench. The pistol came from the pocket, and from the pistol a single shot, which did its deadly work. The defendant walked away and at the corner met his wife who had followed him from the home. The two took a taxicab to Manhattan, where they spent the rest of the night at the dwelling of a friend. On the way the defendant threw his pistol into the river. He was arrested on January 7, 1930, about two months following the crime.

At the trial the vital question was the defendant's state of mind at the moment of the homicide. Did he shoot with a deliberate and premeditated design to kill? Was he so inflamed by drink or by anger or by both combined that, though he knew the nature of his act, he was the prey to sudden impulse, the fury of the fleeting moment? . . . If he went forth from his apartment with a preconceived design to kill, how is it that he failed to shoot at once? How reconcile such a design with the drawing of the pistol later in the heat and rage of an affray? These and like questions the jurors were to ask themselves and answer before measuring the defendant's guilt. Answers consistent with guilt in its highest grade can reasonably be made. Even so, the line between impulse and deliberation is too narrow and elusive to make the answers wholly clear. The sphygmograph records with graphic certainty the fluctuations of the pulse. There is no instrument yet invented that records with equal certainty the fluctuations of the mind. At least, if such an instrument exists, it was not working at midnight in the Brooklyn street when Coppola and the defendant came together in a chance affray. With only the rough and ready tests supplied by their experience of life, the jurors were to look into the workings of another's mind, and discover its capacities and disabilities, its urges and inhibitions, in moments of intense excitement. Delicate enough and subtle is the inquiry, even in the most favorable conditions, with every warping influence excluded. There must be no blurring of the issues by evidence illegally admitted and carrying with it in its admission an appeal to prejudice and passion.

Evidence charged with that appeal was, we think, admitted here. Not only was it admitted, and this under objection and exception, but the changes were rung upon it by prosecutor and judge. Almost at the opening of the trial the people began the endeavor to load the defendant down with the burden of an evil character. He was to be put before the jury as a man of murderous disposition. To that end they were allowed to prove that at the time of the encounter and at that of his arrest he had in his apartment, kept there in a radio box, three pistols and a tear-gas gun. There was no claim that he had brought these weapons out at the time of the affray, no claim that with any of them he had discharged the fatal shot. He could not have done so, for they were all of different caliber. The end to be served by laying the weapons before the jury was something very different. The end was to bring persuasion that here was a man of vicious and dangerous propensities, who because of those propensities was more likely to kill with deliberate and premeditated design than a man of irreproachable life and amiable manners. Indeed, this is the very ground on which the introduction of the evidence is now explained and defended. The district attorney tells us in his brief that the possession of the weapons characterized the defendant as "a desperate type of criminal," a "person criminally inclined." . . . The weapons were not brought by the defendant to the scene of the encounter. They were left in his apartment where they were incapable of harm. In such circumstances, ownership of the weapons, if it has any relevance at all, has relevance only as indicating a general disposition to make use of them thereafter, and a general disposition to make use of them thereafter is without relevance except as indicating a "desperate type of criminal," a criminal affected with a murderous propensity. . . .

If a murderous propensity may be proved against a defendant as one of the tokens of his guilt, a rule of criminal evidence, long believed to be of fundamental importance for the protection of the innocent, must be first declared away. Fundamental hitherto has been the rule that character is never an issue in a criminal prosecution unless the defendant chooses to make it one. . . . In a very real sense a defendant starts his life afresh when he stands before a jury, a prisoner at the bar. There has been a homicide in a public place. The killer admits the killing, but urges self-defense and sudden impulse. Inflexibly the law has set its face against the endeavor to fasten guilt upon him by proof of character or experience predisposing to an act of crime. . . . The endeavor has been often made, but always it has failed. At times, when the issue has been self-defense, testimony has been admitted as to the murderous propensity of the deceased, the victim of the homicide . . . but never of such a propensity on the part of the killer. The principle back of the exclusion is one, not of logic, but of policy. There may be cogency in the argument that a quarrelsome defendant is more likely to start a quarrel than one of milder type, a man of dangerous mode of life more likely than a shy recluse. The law is not blind to this, but equally it is not blind to the peril to the innocent if character is accepted as probative of crime. "The natural and inevitable tendency of the tribunal—whether judge or jury—is to give excessive weight to the vicious record of crime thus exhibited, and either to allow it to bear too strongly on the present charge, or to take the proof of it as justifying a condemnation irrespective of guilt of the present charge." . . .

A different question would be here if the pistols had been bought in expectation of this particular encounter. They would then have been admissible as evidence of preparation and design. . . . A different question would be here if they were so connected with the crime as to identify the perpetrator, if he had dropped them, for example, at the scene of the affray. . . . They would then have been admissible as tending to implicate the possessor (if identity was disputed), no matter what the opprobrium attached to his possession. Different, also, would be the question if the defendant had been shown to have gone forth from the apartment with all the weapons on his person. To be armed from head to foot at the very moment of an encounter may be a circumstance worthy to be considered, like acts of preparation generally, as a proof of preconceived design. There can be no such implication from the ownership of weapons which one leaves behind at home.

The endeavor was to generate an atmosphere of professional criminality. It was an endeavor the more unfair in that, apart from the suspicion attaching to the possession of these weapons, there is nothing to mark the defendant as a man of evil life. He was not in crime as a business. He did not shoot as a bandit shoots in the hope of wrongful gain. He was engaged in a decent calling, an optician regularly employed, without criminal record, or criminal associates. If his own testimony be true, he had gathered these weapons together as curios, a collection that interested and amused him. Perhaps his explanation of their ownership is false. There is nothing stronger than mere suspicion to guide us to an answer. Whether the explanation be false or true, he should not have been driven by the people to the necessity of offering it. Brought to answer a specific charge, and to defend himself against it, he was placed in a position where he had to defend himself against another, more general and sweeping. He was made to answer to the charge, pervasive and poisonous even if insidious and covert, that he was a man of murderous heart, of criminal disposition.

.   .   .

The judgment of conviction should be reversed, and a new trial ordered.

Comment and Questions

As Justice Cardozo points out, it is a general rule of Anglo-American law that the prosecution cannot show the defendant's bad character as evidence making it more likely that he committed the crime charged.

Is the contention of Justice Cardozo that the character of the accused cannot be probative evidence of his guilt? After all, in our own lives we often reason that someone more likely did something because he is just that type of person. Moreover, we recognize the value of character evidence by allowing the defendant to show his *good* character, typically through his reputation or, in some states, through the opinions of those who know him personally.

Can one argue that the character evidence rule is an example of "tenderness" toward the accused? Or are we afraid that the jury, once it hears that the defendant has a bad character, will merely decide that, regardless of his guilt on the particular occasion charged, he should be convicted and punished anyway as a dangerous or otherwise unworthy person?

The legal rules concerning character testimony are quite complex. Very often evidence showing bad character of the accused is admitted because it is introduced for another purpose—such as to show the motive of the criminal (he shot two policemen because he did not wish to be discovered possessing narcotics) or to show the identity of the criminal (he committed five other crimes of exactly the same type in precisely the same way—which earmarks all six crimes as the handiwork of the same person and hence of the accused).

And if the accused takes the witness stand, the prosecution may show that he has been convicted of a felony, on the theory that this may make the truthfulness of his testimony suspect.

Despite the many apparent exceptions to the general rule, it is a hallmark of Anglo-American law that the bad character of the accused cannot be introduced into evidence simply to show that he is the type of person who more likely would commit the crime.

2. CAMUS, THE STRANGER *

[The protagonist is awaiting trial before an Algerian Court on a charge of murdering an Arab in a brawl. The defense is self-defense. His lawyer visits him in jail.] . . . [H]e said that they'd been making investigations into my private life. They had learned that my mother died recently in a home. Inquiries had been conducted at Marengo and the police informed that I'd shown "great callousness" at my mother's funeral.

"You must understand," the lawyer said, "that I don't relish having to question you about such a matter. But it has much importance, and, unless I find some way of answering the charge of 'callousness,' I shall be handicapped in conducting your defense. And that is where you, and only you, can help me."

He went on to ask if I had felt grief on that "sad occasion." The question struck me as an odd one; I'd have been much embarrassed if I'd had to ask anyone a thing like that.

I answered that, of recent years, I'd rather lost the habit of noting my feelings, and hardly knew what to answer. I could truthfully say I'd been quite fond of Mother—but really that didn't mean much. All normal people, I added as an afterthought, had more or less desired the death of those they loved, at some time or another.

Here the lawyer interrupted me, looking greatly perturbed.

"You must promise me not to say anything of that sort at the trial, or to the examining magistrate."

I promised, to satisfy him, but I explained that my physical condition at any given moment often influenced my feelings. For instance, on the day I attended Mother's funeral, I was fagged out and only half awake. So, really, I hardly took stock of what was happening. Anyhow, I could assure him of one thing: that I'd rather Mother hadn't died.

The lawyer, however, looked displeased. "That's not enough," he said curtly.

After considering for a bit he asked me if he could say that on that day I had kept my feelings under control.

* Albert Camus, *The Stranger*, trans. by Stuart Gilbert (New York: Vintage Books, A Division of Random House, 1946), pp. 79–81. © 1946, by Alfred A. Knopf, Inc. Reprinted by permission

"No," I said. "That wouldn't be true."

He gave me a queer look, as if I slightly revolted him; then informed me, in an almost hostile tone, that in any case the head of the Home and some of the staff would be cited as witnesses.

"And that might do you a very nasty turn," he concluded.

When I suggested that Mother's death had no connection with the charge against me, he merely replied that this remark showed I'd never had any dealings with the law.

Comment

Other legal systems than the Anglo-American pay great attention to the character of the accused. In the Soviet Union, the work-record of the accused is extremely important both in determining his guilt or innocence and in determining his sentence, if he is found guilty. In China, a crucial variable is the "class background" of the accused. In most Continental systems, such as the French, parodied in the above excerpt, the character of the accused is of extreme importance in determining his guilt—though not, of course, to the extent implied in the above excerpt.

E. THE FAIRNESS OF THE TRIBUNAL

1. SELECTING THE JURY

a. THE VENIRE

In actual practice, finding persons to sit on the jury in any particular case requires a complicated set of steps. In modern, urban society the process cannot be as simple as in a western movie: the sheriff walks into the Silver Dollar Saloon and gathers twelve locals for a day at the court house.

First, the legislature must decide what kind of citizens will be allowed to serve. For example, jurors must be citizens over 18 years of age, without a felony conviction, in good health, able to speak and write English, and so on.

The second step is a mechanical process whereby a county official (usually called a Jury Commissioner) collects the names of local residents, gathers information about them and applies the legislative standards to them to decide which are legally qualified. He then submits to the court a list of qualified prospective jurors so that they may be subpoenaed to serve in court. As can be gathered, the Jury Commissioner has an administrative chore of no small proportions. In a populous county, thousands of jurors are needed in local courts each year.

Except for the legislative disqualifications, the Jury Commissioner's list should ideally be as close as we can come to the entire population of the area. Considerable dispute exists about how to compile such a list. Most jurisdictions hold that the voting lists are sufficient, despite the fact that a lower percentage of the poor and of ethnic minorities register to vote than do the rest of the population. (Indeed, it is sometimes alleged that one reason why poorer people do not vote is that they are afraid they may be called for jury duty. If this happens, they may have to give up a steady job at perhaps a low wage for the even lower wages that jurors are paid [often $6.00 a day]).

In some jurisdictions, other lists may be integrated with the voting rolls. For instance, in some California counties the list of those who hold drivers' licenses are added to the voting lists—though this presents a severe problem with respect to duplication. In other areas, where automobile driving is not nearly so common, there may be different methods of supplementing the voting lists, better to achieve a cross section of the population.

In any event, once the list of possible jurors is made up, the jury commissioner summons the necessary number (usually about fifty— though for more controversial cases several hundred may be required) picked at random from the list. Excuses may be accepted from members of certain occupations—such as physicians and teachers and from those who have recently performed their jury duty. And those summoned—called the venire (from the Latin, "to come") appear in court at the appointed time so that the next step—the *voir dire*—may begin.

Comment and Questions

How do we reconcile the concept of a fair cross-section of the population with that of a "jury of one's peers"? What does a jury of one's peers mean anyway? Does it mean that one accused of drunkenness should have a jury of drunks? That a terrorist accused of slaying a policeman should have a jury of terrorists? That a policeman accused of slaying a terrorist be tried before a jury of policemen? If not, what does "a jury of one's peers" mean?

b. THE VOIR DIRE *

An American trial jury is something more than twelve good men and true plucked at random from the surrounding community. It is the product of a sometimes lengthy process of questioning and selection by the court and the opposing attorneys. Lawyers call this process the *voir dire*, Norman French for "to tell the truth." During the *voir dire*, the trial judge, through his questioning of prospective jurors, simply seeks persons who are qualified under the laws of the jurisdiction to sit as jurors. The two opposing sides seek something more. The prosecution and the defense each attempts to find jurors who can most easily be convinced of the rightness of its own position.

In England it is done differently. Twelve persons are called indiscriminately from a list of people summoned to court for jury duty and these twelve, subjected to virtually no questioning and without

* John Kaplan and Jon R. Waltz, *The* and Company, 1965, pp. 91–94. © 1965 *Trial of Jack Ruby,* New York: MacMillan (Reprinted by permission).

having revealed either their addresses or their occupations, proceed to decide the case at hand. Occasionally, it is true, a British juror proves to be the defendant's sister or is stone-deaf but, on the whole, this casual approach to the impaneling of juries has worked remarkably well. From time to time efforts have been made in the United States, and especially in the federal courts, to curtail or even eliminate counsel's privilege of examining prospective jurors. They have failed because, as it is carried on today, the *voir dire* constitutes much more than a method of expeditiously deciding which jurors shall hear a case. The right to *voir dire* jurors is one of counsel's most cherished prerogatives and American lawyers have fought vigorously—and largely successfully—against its abolition.

All the other purposes to which the *voir dire* is regularly put, however, should not obscure its main and, in theory, its only legitimate function—developing sufficient information upon which to select the jurors. The actual picking is done by calling prospective jurors, either individually or in groups of up to twelve, and questioning them—first by the judge, then by one side, then by the other. After the questioning the juror may be accepted or he may be challenged or, more politely, "excused." Two types of challenges are recognized in American trial courts: the challenge for cause and the peremptory challenge. The former must be based on a specific, recognized ground, be it statutory or embedded in case law, while the latter, as its name "peremptory" implies, may be for good reason, bad reason, or no reason at all, provided only that the limited number of such challenges allotted each counsel has not been exhausted.

The grounds for challenging a potential juror for cause are manifold. The jury may be unqualified for jury duty in any type of case because, for example, he is mentally incompetent or cannot understand English. Or he may be disqualified because, although qualified in general, he is automatically presumed to be biased either because of a financial interest in the outcome of the case or a relationship to one of the parties or attorneys. Finally, comprising the largest target of challenges for cause are those jurors who, because they are actually biased or hold some fixed notion, cannot fairly judge the case before them. . . .

In theory any number of challenges for cause can be granted, dependent only upon the presence of a specified ground. In fact, however, many of the grounds will be revealed only if the prospective jurors admit to the type of bias which many men are eager to hide. The law, taking this into account, therefore allows each side a set number of peremptory challenges, ... The peremptory challenge has become much more than a device to secure an unprejudiced jury; it is now generally regarded as a method of obtaining jurors who are most likely to be biased in one's favor. It is in this context that a vast body of folklore has been generated concerning the behavior of jurors. Many criminal lawyers adhere almost religiously to an elaborate system of rules in determining what sorts of jurors should be peremptorily challenged and what sorts should be retained. Defense attorneys have long surmised that Irish, Italians, Jews, Eastern Europeans and Negroes make good jurors for their side in criminal cases. Where the juror identifies with a group which at one time or another in American history has been the underdog, he supposedly tends to have sympathy for the defendant. Americans of English, Scandinavian and German extraction are favored by the prosecution since they are thought to be more willing to administer justice untempered by mercy. Occupational groups also occupy an important position in this folklore. Bankers, stock brokers, low-rank white-collar workers and people involved in law-enforcement activity are regarded as good prosecution jurors, while salesmen, artists, musicians, taxi drivers and union men are thought to lean toward the defense. Myriad other rules are bandied about, although they seem to be recognized as less categorical than those based on occupation and ethnic origin. It is sometimes said that, for the defense, young jurors tend to be better than the elderly, women better than men, poor better than wealthy, married men better than single. A substantial part of the questioning of prospective jurors is regularly directed to finding out in which pigeonhole of the folklore they fit.

Not all trial practitioners possess abiding faith in this jury folklore. Every experienced prosecutor has his anecdote about the wealthy, elderly, bachelor Swedish banker who held out for acquittal, and many a defense attorney has seen his cause lost at the hands of a young, married Negro juror of moderate means. It is difficult to get really reliable information on the behavior of jurors. One of the most careful and promising efforts to discover what happens in the jury room, by obtaining the judge's permission and then "bugging" the jury's deliberations, created such an outrage that Congress promptly made it a federal crime.

Questions

Does it make sense, in trying to obtain a fair jury, to set up the system so that the lawyers for the two adversaries each attempts to get the jurors most strongly biased in his favor?

How could one better attempt to get fair jurors? What effect does the fact that a guilty verdict must be unanimous (The Supreme Court in 1972 held that this is not a constitutional command, though almost all states require it anyway) have on the consequences of a mistake by the prosecution in failing to challenge a juror biased against it? Is this balanced by the fact that an acquittal must also be by a unanimous verdict? Why?

c. JURY SIZE

The Sixth Amendment to the Constitution guarantees that "In all criminal prosecutions, the accused shall enjoy the right to a speedy and public trial, by an impartial jury." The Constitution does not, however, require that a jury be of a particular size. Still, until recently, the number twelve had been the fixed size of juries since the mid-fourteenth century. But in 1970, the U.S. Supreme Court declared that the number twelve was an "historical accident, wholly without significance except to mystics." Then the question focused on the lower limit. If not twelve, how about one or two or three or five? The case below offers the answer:

BALLEW v. GEORGIA
Supreme Court of the United States, 1978.
435 U.S. 223, 98 S.Ct. 1029, 55 L.Ed.2d 234.

Mr. Justice BLACKMUN announced the judgment of the Court and delivered an opinion in which Mr. Justice STEVENS joined.

[Ballew was the manager of the Paris Adult Theatre in Atlanta, Georgia. He was charged in a two-count misdemeanor accusation with "distributing obscene materials in violation of Georgia Code Section 26–2101 in that the said accused did, knowing the obscene nature thereof, exhibit a motion picture film entitled 'Behind the Green Door' that contained obscene and indecent scenes." Ballew was brought to trial in the Criminal Court of Fulton County; the practice of this court was to try misdemeanor cases before juries of five persons, pursuant to Georgia law. Ballew's motion that the court impanel a twelve-person jury was denied, and the trial proceeded with the smaller jury panel, which returned guilty verdicts on both counts. Ballew's state appeals, on several grounds, including a Sixth Amendment challenge of the five-person jury, were unsuccessful. The United States Supreme Court granted certiorari.

This case presents the issue whether a state criminal trial to a jury of only five persons deprives the accused of the right to trial by jury guaranteed to him by the Sixth and Fourteenth Amendments. Our resolution of the issue requires an application of principles enunciated in Williams v. Florida, 399 U.S. 78, 90 S.Ct. 1893, 26 L.Ed.2d 446 (1970), where the use of a six-person jury in a state criminal trial was upheld against constitutional attack.

[W]hen the Court in *Williams* permitted the reduction in jury size—or, to put it another way, when it held that a jury of six was not unconstitutional—it expressly reserved ruling on the issue whether a number smaller than six passed constitutional scrutiny. Id., at 91 n. 28, 90 S.Ct., at 1901. The Court refused to speculate when this so-called "slippery slope" would become too steep. We face now, however, the two-fold question whether a further reduction in the size of the state criminal trial jury does make the grade too dangerous, that is, whether it inhibits the functioning of the jury as an institution to a significant degree, and, if so, whether any state interest counterbalances and justifies the disruption so as to preserve its constitutionality.

Williams v. Florida and Colgrove v. Battin, 413 U.S. 149, 93 S.Ct. 2448, 37 L.Ed.2d 522 (1973) (where the Court held that a jury of six members did not violate the Seventh Amendment right to a jury trial in a civil case), generated a quantity of scholarly work on jury size. These writings do not draw or identify a bright line below which the number of jurors would not be able to function as required by the standards enunciated in *Williams.* On the other hand, they raise significant questions about the wisdom and constitutionality of a reduction below six. We examine these concerns.

First, recent empirical data suggest that progressively smaller juries are less likely to foster effective group deliberation. At some point, this decline leads to inaccurate fact-finding and incorrect application of the common sense of the community to the facts. Generally, a positive correlation exists between group size and the quality of both group performance and group productivity. A variety of explanations have been offered for this conclusion. Several are particularly applicable in the jury setting. The smaller the group, the less likely are members to make critical contributions necessary for the solution of a given problem. Because most jurors are not permitted to take notes, see Forston, Sense and Non-Sense: Jury Trial Communication, 1975 B.Y.U.L.Rev. 601, 631–633, memory is important for accurate jury deliberations. As juries decrease in size, then, they are less likely to have members who remember each of the important pieces of evidence or argument. Furthermore, the smaller the group, the less likely it is to overcome the biases of its members to obtain an accurate result. When individual and group decisionmaking were compared, it was seen that groups performed better because prejudices of individuals were frequently counterbalanced, and objectivity resulted. Groups also exhibited increased motivation and self-criticism. All these advantages, except, perhaps, self-motivation, tend to diminish as the size of the group diminishes. Because juries frequently face complex problems laden with value choices, the benefits are important and should be retained. In particular, the counterbalancing of various biases is critical to the accurate application of the common sense of the community to the facts of any given case.

Second, the data now raise doubts about the accuracy of the results achieved by smaller and smaller panels. Statistical studies suggest that the risk of convicting an innocent person (Type I error) rises as the size of the jury diminishes. Because the risk of not convicting a guilty person (Type II error) increases with the size of the panel, an optimal jury size can be selected as a function of the interaction between the two risks. Nagel and Neef concluded that the optimal size, for the purpose of minimizing errors, should vary with the importance attached to the two types of mistakes. After weighting Type I error as 10 times more significant than Type II, perhaps not an unreasonable assumption, they concluded that the optimal jury size was between six and eight. As the size diminished to five and below, the weighted sum of errors increased because of the enlarging risk of the conviction of innocent defendants.

Another doubt about progressively smaller juries arises from the increasing inconsistency that results from the decreases. Saks argued that the "more a jury type fosters consistency, the greater will be the proportion of juries which select the correct (i.e., the same) verdict and the fewer 'errors' will be made." Saks 86–87. From his mock trials held before undergraduates and former jurors, he computed the percentage of "correct" decisions rendered by 12-person and 6-person panels. In the student experiment, 12-person groups reached correct verdicts 83% of the time; 6-person panels reached correct verdicts 69% of the time. The results for the former-juror study were 71% for the 12-person groups and 57% for the 6-person groups. Ibid. Working with statistics described in H. Kalven & H. Zeisel, The American Jury 460 (1966), Nagel and Neef tested the average conviction propensity of juries, that is, the likelihood that any given jury of a set would convict the defendant. They found that half of all 12-person juries would have average conviction propensities that varied by no more than 20 points. Half of all six-person juries, on the other hand, had average conviction propensities varying by 30 points, a difference they found significant in both real and percentage terms. Lempert reached similar results when he considered the likelihood of juries to compromise over the various views of their members, an important phenomenon for the fulfillment of the commonsense function. In civil trials averaging occurs with respect to damages amounts. In criminal trials it relates to numbers of counts and lesser included offenses. And he predicted that compromises would be more consistent when larger juries were employed. For example, 12-person juries could be expected to reach extreme compromises in 4% of the cases, while 6-person panels would reach extreme results in 16%. All three of these *post*-Williams studies, therefore, raise significant doubts about the consistency and reliability of the decisions of smaller juries.

Third, the data suggest that the verdicts of jury deliberation in criminal cases will vary as juries become smaller, and that the variance amounts to an imbalance to the detriment of one side, the defense. Both Lempert and Zeisel found that the number of hung juries would diminish as the panels decreased in size. Zeisel said that the number would be cut in half—from 5% to 2.4% with a decrease from 12 to 6 members. Both studies emphasized that juries in criminal cases generally hang with only one, or more likely two, jurors remaining unconvinced of guilt. Also, group theory suggests that a person in the minority will adhere to his position more frequently when he has at least one other person supporting his argument. In the jury setting the significance of this tendency is demonstrated by the following figures: If a minority viewpoint is shared by 10% of the community, 28.2% of 12–member juries may be expected to have no minority representation, but 53.1% of 6–member juries would have none. Thirty-four percent of 12–member panels could be expected to have two minority members, while only 11% of 6–member panels would have two. As the numbers diminish below six, even fewer panels would have one member with the minority viewpoint and still fewer would have two. The chance for hung juries would decline accordingly.

Fourth, what has just been said about the presence of minority viewpoint as juries decrease in size foretells problems not only for jury decisionmaking, but also for the representation of minority groups in the community. The Court repeatedly has held that meaningful community participation cannot be attained with the exclusion of minorities or other identifiable groups from jury service.

[A]lthough the Court in *Williams* concluded that the six-person jury did not fail to represent adequately a cross-section of the community, the opportunity for meaningful and appropriate representation does decrease with the size of the panels. Thus, if a minority group constitutes 10% of the community, 53.1% of randomly selected six-member juries could be expected to have no minority representative among their members, and 89% not to have two. Further reduction in size will erect additional barriers to representation.

Fifth, several authors have identified in jury research methodological problems tending to mask differences in the operation of smaller and larger juries. For example, because the judicial system handles so many clear cases, decisionmakers will reach similar results through similar analyses most of the time. One study concluded that smaller and larger juries could disagree in their verdicts in no more than 14% of the cases. Disparities, therefore, appear in only small percentages. Nationwide, however, these small percentages will represent a large number of cases. And it is with respect to those cases that the jury trial right has its greatest value. When the case is close, and the guilt or innocence of the defendant is not readily apparent, a properly functioning jury system will insure evaluation by the sense of the community and will also tend to insure accurate factfinding.

Studies that aggregate data also risk masking case-by-case differences in jury deliberations. The authors, H. Kalven and H. Zeisel, of The American Jury (1966), examined the judge-jury disagreement. They found that judges held for plaintiffs 57% of the time and that juries held for plaintiffs 59%, an insignificant difference. Yet case-by-case comparison revealed judge-jury disagreement in 22% of the cases. Id., at 63, cited in Lempert 656. This casts doubt on the conslusion of another study that compared the aggregate results of civil cases tried before 6–member juries with those of 12–member jury trials. The investigator in that study had claimed support for his hypothesis that damages awards did not vary with the reduction in jury size. Although some might say that figures in the aggregate may have supported this conclusion, a closer view of the cases reveals greater variation in the results of the smaller panels, i.e., a standard deviation of $58,335 for the 6–member juries, and of $24,834 for the 12–member juries. Again, the averages masked significant case-by-case differences that must be considered when evaluating jury function and performance.

While we adhere to, and reaffirm our holding in *Williams v. Florida,* these studies, most of which have been made since *Williams* was decided in 1970, lead us to conclude that the purpose and functioning of the jury in a criminal trial is seriously impaired, and to a constitutional degree, by a reduction in size to below six members. We readily admit that we do not pretend to discern a clear line between six members and five. But the assembled data raise substantial doubt about the reliability and appropriate representation of panels smaller than six. Because of the fundamental importance of the jury trial to the American system of criminal justice, any further reduction that promotes inaccurate and possibly biased decisionmaking, that causes untoward differences in verdicts, and that prevents juries from truly representing their communities, attains constitutional significance.

[T]he empirical data cited by Georgia do not relieve our doubts. The State relies on the Saks study for the proposition that a decline in the number of jurors will not affect the aggregate number of convictions or hung juries. Tr. of Oral Arg. 27. This conclusion, however, is only one of several in the Saks study; that study eventually concludes:

> "Larger juries (size twelve) are preferable to smaller juries (six). They produce longer deliberations, more communication, far better community representation, and, possibly greater verdict reliability (consistency)." Saks 107.

Far from relieving our concerns, then, the Saks study supports the conclusion that further reduction in jury size threatens Sixth and Fourteen Amendment interests.

Methodological problems prevent reliance on the three studies that do purport to bolster Georgia's position. The reliability of the two Michigan studies cited by the State has been criticized elsewhere. The critical problem with the Michigan laboratory experiment, which used a mock civil trial, was the apparent clarity of the case. Not one of the juries found for the plaintiff in the tort suit; this masked any potential difference in the decisionmaking of larger and smaller panels. The results also have been doubted because in the experiment only students composed the juries, only 16 juries were tested, and only a video tape of the mock trial was presented. The statistical review of the results of actual jury trials in Michigan erroneously aggregated outcomes. It is also said that it failed to take account of important changes of court procedure initiated at the time of the reduction in size from 12 to 6 members. The Davis study, which employed a mock criminal trial for rape, also presented an extreme set of facts so that none of the panels rendered a guilty verdict. None of these three reports, therefore, convinces us that a reduction in the number of jurors below six will not affect to a constitutional degree the functioning of juries in criminal trials.

With the reduction in the number of jurors below six creating a substantial threat to Sixth and Fourteenth Amendment guarantees, we must consider whether any interest of the State justifies the reduction.

We find no significant state advantage in reducing the number of jurors from six to five.

The States utilize juries of less than 12 primarily for administrative reasons. Savings in court time and in financial costs are claimed to justify the reductions. The financial benefits of the reduction from 12 to 6 are substantial; this is mainly because fewer jurors draw daily allowances as they hear cases. On the other hand, the asserted saving in judicial time is not so clear. Pabst in his study found little reduction in the time for voir dire with the six-person jury because many questions were directed at the veniremen as a group. Total trial time did not diminish, and court delays and backlogs improved very little. The point that is to be made, of course, is that a reduction in size from six to five or four or even three would save the States little. They could reduce slightly the daily allowances, but with a reduction from six to five the saving would be minimal. If little time is gained by the reduction from 12 to 6, less will be gained with a reduction from 6 to 5. Perhaps this explains why only two States, Georgia and Virginia, have reduced the size of juries in certain nonpetty criminal cases to five. Other States appear content with six members or more. In short, the State has offered little or no justification for its reduction to five members.

Petitioner, therefore, has established that his trial on criminal charges before a five-member jury deprived him of the right to trial by jury guaranteed by the Sixth and Fourteenth Amendments.

Mr. Justice POWELL, with whom THE CHIEF JUSTICE and Mr. Justice REHNQUIST join, concurring in the judgment.

I concur in the judgment, as I agree that use of a jury as small as five members, with authority to convict for serious offenses, involves grave questions of fairness. As the opinion of Mr. Justice Blackmun indicates, the line between five- and six-member juries is difficult to justify, but a line has to be drawn somewhere if the substance of jury trial is to be preserved. [I] have reservations as to the wisdom—as well as the necessity—of Mr. Justice Blackmun's heavy reliance on numerology derived from statistical studies. Moreover, neither the validity nor the methodology employed by the studies cited was subjected to the traditional testing mechanisms of the adversary process. The studies relied on merely represent unexamined findings of persons interested in the jury system.

For these reasons I concur only in the judgment.

Question

Do you agree with Justice Powell that Justice Blackmun's opinion is based on "numerology," or do you think the statistical evidence is convincing? Based on Justice Blackmun's opinion, do you think that a six person jury can be representative? If not, why wasn't the number set higher?

d. JURY REPRESENTATIVENESS *

The process through which a trial jury is selected—the voir dire and the challenge system—may be reasonably effective in eliminating those members of the panel who are very strongly biased toward a particular side of the case. But the experience of the Newton trial,** pioneering as it was in the introduction of "racial" questions, suggests that this process is quite ineffective in achieving a jury that is most free of racial bias. In fact, the very procedures by which the twelve final members are selected from the original panel would appear to impose obstacles on the seating of a non-racist or anti-racist jury.

The remarks I made as an expert witness on racism during the pre-trial testimony are relevant here. I began my testimony with the generalization that racism—in the objective sense of the control of the society's institutions by white people and the systematic subordination of people of color and their relegation to the less powerful, prestigious, and rewarding positions—is a basic reality in America. The subjective aspect of this objective or structural pattern is the white group's sense of its own superiority and the inferiority of blacks and other non-whites. This sense of superiority is almost inevitable and it is shared by all white people—on conscious, subconscious, and unconscious levels.

The most effective way to eliminate white racism in the judgment of a racially-relevant case would be to form a jury of citizens from the racial minority groups. Although people of color have also been influenced by the racist assumptions of American culture, their experience as victims of discrimination still make them more aware of the totality of circumstances which motivate black and other non-white defendants. But assuming that the courts are not yet prepared to move this far, one needs to devise new tests or criteria for selecting the least racist whites. Such tests as yet do not exist, and in response to Judge Friedman's * request to propose an improved method, I put forward four tentative criteria along which jury panelists might be evaluated. Granted that my criteria make an extremely tough test and that they are the invention of one sociologist rather than of a commission of social scientists and legal experts, it may yet be informative to use them to evaluate the Newton jury experience.

First, I suggested that the least racist person would not deny racial prejudice, but would be aware that he reflected elements of the society's pervasive racism. He would be sensitive to his racist tendencies, would keep them in his consciousness rather than suppress them, and would strive of course to reduce their impact. During the Newton voir dire,

---

* Ann Fagan Ginger, ed. *Minimizing Racism in Jury Trials,* (Berkeley: The National Lawyers Guild, 1969), pp. 125–128. Reprints available from The National Lawyers Guild, Box 673, Berkeley, California 94703. © 1969 (Reprinted by permission).

** The trial of Huey P. Newton, cofounder and Minister of Defense of the Black Panther party, for the killing of a police officer. Newton was acquitted by a jury after his initial conviction was reversed on appeal.

* The judge in the Newton trial.

most people denied that they had any elements of racism or prejudice within them. Often this closed the discussion, and this denial or "affirmation of purity" made it easier for them to be "passed for cause," that is, seated as a prospective juror. A significant minority of citizens admitted some peripheral prejudices; in some cases the defense appraised this cue as a sign of insight, honesty, and good will—though we may have been fooled in one or two instances in putting too much stock in this criterion.

The second criterion dealt with knowledge. To effectively combat racism, a white person should not see blacks as "invisible" but be attuned to the social circumstances of the present and the forces in the past which have produced our racial crisis. Thus I suggested that the least racist whites would have some substantial knowledge of black or race relations history and a familiarity with the content and character of Afro-American culture. Questions that really test this criterion were not asked during the voir dire. It was clear that almost no one among the 140 white panelists—like American whites in general—knew anything about Negro history and black culture. As we have seen, ignorance about racial discrimination and the black movement was the typical pattern. Such ignorance or indifference actually made it easier for the panelists to be seated, since there was no line of questioning that could be pursued that might lead to a challenge for cause. And because of the system of peremptory challenges, any prospective juror who passed this particular test would have been suspect of pro-black bias and thus dismissed by the prosecuting attorney!

The third point involved contact and experience with members of the minority group. Since the social and cultural barrier between whites and blacks is a keystone of the racist system, leading a life that is primarily segregated in terms of work, residence, and friendship in itself reflects and maintains white racism. Though there were exceptions, the vast majority of whites led such segregated lives. Again, attorney Jensen was free to dismiss those few persons who were committed to racial integration in action.

Finally, I suggested that a non-racist must be involved in efforts to combat discrimination and prejudice. Personal, subjective racism can only be eliminated or diminished in the process of undermining the objective racism in the society and its institutions. Thus, another criterion would be some personal project toward the goal of racial justice. This could be expressed in many possible forms: in local communities, in occupations, professions, or leisure pursuits as well as through organized political groups. Garry employed this standard when he asked persons who said they disapproved of the exclusion of blacks from their fraternal and leisure association whether they had ever acted to end this state of affairs. From the voir dire testimony, it is apparent that the overwhelming majority of the potential jurors had never been involved in combating racism. If any one had testified positively, he would certainly have been challenged.

Thus I have suggested that the logic of the voir dire makes it difficult to minimize white racism in the selection of a jury. This is ultimately a product of the overwhelming presence of racism in our society. People who are somewhere along the line of movement to a non-racist position: the aware, the knowledgeable, the integrated, and the change-oriented, make up only a miniscule proportion of the white population. Such a frequency distribution makes it possible for all such people to be challenged when they appear. The prosecutor need not worry about using up his peremptories against anti-racists, whereas the defense attorney will not have enough challenges to dismiss all the racists.

There is another factor in the logic of the voir dire and challenge system. The assumption is that every citizen has the makings of a fair and impartial juror and the questioning thus takes place solely to locate any negative factors: bias, prejudice, unusual opinions or personal ties, that might vitiate impartiality. But racial bias cannot be dealt with as some negative property that can be detected through the voir dire. It is so omnipresent in American society that the only reasonable means of minimizing it in a predominantly white jury would entail a process of positive selection: setting up a series of qualifications or tests that would locate that minority of *least*-racist, who along with non-whites, would constitute the panel from which the final jury could be drawn.

2. A FLORIDA OBSCENITY TRIAL *

As his trial opened in Fort Lauderdale last week, Luther Campbell, the 29-year-old leader of the rap music group 2 Live Crew, was anticipating a clash of cultures. He said he thought the six jurors, who included three women over age 60 and only one black, might be too old, too white and two middle class to understand his raunchy music.

But the rapper from Miami apparently misjudged the Broward County jurors, who quickly acquitted Mr. Campbell and two other band members of obscenity charges on Saturday.

"He stereotyped us, just as certain people were stereotyping him because of his performance," said David Garsow, the 24-year-old jury foreman, who works as an office clerk and sings in the choir at the Key Biscayne Presbyterian Church. "We were very open."

Indeed, the jurors said they saw artistic merit in the rap music, to the point that some of them were trying their own rap lyrics on trips to and from the courtroom. They found much amusement in the trial, too, especially in the prosecution's bungled tape recording of the band's performance. The recording was so bad that one of the prosecutors said that after he heard it he regarded the trial as a "suicide mission."

* Sara Rimer, "In 2 Live Crew Trial, Cultures Didn't Clash," The New York Times, Monday, October 22, 1990, Sec. B1.

Explaining the verdict, Mr. Garsow said the jurors had accepted much of the testimony of Henry Louis Gates Jr., an American literature professor at Duke University, who testified that the group's lewd lyrics were meant as parody.

"We agreed with what he said about this being like Archie Bunker making fun of racism," the jury foreman said. "But Gates was saying that in order to understand the lyrics you had to be young and black. We didn't buy that."

Mr. Garsow is white and was the youngest juror. If anything, he said, the older members of the jury were the most liberal and the most adamant in insisting that the band members should have the freedom to express themselves.

The jury was sequestered during the trial, and Mr. Garsow said that on the way to the hotel each night, Susan Van Hemert, a 42-year-old assistant middle school principal, would improvise rap songs.

"I thought it would've been cute if we could have come out with the verdict like we were doing a rap song," Mrs. Van Hemert said.

While Mrs. Van Hemert and the other jurors said they laughed at the 2 Live Crew's lyrics, and at the prosecution's continued playing of the garbled tape of the performance that was the only evidence against the band, they said they took seriously the issue of freedom of speech underlying the case.

The senior member of the jury, Helena Bailie, 76, said she had admired what another juror, Beverly Resnick, 65, said in their deliberations. "She said, 'You take away one freedom, and pretty soon they're all gone,' " Mrs. Bailie, a retired sociology professor from New York, recalled.

Questions and Comment

A good deal of attention in recent years has been given to the fact that juries drawn from a cross-section of the population may be found to harbor prejudices against ethnic minorities and hence give them a less fair trial. There are whole categories, other than those of ethnic minorities, who, as any trial lawyer can tell, will often get a trial less fair to one side or the other. Beautiful women and, at least in the past, war heroes or casualties have been treated noticeably more favorably by juries than is the hypothetical average man.

Similarly, those who are physically ugly, homosexuals, or those who practice a lifestyle which the jury may find dissolute or otherwise immoral may be treated less fairly than the average.

Aside from granting an accused who falls into one of the disadvantaged categories the right to waive jury and be tried solely before a judge, what can society do to minimize this problem? Was the Florida jury representative? Was it racist? Was it fair?

3. SOCIAL SCIENCE AND JURY SELECTION

a. THE JOAN LITTLE CASE *

"Do you think male jailers take advantage of female prisoners?" "Do you agree that most women who are raped may have encouraged the attack?" "Do you think that Richard Nixon was treated unfairly during Watergate?" "What magazines do you subscribe to?" And so it went in a dark-paneled courtroom in Raleigh, N.C., last July, as defense attorneys grilled close to 150 prospective jurors. For 10 days, the seven-lawyer defense team tested jurors' attitudes toward race and rape, police and jails, politics and fear—just about anything that might affect a vote on the fate of the defendant, Joan Little, a young black woman accused of fatally stabbing a white jailer 11 times with an ice pick.** The judge was growing impatient; the prosecution objected that the defense was asking irrelevant questions and "psychoanalyzing" the jurors; even some of the jurors began to wonder whether *they* were on trial.

And, in a sense, they were. On a long bench behind the prosecution and the defense sat the jurors' judges—the "Joan Little Fair Jury Project," seven men and women who had come to Raleigh to help defense lawyers select a fair Southern jury for a black defendant—and each candidate was subjected by them to the closest scrutiny. Every answer, gesture, voice inflection, facial expression was noted. In addition, the candidates' personal backgrounds and opinions were rated against criteria compiled on the basis of demographic surveys conducted in the Raleigh area months before. A social psychologist was on the alert for behavioral clues that might offer insight into a juror's personality and feelings toward the defendant. A student of "body language" watched each juror for any hint of anxiety under questioning. Occasionally, the experts would slip a few questions to the lawyers or huddle with them to decide whether to accept or challenge a particular juror. And as each juror gave his age, a self-proclaimed astrologer and psychic judged whether the juror's planet was in conflict with Joan Little's "freedom planet."

[It all started in 1971 when] Jay Schulman, a sociologist who had taught at Cornell University and the City College of New York, was invited by defense lawyers to assist in selecting a jury for the Federal conspiracy trial of a group of Vietnam war protesters known as the Harrisburg Seven. Out of friendship with two of the defendants, Daniel Berrigan and Eqbal Ahmad, Schulman agreed to lend a hand and asked Richard Christie, a social psychologist at Columbia University, to join him.

---

* Edward Tivnan, *Jury by Trial,* New York Times Magazine, Nov. 16, 1975, p. 30 et seq. © 1975 The New York Times. Reprinted by permission.

** The defense was that Ms. Little was resisting a sexual assault by her jailer.

They have continued to revise and perfect their methods since then, and they have racked up an impressive record. Specializing primarily in "political" trials, Schulman and Christie have helped lawyers give jurors an unusually thorough going-over in such celebrated cases as the Camden 28, the Gainesville Eight, the Wounded Knee trial of Indian leaders Russell Banks and Dennis Means and four trials related to the Attica prison revolt. None of these defendants were convicted. At the moment, the high price of this novel technique ($38,992 for the Joan Little *voir dire*) places it out of reach of defendants without personal fortunes or a well-heeled defense committee. But Schulman and Christie are eager to make their methods more accessible for less celebrated trials. To this end, they and a small group of disciples have set up the National Jury Project, a non-profit organization based in Cambridge, Mass., dedicated to spreading social-science jury-selection techniques, with the use of volunteers to lower costs.

In the Little case a team of 20 interviewers called 954 residents of [the county where the trial was to take place], explained their purpose, and asked those willing to cooperate about their income, occupation, political affiliation, reading habits and other matters. They also posed questions designed to elicit opinions on issues related to the trial, including attitudes toward capital punishment, law-enforcement officers, blacks and rape victims. In New York, with the help of a computer, Christie and an associate correlated the demographic data with the responses on trial-related attitudes, and came up with an elaborate picture of the backgrounds and views of [the county's] residents. The computer divided the community into 23 groups, in accordance with factors like age, education, neighborhood, politics, and reading habits, as a way of predicting the characteristics that would be favorable or unfavorable to the defendant.

In the Joan Little case, Christie was surprised to discover that the prospective jurors' choice of magazine fare seemed to make a big difference. "People can start out well," explains Christie. "Their education is right—some college. Their age is right—under 45. Their residence is right—urban. But then they read the wrong magazines—Sports Illustrated, for example, or Ladies' Home Journal, rather than the newsmagazines or Harper's or the Atlantic."

Conceding that some people will not fit neatly in any of the demographic predictions, Schulman and Christie have designed a mechanism to spot the misfits, favorable or not—careful observation of the reactions of each juror during the actual *voir dire*.

In court, Christie is mainly on the lookout for what psychologists call an "authoritarian personality"—not a powerful sort, but eager to please those in authority and willing to go along with their opinions. Christie points to an example in the Joan Little *voir dire:* "There was a guy whose demographics were reasonably good—educated, good job, right age group. We wanted to find out how much he knew about the case, so we asked him to describe what had happened. He omitted any mention of possible rape and said that the jailer was stabbed 16 times, instead of 11. He also said that he was afraid his family would be harassed if he became a juror, because he read about some threatening remarks made by a Black Panther in Toledo." Christie marked him as "a classic authoritarian personality" and, hence, "a real bad apple from the defense point of view." The lawyers agreed and managed to pass him by.

The "body-language" expert at the *voir dire* was David Suggs, 24, a graduate student in psychology and law at the University of Nebraska. What he watched for were signs of anxiety or of "positive affect" on the jurors' part as they were addressed by attorneys for either side. Was the juror looking the defense squarely in the eye as he answered questions? Was he relaxed while responding to the prosecution, or fidgeting as he talked to the defense? What about his speaking tone— was it informal, warm or phony? This field of psychology is relatively new and still experimental, and Suggs concedes that any perceptive lawyer could—and many do—pick up the same signals. But he claims that there is an advantage in being able to focus on one aspect of courtroom behavior, a luxury that a lawyer cannot afford.

Demographic profiles, authoritarian personality, body language. "Generally, if all three agree, you're in pretty good shape," says Christie. "We then feed this information to the lawyers." However, *any* clue to how a juror might vote is useful, so yet another "expert" was on hand in that Raleigh courtroom—Richard Wolfe, 27, astrologer and psychic, invited by the defense committee to add his special brand of sensitivity to the *voir dire*, and paid \$3,000 for his contribution. Wolfe used his arts to "sense" whether jurors were likely to be prejudiced against Miss Little, and members of the defense team were apparently impressed by his powers of observation, feeling that he had discovered genuine bias in some people.

Questions and Comment

Should the law attempt to discourage the use of this type of technique in jury selection? How would it go about doing so?

One serious problem about the use of the technique described is that it is so expensive. It offends our notions of equality that only the rich (or those politically able to command large defense funds) have access to these techniques.

Would it raise different problems if the government attempted to use such techniques while they were denied by financial, or even legal, constraints to the defendant?

Note that the practitioners of the described methods did not attempt to find out anything about the prospective jurors as individuals— except, of course, on the *voir dire* itself. Jury investigations have been done whereby investigators peeped into the garages of potential jurors to see what their bumper stickers said. In some cases, investigators attempted to question friends and relatives of the potential jurors to determine their political convictions. Does this raise different problems than does the technique discussed above?

By the way, Joan Little was acquitted by the jury.

b.   IN PRE–SCIENTIFIC TIMES *

The "social science" techniques of jury selection described were practiced long before the behavioral sciences reached their current prominence.

Shortly after the turn of the century, the nephew of a U.S. senator from South Carolina shot the editor of the state's leading morning newspaper.

In those days, it was not uncommon for citizens of South Carolina to have portraits or photographs of people they admired hanging in their homes (such as Washington, Lincoln, Robert E. Lee, and the like).

Lawyers for the accused identified the veniremen from among whom the jury would be impaneled. They employed persons to pose as salesmen of portraits and photographs to go, door-to-door, to the homes of these individuals. In addition to pictures of Washington, Lincoln, and Lee, a picture of the senator—the uncle of the accused—was included, and comments (positive and negative) about the senator were recorded.

When the case came to trial, the defense lawyers struck from the jury those individuals who did not like the senator and kept those who did. They brought the senator from Washington to sit beside his nephew. The nephew was acquitted.

Question

What kind of a way is this to run a legal system?

F.   THE JURY AS FACTFINDER *

1.   THE RESEARCH FINDINGS

[Lawyers have always been intrigued by the question of what factors in a trial motivate the final verdict of a jury. Two law professors attempted to answer that question by conducting a relatively simple study: a sizable number of judges were asked to fill out questionnaires relating to trials before them, to explain the circumstances surrounding each trial, and to discuss whether they agreed or disagreed with the jury verdict. The hypothesis was that the judges' explanation for disagreement would provide insights into influences upon the jury

---

* "Jury Selection", Saul Lavisky, Letter, *Science,* Vol. 186, p. 302, 25 October 1974. Copyright 1974 by the American Association for the Advancement of Science. (Reprinted by permission).

* Henry J. Friendly, review of *The American Jury,* by Harry Kalven, Jr. and Hans Zeisel, 33 *Univ. of Chicago Law Review* (1966) 884. © 1966 (Reprinted by permission).

decision. The book discussed below, *The American Jury,* is based on those questionnaires.]

The basic data are reports of 3576 criminal jury trials furnished by 555 judges. Attention is focused on 1063 cases, 30% of the total, where the judge would have found otherwise than the jury in some respect. For all but 10% of these disagreements an explanation by the judge was forthcoming. . . .

In 87% of the disagreements the judge would have been more severe than the jury, in 13% the jury more severe than the judge. The disagreements divide into three categories—on guilt [as opposed to innocence], on the charge [or degree of the crime involved], and where the jury hung. Of the cases where the judge was more severe, characterized as "normal" disagreements, 57% were on guilt, 15% were on the charge, and 15% were where the jury hung; of those where the jury was more severe, called "crossovers," 7% were on guilt, 2% were on the charge, and 4% were hung juries. The six categories are then broken down among five major sets of reasons, more than one of which, of course, may exist in any case—sentiments on the law, sentiments on the defendant, evidence factors, facts only the judge knew, and disparity of counsel.

The first roll-call is a resounding triumph for the jury. Evidence factors [differences in weighing specific items of evidence] occurred in 79% of the total disagreements—in these cases the jury was doing precisely the fact finding job it is supposed to do. Next in size come sentiments on the law, present in 50% of the disagreements. The authors proceed from these unweighted ratios to one of their most significant clarifications—a division of disagreements between facts alone, "values" alone, and a combination of "values" and facts. The combination is the winner, 45%, followed by 34% for facts alone and 21% for values alone. This leads to formulation of a "liberation hypothesis"—that the jury gives way to sentiment predominantly when the evidence is in doubt.* "The sentiment gives direction to the resolution of the evidentiary doubt; the evidentiary doubt provides a favorable condition for a response to the sentiment."

One point clearly shown is that in weighing evidence the jury is strongly impressed by a defendant with no criminal record who takes the stand, especially when he has been charged with a serious crime. The figures fail to confirm the supposition that "the jury is differentially skeptical of confessions" or of testimony by an accomplice. As expected, the jury has a somewhat higher threshold of reasonable doubt than the judge, although one cannot determine how far the statistics on this score reflect difference in lay and judicial reaction as compared with the effect of the requirement of unanimity—a factor perhaps not sufficiently taken into account in some of the other analyses. The sympathetic defendant has a significant effect on disagreement, but

* See "The Lecture" p. 327, for precisely this point.

only 19% of defendants are sympathetic, 64% being average and 17% unattractive. Superior defense counsel appears in one of eleven trials and causes normal disagreement once every nine times. . . .

The most fascinating chapters are those which analyze the jury's different views of the law. The jury takes a more liberal attitude toward self-defense, disregarding many of the law's "complex series of restrictions," but often only to the point of reducing the charge rather than acquitting. Somewhat allied to this, it gives weight to the contributory fault of the victim; it does not truly go along with modern law's sharp distinction between crime and tort. A striking example is rape. Although in aggravated rape the jury acquits in only 12% of the cases where the judge convicts, in simple rape the percentage rises to 60%; the jury thinks the woman is in part to blame. So also as to domestic violence if not too violent, and as to the battery which the jury considers a normal incident of overmuch drink. On the other side of the ledger, the jury is likely to take a drastic view of sex offenses on children, finding a higher degree of crime than the judge or occasionally convicting where the judge was not convinced.

The jury applies a principle of *de minimis*. It often refuses to convict not merely for thefts of insignificant amount, but also for such offenses as "the one-punch fight"—as to which its enlarged notion of self-defense and its tort concept are also operative—and in cases where the victim suffers no loss because the crime is detected quickly or displays reluctance to prosecute—both of these again manifesting the criminal jury's affinity for tort equities. More alarmingly, it sometimes will not convict if it thinks the victim was generally "no good"; the unsympathetic victim is a factor for acquittal, or for a lesser charge, just as is the sympathetic defendant. There is a modest list, primarily game and liquor laws, where in many cases the jury simply vetoes the legislature. Sometimes, in disagreement with the more logically minded judge, the jury will acquit or find on a lower charge because it thinks the defendant, in various ways, has already been punished enough or because it regards the threatened punishment as too severe. The jury resents the prosecution's giving a partner in crime, especially a dominant one, soft treatment compared with that proposed for the man before it. Occasionally the jury has taken over what is now increasingly the court's role of protecting against improper police and prosecution practice; it is particularly sensitive to cases where it believes a defendant is being prosecuted *only* because he irritated the police.

As against this long list of instances where the jury tempers the wind to the defendant, there are a few "pro-prosecution equities." I have already mentioned sex offenses against children; another is neglect of them—the American jury loves children. A less attractive instance involves racial factors. A group of cases in which the jury is more severe to an insanity defense than the judge because it doesn't want the accused left free provokes thought in this age when the defense is being liberalized without sufficient provision for civil custody.

· · ·

The book's "single most basic finding is that the jury, despite its autonomy, spins so close to the legal baseline." Rarely does it exercise "the power to bring in a verdict in the teeth of both law and facts." When it does, it generally has some valid reason—often, as the book points out, its verdict would be called for by the law of some other jurisdiction. The jury has indeed completed its slow process of becoming "rationalized" so as to be entitled to be "regarded as a judicial body." It generally uses its freedom to be less "rule-minded" than the judge so as to reach results according with community notions of common sense and decency, and thus of "justice." Yet, for reasons partially indicated above, our applause for the jury's virtuoso performance should not lead us to place undue reliance on it as an agent for keeping the law in touch with reality. While we would probably not like to live in a world in which there was complete congruence between judge and jury determinations in criminal cases, we ought to be able to reduce the divergence.

Comment

As we have seen, the jury has an absolute right to acquit any defendant it wishes. At least, such a decision by a jury cannot be overturned in any way; nor can the jurors be disciplined for returning a verdict which flies in the face of the evidence and the law. It has been argued that since this is the case, it should be made clear to the jury that they have a right to acquit even though they believe the defendant to be factually guilty. Others have argued that the jury has an absolute right to acquit only because we do not know how to restrict that right and still protect the defendant. They argue that, therefore, we should do nothing to encourage the jury to acquit a defendant whom it thinks is really guilty.

Who is correct?

G. RECOMMENDED READING

Bailey, F. Lee. *The Defense Never Rests.* Stein and Day, New York, 1971.

Bush, Chilton R., ed. *Free Press and Fair Trial: Some Dimensions of the Problem.* University of Georgia Press, Athens, 1971.

Frankel, Sandor. *Beyond a Reasonable Doubt.* Stein and Day, New York, 1971.

Friendly, Alfred and Goldfarb, Ronald L. *Crime and Publicity.* Random House, Inc., Westminister, Md., 1975.

Hans, Valerie P. and Vidmar, Neil. *Judging the Jury.* Plenum, New York, 1986. © 1986. Reprinted by permission.

Jacob, Herbert. *Justice in America.* Little, Brown, Boston, 3d ed., 1978.

Kalven, Harry Jr. and Zeisel, H. *The American Jury.* Univ. of Chicago Press (Phoenix Books), Chicago, 1971.

Kaplan, John and Waltz, Jon. R. *The Trial of Jack Ruby.* Macmillan, New York, 1965.

Phillips, Steven. *No Heroes, No Villains.* Random House, New York, 1977.

Simon, Rita James. *The Jury: Its Role in American Society.* Lexington Books, Lexington, Mass., 1979.

Weinreb, Lloyd. *Denial of Justice: Criminal Process in the United States.* Free Press, New York, 1977.

Wellman, Francis L. *The Art of Cross-Examination.* The MacMillan Co., First Collier Books Edition, New York, 1962.

Williams, Glanville. *The Proof of Guilt.* Stevens & Sons, Ltd., London, 1955.

Chapter IX

THE GUILTY PLEA

A. INTRODUCTION

1. THE IMPORTANCE OF THE GUILTY PLEA *

"It is an elementary fact, historically and statistically, that the system of courts—the number of judges, prosecutors, and of courtrooms—has been based on the premise that approximately 90 per cent of all defendants will plead guilty, leaving only 10 per cent, more or less, to be tried.

"The consequences of what might seem on its face a small percentage change in the rate of guilty pleas can be tremendous. A reduction from 90 per cent to 80 per cent in guilty pleas requires the assignment of twice the judicial manpower and facilities—judges, court reporters, bailiffs, clerks, jurors and courtrooms. A reduction to 70 per cent trebles this demand."

Comment and Question

It appears that negotiated settlements are even more common in civil cases than in criminal cases. Up to 98 per cent of all automobile accident cases, and probably even a higher percentage of contract disputes, are settled without trial. Despite this, there has been no outcry against the settlement of civil cases between the parties. Are there any reasons why we should worry more about the settlement of criminal cases via a negotiated guilty plea?

2. THE HISTORY OF THE PLEA BARGAINING SYSTEM

a. ITS RECENCY **

During most of the history of the common law, pleas of guilty were actively discouraged by English and American courts. For centuries, litigation was thought "the safest test of justice." The past one hundred years have, however, seen a revolution in methods of criminal procedure. Today, roughly ninety per cent of all defendants convicted of crime in both state and federal courts plead guilty rather than

---

* Chief Justice Warren Burger, "Address at the American Bar Association Annual Convention," *New York Times,* 11 August 1970, p. 24, Col. 4. © 1970 (Reprinted by permission).

** Albert W. Alschuler, "The Prosecutor's Role in Plea Bargaining", *University of Chicago Law Review,* Vol. 36 (1968), p. 50. © 1968 (Reprinted by permission).

exercise their right to stand trial before a court or jury. Behind this statistic lies the widespread practice of plea bargaining—the exchange of prosecutorial and judicial concessions for pleas of guilty.

The guilty-plea system has grown largely as a product of circumstance, not choice. The volume of crime has increased in recent decades, and the criminal law has come to regulate areas of human activity that were formerly beyond its scope. At the same time, the length of the average felony trial has substantially increased, and a constitutional revolution led by the United States Supreme Court has diverted a major share of judicial and prosecutorial resources from the trial of criminal cases to the resolution of pre-trial motions and post-conviction proceedings. These developments have led in a single direction; there is today an administrative crisis of major proportions in our criminal courts.

In many cities, the criminal caseload has doubled within the past decade, while the size of the criminal bench has remained constant. . . . Only the guilty-plea system has enabled the courts to process their caseloads with seriously inadequate resources. The invisible hand of Adam Smith is at work. Growing concessions to guilty-plea defendants have almost matched the growing need to avoid the burdensome business of trying cases.

As recently as the 1920's, the legal profession was largely united in its opposition to plea bargaining. As America's dependency on pleas of guilty increased, however, attitudes changed. The American Bar Association and the President's Commission on Law Enforcement and the Administration of Justice are among the prestigious observers who have given plea bargaining the remarkably good press that it enjoys today. Most of these observers recognize that the guilty-plea system is in need of reform, but the legal profession now seems as united in its defense of plea negotiation as it was united in opposition less than a half-century ago.

Questions and Comment

Is there anything wrong with the settlement of a case between the prosecutor and the defendant, based upon the litigative probabilities in the case? Certainly in a civil case—say a simple automobile accident—where the damages amount to approximately $100,000, but negligence by the defendant driver is only 50 per cent likely, it is not unreasonable that the plaintiff and the defendant might want to compromise the case for around $50,000. The plaintiff might have good reason for not wishing to gamble and hence might much prefer $50,000 to a 50 per cent chance of $100,000.

Is there any reason why a similar motive should not also exist in the criminal system? Assume a case where the defendant and his attorney decide that the prosecutor has a 75 per cent chance of convicting the defendant (regardless of his factual guilt—if that ever could be known) for armed robbery—for which the maximum sentence is 30 years. Assume further that the prosecutor is willing to accept a plea of guilty to the lesser offense of larceny, for which the maximum sentence is five years. The criminal defendant, like the auto accident plaintiff, might simply not wish to gamble.

If defendants and prosecutors really do wish to minimize the uncertainty in their litigation, is there anything wrong with this? Even if there were something wrong with it, what, as a practical matter, could the court do? Remember that the prosecutor and the defense attorney typically know far more about the facts of the case than does the judge.

b. TRIALS BEFORE THE DEVELOPMENT OF PLEA BARGAINING *

The main historical explanation for the want of plea bargaining in former centuries is, I believe, simple and incontrovertible. When we turn back to the period before the middle of the eighteenth century, we find that common law trial procedure exhibited a degree of efficiency that we now expect only of our nontrial procedure. *Jury trial was a summary proceeding.* Over the intervening two centuries the rise of the adversary system and the related development of the law of evidence has caused common law jury trial to undergo a profound transformation, robbing it of the wondrous efficiency that had characterized it for so many centuries.

The initial point to grasp, and then to explain, is how rapidly jury trials were conducted. The surviving sources show that well into the eighteenth century when the Old Bailey sat, it tried between twelve and twenty felony cases per day, and provincial assizes operated with similar dispatch. Indeed, it was not until 1794 that a trial "ever lasted for more than one day, and [in that case] the court seriously considered whether it had any power to adjourn . . .."

How could the Old Bailey of the 1730s process a dozen and more cases to full jury trial in one day, whereas in modern times the average jury trial requires several days of court time?

(1) The most important factor that expedited jury trial was the want of counsel. Neither prosecution nor defense was represented in ordinary criminal trials. The accused was forbidden counsel; the prosecution might be conducted by a lawyer, but in practice virtually never was. The victim or other complaining witness, sometimes aided by the lay constable and the lay justice of the peace, performed the role we now assign to the public prosecutor, gathering evidence and presenting it at trial. As a result, jury trial was not yet protracted by the motions, maneuvers, and speeches of counsel that afflict the modern trial.

* John H. Langbein, "Understanding the Short History of Plea Bargaining," 13 *Law* *and Society Review,* 1979, pp. 262–265. © 1979 (Reprinted by permission).

(2) There was, for example, no voir dire of prospective jurors conducted by counsel. In practice the accused took the jury as he found it and virtually never employed his challenge rights. Indeed, at the Old Bailey only two twelve-man jury panels were used to discharge the entire caseload of as many as a hundred felony trials in a few days. Each jury usually heard several unrelated cases before deliberating on any. Often the juries rendered verdicts in these cases of life and death "at the bar," that is, so rapidly that they did not even retire from the courtroom to deliberate.

(3) The most efficient testimonial resource available to a criminal court is almost always the criminal defendant. He has, after all, been close enough to the events to get himself prosecuted. In modern Anglo-American procedure we have constructed the privilege against self-incrimination in a way that often encourages the accused to rely entirely upon the intermediation of counsel and say nothing in his own defense. But in the period before the accused had counsel, there could be no practical distinction between his roles as defender and as witness. The accused spoke continuously at the trial, replying to prosecution witnesses and giving his own version of the events.

(4) The presentation of evidence and the cross-examination of witnesses and accused took place in a fashion that was businesslike but lacked the time-consuming stiffness of a modern adversary trial, which has strict rules of sequence and phase preclusion. The trial judge superintended this "altercation" of witnesses and accused, occasionally examining or cross-examining, and he exercised a broad power of comment upon the evidence.

(5) The common law of evidence, which has injected such vast complexity into modern criminal trials, was virtually nonexistent as late as the opening decades of the eighteenth century. The trial judge had an alternative system of jury control that was both swifter and surer than the subsequent resort to rules of admissibility and exclusion. He had unrestricted powers of comment on the merits of criminal cases; he could reject a verdict that displeased him and require the jury to deliberate further; indeed, until 1670 he could fine a jury that persisted in acquitting against his wishes.

(6) In an age before professional police and prosecutors, the problems of controlling such officers and protecting the accused from abuse of their powers lay wholly in the future. The remarkable American exercise of attempting to substitute exclusionary rules of evidence for a direct system of discipline was not yet operating to protract the criminal process.

(7) Finally, there was as yet virtually no appeal in criminal cases.[1] Accordingly, the familiar modern machinations of counsel directed to provoking and preserving error for appeal were unknown.

1. This explains, in part, the prominence of the pardon as an alternative scheme of review.

It should surprise no one that in a system of trial as rough and rapid as this there was no particular pressure to develop nontrial procedure, or otherwise to encourage the accused to waive his right to jury trial. Indeed, the sources reveal an opposite pressure, which we find confirmed by Sir Matthew Hale, a trial judge of long experience, in his *Pleas of the Crown,* written in 1670. He reports that "it is usual" for the judge to discourage an accused from pleading guilty, and "to advise the party to plead [not guilty] and put himself upon his trial . . . ." (1736:225).

We should also not be surprised that this summary form of jury trial perished over the last two centuries. The level of safeguard against mistaken conviction was in several respects below what civilized peoples now require. The hard question, which remains unresearched, is why the pressure for greater safeguards led in the Anglo-American procedure to the common law of evidence and dominance of the trial by lawyers, reforms that ultimately destroyed the system in the sense that they rendered trials unworkable as an ordinary or routine dispositive procedure for cases of serious crime. Similar pressures for safeguard were being felt in the Continental legal systems in the same period, but they led to reforms in nonadversarial procedure that preserved the institution of trial.

B. THE PLEA BARGAIN

1. THE PROSECUTION

a. THE PROSECUTOR'S ROLE IN PLEA BARGAINING *

Variations in the Offers to Guilty-Plea Defendants: The Prosecutor's Basic Motives in Granting Concessions.

When a prosecutor grants concessions in exchange for a plea of guilty, he may be acting in any—or all—of several different roles. First, the prosecutor may be acting as an administrator. His goal may be to dispose of each case in the fastest, most efficient manner in the interest of getting his and the court's work done.

Second, the prosecutor may be acting as an advocate. His goal may be to maximize both the number of convictions and the severity of the sentences that are imposed after conviction. In this role, the prosecutor must estimate the sentence that seems likely after a conviction at trial, discount this sentence by the possibility of an acquittal, and balance the "discounted trial sentence" against the sentence he can insure through a plea agreement. Were a prosecutor to adopt this role to the exclusion of all others, he would accept a plea agreement only when its assurance of conviction outweighed the loss in sentence severity it might entail.

* Albert W. Alschuler, "The Prosecutor's Role in Plea Bargaining," 36 *Univ. of* *Chicago L.Rev.,* (1968) pp. 52–65. ©1968 (Reprinted by permission).

Third, the prosecutor may act as a judge. His goal may be to do the "right thing" for the defendant in view of the defendant's social circumstances or in view of the peculiar circumstances of his crime— with the qualification, of course, that the "right thing" will not be done unless the defendant pleads guilty.

Fourth, the prosecutor may act as a legislator. He may grant concessions because the law is "too harsh," not only for this defendant but for all defendants.

In all of these roles except the last, the prosecutor must determine on a case-by-case basis the concessions that he will offer to guilty-plea defendants; moreover, the importance of each role may vary from one case to the next. For these reasons, "routine" plea agreements are rare. In practice, the benefits of a guilty plea are personalized for each defendant. Indeed, the prosecutorial functions just enumerated suggest only a few of the variables that may affect the sentence differential between guilty-plea and trial defendants in particular cases. Other variables—such as the personal relationship between the prosecutor and the defense attorney, the attitudes of police officers involved in the case, the race of the defendant, and the desires of the victim—are less directly related to the basic goals of the guilty plea process. . . .

Administrative considerations are not simply a background factor equally applicable to every case. Their importance varies, for example, with the length of time a case may require at trial. A Boston attorney recalls a pair of cases that illustrate the point. The first was a simple case that the attorney ultimately tried in less than half a day. When the attorney approached the trial judge in an effort to work out a plea agreement in this case, the judge rebuffed him sharply. "This is not the shopping center, counsel," he said. A month later, the attorney came before the same judge in a case that seemed likely to require a three-week trial. Without a word from either of the attorneys, the judge called them to the bench and said earnestly, "Gentlemen, have you considered a plea in this case?"

. . .

Because calendar considerations are so important a part of the plea-bargaining process, defense attorneys commonly devise strategies whose only utility lies in the threat they pose to the court's and the prosecutor's time. A midwestern prosecutor observes, "All any lawyer has to do to get a reduced charge is to demand a jury trial." It is therefore entirely routine for defense attorneys to file jury demands when they have no desire for trials of any kind. Attorneys commonly go to the point of empanelling a jury in an effort to make their threat to the court's time credible. A string of pre-trial continuances may also be useful, partly because each continuance consumes the court's time.

Pre-trial motions rank with jury demands as the most valuable of the defense attorneys' time-consuming strategies. These motions have their greatest impact in jurisdictions where it is the practice of prosecutors to prepare written briefs in response to procedural and constitutional claims. "It doesn't matter whether the motion has any merit," a San Francisco attorney explains. "Prosecutors naturally want to avoid doing what they are paid to do." A Boston defense attorney reports that he invents some procedural claim in every case. "It takes time to refute even a bad contention," he observes. "Every motion added to the pile helps to secure a better plea."

San Francisco's Chief Assistant District Attorney, Francis W. Mayer, reports that fifteen years ago nothing of importance occurred in most criminal cases until they were tried. "Today," he says, "there are defense attorneys who have never heard of trial. If the case ever gets that far, these attorneys have nothing to do. The usual defense strategy today is to bring in a stack of motions as thick as a Sunday newspaper; defense attorneys hope that we won't have the patience to ride them out. There are, in fact, cases in which that hope may be justified. Sometimes, for example, we know that the defendant will not be sentenced to the state prison even if we spend hours in the courtroom knocking down whatever the other side throws at us. Defense attorneys use the fact that we have to move the unimportant cases as quickly as possible—it's an effective way of doing their job."

Trial strategies, too, may influence the concessions that guilty-plea defendants receive. Houston defense attorney Clyde W. Woody once represented a Negro who had murdered another Negro by shooting him between the eyes. Plea negotiation had broken down. Woody wanted a five-year suspended sentence, but the prosecutor insisted on five years' "hard time." The case came to trial, and the assistant district attorney asked that all witnesses in the case be excluded from the courtroom. Twenty-five defense witnesses stood up and walked slowly toward the exit. The assistant watched them for a moment. Then he came to Woody and said, "That 'five years' suspended' begins to look pretty good." . . . [P]rosecutors are virtually unanimous in their emphasis on another factor that commonly affects negotiation decisions. The overwhelming majority of prosecutors view the strength or weakness of the state's case as the most important factor in the task of bargaining.

When the *University of Pennsylvania Law Review* asked a group of chief prosecuting officials from various states to indicate the considerations that motivated their bargaining decisions, only 27 per cent said that sympathy for the defendant was a relevant factor. Only 32 per cent said that the harshness of the law affected their decisions; and only 37 per cent said that the volume of work was significant. The most frequently listed consideration was the strength of the state's case, and 85 per cent of the prosecutors noted its importance. . . .

[T]he practice of bargaining hardest * when the case is weakest leads to grossly disparate treatment for identical offenders—assuming, for the moment, that they are offenders. Chicago defense attorney J.

* By "bargaining hardest" Professor Alschuler does not mean driving the hardest bargain. Rather he means offering the best bargain to the defendant.

Eugene Pincham comments, "When a prosecutor has a dead-bang case, he is likely to come up with an impossible offer like thirty to fifty years. When the case has a hole in it, however, the prosecutor may scale the offer all the way down to probation. The prosecutors' goal is to get something from every defendant, and the correctional treatment the defendant may require is the last thing on their minds." . . .

Despite the prosecutors' earnest efforts to compromise weak cases, the offer of a favorable sentence is sometimes resisted. Houston prosecutor Sam H. Robertson, Jr. recalls a murder case in which the problems of proof were so substantial that the defendant was offered a five-year sentence. When the defendant rejected this offer, the prosecutor overcame his problems of proof. The defendant was sentenced to a term of thirty-five years' imprisonment. San Francisco defense attorney James Martin MacInnis recalls another "weak" murder case in which the defendant rejected a plea to voluntary manslaughter. He was ultimately put to death in the gas chamber.*

When prosecutors respond to a likelihood of acquittal by magnifying the pressures to plead guilty, they seem to exhibit a remarkable disregard for the danger of false conviction. This apparent disregard is not easy to explain. It might be supposed that when a prosecutor decides to charge a defendant with a crime, he makes a personal judgment concerning the defendant's guilt or innocence. Once the charge decision has been made, the prosecutor may regard trial as a technical obstacle standing between the defendant and the punishment he deserves. To a prosecutor who entertains no doubt of a defendant's guilt, "the best he can get" will usually seem good enough, . . .

A prosecutor's personal opinion seems, in any event, an inadequate safeguard against conviction of the innocent. If trials ever serve a purpose, their utility is presumably greatest when the outcome is in doubt. The practice of responding to a weak case by offering extraordinary concessions therefore represents, at best, a dangerous allocation of institutional responsibility. And when even the minimal safeguard of a prosecutorial judgment of guilt is lacking, as it is in a significant number of cases today, the horrors of the guilty-plea system are multiplied.

The ultimate in a weak case is no case at all, and in this situation plea negotiation commonly becomes a game of bluffing. A typical situation is that in which a critical witness has died, refused to testify,

---

* MacInnis recalls that one of the few pieces of evidence against the defendant was a purported suicide note from one of the two victims of the crime. Handwriting experts could not prove that the note was a forgery, but it contained a curious grammatical error "I am grateful to you, Bart, grateful to what you have done for me." Experts suggested that this sort of error was characteristic of Filipinos, and the defendant was the only Filipino who had been closely associated with the victims.

The defendant's difficulties were aggravated when he asked the court to discharge his appointed attorneys late in his trial. He explained to the judge that his grievance was not personal: "I am grateful to them, grateful to what they have done for me." A mistrial was declared; but by the time of the second trial, the state was able to present a more persuasive case than it had initially.

or disappeared into the faceless city. If a prosecutor hopes to extract a plea of guilty in this situation, he must exude limitless confidence in his ultimate success and keep the defense attorney unaware of the fatal defect in his case.

Sometimes the game is unsuccessful. A Chicago defense attorney says, "There are cases in which I know they can't find their fink— because I know where he is, if you know what I mean." A San Francisco attorney reports that he has sometimes received telephone calls from prostitutes after he had been retained to represent their pimps. "The D.A. bribed me to make a statement," the prostitutes say, "but don't worry. I'm in Las Vegas now."

Moreover, prosecutors may sometimes be inept at bluffing. A Los Angeles defense attorney recalls one negotiating session in which he spotted a written authorization to dismiss the case, signed by the trial assistant's superior. The assistant had foolishly left this paper uncovered in his open briefcase. Oakland's Public Defender, John D. Nunes, says that a defense attorney can usually detect a bluff from the unusually generous character of the prosecutor's offer. And a Pittsburgh public defender refers to "one asinine D.A. in particular. Whenever he wants to talk about a guilty plea, we *know* we should go to trial."

Questions

What is the alternative to entrusting the prosecutor with the right to offer a plea bargain to the defense?

Many persons say they find the system of plea bargaining offensive. If it offends you, can you put your finger on what it is that you find offensive?

Should it be ethical for the prosecutor to "bluff" in plea bargaining?

b. THE PROBLEM OF OVERCHARGING *

Before a prosecutor can reduce the charge against a defendant in exchange for a plea of guilty, he—or someone else—must have formulated the initial charge. The charge is the asking price in plea bargaining, and the drafting of accusations is therefore an integral part of the negotiating process. . . .

The attorneys observe, however, that fifty charges are not usually filed against a single defendant because the prosecutor is interested in securing fifty convictions. The charges may be filed instead in an effort to induce the defendant to plead guilty to a few of the charges, in exchange for dismissal of the rest. A Boston defense attorney says,

"Prosecutors throw everything into an indictment they can think of, down to and including spitting on the sidewalk. They

* Albert W. Alschuler, "The Prosecutor's Role in Plea Bargaining," 36 *Univ. of Chi-* *cago L.Rev.*, (1968) pp. 85–105. ©1968 (Reprinted by permission).

then permit the defendant to plead guilty to one or two offenses, and he is supposed to think it's a victory." . . .

There are two major types of horizontal overcharging. First, a defendant may be charged with a separate offense for every criminal transaction in which he has allegedly participated. When an embezzler has made false entries in his employer's books over a long period of time, for example, it is not difficult for a prosecutor to prepare a fifty-or one-hundred-count indictment. And when a first-offender has passed a dozen bad checks, a prosecutor may file a dozen separate accusations. . . .

Second, prosecutors may fragment a single criminal transaction into numerous component offenses. In Cleveland, "bad check artists" are usually charged, not only with one, but with three separate offenses for each check: forgery, uttering, and obtaining property by false pretenses. In Boston, the pattern is the same, except that a fourth offense is occasionally added; the defendant may also be charged as a "common and notorious thief." . . .

Vincent J. Ziccardi, the First Assistant Public Defender in Philadelphia, once represented a defendant charged with burglary, rape, statutory rape, robbery, and larceny—all for a single transaction with a single victim. The defendant ultimately pleaded guilty to the single crime of statutory rape. . . .

Vertical overcharging, like horizontal overcharging, usually follows a fairly uniform pattern. Defense attorneys in various jurisdictions complain that prosecutors charge robbery when they should charge larceny from the person, that they charge grand theft when they should charge petty theft, that they charge assault with intent to commit murder when they should charge some form of battery, and that they charge the larceny of an automobile when they should charge "joyriding," a less serious offense that does not involve an intention to deprive the car owner permanently of his property. In general, defense attorneys in some cities say that prosecutors charge "the first degree of everything" but accept a guilty plea to "the second degree of any crime" without serious negotiation. . . .

In a sense, overcharging and subsequent charge-reduction are often the components of an elaborate sham, staged for the benefit of defense attorneys. The process commonly has little or no effect on the defendant's sentence, and prosecutors may simply wish to give defense attorneys a "selling point" in their efforts to induce defendants to plead guilty. John W. Miner, a Los Angeles prosecutor, observes: "The number of counts is far less significant in the bargaining session between the prosecutor and the defense attorney than it is in the bargaining session between the defense attorney and his client. Our office usually reduces the number of charges without serious negotiation, because we know that this action will not affect the amount of time the defendant has to serve. But a defense attorney can justify his fee by saying, 'Look, Mr. Defendant, there were four felony charges against you, and I persuaded the prosecutor to go all the way down to one. Now that I've gotten you this special break, please don't blow it.' "

.   .   .

Prosecutors commonly maintain that a reduction in the "level" of a charge, like a reduction in the number of accusations, rarely affects the defendant's sentence. Other observers dispute this contention. A judge may, of course, have the power to impose the same sentence on a reduced charge that he would have imposed had the defendant been convicted of a greater offense, but the existence of this power offers no guarantee that it will be exercised. Charge reduction does occur, and seems relatively unimportant, in jurisdictions where bargaining focuses directly on the defendant's sentence. In jurisdictions like Manhattan, however, where bargaining concerns the level of the charge rather than the prosecutor's sentence recommendation, certain customary sentences seem to be associated with every offense. A judge may even remark from the bench, "Because the prosecutor has chosen to treat this offense as the attempted possession of dangerous drugs in the fourth degree, the sentence will be only six months. Personally, however, I think the defendant deserves a longer term."

Prosecutors, of course, are anxious to discount the effect of charge reduction on sentencing; they want to avoid any suggestion that plea negotiation leads to undue leniency for offenders. Nevertheless, the common contention that charge reduction does not affect the defendant's sentence merely places prosecutors on the opposite horn of a dilemma, for it amounts to a claim that prosecutors dupe defendants [into pleading guilty].

Somewhat analogous to the practice of overcharging is the practice of "overrecommending." In jurisdictions where bargaining focuses on the prosecutors' sentence recommendations, it is common for trial assistants to begin negotiations by suggesting sentences more severe than the ones they actually desire. This practice usually poses fewer dangers than the practice of overcharging. An unknowledgeable defense attorney may, of course, like a tourist at a Latin American bazaar, yield to a suggestion that was made only for effect; and a prosecutor may feel bound to present his extravagant recommendation—or even a higher one—if the defendant insists on a trial.

Nevertheless, while trial judges sometimes encourage the practice of overcharging, they usually take steps to check the practice of overrecommending. Consistently high sentence recommendations may force a judge to assume responsibility for the leniency necessary to induce pleas of guilty, and judges prefer to receive "reasonable" recommendations in every case. When a judge can simply follow a prosecutor's suggestions, public responsibility for sentencing, as a practical matter, is shifted from the courts; no one expects a trial judge to be more severe than the prosecutor.

Questions and Comment

Is it right for prosecutors to charge defendants with very serious crimes, regardless of whether they think that they can prove their cases? Does it matter that the purpose of this is to get defendants to plead guilty to lesser crimes of which they are guilty?

Another facet of the overcharging problem is that prosecutors lobby legislatures to press for statutes which provide the possibility of unrealistically high sentences. Does it matter that, in fact, they do not expect to have these sentences imposed, but rather wish only to use them as threats in the plea bargaining process?

c. THE PROSECUTOR'S BARGAINING POSITION *

Several factors enhance the prosecutor's bargaining position when the defendant is in custody. If the prosecutor believes that the defendant has already been incarcerated for a sufficient period of time and is willing to recommend a "time-in" sentence, the defendant will invariably agree to plead guilty to obtain immediate freedom. Even if the prosecutor does not agree to a "time-in" sentence, an incarcerated defendant, frightened and demoralized by the prospect of an indefinite period of confinement, may be willing to enter a plea and accept a fixed period of imprisonment. Finally, in a "jail room" case, the prosecutor deals almost exclusively with an assistant voluntary defender. Because the defender will probably work with the prosecutor again and will be interested in maintaining a good relationship, he may often be highly receptive to guilty plea negotiations.

The prosecutor's bargaining position is weaker if the defendant is free on bail and he must make substantially greater concessions to induce a guilty plea. Bailed defendants will naturally be reluctant to enter a plea which will result in loss of freedom. Unlike the defendant in prison, the bailed defendant can only profit by postponement of his case. Over time, evidence may disappear, memories may fade, and the defendant may be able to build a record of good behavior to help him at sentencing. Furthermore, a bailed defendant is likely to be represented by a private attorney who deals infrequently with the prosecutor. The private attorney will thus have little incentive to develop a good working relationship with the assistant prosecutor and can concentrate on obtaining the best possible result for his client.

The Trial Prosecutor's Unchecked Discretion

Professor Davis has discussed the problems likely to arise when an administrative agency's powers are not properly defined and controlled. In the present situation, these problems are magnified because each individual trial prosecutor is free to apply plea bargaining policies he considers appropriate and to change these policies from case to case:

* Walsh S. White, "A Proposal for Reform of the Plea Bargaining Process," 119 *University of Pennsylvania Law Review,* (1970) 444–451. © 1970 (Reprinted with permission).

the potential for arbitrariness and inequality of treatment is indeed great.

The low visibility of the present plea bargaining system also creates problems for the prosecutor's office. Plea bargaining should be employed in a manner calculated to maximize the efficient use of available trial resources. The absence of enforceable bargaining standards, however, enables individual prosecutors to reject or accept guilty plea arrangements for reasons unrelated to considerations of office efficiency. The prosecutor's personal desire to try a case may preclude entry of a guilty plea in an otherwise appropriate situation. Conversely, the prosecutor's need to protect his litigation record may lead to unwise acceptance of pleas.

The prosecutor's unrestrained discretion may also reinforce his tendency to take advantage of the relatively ineffective bargaining position of defendants unable to make bail. This practice plays a significant part in perpetuating inequality between the rich and the poor in the criminal process. The jailed defendant, because he is often unable to prepare his defense adequately, may plead guilty in exchange for minor prosecutorial concessions. In addition, as Professor Foote has observed: "It is plausible, at least, that denial of pretrial liberty provides a psychological inducement to plead guilty which would be absent if the defendant were at liberty pending trial." Our commitment to the principle of equal treatment for poor criminal defendants, . . . is subverted when prosecutors take advantage of the jailed defendant's vulnerable position in conducting plea negotiations.

Questions and Comment

Is it not clear that prosecutors have many reasons for accepting guilty pleas? Should we worry then that they will not make good enough deals, and will allow defendants to plead guilty to crimes that are not serious enough, and which result in sentences that are not harsh enough?

But in fact do we really have to worry that prosecutors will make unrealistically soft plea bargains? Are they known for being soft? How might this concern be affected by resources available to the prosecutor's office? The court?

If it is impossible for prosecutors to try a sizable portion of the cases they bring, making deals which do not sufficiently protect the public may be their only alternative to a complete breakdown in operations. In this case the low visibility of the guilty plea may make it difficult to prove that the public is not being sufficiently protected.

2. THE DEFENSE

a. THE DEFENDANT IN CUSTODY *

Ralph and Fred are both 19–year old Black men, residents of the Western Addition and both unemployed, although Fred is a part-time student at City College. One night about 11 P.M. they are waiting for a bus on Geary Street. Because the wind is blowing, they stand in the doorway of a small shop, closed for the night. A police squad car pulls up at the curb, two officers get out to make an investigation, and after some discussion, arrest Fred and Ralph for loitering, trespass, and failure to identify themselves and take them to City Prison at the Hall of Justice. Fred makes a phone call to his family and is told they have no money for bail. The two then spend the night in a cell with 15 to 20 other men.

The next morning, after a breakfast of coffee and mush, they are taken downstairs and placed in a cell adjacent to one of the general Municipal Courts. There are, again, 15 to 20 other men in the cell with them. One man, who is obviously going through heroin withdrawal, gets sick and vomits. Three other men are dressed up as women and look strange because their beards are beginning to show. One other man sits in the corner talking to himself.

At about 9 o'clock, a Deputy Public Defender enters the cell and explains to all the defendants that he will be appointed as their attorney. He also tells them that he will try to get each of them released on O.R. (Own Recognizance) if he can, and he tells them that they have a right to a jury trial. He then interviews each of the defendants briefly, except for the defendant who is sitting in the corner and who cannot talk to him.

Fred and Ralph quickly tell him their story and also protest that they have not done anything wrong. The Public Defender asks them if they can make bail, and they tell him they cannot. Close to 10 o'clock, the attorney leaves the cell and Court convenes. As the case of each defendant is called, he goes into the courtroom before the Judge. Over 70% of these defendants will have their cases dismissed entirely, or will enter guilty pleas, at this first appearance.

When Fred's and Ralph's case is called, they are led out of the cell and into the courtroom. The Public Defender meets them near the attorney's table. He tells them that he has checked the police report and their rap sheet, "Look, I don't think that you guys did anything either, but I can't get you O.R.," he says. "I know this Judge, and he refuses to O.R. anybody with a prior record." Fred and Ralph each have one prior misdemeanor conviction. "I'll talk to the D.A. about dismissing your case, but I can't promise you anything." At this point, the Judge asks if the case is ready, and the Public Defender asks that it

* San Francisco Committee on Crime, "A Report on the San Francisco Public De-   fender's Office" (1970) pp. 7–11. © 1970 (Reprinted by permission).

be passed until after the recess. Fred and Ralph are taken back to the cell.

During the recess, the Public Defender again enters the cell. He tells the defendants that he has talked with the D.A. and that the D.A. will not dismiss the case. However, the D.A. will recommend a 30–day suspended sentence, and probation to the court, in exchange for a guilty plea. Fred and Ralph both ask the Public Defender about going to trial. He tells them that he can get them a trial before a judge in about 10 days, but that they will have to wait for about 20 to 30 days for a jury trial. Fred and Ralph figure out for themselves that they will be in jail during this time. They discuss the problem and decide to take the D.A.'s offer on a guilty plea. The Public Defender again tells them that they have a right to go to trial and that the Public Defender's Office will raise all possible defenses, but they both insist on entering a guilty plea to get out of jail.

After the recess, Court again convenes and their case is again called. They step up to a lectern in front of the Judge, escorted by the Public Defender. The Judge asks them how they plead, and, after a glance at the Public Defender, who nods to them, they each say, "Guilty." The Judge asks them if their plea is "voluntary," and after another glance and another nod, they each reply that it is. The District Attorney then moves to dismiss two of the charges and recommends a 30–day suspended sentence to the Court. The Court accepts the recommendation, puts each of them on probation to the Court (which means that they are not subject to the supervision of the Probation Department) and makes an oral order finding them guilty on the loitering charge. The whole process takes about three minutes.

After picking up their personal belongings in the basement of the Hall of Justice, Fred and Ralph go home.

Questions and Comment

Was the problem faced by Fred and Ralph primarily attributable to any defect in the institution of the guilty plea? Is not the bail system primarily to blame here? On the other hand, the institution of the guilty plea makes it much more difficult to see the true costs of the bail system in such cases. If no guilty plea had been permitted, then Ralph and Fred presumably would have waited in jail for between ten and thirty days before they were tried. If they then were acquitted, the hardship visited upon them by the bail system would be visible to all— as would perhaps the police error. As it happened, however, Fred and Ralph were forced falsely to acknowledge their guilt, and, as a result, the rest of society has no way of becoming aware of the defects in the criminal system.

Can the bail situation and the unhappy result in the case of Fred and Ralph be blamed on the public defender?

Should it be blamed on the district attorney, who refused to dismiss the case? Or should it be blamed on the judge who refused to allow the release on his own recognizance of anyone who had a prior record?

b. THE ROLE OF THE DEFENSE ATTORNEY *

Prosecutors, of course, are not alone in bluffing. "We do it too," says Houston defense attorney Percy Foreman. "Bluffing is an inherent part of any sort of negotiation. Settling cases is a game, like basketball. The only difference is that there are no rules in plea bargaining. Something comes to you, and you try it."

A Boston defense attorney reports a case that illustrates Foreman's thesis. The defendant was charged with manslaughter, and she told a convincing story of self-defense. When the defense attorney investigated the case, however, the story crumbled. Indeed, the attorney realized that if the prosecutor ever got around to talking with his witnesses, he would have a tight, brutal case of first degree murder. The defense attorney therefore sought out the prosecutor and offered to enter a guilty plea in return for probation.

When the prosecutor made a counteroffer, the defense attorney replied, "I'll try it first. I need the practice."

"O.K., try it," the prosecutor said; and the defense attorney walked away with his heart in his throat.

A week later, the defense attorney encountered the prosecutor again and this time the prosecutor was more pliable. He would not recommend probation, but neither would he oppose it. The guilty plea was entered, a pre-sentence report was waived, and the defendant walked home. It is because of cases like this one that Los Angeles defense attorney George L. Vaughn, Jr. describes plea bargaining as "playing Russian roulette with another man's life." . . .

Plea negotiation may thwart the goals of procedural rules in two inconsistent ways, which correspond with two basic, inconsistent approaches that defense attorneys may adopt toward the task of bargaining. Every defense attorney must make a basic strategic judgment concerning the most effective way to win concessions for his clients. Either the attorney can be good—and win concessions because prosecutors fear defeat at trial—or he can be nice—and win concessions because prosecutors are willing to accommodate him in an atmosphere of reciprocity. These two approaches can be combined, but only at the cost of sacrificing some of the benefits of each.

The easier, more comfortable path to success in bargaining lies in cultivating favorable personal relationships with prosecutors and other influential members of the court bureaucracy. When an attorney carries this approach to extremes, he may never advance procedural defenses at all. In the San Francisco Bay area, the plea-negotiation

* Albert W. Alschuler, "The Prosecutor's Role on Plea Bargaining," 36 Univ. of Chi- cago L.Rev. (1968) pp. 67–87 (Reprinted by permission).

process seems to depend on considerations of personal reciprocity to a greater extent than it does elsewhere in the nation. An Oakland defense attorney explains, "I never use the Constitution. I bargain a case on the theory that it's a 'cheap burglary,' or a 'cheap purse-snatching', or a 'cheap whatever.' Sure, I could suddenly start to negotiate by saying, 'Ha, ha! You goofed. You should have given the defendant a warning.' And I'd do fine in that case, but my other clients would pay for this isolated success. The next time the district attorney had his foot on my throat, he'd push too."

Most defense attorneys insist that it is better to be good than to be nice. Some of these attorneys advance every procedural claim that their ingenuity can devise—even claims that lack any chance for success, but which threaten to occupy the court's and the prosecutor's time. Procedural defenses may, indeed, as a class, be more effective than factual defenses in inducing concessions. Legal issues are more likely than claims of innocence to lead to appellate litigation, and appellate litigation increases both the tactical and the administrative problems that prosecutors face.

San Francisco defense attorney Gregory S. Stout observes, "There is a tendency on both sides to walk away from a cloudy point," and in practice most procedural defenses are doubtful. Search and seizure questions, for example, probably constitute the largest single area of procedural litigation at trial. Yet the factual circumstances of search and seizure cases are almost invariably in dispute, and the legal standards by which searches are evaluated are usually less than precise.

Vagaries of judicial personality sometimes contribute to the doubtful character of constitutional defenses. A Houston defense attorney reports that he is quick to sacrifice almost any procedural claim in return for prosecutorial concessions. "Given the attitude of the judges here," he says, "I know that I will have to hit a federal forum before even the simplest constitutional argument will prevail. When I can get something for my client *now*, I take it." The attorney illustrates his contention with a remark that he attributes to a Houston trial judge. "Don't quote that United States Supreme Court opinion to me," the judge is supposed to have said. "It is not the law of Texas until the Court of Criminal Appeals says so."

Comment

A number of studies have indicated that public defenders tend to plead their clients guilty more often than do private attorneys. It has been argued that this indicates that private attorneys are more likely to have their clients' interests at heart than is the bureaucratic public defender's office.

Research also indicates, however, that the clients of public defenders do not do worse in the matter of sentence than the clients of private attorneys, when other variables (such as prior record, type of crime, etc.) are controlled for. Is it possible that, whatever disadvantage the public defenders may labor under, they have one major advantage? Unlike private attorneys, who may have only a few cases in the court, public defenders have a large number. Unless they can be satisfied by prosecutors, they have the power—only to be used, of course, under the most extreme provocation—of completely tying up the court calendar by going to trial on a large number of cases. In some sense prosecutors must "get along" with public defenders in ways that they need not get along with private attorneys.

c. THE DEFENSE ATTORNEY AS A BUREAUCRAT *

Although . . . recently the overzealous role of police and prosecutors in producing pretrial confessions and admissions has achieved a good deal of notoriety, scant attention has been paid to the organizational structure and personnel of the criminal court itself. Indeed, the extremely high conviction rate produced without the features of an adversary trial in our courts would tend to suggest that the "trial" becomes a perfunctory reiteration and validation of the pretrial interrogation and investigation.

The institutional setting of the court defines a role for the defense counsel in a criminal case radically different from the one traditionally depicted. Sociologists and others have focused their attention on the deprivations and social disabilities of such variables as race, ethnicity, and social class as being the source of an accused person's defeat in a criminal court. Largely overlooked is the variable of the court organization itself, which possesses a thrust, purpose, and direction of its own. It is grounded in pragmatic values, bureaucratic priorities, and administrative instruments. These exalt maximum production and the particularistic career designs of organizational incumbents, whose occupational and career commitments tend to generate a set of priorities. These priorities exert a higher claim than the stated ideological goals of "due process of law," and are often inconsistent with them.

Organizational goals and discipline impose a set of demands and conditions of practice on the respective professions in the criminal court, to which they respond by abandoning their ideological and professional commitments to the accused client, in the service of these higher claims of the court organization. All court personnel, including the accused's own lawyer, tend to be coopted to become agent-mediators who help the accused redefine his situation and restructure his perceptions concomitant with a plea of guilty.

Of all the occupational roles in the court the only private individual who is officially recognized as having a special status and concomitant obligations is the lawyer. His legal status is that of "an officer of the court" and he is held to a standard of ethical performance and duty

* Abraham S. Blumberg, "The Practice of Law as Confidence Game: Organizational Cooptation of a Profession," *Law and* *Society Review,* Vol. 1 June, 1967, 115–39. © 1967 (Reprinted by permission).

to his client as well as to the court. This obligation is thought to be far higher than that expected of ordinary individuals occupying the various occupational statuses in the court community. However, lawyers, whether privately retained or of the legal-aid, public defender variety, have close and continuing relations with the prosecuting office and the court itself through discreet relations with the judges via their law secretaries or "confidential" assistants. Indeed, lines of communication, influence and contact with those offices, as well as with the Office of the Clerk of the court, Probation Division, and with the press, are essential to present and prospective requirements of criminal law practice. Similarly, the subtle involvement of the press and other mass media in the court's organizational network is not readily discernible to the casual observer. Accused persons come and go in the court system schema, but the structure and its occupational incumbents remain to carry on their respective career, occupational and organizational enterprises. The individual stridencies, tensions, and conflicts a given accused person's case may present to all the participants are overcome, because the formal and informal relations of all the groups in the court setting require it. The probability of continued future relations and interaction must be preserved at all costs.

This is particularly true of the "lawyer regulars" i.e., those defense lawyers, who by virtue of their continuous appearances in behalf of defendants, tend to represent the bulk of a criminal court's non-indigent case workload, and those lawyers who are not "regulars," appear almost casually in behalf of an occasional client. Some of the "lawyer regulars" are highly visible as one moves about the major urban centers of the nation; their offices line the back streets of the courthouses, at times sharing space with bondsmen. Their political "visibility" in terms of local club house ties, reaching into the judge's chambers and prosecutor's office, are also deemed essential to successful practitioners. Previous research has indicated that the "lawyer regulars" make no effort to conceal their dependence upon police, bondsmen, jail personnel. Nor do they conceal the necessity for maintaining intimate relations with all levels of personnel in the court setting as a means of obtaining, maintaining, and building their practice. These informal relations are the *sine qua non* not only of retaining a practice, but also in the negotiation of pleas and sentences.

The client, then, is a secondary figure in the court system as in certain other bureaucratic settings. He becomes a means to other ends of the organization's incumbents. He may present doubts, contingencies, and pressures which challenge existing informal arrangements or disrupt them; but these tend to be resolved in favor of the continuance of the organization and its relations as before. There is a greater community of interest among all the principal organizational structures and their incumbents than exists elsewhere in other settings. The accused's lawyer has far greater professional, economic, intellectual and other ties to the various elements of the court system than he does to his own client. In short, the court is a closed community. . . .

The hostile attitude toward "outsiders" is in large measure engendered by a defensiveness itself produced by the inherent deficiencies of assembly line justice, so characteristic of our major criminal courts. Intolerably large caseloads of defendants which must be disposed of in an organizational contest of limited resources and personnel, potentially subject the participants in the court community to harsh scrutiny from appellate courts, and other public and private sources of condemnation. As a consequence, an almost irreconcilable conflict is posed in terms of intense pressures to process large numbers of cases on the one hand, and the stringent ideological and legal requirements of "due process of law," on the other hand. A rather tenuous resolution of the dilemma has emerged in the shape of a large variety of bureaucratically ordained and controlled "work crimes," short cuts, deviations, and outright rule violations adopted as court practice in order to meet production norms. Fearfully anticipating criticism on ethical as well as legal grounds, all the significant participants in the court's social structure are bound into an organized system of complicity. This consists of a work arrangement in which the patterned, covert, informal breaches, and evasions of "due process" are institutionalized, but are, nevertheless, denied to exist.

These institutionalized evasions will be found to occur to some degree, in all criminal courts. Their nature, scope and complexity are largely determined by the size of the court, and the character of the community in which it is located, e.g., whether it is a large, urban institution, or a relatively small rural county court. In addition, idiosyncratic, local conditions may contribute to a unique flavor in the character and quality of the criminal law's administration in a particular community. However, in most instances a variety of strategems are employed—some subtle, some crude, in effectively disposing of what are often too large caseloads. A wide variety of coercive devices are employed against an accused-client, couched in a depersonalized, instrumental, bureaucratic version of due process of law, and which are in reality a perfunctory obeisance to the ideology of due process. These include some very explicit pressures which are exerted in some measure by all court personnel, including judges, to plead guilty and avoid trial. In many instances the sanction of a potentially harsh sentence is utilized as the visible alternative to pleading guilty, in the case of recalcitrants.　.　.　.

The defense attorneys, therefore, whether of the legal-aid, public defender variety, or privately retained, although operating in terms of pressures specific to their respective role and organizational obligations, ultimately are concerned with strategies which tend to lead to a plea. It is the rational, impersonal elements involving economies of time, labor, expense and a superior commitment of the defense counsel to these rationalistic values of maximum production of court organization that prevail, in his relationship with a client. The lawyer "regulars" are frequently former staff members of the prosecutor's office and utilize the prestige, know-how and contacts of their former affiliation as part of their stock in trade. Close and continuing relations between the lawyer "regular" and his former colleagues in the prosecutor's office generally overshadow the relationship between the regular and his client. The continuing colleagueship of supposedly adversary counsel rests on real professional and organizational needs of a *quid pro quo*, which goes beyond the limits of an accommodation or *modus vivendi* one might ordinarily expect under the circumstances of an otherwise seemingly adversary relationship. Indeed, the adversary features which are manifest are for the most part muted and exist even in their attenuated form largely for external consumption. The principals, lawyer and assistant district attorney, rely upon one another's cooperation for their continued professional existence, and so the bargaining between them tends usually to be "reasonable" rather than fierce.

.   .   .

The Defense Lawyer as a Double Agent

The lawyer has often been accused of stirring up unnecessary litigation, especially in the field of negligence. He is said to acquire a vested interest in a cause of action or claim which was initially his client's. The strong incentive of possible fee motivates the lawyer to promote litigation which would otherwise never have developed. However, the criminal lawyer develops a vested interest of an entirely different nature in his client's case: to limit its scope and duration rather than do battle. Only in this way can a case be "profitable." Thus, he enlists the aid of relatives not only to assure payment of his fee, but he will also rely on these persons to help him in his agent-mediator role of convincing the accused to plead guilty, and ultimately to help in "cooling out" the accused if necessary.

It is at this point that an accused-defendant may experience his first sense of "betrayal." While he had perhaps perceived the police and prosecutor to be adversaries, or possibly even the judge, the accused is wholly unprepared for his counsel's role performance as an agent-mediator. In the same vein, it is even less likely to occur to an accused that members of his own family or other kin may become agents, albeit at the behest and urging of other agents or mediators, acting on the principle that they are in reality helping an accused negotiate the best possible plea arrangement under the circumstances. Usually, it will be the lawyer who will activate next of kin in this role, his ostensible motive being to arrange for his fee. But soon latent and unstated motives will assert themselves, with entreaties by counsel to the accused's next of kin, to appeal to the accused to "help himself" by pleading.   .   .   .

In effect, in his role as double agent, the criminal lawyer performs an extremely vital and delicate mission for the court organization and the accused. Both principals are anxious to terminate the litigation with a minimum of expense and damage to each other. There is no other personage or role incumbent in the total court structure more strategically located, who by training and in terms of his own requirements, is more ideally suited to do so than the lawyer. In recognition of this, judges will cooperate with attorneys in many important ways. For example, they will adjourn the case of an accused in jail awaiting plea or sentence if the attorney requests such action. While explicitly this may be done for some innocuous and seemingly valid reason, the tacit purpose is that pressure is being applied by the attorney for the collection of his fee, which he knows will probably not be forthcoming if the case is concluded. Judges are aware of this tactic on the part of lawyers, who, by requesting an adjournment, keep an accused incarcerated awhile longer as a not too subtle method of dunning a client for payment. However, the judges will go along with this, on the ground that important ends are being served. Often, the only end served is to protect a lawyer's fee.

The judge will help an accused's lawyer in still another way. He will lend the official aura of his office and courtroom so that a lawyer can stage manage an impression of an "all out" performance for the accused in justification of his fee. The judge and other court personnel will serve as a backdrop for a scene charged with dramatic fire, in which the accused's lawyer makes a stirring appeal in his behalf. With a show of restrained passion, the lawyer will intone the virtues of the accused and recite the social deprivations which have reduced him to his present state. The speech varies somewhat, depending on whether the accused has been convicted after trial or has pleaded guilty. In the main, however, the incongruity, superficiality, and ritualistic character of the total performance is underscored by a visibly impassive, almost bored reaction on the part of the judge and other members of the court retinue.

Afterward, there is a hearty exchange of pleasantries between the lawyer and district attorney, wholly out of context in terms of the supposed adversary nature of the preceding events. The fiery passion in defense of his client is gone, and the lawyers for both sides resume their offstage relations, chatting amiably and perhaps including the judge in their restrained banter. No other aspect of their visible conduct so effectively serves to put even a casual observer on notice, that these individuals have claims upon each other. These seemingly innocuous actions are indicative of continuing organizational and informal relations, which, in their intricacy and depth, range far beyond any priorities or claims a particular defendant may have. . . .

Comment and Questions

There are, as the above excerpt indicates, reasons of their own self interest which might impel defense attorneys to induce their clients to plead guilty. If attorneys get the same fee for going to trial or pleading guilty, the obvious saving of time in the latter course may be financially important to them. Moreover, since the actual reasons why an attorney might choose to advise a guilty plea are extremely difficult to evaluate objectively, there almost certainly are attorneys who sell their clients down the river. Is there any reason to believe that this type of behavior is more common among attorneys than among physicians, who may recommend unnecessary surgery for the financial gain, or among members of a host of other occupational groups who violate the norms of their groups and, indeed, often the law?

Most trial lawyers feel that, in general, more harm is done clients by lawyers who unreasonably refuse to recommend guilty pleas than those who wrongly do so. Remember the two defendants at page 439 in this chapter who did substantially worse after trial than they would have had they pleaded guilty.

Moreover, often criminal lawyers will have an interest in going to trial, even though their clients' interests may be in negotiated settlements. Criminal lawyers who are anxious to gain publicity and attract new clients do not do so by pleading their present clients guilty. Publicity tends to go to the hard fighter in the losing cause more than to the skillful negotiator. In addition, it is a common failing of young defense lawyers to overestimate the strength of their cases and, therefore, more often to choose the more hazardous course of going to trial.

It certainly may be, as the preceding excerpt indicates, that the defense bar has, in a sense, been coopted into the judicial machinery. To that degree, it will make the criminal system look like an administrative, or bureaucratic, method of settling cases rather than the adversary system we usually associate with the criminal process.

Indeed, urban courts reach almost the ultimate in such bureaucratic handling of cases. In some courts one prosecutor and one public defender are assigned to each judge on a semi-permanent basis. Among them, they dispose of 80 per cent of the criminal litigation before that judge. What are the dangers in this type of close work group arrangement?

Does the institution of the guilty plea mean that, in any given case—or over all cases—defendants fare any worse than they would under a situation where both prosecution and defense fight to the bitter end? If not, what disadvantages are there in the process?

d. THE CONVICT'S VIEW OF THE GUILTY PLEA *

After the defendant has been arrested, arraigned, and bond has been set, the stage is set for the crucial activity of the criminal justice system: plea-bargaining. It is, in many ways, a game. There are at least two, perhaps three, "sides," and each possesses resources and goals. The outcome depends largely upon the vigor and skill with which each side exploits its resources.

The vagueness about the number of teams indicates the somewhat anomalous role played by the defendant's attorney. The two obvious sides are the defendant and the prosecution. The lawyer is clearly also

* Jonathan D. Casper, *American Criminal Justice: The Defendant's Perspective* Prentice-Hall, Inc., Englewood Cliffs, N.J., 1972, pp. 77–81. © 1972 (Reprinted by permission).

a crucial participant, but his side in the game is often unclear. In general, if he is a privately retained attorney, he is perceived by the defendant as being on his side; if he is a public defender, he is viewed as a member of the prosecutor's team, or sometimes as a middleman or broker.

Most defendants view the game as one that they cannot, in an absolute sense, "win." It is a game in which they can, should they choose to play and be skillful or lucky, lose less than they would if they failed to play at all. To some extent their ability to play depends upon the prosecutor's willingness to bargain: if the prosecutor refuses to bargain but simply makes an offer and will not budge, then the defendant does not actively bargain; he either acquiesces or goes to trial. This unwillingness appears to occur relatively infrequently. It is most likely to occur when there is strong pressure upon the prosecution to obtain maximum sentences for a particular class of crime: for example, after a notorious case of child rape, the prosecutor may refuse to bargain, for a time, with those charged with sex offenses involving children; after a series of highly publicized drug arrests allegedly involving dealers or pushers, the prosecution may be unwilling, for a time, to engage in reduction of charges from sales to possession, usually a common form of bargain.

But in most cases the defendant will, at some point, be offered a deal—some charge reduction, sentence agreement, or both, in return for a plea of guilty. The prosecutor holds most of the cards in the plea-bargaining game—at least as most defendants see it, for he is viewed as having the power to determine the sentence. Although technically he can only make a recommendation to the judge, his recommendations are usually followed. Occasionally a judge may intervene and impose a higher or lower sentence than is recommended, but usually he will go along. Most defendants believed that the judge is a hidden partner to the agreement; and in many cases the prosecutor does clear the deal with the judge before committing himself to it. Thus, the prosecutor determines the fate of the case: he can dismiss or nolle some or all charges; he can agree to a suspended sentence; he can determine the number of years that the defendant must spend in jail or prison.

Although he is viewed as having this power, he is also perceived to have goals that affect his discretion in its exercise. His major goal, from the defendants' perspective, is to get convictions and turn cases over as quickly as possible. Like the police officer, the prosecutor is viewed as a worker, and his job places constraints upon what he is likely to do in a case. He does not want to go to trial, because this takes time and money.[1] The prosecutor is not viewed as particularly interested in the characteristics of any given defendant or case. The defendants believe that factors such as background, motive, and treat-

---

1. This is clearly a correct perception; the only striking distortion in defendants' perception was that they tended to think that what the prosecutor wanted to avoid was literally the cost of paying the jurors in a trial, rather than the expense in time and manpower of the prosecutor's staff that trials entail.

ment needs are not particularly important in the prosecutor's decisions about what concessions to make. This lack of concern stems, they believe, not from the prosecutor's conscious malevolence, but from the nature of his job. As with their attitude toward policemen, defendants can both resent and sympathize with such behavior.

What resources do defendants possess? The list of potential resources includes money, status, and the credibility that they produce; the ability to demand a trial; fortitude in "waiting them out"; and, often, luck. Most defendants did not possess either of the first two resources in quantities that were of any use. Most could not even afford to hire their own attorney, much less engage investigative resources or make the payoffs that they believe are crucial to success in the legal system. "Money talks" in their view, and any defendant with sufficient resources can buy his way out of almost any trouble. This view was almost unanimous among the men with whom I spoke. When a man mentioned payoffs, he was asked whether he knew of any instance in which this had occurred. A few asserted that they did; the majority simply accepted the premise that everyone has his price. Some defendants were more sophisticated about the power of money: it enables a defendant to make bail and hence wait out the prosecution more effectively; it enables him to hire a good attorney, who will— because he is being paid well—exercise himself vigorously on behalf of his clients. Finally, money, in our society, brings the status which is crucial to one's credibility, both as a witness and in making representations, to prosecutors and judges about future good conduct. Thus, in the defendants' view the crucial resource in the bargaining game is "the big scratch," a resource which they regrettably do not have in great supply.

Defendants lack money and status, but they are not without resources. They still have the ability to demand a trial and to wait "them" out. Demanding a trial is really a bluffer's game: it is a threat and a bargaining counter, but most would be loath to actually go to trial. Thus, the defendant must exploit this resource with great care. He can continue to turn down offers and enter a plea of not guilty and have a trial date set. He may—as two of the men quoted above indicated—get as far as jury selection and perhaps some testimony at his trial. But he wants to avoid having the jury bring in a verdict. Pursuing a strategy of "waiting them out," the defendant can simply refuse offers made to him and have his court appearance continued until a satisfactory deal is offered. The majority of the men interviewed did not have this kind of fortitude. They usually reported rejecting a single offer and then accepting the second one made, which sometimes was identical with the first. Even this strategy sometimes involved fairly long waits, for continuances are often for two weeks, and rejecting an offer could mean a month's delay waiting in jail.

Eventually, whether it took three weeks or three months, the majority of defendants did make a deal and agree to plead guilty. It is crucial to notice that the deal determines the penalty that the offender must pay for his crime. Thus, the decision about what punishment (and "rehabilitation") the defendant receives is not, from his view at least, determined on the basis of characteristics that seem relevant to such a decision: his motives for committing the crime, the nature of the offense and the harm done, his personal history and needs. Rather, it is the product of a kind of game, in which he possesses quite limited resources. Whether he plays the game skillfully and loses less than he might, or whether he plays diffidently or not at all, the outcome is still a matter of the application of resources and power. The prosecutor may, in fact, take account of these individualistic factors in making offers, but the defendants do not see it that way. The deal seems largely determined by systemic factors: how crowded the courts are, whether court officials are highly concerned about a certain kind of crime, personal contacts, or the intervention of luck—the judge or prosecutor had seen a defendant play basketball, or they had misspelled a defendant's name and didn't have his arrest record and realize how extensive it was.

The situation the defendant faces in the period preceding his eventual plea is, in many respects, an extension of his life in the streets. You scuffle around, trying to accumulate a little wealth or power; you con others and are conned by them; you exploit those you can and are exploited by those who are more powerful; you use people for your own ends and are, in turn, used by others. You lie, you cheat, you care little about abstract moral principles. How you make out on the street depends upon what you've got and how you use it. In addition, luck and fate are crucial elements of life in the streets. Often the events that occur are accidental: you come into some money easily; you get burned and lose it. You are to a large extent at the mercy of others and of fate. You try to get what you want, but whether you get it or not often has little to do with your efforts.

These same characteristics seem to the defendants to characterize their experience within the legal system. Their initial arrest is often simply the product of bad luck: they are arrested for an activity that they have been engaging in frequently. Something goes wrong, and they get caught. They then must attempt to make the best of their situation and use the techniques that they already know well in order to attempt to ameliorate their plight. The other participants in the system seem to be doing the same things. They are going about their jobs in fashions that seem to the defendants quite similar to the hypocritical and manipulative ways in which they themselves treat people. And they are probably correct. The attention and care that is paid to the "criminal" after his arrest is quite similar to the attention and care that our society generally pays to its poor and its black; so his belief in the similarity of court and street life is by no means unrealistic.

Questions

Is the convicts' view of the guilty plea one which we wish to encourage? How does it accord with the other materials on plea bargaining between the prosecutor and the defense attorney? Is it possible that the view in the above excerpt differs from that in the excerpt on p. 447 simply because most of the sample of convicts had been represented by the public defender, while most of those interviewed in the earlier excerpt were private attorneys?

Is the convicts' view similar to that in the excerpt on The Defense Attorney as a Bureaucrat on p. 449? Finally, to what extent would you expect an attorney involved in the plea bargaining process to have a very different view of the process from that of a defendant?

e. NOTE ON THE DEFENDANT'S ASSETS IN PLEA BARGAINING

Usually, the only assets defendants have to bargain with are their (usually small) chance of acquittal and their rights to demand trials and hence add to the overcrowding in the courts, and the work of prosecutor's office. Occasionally, however, defendants have more to bargain with.

In the Garrow case (see Chapter VI, p. 341) where the defendant told his lawyers the location of the bodies of two of his victims, the prosecutor alleged that the defense had tried to use this information as a counter in the plea negotiations. According to the prosecutor, one of Garrow's lawyers approached him and offered to reveal the location of the bodies of two of the defendant's other victims in return for accepting a [lesser] plea of manslaughter second-degree" in the case. Garrow's lawyers' version was somewhat different. They said that the authorities had several files on missing girls and that "we told them we might be able to solve some of the open cases if our client got a break." Under either version is this kind of plea bargaining proper?

What about the offer of testimony against another defendant in exchange for a plea bargain? Or cooperation with the authorities to recover stolen property?

Finally consider the following far-fetched hypothetical:

You are the attorney general. You have ultimate responsibility for the prosecution of the vice president of the United States on a tax evasion charge. So far as you can tell, the case is a good one and the chances of acquittal on the facts are quite small. There are two serious legal problems however. The first is whether a vice president can be brought to trial during his term of office. Your legal advisors and you believe that the Supreme Court would permit this and hold that although the wording of the Constitution makes no distinction between an incumbent president and his vice president, the former could not and the latter could be brought to trial during his term without a prior impeachment. You feel, however, that the issue is not free from doubt.

The second issue is whether the vice president will continue to hold office even after conviction, until the long and cumbersome process of impeachment by the House of Representatives and trial before the

Senate is completed. (To complicate the matter further, at this time it is possible, though not very likely, that because of a completely unrelated and bizarre series of events, the impeachment machinery will be needed for the president, himself).

The most important factor preying upon your mind is that if at any time before the final disposition of this case, which may take over a year, the president should die, become disabled or resign, the vice president would then become president, aborting all the legal proceedings against him and plunging the nation into a constitutional crisis the likes of which we have never experienced.

The vice president is talking tough publicly, proclaiming his innocence, and preparing to fight it out. Privately, his attorneys have approached you and said that if a plea bargain were reached whereby he could plead nolo contendere (a plea having the consequences of a plea of guilty for that case, but otherwise not usable as an admission of guilt) and be assured of no jail term, he would resign his office and so plead. Otherwise they will fight. The judge has agreed to go along with the bargain if you accept the defense offer. In this incredibly implausible series of events, what would you do? What would be the effect of a law which forbade plea bargaining?

Note that whatever else one thinks about plea bargaining, the practice makes a statement about the relative power of the citizen and the state. What is this statement?

C. THE ROLE OF THE JUDGE

1. INSURING VOLUNTARINESS

NORTH CAROLINA v. ALFORD

Supreme Court of the United States, 1970.
400 U.S. 25, 91 S.Ct. 160, 27 L.Ed.2d 162.

Mr. Justice WHITE delivered the opinion of the Court.

On December 2, 1963, Alford was indicted for first-degree murder, a capital offense under North Carolina law. The court appointed an attorney to represent him, and this attorney questioned all but one of the various witnesses who appellee said would substantiate his claim of innocence. The witnesses, however, did not support Alford's story but gave statements that strongly indicated his guilt. Faced with strong evidence of guilt and no substantial evidentiary support for the claim of innocence, Alford's attorney recommended that he plead guilty, but left the ultimate decision to Alford himself. The prosecutor agreed to accept a plea of guilty to a charge of second-degree murder, and on December 10, 1963, Alford pleaded guilty to the reduced charge.

Before the plea was finally accepted by the trial court, the court heard the sworn testimony of a police officer who summarized the State's case. Two other witnesses besides Alford were also heard. Although there was no eyewitness to the crime, the testimony indicated that shortly before the killing Alford took his gun from his house, stated his intention to kill the victim and returned home with the declaration that he had carried out the killing. After the summary presentation of the State's case, Alford took the stand and testified that he had not committed the murder but that he was pleading guilty because he faced the threat of the death penalty if he did not do so. In response to the questions of his counsel, he acknowledged that his counsel had informed him of the difference between second- and first-degree murder and of his rights in case he chose to go to trial. The trial court then asked appellee if, in light of his denial of guilt, he still desired to plead guilty to second-degree murder and appellee answers, "Yes, sir. I plead guilty on—from the circumstances that he [Alford's attorney] told me." * After eliciting information about Alford's prior criminal record, which was a long one, the trial court sentenced him to 30 years' imprisonment, the maximum penalty for second-degree murder.

. . .

On appeal, [of a denial of writ of habeas corpus] a divided panel of the Court of Appeals for the Fourth Circuit reversed on the ground that Alford's guilty plea was made involuntarily. 405 F.2d 340 (1968).

. . .

[T]he Court of Appeals ruled that Alford's guilty plea was involuntary because its principal motivation was fear of the death penalty. By this standard, even if both the judge and the jury had possessed the power to impose the death penalty for first-degree murder or if guilty pleas to capital charges had not been permitted, Alford's plea of guilty to second-degree murder should still have been rejected because impermissibly induced by his desire to eliminate the possibility of a death sentence.

. . . We held in Brady v. United States, 397 U.S. 742, 90 S.Ct. 1463, 25 L.Ed.2d 747 (1970), that a plea of guilty which would not have been entered except for the defendant's desire to avoid a possible death penalty and to limit the maximum penalty to life imprisonment or a

---

* After giving his version of the events of the night of the murder, Alford stated:

" * * * I pleaded guilty on second degree murder because they said there is too much evidence, but I ain't shot no man, but I take the fault for the other man. We never had an argument in our life and I just pleaded guilty because they said if I didn't they would gas me for it, and that is all."

In response to questions from his attorney, Alford affirmed that he had consulted several times with his attorney and with members of his family and had been informed of his rights if he chose to plead not guilty.

Alford then reaffirmed his decision to plead guilty to second-degree murder:

"Q. [by Alford's attorney]. And you authorized me to tender a plea of guilty to second degree murder before the Court?

"A. Yes, sir.

"Q. And in doing that, that you have again affirmed your decision on that point?

"A. Well, I'm still pleading that you all got me to plead guilty. I plead the other way, circumstantial evidence; that the jury will prosecute me on—on the second. You told me to plead guilty, right. I don't—I'm not guilty but I plead guilty.

term of years was not for that reason compelled within the meaning of the Fifth Amendment. . . . The standard was and remains whether the plea represents a voluntary and intelligent choice among the alternative courses of action open to the defendant.

. . . That he would not have pleaded except for the opportunity to limit the possible penalty does not necessarily demonstrate that the plea of guilty was not the product of a free and rational choice, especially where the defendant was represented by competent counsel whose advice was that the plea would be to the defendant's advantage. The standard fashioned and applied by the Court of Appeals was therefore erroneous and we would, without more, vacate and remand the case for further proceedings with respect to any other claims of Alford which are properly before that court, if it were not for other circumstances appearing in the record which might seem to warrant an affirmance of the Court of Appeals. As previously recounted after Alford's plea of guilty was offered and the State's case was placed before the judge, Alford denied that he had committed the murder but reaffirmed his desire to plead guilty to avoid a possible death sentence and to limit the penalty to the 30–year maximum provided for second-degree murder. Ordinarily, a judgment of conviction resting on a plea of guilty is justified by the defendant's admission that he committed the crime charged against him and his consent that judgment be entered without a trial of any kind. The plea usually subsumes both elements, and justifiably so, even though there is no separate, express admission by the defendant that he committed the particular acts claimed to constitute the crime charged in the indictment. . . .

Here Alford entered his plea but accompanied it with the statement that he had not shot the victim.

If Alford's statements were to be credited as sincere assertions of his innocence, there obviously existed a factual and legal dispute between him and the State. Without more, it might be argued that the conviction entered on his guilty plea was invalid, since his assertion of innocence negatived any admission of guilt, which, as we observed last Term in *Brady,* is normally "[c]entral to the plea and the foundation for entering judgment against the defendant."

. . .

In addition to Alford's statement, however, the court had heard an account of the events on the night of the murder, including information from Alford's acquaintances that he had departed from his home with his gun stating his intention to kill and that he had later declared that he had carried out his intention. Nor had Alford wavered in his desire to have the trial court determine his guilt without a jury trial. Although denying the charge against him, he nevertheless preferred the dispute between him and the State to be settled by the judge in the context of a guilty plea proceeding rather than by a formal trial. Thereupon, with the State's telling evidence and Alford's denial before it, the trial court, proceeded to convict and sentence Alford for second-degree murder.

.   .   .

.   .   . [W]e perceive [no] material difference between a plea which refuses to admit commission of the criminal act and a plea containing a protestation of innocence when, as in the instant case, a defendant intelligently concludes that his interests require entry of a guilty plea and the record before the judge contains strong evidence of actual guilt. Here the State had a strong case of first-degree murder against Alford. Whether he realized or disbelieved his guilt, he insisted on his plea because in his view he had absolutely nothing to gain by a trial and much to gain by pleading. Because of the overwhelming evidence against him, a trial was precisely what neither Alford nor his attorney desired. Confronted with the choice between a trial for first-degree murder, on the one hand, and a plea of guilty to second-degree murder, on the other, Alford quite reasonably chose the latter and thereby limited the maximum penalty to a 30–year term. When his plea is viewed in light of the evidence against him, which substantially negated his claim of innocence and which further provided a means by which the judge could test whether the plea was being intelligently entered, its validity cannot be seriously questioned. In view of the strong factual basis for the plea demonstrated by the State and Alford's clearly expressed desire to enter it despite his professed belief in his innocence, we hold that the trial judge did not commit constitutional error in accepting it.

.   .   . Alford now argues in effect that the State should not have allowed him this choice but should have insisted on proving him guilty of murder in the first degree. The States in their wisdom may take this course by statute or otherwise and may prohibit the practice of accepting pleas to lesser included offenses under any circumstances. But this is not the mandate of the Fourteenth Amendment and the Bill of Rights. The prohibitions against involuntary or unintelligent pleas should not be relaxed, but neither should an exercise in arid logic render those constitutional guarantees counterproductive and put in jeopardy the very human values they were meant to preserve.

The Court of Appeals for the Fourth Circuit was in error to find Alford's plea of guilty invalid because it was made to avoid the possibility of the death penalty. That court's judgment directing the issuance of the writ of habeas corpus is vacated and the case is remanded to the Court of Appeals for further proceedings consistent with this opinion.

It is so ordered.

Mr. Justice BLACK, concurs.

Mr. Justice BRENNAN, Mr. Justice DOUGLAS, and Mr. Justice MARSHALL dissent.

Questions and Comment

How can we call a plea of guilty "voluntary" if it is motivated by a desire to escape the death penalty?

Is not the *Alford* case a recognition that, as a practical matter, the courts cannot do much about plea bargaining? If the *Alford* decision had been decided the other way, is it not clear that the only difference would have been that the defendant would be told that if he wanted to have his bargain accepted, he would be forced, whether he was guilty or not, to acknowledge his guilt? This type of charade was required in most jurisdictions before *Alford,* and it neither enhanced the dignity of the courts nor inhibited guilty pleas.

It has been argued that it is difficult for judges to pass proper sentences on defendants who have pleaded guilty but affirm their innocence. On the other hand, should this be any more difficult for judges than passing sentence on defendants who, though proclaiming their innocence, have been convicted by a jury? Why?

At least one advantage of the rule in the *Alford* case is that it brings plea bargaining more out into the open, where judges can inquire as to why defendants who claim their innocence should, nonetheless, plead guilty. Presumably, then judges can weigh the strength of prosecution cases to determine whether the defendants have made rational decisions. Is that not, however, the job of defense attorneys?

Finally, if the trial judge had refused to accept Alford's plea of guilty to second degree murder and forced him to go to trial on the first degree murder charge, for whom would he be doing a favor? Himself? Alford? The Prosecutor? Society at large?

2. NOTE ON VOLUNTARINESS

The point in *Alford* is that a guilty plea is proper if defendants enter it with their eyes open, making judgments about what their chances are at trial as opposed to what sentences they are likely to receive on their plea.

What sort of things should defendants be advised of when they plead guilty? Obviously, they should be advised of the fact that they are giving up their right to trial, in most cases a trial by jury, and that they would have a whole panoply of rights in the trial process.

Is it reasonable to expect that defendants should also be advised of the maximum sentence that they might receive if they plead guilty?

Should they be advised also, if they are aliens subject to deportation, that they may be deported if they are convicted or plead guilty; should they be advised that the crimes to which they plead guilty are not ones to which the legislature has allowed parole; should they be advised if it is so that their pleas of guilty will terminate their right to vote, hold office, or to practice a profession? Certainly one would expect that all of these consequences would be important in a rational decision whether to plead guilty to a crime.

Cannot one argue that every plea of guilty is entered in ignorance of its consequences, if defendants do not know what sentences they will receive? Is there any reason why defendants should not be told before they plea?

3. THE INFLUENCE OF THE DEFENDANT'S PLEA ON JUDICIAL DETERMINATION OF THE SENTENCE

a. RATIONALES FOR ADJUSTING SENTENCE *

The reasons why courts feel the defendant's plea is a relevant factor in sentencing may be separated into two major categories. In their answers to the *Questionnaire* ** many judges expressed the belief that an accused pleading guilty was generally less culpable, and thus less in need of punishment, than a defendant convicted after trial. In addition, the view was asserted that a defendant pleading guilty was entitled to some discount in punishment because of the aid of his plea in the efficient administration of justice. Several judges emphasized that the plea was only one of numerous factors taken into consideration in determining sentence, and that the weight given the plea varied from case to case.

The Guilty Plea as Evidence of Repentance

The predominant basis for a court's considering a defendant pleading guilty less culpable than one denying guilt is the belief that a guilty plea demonstrates the readiness of the accused to accept responsibility for his criminal acts. Judges feel that such a confession of wrongdoing evinces a repentant attitude, and thus represents an important step toward rehabilitation of the accused. A few judges added the qualification that a guilty plea would not be considered evidence of reformation unless the accused had no prior criminal record.

A reduction in sentence following a guilty plea is consistent with the rehabilitation theory of criminal punishment only if such a plea is indicative of remorse for prior criminal acts. Although a guilty plea may at times be motivated by repentance, more often it would seem to represent exploitation by the accused of the prosecutor's and court's reaction to such a plea. If a defendant who acknowledged his guilt were aware that the plea could not influence the extent of punishment, then perhaps his action might reflect a renunciation of criminal propensities. But the very fact that a defendant realizes a guilty plea may mitigate punishment impairs the value of the plea as a gauge of character. Faced with convincing evidence of guilt, an accused will probably enter a guilty plea for reasons of expediency, not principle. Moreover, while recidivists, poor prospects for reformation, will not be deterred from admitting guilt by the fear of impeaching their commu-

* Note, "The Influence of the Defendant's Plea on Judicial Determination of Sentence", 66 *Yale Law Journal*, (1956), 209–21. Reprinted by permission of the Yale Law Journal Company and Fred B. Rothman and Company.

** Sent by the Yale Law Journal to every federal district judge.

nal reputations, first offenders, though truly repentant, may well deny guilt in a desperate effort to avoid the stigma of conviction.

Nor can lenient treatment of defendants pleading guilty be justified in terms of a deterrence theory of criminal punishment. It seems evident that the goal of discouraging future criminal activity by punishing past offenders is not served by awarding a reduced sentence to a person willing to admit his crime. Indeed, the awareness that a guilty plea will probably result in clemency may seriously undercut the deterrent effect of criminal prosecutions.

Commission of Perjury at Trial

A second reason why judges award a defendant convicted at trial a more severe sentence than one pleading guilty is the belief that the former has usually committed perjury in his defense. Of course this inference is drawn only when the defendant has taken the stand. While some judges indicated that an implied finding of perjury is predicated upon a review of the facts and circumstances of each case, other judges appear to presume the occurrence of perjury from the mere fact of conviction. Regardless of the chain of reasoning employed, judges agreed that a defendant who was also a perjurer deserved additional punishment.

The perjury rationale for increasing sentence may be viewed from two different perspectives. It may be said that the judge is awarding the defendant a given punishment for the crime of which he has been convicted, and then, within the limits of his discretion to fix punishment for this offense, is imposing an additional sentence because the defendant has committed the second crime of perjury. Or the court may be said to consider the occurrence of perjury as a culpable act bearing upon the character of the accused; accordingly, the defendant is given a longer sentence for the crime of which he stands convicted because his perjurious conduct increases the difficulty of reformation. Both of these justifications seem unsound.

Penalizing the defendant for the substantive crime of perjury by increasing the sentence for another offense contradicts basic tenets of criminal law. . . . [P]erjury is properly punishable in a separate criminal proceeding. Summary adjudication by the court of the defendant's guilt is an inadequate substitute for the constitutional safeguards inherent in a new indictment and jury trial. Moreover, even though the defendant's conviction must be taken as a repudiation of his testimony, the judgment in the initial case would undoubtedly be inadmissible evidence in a subsequent perjury proceeding. In light of this doctrine, the practice of conclusively presuming the commission of perjury from the fact of conviction is particularly suspect.

. . .

Assertion of Frivolous Defense

Some judges reported that a defendant pleading not guilty was awarded a more severe sentence than a defendant pleading guilty only if the court felt that the demand for trial was not made in good faith but was essentially a dilatory tactic. The view was expressed that a defendant faced with overwhelming evidence of guilt who presented a frivolous defense in a desperate gamble to sway a jury deserved additional punishment. In contrast, an accused whose defense raised a substantial question of law or fact was accorded the same sentencing treatment as was given defendants pleading guilty. Since the Sixth Amendment guarantee of trial by jury does not distinguish between dilatory and substantial defenses, the defendant whose punishment has been increased for demanding what the court considers a useless trial is in effect being penalized for asserting his constitutional rights. It is questionable whether a not guilty plea can ever be fairly deemed "dilatory," since it accords with the presumption of innocence which the prosecution must rebut beyond a reasonable doubt. In addition, the judicial determination that a defense was frivolous is made when the accused has already been convicted; any defense appears less meritorious after it has been rejected.

Revelation of Circumstances of Crime

Four judges answering the *Questionnaire* suggested that a guilty plea may contribute to a shorter sentence because the brutal circumstances frequently accompanying criminal activity are not emphasized by the prosecution, and vividly recounted at trial. Such a position implies that the pre-sentencing report on a defendant pleading guilty either does not describe the details of the crime or lacks the dramatic thrust inherent in testimony. Though judges are naturally swayed by emotional responses, the means by which a defendant is convicted cannot alter the actual nature of his criminal conduct. Theoretically, the circumstances of the crime should be given the same weight in evaluating the character of the accused regardless of his plea.

Sentencing Policy and the Innocent Defendant

The greatest danger inherent in the policy of utilizing the plea as a factor in sentencing is that innocent men will be influenced to plead guilty. Confronted with the probability that conviction after trial will substantially enhance punishment, a defendant may decide that assertion of his innocence entails too much of a risk. The greater the potential discrepancy in the sentence to be imposed following trial convictions and guilty pleas, the more will be magnified the fear of standing trial. A defendant may be especially reluctant to plead not guilty when he has a criminal record, for then his chances of successfully establishing innocence are considerably diminished. Under prevalent evidentiary rules, the defendant's criminal past may be brought out at trial by one means or another, with consequent prejudice to his defense. In addition the accused may have a weak alibi, corroborated only by witnesses of questionable character.

The judicial practice of reducing sentence following guilty pleas works a subtle coercion upon the defendant, incompatible with the constitutional guarantee of due process. The Supreme Court has held that a conviction will be invalidated if based upon a guilty plea which is the product of mental coercion. While it is doubtful that a guilty plea could successfully be voided on the ground that sentencing procedure discriminated against the defendant demanding trial, nevertheless the pleader's freedom of choice is seriously inhibited when he is aware of such differentials in punishment.

Comment and Questions

We will discuss the many variables which go into the judicial determination of sentence in the next chapter. At this point, however, it is necessary to note that, even if there were no plea bargain, in which the prosecutor offered a lessor included offense to which the defendant might plead guilty, the defendant could still attempt to secure a reduced sentence from the judge by pleading guilty. In determining whether this is a practice to be encouraged, does it matter whether the judge specifically offers the defendant a reduced sentence if he or she pleads guilty, or whether the defendant pleads guilty, relying on a known judicial policy to give reduced sentences to those who plead guilty?

If there is a difference, which of the two procedures should the law favor?

Finally, is the thrust of the above excerpt that the judge should not give a reduction in sentence as a result of a guilty plea? Or is it that no one should—including the plea-bargaining prosecutor?

b. BORDENKIRCHER v. HAYES

Supreme Court of the United States, 1978
434 U.S. 357, 98 S.Ct. 663, 54 L.Ed.2d 604.

In 1973, Paul Lewis Hayes was indicted by a Kentucky grand jury for forgery of a check for $88.30, then a felony offense punishable by a term of two to ten years (a penalty that was subsequently repealed in 1975). After arraignment, Hayes' attorney met with the prosecutor to discuss a possible plea agreement. During these conferences the prosecutor offered to recommend a sentence of five years if Hayes would plead guilty and "save the court the inconvenience and necessity of a trial." He also indicated that if Hayes would not plead guilty he would return to the grand jury and seek an indictment under the state's Habitual Criminal Act (also repealed in 1975), which would subject Hayes to a mandatory life sentence since he had two prior felony convictions. The first conviction was in 1961, when Hayes was seventeen, for "detaining a female," for which he served five years in a reformatory; the second in 1970, for robbery, for which he received a five-year suspended sentence and probation.

Hayes refused to plead guilty. In turn, the prosecutor secured the additional indictment under the habitual criminal statute, and Hayes was subsequently convicted and sentenced to life imprisonment.

The Kentucky Court of Appeals rejected Hayes' contention that the enhancement charge for habitual felony, initiated solely because he had refused to plead guilty, constituted a violation of his constitutional right to due process. The United States District Court denied his writ for a petition of habeas corpus, holding that it found no constitutional defects in the indictment and sentencing process. The United States Court of Appeals reversed, reasoning that the prosecutor's conduct during the pretrial process violated principles that "protected defendants from the vindictive exercise of a prosecutor's discretion," and ordered that Hayes be discharged from prison once he had completed the lawful term for forgery. The State of Kentucky, acting through its penitentiary superintendent, Bordenkircher, successfully petitioned the United States Supreme Court for a writ of certiorari.

Mr. Justice STEWART delivered the opinion of the Court.

To punish a person because he has done what the law plainly allows him to do is a due process violation of the most basic sort, . . . and for an agent of the State to pursue a course of action whose objective is to penalize a person's reliance on his legal rights is "patently unconstitutional." . . . But in the "give-and-take" of plea bargaining, there is no such element of punishment or retaliation so long as the accused is free to accept or reject the prosecution's offer.

Plea bargaining flows from "the mutuality of advantage" to defendants and prosecutors, each with his own reasons for wanting to avoid trial. . . . Defendants advised by competent counsel and protected by other procedural safeguards are presumptively capable of intelligent choice in response to prosecutorial persuasion, and unlikely to be driven to false self-condemnation. . . . Indeed, acceptance of the basic legitimacy of plea bargaining necessarily implies rejection of any notion that a guilty plea is involuntary in a constitutional sense simply because it is the end result of the bargaining process. By hypothesis, the plea may have been induced by promises of a recommendation of a lenient sentence or a reduction of charges, and thus by fear of the possibility of a greater penalty upon conviction after a trial. . . .

While confronting a defendant with the risk of more severe punishment clearly may have a "discouraging effect on the defendant's assertion of his trial rights, the imposition of these difficult choices [is] an inevitable"—and permissible—"attribute of any legitimate system which tolerates and encourages the negotiation of pleas." . . . It follows that, by tolerating and encouraging the negotiation of pleas, this Court has necessarily accepted as constitutionally legitimate the simple reality that the prosecutor's interest at the bargaining table is to persuade the defendant to forgo his right to plead not guilty.

It is not disputed here that Hayes was properly chargeable under the recidivist statute, since he had in fact been convicted of two previous felonies. In our system, so long as the prosecutor has probable cause to believe that the accused committed an offense defined by statute, the decision whether or not to prosecute, and what charge to file or bring before a grand jury, generally rests entirely in his discretion. Within the limits set by the legislature's constitutionally valid definition of chargeable offenses, "the conscious exercise of some selectivity in enforcement is not in itself a federal constitutional violation" so long as "the selection was [not] deliberately based upon an unjustifiable standard such as race, religion, or other arbitrary classification." . . . To hold that the prosecutor's desire to induce a guilty plea is an "unjustifiable standard," which, like race or religion, may play no part in his charging decision, would contradict the very premises that underlie the concept of plea bargaining itself. Moreover, a rigid constitutional rule that would prohibit a prosecutor from acting forthrightly in his dealings with the defense could only invite unhealthy subterfuge that would drive the practice of plea bargaining back into the shadows from which it has so recently emerged. . . .

There is no doubt that the breadth of discretion that our country's legal system vests in prosecuting attorneys carries with it the potential for both individual and institutional abuse. And broad though that discretion may be, there are undoubtedly constitutional limits upon its exercise. We hold only that the course of conduct engaged in by the prosecutor in this case, which no more than openly presented the defendant with the unpleasant alternatives of forgoing trial or facing charges on which he was plainly subject to prosecution, did not violate the Due Process Clause of the Fourteenth Amendment.

Accordingly, the judgment of the Court of Appeals is

Reversed.

[Mr. Justice BLACKMUN, with whom Mr. Justice BRENNAN and Mr. Justice MARSHALL joined, wrote a dissenting opinion.]

Mr. Justice POWELL, dissenting.

Although I agree with much of the Court's opinion, I am not satisfied that the result in this case is just or that the conduct of the plea bargaining met the requirements of due process.

Respondent was charged with the uttering of a single forged check in the amount of $88.30. Under Kentucky law, this offense was punishable by a prison term of from 2 to 10 years, apparently without regard to the amount of the forgery. During the course of plea bargaining, the prosecutor offered respondent a sentence of five years in consideration of a guilty plea. I observe, at this point, that five years in prison for the offense charged hardly could be characterized as a generous offer. Apparently respondent viewed the offer in this light and declined to accept it; he protested that he was innocent and insisted on going to trial. Respondent adhered to this position even when the prosecutor advised that he would seek a new indictment under the State's Habitual Criminal Act which would subject respondent, if convicted, to a mandatory life sentence because of two prior felony convictions.

The prosecutor's initial assessment of respondent's case led him to forgo an indictment under the habitual criminal statute. The circumstances of respondent's prior convictions are relevant to this assessment and to my view of the case. Respondent was 17 years old when he committed his first offense. He was charged with rape but pleaded guilty to the lesser included offense of "detaining a female." One of the other participants in the incident was sentenced to life imprisonment. Respondent was sent not to prison but to a reformatory where he served five years. Respondent's second offense was robbery. This time he was found guilty by a jury and was sentenced to five years in prison, but he was placed on probation and served no time. Although respondent's prior convictions brought him within the terms of the Habitual Criminal Act, the offenses themselves did not result in imprisonment; yet the addition of a conviction on a charge involving $88.30 subjected respondent to a mandatory sentence of imprisonment for life. Persons convicted of rape and murder often are not punished so severely.

No explanation appears in the record for the prosecutor's decision to escalate the charge against respondent other than respondent's refusal to plead guilty. The prosecutor has conceded that his purpose was to discourage respondent's assertion of constitutional rights, and the majority accepts this characterization of events. . . .

The plea-bargaining process, as recognized by this Court, is essential to the functioning of the criminal-justice system. It normally affords genuine benefits to defendants as well as to society. And if the system is to work effectively, prosecutors must be accorded the widest discretion, within constitutional limits, in conducting bargaining. This is especially true when a defendant is represented by counsel and presumedly is fully advised of his rights. Only in the most exceptional case should a court conclude that the scales of the bargaining are so unevenly balanced as to arouse suspicion. In this case, the prosecutor's actions denied respondent due process because their admitted purpose was to discourage and then to penalize with unique severity his exercise of constitutional rights. Implementation of a strategy calculated solely to deter the exercise of constitutional rights is not a constitutionally permissible exercise of discretion. I would affirm the opinion of the Court of Appeals on the facts of this case.

Question

Apart from the severity of his sentence, how does Hayes' position differ from a great many other defendants? Does Justice Powell offer a convincing reason for making a distinction in this case?

D. IMPROVING THE PROCESS

1. RESTRUCTURING THE PLEA BARGAINING SYSTEM *

I hear no principled argument for . . . plea bargaining. There are, to be sure, principled reasons for pre-trial settlement of criminal charges in many cases, but charge or plea or punishment concessions to purchase such settlements are defended primarily in terms of expediency. Predominantly what is offered by the supporters of plea bargaining are arguments as to its unavoidability in the present circumstances of the courts, particularly the city courts, together with a proliferation of rules of practice and procedure, such as those offered by the American Bar Association Minimum Standards Project or required by federal or state Rules of Court, designed to avoid the grosser injustices and improprieties in plea bargaining. What such reformist efforts seem to amount to is, in the language of diplomacy, the rejection of secret covenants secretly arrived at and the advocacy of open covenants secretly arrived at. The judiciary seems more interested in protecting its trailing robes from the dirt of the market place than in overturning the tables or regulating the market.

Prisoners are, I assure you, amply aware that plea bargaining is another name for sentencing. They are aware that the most effective defense counsel is not the counsel who can adduce the best defense but is rather that counsel who can obtain the best deal. The more experienced in crime the prisoner is, the more he has come to appreciate the negotiative quality of the American criminal justice system. "Get me Agnew's lawyers," they all plead.

At last a national commission, the National Advisory Commission on Criminal Justice Standards and Goals, has recommended the abolition of plea concessions. Their recommendation has been met with outrage by many criminal law practitioners and has almost sunk in the turbulence of prejudiced debate. It has not proved easy to persuade the legal profession, in particular the criminal bar, that the abolition of plea concessions does not mean the abolition of pre-trial settlement of criminal charges. What corrupts is the concession for the plea, not the pre-trial settlement.

At present, there are two parties to the plea bargaining: the prosecutor and the defense counsel. Allegedly the defense counsel advises his client with precision of a possible settlement and of the likely sentence which will flow from alternative trial procedures. But, as every practitioner knows, there are many pressures upon defense counsel to narrate those facts inaccurately. For example, some acquaintance with the operation of plea bargaining in the crowded city courts of this country has led me to the conclusion that it is in the interests both of the prosecution and of the defense counsel for the

---

* Norval Morris, *The Future of Imprisonment* (Chicago, U. of Chicago Press, 1974) pp. 51–55. © 1974 Reprinted with permission.

prosecution to "overcharge" the accused. There is then available something by way of charge "concession" for the defense counsel to get for his client and, obviously, the prosecutor's bargaining position is strengthened by overcharging. Likewise, it is in the interests of both counsels to tend to exaggerate the severity of the sentence which might be imposed pursuant to conviction after a bench trial or a jury trial. Again, defense counsel's interests differ from those of his client; again he can more likely win something, if only a lesser sentence than was feared. And obviously, if defense counsel has reasonable expectations of settling a plea, there is substantial pressure on him to exaggerate to his client the risks of bench and jury trial and to overstate the likely disadvantages of not accepting a bargain which counsel thinks wise.

The judge also becomes a mere secondary party, advised by the first two parties of the conclusions of their negotiations, having only a veto power over them, a veto power he can exercise only rarely if the trial system is not to break down. I recognize that in some jurisdictions judges participate to varying degrees in plea bargaining discussions and that there are a few official recommendations that they should do so, but I have stated the general pattern.

So, as a first and obviously essential reform we start with the requirement of the presence of at least four parties for any sound pre-trial dispositive process: judge (clearly not the trial judge, if the matter goes to trial), prosecutor, defense counsel, and accused.* Apart from other reasons, the constitutional right to presence at trial can only be given reality if the accused is allowed to attend those aspects of the pre-trial processes that are of significance to him. Now he is present only for the formalities, the signing of the treaty, not its negotiation.

A pre-trial hearing should be called by a judicial officer in respect of every criminal charge for which a true bill has been found or an equivalent preliminary hearing process completed. It is important that the pre-trial hearing be called in every case and that no report of such pre-trial discussion should be available in any case to a trial judge if the matter subsequently goes to trial. There must be no record kept of the pre-trial discussions, and no statements made there must be admissible either in examination-in-chief or in cross-examination if the matter goes to trial. The pre-trial hearing has two purposes. First, if the matter is set down for trial, to lay out a timetable of preliminary motions and trial hearings so that at least we may begin to give reality to the promise of speedy trial. The second purpose is to explore what might be feasible by way of a settlement of all issues in dispute, acceptable to the state and the accused alike, including questions of compensation of victims, and everything that is now properly relevant to plea bargaining.

Complementary to such a pre-trial dispositional hearing would be a professional ethical prohibition on private consultation between prose-

---

* The author also argues for inclusion of
the victim in plea negotiations.

cutor and defense counsel regarding any matters at issue in the pending case, akin to the prohibition on private consultation between judge and counsel concerning pending litigation in which they are both involved. In effect, all charge and plea bargaining would be pursued in the controlled setting—and only there.

It would seem to me that in such a setting everything that is good in our present plea bargaining processes can be retained and much that is evil in them can be eliminated. It is obvious that the accused has an unfettered right to go to trial and to refuse to accept any product of such a pre-trial discussion. Likewise, a veto power must be held by the judge, though for different and distinct reasons. But absent the exercise of either of these two veto powers, a prison sentence based on such a pre-trial discussion and settlement of the issue can hardly be regarded by the prisoner as other than one in which he has been fairly and justly treated.

Questions and Comments

Is it not an elementary rule of fairness that the same judge who has attempted unsuccessfully to work out a guilty plea should not preside over the trial itself? Is this because the judge, through the guilty plea negotiations, might become aware of a good deal of inadmissible evidence which he or she may hold against one party (most often the defense); or is the more serious problem that if the defendant is found guilty after trial, the judge might be resentful that the defendant was unreasonable not to bargain and put the court to extra work? Should this affect a judge's sentence?

Is the situation much better when the judge trying the case merely knows that another judge has attempted to bring about a settlement and failed? Will this not always be the case if a multi-judge court system (as we have in all our urban areas) routinely attempts to work out plea bargains?

Does the proposal advanced in the above excerpt solve many of the problems inherent in the institution of the guilty plea? Who is expected to make the concessions necessary to induce the defendant to help reduce overcrowding in the courts by pleading guilty?

Finally, isn't it clear that we have simply too many criminals to process in the criminal system? What can we do to lower the number? See Chapters I and IV. Alternatively, maybe we should spend much more money on the criminal process. If we spend more on the police, won't they just catch more criminals, thus overburdening the system even more?

2. DOING AWAY WITH PLEA BARGAINING

a. PLEA BARGAINING IN ACADEME *

I think that the appeal that plea bargaining has is rooted in our attitude toward bargains in general. Where both parties are satisfied with the terms of an agreement, it is improper to interfere. Generally speaking, prosecutors and defendants are pleased with the advantages they gain by negotiating a plea. And courts, which gain as well, are reluctant to vacate negotiated pleas where only "proper" inducements have been applied and where promises have been understood and kept. Such judicial neutrality may be commendable where entitlements are being exchanged. But the criminal justice system is not such a context. Rather it is one in which persons are justly given, not what they have bargained for, but what they deserve, irrespective of their bargaining position.

To appreciate this, let us consider another context in which desert plays a familiar role; the assignment of grades in an academic setting. Imagine a "grade bargain" negotiated between a grade-conscious student and a harried instructor. A term paper has been submitted and, after glancing at the first page, the instructor says that if he were to read the paper carefully, applying his usually rigid standards, he would probably decide to give the paper a grade of D. But if the student were to waive his right to a careful reading and conscientious critique, the instructor would agree to a grade of B. The grade-point average being more important to him than either education or justice in grading, the student happily accepts the B, and the instructor enjoys a reduced workload.

One strains to imagine legislators and administrators commending the practice of grade bargaining because it permits more students to be processed by fewer instructors. Teachers can be freed from the burden of having to read and to criticize every paper. One struggles to envision academicians arguing for grade bargaining in the way that jurists have defended plea bargaining, suggesting that a quick assignment of a grade is a more effective influence on the behavior of students, urging that grade bargaining is necessary to the efficient functioning of the schools. There can be no doubt that students who have negotiated a grade are more likely to accept and to understand the verdict of the instructor. Moreover, in recognition of a student's help to the school (by waiving both the reading and the critique), it is proper for the instructor to be lenient. Finally, a quickly assigned grade enables the guidance personnel and the registrar to respond rapidly and appropriately to the student's situation.

What makes all of this laughable is what makes plea bargaining outrageous. For grades, like punishments, should be deserved. Justice

* Abraham Blumberg, *Ethics,* Vol. 86, No. 2, Jan. 1976. © 1976 (Reprinted with permission).

in retribution, like justice in grading, does not require that the end result be acceptable to the parties. To reason that because the parties are satisfied the bargain should stand is to be seriously confused. For bargains are out of place in contexts where persons are to receive what they deserve. And the American courtroom, like the American classroom, should be such a context.

Questions

Is the analogy drawn in the above excerpt a good one? If it is not, what is wrong with it? If it is, should we simply do away with plea bargaining?

b. ATTEMPTED RESTRICTIONS ON PLEA BARGAINS

(1) NEW YORK *

New York State's draconian Rockefeller drug and sentencing laws resulted in fewer dispositions, convictions and prison sentences for drug offenses in 1974 and 1975 than in 1973, the last year of the old drug laws.

These are findings from an interim evaluation report prepared by the Committee on New York Drug Law Evaluation (the adverse findings are reminiscent of an earlier report by State University of New York researchers on the effects of the mandatory sentencing [and plea bargaining] provisions in the statutes).

By increasing the penalties and mandating terms of imprisonment, the Rockefeller drug laws were supposed to deter drug abuse and/or incarcerate drug offenders. But the new study found no difference in the risk of prison faced by drug offenders under the new laws: "That risk is still less than one chance in a hundred. . . ."

In fact, the number of drug offenders sentenced to prison declined from 1,561 in 1973 to 1,074 in 1974, and only part of the way back up to 1,433 last year.

Convictions Drop. Though the chances of a convicted drug offender being sentenced to prison increased from 41% to 56% under the new laws, conviction rates dropped simultaneously from 85% to 75%, due to an increase in dismissals.

The stringent laws had a dramatic impact on the courts. While upstate courts adjusted to the extra caseload in about a year, New York City courts at one point developed a backlog equivalent to 10 months' worth of drug indictments—despite assignment of 31 new judges to drug cases.

Future reports from the committee will render judgment on whether the Rockefeller laws reduced drug abuse and drug-related crime.

* *Criminal Justice Newsletter*, Sept. 13, 1976, p. 3. © 1976 Reprinted with permission.

Comment

New York's Rockefeller drug law was widely touted as a "hard line" approach to the drug problem. To cope with the problem of "too lenient" sentences, restrictions were placed upon the judge's discretion in sentencing and the prosecutor's ability to give concessions in plea bargaining. Is it not clear that preventing one of these methods of granting concessions without preventing the other would have accomplished very little? The above excerpt indicates what the law did accomplish.

Two other facts about the Rockefeller drug law are also of interest. First, the police, faced with overcrowding in the courts and the threat of sentences they felt were out of proportion to the drug offenses, cut down the number of drug arrests they made and reached more "deals" on the street.

Second, after two years of experience with the restrictions on plea bargaining, New York loosened the restrictions considerably with respect to sale of small amounts of heroin.

(2) CALIFORNIA *

Proposition 8 added Section 1192.7 to the California Penal Code. It reads:

> (a) Plea bargaining in any case in which the indictment or information charges any serious felony or any offense of driving while under the influence of alcohol, drugs, narcotics, or any other intoxicating substance, or any combination thereof, is prohibited, unless there is insufficient evidence to prove the people's case, or testimony of a material witness cannot be obtained, or a reduction or a dismissal would not result in a substantial change in sentence.

> (b) As used in this section, "plea bargaining" means any bargaining, negotiation, or discussion between a criminal defendant, or his or her counsel, and a prosecuting attorney or judge, whereby the defendant agrees to plead guilty or *nolo contendere*, in exchange for any promises, commitments, concessions, assurances, or considerations by the prosecuting attorney or judge relating to any charge against the defendant or to the sentencing of the defendant.

This new Penal Code section also contains a list of 25 "serious felonies" to which the prohibition applies. This list includes such crimes as murder, rape, robbery, arson, various sexual assault crimes, and residential burglary. Currently, these "serious felonies" account for approximately one-fourth of all felony arrests in California.

* Candace McCoy and Robert Tillman, "Controlling Felony Plea Bargaining in California," California Department of Justice (1986) pp 3, 69, 79. © 1986 (Reprinted by permission).

Another provision of Proposition 8 added Section 667(a) to Penal Code which states: Any person convicted of a serious felony who previously has been convicted of a serious felony in this state or of any offense committed in another jurisdiction which includes all of the elements of any serious felony, shall receive, in addition to the sentence imposed by the court for the present offense, a five-year enhancement for each such prior conviction on charges brought and tried separately. The terms of the present offense and each enhancement shall run consecutively.

[According to the study, Proposition 8, by restricting plea bargaining in cases where there was an "indictment or information," was not held to interfere with the process before indictment or information—i.e. in the municipal court. As a result all that happened was that the bargaining had to be done earlier in the criminal processing].

Did Proposition 8 end plea bargaining in serious felony cases? Unequivocally: no. On the basis of our qualitative and quantitative data in three jurisdictions and on the basis of statewide quantitative data, we conclude that plea bargaining is just as essential to criminal prosecution as it ever was. While the location of this bargaining and the procedures surrounding it changed in response to the law, overt negotiation over case dispositions among defense attorneys, prosecutors and judges remains the predominant method for disposing of criminal cases in California. These discussions usually occur in informal meetings between counsel or in more formal give-and-take in [municipal court] judges' chambers. Actual court hearings accomplish little in the guilty plea process except in those cases that proceed through a municipal court preliminary hearing, where witnesses and evidence are presented and evaluated; or cases that proceed to superior court, where evidentiary motions may be made.

Did the habitual offender enhancements mandated by Proposition 8 result in longer, more severe sentences for recidivists? With less certainty: probably not. We remain somewhat cautious in this conclusion because we were unable to determine exactly how many offenders were eligible for the Penal Code 667(a) five-year sentencing enhancement. However, available data suggest that many of those eligible are not charged with the enhancement, and that when the enhancement is charged, it is frequently not imposed. For that very small proportion of offenders against whom the enhancement is actually imposed, however, it is plausible that the legislation may have increased.

(3) A MODEST PROPOSAL—REPLACING THE BAZAAR WITH THE DEPARTMENT STORE *

Norval Morris ** has suggested that we require all plea bargaining to be done in open court and that we make it unethical for the prosecutor and the defense attorney to talk about a plea bargain privately. At the bargaining session the prosecutor, the defense law- yer, the defendant, and the judge should all be present. (By the way, Professor Morris would also invite the victim—a most interesting idea.) Professor Morris has pointed out that presently plea bargains are secret covenants secretly arrived at, and that the improvements that are routinely suggested by bar associations, committees, and the like would simply require that details of the plea bargain be spread on the table before the judge. Professor Morris points out that this would amount to open covenants secretly arrived at. He, however, would go a step further and require open covenants openly arrived at.

Of course, this does not hit at the major problem of plea bargain- ing, which is that the defendant has a right to trial which he can sell to the prosecutor and judge for more lenient treatment. So long as the system has to buy, he will be able to do this. Nonetheless, Professor Morris' plan will reduce some of the abuses inherent in plea bargaining as practiced today. For instance, it will make it much more difficult for the defense attorney to misrepresent the prosecution's position and the likely consequence to the defendant should he reject the bargain. And it will make less likely the more flagrant examples of overcharg- ing. Nonetheless, even under Professor Morris' system where every- thing is out in the open, we will just be treated to the spectacle of the Turkish bazaar and its haggling. Just as in the bazaar different purchasers will pay different prices, different defendants will receive different treatment for the same crime—depending on the strength of the prosecution's case, the length of time the trial would take, the state of the prosecutor's backlog, and the skill of the defense attorney at getting concessions from the prosecutor—or his client, to name only the most common reasons. In any event, the difference produced by this process among similarly situated defendants is an affront to our ideals of equality as well as a serious practical problem.

I would like to propose a more sweeping improvement. I am convinced that we must still buy our pleas of guilty and that nothing we can do in the foreseeable future will change that. So I would take advantage of the mandatory sentence, or flat time, proposals to replace the Turkish bazaar with America's distinctive contribution to merchan- dising, the one-price department store—Macy's, Gimbel's, Scarbor- ough's, if you will. We will use a system providing flat time for each crime, with variations for specific aggravating factors such as prior

* John Kaplan, "American Merchandis- ing and the Guilty Plea: Replacing the Bazaar with the Department Store", *Amer- ican Journal of Criminal Law*, Vol. 5, No. 2

(1977), pp. 215–224. © 1977 (Reprinted by permission).

** See pp. 471–473.

criminal record, use of violence, and the like. The problem, however, with all the flat time proposals today is that while they freeze the judge's ability to reward the defendant for forsaking his right to trial, they leave plea bargaining untouched. As a result, the prosecutor has to take up the slack, and he must give whatever rewards are necessary to make the system work.

My proposal is startling in its simplicity. Let us simply and aboveboard consider a plea of guilty as a mitigating factor in a flat time sentence scheme. As a first approximation, a plea of guilty should reduce the sentence by, say, 50%. This figure might be determined by the legislature—presumably on a county by county basis, but it would seem less of a departure from present practice for the prosecutor, who presently awards the concessions, to determine the discount which will bind him. Arguments can be made that the discount rate should be a fixed, across the board, rate for all crimes or, alternatively, that the prosecutor, as he does now should be able to bargain differently depending upon the crime involved.

In either case, the instant reaction to such a scheme would be that it is unconstitutional. It amounts to a penalty for the exercise of a constitutional right—and so it does. Yet it would be an especially hypocritical Court which would invalidate such a plan. After all, we do exactly this now. We do pay the defendant for giving up his right to trial, but we do it in an uncontrolled, below-the-table way, and we will have to continue doing so unless we bring things out into the open where everyone can see what is going on. Not only will defendants be treated far more equally but it will be much harder for a defendant to complain that the prosecutor was out to get him and drove an especially hard bargain, or that his defense attorney sold him down the river and did not drive a hard enough bargain.

Of course, the system must be a little bit more complicated than this. We would also have to adopt Professor Morris' guilty plea-hearing procedure for various reasons. The defendant, though he is usually simply giving up his right to clog up the system and demand a trial, sometimes is giving up more. In the rare case where the defendant is giving up more than his right to trial we should, perhaps, offer more to him. Thus, in those rare cases where the defendant knows where the loot is stashed and can trade this knowledge for leniency, we may not be able to prevent ad hoc bargaining. But at least the deal should be acknowledged rather than under-the-table, and the judge should make a specific finding that this is why he is allowing extra leniency. A similar situation would be presented in the extremely improbable case of a Spiro Agnew, who could trade the credible threat of his becoming president of the United States should the president die, resign, or be impeached. For these special situations, the judge would have discretion to accept a better bargain. But where this is done it should be done on the record, if not publicly, then at least subject to the judge's supervision. Most important, a bargain based on the chance of the defendant's innocence would simply not be permissible. The reason is that those are just the cases we most wish to have tried.

This system, moreover, can build in checks against the prosecutor's overcharging. Thus the prosecutor who has charged a crime may simply have to reveal what his evidence is in the guilty plea discussion. The judge then would be expected to say: "Well, you really don't expect to get a burglary first out of that. That's almost certainly a burglary second." So the charge will be changed; now the defendant can plead or not as he wishes. If he pleads, he gets the statutory 50% off, and, if he doesn't that is his decision.

Now it may be that 50% of the sentence would be too great a discount, or it may be that it would be too little to "clear the market," as it were, in economic terms. If the former, political pressures, the role of the prosecutor and a sudden drop in the number of trials will tend to force a lower discount. If the latter and the discount were too little to clear the market, the legislature could add to the resources of the court system, the prosecutor could simply have to raise the percentage discount, or the backlog could grow. (By the way, one advantage of the flat time proposal is that it gives the legislature another opportunity for an openly-made choice. That is, if the prisons are overcrowded, the legislature publicly must make the choice of either building more space at considerable expense or of lowering sentences.) In both cases, and in the case of the statutory discount the responsibility will be brought out in the open and placed where it belongs. It will not be possible to blame plea bargaining on lenient judges.

Hopefully, too, the legislature and prosecutors will, over time, be able to lower the discount for pleading guilty. After all, even if it is necessary to pay the defendant for giving up his right to trial, this is a regrettable necessity and, perhaps, when it is brought out into the open, we can better work to eliminate it. When the legislature works in the sunlight, it tends to work better and more fairly. It should be noted that whatever improvements have already been made—or will be made—in the guilty plea came when we stopped indulging in the pious fiction that no inducements had been extended to the defendant as exchange for his plea and finally acknowledged that plea bargaining existed and it is likely that once we expose the magnitudes of the inducements we may find some action taken there as well.

E. IS PLEA BARGAINING INEVITABLE? *

In most criminal cases, plea bargaining is necessary and inevitable—at any rate, that is the view of nearly all knowledgeable scholars and practitioners and much of the public at large. In this Article, I suggest that this pervasively important assumption is erroneous. I shall argue that effective containment of plea bargaining is realistically possible for American criminal courts, and that in fact this goal has

* Stephen J. Schulhofer, "Is Plea Bargaining Inevitable?" Harvard Law Review, Vol. 97, No. 5, March 1984 (Reprinted with Permission).

already been achieved in one large, heterogeneous, crime-conscious urban jurisdiction. By plea bargaining I mean any process in which inducements are offered in exchange for a defendant's cooperation in not fully contesting the charges against him. Thus, I am asserting the feasibility of restricting or even eliminating not only formal, officially sanctioned plea bargaining, but also the wide variety of informal, sub rosa behavior patterns in which indirect inducements, unspoken commitments, and covert cooperation create the functional equivalent of explicit bargaining. The mechanism for realizing this ostensibly utopian vision is the Philadelphia bench trial, an institution I will undertake to describe and then assess.

In offering the Philadelphia bench trial as a model, I am claiming not only that it is feasible in the narrow administrative sense, but also that it is compatible with the complex of values that should inform the choice of procedural arrangements for ascertaining guilt. The normative argument for the bench trial model includes both an appeal to adjudication over negotiation and an appeal to judicial adjudication over lay participation. In both respects, the normative argument poses a challenge to widely accepted procedural traditions. The descriptive argument for the bench trial model is at least equally problematic. In claiming that bargaining can be and *has been* successfully restricted, I am denying the deeply held belief that plea bargaining in one form or another is universal and inevitable. I will therefore be obliged to examine the conceptual and empirical foundations of that belief and to present the evidence supporting a contrary conclusion—an empirical study of Philadelphia bargaining and trial practice—in enough detail to satisfy readers who will be and should be extremely skeptical of my claim.

The Court of Common Pleas, consisting of roughly seventy-five judges, handles appeals from the Municipal Court and initial trials in cases involving more than five years' potential imprisonment. The court also handles all significant civil matters, including juvenile prosecutions and other family court cases. The caseload is large and growing. On the criminal side alone (the discussion throughout will refer to adult prosecutions only), there were 10,539 new filings and 9458 dispositions in 1981. Because nearly all these cases had been screened by preliminary hearing or trial in Municipal Court, relatively few cases (21%) were diverted or dismissed at the Common Pleas stage. Of the remaining 7510 cases, 45% were disposed of by guilty plea, 49% by bench trial, and 6% by jury trial.

For administrative purposes, the criminal docket of the Court of Common Pleas is divided into three "programs"—the homicide program, the "Calendar" program (major or complex cases other than homicide), and the "List" program (all other cases). At the time of our study, thirty-five courtrooms were allocated for conducting criminal trials and taking pleas—ten in the homicide program, seventeen in the Calendar program, and eight in the List program.

The Procedure in Court.—Bench trials always begin with a colloquy designed to ensure that the defendant's waiver of his jury trial right was knowing and voluntary. The colloquy usually followed the standard format for the guilty plea colloquy: discussion focused on the elements of the offense and the maximum sentence, the defendant's state of mind, and the rights being waived. A few judges and prosecutors conducted virtually identical colloquies for bench trials and for guilty pleas. More often, however, rights unaffected by the jury waiver were not discussed. For the List cases in our sample, the waiver colloquy lasted an average of five minutes; some colloquies took as long as ten or fifteen minutes, but several others lasted only one or two minutes.

After the colloquy and acceptance of the jury waiver, the prosecution immediately called its first witness; we never observed an opening statement. Trial procedure followed the usual course, with cross-examination (if any), demurrers at the close of the Commonwealth's case, and testimony by defense witnesses (if any). Attorneys presented closing arguments in virtually every case, though the judge sometimes limited argument to one or two issues or heard argument only from the defense. The judge then announced a decision and—sometimes—a brief reason for it.

The time consumed by such proceedings was typically rather short. As Table II indicates 64% of the Calendar trials in our sample were completed in less than two hours. List program trials tended to be even shorter; the typical List room trial lasted about forty-five minutes, and 69% were completed in less than one hour. Allowing for the waiting time attributable to each disposition, the total courtroom time consumed by the typical List program bench trial was approximately one hour and twenty minutes, compared to the fifty-five minutes of total courtroom time spent on a typical guilty plea.

Table II
Time for Trial

	List		Calendar	
	N	**%**	**N**	**%**
Less than 30 minutes	27	18	1	4
30–59 minutes	78	51	5	20
1–2 hours	43	28	10	40
2–3 hours	2	1	5	20
Over 3 hours	3	2	4	16
Total	153	100	25	100

To what extent were these trials genuine adversary proceedings? Analysis of the procedures followed and of the time consumed points in two directions. The traditional procedural requisites of a contested trial were normally present, and in many instances they required considerable courtroom time. On the other hand, 18% of the List room trials were completed in about the same amount of time as was a typical guilty plea case, and most of the List cases required only a little more time—just twenty to thirty minutes more than a guilty plea. Were these "trials" really the functional equivalent of guilty pleas? The following subsections present qualitative and quantitative material bearing on that question.

"Adversariness": Behavior of the Attorneys.—In their trial preparation and their advice to their clients on the jury waiver decision, defenders generally seemed to assume that bench trials would be genuinely contested. Nearly all defenders directly confirmed this impression by stressing that they press hard for acquittals, that their relationship with the prosecutor is quite adversarial, and that the judges decide cases on the basis of the evidence. But there were exceptions. Three defenders told us that in all but a few cases, the List room trial is nothing but a slow guilty plea. Defender HI explained that the system is geared toward sentencing and not toward determining guilt or innocence. RO said that the bench trial is "just a charade . . . . The parties go through the motions." VO claimed that the List program is not designed to give fair verdicts, but only to dispose of cases quickly; because of lenient sentencing, defendants are not really hurt, but "it has nothing to do with justice."

We observed wide differences in the style and demeanor of the public defenders. We were able to make extended observations of two of the three defenders who saw the process as simply a "slow plea," and the courtroom performance of these lawyers was particularly revealing. When interviewed, HI had been the epitome of worldly cynicism, and the researchers had been grateful to learn from this experienced and articulate practitioner what the "real world" was actually like. In court, however, HI was extremely vigorous.

VO's approach, in contrast, seemed more consistent with his own portrayal of defenders' behavior. He was by far the most "low key" attorney we observed. He often declined to cross-examine, and when he did ask questions, he kept them to a minimum. Although we did once see VO put some energy into a cross-examination, on every other occasion he asked his questions in a monotone and showed no sign of emotion.

However one chooses to regard the performance of VO, he was a distinct exception among the attorneys we observed. Many other defenders might also be described as "low key," but they were far less cynical. These lawyers were calm and unemotional, unintimidating to witnesses, and generally respectful toward the judge. Nonetheless, they cross-examined thoroughly and pressed available points firmly. Their somewhat understated style enhanced the impression that their arguments were sincere and reasonable, just as it would have in a jury trial. These were very capable attorneys, thoroughly adversarial in their approach to trial.

When defense tactics seemed to us unwise or ineffective, the problem most often was not that the attorney was too "low key," but rather that he went to the opposite extreme. Whether by temperament or by choice, several defenders were highly assertive, flamboyant in style, and frequently emotional.

Private defense attorneys were even more likely to "go overboard" by pursuing unproductive cross-examination that only tended to reinforce the witness' story, using the closing argument for a speech about the reasonable doubt requirement, or making the same point repeatedly until the judge asked them to sit down. Although there were notable exceptions, private attorneys generally seemed less capable and less seasoned than the public defenders, and these factors may explain the private attorneys' frequent use of such counterproductive tactics. Possibly the private attorneys were more interested in impressing their clients than in persuading the judge (especially if the case was hopeless). A perceptive observer of attorney behavior would find much to question or criticize, but an insufficiently adversarial stance was seldom the problem.

"Adversariness": Judicial Behavior.—Judges typically played an active role at trial. Nearly all the judges questioned witnesses at least occasionally. A few questioned witnesses in virtually every case. Sometimes a judge sought to clear up an important point after direct and cross-examination had been completed; in No. 3087, a burglary case, Judge WO even recalled two witnesses to the stand after both sides had rested. Some of the judges also interrupted direct or cross-examination to put their own questions to the witnesses. Judge VT frequently intervened to ask even the most routine questions ("What happened next?"); he seemed to prefer to conduct direct examination himself. The judges also freely interrupted questioning that they considered irrelevant or repetitive. Attorneys were sometimes forcefully told to stop wasting time or to hurry up.

Given the lengthy and repetitive questioning that seemed a habit with some attorneys, judicial badgering of this kind was not always unwarranted.

Closing statements were almost always a time for active participation by the judge.

Interchanges with the judge usually covered the main points very rapidly. The parties used a great deal of verbal shorthand that would no doubt mystify a casual observer (or first offender), and judges seldom seemed to ponder or agonize over an issue. On the other hand, most of the judges did appear to focus conscientiously on the law and the evidence. Though they made up their minds in short order, most of them took the decision seriously and showed concern.

Following oral argument, judgment was rendered immediately; we never saw a case taken under advisement. The judges often gave no explicit reasons for their rulings, but many times they briefly referred to a critical weakness in the prosecution's or defense's theory of the case. Not all the decisions seemed completely logical. Particularly in cases arising out of fights among neighbors or acquaintances, judges sometimes seemed to find fault on both sides; under these circumstances a decision might be something of a compromise. In several cases, Calendar Judge VT explained his decision by stating simply, "This is a 'jury verdict.' "

To describe the judges' behavior as "adversarial" would risk confusion, because the adversary model is often identified with a system in which the parties assume absolute control over facts and issues while the judge remains wholly passive. The Philadelphia judges certainly were not "adversarial" in this sense. Our central concern, however, was to determine the extent to which the bench trials were *genuinely contested*, with vigorous efforts by opposing counsel and decisions based on applicable law and the testimony given in court. These features (which are said to be characteristic not only of jury cases, but also of trials within the nonadversary systems of continental Europe) seemed fully present in the Philadelphia bench trials we observed. In their relative activism, the judges may have taken a step toward the nonadversary role of the continental judge, but in no relevant sense could the proceedings be described as the functional equivalent of a guilty plea. With rare exceptions that will now be described, these trials were not "slow pleas." . . . In the course of eight weeks of observation by four full-time researchers, we found seven trials that might be considered candidates for the "slow plea" designation.

"Adversariness": The Data.—Our observations led us to conclude that a very few trials were perfunctory but that most were vigorously contested. Previous studies have almost uniformly asserted the opposite proposition—that a few bench trials may be contested but that most are not. Plainly, the choice between these two views depends critically on assessments of the relative frequency of "slow pleas." Under these conditions, one may too easily conclude that such assessments are simply a matter of subjective impression and that the "other side" has not carried its burden of proof. The qualitative information we have developed for Philadelphia provides such a clear, unequivocal picture that this problem should not arise. Nonetheless, quantitative material less dependent on evaluation and impression would furnish a useful supplementary perspective. Can we therefore develop an "objective," quantitative measure of "adversariness" and use it to gauge the vigor of the Philadelphia trials?

The difficulties of such an endeavor are not small. The elements of vigorous trial advocacy do not come in measurable units of intensity. A short, pointed cross-examination may be more effective than a long one; sometimes defense counsel may wisely prefer none at all. Even stipulations, which seem on their face the essence of cooperation rather than challenge, may be chosen as part of a carefully considered, vigorous defense strategy. One could, of course, compare the incidence of cross-examination, stipulations, or other defense tactics in bench trials and in jury trials, on the assumption that the latter provides a workable benchmark of genuine adversariness. But the two groups of cases differ systematically, in part because the very tactical concerns we want to study will affect the threshold decision whether to demand a jury. And even in otherwise "identical" cases, the tactics of vigorous defense differ when the trier of fact is a judge.

Despite these obstacles, we can develop useful "objective" indications of adversariness, provided that we recognize their limitations and do not forget their role as a supplement to the essential qualitative material. We may begin by examining the outcome of the trials. According to published court statistics, approximately 30% of all Philadelphia bench trials end in acquittal. Because this acquittal rate is somewhat higher than the one for jury trials, one might conclude that bench trials are the more effectively contested. Such a comparison, however, is quite misleading. Not only are the bench and jury cases dissimilar, but the published 30% acquittal rate for bench trials may be inflated by factors that are not relevant to adversariness. In our own sample, the bench trial acquittal rate was only 20% for List cases and 24% for Calendar cases, figures that by themselves say very little about whether the trials were perfunctory or genuine.

In addition to the acquittals, many bench trials ended in conviction only on charges significantly less serious than the principal counts. In the List program sample, significant charge reduction occurred in only 20% of the guilty plea cases but in 25% of the bench trial cases; moreover, significant charge reduction was present in 31% of the 128 bench trial *convictions*—55% more often than in guilty plea cases. Of course, the guilty plea and bench trial cases are not strictly comparable, because the former group presumably contains many more open-and-shut cases. But this is, in part, the point. When a case involves debatable issues, the defendant goes to trial and often wins significant charge reduction, a result normally unobtainable in Philadelphia plea bargaining. Thus, even the relatively simple criterion of case outcome suggests that a bench trial is not the functional equivalent of a guilty plea.

The outcome criterion cannot tell us whether the bench trials resulting in major convictions were genuinely contested. Fifty-two percent of the List cases ended in conviction on all the principal charges—the same outcome as in the typical guilty plea case. Many of these cases conceivably could have been "slow pleas." To refine the analysis further, we need to measure adversariness in terms of effort as well as result.

For the great bulk of the cases, stipulations alone do not provide an adequate measure of the vigor of the defense. Demurrers and reasonable doubt arguments also are unsatisfactory, because one or the other is almost always present and because there is no strictly objective way to distinguish serious from perfunctory efforts in these areas. We therefore chose to focus on the extent to which a factual defense was developed. We recorded for each case the nature of any cross-examination and the use of witnesses in defense. As Table IV indicates, only 11% of the List cases lacked any apparent challenge to the prosecution's factual allegations, and in only 30% of the List trials was the defense confined to cross-examination. Sixty percent involved both substantial cross-examination and an affirmative defense case, and the defense called witnesses other than the defendant.

Table IV
Characteristics of Defense

Defense Code	Defense Description	List N	List %	Calendar N	Calendar %
A	No substantial cross-examination; no defense witnesses	18	11	1	3
B	Cross-examination; no defense witnesses	48	30	6	21
C	Cross-examination; defendant testifies	56	35	3	10
D	Cross-examination; third-party defense witnesses	13	8	4	14
E	Cross-examination; defendant and other defense witnesses testify	27	17	15	52
	Total	162	100	29	100

Because proponents of plea bargaining often assert that nearly all criminal cases (up to 90%) are devoid of triable issues, it seems important to try to assess that claim empirically. Any attempt to gauge the frequency of such cases quantitatively and "objectively" is of course fraught with difficulty, but . . . the cases ending in acquittal or significant charge reduction (45% of the List program total) can safely be treated as triable ones. I believe that the same is true of the nineteen cases (an additional 12% of the total) in which unsuccessful defense efforts included testimony from third-party defense witnesses. Thus, roughly speaking, at least 57% of the List program cases involved legitimately triable issues.

CONCLUSION

From repeated pronouncements of the Supreme Court and a near-unanimity of scholarly opinion, we have learned that most felony cases are devoid of triable issues of fact or law; that a contested trial in such cases is therefore a needless waste of resources; that affording most defendants a contested trial is in any event wholly beyond the capacity of any American urban jurisdiction; and finally that even if we could somehow, heroically, make genuine trials available, opposing attorneys would nonetheless find ways to cooperate and would settle cases by negotiation anyway. It follows from all this that plea bargaining need not clash with due process values, that it is in any event inevitable, and that one had best accept this reality, make one's peace with it, and work to legitimate the plea bargaining process and to ameliorate its harshest effects.

The present study throws each of these assumptions into question. It shows that in America's fourth-largest city, no concessions of any kind are offered for guilty pleas in the great majority of felony cases. In the absence of concessions, most felony defendants do in fact demand a trial, and their cases are resolved in genuinely contested adversary proceedings. Many of these cases turn out to involve difficult, debatable questions of fact or law, and many defendants win acquittal or substantial charge reduction—results that in nearly all cases reflect not intuitive or off-the-cuff compromise, but the considered application of law to facts proved in open court.

Plea bargaining is not inevitable. In most American cities, judges and attorneys have *chosen* to process cases that way. The Supreme Court has chosen to tolerate, to legitimate, and finally to encourage the plea bargaining system. We can instead choose, if we wish, to afford criminal defendants a day in court. We can cease imposing a price, in months or years of incarceration, upon defendants who exercise that privilege, and can instead permit or even encourage defendants to ask for a hearing in which they may put the prosecution to its proof. We can make available a formal bench trial that permits the expeditious but fair and accurate resolution of criminal cases on the basis of public testimony, tested and challenged with the traditional tools of American adversary procedure. If we nevertheless continue to tolerate plea bargaining, that choice will not tell us that resources are too scarce or that *other* lawyers, those over there in court, are impatient with zealous advocacy and uncontrollably drawn to more comfortable modes of work. A choice to prefer plea bargaining to an inexpensive, feasible adversary trial will instead tell us a great deal about ourselves.

Comment and Question

The Philadelphia bench trial system described by Schulhofer is not quite the panacea it appears to be. It works because the City's toughest judges are assigned to the jury trial parts of the court. In effect defendants are given the choice of taking their chances before these tough judges who may impose a surcharge in the form of a harsher sentence, or opting for a guilty plea or bench trial without the fear of such a surcharge. Under the circumstances few opt for a jury trial and a great many opt for a bench trial. Although he does not condone this form of pressure to avoid lengthy jury trials, nevertheless Schulhofer thinks that Philadelphia's bench trials are truly adversarial and are a great advance over plea bargaining. Is he convincing? What in particular does he see as the advantage of the short but vigorous bench trial? If you are convinced, how might we institutionalize such a system—abolish the right to jury trial?

Some have said that the problem with American criminal trial system is that it is a Rolls Royce of a system—near perfect in its operation, but beyond the reach of most people—and that what we need is a trial that is the equivalent of a Ford Fiesta, not the best that can be built, but reliable enough under most circumstances. Has Schulhofer described this system?

F. RECOMMENDED READING

Heumann, Milton. *Plea Bargaining.* University of Chicago Press, Chicago, 1977.

Law and Society Review. Vol. 13, no. 2, Winter 1979. (Includes extensive bibliography).

Maynard, Douglas. *Inside Plea Bargaining: the Language of Negotiation.* Plenum Press, New York, 1984.

Rossett, Arthur and Cressey, Donald R. *Justice by Consent: Plea Bargains in the American Courthouse.* Lipincott, Philadelphia, 1976.

Utz, Pamela. *Settling the Facts.* Lexington Books, Lexington, Mass., 1978.

Chapter X

THE CORRECTIONAL ENTERPRISE

Introduction

The correctional enterprise is the most hidden and, in many ways, the least understood part of the criminal justice system. Yet what happens to a person who has been assigned to an institution or correctional program is terribly important, since it is here—in real life—that the purposes of the criminal law are transformed into a meaningful reality. In that sense, the correctional enterprise carries the burden of justifying the entire criminal process.

Correctional measures are of two kinds—institutional corrections, consisting of prison and jail; and community corrections—probation, parole and, in recent years, diversion. Prisons are state and Federal institutions, which house offenders serving relatively long term sentences—generally those of over a year. Jails are more complicated. They are under the authority of counties or cities, and typically hold persons serving short terms, usually less than one year, plus those awaiting trial who have not made bail.

Parole and probation are often confused and are quite similar in that both involve a degree of liberty in the community, under supervision, and both involve a threat of incarceration by a summary proceeding, far short of a trial, for violation of the conditions of liberty. Parole, however, is granted to one who has already served time in a penal institution and is conceived of as part of a prison term, while probation is used prior to incarceration and is conceived of as an alternative to imprisonment.

Diversion is another alternative to incarceration—indeed, it is an alternative to the trial or guilty plea as well. In return for a defendant's consent to postpone proceedings, he or she will not be prosecuted, but rather "diverted" to a correctional or educational program or facility in the community. There they may receive drug counselling, mental health therapy, job training, or simply the live-in guidance of a "halfway house." Probationers, parolees and those who have been diverted often may attend the same programs.

Although, at any one time, far more people are under some state control through diversion, probation or parole than are incarcerated, we will spend most of this chapter on the administration of our prisons and jails. These are far more expensive and politically they have been the most sensitive areas of our criminal system. In many ways these cry out most loudly for change—even though it is arguable that the community corrections systems are more important because of the far larger number of people they affect.

Taken together, these institutional and community corrections measures—diversion, probation, jail, prison, parole—fairly well exhaust the range of alternatives in the U.S. correctional enterprise. But these are not the only possible "correctional" measures. Throughout human history, "corrections," usually in some form of public torture—whipping, branding, stocks, pillory—has been a frustrating enterprise, often degrading to both punishers and the punished.

In the first two editions of this book, the corrections chapter followed the chapter on sentencing, since, in the criminal justice process, sentencing precedes "corrections." The two topics are, of course, inextricably linked, and it would be perfectly sensible to study this chapter after the one on sentencing. We have changed the order here to highlight the decision-making dilemmas of sentencing. If a convicted offender is to be sentenced, what do days, months, years of probation, jail, prison, parole, mean? This chapter attempts to convey that reality so that when sentencing is discussed, the student might consider how well the realities of the correctional enterprise concur with theories of sentencing.

A. CORRECTIONS IN HISTORY

1. CORPORAL PUNISHMENT *

Eighteenth-century criminal codes fixed a wide range of punishments. They provided for fines, for whippings, for mechanisms of shame like the stocks, pillory, and public cage, for banishment, and for the gallows. They used one technique or a combination of them, calling for a fine together with a period in the stocks, or for a whipping to be followed by banishment. The laws frequently gave the presiding magistrate discretion to choose among alternatives—to fine or to whip—or directed him to select the applicable one—to use the stocks if the offender could not pay his fine. They included some ingenious punishments, such as having a convicted felon mount the gallows, remain for an hour with a noose around his neck, and then go free. Rarely, however, did the statutes rely upon institutionalization. A sentence of imprisonment was uncommon, never used alone. Local jails held men caught up in the *process of judgment,* not those who had completed it: persons awaiting trial, those convicted but not yet punished, debtors who had still to meet their obligations. The idea of serving time in a prison as a method of correction was the invention of a later generation.

* David Rothman, "Correction in the Eighteenth Century," *The Discovery of the* *Asylum,* Little, Brown, Boston, 1971, p. 48. © 1971 (Reprinted by permission).

Questions

What purposes of punishment are served by corporal punishment? Does corporal punishment serve the purposes of deterrence? Rehabilitation? Incapacitation? Retribution? Inasmuch as corporal punishment is so much cheaper than imprisonment, why do we not use it more? Is it that in all likelihood we would simply use it in addition to imprisonment? Or is it that corporal punishment is much more threatening to people who have not grown up in families which constantly use corporal punishment anyway? Or, is it simply that we feel it is wrong?

2. CORPORAL PUNISHMENT vs. IMPRISONMENT *

In 1847, seventy-two soldiers who deserted from the United States Army and fought for Mexico during the Mexican-American War were tried for desertion. After all appeals, fifty were sentenced to be executed and fifteen to be lashed and branded. As for the latter:

> Lashing and branding was no mild form of retribution, according to descriptions. There were 50 lashes per man, and they were laid on with rawhide whips by brawny Mexican muleteers. The backs of those lashed "had the appearance of a pounded piece of raw beef, the blood oozing from every stripe as given." The brand was a capital "D" two inches high burned into the cheekbone with a red-hot iron. Those sentenced to this punishment were also required to dig the graves of the men who were hanged. . . .

Today, most people would react with outrage and disgust to the imposition of such physical abuse. Modern America has reached a point at which "[p]unitive mutilation has become unacceptable even as retaliation for irreversible bodily injury. Indeed, we have become repelled altogether by any form of corporal punishment." Professing humanitarian purposes, imprisonment has been substituted for whipping, mutilation, branding, impaling, and disemboweling. But is imprisonment really so different from or superior to the tortures of the past? Are the pain and suffering, degradation, and humiliation occasioned by flogging and branding truly more onerous than that resulting from an average prison term? How many days in a cage does it take to achieve a quantum of misery comparable to that suffered during the whipping and branding of the deserters?

Comment

Regardless of their faults, the prisons, it should be remembered, were developed because of a dissatisfaction with corporal punishment. To what extent are we better off today?

* M. Kay Harris and Frank M. Dunbaugh "Premise for a Sensible Debate: Giving Up Imprisonment" *Hofstra Law Review* Vol. 7, 1979 pp. 418–419. © 1979 (Reprinted by permission).

3. THE DEVELOPMENT OF THE PRISON **

The American prison system as we know it began in New York in the early 19th century. The founders of this system were men of high purpose, who conceived of prisons as more than simple warehouses of convicted criminals. "Reformation" was their goal, and, as rational men, they developed a concept of imprisonment which was consistent with their beliefs concerning the causes of crime in the simple society of that time. The prisons which these reformers built almost 150 years ago to put their theories into practice survive physically throughout the country and conceptually in maximum security prisons like Attica. . . .

When the doors of Auburn Prison opened in 1819, America had the model and prototype of its maximum security prison. . . .

For economic reasons, most American prisons came to be patterned after Auburn and were as much silent factories and involuntary labor pools as they were bleak prisons. Auburn Prison, in fact, turned a profit in the early years of its existence.

It was an article of faith that these prisons would not only be successful in transforming idle and corrupt men into virtuous laborers, but that they were examples of model communities from which the larger society could benefit as well. . . .

Discipline was regarded as the key to success of the congregate prison, and one rule soon emerged as the key to discipline. That rule was silence, a silence so profound and so pervasive that it became the most awesome and striking feature of the fortresslike prisons of America. From their tour through Auburn, de Beaumont and de Tocqueville wrote, "We felt as if we traversed catacombs; there were a thousand living beings, and yet it was a desert solitude."

In order to maintain silence and order in the movement of large numbers of inmates about the prison, Auburn devised the silent, lockstep shuffle. Inmates stood in line, each with the right foot slightly behind the left and the right arm outstretched with the hand on the right shoulder of the man in front of him. They moved in a shuffle, sliding the left foot forward, then bringing the right foot to its position just behind the left, then the left again, then the right. This awkward locomotion, coupled with the striped uniforms in New York, was considered therapeutic. Prisoners were not in a state of grace with society, and their condition was made as graceless as possible, lest they forget their corrupt condition. As the prisoners moved, they were not permitted to hold their heads up, as would befit free men, and their shameful pose with their heads turned to the right and their eyes cast to the floor kept them ever mindful of their low estate and the wickedness that had brought them there. The guard watching such a

** The New York State Special Commission on Attica, 1972. Reprinted with permission.

group shuffling across a prison area could readily spot any unauthorized conversation or activity.

Solitary confinement in a bare cell with one meal a day was introduced as a punishment for breaking the rules. But solitary had the disadvantage of removing prisoners from the labor force necessary to support the institution. Physical punishment, which had a less disruptive effect on inmate labor, was authorized. Soon, the very punishments that prisons were supposed to have eliminated were widely used within the prisons themselves, and the whip was the most common. Water "cures," stocks, "stretchers," and sweatboxes were all widely used in American prisons well into the 20th century. By the 20th century, the old concept of "reformation" had largely disappeared, and most prison administrators viewed the goal of prisons as simply to keep prisoners securely in custody. Indeed, the warden's first assistant, who was responsible for the day-to-day operation of the prison, was known as the "principal keeper."

In New York, as one prison became overcrowded, another was built, always on the Auburn principle. In 1825, Sing Sing was built along the Hudson River north of New York City by a hundred inmates from Auburn who were transported down the Hudson by boat, shackled in irons. When the swelling prison population threatened the silent program and the individual cell policy, additional cellblocks were added to Auburn and Sing Sing. In 1844, the construction of Clinton Prison was authorized.

The construction of all these prisons followed the same basic plan. In fact, prison construction in the United States did not change until well into the 20th century, and even then variations were usually minor and often shortlived. From the beginning the American prison has been a maximum security institution.

As new Auburns were built throughout the country, the severity of the prison routine became the subject of criticism by a new generation of penal reformers. In 1870, the National Prison Association, at its founding meeting in Cincinnati, reminded the authorities that "reformation, not vindictive suffering, should be the purpose of penal treatment of prisoners." The means toward that end, which the Cincinnati prison congress of 1870 advocated in its Declaration of Principles, included:

> The prisoner should be made to realize that his destiny is in his own hands.

> Prison officials should be trained for their jobs.

> Prison discipline should be such as to gain the will of the prisoner and conserve his self-respect.

> The aim of the prison should be made industrious freemen rather than orderly and obedient prisoners.

A more adequate architecture should be developed, providing sufficiently for air and sunlight, as well as for prison hospitals, school rooms, etc.

The social training of prisoners should be facilitated through proper association, and the abolition of the silence rules. . . .

. . . At the turn of the century, New York made efforts to actually implement some of the specific proposals of the Cincinnati Congress of 1870. The first such effort was Elmira Reformatory, opened in 1876 for young first offenders. Built on the same architectural principle as Auburn, however, it soon proved to be only another prison in the style of Auburn, but with younger inmates—a maximum security reformatory. In 1911, Great Meadow, a new prison without a wall around it, was built for young first offenders. The striped uniforms and the silent lockstep were discontinued. The rule of silence continued in actual practice in most institutions, but at Great Meadow movies were presented to the inmates once every two weeks. The dining area provided small tables with chairs in order that the young inmates could dine in a more natural atmosphere than that provided by immovable tables and stools in the other prisons.

Due to the overcrowding elsewhere, however, it was not many years before Great Meadow began receiving second offenders and other first offenders who were deemed by the authorities to require close supervision. Discipline tightened at Great Meadow; enforcement of silence appeared in the routine, and a prison factory, like those at Auburn, Sing Sing, and Clinton, was started. By 1928, a wall had been erected around the once medium security prison of Great Meadow, and it was added to the list of adult male maximum security prisons of the state.

The architecture of prisons had become a self-engendering style. The major improvements in the construction of prisons were the introduction of escape-proof cells and unbreakable toilets and washbasins. This escalating process of constructing ever more secure prisons reached its pinnacle in 1931, when the most secure, escape-proof prison ever built opened in the little upstate village of Attica, New York. With such dedication poured into its construction, Attica was, at the time, the most expensive prison ever built. . . .

In the late 1920s there had occurred the first "wave" or widespread outbreak of prison riots in this country. In July 1929, some 1,600 inmates of Clinton Prison rioted in protest of overcrowding there; three inmates were killed when the state put down the uprising. In the same year, Auburn Prison exploded when a trusty threw acid into a guard's face, overpowered him, and secured the keys to the prison arsenal. Guns were passed out to several inmates and a general riot ensued in which four inmates escaped. Six shops were burned, the assistant warden was killed, and the prison was wrecked before the prisoners were subdued by rifles, machine guns, and tear gas. Then, as now,

New York's immediate response to the uprisings in its prisons was the appointment of official investigators and commissions to determine the causes of the sudden uprisings.

Attica State Prison in New York was to be the solution to the recent problem of prison uprisings and the response to the commissions that investigated them.

When Attica opened, it was widely hailed as the ultimate prison. Its wall alone, enclosing 55 acres, was 30 feet high, extended 12 feet into the ground, and cost $1,275,000 to erect. The prison contained four separated cellblocks, each of which could house some 500 men in individual cells. The total cost of the prison eventually reached the sum of "approximately $9,000,000." . . .

. . . [No] other prison since Auburn has created the interest that Attica did when it was built. Shortly before it opened, Attica was hailed in the following article, which appeared in the *New York Times* on August 2, 1931:

Attica Prison To Be Convict's Paradise

Condemned by the Wickersham Commission for its maintenance of Auburn and Clinton prisons, New York State will have an answer to charges of inhuman penal conditions when the new State Prison opens at Attica within the next few months with its full quota of 2,000 convicts. Said to be the last word in modern prison construction, the new unit in the State's penal system will do away with such traditions as convict bunks, mess hall lockstep, bull pens, and even locks and keys.

In their places will be beds with springs and mattresses, a cafeteria with food under glass, recreation rooms and an automatic signal system by which convicts will notify guards of their presence in their cells. Doors will be operated by compressed air, sunlight will stream into cells and every prisoner will have an individual radio.

Perhaps because of the depression economy, perhaps for other reasons as well, no Attica inmate has ever seen the institution described above. When Attica opened, there was no cafeteria with food under glass, no recreation room, no automatic signal system, and no sunlight streaming into the cells. There was, in fact, nothing but another huge, foreboding prison. With the unprecedented emphasis on security visible in every brick and every door, this "last word in modern prison construction," far from doing away with locks and keys, made them the focal point around which all life revolved.

When Attica opened, over 130 years had passed since Auburn Prison was built; the population of New York State had changed vastly; the entire social structure of the nation had been dramatically altered; new laws and social conditions had altered the very nature of crime itself; theories of human behavior had been radically modified by the developing social sciences. In fact, everything had changed—everything but the prisons. They were still being built in the silent congregate style of Auburn.

Questions and Comment

Jeremy Bentham argued in his treatise on prisons, *Panopticon: or the Inspection House (1791)* that every penal system must observe the rule of "severity," that is, that the standard of living of "a convict doomed to punishment" must be less desirable than that enjoyed by "the poorest class of subjects in a state of innocence and liberty." Herman Mannheim was later to cite this "rule" as a realistic limit to the possibilities of penal reform. He restated it somewhat as follows: "Every deterioration in economic conditions as well as every improvement in prison conditions is bound to lead to an equality that will be unacceptable to the population at large." In other words, prisoners must always be worse off in comparison to the most impoverished portion of the free citizenry. What do you think might happen if prisoners were better off?

Might this "rule" explain why Attica was not built according to the original plan calling for a model prison? Recall that Attica was opened during the economic depression of 1931. What explanation would you suggest if you do not find this one plausible?

B. INSTITUTIONAL CORRECTIONS

Introduction

Throughout the 1980s prison systems in most all of the states and the federal system experienced unprecedent growth, and reached record highs. Indeed the nation's prison population more than doubled during the 1980s, making it the fastest growing public sector service area in the nation. Consider the implications of this boom, as you read about the current state of America's prisons.

1. THE CONTEMPORARY PRISON

a. LITTLE v. WALKER

United States Court of Appeals, Seventh Circuit, 1977.
552 F.2d 193.

CUMMINGS, Circuit Judge.

Plaintiff, then an inmate of the Illinois State Penitentiary in Stateville, Illinois, filed this civil rights class suit. . . .

. . . Plaintiff alleged that he and other inmates at Stateville "repeatedly suffered acts and threats of physical violence, sexual assaults, and other crimes perpetrated by other inmates from whom plaintiffs were not reasonably protected by defendants." . . .

. . . The complaint alleged that plaintiff and fellow inmates lived in constant and imminent fear of physical violence and sexual assaults, "especially when inflicted by gang-affiliated inmates."

Defendant Chairman of the Institutional Assignments Committee of the prison supposedly ordered plaintiff and others to work in certain areas of the penitentiary that were controlled by gang-affiliated inmates. Because of fear for their personal safety, plaintiff and others refused to comply with such work assignments and were then committed to isolation and other grievous punishment "at the direction of the Disciplinary Committee." To avoid violence-prone and gang-affiliated inmates as well as Disciplinary Committee punishment for refusal to accept work assignments in gang-controlled areas, plaintiff and other inmates accepted placement in "Segregation-Safekeeping" status, sometimes in excess of one year. Such status resulted in:

"(a) Denial of access to religious services, ministrations, and sacraments;

"(b) Denial of all opportunities of a rehabilitative nature, including educational and vocational instruction;

"(c) Denial of adequate medical and dental treatment;

"(d) Denial of adequate means with which to maintain their cells in a clean and sanitary condition;

"(e) Denial of essentials necessary for personal hygiene, including access to shower facilities at least once a week;

"(f) Denial of access to the prison dining room or to warm food served in a sanitary manner;

"(g) Denial of all indoor or outdoor recreational activity;

"(h) Denial of effective access to the prison law library and legal materials contained therein;

"(i) Denial of opportunities for parole, work release program or transfer to a minimum security unit or institution."

Defendants made no distinction between disciplinary and protective segregatees, thereby subjecting plaintiff to the same restrictions and deprivations imposed on inmates who had committed disciplinary infractions.

Those placed in Segregation-Safekeeping status were confined by defendants in gallery 6 of cell-house B where the inmates most prone to violence are also housed. Those in Segregation-Safekeeping status had meals served to them in their cells by gang-affiliated inmates who "withhold meals from plaintiffs unless plaintiffs perform unnatural sexual acts through the cell bars." Defendants ignored plaintiff's entreaties to remedy the situation.

According to the complaint, on September 6, 1973, through defendants' failure to afford reasonable protection, cell-house B was seized by a group of rebellious inmates for nine hours while gang rapes were inflicted on other inmates. Plaintiff's personal property, including legal materials, was destroyed and confiscated. After the rebellion, defendants nevertheless continued to confine plaintiff in the same area with those inmates in disciplinary segregation who had instigated the uprising.

The complaint alleged that Little and other inmates were deprived of their constitutional rights to due process of law, equal protection of the laws [and] freedom from cruel and unusual punishment, . . . and that defendants acted with malice or reckless disregard for the rights of Little and others. Plaintiff asserted that defendants knew or should have known of these abuses and failed to correct them. In sum, the plaintiff maintains these officials failed to provide him reasonable protection from violent inmates and that they subjected him to impermissible privations while in protective segregation. Numerous affidavits were filed to substantiate the charges, . . .

In Breeden v. Jackson, 457 F.2d 578, 580 (4th Cir.1972), the petitioner was voluntarily transferred from the general prison population to maximum security because of threats of bodily harm from other inmates. The majority opinion denied him equitable relief or damages because his complaints only "related to limited recreational or exercise opportunities, the prison menu and restricted shaving and bathing privileges." In sharp contrast, Little's alleged treatment was so unreasonable as to be characterized as vindictive, cruel or inhuman or so intolerable in fundamental fairness that even the *Breeden* majority would have found a violation of his constitutional rights. In any event, Judge Craven's dissenting opinion in *Breeden* now appears to have been the rule in the Fourth Circuit since July of 1973. . . .

. . . By May 1972, it was already well settled that the treatment Little received while in Segregation-Safekeeping status was cruel and unusual punishment. . . . And there is no doubt of the continuing validity of Chief Judge Fairchild's stricture in Knell v. Bensinger, 522 F.2d at 725:

> "[I]n exercising their informed discretion, officials must be sensitive and alert to the protections afforded prisoners by the developing judicial scrutiny of prison conditions and practices."

. . .

. . . It has been both a settled and first principle of the Eighth Amendment, long before the relevant 1972–1974 period in the instant case, that penal measures are constitutionally repugnant if they "are incompatible with 'the evolving standards of decency that mark the progress of a maturing society,' or [if they] 'involve the unnecessary and wanton infliction of pain.'" . . . Violent attacks and sexual assaults by inmates upon the plaintiff while in protective segregation are manifestly "inconsistent with contemporary standards of decency." "Deliberate indifference" to these happenings "constitutes the 'unnecessary and wanton infliction of pain' proscribed by the Eighth Amendment." Moreover, in the highly publicized landmark case of Holt v. Sarver, . . . it was held that under the Eighth Amendment prisoners are entitled to protection from the assaults of other prisoners. . . . Therefore, it is immaterial that Little himself sought refuge in the segregated part of Stateville for bodily protection.

Questions

Note the rights which inmate Little gave up in Segregation-Safe-keeping status. Which of these do you think that such prisoners should be made to give up? Which of these should be denied to all prisoners? Why?

If Little had escaped to avoid the attacks by other inmates, would he have a "necessity" defense to a prosecution for escape? What if he escaped to avoid the measures the prison authorities took to "protect" him?

b.   GROWTH IN CORRECTIONS

(1) AMERICA'S IMPRISONMENT BINGE *

Since 1880, the year criminologists began keeping track of prison populations, the number of people locked up in America's jails and prisons has steadily increased. A century ago, the daily imprisonment rate (i.e., the number of persons imprisoned on any given day) was about 120 per 100,000 citizens. Today it is more than 300 per 100,000—*almost a threefold increase* (Figure 1).

In absolute numbers, there are almost 530,000 people in state and federal prisons, 235,000 people in jail, and another 85,000 children in juvenile facilities (Figure 2). The total number of people confined, 850,000, would compromise a city larger than most of the nation's

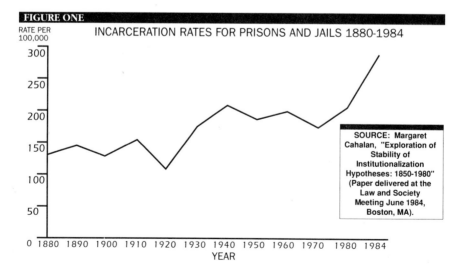

FIGURE ONE

RATE PER 100,000   INCARCERATION RATES FOR PRISONS AND JAILS 1880-1984

SOURCE: Margaret Cahalan, "Exploration of Stability of Institutionalization Hypotheses: 1850-1980" (Paper delivered at the Law and Society Meeting June 1984, Boston, MA).

* John Irwin and James Austin, It's About Time: Solving America's Prison Crowding Crisis, The National Council on   Crime and Delinquency, pp. 7–9, 1987 (Reprinted with Permission).

FIGURE TWO

AMERICANS UNDER CRIMINAL JUSTICE CONTROL

Adults	Annual Admissions	Annual Population
Jail [1]	8,084,344	234,500
Prison [2]	173,289	528,945
Probation	766,488[3]	1,711,190[4]
Parole	132,562[3]	268,515[4]
ADULT TOTAL	9,156,683	2,743,150
Juveniles		
Public Institutions [5]	521,607	49,322
Private Institutions [5]	88,806	34,000
Probation [6]	337,000	337,000
Parole	33,500	33,500
JUVENILE TOTAL	980,913	453,822
TOTALS	10,137,596	3,196,972

SOURCES:
1. **U.S. Dept. of Justice.** *Jail Inmates, 1984.*
2. **U.S. Dept. of Justice.** *Prisoners in 1984 and Prisoner Count, 1986.*
3. **Criminal Justice Institute.** *The Corrections Yearbook, 1986.*
4. **U.S. Dept. of Justice.** *Probation and Parole, 1984.*
5. **U.S. Dept. of Justice.** *Children in Custody, 1982 and 1984.*
6. **National Center for Juvenile Justice.**

major cities including San Francisco, Cleveland, Denver, San Diego, and St. Louis. There are another 2.5 million adults and juveniles on probation or parole. On any given day, therefore, the criminal justice system supervises 3.2 million people.

But such large figures fail to reflect the tremendous scope of imprisonment and correctional supervision. The U.S. Justice Department reports that more than 8 million people, most of them arrested but not convicted of misdemeanor crimes, are booked into jails each year. The number of people admitted to jails plus the large numbers of adults and children admitted to prison and juvenile facilities, makes a total of close to 9 million people put in jail or prison each year.

What is particularly disturbing, however, is the recent rapid expansion of state prison populations. In 1970, there were less than 200,000 people in state and federal prisons. Now, more than 500,000 inmates are jammed into the nation's bulging prisons (Figure 3).

According to the U.S. Department of Justice, an additional 750 prisoners are being added to prison populations *each week*. Some states are experiencing explosive increases. California's prison population, which is the largest in the country, rose 33 percent in one year (1986). By 1995, California officials project that the adult prison population will surpass 110,000. Another 100,000 will be held in California's jails and juvenile facilities. Nevada, which has the highest incarceration rate in the nation (420 per 100,000 citizens) is expected to double its prison population by 1995, at which time Nevada's imprisonment rate will approach 700 per 100,000.

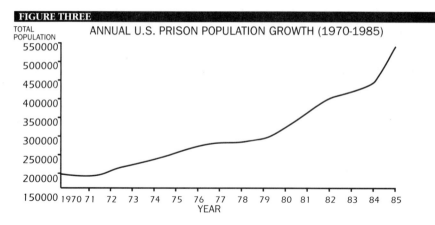

FIGURE THREE

ANNUAL U.S. PRISON POPULATION GROWTH (1970-1985)

While most states will not experience the astronomic increases of California and Nevada, they will continue to grow at rates that far exceed population increases. The National Council on Crime and Delinquency (NCCD), which provides forecasts for seven states that incarcerate almost one-third of the nation's prison population, projects that inmate populations will increase by 50 percent in the next 10 years.

What is causing these recent phenomenal increases? It is not increases in the nation's population, which has grown by about 10 percent since 1975, nor crime rates, which have been fairly constant for the last 10 years. Prison populations have more than doubled in the same period. [See Figure 4.]

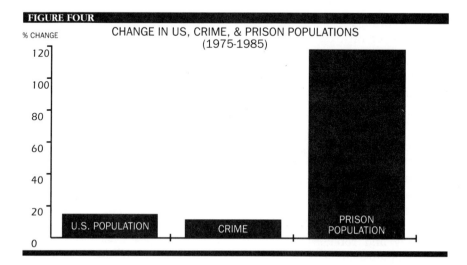

FIGURE FOUR

CHANGE IN US, CRIME, & PRISON POPULATIONS
(1975-1985)

The evidence suggests that *sentencing legislation,* approved by elected officials, has resulted in courts sending a higher percentage of persons convicted of felonies to prison and for longer terms of imprisonment. For example, 18 percent of California's felony convictions in 1976 resulted in imprisonment. In 1986, the proportion of felons convicted and sentenced to prison approached 35 percent. In addition, prison terms are much longer, especially for those convicted of burglary, drug dealing, and crimes of violence. Federal courts have increased prison sentences by almost 33 percent according to a recent study by the U.S. Department of Justice. In Illinois, prison terms for many crimes of violence are several years longer than sentences given out for similar crimes less than a decade ago.

(2) CALIFORNIA DEPARTMENT OF CORRECTIONS POPULATION PROJECTIONS 1990–1996 *

Factors Affecting Prison Population Increases

Over the last ten years, the population in California Department of Corrections institutions has increased considerably. On June 30, 1990, the population was 93,810 compared to 23, 511 on June 30, 1980, an annual compound increase of 14.8 percent. The increase over the June 30, 1989 population of 82,872 was 13.2 percent. The increases in population are due to continuing increases in new admissions and parole violators returning to prison.

The increase in new admissions is due primarily to the impact of legislative changes and an increase in reported crime, especially drug-related crime. The increase in parole violator returns results from a combination of factors, including severe crowding in local jails and court orders against such crowding, a larger parolee population, and a high rate of returning parolees with new terms.

Over the years, voter initiatives, court decisions, legislation and administrative policy have played, and continue to play, key roles in affecting the population level of California's prisons.

Voter initiatives and legislation enacted since 1976 have significantly limited the ability of the courts to sentence certain offenders to local disposition rather than state prison, as well as increased the penalties for a great number of felony offenders. Some of the major offenses for which the possibility of probation has been restricted or eliminated include residential burglary, child molestation, specific sex offenses, arson and other offenses involving the use of a firearm. Legislation has increased sentences for committing murder, residential burglary and robbery, manslaughter, certain drug and sex offenses, crimes against defenseless victims, other crimes involving the use of a firearm, and many others.

* California Department of Corrections, Fall 1990 Population Projections 1990–1996, Sacramento 1990.

Recent administrative policy and court decisions have also translated into stronger law enforcement and more severe criminal sanctions. Given the current tenor of the Legislature, the court system and the public-at-large, California's prison population can be expected to continue to grow in the foreseeable future.

Figure 1 graphically displays the Fall 1990 projections for total institution population.

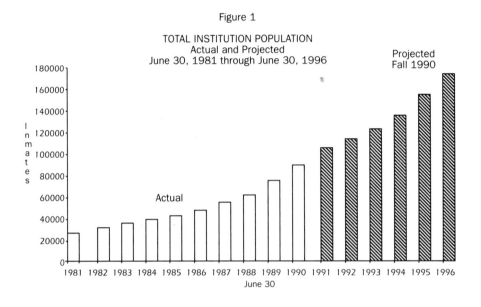

Figure 1

(3) THE MILLION DOLLAR CELL *

Most people are aware that prisons are expensive to build and operate, but few understand just how expensive. Indeed, previous estimates routinely cited by public officials have dramatically underestimated the amounts of money spent on housing prisoners and building new prisons.

Prison and jail administrators typically calculate operating costs by dividing their annual budget by the average daily prison population. However, this accounting practice is quite misleading and produces patently low estimates of the true costs of imprisonment. For example, agency budgets often exclude contracted services for food, medical care, legal services, and transportation provided by other government agencies. According to two studies conducted in New York, these additional expenses increased the official per diem operating costs by 20 to 25 percent. An independent audit of the Indiana prison system found that

---

* John Irwin and James Austin, It's About Time: Solving America's Prison Crowding Crisis, The National Council on Crime and Delinquency, pp. 9–11, 1987 (Reprinted with Permission).

actual expenditures were one-third higher than those reported by the agency. Besides the "hidden" direct expenditures, there are other costs which are rarely included in calculations of imprisonment costs. For instance, the state loses taxes that would be paid by many of the imprisoned, pays more welfare to their families, and maintains spacious prison grounds that are exempt from state and local real estate taxation. In the New York study conducted by Coopers and Lybrand in 1977, these costs amounted to over $21,000 per inmate.

While there is considerable variation among the states, on the average, prison officials claim that it costs about $20,000 per year to house, feed, clothe, and supervise a prisoner. Because this estimate does not include indirect costs, the true annual expenditure probably exceeds $30,000 per prisoner.

The other enormous cost is prison construction. Prisons are enclosed, "total" institutions in which prisoners are not only housed, but guarded, fed, clothed and worked. They also receive schooling and medical and psychological treatment. These needs require—in addition to cellblocks or dormitories—infirmaries, classrooms, laundries, offices, and kitchens. Dividing the total construction costs of one of these institutions by the number of prisoners it houses, produces a cost per "bed" as low as $7,000 for a minimum security prison, to $155,000 for a maximum security prison.

However, instead of using current tax revenues to pay directly for this construction, the state does what most citizens do when buying a house—they borrow the money, which must be paid back over several decades. The borrowing is done by selling bonds or using other financing instruments that may triple the original figure. The costs of prison construction are further increased by "errors" in original bids by contractors and cost overruns due to delays in construction, which seem to be the rule rather than the exception. A recent survey of 15 states with construction projects revealed that cost overruns averaged *40 percent* of the original budget projections.

Consequently, when a state builds and finances a typical medium security prison it will spend approximately $268,000 per bed for construction alone. However, operating costs will greatly surpass construction costs in a little more than 10 years. Assuming a *conservative* $25,000 yearly operating cost per inmate with a two percent inflation factor, taxpayers will spend over one *million dollars* for each prisoner they incarcerate over a 30–year period (Figure 5).

The enormous increases in the cost of imprisonment are just beginning to be felt by the state. For example, in California a $300 million state expenditure deficit, caused, in part, by the uncontrolled rising costs of the prison system, resulted in a cutback in funds for public education and medical services for the poor. Budgetary battles have begun in which important state services for children, the elderly, the sick, and the poor are gutted to pay for prisons.

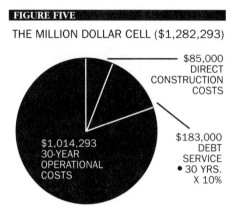

FIGURE FIVE

THE MILLION DOLLAR CELL ($1,282,293)

$85,000
DIRECT
CONSTRUCTION
COSTS

$1,014,293
30-YEAR
OPERATIONAL
COSTS

$183,000
DEBT
SERVICE
● 30 YRS.
X 10%

(4) THE COURTS AND UNCONSTITUTIONAL CONDITIONS *

Modern prisoners' rights litigation began in the 1960s as a natural adjunct to the civil rights movement and society's increasing interest in the plight of the poor and disenfranchised. Prior to that time, the courts had a policy of refusing to entertain claims by prisoners that their constitutional rights were being violated. This hands-off doctrine was based on the notion that elected officials and the citizenry were entitled to make decisions about the treatment of prisoners and that, in any event, the management of a prison required an expertise in penology that was beyond the ken of the federal courts. Beginning in the 1960s, inmate advocates began to make incursions in this policy of non-interference, and they established limited rights for prisoners in such areas as religious freedom and freedom of expression.

Litigation challenging overcrowded prison conditions grew along with the prisoners' rights movement and the prison population. The earliest cases involved such notorious prison systems as those in Arkansas and Alabama, where overcrowding and a host of other deplorable conditions and practices were pervasive and evident. Citing violence, malnutrition, inadequate medical care, filth and infestation, and, of course, severe overcrowding, lawyers for the prisoners argued that the combination of these factors, the "totality of conditions" in such institutions, amounted to a violation of the Eighth Amendment's prohibition against "cruel and unusual punishment."

Lawsuits proliferate and plaintiffs continue to achieve remarkable success. Prisoners' advocates have learned to identify and document the onerous conditions their clients suffer as a consequence of overcrowding. They succeed because so many prisons and jails are deficient in so many ways.

* Claudia Angelos and James B. Jacobs, "Prison Overcrowding and The Law," Annals, *AAPSS,* Vol. 478, March, 1985. Pp. 100–112 ©1985. Reprinted by permission of Sage Publications, Inc.

In hearing the Eighth Amendment complaints of sentenced convicts, the lower courts must examine a broad range of prison conditions to determine whether their sum amounts to an unconstitutional totality. Almost invariably, overcrowding is one of those conditions. Since crowding alone is not unconstitutional, courts must, in each of these cases, determine whether, and to what extent, crowding has caused "deprivation of basic human needs" before they can order relief from the offending conditions. "Basic needs" are those needs which, if not met, result in "wanton pain." Courts must consider medical and mental health services, violence, food preparation and quality, sanitary conditions, hygiene, and recreational opportunities.

In determining the extent to which deficiencies in these areas are the consequence of crowding—as distinct from inadequate funding, poor administration, or sheer indifference—the lower courts hear a wide range of evidence, including testimony from corrections officials, inmates, and experts. Not surprisingly, correctional administrators themselves often blame their failure to meet minimum standards of humane treatment on crowded conditions; this explanation is more appealing than poor or indifferent administration. Expert witnesses in the fields of penology, public health, psychology, and medicine testify about the connection between overcrowding and a facility's ability to meet basic needs. The statistics purport that, for example, the increased assault rate is associated with double-celling. Inmates testify about the misery of cramped cells, sleeping on cement floors, clogged toilets, overtaxed health care and recreational services, and their inability to protect themselves from other inmates.

A leading formulation postulates four factors for consideration:

—the actual level of crowding, that is, the square footage of living space designated for each inmate;

—the location of the inmates' beds, for example, whether mattresses are placed on the floors of cells, dayrooms, corridors, or elsewhere;

—how much time away from their sleeping quarters inmates are afforded on a daily basis, and how much space these and other areas provide; and

—the duration of pretrial confinement.

If crowding is extreme, if the sleeping arrangements are unsanitary, and if deprivations endure for many weeks and for the greater portion of the day, a finding of unconstitutional crowding is likely.

Because the courts have great latitude in interpreting the Supreme Court's crowding jurisprudence and in applying constitutional standards to individual cases, overcrowding and totality litigation is unpredictable, especially when some deprivational conditions exist but not others. In each case, the courts confront a number of difficult questions: How many detainees, in what size cell, for how long a period, constitutes "genuine privations and hardships over an extended period of time"?   How many and what prison conditions must cause the inmates "pain" before they aggregate to an unconstitutional "totality"? What weight should the court assign each factor in determining whether the "totality" violates the Eighth or Fourteenth Amendment?

It is unlikely that precise answers can ever be provided. Each institution is to some degree unique. Housing facilities, medical care, cleanliness, degree of violence, and administrative practices vary widely. The discretion afforded the lower courts to sort through, weigh, and balance the many factors that they must consider in deciding these wide-ranging and time-consuming cases leads inevitably to subjective decision making. Each judge necessarily infuses some of his or her own values into the ultimate findings of fact and conclusions of law. The outcome of each case depends on the facts presented in the lower court, not on the legal formulae promulgated by appellate courts and the Supreme Court.

c. RESPONSES TO UNCONSTITUTIONAL CONDITIONS

(1) THE IMPACT OF LITIGATION *

The case came to trial in August 1975. Testimony for prisoners was studded with horror stories of murder, assault with knives and other prison-made weapons, and rape. It was shown that weapons were in widespread use by prisoners, if not for attacks on others then for purposes of self-defense. The prison authorities had abdicated their responsibilities for the prevention of violence and the maintenance of order.

An expert sanitarian reported on the numerous indicia of rodents in the food preparation areas and on the presence of weevils in the flour, bedbugs in the dormitory, and cockroaches in unobstruced circulation throughout the facilities. Toilets overflowed or were otherwise inoperable. In the sanitarian's opinion, regardless of any other charges that might be made against the prison administration, these facilities were unfit for human habitation. Six expert witnesses were called to testify to the deficiencies in custodial and administrative management. The state's defense was overwhelmed, and its attorneys virtually conceded defeat.

.   .   .

At the conclusion of the trial in August 1975, Judge Johnson ordered an immediate end to the use of the "doghouse" and other cells unsuitable for the punitive segregation of prisoners. The remaining remedies were deferred until a detailed decree could be prepared.

On January 13, 1976, Johnson issued his decree. He found that the State of Alabama was in violation of its constitutional duty to provide prisoners with "reasonable protection from the constant threat

* John P. Conrad, "From Barbarism Toward Decency: Alabama's Long Road To Prison Reform," Journal of Research in   Crime and Delinquency, Vol. 26, No. 4 November 1989, c. 1989 Sage Publications, Inc. (Reprinted with Permission).

of violence." Further, its "penal system cannot be operated in such a manner that it impedes an inmate's ability to attempt rehabilitation, or simply to avoid physical, mental or social deterioration."

The court enjoined the governor and other officers of the state government from failing to implement the specific requirements set forth in an appendix to the order and within the specified time limits. The appendix contained a statement of the "Minimum Constitutional Standards for Inmates of the Alabama Penal System." In response, Governor Wallace charged that "thugs and judges" were now in charge of the prisons, thereby keynoting a resistance to reform that has to this day been a persisting theme in Alabama political discourse. In the Minimum Constitutional Standards set forth by Judge Johnson, there were 11 categories of requirements, ranging from overcrowding to staffing. Each category included a great deal of detail for which officials would be held accountable.

To monitor the implementation of the order, Judge Johnson appointed a Human Rights Committee. . . .

This was the beginning of a process that was to continue for 12 years. All concerned were to discover that it is one thing for the court to issue a wise and necessary injunction but that in Alabama it was an arduous, expensive, and interminable matter to implement the requirements of the injunction.

The implementation of *Newman* was left to Commissioner Sullivan, and the court set a deadline of six months for the first report of progress. Commissioner Sullivan faithfully submitted monthly reports. However, little actual progress was made, mainly because there were insufficient funds. . . .

The population issue was the most intractable of the Minimum Standards required in Judge Johnson's order. The requirement that the system's population should be limited to the actual capacity of the prisons resulted in immediate and predictable population explosions in the county jails of Alabama. Efforts to induce the Parole Board, which was, and still is, independent of the department, to liberalize parole policies were intransigently resisted. . . .

To circumvent the Parole Board, legislation was introduced to provide for "good time" for prisoners serving short sentences—less than 10 years—and passed both houses of the legislature. . . .

Britton [the Commissioner] started an ambitious prison building program in hopes that he could solve the long-standing overcrowding. Two new prisons were built in the northern section of the state, in spite of vigorous resistance in communities in which it was felt that prisons should be situated in the southern part of the state, where they had always been.

The security of prisoners was much improved by suspension of normal civil service procedures, made possible by Governor James's receivership. Incompetents and recalcitrants could be removed without extended proceedings. The salaries for correctional officers had already been dramatically increased to parity with state police. It was now possible to recruit for these positions college graduates who wanted to make a career in corrections.

To reform medical services, Britton instituted a medical advisory committee to develop a satisfactory plan. It was decided to contract medical services with a Birmingham hospital. The Department of Corrections still contracts out the medical service, though no longer to an Alabama health maintenance organization.

Classification, for so long a battleground between competing groups of experts, was settled for good. A computerized system was installed and personnel were trained in its use and in the considerations that would have to be weighed to override computer determinations. The results are arguable at best. Claims were made that inmate security was improved and the number of escapes reduced.

Finally, much attention was given to putting convicts to work on the extensive agricultural lands owned by the Department of Corrections. Employment at canneries and food-preserving plants, together with a new educational and vocational training program, greatly reduced but did not eliminate the idleness of prisoners.

In December 1982 I was invited to revisit the Alabama prisons. That was a scant seven years since my inspection of the system before the trial of *James v. Wallace*. I met spruce, uniformed young correctional officers who seemed to be interested in their work instead of merely enduring it. There was clear evidence of professionalism in the management of the institutions. Classification was a reality rather than the fiction that I had seen before. The prisons were still more crowded than they should have been, but there was nothing like the truly infernal North Dorm of Mount Meigs in 1975. The transformation was impressive, and I wondered how it was done.

The answer began with money. In 1981, oil was discovered off the narrow Alabama shoreline and the state received $450,000,000 for leases for further exploration and drilling. This made possible significantly more liberal budgeting for the prisons as well as for other state services. Competent management was obviously in evidence. There was continued pressure from Judge Robert Varner, to whom *Pugh v. Locke* had been reassigned when Johnson was elevated to the Fifth Circuit Court of Appeals, to reduce the population in the prisons so that the hundreds of men and women confined in the county jails awaiting prison space could be moved out of conditions which, in most cases, were about as bad as those prevailing in the prisons in 1975.

.   .   .

The Alabama story diverges from that hardest of lines. Moving from the barbaric conditions of 1975, it was possible for the Department of Corrections, on the initiative of the commissioner, to improvise program(s) as part of the solution to the wretchedness of overcrowding. Not everyone is pleased with them or with the accelerated release of prisoners on parole, but so far these elements of the reform of corrections have been accepted.

To sum up this narrative, the ascent from 1975 was made possible by the following necessary ingredients:

1. Judges who were willing to issue unpopular orders and stand by them. Without the firm hands of Judges Johnson and Varner, the reforms might have eventually taken place—the conditions to be remedied were too intolerable to continue forever—but delay and uncertainty would have been inevitable.

2. Support from the state's executive branch. Governor Fob James conceded that he knew little about the administration of criminal justice but was sure that good management would solve most of the state's correctional malaise. He took the necessary steps to change correctional management from top to bottom.

3. Competent management. Until the appointment of Commissioner Britton, progress toward compliance with the court's reforming orders was partial and slow. With emphasis on the centralization of correctional authority and the power of the governor, as receiver, to make sweeping changes in the system, reforms gathered momentum. Some of them, at least, have become irreversible.

4. Continuous monitoring. It is clear that when sustained observation of the system lapsed, little progress took place. The Human Rights Committee was not an ideal monitoring agency, but it laid a necessary foundation. When it was ruled out by the appellate court, progress stopped. The role of Governor James as receiver, followed by the activity of the Implementation Committee, were crucial to continued change.

All of the above elements were affected by political crosscurrents, an unavoidable aspect of any prison reform. Imprudent administrators, impatient with continued surveillance by the federal court—and quite rightly viewing themselves as impotent subjects of coercion—hoped to enlist enough political support to liberate themselves from supervision. It is fair to say that reform was impeded to the extent that they were successful in challenging the orders of the court, but the coercive processes implicit in the consent decree prevailed.

Some participants in the process were disappointed that the reforms involved prison construction rather than the adoption of policies that would rationalize the sentencing structure and rely increasingly on innovative community-based corrections. One can sympathize with their humane aspirations, but recognize at the same time that a correctional revolution would be neither desirable nor attainable. Incremental change, carefully planned, will survive. The world is cluttered with failed revolutions. American institutions fortunately provide neither the means nor the encouragement to make unpredictable leaps forward. In the words of the Roman poet, Virgil, ". . . to climb back again, to retrace one's steps to the upper air, that is the task, the labor." Step by careful step, with no reckless leaps to the upper air.

Comment and Questions

In Rhodes v. Chapman the U.S. Supreme Court was asked to rule whether doubling up of inmates in cells designed for one was "cruel and unusual punishment." The prison in question was an Ohio maximum security prison which, when opened in 1972, was hailed as a model for such institutions. After reviewing the overall conditions at the prison, the Supreme Court found (June 15, 1981) that, taking all the circumstances into account, double celling did not inflict "unnecessary or wanton pain," nor was it "grossly disproportionate to the severity of crimes warranting imprisonment," the two tests the Court has come to rely upon as indicia of "cruel and unusual punishment." But however the Court would have ruled would not have resolved the underlying dilemma of the American prison system. Given that double celling is Constitutionally permitted, it is unlikely that states will be moved to build new prison space. But if they don't, how will they deal with the worsening threat of violence? On the other hand, if double-celling had been found to be unconstitutional, and states were required to build more prisons, where would they put them and how would they afford it? Do you think the Supreme Court might have had that in mind when it found double-celling constitutional? How would you resolve the dilemma of prison overcrowding?

Suppose you or one of your closest relatives was the prisoner? Suppose the prisoner was formerly Attorney-General of the United States? Would your answer regarding minimal or maximal entitlement be different in either of those instances? Should it be different? Why? Why not?

(2) IS PRIVATIZATION THE ANSWER?

(a) Yes *

When first proposed, privatization of the prison industry seemed a dramatic and thought-provoking concept. In retrospect, however, it was a natural and inevitable development. While the demand for criminal incarceration is growing, the supply of prison space is not keeping pace. Prison overcrowding demonstrates the need for new facilities, but the cost of prison construction and operation is high. Although the public demands that criminals be incarcerated, the public refuses to pay the price for such services. Privatization of prisions, therefore, represents an influx of new suppliers who are attempting to satisfy these needs, and earn profits in the process.

* E.S. Savas, "Privatization and Prisons," Vanderbilt Law Review, Vol. 40, pp. 895–896, 1987 (Reprinted with Permission).

The private sector can perform several distinct functions with respect to prisons: (1) finance and construct prisons; (2) operate facilities for juveniles; (3) operate facilities for adults; (4) provide work for prisoners; and (5) provide specific contractual services to prisons, for example, health care and vocational education for the inmates and training for the staff. Public interest focuses on the role of private firms in the first three of these areas, the construction and operation of various types of correctional facilities. Private organizations, particularly not-for-profit ones, have operated halfway houses for criminal offenders for many years. Now, however, they also operate detention facilities. Private, for-profit firms are planning maximum-security prisons. In 1985 private firms were building or operating some two dozen adult prisons, most of them for illegal aliens and protective-custody prisoners.

Interest in prison privatization stems from the perception that private prisons are more cost effective and efficient, constructed more quickly, and operated under more flexible and innovative management. Although public costs are said to be twenty to forty percent greater than private costs, the evidence is not yet persuasive because public costs omit various factors and private costs may or may not cover the construction costs of new facilities. A definitive study of the relative costs of private and public prison service provision cannot be completed until more private prisons are operating and uniform cost frameworks are established.

The private-sector advantage in speed and flexibility of construction has merit. State governments find private financing and construction attractive, in part because it permits them to evade voter approval of bond issues. Typically, the state does not have to raise the capital to build the prison. The private sector builds the prison with private financing and operates it. The state then makes annual payments to the private owner under a lease-purchase contract. Although the validity of this arrangement has been questioned because it bypasses express voter approval, it saves time and money for state governments.

Private companies already provide extensive contract services in *existing* prisons. Sixty-six correctional agencies in thirty-nine states plus the District of Columbia spent about 200 million dollars 1983 on 3215 contracts with private firms for thirty-two different services and programs. These services consisted mostly of health and mental-health care, drug treatment, counseling, education, vocational training, college programs, and staff training. The agencies reported that contract services were more cost effective than those that the agency could provide, that advantages outweighed disadvantages, and that most of the agencies planned to expand their use of contracts for specific services.

(b) No *

For the sake of argument let us suppose that, private firms can operate successfully on a wide-scale, constructing and managing everything from community corrections centers to maximum-security prisons. For the sake of discussion, let us concede, without any qualifications, that private firms can maximize services while minimizing costs in an abuse- and corruption-free environment, unimpeded by political, judicial, or other such constraints. In other words, let us grant for the sake of argument that private prisons are eminently feasible. Must it then follow that private prisons are desirable? Philosophically, is the privatization of corrections, however instrumental it may prove to be in reducing costs and bettering services, consistent with the public interest, the common good?

It is less difficult to persuade people that privatization is philosophically right or wrong than to first persuade them that such philosophical questions have any place at all, let alone a central place, in this debate. There are those who simply reject the importance of philosophy: "If you grant that private prisons can work well and save us buckets of money you'd have to be crazy to argue against them." In this view, philosophizing on such matters is for tenderminded professors unschooled in the hard-bitten realities faced by policymakers, administrators, and those who pay the bills. There are others who, while not denying the importance of philosophy, maintain that the "public interest" or "common good" is in the eye of the beholder: "One person's opinion on privatization is no better or worse than any other's." In this view, if there is a public good it cannot be objectively determined nor can its relation to any given policy be reckoned with precision. From this perspective, privatization can be neither absolutely right nor absolutely wrong, neither positively good nor positively bad, neither moral nor immoral.

But the debate over the privatization of corrections ought not to take place on unphilosophical or pseudo-philosophical grounds. What is the proper scope of governmental authority? Where does government's responsibility begin? Where does it end? In this case, should the government's responsibility to govern end at the prison gates? Or is not imprisonment the most significant power that the government must exercise, on a regular basis, over a large body of citizens? Ultimately, any case for (or against) privatization must rest on unequivocal answers to these and related questions of political philosophy.

In my judgment, the philosophical considerations weigh decisively against privatization. Regardless of what penological theory is in vogue, the being of every correctional facility contains the message "Those who abuse liberty shall live without it." That message is to be

* Jon Dilulio, Jr., "Prisons, Profits, and the Public Good: The Privatization of Corrections," Criminal Justice Center Research Bulletin, No. 1, Sam Houston State University, 1986.

conveyed by the offended community of law-abiding citizens, through its duly constituted public agents, to the incarcerated or detained individual. It is precisely because corrections involves the deprivation of liberty, precisely because it involves the legally sanctioned exercise of coercion by some citizens over others, that it must remain wholly within public hands. The badge of the arresting police officer, the robes of the judge, and the state patch of the correctional officer are symbols of the inherently public nature of crime and punishment.

John Locke, who so much influenced American political and legal traditions, defined legitimate political power as "a Right of Making Laws with Penalties of Death, and consequently all less Penalties, for the Regulating and Preserving of Property . . . and all this only for the Publick Good," By "Property" Locke understood the citizen's natural right to life, liberty, and the pursuit of well-being. The power to punish those who transgress on our rights must, if it is to remain legitimate, reside in the hands of duly constituted public authorities. This power may not be freely delegated to contractually deputized private individuals or groups. Yet the privatization of corrections is predicated on just such an illegitimate delegation of state authority.

Adam Smith, that champion of limited government and free enterprise whose name is so often invoked in favor of such privatization schemes, insisted that government can and should perform three main functions: defense from attacks by foreign enemies, maintenance of a few vital public works, and the administration of justice. Concerning the last function, Smith would have understood what his false disciples do not; namely, that the private performance of certain key public functions, from trash collection and transportation to health care and education, is not to be compared as such to the private administration of justice. Trash collection and these other functions are not the normal equivalents of imprisonment.

Contrary to what some have argued, from a philosophical standpoint the profit motive of privatizers is irrelevant. The question is whether the authority to deprive others of their liberty and to coerce (even kill) them ought to be delegated to private, non-governmental entities, not whether such persons or groups ought to be paid or to profit financially from their services. Thus, in the unlikely event that private prison firms were to offer their services for free, the philosophical case against privatization would not be affected in the least. By the same token, the number and kind of facilities in private hands is philosophically irrelevant. The dispute over principle would be just as sharp whether one halfway house or every prison in the country were privately owned and operated. . . .

There are many things which government has neither the right nor the ability to do. The administration of criminal justice, however, is not among them. Whether government can or should run cost-effective railroads, engineer economic growth, or negotiate us to international security may all be open questions. But government can and should run safe, humane, productive prisons at a reasonable cost to the taxpayers.   No self-respecting constitutional government would abdicate so central a responsibility.   We are most likely to improve our prisons if we approach them not as a private enterprise to be run in the pursuit of profit, but as a public trust to be administered in the name of civility and justice.

(3) PRISON RIOTS—MAXIMUM INSECURITY *

When 11 inmates escaped last December from the Penitentiary of New Mexico in Santa Fe, the state called in Ramond K. Procunier, former director of the California prison system to look at the prison's security system.   On Jan. 14, Procunier issued a scathing indictment of the penitentiary, saying that the prison was overcrowded, understaffed, and, worst of all, that the guards, most of whom were recent high school graduates, had absolutely no training.   By failing to staff the prison properly and train the guards, he wrote, New Mexico state officials were "playing Russian roulette with the lives of inmates, staff and the public."

On Feb. 2, New Mexico lost the game of Russian roulette.   The penitentiary exploded in the most violent and destructive riot since 43 inmates and hostages were killed at the Attica Correctional Facility in New York in 1971.

At Attica, the disturbance was tightly controlled by a small group of powerful inmates.   But in New Mexico, the inmates, leaderless and uncontrolled, went berserk.   Fourteen guards were held hostage while hundreds of prisoners roamed the prison smashing and burning everything in sight.   At least seven of the hostages were severely beaten; several were repeatedly raped.   But the inmates reserved the brunt of their rage for each other; 33 inmates were killed, some of them after being brutally tortured and mutilated.   As many as 200 other inmates were beaten and raped.   The terror was so pervasive and uncontrolled that the majority of the 1,136 inmates fled and sought safety among the state police and National Guardsmen ringing the penitentiary.   Such inmate-to-inmate violence was unprecedented in any prison riot in memory.   Both New Mexico officials and outside experts found it difficult to explain.

When the bloody riot was over, officials remorsely acknowledged that the New Mexico corrections system had long been neglected.   For more than five years, everyone—inmates, guards, prison administrators, legislators, outside critics—had complained that the Penitentiary of New Mexico (PNM) was dangerously overcrowded and understaffed. Most of the inmates were idle.   Maximum-custody inmates, including some labeled psychotic, were mixed together with young and vulnerable first offenders, often in dormitories holding as many as 90 men each.

---

* Michael S. Serrill and Peter Katel, "New Mexico: The Anatomy of a Riot," *Corrections Magazine*, Vol. 6, No. 2, April 1980, pp. 6–7.   © 1980 (Reprinted with permission).

The people running the prison never had enough time to deal with these problems. In the last five years, there have been five corrections directors in New Mexico and five penitentiary wardens.

In the wake of the riot, Gov. Bruce King quickly put together a package of legislation appropriating $82 million for the corrections system—an extraordinary amount of money for a state with 1.2 million people and a total state budget of $1.7 billion. But the legislation was hardly reformist. While it increased the size of the guard force at PNM and raised correction officers' base pay from $728 to $1,002 a month, the legislation's centerpiece was $44 million for a new "super-max" prison.

There is little sympathy for criminals in New Mexico. One of the explanations offered for the extreme violence of the riot was that many inmates are serving sentences so long—many of them number in the hundreds of years—that they are bitter and desperate.

But a Santa Fe district attorney offered a harsher analysis. "They're just a bunch of f- - -ing animals," he muttered to a reporter as the bodies of the dead and injured were carried out of the prison.

One of the strangest phenomena in the aftermath of the blood-soaked riot was that state officials congratulated each other on how well it had been handled. Some even seemed to forget that inmates had died. During a television talk show three days after the riot, state senate majority leader C.B. Trujillo remarked: "The fact that nobody was killed in this major uprising is certainly a credit to the governor of the state of New Mexico."

Comment and Questions

Correctional authorities believe that the potential for uprisings exists in more than a few state institutions. Should we simply build more prisons? At what cost?

Given the continuing possibility of riots and continued crowding, isn't it reasonable to turn to the private sector to build and run new facilities? By almost all accounts they can construct them faster and cheaper and manage them more efficiently than can the public sector.

d. THE SOCIAL SIGNIFICANCE OF CORRECTIONAL PRACTICES

(1) 23% OF YOUNG BLACK MEN UNDER CRIMINAL SANCTIONS *

Nearly one out of four black men between the ages of 20 and 29 nationwide is in prison or jail or on probation or parole on a given day, according to a new study based on records of the Justice Department and the Bureau of the Census. The 23.0-percent "criminal justice control rate" for young black men compared to 6.2 percent for white

* Criminal Justice Newsletter, Vol. 21, No. 5, March 1, 1990.

males in their 20s, and 10.4 percent for Hispanic males in that crime-prone age bracket.

"These new findings should be disturbing to all Americans," said Marc Mauer, assistant director of the Sentencing Project, the Washington, D.C.-based organization that conducted the study. "We now risk the possibility of writing off an entire generation of black men from leading productive lives." The Sentencing Project promotes development of sentencing options other than incarceration, through projects such as defense-based sentencing advocacy for individual offenders.

The findings understate the impact of criminal justice policies on young black men, Mr. Mauer said, because they are based on population counts and estimates for prisons, jails, and probation and parole agencies for a single day in mid–1989. If all offenders who were processed through the system at any time during 1989 were counted, the proportion of black males subjected to criminal sanctions would be even higher, he said.

The national "war on drugs," as outlined in the strategies developed by the Office of National Drug Control Policy, continues an emphasis on law enforcement and corrections, so it will likely result in even higher rates of incarceration for blacks and Hispanics, Mauer said, because minority groups are especially overrepresented in drug cases. In Florida, for example, blacks make up 73 percent of all drug offenders, but they make up a smaller share—54 percent—of prison admissions for other types of offenses.

The Sentencing Project said it did not attempt to determine whether young black men are disproportionately involved in the criminal justice system, that is, whether blacks commit more crimes or different types of crimes than non-blacks, or merely are treated more harshly by the system. Regardless of why blacks are overrepresented, the Sentencing Project found the results of the study a matter of concern.

"Few would claim that today's overcrowded corrections systems do much to assist offenders in becoming productive citizens after release," Mauer wrote. "For the black community in general, nearly one-fourth of its young men are under the control of the criminal justice system at a time when their peers are beginning families, learning constructive life skills, and starting careers. . . . Unless the criminal justice system can be used to assist more young black males in pursuing these objectives, any potential positive contributions they can make to the community will be delayed, or lost forever."

The Sentencing Project said that "jail and prison should be sanctions of last resort for offenders who cannot be diverted from the system," and urged wider use of intensive-supervision probation and other community corrections programs.

Question

What are the social policy implications for a prison population that is increasingly African American? To what extent do these figures suggest that our correctional system is not so much "punishing" criminal offenders as it is "managing" a disenfranchised segment of the underclass?

(2) PRISON RECIDIVISM

(a) The Figures *

One-fourth of prisoners released from state institutions return to prison within two years of release, and almost a third are imprisoned again within three years, according to a study by the Bureau of Justice Statistics. The findings are based on a study of recidivism rates in 14 states. The three-year recidivism rate of 31 percent did not vary greatly among the states studied, according to BJS.

At least half the people sent back to prison were sentenced for new crimes, as opposed to technical violations of parole rules, the Justice Department agency said. As might be expected, the longer a former prisoner remains in the community without reincarceration, the less the likelihood of recidivism. With some exceptions, the highest risk of recidivism occurs during the second half of the first release year.

The highest overall recidivism rates occurred among burglars, followed by those convicted of robbery. The lowest recidivism rates occurred among those convicted of drug offenses, followed by homicide, forgery, fraud or embezzlement, and sexual assault.

The younger the age at release, the higher the likelihood of recidivism within three years, the report said. For example, 31 percent of Massachusetts inmates released before their 25th birthday returned to prison within three years, while only 17 percent of those age 30 or older were recidivists.

Recidivism rates used in the study included only new convictions, not arrests that did not result in conviction. Thus the report "dramatically understates the problem of repeat offending," according to Jeffrey L. Sedgwick deputy director for data analysis at BJS.

Comment

There are enormous problems in determining the recidivism rate of discharged prisoners. Typically, all we ask is the percentage of those who have been rearrested. The percentage committing new crimes is of course much higher. On the other hand, it is possible that those with a criminal record are more likely to be arrested for crimes they have not committed and hence recidivism figures based on rearrests may actually be an overestimation. It is true, perhaps, that our restrictions on character testimony make it less likely that ex-convicts will be wrongfully convicted at trial, but a revocation of parole may

* Criminal Justice Newsletter, Jan. 16, 1985 p. 8. © 1985 (Reprinted with permission).

occur on far less evidence than a conviction, and hence the inclusion of parole revocations may also overstate the amount of recidivism.

Not only are legal dispositions a poor guide to subsequent criminality, but it is even arguable that criminality is not a very good guide to the effectiveness and rehabilitative effects of prison. Prisons, after all, receive many of the failures of society's other institutions, such as, the schools, the job market, the family, etc., and it is unreasonable to expect the prisons to repair the damage in a very high percentage of cases. It may be that a corrections system has done quite well if it is able to turn major offenders into minor ones or turn frequent offenders into infrequent ones.

(b) Treatment Programs: Some Help, Some Harm *

Any conclusion in scientific inquiry is held provisionally, subject to further evidence. My original conclusion concerning the importance of treatment programs in criminal justice was derived from a survey accomplished for the State of New York covering the period 1945–1967. This survey led to a book, *The Effectiveness of Correctional Treatment (ECT),* which summarized research from 231 studies. I coauthored *ECT.* The conclusion I derived from *ECT* is supplied in an article which has been widely quoted and reprinted. However, new evidence from our current study leads me to reject my original conclusion and suggest an alternative more adequate to the facts at hand. I have hesitated up to now, but the evidence in our survey is simply too overwhelming to ignore.

Different procedures were used in the two surveys. *ECT* is based primarily on the findings of evaluation research—a special kind of research which was applied to criminal justice on a wide scale for the first time in California during the period immediately following World War II. This research is experimental—that is, offenders are often randomly allocated to treatment and nontreatment groups so that comparison can be made of outcome. Our current study, however, compares the reprocessing rates of groups receiving treatment with roughly comparable groups who receive the "standard processing" given to most offenders across the United States.

ECT excluded about ninety percent of the research it had available because it was not evaluation research. Only evaluation studies were included on the ground that only this kind of study can truly unearth causality. Our current survey, on the other hand, includes any study which contains a verifiable reprocessing rate for a group of at least ten sentenced offenders. By including annual follow-up studies we increase the number of rates for persons given standard processing. In comparison to *ECT,* our sample is much more representative of criminal justice nationally.

* Robert Martinson, "New Findings, New Views: A Note of Caution Regarding Sentencing Reform, *Hofstra Law Review*   Vol. 7, No. 2, Winter 1979 pg. 252–255. ©1979 (Reprinted by permission).

In brief, *ECT* focused on summarizing evaluation research which purported to uncover *causality;* in our current study we reject this perspective as premature and focus on uncovering *patterns* which can be of use to policymakers in choosing among available treatment programs. These patterns are sufficiently consistent to oblige me to modify my previous conclusion.

The authors of *ECT* laboriously summarized hundreds of evaluation studies, but astonishingly the book itself contains no general conclusion. It is a compendium of findings displayed in hundreds of subparagraphs, and, in my opinion, it defies summary as a whole. I undertook, on my own responsibility, to supply what the authors of this work could not or would not supply—a conclusion. I limited my summary to recidivism, and included with the summary brief discussion and analyses of the research on which the summary was based. My conclusion was: "With few and isolated exceptions, the rehabilitative efforts that have been reported so far have had no appreciable effect on recidivism."

This conclusion takes the usual form of rejecting an hypothesis, i.e., the hypothesis that treatment *added* to the networks of criminal justice does in fact have an *appreciable* effect. The very evidence presented in the article indicates that it would have been incorrect to say that treatment had *no* effect. Some studies showed an effect, others did not. But, all together, looking at this entire body of research, I drew this conclusion, and thought it important that the conclusion be made public and debated. It surely was debated.

On the basis of the evidence in our current study, I withdraw this conclusion. I have often said that treatment added to the networks of criminal justice is "impotent," and I withdraw this characterization as well. I protested at the slogan used by the media to sum-up what I said—"nothing works." The press has no time for scientific quibbling and got to the heart of the matter better than I did.

But for all of that, the conclusion is not correct. More precisely, treatments will be found to be "impotent" under certain conditions, beneficial under others, and detrimental under still others. The current study, by enabling us to uncover a major category of *harmful treatment* is an advance on *ECT.* It enables us to indicate, at least roughly, the conditions under which a treatment program will fall into one of three categories: (1) beneficial (the program *reduces* reprocessing rates); (2) neutral (*no impact,* positive or negative, can be determined); and (3) detrimental (the program *increases* reprocessing rates).

The most interesting general conclusion is that no treatment program now used in criminal justice is inherently either substantially helpful or harmful. The critical fact seems to be the *conditions* under which the program is delivered.

Comment

Martinson's original article had a major, and as he himself suggests, unmerited impact. From an earlier naive belief in the efficiency of rehabilitation—in a sense, indeterminate sentencing might have been taken to imply that "everything works"—there was gradual disenchantment with rehabilitation as a goal. Martinson's original slogan "nothing works" had a major impact because people were disenchanted with the rehabilitative ideal, and were prepared to accept a seemingly definitive study.

As the above indicates, Martinson deeply regretted the simplicity of the conclusions drawn from his earlier work and understood that social scientific questions are more properly stated as follows: "What does and doesn't work, under what conditions? What evidence, based on what methodology, can we count on to support our conclusions?" If these are the questions, do we have any good answers?

(c) *"Experience to Let"* *

Experience is a futile teacher,

Experience is a prosy preacher,

He who has never tasted jail

Lives well within the legal pale,

While he who's served a heavy sentence,

Renews the racket, not repentance.

Questions

Is this surprising, seeing how we make it impossible for many of those released from incarceration to earn an honest living? For example, if employers hire ex-convicts who then victimize them, who will compensate them? Should we as a society be willing to provide insurance for those who provide jobs to convicted criminals?

2. JAILS

a. THE JAILS: MANAGING RABBLE **

In a legal sense, the jail is the point of entry into the criminal justice system. It is the place where arrested persons are booked and where they are held for their court appearances if they cannot arrange bail. It is also the city or county detention facility for persons serving misdemeanor sentences, which in most states cannot exceed one year. The prison, on the other hand, is a state or federal institution that

---

* Ogden Nash, *I'm a Stranger Here Myself,* Little Brown & Co. © 1935 (Reprinted with permission).

** John Irwin, The Jail: Managing the Underclass in American Society, University of California Press, Berkeley, 1985 (Reprinted with Permission).

holds persons serving felony sentences, which generally run to more than one year.

The public impression is that the jail holds a collection of dangerous criminals. But familiarity and close inspection reveal that the jail holds only a very few persons who fit the popular conception of a criminal—a predator who seriously threatens the lives and property of ordinary citizens. In fact, the great majority of the persons arrested and held in jail belong to a different social category. Some students of the jail have politely referred to them as the poor: "American jails operate primarily as catchall asylums for poor people." Some have added other correlates of poverty: "With a few exceptions, the prisoners are poor, undereducated, unemployed, and they belong to minority groups." Some use more imaginative and sociologically suggestive labels, such as "social refuse" or "social junk." Political radicals sometimes use "lumpen proletariat" and argue over whether its members are capable of participating in the class struggle. Some citizens refer to persons in this category as "street people," implying an excessive and improper public presence. Others apply such labels as "riff-raff," "social trash," or "dregs," which suggest lack of social worth and moral depravity. And many police officers, deputies, and other persons who are familiar with the jail population use more crudely derogatory labels, such as "assholes" and "dirt balls."

In my own research, I found that beyond poverty and its correlates—undereducation, unemployment, and minority status—jail prisoners share two essential characteristics: detachment and disrepute. They are detached because they are not well integrated into conventional society, they are not members of conventional social organizations, they have few ties to conventional social networks, and they are carriers of unconventional values and beliefs. They are disreputable because they are perceived as irksome, offensive, threatening, capable of arousal, even protorevolutionary. In this book I shall refer to them as the *rabble,* meaning the "disorganized" and "disorderly," the "lowest class of people."

I found that it is these two features—detachment and disrepute—that lead the police to watch and arrest the rabble so frequently, regardless of whether or not they are engaged in crime, or at least in serious crime. (Most of the rabble commit petty crimes, such as drinking on the street, and are usually vulnerable to arrest.)

These findings suggest that the basic purpose of the jail differs radically from the purpose ascribed to it by government officials and academicians. It is this: the jail was invented, and continues to be operated, in order to manage society's rabble. Society's impulse to manage the rabble has many sources, but the subjectively perceived "offensiveness" of the rabble is at least as important as any real threat it poses to society.

The contemporary jail is a subsidiary to the welfare organizations that are intended to "regulate the poor." Frances Fox Piven and

Richard Cloward have pointed out that when masses of occupationally dislocated people pose a threat, society applies social control devices, such as relief programs:

> When large numbers of people are suddenly barred from their traditional occupations, the entire structure of social control is weakened and may even collapse. There is no harvest or paycheck to enforce work and the sentiments that uphold work; without work, people cannot conform to familial and communal roles; and if the dislocation is widespread, the legitimacy of the social order itself may come to be questioned. The result is usually civil disorder—crime, mass protests, riots—a disorder that may even threaten to overturn existing social and economic arrangements. It is then that relief programs are initiated or expanded.

However, from among the poor there will also emerge a rabble who are perceived as a more serious and constant threat to the social order, a group in need of the more direct forms of social control delivered by the criminal justice system. Usually the more violent and rapacious rabble are arrested, convicted, and sent to prison; the merely offensive are held in jail. The jail was devised as, and continues to be, the special social device for controlling offensive rabble.

Comment

Interestingly, John Irwin characterizes the jail as an institution for managing the most unruly portion of society's "rabble." More conventional observers might describe it as an institution for "holding people unable to post bond prior to trial" or for "housing sentenced offenders serving short terms." As you read the following materials on the jails and consider them in light of materials presented in earlier chapters, ask yourself which is the more accurate characterization of jails. How does this portrait of the jail square with the finding presented in the previous reading, that nearly one quarter of all young African American men are in some form of correctional custody?

b. PORTRAITS OF JAILS

(1) LOS ANGELES *

It is size—sheer immensity—that is the first and the last principle of the Los Angeles County Central Jail. It is this simple, stunning fact that sparks both the pride of the men and women who run it and the problems that today beseige what is said to be the largest jail in the world.

The operation of the Central Jail's morning "court line," in which up to 1,000 inmates are awakened, fed, given civilian clothes, chained and shepherded into 30 buses during a two-hour period, has been called

* William Hart, "L.A.'s Giant Jails: A Giant Headache," *Corrections Magazine,*   Vol. 6, No. 6, December 1980, pp. 32–35, 37. © 1980 (Reprinted by permission).

"the daily miracle" by Art Stoyanoff, chief of the Custody Division of the L.A. Sheriff's Department.

But the huge concrete bunker squatting near the center of L.A., is an unlikely setting for a supernatural event. The jail dwarfs every other pretrial facility and almost every prison in the country. Its count in November of about 5,100 inmates was under its design capacity of 5,580. The vast majority of its charges are pretrial detainees, many of whom must be bused daily to some 30 separate courts located from one to 75 miles away.

The inmates range from maximum-security street gang leaders to overnight guests on their way to a dismissal. They are housed in 27 multi-cell "modules" stacked on four floors. The modules, which are conventional cellblocks, include 1,080 one-bed cells and hundreds of multi-bed cells each holding from four to ten inmates. Including corridors, escalators, cafeterias and other areas, the facility spreads over some 935,000 square feet within its tall, windowless walls.

The jail's medical staff make some 2,000 patient-contacts a day. Two thousand outsiders come daily for 20–minute social visits. The annual expense of running the jail and its adjacent Inmate Reception Center (IRC) is nearly $30 million. It is a very big, very busy place—a fact not lost on the staff who operate it.

Over the past several years the mammoth facility has been accused of a striking range of deficiencies, from overcrowding and insufficient recreation to inadequate medical care, harassment of prisoners and brutality. The jail remains embroiled in dealing with a federal court decision that found many of the charges to be accurate; the court ordered nearly a dozen changes in the facility's operation. . . .

. . . [I]n February . . . 1979 . . . U.S. District Court Judge William Gray, . . . found conditions within the facility "intolerable" and unconstitutional in ruling for inmate plaintiffs in a class-action lawsuit. Gray's sweeping order sustained the plaintiffs' allegations that inmates were awakened too early, were not given enough time to eat, were crammed into holding tanks with nowhere to sit for long periods, were forced to sleep on mattresses on corridor and dayroom floors, and did not get adequate recreation, access to telephones, or changes of clothing. Many of these problems stemmed from overcrowding. While the jail population has recently been below its 5,580–bed design capacity, the population frequently exceeds that number after a spate of new admissions.

In addition to ordering remedies for these deficiencies, Judge Gray also directed officials to allow contact visits, to permit inmates to be present during cell-searches, and to remove the steel sheets bolted over jail windows in 1972 so that inmates would be able to see "the sun, the sky, or the outside world."

These last three orders are currently being appealed by the department.

A related lawsuit charges the jail with having inadequate resources for handling the large numbers of mentally disturbed inmates who pass through the facility. The federal trial on that issue has been postponed; the plaintiffs' attorney acknowledged that psychiatric care at the jail has improved since the suit was filed.

. . . [According to] ACLU attorney Terry Smerling, who has directed the federal lawsuit for several years, . . . "the place is so big that it brings on a callous, impersonal atmosphere; nobody has the opportunity or incentive to get to know anyone else." The result, he claimed, is that inmates' access to court-ordered services frequently depends on the personality or mood of the deputy in charge of a module or group of cells. "The deputies' job there is a terribly difficult one. When they get pressed—which they often are—they just cut out what they consider optional."

The consensus is that the L.A. Central Jail works because it has to, and because it is staffed from a department known for its emphasis on training and discipline. But it also works because the prisoners permit it to, officials said. "There are a lot of very bad people in here," one sergeant said in a typical comment. "But most of them pretty much go along with the program. Most of them don't expect to be here very long, or are hoping to get a break in court, so they think twice about messing up."

The inmates are mostly black and Hispanic defendants unable to make bail, and they are everywhere, trudging along the halls in single or double file, lying on bunks or hanging around on the "free-ways" * manning the food lines, the medical lines, the court lines, peering at the signs, listening to the loudspeakers, or just following whoever is ahead of them.

"We do it every day, and after a few times they [inmates] learn the system," said Lt. Grand Johnson. "Once they do, they'll tell you if you're trying to put them in the wrong line or holding cell.

"The surprising thing was that when I first came here, I heard all the [loudspeaker] announcements and wondered who they were aimed at," Johnson said with a smile. "I found out that it's not the deputies they're talking to, it's the inmates."

Questions

What are the most important differences between a large jail such as this one and a large prison such as Stateville? It is generally agreed that by and large conditions in our jails are worse. Why should this be?

* The corridors in front of the cells.

(2) RIKERS ISLAND *

New York's Rikers Island, the nation's most populous penal complex, undergoes a daily battle for control between guards and inmates, corrections experts say. Violence occurs every day, inmates come and go continually and, sometimes, only a thin line separates the guards from the men they are supposed to keep in line.

Just how explosive Rikers can be was shown by the bloody disturbance last month and subsequent inquiries by state and city correction agencies. Now some correction officials are asking if conditions have deteriorated to the point where the 440–acre penal island cannot be governed without bloodshed.

Allyn R. Sielaff, the city's new correction commissioner, is gambling his career and his reputation as a prison reformer that the answer lies in long-range programs aimed at reducing violence.

"People say Rikers is hopeless," Mr. Sielaff said in a recent interview. "I don't belive that. We just haven't instituted the programs that will work."

Mr. Sielaff says his plans include four major programs: screening to identify violent inmates and separate them from other prisoners at the outset; isolation to punish inmates who break rules; drug-treatment, educational and calisthenics programs to help reduce jail violence bred by boredom; and closer scrutiny of prospective guards to weed out those prone to corruption and violence.

Mr. Sielaff acknolwedges that it may take some time to put these programs in place, especially given New York's budgetary troubles. Mr. Sielaff's critics contend that Rikers needs to enact immediate programs and that Mr. Sielaff has virtually overlooked his most pressing problem: a brutal, poorly trained staff.

"I agree with all his programs," said William G. McMahon, chairman of the state Commission on Corrections, which recently determined that there had been widespread misconduct by Rikers guards during and following last month's disturbance. "But what about today? His plans may work, but only if the whole place doesn't blow up on him."

Mr. McMahon said Mr. Sielaff needs tear-gas masks and other riot gear right away, as well as wardens trained to handle riots who would control the most violent sections of the jail. Mr. McMahon also said that instead of waiting for the city to conclude its current inquiry of the Rikers upheaval, the commissioner must conduct his own investigation and severely punish guards who beat inmates without provocation.

"I'm worried that he does not realize the crisis he's in," Mr. McMahon said.

* Dean Baquet, "Can Rikers Island Become Anything but Worse?" The New York Times, Sunday, September 2, 1990.

Set in the East River, Rikers Island is a jail with a rapid turnover, not a prison with a relatively stable population. That is the main reason, many experts say, why the complex is so tough to govern. The majority, or 65 percent of its nearly 14,000 inmates, known as detainees, are merely awaiting trial; the remainder include those serving time of less than a year and those accused of violating parole who are awaiting hearings. Some inmates will be found innocent of the charges against them. Federal judges, aware of this distinction, have laid down 20 orders addressing overcrowding and brutality that are supposed to protect the inmates from being treated like convicts.

Rikers became more explosive with a dramatic surge in the inmate and guard populations, as drug arrests soared and politicians, responding to the public outcry over crime, pushed for more and bigger jails.

The fastest, cheapest solution was to expand Rikers, with huge dormitory-like structures similar to those elsewhere in the country that corrections officials now agree are a major mistake. The housing, open rows of bunk beds, gave rise to violence. "If somebody plays a radio too loud, tempers flare, and you have a problem," sad Robert Gangi, executive director of the Correction Association of New York, a private research group.

The guards, who are unarmed, must walk the aisles between the rows of beds, and they complain they are constantly on the defensive.

In 1981, the city had 4,500 guards for its jails. Today, there are 11,000. So many guards were hired so quickly that the standards were relaxed and training reduced, said Mr. Sielaff, who has run state prison systems in Illinois, Virginia, Wisconsin and Pennsylvania. Some jail officials say the guards are worse than ever and that some smuggle in drugs.

Critics contend that Commissioner Sielaff's programs, while suited to state prisons, are not appropriate for the short-term inmates at Rikers. For example, the detailed psychological testing of inmates to separate the most violent from the rest can take weeks, which is not of much apparent value for the average stay of 40 days on Rikers. But Mr. Sielaff's point is that the test results will then be on file if an inmate returns. "And let's face it," he said, "many of these guys come right back."

Short stays will not affect his plans for education programs and community service projects for inmates like cleaning streets in nearby Queens, Mr. Sielaff said. An intensive program can be designed to enable an inmate to win a high-school equivalency diploma in six weeks, he said, and drug treatment will be available.

The commissioner has already started expanding a building for prisoners who must be punished by isolation. His tougher screening for guards has already exposed 36 crack dealers who had applied.

Some present and former jail officials, including Bonnie Nathan, formerly associate commissioner in charge of investigations, said Mr.

Sielaff, who has been in his post since March, has spent so much time on such programs that he has permitted the guards free reign.

"He's lost control of the guards," said Ms. Nathan, who was fired by Mr. Sielaff.

The commissioner countered by saying that he intends to discipline guards who violate the rules, but that Ms. Nathan was too severe and focused on trivial violations like tardiness. "The guards were being treated like criminals," he said.

Robert Kasanof, chairman of the city's Board of Correction, an advisory group that monitors city jails, said Mr. Sielaff's proposals may be the long-term answer for Rikers, but they will fail unless the commissioner makes the jail a "stable environment" where teachers, psychologists and others needed for his programs will be willing to work.

"Many of us who are concerned with prison reform were elated with the selection of Mr. Sielaff because he does have solid long-range ideas." Mr. Kasanof said, reflecting the view of many corrections officials. But the basis for prison reform is public confidence in the basic safety of the prisons. And on that issue, the jury is still very much out."

Comment

The account of Rikers Island describes a city's jail system that has been under court order for over ten years. Imagine what the problems and conditions would have been like if a federal court judge had not issued orders to improve conditions and expand staff.

(3) CHOCTAW COUNTY JAIL *

FINDINGS OF FACT

Donald Lolley is the Sheriff of Choctaw County, Alabama, and under the laws of the State of Alabama is the person responsible for the administration, operation and maintenance of the county jail.

.   .   .

The Choctaw County Jail was built in 1964, and was designed to house 52 inmates.   .   .   .

.   .   .

The overcrowding at the jail in 1977 was a result of federal court orders concerning the conditions in the state prison system. As a result of those orders the state transferred some of its inmates to county jails, including the Choctaw County Jail. This condition ended several months ago, and the jail population presently runs around 11 or 12 inmates.   .   .   . The jail serves a small rural county with a popula-

* Nicholson v. Choctaw County, Alabama, 498 F.Supp. 295 (S.D.Ala.1980).

tion of 16,589 persons (1970 Census). It is located in a small town.
. . .

Health Care

There are no medical facilities at the jail other than medicine
prescribed by doctors for the inmates, and a first aid kit. There is no
sick bay. No medical personnel have been to the jail since September
20, 1979, in violation of the preliminary injunction order. The sheriff's
effort to obtain medical personnel in compliance with the court order
was to ask the Probate Judge and County Commission to get a Registered Nurse or a Licensed Practical Nurse to come to the jail. The
Probate Judge and the County Commission have not hired medical
personnel to go to the jail. The County Commission has appropriated
no funds to hire medical personnel. . . .

Fire Safety

The May 16, 1977, inspection of the Choctaw County Jail by the
Deputy State Fire Marshal John W. Hammac stated that the lack of a
fire escape from the second floor "poses a serious hazard to the safety of
inmates housed there and should be corrected immediately by providing
a second means of egress from that area." The October 25, 1977,
inspection of Mr. Hammac found that the fire escape deficiency still
existed and had not been corrected. . . . No fire escape from the
second floor of the jail has been constructed. There have been no plans
drawn nor any cost estimates of constructing a fire escape from the
second floor. . . .

Trust System

. . . (T)rusties continue to perform the jobs of a jailer when the
jailer is on leave.

As of March 23, 1979, jailer Joseph G. Campbell had been on sick
leave for six weeks. Inmate trusty Tony Ward has served as the jailer
in Mr. Campbell's place. Inmate trusty Tony Ward has also served as
jailer on another shift during this same period since Charlie Ezell, Jr.
terminated his employment in January 1979. Thus inmate trusty Tony
Ward serves as jailer sixteen hours per day. Inmate trusties who are
serving as jailer have the duties and responsibilities for the overall
running of the jail. These duties include:

(a) communicating by radio and telephone with the deputies' cars across the county;

(b) receiving, handling and dispatching complaints by radio to the deputies across the county from 5:00 p.m. to 8:00
a.m.;

(c) handling other telephone calls to the jail;

(d) custody of the keys; and

(e) hourly patrol of the cells. . . .

Recreation

Prisoners are confined to their cells 24 hours a day. There is no organized recreation for prisoners when they are in their cells.

Adjacent to the jail and immediately behind it is a large area which could be fenced in and used for a recreation area for the jail. The estimated cost to fence the area is $14,000–$15,000.

. . .

Ms. Carrie Turner is employed as a cook for the jail through the CETA program. Ms. Turner has no training in nutrition. The menus for the meals at the jail are prepared by Sheriff Lolley. Sheriff Lolley has no formal training in nutrition and consults with no person who has training in nutrition in preparation of the menus.

. . . Despite the deficiencies noted in a Health Department report, the jail continues to serve inmates uninspected beef which has been slaughtered by inmates from cows killed on the highway and uninspected deer killed in hunting accidents or killed on the highway.

Discipline

The sheriff revised the disciplinary rules pursuant to the preliminary injunction order of September 20, 1978, by abolishing the rules. The inmates are still given a set of the abolished disciplinary rules, but are not told that the rules no longer apply. . . .

When a person is moved to another cell or to a cell by himself, he is not allowed to state his position or to have a hearing. . . .

Visitation

Visiting hours are Monday and Thursday from 2:00–4:00 p.m. Visits are not held in private, but take place with the visitor talking to the inmate through the bars. Thus, an inmate can kiss or embrace a visitor only if he does so through the bars.

The sheriff determines whether an inmate is allowed to leave the jail to attend a funeral or to visit a sick relative. . . .

Pretrial Detainees

. . . Persons held at the Choctaw County Jail pending trial are treated no differently than convicted persons. . . .

Religious Services

Inmates are not allowed to attend religious services outside the jail. The only religious guidance provided to plaintiffs and other inmates is provided on a sporadic basis by laymen and/or ministers who may come to the jail of their own volition or at the request of an inmate. In addition, plaintiffs and other inmates are not consulted about their religious needs by Sheriff's Department personnel.

Legal Materials

The jail does not have a facility for housing legal materials, nor does the jail have legal textbooks, case law books, statutory materials, a writing room, a notary public, or typewriters to assist inmates in the preparation of their pretrial or post-trial proceedings.

Bathing Facilities

There are four cells on the second floor of the jail without showers. There is one cell on the first floor of the jail without a shower.

Classification of Inmates

There is not a classification system at the jail. With the exception of juveniles and females, pretrial detainees, misdemeanants, and persons being held on mental illness charges are housed with inmates convicted of felonies. In addition, pretrial detainees are not treated differently from convicted detainees.

Jail Staff

The only training the staff of the jail has had is on-the-job training. They have not had any formal training of any kind. . . .

Comment and Questions

If you had to be confined to a jail, which would you choose, the L.A. County jail, Rikers Island, or the Choctaw County jail? Notice that all are operating under federal court orders. Although traditionally, adjudication has been understood to be a process for resolving disputes between private parties, the Federal Courts are being asked in these cases to serve as a regulatory agency, overseeing the operation of a County governmental institution. Do you think that they can adequately perform such a task? If federal courts cannot, what part of government can—or cares enough to do so? To what extent do problems in jails raise different issues than those in prisons?

C. INTERMEDIATE SANCTIONS

1. EXPANDING OPTIONS FOR CRIMINAL SENTENCING *

Routine Probation: Unsuccessful for Felony Offenders

Most criminal justice personnel agree that prison should serve the ends of "just desserts" (making the punishment fit the crime) and "incapacitation" (keeping offenders from committing crime in the community). But how can either of these objectives be served when a

* Joan Petersilia, Expanding Options for Criminal Sentencing, RAND Corporation, Santa Monica, 1987.

convicted felon sees his probation officer once a month and is otherwise free to do what he wants in the community he has already victimized?

Actually, even once-a-month "supervision" is more stringent than probation supervision in many jurisdictions. And that presents another irony: Probation agencies all over the country have been asked to supervise more criminals, and more serious criminals, yet their budgets are being cut. The justification for the budget cuts has been that probation agencies serve less serious offenders and can therefore manage with less funding. The greatest irony is that most of the cuts were made to free more resources for prison construction and operation. The result has been a staggering increase in some probation agencies' caseloads. In many urban jurisdictions, "low-risk" probationers have virtually no supervision; they only have to mail in a postcard at specified intervals.

Needed: Appropriate Alternatives

With less than enthusiastic public support to build additional jails and prisons, with a continuing public demand to punish criminal offenders severely, and with probation's unsuitability as a felony sentence, policymakers find themselves facing a serious dilemma. These realities are encouraging state legislatures to consider alternative sanctions that punish but do not involve incarceration. These strategies require finer distinctions among criminal offenders and create, de facto, a range of sanctions that reflect the range of criminality.

The Search for Intermediate–Sentencing Options

Policymakers and managers across the country are looking for "intermediate" or "middle-range" sentencing options that are tougher than traditional probation but less stringent—and less expensive—than imprisonment. The prisons in some states are crowded partly because all convicted offenders, from first-time welfare cheats to repeat robbers, are sent to prison, without consideration of the different risks they present to the community. Recent national statistics show that the majority of offenders admitted to prison each year were convicted of property or public-order offenses, not violent crimes.

While nonviolent offenses must be taken seriously, it is not obvious that they require a prison term. Lawmakers are finding that when properly structured, intermediate sanctions can prevent new crimes, without the high cost of prison.

Intermediate sanctions have become especially popular in the South, the region of the nation that incarcerates the highest proportion of offenders. In addition, jurisdictions in other parts of the country have recently begun to design such programs. While the dimensions, degree of formality, and other specifics of these programs differ from jurisdiction to jurisdiction, all are designed to be safe, punitive, and inexpensive:

- Intensive-supervision probation (ISP) programs have been implemented in at least one county in 40 states. Offenders sentenced to these programs are closely supervised on small caseloads; in most, they must pay victim restitution and perform community service, hold a job, submit to random urine and alcohol testing, and pay a probation supervision fee. Statewide programs are now operational in Arizona, Connecticut, Florida, Georgia, New Jersey, Illinois, Oklahoma, Virgina, Utah, Vermont, Massachusetts, Texas, and New York.

- Intermediate-sanctions programs in Florida, Oklahoma, and Alabama rely heavily on house arrest. In these programs, offenders are legally ordered to remain in their residences for the duration of their sentences. House arrestees may leave their homes for medical reasons, employment, and approved treatment programs.

- California, Florida, Kentucky, Michigan, Oregon, and Utah have begun experimenting with electronic monitoring devices to verify that probationers and parolees are really where they are supposed to be. These devices are usually used as complements to house arrest sentences.

- In Long Beach, California, probation officials are teaming up with police to provide greater surveillance of probationers. Police officers carry laminated cards listing the names and addresses of felony probationers residing in the community, along with their probation conditions. Police who observe any violations detain the offenders and immediately call the probation officer.

- In New York, the Vera Institute of Justice supervises more than a thousand jail-bound recidivists who are performing court-ordered, unpaid labor for the benefit of community groups.

- In Georgia, Oklahoma, and Mississippi, young first offenders are sentenced to "boot camp" correctional facilities, where they are confined for short periods under rigid standards and strict military discipline. After they have completed their sentence, they return to their communities under intensive probation supervision.

- Texas is expanding its "quarter-house"/halfway house facilities. These residential centers, which currently house mentally retarded convicts, will soon begin accepting offenders who violate technical probation and parole conditions.

- In New Jersey and California, members of the community are being asked to sign formal contracts with probation and/or parole departments stating that they will serve as "community sponsors." Community sponsors assume some responsibility for assuring that the probationer is adhering to his court-ordered conditions and agree to notify the court if violations are observed.

The Advantages and Disadvantages of Intermediate Sanctions

The financial appeal of intermediate and middle-range sentencing programs is seen by many as the primary reason for the surge of interest in such programs. If the program participants are truly the prison-bound, the programs not only save the state the cost of housing offenders, they also reduce the pressure to build new prisons. Also, the state may save the welfare costs required to support the offender's family while he is incarcerated. And since the offender continues to be employed, he pays state and local taxes and can be ordered to pay probation supervision fees a well.

A second advantage of intermediate-sanction programs is that they are "socially cost-effective," because they allow the offender to remain in the community, thereby avoiding the breakup of community and family networks. Furthermore, the offender is not subjected to the corrupting or stigmatizing effects associated with prison. This is particularly desirable for first-time offenders who may not have committed themselves to a life of crime. They are not exposed to being "educated" by career criminals in prison or to physical or sexual assault. Avoiding the criminogenic effects of prison was one of the major rationales for the Kentucky and Oregon house arrest programs for drunk drivers.

Third, these programs provide a flexibility that does not now exist in criminal sentencing. They can be used at almost any point in the criminal justice process—before an offender serves any jail time, after a short term in jail, after a prison term (usually joined with work release), or as an add-on condition for probation and parole. In addition, some of the programs can be limited to particular times of the day or particular types of offenders. This is especially attractive for offenders who are situationally dangerous. The drunk driver, the alcoholic who becomes assaultive, and the drug addict may all be likely candidates for programs such as house arrest and electronic minitoring.

Opponents of alternative sentencing, on the other hand, have begun to voice opposition to these programs. Some victims' rights groups—for example, Mothers Against Drunk Drivers (MADD)—believe that such community-based programs, however stringent, are too lenient for convicted offenders.

Many probation and parole officers, too, are critical of such programs, because the programs clearly focus on guarding people instead of helping them. Civil rights groups fear that the technology will be abused, particularly in programs that use electronic monitoring, and that the programs set a dangerous precedent by violating the sanctity of the private residence.

Nearly everyone is concerned with the public safety issue: Will offenders simply run criminal operations out of their homes? Will they escape? To date, participants in community-based programs are behaving extremely well. Less than 10 percent of offenders are being rearrested while in these programs—as compared with about 50 percent of such offenders who are sentenced to regular probation or parole supervision. However, as the programs expand and a wider array of offenders becomes eligible, the question of public safety will undoubtedly become more critical.

There is also some concern that the programs may simply widen the scope of social control. The prime candidates for these programs— nonviolent and low-risk offenders—are the ones who are least likely to be sentenced to prison in the first place. As judges become more familiar with the programs, they may use them for defendants who would normally have been sentenced to probation with nominal supervision. Hence, rather than reducing crowding, the programs may in fact widen the net of social control. If this happens, the programs will have increased, rather than decreased, the total cost of criminal sanctions.

2. PROBATION

a. NOTE

The theory of probation is that, instead of being sentenced to a correctional institution, a convicted defendant may be more humanely and economically subjected to lesser, but more flexible, controls within the community.

The supervised freedom of a man on probation is subject to specific conditions. A typical condition of probation is that the probationer violate no state or federal law. Other conditions may be shaped to the particular problems which are felt to have caused the original offense. Thus, a defendant accused of assaulting his estranged wife may be placed on probation with the condition that he not visit, call, or bother her in any way. Another common condition of probation is that the defendant refrain from the use of alcoholic beverages during the period of probation.

Where conditions of probation trench upon constitutional rights, they should be, and are, more carefully supervised. Should a condition of probation be valid where it provides that the probationer must submit himself to search by law enforcement authorities under conditions which would violate the Fourth Amendment rights of an ordinary citizen? That he attend church regularly? Or, that he not participate in political activities?

Should it matter whether these conditions can be shown to be related to his future observance of the law?

In any event, if one on probation violates the conditions of his probation, he may have his probation revoked by a judge at a relatively summary hearing, similar to the hearing he would receive on his initial sentencing. Though he has a right to an attorney at a probation revocation hearing, he certainly would have no right to trial by jury and in most cases he would not even be permitted to confront and cross-examine the witnesses against him.

On revocation of probation, the defendant may usually be given any sentence he might have received when initially convicted. Sometimes, however, the sentencing judge at the time he places a defendant on probation, will specify a particular sentence to be imposed if probation is revoked. Some judges do this to make the consequences seem more real to the defendant. "I sentence you to two years imprisonment, (then perhaps they pause for breath before continuing) the sentence to be suspended, on condition that you successfully complete 4 years on probation." On revocation of probation then, the defendant will be sentenced automatically to the two-year prison term specified.

In theory, one of the major advantages of probation in the rehabilitation of offenders is that they will be subject to supervision, in the social work sense, by experienced case workers, who have the time and ability to help them lead law-abiding lives.

b.   HISTORY AND PROBLEMS OF PROBATION *

Probation began in Boston in 1841, as a result of the work of a Boston shoemaker, John Augustus. Courts had already established the practice of release on bail. Augustus decided to stand bail for men charged with drunkenness, although he had no official connection with the court. Soon he extended his voluntary services to women and children. Until his death in 1859, Augustus supervised almost 2,000 persons in lieu of confinement in the Boston House of Corrections. He generally limited his guardianship to first offenders and conducted detailed examinations into the history and character of offenders before selecting them for his caseload. Probation supervision covered oversight of the client's schooling and work responsibilities as well as sometimes securing housing for probationers. The work of John Augustus was carried on by a number of volunteer "probation officers" who sought to "rescue youthful offenders" from the evils of confinement with hardened criminals.

In 1869, the state of Massachusetts established by statute a system by which agents of the Board of the State Charities took charge of delinquents before they appeared in court. The youths were often released on probation subject to good behavior in the future. An 1878 law permitted Massachusetts to appoint paid probation officers for Boston's criminal courts. This law specified that probationers should be "such persons as may reasonably be expected to be reformed without punishment" but did not limit probation to any particular class of offenders. Massachusetts established a statewide system of probation in 1891. California empowered courts to employ probation in 1903 and

* Barry A. Krisberg and James F. Austin, "The Unmet Promise of Alternatives to Incarceration," unpublished paper, National Council on Crime and Delinquency Research Center, San Francisco, CA, 1981, pp. 8–11. © 1981 (Reprinted with permission).

Pennsylvania in 1909. Early observers celebrated probation's great promise but also noted potential problems. Barnes (1926) argued that probation:

> . . . saves the person from the stigma, humiliation, degradation, and demoralizing association which is everywhere to be found in our penal and correctional institutions. For the time being, the extension of probation is one of the most promising immediate steps which can be taken in criminal science and jurisprudence.

He also noted that wide variation existed in the application of the new sanction by Pennsylvania judges. Barnes advocated either compulsory probation for certain classes of minor offenders or "a more universally intelligent judiciary."

In California, too, concern was expressed about large variations in the number and types of offenders placed on probation in different counties. Attempts to better regulate probation included efforts to upgrade the quality and salaries of probation officers as well as legislation to restrict probation eligibility. A 1923 law denied probation to:

> persons in cases of murder, robbery, burglary, or rape, where in the perpetration of such crimes a deadly weapon was used or where the perpetrator was armed with a deadly weapon . . . (and) to any person previously convicted of any of the above crimes, (and) to any public official who offered or took a bribe.

Limits on the use of probation were further extended to prior felony convictions and all persons possessing weapons during their crimes or arrests. A 1929 California Crime Commission noted the anger by law enforcement officials that courts were circumventing legislative restrictions on probation. The Commission cited problems of weak local administration, inadequate training of judges and probation officers, and a "tenderheartedness and sympathy to appeals made by effective pleaders." Another issue was the growing practice of sentencing felons to terms in county jails as one of their conditions of probation. Some felt this split sentence complicated jail administration, introduced further disparities in sentencing, and undermined the state's indeterminate sentencing law. [Nonetheless] probation and especially the split sentence expanded throughout the next several decades.

c. THE POLITICS OF PROBATION *

Probation—or any other aspect of criminal justice, for that matter—was hardly a prominent issue in the 1980 presidential campaign, but the question certainly seems worth asking: Will local probation policy and practice shift to the right—favoring law-enforcement rather than social work—in the new political climate?

* John Blackmore, "A Swing to the Right," *Corrections Magazine*, Vol. 7, No. 1, February 1981, p. 14. © 1981 (Reprinted with permission).

. . . There is much evidence that most probation authorities believe that the traditional model of probation, involving an integration of the law enforcement and social service functions, remains the appropriate path. . . . A recent study wrote: "Decisions constantly must be made between the relative risk of law violation at the present time and the probable long-term gain if a probationer is to be allowed the opportunity to develop an improved life style. . . ."

But the traditional view is not unchallenged. David Fogel and his associates at the University of Illinois propose that "simple justice urges us to redirect [the mission of probation] to correct the imbalance which occurred as a result of . . . the crime." This, they say, involves "making the victim, rather than the offender, whole," and "requires an emphasis on surveillance and supervision."

According to Milton Rector, executive director of the National Council on Crime and Delinquency, probation departments around the country were already drifting toward a surveillance emphasis before the "just deserts" theorists provided the justification. "I've been observing the trend," he said in a recent interview, "and it seems to me that probation is rapidly developing into an extension of the coercive arm of the correctional system. I'm really shocked at how things have changed.

"In the old days, P.O.s (Probation Officers) used to be able to go in and take an armed offender when the police couldn't because that offender would have some respect for the P.O. and know that he wasn't armed. Nowadays, P.O.s are making calls in dangerous neighborhoods. They're frightened and want to be armed. But I would still guess that the majority of P.O.s in the country don't see themselves as cops or gun-carrying officers."

On the official end, the drift to surveillance and control in probation "fits more with the call for retribution and deterrence than with the repair-the-man concept," according to Rector. "This is what the public wants. I know of no other field where so much money is expended and where decisions are made on the basis of public sentiment, real or imagined."

"The conservative swing in public attitudes affects all of us," said Tim Fitzharris, executive director of the California Probation, Parole and Correctional Association. "Judges, cops, D.A.s, public defenders are part of the community and reflect that community. So are probation officials. . . . You have to look at the survival issues too. There's a visceral reaction out there [in the probation field] that if we look more like cops, whom the public likes, maybe they'll give us the funding we need."

Questions

According to the above excerpt, the "justice model" of corrections requires that probation officers be "neither cops nor counselors" but rather that they be "compliance officers." What is the difference between enforced compliance with an order and law enforcement? Is not a compliance officer merely another name for a law enforcement officer? Does this mean the above excerpt is wrong? Do you think that probation officers will readily accept this change of orientation? Why?

3.   FINES: PROS AND CONS *

The fine is one of the oldest forms of punishment and is widely used in Western Europe as the sole sanction for the major portion of cases coming before the criminal courts, Sweden, England, and West Germany all report that more than three-quarters of cases result in a fine. In the United States, recent studies for the National Institute of Justice have shown that although the fine is widely used, the amounts levied tend to be relatively small and are used in combination with other sanctions, notably probation.

Proponents of greater fine use have argued that this monetary sanction offers a number of advantages. The amount of the fine can be adjusted to a level appropriate to the individual offender and the seriousness of the crime. Because it is a community-based punishment, it does not destroy the essential economic and social ties of the offender. Fines are relatively inexpensive to administer and can be financially self-sustaining. In short, fines can be an effective punishment for offenders who have committed crimes of varying degrees of severity.

Critics, on the other hand, cite these drawbacks: given the poverty of most offenders, fines cannot be collected; they are difficult to enforce; and their use adds to the courts' administrative burdens.

Usually probation officers are charged with pressing offenders to pay their fines. Given heavy probation caseloads, however, some departments have hired other employees to monitor fine payments as a way of reducing the burden on trained probation officers.

Judges have a special responsibility to make known to the offender the seriousness of the sentencing order and the fact that additional sanctions will follow if the fine is unpaid. The legitimacy of the court in the eyes of both the offender and the community requires that sentences are seen to be carried out.

Collection and enforcement innovations

Despite the problems noted in this article, there are courts where fine collection and enforcement are taken seriously, and where new methods have resulted in a high proportion of fines being paid. What are some of these techniques, and how can they be applied more generally? The following are five methods used in various State and local courts, their advantages, and their disadvantages.

* George Cole, "Innovations in Collecting and Enforcing Fines," National Institute of Justice Reports, July/August 1989, No. 215.

Installment payments. Increasingly, courts are allowing offenders to pay their fines on the installment plan. The number of payments is usually worked out by the clerk, taking into account the means of the offender and the total amount due. In some courts, fine coordinators are employed to counsel offenders on their obligation and to draw up payment schedules. In the Phoenix Municipal Court, offenders consult a coordinator if they cannot pay the fine immediately.

Credit cards. The potential for a "cashless society" has encouraged courts to allow offenders to make fine payments with credit cards. Administrators have viewed the credit card as a way to receive fine payments while the banks do the actual collecting. Unfortunately, credit cards have not proved as useful to courts as originally projected. For some offenders, especially those from the middle and upper classes, the credit card serves as a convenience in court. Other fine payers either do not own credit cards or recognize that this payment method may result in an 18- to 20-percent interest charge.

Computerized recordkeeping systems. The advent of computers has given court administrators effective tools for maintaining fine-payment records and automatically notifying offenders when payments are due. Typically, a computer system will create a case record listing offender information, the amount of money owed the court, and the payment schedule. When a payment is overdue beyond a certain time period, the computer automatically sends a warning letter to the delinquent offender.

Telemarketing. Private businesses also routinely use the telephone to remind customers of installment payments due. Some courts have found that they can enhance fine collection by using their own employees or by contracting with private telemarketing firms to provide such reminder services. Modern technology provides for automatic dialing, screening of busy signals or no answers with automatic redialing at a later time, use of live or pre-recorded messages, and recording of an offender's response to a question about when a fine payment will be made. All these technological innovations have proved useful to courts in their collection efforts.

Collection agencies. Courts are increasingly looking to the private sector for assistance with fine collection, and a number of jurisdictions have contracted with private collection agencies. In most States, collection firms are licensed and must conform to certain approved practices. These companies are able to pursue debtors across State lines and often have access to data bases that allow them to track offenders' whereabouts. Many collection agencies routinely notify credit bureaus of delinquent accounts. Communicating this fact to offenders seems to be a major factor in recovering overdue fines.

The future of fine collection

Fines have proved to be a useful sentencing option for a sizable number of cases in courts of both general and limited jurisdiction. As jurisdictions search for ways to ensure appropriate sanctions in light of jail crowding and record numbers of probationers, the experience of these courts demonstrates that the technology exists for effective fine enforcement and collection.

If courts were to avail themselves of these techniques, they would be able to reduce the number and size of delinquent accounts. This would achieve two key goals. It would clearly signal to offender and community alike that judicial orders will be obeyed. And, by making this form of punishment more certain, judges might be inclined to make greater use of the fine as the sole sanction for many criminal offenses.

4. ELECTRONIC MONITORING OF OFFENDERS INCREASES *

Officials in 33 States were using electronic monitoring devices to supervise nearly 2,300 offenders in 1988—about three times the number using this new approach a year earlier, according to a National Institute of Justice survey.

In 1988, most of those monitored were sentenced offenders on probation or parole, participating in a program of intensive supervision in the community. A small portion of those being monitored had been released either pretrial or while their cases were on appeal.

The first electronic monitoring program was in Palm Beach, Florida, in December 1984. Since then an increasing number of jurisdictions have adopted electronic monitoring to better control probationers, parolees, and others under the supervision of the criminal justice system.

Survey results show that offenders monitored in 1988 were convicted of a wide range of criminal violations.

A quarter (25.6 percent) of offenders were charged with major traffic offenses. Most of the offenders in this group (71 percent) were charged with driving under the influence or while intoxicated. The other offenses in this category reflect primarily current or previous drunk driving convictions such as driving on a revoked or suspended permit.

Property offenders were strongly represented. They committed a few closely related offenses—burglary (28 percent), thefts or larcenies (39.6 percent), and breaking and entering (16.6 percent).

Drug law violators constituted 15.3 percent of monitored offenders, with slightly over half of these charged with possession of drugs and the rest charged with distribution.

How are the offenders monitored?

The monitoring equipment used can be roughly divided into two kinds: continuously signaling devices that constantly monitor the pres-

* Annesley K. Schmidt, "Electronic monitoring of offenders increases," National Institute of Justice Reports, January February 1989, No. 212.

ence of an offender at a particular location, and programmed contact devices that contact the offender periodically to verify his or her presence.

How electronic monitoring equipment works

A continuously signaling device has three major parts: a transmitter, a receiver-dialer, and a central computer.

The transmitter, which is attached to the offender, sends out a continuous signal. The receiver-dialer, which is located in the offender's home and is attached to the telephone, detects the signals sent by the transmitter. It reports to the central computer when it stops receiving the signal and again when the signal begins.

A central computer at the monitoring agency accepts reports from the receiver-dialer over the telephone lines, compares them with the offender's curfew schedule, and alerts correctional officials about any unauthorized absences. The computer also stores information about each offender's routine entries and exits so that a report can be prepared.

Programmed contact devices use a computer programmed to telephone the offender during the monitored hours, either randomly or at specified times. The computer prepares a report on the results of the call.

Most but not all programs attempt to verify that the offender is indeed the person responding to the computer's call. Programmed contact devices can do this in several ways. One is to use voice verification technology. Another is to require the offender to wear a wristwatch device programmed to provide a unique number that appears when a special button on the watch device is pressed into a touchtone telephone in response to the computer's call.

A third system requires a black plastic module to be strapped to the offender's arm. When the computer calls, the module is inserted into a verifier box connected to the telephone. A fourth system uses visual verification at the telephone site.

Programs surveyed in 1988 varied in the way they paid for the sanction, the intensity of supervision, and failure rates.

Who pays? The survey answers show that in most programs the offenders do, with the exception of the Florida Department of Corrections. Charges are based on a sliding scale, with a maximum fee of $15 a day.

How do offenders fare in these programs? Some programs reported that few participants had failed to complete the program successfully while others reported that almost half had not completed the program. Most of the failures resulted from infractions of program rules such as not abiding by curfew hours or using alcohol or drugs.

Survey respondents noted a variety of problems that they had for the most part resolved. Some programs, for instance, initially had difficulty gaining acceptance within their agencies for either the program or the equipment that would be used. After proper training and successful tests of the program, however, confidence grew.

Electronic monitors have been available commercially for only a short time, but their use has grown rapidly. Recent discussions with manufacturers suggest the growth continues.

5. RETRIBUTION AND TREATMENT *

California's Blue Ribbon Commission on Inmate Population Management issued its *Final Report* in January 1990.

Of the Commission's recommendations, the single most important one is a Community Corrections Act. Such an act would provide state funds to localities through grants and contracts for the expansion of community-based programs such as drug treatment, mother-infant care, intensive probation, house arrest and expanded pretrial release options.

One of the alternatives recommended by the Commission was the use of "Offender Specific Planning"—having a nonprofit organization provide highly specific, rigorous reports to courts at sentencing which develop alternatives to prison, jail or Youth Authority commitments. The following are two case examples of prison bound offenders who were effectively diverted by alternative sentencing proposals.

Case #1—John B.

In September 1987, John B., 20, and several friends drank eight to ten glasses of beer at a fraternity party. Feeling fully in control to drive, John set off with his best friend. As he rounded a curve on a canyon road, John lost control of his car, veered up an embankment and overturned. John's friend was killed instantly.

John's blood alcohol tested 0.16%. He was charged with voluntary manslaughter with gross negligence. A college student and an athlete, a first-time offender, faced with the probability of imprisonment, John was devastated.

What followed was "client specific planning." With the cooperation of the victim's family, John's defense team put together a program which included active participation in SADD (Students Against Drunk Driving), restitution to the family and community service.

When the judge read the proposed sentencing plan, he commented that it was more rigorous than imprisonment in that it required John to truly face up to and atone for what he had done.

In study after study, imprisonment has been proven to be an ineffective deterrent to drunk driving. Analysis of data in seven countries, including the United States, Australia, Norway, Sweden, Denmark and the Netherlands, revealed that neither the overall per-

* Vincent Schiraldi, "The Prison Dilemma: Should We "Lock 'em All Up" San Francisco Attorney, Vol. 16, No. 5, October/November 1990. (Reprinted with permission).

centage of DUI accidents nor the percentage of DUI injury and fatal accidents per number of reported DUI arrests declined with tougher sentencing laws.

Case #2—Alex R.

By the time Alex R. obtained legal counsel his chances of staying out of the California state prison system looked dismal. Charged with molesting four boys under the age of 14 and having given taped confession to one of the parents, he was facing mandatory imprisonment of up to 22 years.

In Alex R.'s case, the parents of the children were brought into the process early to assist in the development of a sentencing plan that would meet the often conflicting goals of punishment, restitution and rehabilitation. With the cooperation of the parents, an earnest effort on Alex's part to save restitution for counseling for the victims, rigorous residential therapy with aftercare, and mandatory Depo Provera (sex drive inhibitor) injections, a plan was prepared which met with the court's concerns in Alex's case.

Unfortunately, sexually disordered offenders stand less than 1% chance of receiving treatment in the California Department of Corrections.

The battle for creative, non-incarcerative sentences for child molesters is both a worthy and a difficult one. While most therapists recognize that the crime of child molestation is synonymous with the disease of pedophilia, the moral repugnance for such acts, reflected by society, the courts and even prison inmates, can often land treatable defendants in prison.

Will the public accept alternatives to prison?

The oft-touted "will of the people" that all offenders should be locked up for as long as possible was shown to be more perception than reality in many cases. Sophisticated public surveys indicate that, when respondents are provided with basic information about the availability of alternatives to incarceration for offenders, the likelihood that interviewees would choose imprisonment for hypothetical offenders drops dramatically.

The Commission reported the results of a study recently commissioned by the California Department of Corrections. In it, the respondents were asked to respond to 25 hypothetical cases from petty theft to rape choosing whether the offenders should be incarcerated or placed on probation. Respondents then read short descriptions of the costs of imprisonment, prison overcrowding, and the nature of a variety of alternative options. Initially, respondents placed about 63% of offenders in prison. When given more options and better information, they sent about 27% to prison. This study was replicated in Alabama with even more dramatic results with the number of hypothetical cases "jailed" dropping from 78% to 17%.

Unfortunately, policy makers continue incorrectly to perceive the public's attitudes to be more punitive then they actually are.

6. PAROLE

a.   INTRODUCTION

Parole is in theory a continuation of a prison sentence, under the supervision of a parole officer, in the community. We will discuss the restrictions and reality of the parole experience in the next excerpt.

The decision to release a prisoner on parole is a vital one for the prisoner. Whatever his problems with parole supervision, he vastly prefers it to life in prison.

The parole system is founded on several principles. First, as in the theory of probation, if supervision in the community will prevent an individual from committing further crimes, it is far cheaper than continuing to imprison him for the same purpose. Second, since parole follows a prison term, the retributive and deterrent purposes of the law are not compromised. Third, perhaps the most important reason for parole is that studies have shown that, no matter how likely a type of offender is to repeat criminal activity, he will do better if, instead of being released at the expiration of his sentence, the transition between prison and freedom is made less abrupt by a period of parole.

The decision to parole is, at the very least, a most difficult one, involving a prediction as to the likelihood of the prisoner's future criminal activity. There is sizeable literature on parole prediction—the use of characteristics, such as age, education, work experience, family ties, availability of employment, previous criminal record and the like to determine which inmates are the best candidates for parole. Though research seems to have increased somewhat the possible accuracy of parole prediction in recent years, it still remains, in each case, a guess. The guess, however, is forced upon us simply because both humanity and expense prevent us from retaining all prisoners for the rest of their lives.

We will discuss the decision to release or parole in the next chapter because it is so intimately tied up with the issue of sentencing.

b.   RELEASE *

. . . It is impossible or at best extremely difficult to live strictly within the limits set by the conditions of parole—the formal parole status. This proves difficult for various reasons: (1) In order to become viable, to meet the bare citizen exigencies it is often necessary to break some of the conditions. For instance, condition IX states that the parolee must have written permission from the parole agent before he

* John Irwin, *The Felon* © 1970 pp. 155–183. Reprinted by permission of Prentice Hall Inc., Englewood Cliffs, New Jersey.

may drive a motor vehicle. Before the agent can grant this permission, however, the parolee must show that he has a valid driver's license and bodily injury and public-damage insurance coverage (which is expensive for parolees since they are placed in a high-risk category). Often the parolee, before he can afford the insurance, must drive to maintain employment. . . . Forty-seven per cent of those interviewed admitted that they drove a car before receiving written permission to drive.

Second, in some instances it is, in all practicality, impossible to live according to the conditions of parole. For instance, condition II states that the parolee must have permission to leave the county of residence. The San Francisco Bay Area is in many ways one large sprawling community which covers six counties— . . .

Condition III states that it is necessary for the parolee to maintain gainful employment. For many parolees who are unskilled, members of racial minorities, older, or have no work history, maintaining employment is next to impossible, especially in times of high unemployment. . . . Condition VIII states that the parolee "must avoid association with former inmates of penal institutions unless specifically approved by your parole agent, and you must avoid association with individuals of bad reputation." This as it is written is impossible to follow for a sizable proportion of parolees. Sixty per cent of those interviewed after a year indicated that they had violated this condition. Parolees, even the most conventionally oriented, make close friends in prison whom they usually plan to meet on the outside—if only for one or two short visits. More often, convicts make some lasting friendships which they intend to maintain. Furthermore, parolees often discover that other parolees are one of the best resources for finding jobs and residences and for supplying money, tools, and transportation which the recently released parolee desperately needs. Other parolees who are passing or have passed through similar difficulties and who are closer in all ways to the individual's problems are more willing and at times more able to extend help.

Beyond these more or less planned incidents of association, it would be virtually impossible for some parolees not to associate with ex-inmates or persons with bad reputations unless they went to live in a new city or perhaps a new state. These are persons who have been raised in locations such as the Negro or Mexican-American lower-class neighborhoods—the "ghettos"—where many of one's friends and relatives are either ex-convicts or persons who by conventional criteria are "individuals of bad reputation"; that is, they have long arrest records. . . .

Disparate Perspectives of Agent and Parolee

The parole conditions reflect the influence of an extremely conservative and puritanical segment of society. It has been suggested that the state legislature and governmental agencies are extremely vulnerable to the "crusades" of "moral entrepreneurs."

Because of their zeal and dedication and because of a tendency of the public to be stirred or cowed on issues involving "sin" and public "decency," these "moral entrepreneurs" have had considerable influence upon laws and official policies of agencies in matters related to drugs, sex, crime, and abortion. The legal and official status of the parolee has, therefore, been unduly influenced by a conservative and puritanical perspective. . . .

The System's Flaw

In effect, the parole social system has brought into close contact, in an agent-client relationship, two people who represent different social worlds—one, the parole agency, which is unduly influenced at the formal level by conservative segments of society; and the other, a deviant sub-society. Officially, the agent is to demand that the parolee live according to a set of conditions which originate from the dominant and conservative segments of society, membership in which is barred to and/or rejected by the parolee. The parolee, especially if he is an ex-criminal, usually returns to segments of society which, even though they be noncriminal, such as the lower working class, do not share the conservative perspective underlying these conditions. This is an inherent disrupting factor which must be withstood if any equilibrium in the system is to be achieved. Though both role incumbents are involved in dealing with this potential disruption, the degree to which each makes adjustments and the styles of these adjustments are usually dominated by the performance of the agent as it is seen by the parolee.

The Fragility of System

. . .

Except in the few cases where the parolee has a strong commitment to conventional norms and has no "problem," such as alcoholism or sexual perversion, which he cannot control, the equilibrium established in the parolee-agent relationship is precarious. This is because (1) the amount and types of deviant behavior in which the parolee engages remain beyond the limits of the official system and often beyond the legal limits of the community and (2) the actual performance of the parolee, although he has a tolerant agent and is successful in presenting a deceitful performance which is within the informal limits set by the agent, is usually outside the agent's tolerance limits. Because of this inherent flaw in the system, it remains fragile until the parolee is discharged. At any time a minor event may shatter it. This may mean a return to prison through cancellation of parole or a new prison sentence, a short disruptive stay in city jail—which results in loss of employment, perhaps loss of a particular employment career—or at least a major reorganization of his parole status—a change of residence, perhaps a move back into a halfway house, a change of jobs, assignment to special programs, such as the nalline (narcotics testing) clinic, the out-patient clinic, or group counseling.

. . .

Disruption of the System

. . . The disruption of the system, which always involves a shift in the definitions operative in the system, can be precipitated and proceed in several different ways. First the agent, because of some discovery, some event or a spontaneous reevaluation, changes his conception of the parolee's performance. He believes that the parolee has stepped over the boundaries. Some event or behavior is brought to his attention or the parolee is arrested and the agent sees through the screens of deceit and distance erected by the parolee. When this occurs the agent usually conducts an investigation—he searches the parolee, searches his room, makes inquiries, questions employers, relatives and friends, and discovers a great deal of behavior that is beyond the official and his own limit of tolerance and rediscovers or reassesses behavior which he had been aware of and perhaps had tacitly or opening approved but which now, in sight of his new evaluation, takes on new contours. Sometimes the investigation uncovers criminal acts, such as possession of drugs or drug paraphernalia, or possession of a weapon.

. . . A second manner in which the agent-parolee equilibrium can be disrupted and the definitions shifted is when the agent does not change his conception of the parolee's performance, but in view of the possible intrusion of demands and expectations from other sources, shifts his performance toward the parolee. Because the deviant acts of the parolee have become visible or are in danger of becoming visible to persons other than the agent and because of shifts in department formal or informal policies, the agent deems it necessary to protect himself by moving toward the official perspective. . . . A third way that the system can be threatened is from a change of parole agents. This can be quite serious to a parolee who has settled into a relationship with an agent who was tolerant and not intense and is then placed under the supervision of an intense and intolerant agent. To reestablish equilibrium he must make major revisions in his performance. This can be especially difficult as many parolees confuse the informal status—the expectations that emerge in their interaction with the particular agent—with the formal status. The tightening of restrictions and the intensification of surveillance which follows the change of the parole agent may seem extremely unfair and precipitate action which introduces additional strains in the new relationship.

Question and Comments

The above excerpt is obviously quite critical of the way parole works in practice. What kinds of reforms would lessen these problems?

It has been argued that parole, like probation, should serve two very distinct functions. First, it should be a service to the prisoner to enable him to adjust to the outside society. One of the functions of the parole agent, then, is to offer help to the prisoner during his cultural shock on re-entering the world from a period of long confinement. A number of prisons in an effort to solve this problem have allowed short weekend furloughs for prisoners close to the parole time so that they can adjust, without undue shock, upon their release.

Even more important, in most cases, would be the aid of a parole officer in getting employment for the prisoner. Often parole authorities will not release a prisoner until he is assured of some job, but unfortunately these jobs, perhaps because they are often offered only as a means of getting the prisoner out of prison, may not last very long. The prisoner will then need to turn somewhere to find employment, and it is arguable that parole's greatest benefit to the prisoner would be to give him meaningful help in finding a job—something which, regrettably, most parole departments barely attempt to do.

The other function of parole—the protection of society—has also come in for a considerable amount of criticism. According to the above excerpt, it is really not very effective because, among other things, it asks too much of parolees. In addition, it may be less effective because of the wide gulf in understanding between the prisoner and his parole officer, which seems to contribute to the ability of the parolee to mislead his parole officer about what actually is happening in his life.

A number of arguments have been made against parole, as an institution, on the grounds that it is anti-rehabilitative. Some have argued that giving some men so much power over the lives of others exerts changes for the worse in both of them. This, as yet, is clearly a minority view. It does seem that those released from prison are, as a group, more likely to commit further crimes than is the citizenry at large. If controls can be exerted over them to increase the likelihood of their apprehension should they commit other crimes—and indeed if special restrictions can be placed upon them to make crime less likely— this, in theory, might justify the parole system. Finally, even if the supervision and restrictions do no good at all, is it arguable that, but for an effort in this direction, the whole parole system would become politically unacceptable to the majority of law-abiding citizens?

Two factors account for the dramatic growth of California's parole violation and return to custody rate. First, in the 1980s reliable and inexpensive drug tests were developed and testing quickly became a routine condition of parole. One result has been that an increased number of parolees are found in violation of their conditions of parole. Second, increasingly police and prosecutors find it more convenient to process new arrestees by violating them for conditions of parole on old convictions rather than prosecuting them for new offenses. Indeed this has led to a new form of plea bargaining; arrestees waive their right to a revocation hearing and immediately return to custody to serve the balance of their parole term. In exchange prosecutors agree not to prosecute the new charges. Police and prosecutors like this because they can get people back into prison within a matter of hours without even having to meet the lower standards of proof at an administrative (rather than criminal) parole revocation hearing. Arrestees like it because it minimizes their exposure to prison; they serve only the balance of their parole time, often only a few months. And with so many prisons under court-ordered population caps, this time may be reduced, at times to just a few weeks.

This growth in a return to custody population led, James K. Rowland, Director of the California Department of Corrections, to comment, "I run the world's largest county jail." By this he meant that although his Department is organized to handle long term inmates, in fact it is spending an increasing amount of its efforts at managing short term detainees, a group with which traditionally corrections has not had to deal and for which it lacks programs. Furthermore although most corrections officials do not believe that such short term inmates pose much of a security risk, they nevertheless often take up valuable space in high security prisons. For instance as of 1990 a substantial portion of the inmates in California's high security prison, San Quentin, were there for violating conditions of parole. In response to this problem several states, Texas among them, are turning to private contractors to build cheaply constructed and inexpensive to operate low security, return to custody facilities to house this burgeoning new type of inmate population.

c. INCREASED EFFICIENCIES LEAD TO NEW PROBLEMS *

Parole violations are a significant and dramatically increasing contributing factor to prison population increases. Parole violators are those returned to prison by parole authorities for a violation of their parole conditions or a violation of law which parole authorities have found to occur based on administrative review and a "preponderance of evidence" finding. California leads the nation by a significant margin in the number of parole violators returned to prison. The felon parole population increased from approximately 9,000 in 1978 to in excess of 55,000 today and is projected to increase to almost 97,000 by 1994. Parole violators returned to prison in 1978 totaled 1,011, increased to 34,014 in 1988, and are projected to increase to over 83,000 by 1994. Thus, the parole population is increasing at a rate far exceeding prison population and parole violators returned to prison are accelerating at a rate far exceeding the increases in the parole population. In 1978, parole violators accounted for 8 percent of the admissions to prison. By 1988, this had increased dramatically to 45 percent. As of August 31, 1989, parole violators returned to custody represented about 16 percent, or approximately 13,500, of the CDC inmate population.

* Blue Ribbon Commission On Inmate Population Management, Final Report, pp. 24–25, The State of California, January 1990.

Parole violators represent not only a state prison population increase impact but also a processing problem in that over 81 percent of all parole violators spend less than six months in prison; over 52 percent spend less than three months.

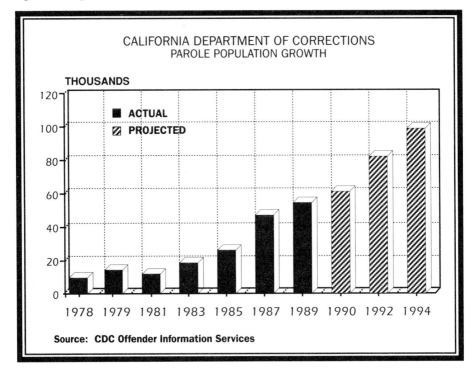

CALIFORNIA DEPARTMENT OF CORRECTIONS
PAROLE POPULATION GROWTH

Source: CDC Offender Information Services

Questions

How long do you think this projected trend can continue? Will costs associated with it cut into funds available for education, health care, highways and mass transit? Do you think the public will accept the trade-offer of increased incarceration for decreased support for these other services? Should the issues be framed in this way?

D. RECOMMENDED READING

Alpert, Geoffrey P., ed. *Legal Rights of Prisoners.* Sage Publications, Beverly Hills, 1980.

DiIulio, John J. *Governing Prisons: A Comparative Study of Correctional Management.* Free Press, New York, 1987.

DiIulio, John J., ed. *Courts Corrections, and the Constitution.* Oxford U.Press, 1990.

Foucault, Michel. *Discipline and Punish: The Birth of the Prison.* Translated by Alan Sheridan. Pantheon Books, New York, 1977.

Garland, David. *Punishment and Modern Society.* University of Chicago Press, Chicago, 1990.

Greenberg, David F., ed. *Corrections and Punishment.* Sage Publication, Beverly Hills, 1977.

Irwin, John. *Prisons in Turmoil.* Little, Brown & Co., Boston, 1980.

Irwin, John. *The Jail.* University of California Press, Berkeley, 1986.

McCarthy, Belinda, (ed.) *Intermediate Punishments.* Monsey, N.Y., Criminal Justice Press, 1987.

Morris, Norval and Tonry, Michael. *Between Prison and Probation.* University of Chicago Press, Chicago (1990).

Morris, Norval. *The Future of Imprisonment.* University of Chicago Press, Chicago, 1974.

Rothman, David. *The Discovery of the Asylum: Social Order and Disorder in the New Republic.* Little, Brown & Co., Boston, 1971.

Stanley, David T. *Prisoners Among Us: The Problem of Parole.* Brookings Institute, Washington, D.C., 1976.

Sykes, Gresham. *The Society of Captives: A Study of a Maximum Security Prison.* Princeton Univ. Press, Princeton, N.J., 1958.

Wicker, Tom. *A Time to Die.* Quadrangle/New York Times Book Co., New York, 1975.

Chapter XI

SENTENCING

A. INTRODUCTION

THREE MODELS OF CRIMINAL SENTENCING *

The history of criminal sentencing in the United States has been a history of shift in institutional power and in the theories that have guided the exercise of such power. In each period, one of three sentencing models has predominated, either the legislative, judicial, or administrative model. These are so called in recognition of the institution or the group of policy makers which exercises the power to imprison and to determine the length of imprisonment. Although incarcerative powers usually are shared by several persons or agencies, it is nevertheless possible to postulate pure sentencing models.

In the *legislatively fixed model,* the legislature determines that conviction for a given crime warrants a given term of imprisonment. For example, a first offender convicted of armed robbery must be sentenced to five years' imprisonment. There is no judicial or administrative discretion under this model; the legislature has authorized but one sentence.

In practice, there is still discretion at various points in this process. The police and prosecutor generally have wide discretion to determine the charge—whether the taking was a robbery or some lesser form of larceny, for example, or whether the means of committing the crime included the requisite type of weapon. Also, the executive generally has discretion to commute or pardon. In theory, however, the legislatively fixed sentence model is the least discretionary in the sense that the sentence is determined in advance of the crime and without knowing the identity of the criminal. But since the legislature has enormous discretion to determine which crimes deserve what punishments and since it is widely known what kinds of persons generally commit what kinds of crimes, racial and other kinds of prejudice tend to play a role in determining punishments for different typical crimes.

In the *judicially fixed model,* the legislature determines the general range of imprisonment for a given crime. For example, a first offender convicted of armed robbery shall be sentenced to no less than one and no more than 10 years' imprisonment. The sentencing judge must fix a determinate sentence within that range: "I sentence the

---

* Alan Dershowitz, Background Paper; on Criminal Sentencing 79–80 (1976). Fair and Certain Punishment: Report of © 1976 (Reprinted by permission). the Twentieth Century Fund Task Force

defendant to five years' imprisonment." Once this sentence is fixed, it cannot be increased or reduced by any parole board or adult authority; the defendant must serve for five years. (This model does not consider good-time provisions or other relatively automatic reductions, nor does it consider commutation or pardon.)

Under this model, discretion is vested in the sentencing judge; how much is vested depends on the range of imprisonment authorized by the legislature. On the day he is sentenced, however, the defendant knows precisely how long he will serve; there is no discretion vested in the parole board or prison authorities.

In the *administratively fixed model*, the legislature sets an extremely wide permissible range of imprisonment for a given crime. A first-offense armed robber, for example, shall be sentenced to a term of one day to life. The sentencing judge must—or may—impose the legislatively determined sentence: "You are sentenced to one day to life." The actual duration of the sentence is decided by an administrative agency while the prisoner is serving his sentence. For example, after five years of imprisonment, the adult authority decides that the prisoner is ready for release.

Under this model, vast discretion is vested in the administrative agency and in the prison authorities. On the day he is sentenced, the defendant does not know how long he will have to serve, although he probably can make an educated guess based on past practices.

Comment

As a practical matter, the sentencing of those convicted is probably the most important part of the criminal process. It is here that the criminal law has its "bite" on the individual. Further, as we have seen, the great majority of those charged with a crime plead guilty, and most of those who plead not guilty are convicted at trial. For them, the most important issue on entering the criminal process is what will be their punishment.

Sentencing also presents some of the most complex issues in the operation of the criminal system. As we noted in Chapter II, the criminal system serves a variety of purposes including deterrence, rehabilitation, isolation and perhaps retribution. It is at the point of sentencing that these aims must be balanced against one another in reaching a concrete decision as to what should be done with a particular individual. If all of the aims of the criminal law pointed in the same direction, the decision would be easily made. In fact, however, things are not nearly that simple. The kind of sentence which will most deter others and which will wreak vengeance upon the defendant for his crime, may also be the one least likely to rehabilitate him and most expensive, in simple money terms, to carry out.

Finally, the legal standards in sentencing are less developed than those in other areas of the criminal process. Although at other stages of the process, the legal rights of the parties are defined fairly clearly and enforced by a host of guarantees, perhaps because of the complexity of the sentencing process, we have developed fewer rules to insure regular procedures, rationality of decisions, and fairness in sentencing.

B. SENTENCING BY THE JUDGE

1. JUDICIAL DISCRETION

a. THE JUSTICE OF DISCRETION *

. . . Criminal justice is preeminently the process through which society pronounces moral judgment on those who have offended its laws. When in our everyday lives we judge or condemn those whom we know well, we do so in a context thick with circumstances we consider relevant and important. There is no reason why these surrounding circumstances become less relevant in the criminal arena. Therefore, when society pronounces the moral judgment of criminal conviction, it must be done within the rich context of an offender's background. This includes social, educational, familial, vocational, psychological, and even physiological factors. The availability of this information is a necessary prerequisite for using the criminal justice system as a means of educating ourselves about the social origins of crime.

This information is necessary not only for determining responsibility or *mens rea* for a criminal conviction, but also for the sentencing process after conviction. In sentencing, John Winthrop pointed out in 1644: "Justice ought to render to every man accordinge to his deservinge." When a sentence of death is at issue, the Supreme Court has given this principle constitutional grounding. In Woodson v. North Carolina, for example, Justice Stewart stated, announcing the judgment of the Court:

> A process that accords no significance to relevant facets of the character and record of the individual offender or the circumstances of the particular offense excludes from consideration in fixing the ultimate punishment of death the possibility of compassionate or mitigating factors stemming from the diverse frailties of humankind. It treats all persons convicted of a designated offense not as uniquely individual human beings, but as members of a faceless, undifferentiated mass to be subjected to the blind infliction of the penalty of death.

In Roberts v. Louisiana, the Court noted some of the myriad of factors to be considered at sentencing: "Circumstances such as the youth of the offender, the absence of any prior conviction, the influence of drugs, alcohol, or extreme emotional disturbance, and even the existence of circumstances which the offender reasonably believed provided a moral justification for his conduct are all examples of mitigating facts . . . ."

---

* David L. Bazelon, "Missed Opportunities in Sentencing Reform," *Hofstra Law* *Review*, Vol. 7, 1978–79, pp. 60–61. © 1978 (Reprinted by permission).

Questions

Is it not clear that, among other variables, a judge's sentence will be influenced by his perception of the utility of different correctional alternatives; by the importance he attaches to the varying purposes of the criminal law; by his view of the seriousness of different types of crime—sex offenses, offenses against property, violent offenses, fraud, and drug offenses, for instance; by his views of particular types of defendants, and by a host of other factors conscious and unconscious?

Moreover, and perhaps most important, does it make any sense talking about the proper criteria for sentence in a criminal system where so many sentences are in fact determined by plea bargains reached because of entirely different criteria?

b.   THE INJUSTICE OF DISCRETION *

Sentencing is an example of a decisionmaking process in which decisions are made not directly about people, but about information about people.   Such a process cannot outperform its informational inputs: garbage in, garbage out.   Uniformly, social scientists studying dispositional decisionmaking have commented on the nearly hopeless unreliability of the data used in the process.   Even more important than the level of inaccuracies identified, however, is the level of inconsistency found.   Often, factors deemed significant in one presentence report may be omitted and ignored in another, although present in both cases.   Compounding the problematic character of the actual data is an approach to data presentation that stresses not a standardized comparative assessment, but an individualized understanding of each offender on his own terms.   Here, then, is an impressionistic methodology uniquely ill-suited to the elimination of disparities, because it focuses on the uniqueness of each case and not on the similarities among cases.   Put simply, if we wish the sentencing judge to treat "like cases alike," a more inappropriate technique for the presentation of information could hardly be found than one that stresses a novelistic portrayal of each offender and thereby overloads the decisionmaker in a welter of detail.

Questions

It is clear, is it not, that the authors of the two previous excerpts, Judge Bazelon and Professor Coffee, sharply disagree?   If so, what is the focus of their disagreement?   Would it be fair to conclude that Judge Bazelon perceives the moral importance of individualizing sentences based on the context of an offender's background, while Professor Coffee sees the impossibility of rendering decisions based upon the sort of information normally available to judges?

* John C. Coffee, "Repressed Issues of Sentencing," 66 *The Georgetown Law Journal,* 1978, pp. 986–987. (Reprinted with the permission of the publisher © 1978 by the Georgetown Law Journal).

c. THE JUDGE'S OPTIONS *

The common form of criminal penalty provision confers upon the sentencing judge an enormous range of choice. The scope of what we call "discretion" permits imprisonment for anything from a day to one, five, 10, 20, or more years. All would presumably join in denouncing a statute that said "the judge may impose any sentence he pleases." Given the mortality of men, the power to set a man free or confine him for up to 30 years is not sharply distinguishable.

The statutes granting such powers characteristically say nothing about the factors to be weighed in moving to either end of the spectrum or to some place between. It might be supposed by some stranger arrived in our midst that the criteria for measuring a particular sentence would be discoverable outside the narrow limits of the statutes and would be known to the judicial experts rendering the judgments. But the supposition would lack substantial foundation. Even the most basic sentencing principles are not prescribed or stated with persuasive authority. There is, to be sure, a familiar litany in the literature of sentencing "purposes": retribution, deterrence ("special" and "general"), "denunciation," incapacitation, rehabilitation. Nothing tells us, however, when or whether any of these several goals are to be sought, or how to resolve such evident conflicts as that likely to arise in the effort to punish and rehabilitate all at once. It has for some time been part of our proclaimed virtue that vengeance or retribution is a disfavored motive for punishment. But there is reason to doubt that either judges or the public are effectively abreast of this advanced position. And there is no law—certainly none that anybody pretends to have enforced—telling the judge he must refrain, expressly or otherwise, from trespassing against higher claims to wreak vengeance.

Moving upward from what should be the philosophical axioms of a rational scheme of sentencing law, we have no structure of rules, or even guidelines, affecting other elements arguably pertinent to the nature or severity of the sentence. Should it be a mitigating factor that the defendant is being sentenced upon a plea of guilty rather than a verdict against him? Should it count in his favor that he spared the public "trouble" and expense by waiving a jury? Should the sentence be more severe because the judge is convinced that the defendant perjured himself on the witness stand? Should churchgoing be considered to reflect favorably? Consistently with the first amendment, should it be considered at all? What factors should be assessed—and where, if anywhere, are comparisons to be sought—in gauging the relative seriousness of the specific offense and offender as against the spectrum of offenses by others in the same legal category? The list of such questions could be lengthened. Each is capable of being answered, and is answered by sentencing judges, in contradictory or conflicting, or

* Frankel, Marvin E., (U.S. District Judge) Lawlessness in Sentencing, *University of Cincinnati L.Rev.,* Vol. 41 No. 1 (1972), pp. 4–24. © 1972 (Reprinted by permission).

at least differing, ways. There is no controlling requirement that any particular view be followed on any such subject by the sentencing judge.

With the delegation of power so unchanneled, it is surely no overstatement to say that "the new penology has resulted in vesting in judges and parole and probation agencies the greatest degree of uncontrolled power over the liberty of human beings that one can find in the legal system." The process would be totally unruly even if judges were superbly and uniformly trained for the solemn work of sentencing. As everyone knows, however, they are not trained at all.

Questions and Comments

For an example of how Judge Frankel, the author of the above excerpt used his discretion in a concrete case, see p. 562.

Can we really eliminate judicial discretion? Consider the following six cases of an identical offense, kidnapping, in light of whether each of the offenders should receive a mandated fixed sentence:

(1) A woman's baby dies, and she takes another woman's baby from the hospital. (2) A young man's girlfriend breaks up with him. He invites her into his car and then, against her protests, drives her around for 24 hours trying to persuade her to change her mind. In the meantime, her parents are worried sick over her disappearance. (3) A divorced father takes his own child on a weekend fishing trip without telling the child's mother, who has legal custody. The mother is frantic, since the child did not return home from school on Friday, and, unknown to the father, parents of school children have been alerted to the presence of a child molester lurking about the playground. (4) A man abducts a child as the youngster returns from school. He buries the child in a box fitted with air tubes for breathing, and in the meantime demands a half million dollars from her wealthy father for her return. (5) A woman assists in the kidnapping of the girl in the box because she loved the kidnapper and also was afraid of him. She did everything she could to keep the buried girl alive and comfortable. (6) Loving parents, with the aid of a "deprogrammer," carry off their 22–year-old daughter against her will. Their daughter has joined [a religious cult] and the parents are terribly upset.

The same crime, kidnapping, is involved in each of the above cases. Do you think the same harm is involved? Do the same considerations of deterrence, isolation and retribution apply to all parties involved in the crime? If not, why not? Do you still think, if you ever did, that the sentence for kidnapping should be mandated by the legislature? Or should the sentence be ultimately decided, if not by the judge, by a sentencing authority? If the judge decides, should his or her sentence be subjected to appellate review?

d.   "FACTS–OF–LIFE" JUDGE FACES INVESTIGATION *

CHICAGO (UPI)—A suburban judge who allegedly spelled out the "facts of life" in no uncertain terms to offenders has been called on the carpet.

Judge John Teschner of Wheaton has confirmed that the Illinois Judicial Inquiry Board is investigating him.

In one case Teschner allegedly told a 17–year-old boy:

> "The facts of life are you're a slight white male. And the prisons are full of big, black people."

Then, the complaint charges, Teschner went on to detail the "facts of life" about sexual assaults in prison and admonished the youth to get his life in order or face the unseemly consequences.

The Judicial Inquiry Board is empowered to investigate any allegations that "bring the judicial office into disrepute."

If it finds the allegations are substantiated, the board could file charges with the Illinois Courts Commission, which has power to reprimand, suspend or remove judges from office.

Questions

Should the sentencing judge in exercising his or her discretion consider what life inside the prisons is really like? Should the judge consider the cost of imprisonment—running around $20,000 per year per prisoner? Should he consider the likely effectiveness of the prisons in preventing recidivism? How can the judge not do so and still exercise his or her discretion?

2.   THE CHOICE OF SENTENCE

a.   IN VERSE

A More Humane Mikado **

It is my very humane endeavour to make to some extent
Each evil liver a running river of harmless merriment.
My object all sublime I shall achieve in time
To let the punishment fit the crime, the punishment fit the crime;
And make each pris'ner pent unwillingly represent
A source of innocent merriment, of innocent merriment.
All prosy dull society sinners, who chatter and bleat and bore
Are sent to hear sermons from mystical Germans who preach from
     ten till four.
The advertising quack who wearies with tales of countless cures

---

* San Jose Mercury News, June 3, 1981, p. 2A. Reprinted by permission of United Press International.

** William S. Gilbert and Arthur Sullivan from "The Mikado".

His teeth I've enacted shall all be extracted by terrified amateurs.

The billiard sharp whom anyone catches, his doom's extremely hard

He's made to dwell in a dungeon cell on a spot that's always barred.

And there he plays extravagant matches in fitless finger stalls.

On a cloth untrue with a twisted cue and elliptical billiard balls.

b. SAMPLE DISPOSITIONS *

1

In sentencing a narcotics addict the judge explained, "For your own protection I am forced to send you into a period of confinement, so that you will be able to lose the habit of taking narcotics. You may then become a worthwhile citizen. I sentence you to from one to five years in the state prison."

2

Two elderly, shabbily dressed women were brought before the court, charged with drunkenness. The probation officer indicated to the judge that these two women had no place to go and were not well. The judge sentenced them to thirty days in the house of corrections, saying that they would be better off there than on the street.

3

A man was charged with being drunk and entered a plea of guilty. The defendant said that this was his first offense. The arresting officer described the man's belligerency and his resistance to arrest. The judge said that he would ordinarily suspend sentence in a case like this were it not for the difficulties with the officer. The judge asked how much money the defendant had, and he replied, "$30." The judge said, "All right, $30 or 30 days."

4

A twenty-year-old man was in court for the first time on a charge of possessing narcotics. Ordinarily the judge would have put a first offender on probation. During the trial the judge noticed that a group of young men were in the courtroom. During a recess he asked one of the detectives who the men were. The detectives told him they were members of a gang and the defendant was their leader. This decided the judge to impose a jail sentence.

* Remington, Newman, Kimball, Melli, Goldstein, *Criminal Justice Administration, Materials and Cases.* Indianapolis, Bobbs Merrill Co., Inc., 1969, pp. 712–713. ©1969 (Reprinted by permission).

5

A 25–year-old woman was charged with vandalism in breaking a window of a house bought by a black family in a white neighborhood. This was one of a series of acts by whites against the family. The judge imposed a ten-day jail sentence, saying "This sort of thing is going to stop. I want you to tell all your friends what happens here."

6

A man with a long narcotics record was arrested for sale of narcotics to a police undercover agent. He immediately expressed a desire to "do himself some good." He helped the police set up a case against his supplier. As a result he was charged with possession rather than sale, and the judge, having been informed privately that the informer had been responsible for making an important case, imposed a very light sentence.

Questions

Which of the purposes of the criminal law seems to be most clearly reflected in each of the sentences in the above excerpt?

Do you disagree with any of the sentences? What would you have done if you were the judge?

c. UNITED STATES v. BERGMAN
United States District Court, Southern District of New York, 1976.
416 F.Supp. 496.

FRANKEL, District Judge.

Defendant is being sentenced upon his plea of guilty to two counts of an 11–count indictment. The sentencing proceeding is unusual in some respects. It has been the subject of more extensive submissions, written and oral, than this court has ever received upon such an occasion. The court has studied some hundreds of pages of memoranda and exhibits, plus scores of volunteered letters. A broad array of issues has been addressed. Imaginative suggestions of law and penology have been tendered. A preliminary conversation with counsel, on the record, preceded the usual sentencing hearing. Having heard counsel again and the defendant speaking for himself, the court postponed the pronouncement of sentence for further reconsideration of thoughts generated during the days of studying the briefs and oral pleas. It seems fitting now to report in writing the reasons upon which the court concludes that defendant must be sentenced to a term of four months in prison.

I. *Defendant and His Crimes*

Defendant appeared until the last couple of years to be a man of unimpeachably high character, attainments, and distinction. A doctor of divinity and an ordained rabbi, he has been acclaimed by people around the world for his works of public philanthropy, private charity, and leadership in educational enterprises. Scores of letters have come to the court from across this and other countries reporting debts of personal gratitude to him for numerous acts of extraordinary generosity. (The court has also received a kind of petition, with 50–odd signatures, in which the signers, based upon learning acquired as newspaper readers, denounce the defendant and urge a severe sentence. Unlike the pleas for mercy, which appear to reflect unquestioned facts inviting compassion, this document should and will be disregarded.) In addition to his good works, defendant has managed to amass considerable wealth in the ownership and operation of nursing homes, in real estate ventures, and in a course of substantial investments.

Beginning about two years ago, investigations of nursing homes in this area, including questions of fraudulent claims for Medicaid funds, drew to a focus upon this defendant among several others. The results that concern us were the present indictment and two state indictments. After extensive pretrial proceedings, defendant embarked upon elaborate plea negotiations with both state and federal prosecutors. A state guilty plea and the instant plea were entered in March of this year. (Another state indictment is expected to be dismissed after defendant is sentenced on those to which he has pled guilty.) As part of the detailed plea arrangements, it is expected that the prison sentence imposed by this court will comprise the total covering the state as well as the federal convictions.

For purposes of the sentence now imposed, the precise details of the charges, and of defendant's carefully phrased admissions of guilt, are not matters of prime importance. Suffice it to say that the plea on Count One (carrying a maximum of five years in prison and a $10,000 fine) confesses defendant's knowing and willful participation in a scheme to defraud the United States in various ways, including the presentation of wrongfully padded claims for payments under the Medicaid program to defendant's nursing homes. Count Three, for which the guilty plea carries a theoretical maximum of three more years in prison and another $5,000 fine, is a somewhat more "technical" charge. Here, defendant admits to having participated in the filing of a partnership return which was false and fraudulent in failing to list people who had bought partnership interests from him in one of his nursing homes, had paid for such interests, and had made certain capital withdrawals.

The conspiracy to defraud, as defendant has admitted it, is by no means the worst of its kind; it is by no means as flagrant or extensive as has been portrayed in the press; it is evidently less grave than other nursing-home wrongs for which others have been convicted or publicized. At the same time, the sentence, as defendant has acknowledged, is imposed for two federal felonies including, as the more important, a knowing and purposeful conspiracy to mislead and defraud the Federal Government.

II. *The Guiding Principles of Sentencing*

Proceeding through the short list of the supposed justifications for criminal sanctions, defense counsel urge that no licit purpose could be served by defendant's incarceration. Some of these arguments are plainly sound; others are not.

The court agrees that this defendant should not be sent to prison for "rehabilitation." Apart from the patent inappositeness of the concept to this individual, this court shares the growing understanding that no one should ever be sent to prison *for rehabilitation.* That is to say, nobody who would not otherwise be locked up should suffer that fate on the incongruous premise that it will be good for him or her. Imprisonment is punishment. Facing the simple reality should help us to be civilized. It is less agreeable to confine someone when we deem it an affliction rather than a benefaction. If someone must be imprisoned—for other, valid reasons—we should seek to make rehabilitative resources available to him or her. But the goal of rehabilitation cannot fairly serve in itself as grounds for the sentence to confinement.

Equally clearly, this defendant should not be confined to incapacitate him. He is not dangerous. It is most improbable that he will commit similar, or any, offenses in the future. There is no need for "specific deterrence."

Contrary to counsel's submissions, however, two sentencing considerations demand a prison sentence in this case:

First, the aim of *general deterrence,* the effort to discourage similar wrongdoing by others through a reminder that the law's warnings are real and that the grim consequence of imprisonment is likely to follow from crimes of deception for gain like those defendant has admitted.

Second, the related, but not identical, concern that any lesser penalty would, in the words of the Model Penal Code, § 7.01(1)(c), "depreciate the seriousness of the defendant's crime."

Resisting the first of these propositions, defense counsel invoke Immanuel Kant's axiom that "one man ought never to be dealt with merely as a means subservient to the purposes of another." In a more novel, but equally futile, effort, counsel urge that a sentence for general deterrence "would violate the Eighth Amendment proscription against cruel and unusual punishment." Treating the latter point first, because it is a short subject, it may be observed simply that if general deterrence as a sentencing purpose were now to be outlawed, as against a near unanimity of views among state and federal jurists, the bolt would have to come from a place higher than this.

As for Dr. Kant, it may well be that defense counsel mistake his meaning in the present context. Whether or not that is so, and without pretending to authority on that score, we take the widely accepted stance that a criminal punished in the interest of general deterrence is not being employed *"merely* as a means. . . ." Reading Kant to mean that every man must be deemed *more* than the instrument of others, and must "always be treated as an end in himself," the humane principle is not offended here. Each of us is served by the enforcement of the law—not least a person like the defendant in this case, whose wealth and privileges, so long enjoyed, are so much founded upon law. More broadly, we are driven regularly in our ultimate interests as members of the community to use ourselves and each other, in war and in peace, for social ends. One who has transgressed against the criminal laws is certainly among the more fitting candidates for a role of this nature. This is no arbitrary selection. Warned in advance of the prospect, the transgressor has chosen, in the law's premises, "between keeping the law required for society's protection or paying the penalty."

But the whole business, defendant argues further, is guesswork; we are by no means certain that deterrence "works." The position is somewhat overstated; there is, in fact, some reasonably "scientific" evidence for the efficacy of criminal sanctions as deterrents, at least as against some kinds of crimes. Moreover, the time is not yet here when all we can "know" must be quantifiable and digestible by computers. The shared wisdom of generations teaches meaningfully, if somewhat amorphously, that the utilitarians have a point; we do, indeed, lapse often into rationality and act to seek pleasure and avoid pain. It would be better, to be sure, if we had more certainty and precision. Lacking these comforts, we continue to include among our working hypotheses a belief (with some concrete evidence in its support) that crimes like those in this case—deliberate, purposeful, continuing, non-impulsive, and committed for profit—are among those most likely to be generally deterrable by sanctions most shunned by those exposed to temptation.

The idea of avoiding depreciation of the seriousness of the offense implicates two or three thoughts, not always perfectly clear or universally agreed upon, beyond the idea of deterrence. It should be proclaimed by the court's judgment that the offenses are grave, not minor or purely technical. Some attention must be paid to the demand for equal justice; it will not do to leave the penalty of imprisonment a dead letter as against "privileged" violators while it is employed regularly, and with vigor, against others. There probably is in these conceptions an element of retributiveness, as counsel urge. And retribution, so denominated, is in some disfavor as a reason for punishment. It remains a factor, however, as Holmes perceived, and as is known to anyone who talks to judges, lawyers, defendants, or people generally. It may become more palatable, and probably more humanely understood, under the rubric of "deserts" or "just deserts." However, the concept is formulated, we have not yet reached a state, supposing we ever should, in which the infliction of punishments for crime may be divorced generally from ideas of blameworthiness, recompense, and proportionality.

III. *An Alternative, "Behavioral Sanction"*

Resisting prison above all else, defense counsel included in their thorough memorandum on sentencing two proposals for what they call a "constructive," and therefore a "preferable" form of "behavioral sanction." One is a plan for Dr. Bergman to create and run a program of Jewish vocational and religious high school training. The other is for him to take charge of a "Committee on Holocaust Studies," again concerned with education at the secondary school level.

A third suggestion was made orally at yesterday's sentencing hearing. It was proposed that Dr. Bergman might be ordered to work as a volunteer in some established agency as a visitor and aide to the sick and the otherwise incapacitated. The proposal was that he could read, provide various forms of physical assistance, and otherwise give comfort to afflicted people.

No one can doubt either the worthiness of these proposals or Dr. Bergman's ability to make successes of them. But both of the carefully formulated "sanctions" in the memorandum involve work of an honorific nature, not unlike that done in other projects to which the defendant has devoted himself in the past. It is difficult to conceive of them as "punishments" at all. The more recent proposal is somewhat more suitable in character, but it is still an insufficient penalty. The seriousness of the crimes to which Dr. Bergman has pled guilty demands something more than "requiring" him to lend his talents and efforts to further philanthropic enterprises. It remains open to him, of course, to pursue the interesting suggestions later on as a matter of unforced personal choice.

IV. *"Measuring" the Sentence*

In cases like this one, the decision of greatest moment is whether to imprison or not. As reflected in the eloquent submissions for defendant, the prospect of the closing prison doors is the most appalling concern; the feeling is that the length of the sojourn is a lesser question once that threshold is passed. Nevertheless, the setting of a term remains to be accomplished. And in some respects it is a subject even more perplexing, unregulated, and unprincipled.

Days and months and years are countable with a sound of exactitude. But there can be no exactitude in the deliberations from which a number emerges. Without pretending to a nonexistent precision, the court notes at least the major factors.

The criminal behavior, as has been noted, is blatant in character and unmitigated by any suggestion of necessitous circumstance or other pressures difficult to resist. However metaphysicians may conjure with issues about free will, it is a fundamental premise of our efforts to do criminal justice that competent people, possessed of their faculties, make choices and are accountable for them. In this sometimes harsh light, the case of the present defendant is among the clearest and least relieved. Viewed against the maxima Congress ordained, and against the run of sentences in other federal criminal cases, it calls for more than a token sentence.

On the other side are factors that take longer to enumerate. Defendant's illustrious public life and works are in his favor, though diminished, of course, by what this case discloses. This is a first, probably a last, conviction. Defendant is 64 years old and in imperfect health, though by no means so ill, from what the court is told, that he could be expected to suffer inordinately more than many others of advanced years who go to prison.

Defendant invokes an understandable, but somewhat unworkable, notion of "disparity." He says others involved in recent nursing home fraud cases have received relatively light sentences for behavior more culpable than his. He lays special emphasis upon one defendant whose frauds appear indeed to have involved larger amounts and who was sentenced to a maximum of six months' incarceration, to be confined for that time only on week nights, not on week days or weekends. This court has examined the minutes of that sentencing proceeding and finds the case distinguishable in material respects. But even if there were a threat of such disparity as defendant warns against, it could not be a major weight on the scales.

Our sentencing system, deeply flawed, is characterized by disparity. We are to seek to "individualize" sentences, but no clear or clearly agreed standards govern the individualization. The lack of meaningful criteria does indeed leave sentencing judges far too much at large. But the result, with its nagging burdens on conscience, cannot be meaningfully alleviated by allowing any handful of sentences in a short series to fetter later judgments. The point is easy, of course, where Sentence No. 1 or Sentences 1–5 are notably harsh. It cannot be that a later judge, disposed to more leniency, should feel in any degree "bound." The converse is not identical, but it is not totally different. The net of this is that this court has considered and has given some weight to the trend of the other cited sentences (though strict logic might call for none), but without treating them as forceful "precedents" in any familiar sense.

How, then, the particular sentence adjudged in this case? As has been mentioned, the case calls for a sentence that is more than nominal. Given the other circumstances, however—including that this is a first offense, by a man no longer young and not perfectly well, where danger of recidivism is not a concern—it verges on cruelty to think of confinement for a term of years. We sit, to be sure, in a nation where prison sentences of extravagant length are more common than they are almost anywhere else. By that light, the term imposed today is not notably long. For this sentencing court, however, for a nonviolent first offense involving no direct assaults or invasions of others' security (as in bank robbery, narcotics, etc.), it is a stern sentence. For people like Dr. Bergman, who might be disposed to engage in similar wrongdoing, it should be sufficiently frightening to serve the major end of general deterrence. For all but the profoundly vengeful, it should not depreciate the seriousness of his offenses.

V. *Punishment in or for the Media*

Much of defendant's sentencing memorandum is devoted to the extensive barrage of hostile publicity to which he has been subjected during the years before and since his indictment. He argues, and it appears to be undisputed, that the media (and people desiring to be featured in the media) have vilified him for many kinds of evildoing of which he has in fact been innocent. Two main points are made on this score with respect to the problem of sentencing.

First, as has been mentioned, counsel express the concern that the court may be pressured toward severity by the force of the seeming public outcry. That the court should not allow itself to be affected in this way is clear beyond discussion. Nevertheless, it is not merely permissible, but entirely wholesome and responsible, for counsel to bring the expressed concern out in the open. Whatever our ideals and mixed images about judges, it would be naive to doubt that judges have sometimes been swept by a sense of popular demand toward draconian sentencing decisions. It cannot hurt for the sentencing judge to be reminded of this and cautioned about it. There can be no guarantees. The sentencer must confront and regulate himself. But it bears reaffirmance that the court must seek to discount utterly the fact of notoriety in passing its judgment upon the defendant. Defense counsel cite reported opinions of this court reflecting what happens in a large number of unreported cases, by the present sentencer and many others, in which "unknown" defendants have received prison sentences, longer or shorter than today's, for white collar or comparably nonviolent crimes. The overall run of cases, with all their individual variations, will reflect, it is hoped, earnest efforts to hew to the principle of equal treatment, with or without publicity.

Defendant's second point about his public humiliation is the frequently heard contention that he should not be incarcerated because he "has been punished enough." The thought is not without some initial appeal. If punishment were wholly or mainly retributive, it might be a weighty factor. In the end, however, it must be a matter of little or no force. Defendant's notoriety should not in the last analysis serve to lighten, any more than it may be permitted to aggravate, his sentence. The fact that he has been pilloried by journalists is essentially a consequence of the prestige and privileges he enjoyed before he was exposed as a wrongdoer. The long fall from grace was possible only because of the height he had reached. The suffering from loss of public esteem reflects a body of opinion that the esteem had been, in at least some measure, wrongly bestowed and enjoyed. It is not possible to justify the notion that this mode of nonjudicial punishment should be an occasion for leniency not given to a defendant who never basked in such an admiring light at all. The quest for both the appearance and the substance of equal justice prompts the court to discount the thought that the public humiliation serves the function of imprisonment.

Writing, as judges rarely do, about a particular sentence concentrates the mind with possibly special force upon the experience of the sentencer as well as the person sentenced. Consigning someone to prison, this defendant or any other, "is a sad necessity." There are impulses of avoidance from time to time—toward a personally gratifying leniency or toward an opposite extreme. But there is, obviously, no place for private impulse in the judgment of the court. The course of justice must be sought with such objective rationality as we can muster, tempered with mercy, but obedient to the law, which, we do well to remember, is all that empowers a judge to make other people suffer.

Questions and Comment

Do you think that Judge Frankel used his discretion wisely in sentencing Mr. Bergman? Would it have been more desirable for the judge not to have had discretion in this case? Suppose that the defendant's plea of guilty to count 1 required that the judge sentence him to 2 years in prison? Would such a sentence have been more just? Would such a mandated sentence be more likely to deter others contemplating frauds involving nursing homes?

The defendant asked the judge for a lighter sentence on grounds that others involved in recent nursing home fraud cases have received relatively light sentences for behavior more culpable than his. Might it not be argued that such light sentences invite fraud, and that Bergman's criminal acts would not have occurred had there been a heavier mandatory sentence? If you thought that judicial discretion was wisely employed in this case, do you still think so or do you think consideration of deterrence should necessitate a policy of mandatory sentencing? Would it surprise you to learn that the sentence of four months' imprisonment was highly criticized by New York newspapers for its leniency?

d. MAYOR SENTENCED TO PRISON *

Washington D.C. Mayor Marion Barry was sentenced yesterday to six months in prison and fined $5,000 on his one-count misdemeanor conviction for drug possession.

U.S. District Judge Thomas Penfield Jackson, in passing the stiff sentence, rejected Barry's plea for leniency. He told the mayor that there were "aggravating circumstances" to his conviction, including his "frequent and conspicuous drug use . . . which gave aid, comfort and encouragement to the drug culture at large."

---

* Robert L. Jackson, "Judge Gives D.C. Mayor 6–Month Term," San Francisco   Chronicle, Saturday, October 27, 1990, Sec. A, p. 1.

The mayor's chin dropped and shoulders slumped as the judge told him that he found Barry had taken part in "a willful attempt to obstruct justice" by lying to a federal grand jury investigating his use of cocaine.

"Having failed as the good example he might have been, the defendant now must become an example of another kind," the judge said.

Barry, 54, bitterly told reporters outside the U.S. Courthouse that "there are different sets of standards for different people. That's the American injustice system."

He referred to the fact that most first-time drug offenders who are convicted of a misdemeanor receive probation rather than jail time.

The 10–week trial of the black chief executive, which ended nearly three months ago, had transfixed the capital throughout the summer and strained race relations in this city, where 70 percent of the residents are black.

Black leaders across the United States accused the U.S. attorney's office of a vendetta against black elected officials because of leaks about investigations involving other black officials and the sting operation that was mounted to gain evidence to prosecute Barry. The Department of Justice vehemently denied those charges.

U.S. Attorney Jay B. Stephens, who earlier had recommended the maximum penalty of a year in prison, told reporters at a news conference later that Barry's sentence is appropriate and "well within the range of the maximum sentence provided by law. Mr. Barry contributed to this city's and this nation's most devastating problem."

The mayor's attorney, R. Kenneth Mundy, noted to reporters after the sentencing that several aides to former President Ronald Reagan had received community service instead of jail time for first offenses, including Iran-Contra figure Oliver North and former deputy chief of staff Michael Deaver.

Jackson, appointed to the bench by Reagan, fined Deaver $100,000 and gave him 1,500 hours of community service two years ago on his felony perjury conviction.

Under new sentencing guidelines for the federal courts, Barry must serve his full six months behind bars with no time off for good behavior. Upon completion of that term, Jackson put him on supervised probation for a year, meaning that he must report regularly to a probation officer and be subject to periodic drug tests.

Federal prosecutors urged Jackson before sentencing to consider Barry's conviction an "aggravated" one—and thus subject to a heavier penalty—because he has since admitted to repeated use of cocaine and only Thursday acknowledged in a court filing that he was an addict.

In court, Barry told Jackson that he had been free of alcohol and drugs for 279 consecutive days since he spent seven weeks in substance-abuse treatment centers in Florida and South Carolina after his arrest in an FBI "sting" operation last January.

Barry told the court yesterday that his drug activities were "out of character," adding that "my wife, Effi, would not have married such a man 10 years ago."

"I stand here truly remorseful," he said, "and I ask this court to impose community service as a sentence."

"The defendant has not owned up to what he has done for a period of over five years," Assistant U.S. Attorney Judith E. Retchin told Jackson. "There is a pattern to his use of illegal drugs, and he used his position to obtain those drugs. This is hardly a simple misdemeanor committed by a first-time offender."

Jackson agreed that Barry had abused "his public trust," adding that "his conduct has inspired others to emulate him." At the same time, the judge said, there were "some mitigating circumstances."

"He has admitted his alcoholism and his compulsive use of cocaine, and he appears to be making significant progress in rehabilitating himself," Jackson said.

Question

Consider the examples of client specific sentencing discussed earlier (pp. 544–546). Why shouldn't Mayor Barry have been a candidate for community service as his defense counsel argued? Should famous people be used as examples in sentencing? If so, why did not President Reagan's advisors receive harsher sentences?

e. JUDGE WOOD'S EXPLANATION OF THE MILKEN SENTENCING *

[*Following is an excerpt from comments by Judge Kimba M. Wood about her sentencing of Michael R. Milken in Federal District Court in Manhattan:*]

Because of the extraordinary interest that has been expressed in this case and the fact that many letters to the court reflect misconceptions about what it is that Michael Milken is being punished for, I believe that I should briefly attempt to dispel those misconceptions, many of which were alluded to by Mr. Liman.

The letters reflect a perception that we as a society must find those responsible for the alleged abuses of the 1980's, economic harm caused savings and loan associations, take-over targets and those allegedly injured by the issuance of junk bonds as well as by insider trading and other alleged abuses, and punish these criminals in proportion to the losses believed to have been suffered. These writers ask for a verdict on a decade of greed.

* The New York Times, Thursday, November 22, 1990.

While I sympathize with the anxiety expressed in these letters, the suppositions upon which these views are based cannot enter into sentencing defendant on the six counts of wrongdoing to which he pled guilty. Our system of justice protects everyone from being sentenced on supposition and it is this court's responsibility to insure that defendant receives that same protection here.

It is important to note as well that although many of those who wrote to the court believe that defendant should be treated harshly because they believe that he is the one responsible for the massive job losses and the financial failure of savings and loan associations, the Government did not charge him with responsibility here for those losses. For the Government to prove such charges would have required the Government to try to isolate the effect of defendant's actions from all of the other forces acting in the marketplace.

For similar reasons, the court cannot take into account the claims of those who urge leniency for defendant because he allegedly created jobs and business opportunities or drew capital to its most productive uses. Determinations such as these would require information not before the court and would, for example, require the court to speculate on how defendant's clients would have invested their money absent his advice, and what effect those actions would have on job creation or loss, business opportunities and productivity.

I note that these letters also reflect a legitimate public concern that everyone, no matter how rich or powerful, obey the law as alluded to by Mr. Fardella, and that our financial markets in which so many people who are not rich invest their savings be free of secret manipulation. This is a concern fairly to be considered by the court.

Looking at Milken's Conduct

I will turn now to the conduct for which defendant is being sentenced.

You are being sentenced for six counts of criminal activity spanning approximately three years in participation with several other people involving several different transactions that violated securities laws, tax laws and other laws.

You have attempted to mitigate these crimes by claiming they represented no more than overzealous service to your clients, that they involved mere technicalities and that they did not represent the core of how you did business.

I will speak to these points briefly before moving to the factors influencing sentencing.

To the extent that your crimes benefited your clients, that is, of course, no excuse for violating the law. In addition, there is no escaping the fact that your crimes also benefited you, not necessarily by lining your pockets directly and immediately, but by increasing your clients loyalty to you, hence, increasing your edge over competitors and increasing the likelihood that your clients would pay for your services in the future.

It has also been argued that your violations were technical ones to be distinguished from accumulating profits through insider trading and that your conduct is not really criminal or that it is only barely criminal.

It was suggested that if you were truly disposed to criminal conduct, you could have made much more money by committing more blatant crimes such as repeatedly misusing insider information.

Pattern of Skirting the Law

These arguments fail to take into account the fact that you may have committed only subtle crimes not because you were not disposed to any criminal behavior but because you were willing to commit only crimes that were unlikely to be detected.

We see often in this court individuals who would be unwilling to rob a bank, but who readily cash Social Security checks that are not theirs when checks come to them in the mail because they are not likely to be caught doing so.

Your crimes show a pattern of skirting the law, stepping just over to the wrong side of the law in an apparent effort to get some of the benefits from violating the law without running a substantial risk of being caught.

In this regard, your post-Nov. 14, 1986, comments to other employees about subpoenas are of the same character as the six admitted offenses. You did not order employees to destroy or remove documents, but you communicated the advisability of their doing so in subtle terms that preserved some deniability on your part.

Your attorneys also argue that most of your business was conducted lawfully and that you would have prospered even absent the unlawful practices you admitted.

The evidence before the court on this point is sparse and equivocal. I do not know, for example, whether some of your biggest clients would have made their funds available to you repeatedly without the benefits fund managers personally received from Drexel. Statements to the contrary made by fund managers at the Fatico hearing were unpersuasive, given their self-serving nature.

There may some day be enough information for another entity, be it a court, or, as Mr. Liman suggested, a historian, to judge whether most of your business was conducted lawfully, but I cannot make that judgment today either way.

The Need for Deterrence

Let me turn then to the purposes of sentencing and their application here. As was pointed out, purposes are generally thought to be individual deterrence, general deterrence, punishment or just deserts, retribution and rehabilitation.

Taking them one by one, deterring you as an individual from breaking the law again has already been furthered in part by your being barred from ever again working in the securities industry, by your $200 million fine, by the $400 million restitution fund that you have funded and by the fact that you face numerous civil lawsuits that could result in your paying even more than the $400 million that you have already paid to the restitution fund.

I am sensitive to the view that you and your family have already been punished by the sanctions I have just mentioned and by the emotional stress of living with the uncertainty of your status and your sentence since the prosecution began.

I have given considerable thought to whether a sentence of lengthy community service would be an adequate penalty here. It would have the advantages of permitting you to work productively with others which I believe you could do well rather than having you be warehoused in a prison. Nevertheless, I believe that a prison term is required for the purposes of general deterrence; that is, the need to deter others from violating the law and the possibility that the sentence given in one case will prevent others from violating law.

Prison sentences are viewed as one of the most powerful deterrents to the financial community. This view is reflected in the legislatively mandated sentencing guidelines which punish white-collar crimes with more prison time than was common before their adoption, and I have looked to those guidelines for some guidance in connection with this sentencing.

When a man of your power in the financial world at the head of the most important department of one of the most important investment banking houses in this country repeatedly conspires to violate and violates securities and tax laws in order to achieve more power and wealth for himself and his wealthy clients and commits financial crimes that are particularly hard to detect, a significant prison term is required in order to deter others.

This kind of misuse of your leadership position and enlisting employees who you supervised to assist you in violating the law are serious crimes warranting serious punishment and the discomfort and opprobrium of being removed from society.

Although community service can further the goals of punishment and retribution in cases whereby requiring a defendant to forego remunerative employment for a while, it causes defendant to suffer financially, such would not be the case here. In this case both the sanctions already imposed and imprisonment will further the goals of punishment and retribution.

The goal of rehabilitation is likely to be furthered by your providing community service after your incarceration.

I turn now to the sentence that is appropriate.

In deciding how long a prison term is appropriate and how much community service is appropriate, I have taken into account that long before your current legal problems you took a significant amount of your own personal time to serve the community by working with disadvantaged children rather, for example, than using all of your personal time to acquire possessions. You also successfully encouraged your colleagues at work to do the same.

I have also taken into account the emotional support that you have provided to your family, neighbors, co-workers, and the fact that many colleagues and competitors found you to be forthright, honorable and honest in your dealings with them over the years.

On the other side of the scale, I must also take into account that you were head of your department and that you used others in your department to effect unlawful schemes. By your example, you communicated that cutting legal and ethical corners is, at times, acceptable.

You also committed crimes that are hard to detect, and crimes that are hard to detect warrant greater punishment in order to be effective in deterring others from committing them.

Question of Cooperation

I should also note, for the benefit of those who urge the court to sentence you to the full 28 years in an effort to force you to cooperate with the Government in its investigation in the future, that a court is not permitted to do that. Instead, a court is required to select a fair sentence for the crimes that occurred, and, only after making that decision, consider whether a defendant's cooperation with the Government warrants lightening the sentence.

Where a defendant cooperates with the Government fully and is of assistance to the Government, the defendant deserves a significant reduction in sentence for assisting the Government to uncover crimes that are otherwise very resistant to discovery.

So it is that Ivan Boesky, whose cooperation was characterized by the Government as the most extensive and remarkable in the history of the securities laws and who also persuaded his former staff to assist the Government in its investigation, was permitted to plead guilty to only one count of conspiracy to file a false statement that carried a maximum prison term of five years.

As I mentioned earlier, I have no way to evaluate now the value of any cooperation you may offer the Government in the future. I have never given a defendant credit for cooperation without knowing the extent of the cooperation and without knowing how useful the information was to the Government and I will not deviate from that practice now.

If you cooperate, and if the Government moves for a reduction in your sentence based on your cooperation, the court can adjust your sentence accordingly.

Disregarded Statements

Given that defense counsel objected to the portion of the Government's sentencing memorandum that urges the court to consider imposing a sentence as long as that given to the lead defendant in the Send [a similar, related] case [another securities fraud case], which defense counsel views as a violation of the Government's undertaking in the plea agreement not to make any recommendation as to a specific term of incarceration, I note that I have totally disregarded all statements by that Government that relate to specific terms of incarceration as well as the Government's comparison of Mr. Boesky to Mr. Milken.

I made my own independent evaluation of the conduct of and sentences given to Mr. Boesky . . . and others based on my reading of their presentence reports and the transcripts of sentencing arguments and I arrived at my own conclusion as to the appropriate proportionality among them.

With respect to the community service component of the sentence that I will shortly pronounce, I note your expressed desire to spend any community service working with disadvantaged children. Because changes are likely to take place in community programs between today and the day you are released from prison, it would be inappropriate to select a particular program for you today. The court and probation will work with you to select a program that will make maximum use of your skills.

For those who have written to the court expressing concern at your suggestion that you be assigned to Project DARE, which concern is apparently motivated, in part, by distrust of the judgment shown by Commissioner Gates, I note that before selecting a community-service program for you the court will carefully scrutinize the quality of the supervision that the program offers for those performing community service.

Details of the Prison Term

Mr. Milken, please rise.

You are unquestionably a man of talent and industry and you have consistently shown a dedication to those less fortunate than you. It is my hope that the rest of your life will fulfill the promise shown early in your career. However, for the reasons stated earlier, I sentence you to a total of 10 years in prison, consisting of two years each on counts two through six to be served consecutively, and I also sentence you to three years of probation on count one. A special condition of your probation is that you serve full-time community service, 1,800 hours per year for each of the three years, in a program to be determined by the court, I also impose the mandatory statutory assessment of $50 on each count for a total of $300.

I advise you that you have a right to appeal this sentence.

You may be seated at this point.

Comment and Questions

Michael Milken's sentence was harsher than those of either Mr. Bergman and Mr. Barry. Indeed it was several times longer than either of their sentences. Was his offense that much more serious? Mr. Bergman's offense involved stealing funds from nursing homes in ways that may have deprived old and infirm people of resources and thus affected their health. Mr. Barry's offense was a so-called "victimless" crime. But he was, after all, in a position of trust and leadership in a city plagued by drug use and crime. In contrast, Mr. Milken generally stole from the relatively well to do, and indeed he gave away to charity much of what he took.

Presumably sentencing should be a rational and principled process leading to fairness and consistency in outcome. Indeed the judges in all three cases—and especially Bergman's and Milken's—go to great lengths to review the basis for fairness in sentencing and to justify their sentences. However, is there any indication that these general principles actually decide concrete cases? Was Milken's behavior worthy of a sentence several times that of Bergman's? What do you think would have occurred if Bergman and Milken had ended up with each other's judges? Is it fair that prominent people should be sentenced severely simply because they are prominent and thus can serve as an example by publicizing the wrong-doing? Did this happen in any of these cases—or alternatively, did these men receive lighter sentences because they were well known and had resources to buffer themselves from the full force of the law? Jumping ahead in the book for a moment, ask yourself whether some sort of sentencing guidelines might help in cases like this.

Finally, note that in the Milken case it is not really clear that his sentence will remain ten years. Towards the end of her statement, Judge Wood suggests that the court "can adjust your sentence" downward if Milken "cooperates" with prosecutors in related matters, that is if like another big time securities law violator, Ivan Boesky, he informs on his friends and associates. Although we recognize that in setting charges prosecutors often pressure defendants to cooperate, is it appropriate for judges to do so? If not, why is it OK for prosecutors? Or is it?

Before you answer, you may recall that Judge John Sirica used this technique successfully in sentencing some of the Watergate defendants. After receiving extremely harsh sentences several minor participants in the affair decided to cooperate with the prosecution in ways that implicated the White House in the break-in and cover-up. This in turn eventually led to the conviction of several key White House officials and the resignation of the President of the United States, Richard M. Nixon. If Judge Wood is inappropriately pressuring Mr. Milken, was Judge Sirica wrong? In light of what we now know occurred, was it a good thing he did this?

3. THE OTHER ACTORS IN JUDICIAL SENTENCING

a. THE PROBATION OFFICER

(1) THE BUREAUCRATIZATION OF SENTENCING *

Recent decades have seen a quiet and not adequately recognized transformation in the sentencing process. The key event in this process has been the professionalization of the probation staff. In a phrase, the simple turnkey of an earlier era has given way to the modern, highly trained probation officer, equipped with a master's degree in criminology, a manual of standard operating procedures, and a highly developed sense of the importance of his role in the sentencing drama. A by-product has emerged, however, from this process of professionalization: a developing bureaucracy that defends its institutional turf zealously. Indeed, some evidence exists that probation officers throughout the country tend to define their success in terms of their ability to obtain acceptance of their sentencing recommendations from judges; the higher the percentage of concurrence between the judicial decision and their recommendation, the greater the evidence, in their view, of their recognition as true "professionals." On the whole, probation officers have been extraordinarily successful in winning acceptance of their recommendations. In part, this success is unrelated to the quality of their work, but instead is due to the judge's need to be perceived as fair and to his desire to diffuse responsibility for a decision provoking anxiety and even guilt.

Of what relevance is this phenomenon? Some social scientists, after studying the sentencing process, have concluded that the truly operative decisionmaker often is the probation officer. Although the judge holds the legal power, he tends to ratify decisions made earlier in the process by these new sentencing bureaucrats. Tension always exists between sovereigns and bureaucracies. The modern day sentencing judge is like the 17th–century monarch, who possessed absolute power in theory but in practice was frequently manipulated by the ministers who stood quietly behind the throne and controlled the flow of information to him. Today the judge must operate in a system that processes a high volume of criminal cases, and therefore he must rely heavily on his own ministers, the probation staff. Not unexpectedly, some social scientists have pointed to the probation staff—and to the differences in techniques and attitudes among individual probation officers—as a likely major cause of disparities.

* John C. Coffee, Jr., "Repressed Issues of Sentencing," *The Georgetown Law Jour-* *nal,* Vol. 66, pp. 982–984. © (Reprinted with permission).

Why have recent proposals not sought to deal with this problem? I suggest . . . that . . . lawyers as a class tend to share an unconsciously egotistical vision of the legal process that makes it difficult for them to recognize that nonlawyer participants could have a greater effect on the outcome of a judicial proceeding than the lawyers themselves. In any event, a kind of false consciousness has persisted: Both legislative and judicial efforts to reform have continued to focus on the interchange among the court, the defense counsel, and the prosecutor on the day of sentencing. By this time, however, the outcome frequently has become a *fait accompli*. . . .

Questions

Who do you think is more important in the reality of criminal justice administration, the judge or the probation officer preparing the presentence report? Is it possible that one reason why probation officers secure a high level of agreement from sentencing judges is that the probation officer recommends the sentence he thinks the judge will give?

(2) THE PRE-SENTENCE REPORT

(a) By the Probation Officer *

The probation officer plays a crucial role in this process by gathering and evaluating information about the defendant. To fulfill this role properly, the probation officer must evaluate the information received from many sources both for content and reliability, which requires that he develop a relationship of trust with the defendant, establish a neutral position between the defense and prosecution, and maintain the court's confidence. Because the probation officer develops a "feeling" about the defendant through investigation and personal interviews, most federal courts require him either to include a character evaluation of the defendant in the presentence report or to discuss the defendant's character with the judge in chambers. Almost all courts require the presentence report to include an evaluative summary containing the officer's subjective evaluation of the report's contents and the defendant's character. Moreover, he is often viewed as a "professional sentencer," and most judges require him to include a sentencing recommendation in the presentence report.

Comments and Questions

Is not the pre-sentence report especially important in a legal system where most of the cases are disposed of by pleas of guilty and the judge does not get a chance to hear about the crime and observe the defendant at trial?

* Stephen A. Fennell and William N. Hall, "Due Process at Sentencing: An Empirical and Legal Analysis of the Disclosure of Presentence Reports in Federal Courts," 93 *Harvard Law Review*, 1980, pp. 1666–1668. Copyright 1980 by the Harvard Law Review Ass'n. (Reprinted with permission).

If the pre-sentence report is that important should not defendants and their attorneys get to see it so they can correct any errors or misconceptions? In about half the states defendants have no such right. If they do have such a right how is this going to affect the flow of confidential information to probation officers from people who may not want defendants to know what they have said? How will this affect the working relationship between offenders on probation and probation officers who investigate their cases and recommend that they be sent to prison?

(b) The Alternative Sentencing Report **

The defendant stood nervously before U.S. Northern District Judge Marilyn Hall Patel. He was being sentenced for a string of unarmed bank robberies that netted him $5,000 in five days.

With two prior convictions, a stretch at the federal prison on Terminal Island in Southern California, two years in a drug diversion program and a 15–year heroin habit, the 36–year-old defendant was a prime candidate for prison.

"I reviewed both reports, the bound one and the unbound one," Patel said in court with a wry smile. The unbound copy—a probation report—is what routinely guides judges in setting sentences for criminals. The bound volume was prepared by a private alternative sentencing group, the San Francisco office of the National Center for Institutions and Alternatives (NCIA).

Although both reports reached similar conclusions, the alternative sentencing report was more comprehensive, and Patel adopted its recommendations. The defendant was ordered to stay at a long-term drug treatment facility, make full restitution, donate his services as a chef, speak before young adults about the dangers of drugs, submit to random urinalysis testing after completing the treatment program and find employment.

Patel hung a 10–year suspended sentence over his head. "I don't get any pleasure in sending someone to prison," Patel said to the defendant. "But if you fail this time, I'll do it. I want you to succeed on this, but I also mean business."

Alternative sentencing reports like the one used by Patel are showing up with greater frequency in criminal courts in California and around the country. The current and unprecedented prison crowding and an overburdened probation system have spawned a growth indus-try in private organizations appearing under the general rubric of alternative sentencing advocates. These organizations, which range from one-man operations to nationwide services, work directly with defense attorneys to develop individualized, highly structured sentenc-ing plans for convicted criminals.

** Michael A. Kroll, "Getting Another Chance," *California Lawyer,* Sept 1986, p 27. © 1986 (Reprinted with permission).

Tailored plans

Plans prepared by alternative sentencing services are tailored to fit the individual. Beyond identifying problems—as probation officers do—the sentencing services focus on detailed solutions. The NCIA, for example, will contact a therapy center and reserve a slot for the client in case the court accepts the plan. Plans generally include some or all the following: residential or out-patient treatment for medical or psychological problems, community service, financial restitution, employment, education, supervision and third-party monitoring.

To be effective, the alternative sentencing groups say they should be involved at the start of a criminal proceeding. "We get our best results when we get a client right after arrest," says Sickler. "We'll start digging up background for the bail hearing. We'll structure a release plan for when he's out on bail that addresses his criminal behavior, like getting him into Alcoholics Anonymous or Gamblers Anonymous. We'll get him back on the job working, so by the time of sentencing eight or 10 months down the line, not only can the client begin to pay restitution, but we've established a track record for the court."

Many criminal lawyers have been impressed by sentencing advocacy groups. When Patel adopted the NCIA's recommendations, for example, the defendant's attorney, Dennis Roberts of Oakland, stood up and said, "I want to thank [NCIA's Vincent] Schiraldi, Your Honor. I consider myself good at sentencing, but he put me to shame. He put in incredible hours." Later, after leaving the courtroom, Roberts said Schiraldi, who charged $50 an hour, put in four times as many hours as he billed.

California Attorney General John Van de Kamp believes the private providers can operate in ways the probation department cannot. "The case loads make probation like a cafeteria service," he says. "There's very little personal contact on a direct basis."

Questions

Consider two other examples of client specific sentencing discussed on pp. 544–546. Do you think the alternative sentencing report is a good idea? Why shouldn't the judge be able to select between the official probation report and a privately drawn alternative? Does the latter offer an unjust advantage to the wealthy defendant?

b. THE PROSECUTOR

(1) THEIR POWERS *

The *prosecutor* is not normally thought of as an official who has, or exercises, the power to determine punishment. In practice, however,

* Franklin E. Zimring, "Making the Punishment Fit the Crime: A Consumer's Guide to Sentencing Reform," in *Sentenc-* *ing,* ed. by Hyman Gross and Andrew von Hirsch (New York: Oxford University

the prosecutor is the most important institutional determinant of a criminal sentence. He has the legal authority to drop criminal charges, thus ending the possibility of punishment. He has the legal authority in most systems to determine the specific offense for which a person is to be prosecuted, and this ability to select a charge can also broaden or narrow the range of sentences that can be imposed upon conviction. In congested urban court systems (and elsewhere) he has the absolute power to reduce charges in exchange for guilty pleas and to recommend particular sentences to the court as part of a "plea bargain"; rarely will his recommendation for a lenient sentence be refused in an adversary system in which he is supposed to represent the punitive interests of the state.

(2) PLEA BARGAINS, GOING RATES, AND SENTENCING **

Analysis of the ninety most frequently appearing charges, accounting for two-thirds of guilty pleas, . . . points to the dominance of consensus pleas. We examined the distribution of sentences for each charge category separately because the type of offense determines more than anything else the general range of the sentence. Armed robbers receive harsher sentences than pickpockets.

What can the distributions of these sentences tell us? If going rates reflecting a consensus rather than individually negotiated deals involving exchange of concessions lead to pleas, then sentences for individual crimes should fall into just a few categories. In other words, a standard formula for determining sentences will produce two or three clusters of sentences. On the other hand, if concessions shaped by such factors as strength of evidence, skill of the attorneys, condition of the docket, and characteristics of the defendant result in pleas, the sentences should be more scattered. The distribution of sentences would then reflect the trading of concessions that individually calibrate penalties to the specifics of the case.

Examining the distribution of sentences revealed striking evidence that consensus pleas predominate. A huge number of sentences fell into the same cluster. Specifically, as mentioned earlier, probation or diversion stands out as the going rate for many defendants in each jurisdiction. In fact, among the 4,000 guilty-plea defendants arrested for the ninety most common charges, nearly two thirds (65.8 percent) received probation or diversion.

This figure is significant. Defendants care *far* more about whether they will be sentenced to any time in jail or prison than about the amount of fines and costs or the terms of probation. Though we did not analyze in detail the amount of fines imposed, our conclusion is that they too are calculated using going rates. Set amounts for court costs

Press, 1981), pp. 327–329. © 1981 (Reprinted by permission).

** Eisenstein, James, Flemming, Roy, and Nardulli, Peter, The Contours of Justice: Communities and Their Courts, Little, Brown and Company, Boston, 1987, pp. 246–248 (Reprinted with Permission).

and program fees for diversion programs add to the predictability of monetary penalties. Even if some haggling occurred over the amount of a fine, it would not involve concessions on matters regarded as very important compared to length of incarceration.

In every county, then, many cases ended routinely in probation. After all, many crimes involved garden-variety property offenses and defendants with no prior criminal record. That the court community did not get excited about them, and that it relied on routine dispositions for routine cases, is no surprise. Nor is it surprising that the defendants under such circumstances were willing to enter a plea without haggling over the details. The question most on their minds, "Will I have to go to jail, or will I be able to stay on the street," had been answered. The combination of their offense and prior record meant that probation would be the outcome. Going to trial would prolong uncertainty and carry the risk of some jail time.

Although this analysis clearly suggests that most pleas result from consensus, it also provides evidence that some do not. Twenty percent of the 4,000 guilty-plea defendants examined received sentences that fell outside the cluster. Going rates do not completely dictate sentences. Though the guilty-plea process does not resemble a huge bazaar, in places trading of concessions does take place for a small but significant minority of defendants.

(3) THE CONVICT'S VIEW OF THE PROSECUTOR'S POWER *

The judge is, in common stereotypes, a semireligious figure, handing down evenhanded justice and symbolizing the majesty of the law. He is the power in the courtroom, determining the fate of the accused. He is a man whose job is, in many ways, to "play God," to pass judgment on the past and future of men's lives.

In fact, in the defendants' eyes the judge is usually a relatively peripheral figure in the criminal justice system. He is something of a figurehead, possessing power but delegating it to the prosecutor. His is among the easiest jobs in the system, for he takes his cues about what he ought to do from the prosecutor and acts something like a rubber stamp—stamping "legitimate and final" upon the deal that has been worked out.

> *What about the judge who sentenced you? Did he seem concerned about your welfare? Hostile to you? Matter of fact?*
>
> I feel that a judge really ain't shit, you know. He's just put up there—he's supposed to be the head of the show, but he ain't nothing.
>
> *Who runs the show?*
>
> The person who runs the show is the prosecutor.

* Jonathan D. Casper, *American Criminal Justice: The Defendant's Perspective*, Prentice-Hall, Inc., Englewood Cliffs, N.J. 1972, pp. 135–6, 142–44. © 1972 (Reprinted by permission).

Well, what's the judge's job?

The judge's job is to sit on his ass and do what the prosecutor tells him to do.

. . .

How did the judge seem? Did he seem concerned with your welfare? Hostile? Matter of fact?

No, the judge that sentenced me was like—see, the prosecutor is the fellow that gives you the time.

. . .

Well, did you get the feeling that the judge was neutral or that he was on one side or the other?

I think he was neutral. To me, man, it seemed like the judge, he up there, it don't seem like sides. You see him sitting up there like this . . . and the prosecutor and everybody—like your lawyer is talking toward the judge, but he's talking to the prosecutor; and the prosecutor is talking toward the judge, but he's talking to your lawyer, you know. That's just all, the way the thing goes.

The general view of the judge as a figurehead flies in the face of most of our presumptions about the role of the judge and is among the most significant aspects of the defendant's view of criminal justice. As we have stressed before, the system appears to the defendant to have no real neutral or principled figures in it. Everyone has a job to do and an axe to grind or is, like the judge, viewed as primarily indifferent. The determinants of the disposition of the case are largely similar to the determinants of a defendant's own behavior on the street. Short-run self-interest or indifference seems to the defendant to characterize the activities of the prosecutor and the judge. The only really "personal" characteristic of great consequence is the defendant's past criminal record. Most believe that, in the abstract at least, this criterion ought to be of relevance, but that much more ought to be taken into account. The defendants want someone to do them some good, for most are not particularly satisfied with their lives or content with the crimes they commit. At the very least, even if no one is wise enough to decide upon some treatment that will really improve him and his lot, at least someone ought to *care,* ought to agonize over the decisions that will affect the defendants' lives. As they view it, though, no one even agonizes, much less comes up with solutions to his problems. The police, the prosecutor, the public defender are all simply doing their jobs, are working under constraints placed by the production ethic that make attention to particular defendants' needs either too much work or irrelevant to their functions.

The perceived behavior of the judge is the ultimate failure of the system in their eyes. He is the one man whose job *might* involve caring and attention to the individual. He has, in their eyes, reached the pinnacle of his career, for he has attained the prestigious position that members of the legal community are thought to covet. He is fixed for life. He is, putatively, indebted to no one. Moreover, the defendants, like the rest of us, have been imbued with the myth of the judge as the independent figure—removed from petty and partisan concerns—meeting out justice in some kind of evenhanded manner. He embodies the majesty and authority of the law. He embodies the principles of right conduct that the law itself is supposed to exemplify and that the defendants themselves are in many ways eager to accept.

His apparent abdication, his betrayal of authority, his willingness to appear to turn things over to just another "worker"—the prosecutor—epitomize the failure of the system in the defendants' eyes. The activities of the other actors—their lack of concern, their pressuring, conning, lying—are, to the defendants, a product of the job, something they can understand. The indifference of the judge is more difficult to swallow, for they perceive that he potentially suffers from far fewer constraints than the others. He can be *God*. If he can't necessarily straighten them out, at least he can *care*. But he doesn't. Therefore, no one does. The administration of justice is very much like the street, for no one is in fact truly disinterested or authoritative. The production ethic infects everyone, even the man who might potentially be immune to it. The irrelevance of the judge is, from the defendants' perspective, the ultimate failure of American criminal justice.

Questions

Do you think most judges know how convicts see them? Do you think that they care? If they do care, what excuse is there for their not knowing? If they do not care, shouldn't they?

Interestingly, a recent study confirms in part, the convict's view. Of the 10 felony court judges in Houston, Texas, 3 followed the prosecutor's recommendation in 100% of the guilty plea cases; one in 99% and two in 98%. The most "independent of the judges followed the prosecutor's recommendation in 88% of the cases." Note, though, that the prosecutor and the defense had already reached their bargain, and the judge was merely ratifying it.

c. THE ROLE OF THE DEFENSE ATTORNEY IN SENTENCING

(1) **Martin v. United States**
United States Court of Appeals, Fifth Circuit, 1950.
182 F.2d 225.

RUSSELL, Circuit Judge. [Petitioner's complaint was that] his appointed counsel had been excused by the Court and consequently was not present when sentence was imposed upon him.

It may be safely said that at this time there is no question of constitutional law any more firmly established than the oft enunciated and applied principle that, in the trial of criminal cases in the federal courts, the defendant is entitled to have the guiding hand of counsel at every stage of the proceeding.

The very nature of the proceeding at the time of imposition of sentence makes the presence of defendant's counsel at that time necessary if the constitutional requirement is to be met. The advisability of an appeal must then, or shortly, be determined. Then is the opportunity afforded for presentation to the Court of facts in extenuation of the offense, or in explanation of the defendant's conduct; to correct any errors or mistakes in reports of the defendants' past record; and, in short, to appeal to the equity of the Court in its administration and enforcement of penal laws. Any Judge with trial Court experience must acknowledge that such disclosures frequently result in mitigation, or even suspension, of penalty. That it is also true that such discussion sometimes has a contrary result, does not detract from the fact that the nature and possibilities of this important stage of the proceedings are such as make the absence of counsel at this time presumably prejudicial. . . . That judgment is reversed, and the cause remanded for imposition of the sentence of the Court upon the defendant in proceedings had with his counsel present.

Judgment reversed.

(2) DUTIES OF DEFENSE COUNSEL *

The important role of defense counsel in helping to achieve the most appropriate disposition for his client [must be] emphasized. This role extends to the gathering and evaluation of facts relevant to sentencing, and most important, to their presentation in court at the time of sentencing. Certainly in view of the shortage of competent lawyers to perform all the legal tasks in the criminal process, it would be unwise to rely exclusively on defense counsel to gather and evaluate sentencing facts. However, the ultimate responsibility for ensuring that facts are gathered and evaluated and for persuasively presenting them to the court rests with counsel.

Too many attorneys appear to believe their task to be fulfilled when the issue of guilt or innocence has been decided. Their assistance in the preparation of the presentence report and their presentation to the court on sentence often are perfunctory. In part this may reflect the failure of law school training to make defense counsel sensitive to these issues. Financial considerations also may discourage counsel from investing the necessary time and effort in the problem of sentencing.

* President's Commission on Law Enforcement and the Administration of Justice, *Task Force Report: The Courts,* Washington D.C., GOP, 1967, pp. 19–20. © 1967 (Reprinted with permission).

. . .

Defense counsel's primary duty is to ensure that the court and his client are aware of the available sentencing alternatives and that the sentencing decision is based on complete and accurate information. Counsel must familiarize himself with possible dispositions and with the sentencing practices of the court so that he can make an intelligent and helpful presentation. In jurisdictions where the presentence report is disclosed to the defense, counsel should attempt to verify the important information in the report. He should be prepared to supplement it when it is incomplete and to challenge it when it is inaccurate. When the presentence report is not disclosed, the only way in which counsel can ensure that the sentencing decision is based on adequate facts is to gather and present information to the court himself, although this may involve wasteful duplication of effort if a presentence report has been prepared for the court.

When counsel believes that probation would be an appropriate disposition for his client, he should be prepared to suggest a positive program of rehabilitation. He should explore possibilities for employment, family services, educational improvement, and perhaps mental health services and attempt to make specific and realistic arrangements for the defendant's return to the community.

Finally, defense counsel should explain to his client the consequences of the various types of sentences which he may receive. Most defendants are unaware of the effects of imprisonment or probation on their families or their own future. A defendant who understands the adjustments which his sentence demands is more likely to respond favorably.

Questions

Is it the duty of the defense counsel to help the court reach the most enlightened and societally beneficial decision as to the sentence of the accused? If so, this represents a dramatic departure from the defense counsel's role in the determination of guilt or innocence.

If it is the defense counsel's duty to help the court to reach the most enlightened decision, should this decision be concerned solely with the rehabilitation of the defendant? Or should the defense counsel also do his best honestly to appraise the deterrent effect upon others of the severe punishment for his client?

Is it arguable that neither of these issues is really a serious problem since most defense attorneys honestly believe that the lowest possible penalty is the one that rehabilitates best, and that the deterrent effect of the criminal law, at least in the case of any one person caught in the system, is minimal?

C. SENTENCING BY CORRECTIONAL AUTHORITY

1. HISTORY OF THE INDETERMINATE SENTENCE *

. . . Americans in the Progressive period (1900 to 1920) believed that they had discovered a new method of rehabilitation, one with basic implications for incarceration. Put most simply, they discovered social case work, or more broadly, the therapeutic encounter. The deviant, in dialogue with a trained case worker or psychiatrist, would learn the error of his ways. The criminal was defined as the maladjusted, and therapy would teach him to conform. As one outgrowth of this attitude, Americans created a probation and parole system. Another outgrowth was that the prison system itself underwent change. During these years, such amenities as prison commissaries, privileges of the yard, prison bands, and sports for the first time entered the institutions. The silent system and lock step gave way to mingling inmates and new privileges. These innovations, according to proponents, were to make the prisons more like the society. They were, in essence, to help prepare inmates for life outside, reward them for good behavior, and punish them for bad behavior by manipulating privileges. The institution was not to be, as it had been in the 1830s, a utopian alternative to the society, but rather a reflection of it. It was a testing ground for society, and ostensibly the prisoner who left the institution was prepared to reenter the community.

Both the case work model and the idea of prison as society in miniature contributed to the spread and popularity of a new mode of sentencing: the indeterminate sentence. Previously, legislators had set down for the judge a range of imprisonment for each crime category: he could pass a sentence for this particular offense that ranged between, say, two and six years. The judge then settled on two years or four years, or five years, and the inmate served just that time. Under the indeterminate sentence, the legislature established a wider range of options for the judge, and most important, the judge no longer passed a fixed sentence. Now he gave the offender a term of three to nine years, or seven to twelve years, and left it to the parole board to set the moment of release. During the first decades after its introduction, the indeterminate sentence appears to have actually lengthened the time inmates served in prison. And even after 1945, when time served began to lessen, the indeterminate sentence became the feature of the incarceration system that inmates most detested.

Ultimately, these changes took hold because of the appeal of a rehabilitation ethic—here was a new way to reform the criminal, a method worthy of implementation. The metaphor constantly used to support the innovation was a medical one. Just as the doctor needed discretion to decide when a patient was cured, so wardens and parole officers needed discretion to decide when an offender was cured. Just

* David J. Rothman, "Doing Time: Days, Months and Years in the Criminal Justice System," in *Sentencing*, edited by Hyman Gross and Andrew Von Hirsch, New York, Oxford University Press, 1981, pp. 379–380. ©1981 (Reprinted with permission).

as a doctor needed a wide range of information in order to decide on the right diagnosis and treatment, so in the field of criminal justice it was necessary to know about an offender's home life, his feelings, his childhood, and his marriage. Under the rubric of treatment, then, the criminal justice system expanded and ballooned out. More information, more time, more discretion—these became its central features. . . .

2. THE CALIFORNIA EXPERIENCE *

. . . California pioneered in the adoption of the indeterminate sentence for felony offenders. Under this system the legislature set the minimum and maximum term for each offense (for example, burglary, second degree, one to fifteen years; robbery, five years to life; sale of marijuana, five years to life), and the judge, instead of sentencing the defendant to a specific term, simply remanded him to the state prison "for the term prescribed by law." **

As conceived by its advocates among the early reformers, the indeterminate sentence was integral to rehabilitation. The idea was to grant an earlier discharge than would be possible under a determinate sentence to those prisoners who demonstrate by their behavior a readiness to return to the community. The sentencing power would be removed from a possibly prejudiced trial judge and placed in the hands of skilled experts in human behavior. These experts would look at the man rather than his crime, take into account all the circumstances, and make a prognosis for his rehabilitation via "excellent programs of work, education, vocational training."

But there was another side to this coin. To prison administrators, the indeterminate sentence was a potent instrument for inmate control. "The Corrections people never lost sight of its punitive advantages; in fact, they seized on it as the best control measure ever handed to them," a sociologist told me.

> It's a hell of a lot more effective for maintaining discipline than the whip. In effect, the message to the prisoners is: "Keep this joint running smoothly and we'll let you out earlier." Conversely, they can keep the really "dangerous" criminal in almost indefinitely. Yet, who is to decide which is the "dangerous" man? This category is elastic enough to embrace political nonconformists, inmate leaders of ethnic groups, prison troublemakers. From the vindictive guard who sets out to build a record against some individual, to the parole board, the indeterminate sentence grants Corrections the power to play God with the lives of inmates.

---

* Jessica Mitford, *Kind and Usual Punishment,* Alfred A. Knopf, Inc., 1971; pp. 80–87. Copyright 1971 (Reprinted with permission).

** For most offenses the judge could also sentence the offender to probation, or a short jail term.

While the indeterminate sentence implied a policy of early release for the rehabilitated offender, it was also a means of assuring much longer sentences for the troublesome element than would normally be imposed by judges; the theme that judges do not give long enough sentences, that under the determinate sentence system miscreants are let out too soon, recurs in the writings of nineteenth-century penologists. The indeterminate sentence reassured the public on both counts: by promising a benevolent prison system wherein criminals will be dealt with as fairly as their fallen state deserved, and by offering the assurance that only those who were thoroughly "safe" would be loosed on the community.

In California, sentencing and paroling of male convicts was entrusted to a nine-member Adult Authority, according to its published literature "composed of persons who have demonstrated skills, abilities, and leadership in many fields."

Its members were appointed by the governor for four-year terms. The composition of the latest board was not easily squared with its self-appraisal. It was, with the lone exception of a retired dentist, drawn from the ranks of law enforcement and Corrections: former policemen, prosecutors, FBI and prison personnel. This board wielded total, arbitrary, despotic power over the destinies and liberties of California's state prison population, not only while they were in custody but also after they had been released on parole.

Under cover of the indeterminate sentence, the median term served by California's "felony first releases" had by 1968 risen to thirty-six months, highest in the nation and probably the world. Without exception, prisoners in jurisdictions that adopted the indeterminate sentence served more time month-for-month than those in jurisdictions where the judge set the maximum term of imprisonment and the parole board had to operate within that maximum.

At a meeting of ex-convicts, I asked what they conceived to be the major grievances of California prisoners. There was near unanimity: surprisingly, the wretched physical conditions of prison life were by no means their major concern. The food, they said was generally lousy. Medical treatment amounted to criminal neglect in many instances. Overcrowding, which led to every sort of problem from aggravated homosexual assaults and inmate fights to filthy living conditions was endemic in most of the "correctional facilities." The highly touted vocational training was a fraud; in San Quentin there were 350 places in the trade programs for a population of over 3,500 (you had to be on a waiting list for eighteen months or more to get in), and even in the minimum-security conservation camps there was little opportunity to learn skills that would be useful on the outside.

But these features of prison existence, disheartening, degrading, and dangerous though they were, paled in importance, said the former convicts, beside the total arbitrariness of the bureaucracy that ruled every aspect of their existence. One former inmate summed it up:

"Don't give us steak and eggs; get rid of the Adult Authority! Don't put in a shiny modern hospital; free us from the tyranny of the indeterminate sentence!" . . .

3. PAROLE PREDICTION *

Let me be plain. I do not argue that parole decision making should be more equitable. I do not argue that applicants for parole should have their cases thoughtfully and carefully considered, or that parole revocation procedures should responsibly incorporate constitutional due process protections, or that parole boards should "be taken out of politics," whatever that means. All these are obviously desirable but they leave the fundamental flaw in the parole process untouched. My assertion is simpler. The link between release on parole and involvement in prison programs must be broken. The best and fairest way to do this is to determine the parole date early. If parole is to be retained, and there are practical reasons why it is likely to be, then the date of the prisoner's first release on parole must be settled and disclosed to him within the first few weeks of his imprisonment.

It would be redundant to rehearse my critique of the rehabilitative ideal as the determinant of the prison term. And the relationship between parole and the individualized treatment model that reflects that ideal is equally clear: give the medicine of treatment, allow release on parole when it takes. Protracted empirical analysis has demonstrated, however, that *predictions of avoidance of conviction after release are no more likely to be accurate on the date of release than early in the prison term.* Neither the prisoner's avoidance of prison disciplinary offenses nor his involvement in prison training programs is correlated with later successful completion of parole or with later avoidance of a criminal conviction. Put another way: thirty years of careful compilation of base expectancy rates for parole revocation risk and later conviction risk reveal that only three possible changes in the life of the prisoner during his incarceration are correlated with his later conformity to the conditions of his parole and with his avoidance of conviction for crime after his release—the availability of a family or other supportive social group for him to join on release; the availability of a reasonable supportive job; and the process and duration of aging itself. All three are largely extrinsic to the treatment aspects of prison programs.

Getting a job and preserving or creating social relationships are exactly what prison most interferes with; although time for aging it does provide. We cage men, it is clear, not to treat them; indeed, the caging is likely to preclude self-change toward social conformity; we confine for other reasons. We delude ourselves in thinking that we possess predictive capacities derived from observation of the prisoner's success in prison programs and the time-treatment link we forge on this

---

* Norval Morris, The Future of Imprisonment, U. of Chicago Press, Chicago 1974, pp. 35, 36. © 1974 (Reprinted with permission).

delusion effectively inhibits the prisoner's relating appropriately to those programs.

On the other hand, if the legislature retains minimum-maximum sentencing, we are wise to determine the parole release date in relation to our knowledge of the risk of serious crime after release by that prisoner. But this can be done early in the prison term as well as later; nothing relevant to the assessment of the risk changes except the prisoner's preservation or formation of social ties or his obtaining a job to go to upon release, and these are matters best handled by a furlough program, by work release, by pre-release opportunities for job finding, by our intelligent support of him in his efforts to create these social and vocational ties. They are certainly better ascertained by testing than by predicting.

4. THE UNITED STATES SINCE 1970 *

Prior to 1970 the indeterminate sentence was accepted by leading jurists and penologists as the most effective and humane approach to the problems of sentencing offenders. Since that time the climate of opinion has shifted radically. Most commentators now call for some form of determinacy in sentencing, and even defenders of the parole board's role in sentencing argue that parole discretion should be confined and structured by decisionmaking guidelines. The reasons for this sudden turnabout are varied. First, there was much criticism of the way in which parole boards exercised their discretion, with several extreme cases of arbitrary and capricious use of discretion pointing to a lawless system. Analysis of unfettered parole discretion soon led to indeterminate sentence laws as the source of this problem. Furthermore, as numerous middle class persons entered prisons in the late 1960's for drug offenses and various kinds of protest-related crimes, and as more middle class persons became interested in prisoners' rights, they heard for the first time the gripes of "real" prisoners.

And much to the surprise of many civil libertarians, the foremost gripes were directed against rehabilitation in general and indeterminate sentencing in particular. Indeed, the Attica Report concluded that "the operation of the parole system was a primary source of tension and bitterness within the walls."

These concerns were then addressed to the larger public in the news media and popular works. The gist of these books and articles was that parole and indeterminate sentencing were arbitrary, highhanded and unfair, hypocritically masking retribution and capriciousness behind the mask of scientific objectivity.

Comment

Note how well parole prediction fitted in with the rehabilitative, almost medical, model. The parole authorities could, like the physi-

---

* Michigan Felony Sentencing Report, 1979. Reprinted with permission.

cian, tell when their charge was "cured" and released him. As the above excerpt indicates we simply do not know how to do this. As a result along with the decline of the rehabilitative ideal, the indeterminate sentence began to lose support.

D. SENTENCING BY THE LEGISLATURE

1. DISCRETION AND DISPARITY *

Criticisms of sentencing and parole structures in the United States have focused on the problem of disparity, or unwarranted variation, in penalties imposed on offenders convicted of similar crimes. Three types of structural changes have been proposed as remedies, and each has been adopted in various jurisdictions. First, there are advocates of mandatory sentencing—with specific, unvarying penalties for specific crimes. Second, there are proposals for "presumptive sentencing," according to which punishments would be set for the "normal" case within much narrower bounds than has been customary under the previously prevailing philosophy of indeterminacy. (Some deviation ordinarily would be allowed for unusual cases involving aggravating or mitigating circumstances.) Third, systems of "guidelines" have been developed, with sentences determined according to an explicit policy intended to structure and control, but not eliminate, the exercise of discretion. Specific ranges of penalties are provided for combinations of offense and offender characteristics, with some discretion permitted within the prescribed range and also with provision for further deviation for specified reasons. Each of these models (including the latter, although to a lesser extent) reduces the discretion of the sentencing judge.

The sentencing trends now in progress thus may be summarized as tending toward more definite sentences, according to desert principles, with markedly reduced discretion by the relevant authorities. The word "discretion" has interesting ambiguities. It may mean either being discrete (making distinctions) or being discreet (being prudent or careful). It may also mean the "liberty or power of deciding or acting without other control than one's own judgment." Current debates focus, of course, on issues of the judge's discretion in the latter meaning of the word. Although the making of careful distinctions seems desirable in a judge, the proper degree or amount of uncontrolled freedom in judicial decisionmaking is a subject of considerable controversy.

But discretion in sentencing, in the sense of freedom to exercise judgment, may be justified on the grounds that it allows for individual handling of each offender. Thus, if each person is unique (as must be agreed) or if each criminal act is in some way different from all others (as must certainly be the case), then it may be expected that sentences

* Gottfredson and Gottfredson, *Decisionmaking in Criminal Justice*, Ballinger Publishing Co., Cambridge, Mass.1980, pp. 191– 192. Reprinted with permission from *Deci-* *sionmaking in Criminal Justice: Toward the Rational Exercise of Discretion*, Copyright 1980, Ballinger Publishing Company.

will be disparate (that is, variable). The word "disparity" in sentencing, however, has acquired a surplus meaning. It has come to be a
pejorative referring to variation in sentences that is perceived as
inequitable and, hence, unfair and unjust. (It may also be used to refer
to sentences that are claimed to be irrational in the sense that they
lack an appropriate proportionality or severity of sanction commensu-
rate with the offense seriousness, as when two offenders' crimes seem
obviously different in seriousness but the same sanction is imposed.) If
some discretion is justified on grounds of individual differences and it is
not assumed that all variation in sentencing outcomes for ostensibly
similar "cases" (offenders and criminal events) is based on invidious
factors, then some disparity (that is, variation) may be warranted.
(Therefore, it is undoubtedly preferable to refer not to the problem of
"disparity" but to that of "unwarranted" disparity.)

Proposals for dealing with the problems of sentencing discretion,
and particularly of unwarranted variation, have emphasized the need
for consistent policy. At the same time, the appropriate range or
license for discretion has been noted widely as a significant problem at
each decision point in the processing of offenders. Remington et al.
have summarized the principal object for research about discretionary
decisions as follows: "For every government decision there is an optimal point on the scale between the rule-of-law at one end and total
discretion at the other end. The task of research is to find that
optimum point and to confine discretion to the degree which is feasible." Thus, although most of the current discussions about sentencing
focus on the problems associated with too much discretion, there is also
the danger in overly rigid decision rules that do not permit the taking
into consideration of legitimate individual differences. It should be
noted that the latter also involves a sacrifice of justice: rigid, discre-
tionless systems may produce "equity" only at the expense of treating
unequal cases alike. . . .

Questions

The authors are arguing, are they not, that disparity can result
from too little discretion as well as too much. How is that possible? Is
not the purpose of reducing judicial discretion to diminish disparity?

2. EXPANDING PROSECUTORIAL POWER *

In the American system of criminal justice, power over punishment
is allocated primarily among four types of governmental decisionmakers—legislatures, prosecutors' offices, courts, and correctional
agencies (including, most notably, parole boards). The thrust of many
recent proposals for sentencing reform has been to reduce or eliminate
the discretion of both courts and correctional agencies and to increase

* Albert W. Alschuler, "Sentencing Reform and Prosecutional Power: A Critique
of Recent Proposals for 'Fixed' and 'Presumptive' Sentencing," 126 *University of
Pennsylvania Law Review* 1978, pp. 550–
551. © 1978 (Reprinted with permission).

the extent to which legislatures specify criminal penalties in advance. In "fixed" sentencing schemes, statutes specify the exact penalty that will follow conviction of each offense; in systems of "presumptive" sentencing, statutes specify a "normal" sentence for each offense but permit limited departures from the norm in atypical cases. Although prosecutors' offices, in practice, have probably had a greater influence on sentencing than any of the other agencies (including state legislatures), the call for sentencing reform has largely ignored this extensive prosecutorial power. In my view, fixed and presumptive sentencing schemes of the sort commonly advocated today (and of the sort enacted in California) are unlikely to achieve their objectives so long as they leave the prosecutor's power to formulate charges and to bargain for guilty pleas unchecked. Indeed, this sort of reform is likely to produce its antithesis—a system every bit as lawless as the current sentencing regime, in which discretion is concentrated in an inappropriate agency, and in which the benefits of this discretion are made available only to defendants who sacrifice their constitutional rights.

Question

How can a legislative reform intended to reduce discretion, not reduce it? Do you think that legislatures, when mandating fixed or presumptive sentencing schemes, intended to give so much power to the prosecutor?

3.　AN ILLUSTRATION OF LEGISLATIVE SENTENCING—INDIANA *

The most serious concern is that the new sentencing codes will lead to the imposition of sentences that could result in doubling, tripling or quadrupling time actually served. The authorized maxima are high, aggravating factors make those authorized maxima even higher, and the mandatory consecutive and habitual offender provisions make matters even worse. Moreover, there is no reason to assume that legislatures will hold the present line and not, in response to particularly outrageous crimes, raise the maxima even higher.

Making Uniformity Unlikely

Such mandatory sentencing terms are [already] far too high. Moreover, while the Indiana Code, like its counterparts in other jurisdictions, provides the sentencer with a list of statutory aggravants and mitigants, there is no reason to believe that these will be applied consistently by sentencing judges in the absence of appellate review of sentence. In fact, the effective fixed sentencing range permitted by statutory aggravants and mitigants makes uniformity unlikely.

Moreover, Indiana's abandonment of rehabilitation is curiously incomplete. The judge is permitted to increase (but not decrease) a

* Leonard Orland, "Is Determinate Sentencing an Illusory Reform?," 62 *Judica-* *ture* 1979, pp. 386–389. ©1979 (Reprinted with permission).

sentence on rehabilitative grounds, i.e., if the defendant is "in need of
. . . rehabilitative treatment that can best be provided by his commitment to a penal facility." This is statutory reform with a vengeance.
High flat sentences, presumptive consecutive sentences, and habitual
offenders sentences are enacted in the name of abandonment of rehabilitation; then rehabilitation reemerges as an aggravant to increase
length of time if the judge is so inclined.

Catch 22: Good Time

Reformers were concerned that the substantial disparity of judge-
imposed sentences would be further increased by the arbitrariness of
parole boards who could not rationally decide when a defendant was
rehabilitated. But the new sentencing codes raise the possibility that
the tyranny of arbitrary parole boards will be replaced by the tyranny
of arbitrary prison discipline committees when they take away good
time.

Under the new Indiana code, all inmates are assigned to class I and
receive one day of credit for each day of imprisonment. The discipline
hearing committee can reassign an inmate to class II; in that event the
inmate will receive only one day of good time credit for each two days
served; or the committee can reassign to class III, where the inmate
will receive no credit time.

But are there substantive standards for misconduct? No! The
basis for reassignment between classes is literally open ended: "A
person may be reassigned to class II or class III if he violates a rule or
regulation of the Department of Correction" and the committee finds
that "reassignment is an appropriate disciplinary action for the violation."

Quite apart from the potential pernicious consequences of reassignment is the open ended authority of the commissioner of corrections to
take away credit time for violation of disciplinary rules: "A person may
be deprived of any part of the credit time he has earned if he violates a
rule or regulation of the Department of Correction".

An Illusory Reform

This statutory credit time structure makes a substantial impact on
disparity of time served. For example, two inmates, each with a fixed
flat sentence of 30 years, could end up actually serving 15 and 30 years
respectively. Thus, the notion that sentencing code reform will lead to
equality of time served is illusory. All that Indiana has really accomplished is to shift arbitrary power from the parole board to the prison
disciplinary committee. And, Indiana is not alone; similar, but less
severe problems exist under the Illinois code.

Some Tentative Conclusions

As this necessarily brief examination of the Indiana legislation indicates, the return to determinate sentencing is not the panacea many believed. On the contrary, it is subject to many serious concerns:

- Well trained treatment staffs and good treatment programs may be jeopardized by the intellectual purity of a sentencing code which declares that rehabilitation is dead and that the purpose of sentencing is to punish.

- Sentencing legislation that purports to create sentencing equality will not; rather, it creates grave risks of higher unequal sentences in place of lower unequal sentences.

- Discretionary release on credit time by prison discipline committees is at least as bad, if not worse, than release by parole boards. There is every reason to assume prison disciplinary committees will act as arbitrarily and unfairly as parole boards.

- The structure of the new sentencing codes, the provisions for consecutive sentences and long recidivist sentences, and the discretion given prosecutors to threaten invocation of those provisions, raises grave risks that uncontrolled judicial sentencing discretion will simply be replaced by uncontrolled prosecutorial plea bargained sentencing.

- These new sentencing codes may well lead to substantial increases in the prison population. But, since the federal courts have made fairly clear that they will not tolerate massive overcrowding or unsafe penal institutions, states which adhere to unrealistic sentencing legislation may well have to embark upon a massive prison construction program. But, does America want or need to double the prison population from 400,000 to 800,000? And, will taxpayers be willing to pay the costs, presently estimated at $50,000 for each new prison bed?

Despite rehabilitation's considerable shortcomings, it is a profound mistake to legislate it out of existence and, in its place, substitute a Draconian system of sentencing which will substantially increase time served in prisons in the United States. American prison sentences already exceed those of most other western nations, and to embark upon reforms which may catapult the nation still further into the lead in terms of how we confine our citizens in penal institutions is both unwise and ill-considered.

Question

Do you think the author's criticisms are justified? If not, why not?

4. SENTENCING GUIDELINES

a. OREGON'S SENTENCING GUIDEILINES *

A dozen states and the federal government now use systems for the sentencing of felony offenders which they call sentencing guidelines. The guidelines vary considerably: Many are voluntary rather than mandatory, some cover a limited group of felonies only, and most are developed independently of any consideration of existing state correctional capacity. In 1989, Oregon developed felony sentencing guidelines for a state with already overcrowded corrections facilities.

An essential part of Oregon's guidelines was the choice to develop guidelines tied to expected prison capacity and to make them mandatory. The language of the enabling legislation provided that "Factors relevant to appropriate sentencing include . . . effective capacity of state and local corrections facilities and other sentencing sanctions available" (619 O.L. § 2 [2][b][1987]). In taking this approach, Oregon chose to model its felony guidelines after the mandatory capacity-linked guidelines of Minnesota and Washington.

The committee focused first on the two major components of traditional sentencing guidelines systems. One axis of a sentencing guidelines grid is usually a crime seriousness scale, which ranks all offenses subject to the guidelines in order of relative seriousness; the second is an axis that arrays offenders' criminal histories. The interaction of these two variables places the offender in a sentencing guidelines grid classification that sets an appropriate sentence for a given crime and criminal history. The council formed separate subcommittees to work on the crime seriousness and criminal history issues, and these groups began work at once.

Crime Seriousness Scale

The Oregon crime seriousness scale classifies 100 of the 150 felonies in the state criminal code into an 11–level scale. The sentencing grid itself displays roughly 50 offenses; the full ranking of offenses is included in an appendix to the guidelines rules. Drug offenses are classified in a separate appendix. Oregon's criminal code, which the Criminal Justice Council chose not to amend, but to work within, defines felonies at three levels: Class A, B, and C. Each of the classes has a maximum statutory sentence but no minimum. Because in many instances the statutory definition of a given offense captured such a wide array of conduct, Oregon "subcategorized" statutory offenses in its rankings. For instance, Burglary I, a Class A felony, is classified at crime seriousness level 9 on the Oregon guidelines crime seriousness scale if it involves a deadly weapon or a threat of physical injury, at crime seriousness level 8 if it is committed in an occupied dwelling

* Kathleen M. Bogan, "Constructing Felony Sentencing Guidelines in an Already Crowded State: Oregon Breaks New Ground," Crime & Delinquency, Vol. 36, No. 4, October 1990, c. 1990 Sage Publications, Inc. (Reprinted with Permission).

without the facts to justify the classification at level 9, and at crime seriousness level 7 in all other cases meeting the statutory definition of Burglary I.

Criminal History Scale

Oregon was also innovative in the development of sentencing guidelines criminal history scale. Because each prior conviction was critical in moving offenders from one criminal history classification to another, disputes over the accuracy of each and every reported conviction could be a major issue at sentencing.

Oregon wanted a scale that was simpler, reducing disputes at sentencing, and more sensitive, in that it considered the type of prior offenses. The scale devised was not ordinal, but had nine criminal history classifications, each of which set a threshold for the number and type of prior convictions related to that classification. A distinction is made between prior person felonies and nonperson felonies, as well as between misdemeanor and felony convictions. Person and nonperson felonies are defined in the guidelines rules.

In Oregon, an offender is in the most serious criminal history category with three or more prior person felony convictions. Historical data indicated that only 4% of felony offenders in the state had three or more convictions for person felonies. Thus the number of offenders that would be eligible for the longest sentences in the most serious criminal history classification would be small.

Under the Oregon criminal history scoring system, once an offender has the requisite number of prior person or nonperson felony convictions to justify the threshold of a criminal history classification, the number of convictions in excess of that does not change the classification. Oregon is thus hopeful that, with its criminal history scale, disputes at sentencing over exact numbers and the validity of prior convictions will be somewhat reduced.

Grid Structure and Dispositional Line

In Oregon's sentencing guidelines grid there are 99 cells; 53 of them are presumptive prison cells, 46 are presumptive probationary cells. Through the use of detailed data on preguidelines sentencing practices, the council was able to determine that the dispositional policy of the guidelines would shift Oregon from an 18% preguidelines prison commitment rate to a 22% prison commitment rate under guidelines. The data were also able to document which type of offenders would be shifted, either from preguidelines probationary sentences to prison (sex offenders and other person offenders), or from preguidelines prison sentences to probation (driving offenders, drug possession for personal use).

The guidelines structure a judge's sentencing discretion within narrow sentence ranges, but the policy allows judges two avenues for imposing a sentence other than presumptive sentence under the guidelines. One is a formal "departure," similar to the process used in the Washington and Minnesota systems. In these cases, based on findings on the record, the judge may impose a shorter or longer sentence, or differ from the dispositional policy. As in Washington and Minnesota, a departure sentence may be appealed by either the defendant or the prosecutor.

A second option allows the use of probation rather than prison for a limited group of offenders. "Optional probation" also requires findings, but its imposition is not an appealable issue. In adopting an optional probation approach Oregon considered the first offender and sexual offender sentencing options that Washington had built into its initial guidelines but selected another approach. Under the Oregon option, offenders in three designated grid cells, at a fairly high level of crime seriousness, but with relatively minor criminal records (generally sex and drug offenders) are eligible for a sentence to a community program. The judge may impose the community sanction on finding that three conditions are met: (a) that the program is available, (b) that it will be more effective than prison at preventing this offender's recidivism, and (c) that the offender was not on supervision status or armed with a firearm at the time of the offense.

b. APPELLATE REVIEW OF SENTENCNG UNDER GUIDELINES *

Both defendants and the government may appeal a guidelines sentence on grounds that it was imposed in violation of law, resulted from an incorrect application of the guidelines, constitutes an unfavorable departure, or, if imposed for an offense for which there is no applicable guideline, constitutes a plainly unreasonable sentence. The circuit courts that considered the issue during 1989 have held that the appellate review statute does not authorize review of a district court's discretionary refusal to depart from a properly determined guideline range, nor does it authorize an appeal on the basis that the extent of the departure was insufficient. Appellate courts have also declined to review disputes over the applicable guideline range where it is clear on the record that the same sentence would be imposed under either of several overlapping ranges. The statutory scheme for appellate consideration of guideline sentences and sentences outside the applicable guideline range is set forth at 18 U.S.C. § 3742(e), which provides:

> Upon review of the record, the court of appeals shall determine whether the sentence—
>
> (1) was imposed in violation of law;
>
> (2) was imposed as a result of an incorrect application of the sentencing guidelines;

* United States Sentencing Commission, Annual Report, 1989.

(3) is outside of the applicable guideline range, and is unreasonable;

(4) was imposed for an offense for which there is no applicable sentencing guideline and is plainly unreasonable.

The court of appeals shall give due regard to the opportunity of the district court to judge the credibility of the witnesses, and shall accept the findings of fact of the district court unless they are clearly erroneous and shall give due deference to the district court's application of the guidelines to the facts.

Review of Guideline Application

In reviewing the "correctness" of guideline determinations, 18 U.S.C. § 3742(e) requires the court of appeals to give due regard to the district court's assessment of the credibility of witnesses, to accept the court's findings of fact unless they are clearly erroneous, and to "give due deference to the district court's application of the guidelines to the facts." Courts have reviewed the legislative history surrounding the adoption of the "due deference" standard and have interpreted it to be the standard courts have "long employed when reviewing mixed questions of fact and law"—a sliding scale that "varies with the 'mix' of the mixed question." If the question is essentially factual, such as assessing the defendant's role in the offense or acceptance of responsibility, the standard of review is "clearly erroneous; " if the question requires consideration of legal concepts and values, such as interpretation of a guideline term, the standard is closer to *de novo* review.

Review of Departures

The appellate review statute provides that district court departure decisions are to be reviewed using a standard of "reasonableness." During 1989, several circuits gave further content to this statutory criterion by establishing a multi-prong standard of review for general departure sentences. The standard requires a reviewing court to address several issues:

- Was the circumstance identified by the district court "of a kind or to a degree" not adequately considered by the Commission in drafting the guidelines?
- Did the circumstance identified by the district court as warranting departure actually exist in the instant case?
- Was the extent of departure reasonable?

If the answer to all three questions is "yes," courts have held that the departure generally will be upheld on appeal. In reviewing these questions, the appellate courts have applied a *de novo* standard of review to the first question, a clearly erroneous standard of review to the factual determination of whether the circumstance exists in the present case, and a deferential or abuse of discretion standard of review in assessing the reasonableness of the extent of the departure. In determining whether a particular factor has been "adequately considered" by the Commission for a particular offense and offender, the statute requires the court to look only to the guidelines, policy statements, and official commentary of the Sentencing Commission. Courts generally have afforded wide latitude to sentencing judges with respect to the extent of departure once a valid factor has been identified.

Adequacy of Criminal History

For departures under guideline 4A1.3 (Adequacy of Criminal History), appellate courts have followed the directive in this policy statement and more closely scrutinized the extent of departure by requiring the district court to refer to the range applicable to an offender in the next higher or lower criminal history category prior to departing beyond that point. In essence, the appellate courts have required the district courts, where possible, to assign points to the under- or overstated criminal history score and determine a new range for the departure sentence that more adequately reflects the seriousness of the defendant's criminal history as compared to typical offenders in the various criminal history categories.

Comment and Questions

Contrast the process of sentencing under guidelines with the discretionary sentencing that appears to be called for with the use of "alternatives" such as community service or sentencing to treatment programs and with sentencing by correctional authority.

Are sentencing guidelines compatible with the search for new and flexible sentencing alternatives?

Note that appellate review of guidelines sentencing allows both the defendant and the prosecution to appeal. Is it likely that the prosecution would ever appeal because the sentence was too harsh? Is it fair to allow the prosecution to appeal a lenient sentence in order to try again to secure a harsher sentence?

5. LEGISLATIVE SENTENCES IN ACTION *

Statute Outlined. New York's Second Felony Offender Law was passed as a "sleeper" bill in August, 1973 while the philosophically-related "Rockefeller" drug legislation occupied center stage.

The law stipulates that most serious, second felony offenders must be sentenced to a minimum prison sentence of one-half the maximum term set by statute.

"Counterproductive" effects of the Second Felony Offender Law during its first 19 months of operation, according to the study, included:

• *Soaring Prison Populations*—the number of inmates at state institutions was up from 12,444 on Jan. 1, 1973 (before

* *Criminal Justice Newsletter,* Vol. 6, No. 17, Sept. 1, 1975, p. 2. ©1975 Reprinted with permission.

the law) to about 16,000 now; the male incarceration rate per 100,000 New York residents jumped from 533.8 in 1972 to 570 in 1973; state institutions are due to reach capacity in one to two years.

• *Congested Courts*—the backlog of cases in New York City increased by 8.7% in the first year of the new law, while case processing time in the state's busiest district (Brooklyn) has at times doubled and is still rising, despite increased court resources and personnel.

• *More Trials*—the rate of cases going to trial increased from 4.6% to 9.6% between 1971 and 1974; it reached 12% in New York City in the last two months of 1974, and has hit 25% in some districts.

• *Fewer Guilty Pleas*—down from 74.8% of convictions in 1973 to 65.6% in 1974.

• *Fewer Convictions*—down from 83.4% of felony trials in the first quarter of 1974 to 77.2% in the final quarter.

• *Longer Sentences*—the proportion of sentences of five years or more increased from 31% of the felony total in 1972 to 40% of the total in 1973.

Finding ". . . strong indications that the measure has failed to deter criminals or reduce recidivism . . .," the study team recommended repeal of the Second Felony Offender Law and less use of incarceration in New York. While all of the negative trends cannot be laid solely at the door of the law, it can hardly be said not to deserve a major portion of the blame.

Question

Was the problem here that there were legislatively fixed sentences, or that the sentences were too high, considering the capacities of the courts and prisons?

E. RECOMMENDED READING

Forer, Lois G. *Criminals and Victims: A Trial Judge Reflects on Crime and Punishment.* Norton, New York, 1980.

Frankel, Marvin E. *Criminal Sentences: Law Without Order.* Hill and Wang, New York, 1973.

Garland, David. *Punishment and Welfare: A History of Penal Strategies.* Gower, London, 1985.

Gaylin, Willard. *Partial Justice: A Study in Sentencing.* Random House, New York, 1974.

Gross, Hyman and von Hirsch, Andrew, eds. *Sentencing.* Oxford University Press, New York, 1981.

Menninger, Karl M.D. *The Crime of Punishment.* The Viking Press, Inc., New York, 1968.

Mitford, Jessica. *Kind and Usual Punishment.* Alfred A. Knopf, Inc., New York, 1971.

Singer, Richard G. *Just Desserts: Sentencing Based on Equality and Dessert.* Ballinger Publishing Co., Cambridge, Mass., 1979.

Tonry, Michael and Zimring, Franklin (eds.). *Reform and Punishment: Essays on Criminal Sentencing.* University of Chicago Press, Chicago, 1983.

Wheeler, Stanton, Mann, Kenneth, and Sarat, Austin. *Sitting in Judgment: The Sentencing of White Collar Criminals.* Yale University Press, New Haven, 1988.

Chapter XII

CAPITAL PUNISHMENT

A. INTRODUCTION

1. WORLDWIDE *

LIST OF ABOLITIONIST AND RETENTIONIST COUNTRIES

Attached is a list of countries, indicating whether or not their laws provide for the death penalty. This list has been compiled on the basis of information available to Amnesty International as of February 1986.

ABOLITIONIST BY LAW FOR ALL CRIMES

(Countries whose laws do not provide for the death penalty for any crime)

ANDORRA	HAITI	NORWAY
AUSTRALIA	HONDURAS	PANAMA
AUSTRIA	ICELAND	PHILLIPINES
CAMBODIA	IRELAND	PORTUGAL
CAPE VERDE	KIRIBATI	ROMANIA
COLOMBIA	LIECHTENSTEIN	SAN MARINO
COSTA RICA	LUXEMBOURG	SOLOMON ISLANDS
CZECHOSLOVAKIA	MARSHALL ISLANDS	SWEDEN
DENMARK	MICRONESIA	TUVALU
DOMINICAN REPUBLIC	MONACO	URUGUAY
ECUADOR	NAMIBIA	VANUATU
FINLAND	NETHERLANDS	VATICAN
GERMANY	NEW ZEALAND	VENEZUELA
FRANCE	NICARAGUA	

Total: 42 countries

* "The Death Penalty," Amnesty International Publications, 1990 (Reprinted by permission).

ABOLITIONIST BY LAW FOR ORDINARY CRIMES ONLY

(Countries whose laws provide for the death penalty only for exceptional crimes such as crimes under military law or crimes committed in exceptional circumstances such as wartime)

ARGENTINA	ITALY	PERU
BRAZIL	MALTA	SEYCHELLES
CANADA		
CYPRUS	MEXICO	SPAIN
EL SALVADOR	NEPAL	
FIJI		SWITZERLAND
ISRAEL	PAPUA NEW GUINEA	UNITED KINGDOM

Total: 17 countries

COUNTRIES WHICH HAVE ABOLISHED THE DEATH PENALTY SINCE 1976

PORTUGAL (1976)

CANADA (1976)

SPAIN (1978)

DENMARK (1978)

LUXEMBOURG (1979)

NICARAGUA (1979)

NORWAY (1979)

BRAZIL (1979)

FIJI (1979)

PERU (1979)

FRANCE (1981)

NETHERLANDS (1982)

CYPRUS (1983)

EL SALVADOR (1983)

ARGENTINA (1984)

AUSTRALIA (1984)

THE PHILIPPINES (1987)

HAITI (1987)

LIECHTENSTEIN (1987)

GERMAN DEMOCRATIC REPUBLIC (1987)

CAMBODIA (1989)

NEW ZEALAND (1989)

ROMANIA (1989)

ANDORRA (1990)

CZECH AND SLOVAK FEDERATIVE REPUBLIC (1990)

IRELAND (1990)

NAMIBIA (1990)

NEPAL (1990)

Total: 28 countries

FEDERATED COUNTRIES WITH DIVIDED JURISDICTIONS

(Countries in which the law in some states provides for the death penalty while that in others does not)

UNITED STATES OF AMERICA

Total: 1 country

Questions

How many of these nations are like the United States? How have they been able to get along without capital punishment?

2. IN THE U.S.

a. HISTORICALLY *

Prisoners Executed Under Civil Authority, by Race and Offense: 1930 to 1970

Year	Murder Total	Murder White	Murder Negro	Rape Total	Rape White	Rape Negro
1970	—	—	—	—	—	—
1969	—	—	—	—	—	—
1968	—	—	—	—	—	—
1967	2	1	1	—	—	—
1966	1	1	—	—	—	—
1965	7	6	1	—	—	—
1964	9	5	4	6	3	3
1963	18	12	6	2	—	2
1962	41	26	15	4	2	2
1961	33	18	15	8	1	7
1960	44	18	26	8	—	8
1959	41	15	26	8	1	7
1958	41	20	20	7	—	7
1957	54	32	22	10	2	8
1956	52	20	31	12	—	12
1955	65	41	24	7	1	6
1954	71	37	33	9	1	8
1953	51	25	25	7	1	6
1952	71	35	36	12	1	11
1951	87	55	31	17	2	15
1950	68	36	32	13	4	9
1949	107	49	56	10	—	10
1948	95	32	61	22	1	21
1947	129	40	89	23	2	21
1946	107	45	61	22	—	22
1945	90	37	52	26	4	22
1944	96	45	48	24	2	22
1943	118	54	63	13	—	11
1942	115	57	58	25	4	21
1941	102	55	46	20	4	16
1940	105	44	61	15	2	13
1939	145	79	63	12	—	12
1938	154	89	63	25	1	24
1937	133	67	62	13	2	11
1936	181	86	93	10	2	8
1935	184	115	66	13	2	11

* *Historical Statistics of the United States, Colonial Times to 1970*, U.S. Department of Commerce, Bureau of the Census, 1975.

Prisoners Executed Under Civil Authority, by Race and Offense: 1930 to 1970

	Murder			Rape		
Year	Total	White	Negro	Total	White	Negro
1934	154	64	89	14	1	13
1933	151	75	74	7	1	6
1932	128	62	63	10	—	10
1931	137	76	57	15	1	14
1930	147	90	57	6	—	6

Comment

In addition to the executions for murder and rape, a relatively small number of executions have been held under laws permitting capital punishment for other crimes. Since 1930, 25 persons were executed for armed robbery, 20 for kidnapping, 11 for burglary, 6 for sabotage, 6 for aggravated assault and 2 for espionage. Of those executed for all crimes, by the way, all were men except for 32 women.

The executions for rape are now primarily of historical interest. In Coker v. Georgia, 433 U.S. 584 (1977), the Supreme Court held that the infliction of the death penalty was unconstitutional where the crime was a "non-aggravated rape of an adult woman." By then, the number of states permitting this penalty had dropped to only 3, Georgia, Louisiana, and North Carolina.

Capital punishment for rape, however, is of interest because it was here that the only satisfactorily clear judgment possible was that the infliction of capital punishment was racially biased. One study, for instance, showed that 38% of the black men who raped white women were sentenced to death, while in the cases involving other combinations of defendants and victims only 5% of those convicted received death sentences. Not only that, but the study was able to show that even accounting for other variables also related to the sentence—(1) the commission of an offense contemporaneous with the rape, (2) the display of a weapon by the defendant at the time of the offense of rape, (3) the defendant's relationship to the victim, (4) length of the defendant's trial and (5) the defendant's plea—the demonstration of racial discrimination was still strong. No such clear showing has been made concerning the death penalty for murder.

b. EXECUTION UPDATE *

Total executions to May 30, 1990 since 1976 reinstatement of capital punishment: 128.

* Compiled by the NAACP Legal Defense Fund, Sept. 1990 © 1990 (Reprinted by permission).

c. CAPITAL PUNISHMENT LAWS *

As of 1990 38 states had laws that provided for capital punishment. Of these, two had not sentenced anyone to death since 1973.

The states which have death penalty statutes are as follows:

Alabama, Arizona, Arkansas, California, Colorado, Connecticut, Delaware, Florida, Georgia, Idaho, Illinois, Indiana, Kentucky, Louisiana, Maryland, Mississippi, Missouri, Montana, Nebraska, Nevada, New Hampshire, New Jersey, New Mexico, North Carolina, Ohio, Oklahoma, Oregon, Pennsylvania, South Carolina, South Dakota, Tennessee, Texas, Utah, Virginia, Washington, Wyoming, U.S. Government, U.S. Military.

The following jurisdictions had no capital punishment statutes in 1990:

Alaska, District of Columbia, Hawaii, Iowa, Kansas, Maine, Massachusetts, Michigan, Minnesota, New York, North Dakota, Rhode Island, Vermont, West Virginia, Wisconsin.

d. RECENT HISTORY **

Death Row Inmates

Race of Defendant:

White	1,180	(50.27%)
Black	946	(40.30%)
Hispanic	156	(6.64%)
Native American	42	(1.78%)
Asian	15	(.63%)
Unknown at this issue	8	(.34%)

Sex:	Male	2,317	(98.72%)
	Female	30	(1.27%)

DISPOSITIONS SINCE JANUARY 1, 1973:

Death sentences vacated under unconstitutional statutes: 558 (rev. est.)

Convictions reversed or sentences vacated on other grounds: 992 (est.)

Executions: 128

Suicides: 28

Commutations: 51 (including those by the Governor of Texas resulting from favorable court decisions)

Died of natural causes, or killed while under death sentence: 52

* Compiled by the NAACP Legal Defense Fund, Sept. 1990 © 1990 (Reprinted by permission).

** Compiled by the NAACP Legal Defense Fund, Sept. 1990 © 1990 (Reprinted by permission).

B. THE ADMINISTRATION OF CAPITAL PUNISH-MENT

1. THE EVOLVING LAW *

A. *Furman*

In 1972 the Supreme Court announced its per curiam decision in Furman v. Georgia, which invalidated standardless, discretionary jury sentencing in capital cases. Because none of the five concurring Justices could agree upon a single rationale, the exact meaning of *Furman* is difficult to decipher. Indeed, the Court's recurrent inability since *Furman* to agree upon a majority opinion when vacating sentences of death because they violate the eighth amendment underscores the diversity of views reflected in *Furman*.

In *Furman* Justice Brennan and Justice Marshall both concluded, but for somewhat different reasons, that imposition of the death penalty under any circumstances would violate the eighth amendment. The remaining three members of the *Furman* plurality—Justices Douglas, Stewart, and White—chose to decide the case on more narrow grounds. They all agreed that standardless discretionary jury sentencing was unconstitutional because the death sentences which resulted reflected qualities or characteristics which offended the eighth amendment. But each Justice described that constitutionally impermissible quality or characteristic in a substantially different way. For example, Justice Douglas concluded that standardless, discretionary sentencing violated the eighth amendment because it permitted juries to discriminate between defendants for reasons that offended the equal protection clause. In particular, he believed black or impoverished defendants suffered the death penalty to a disproportionate degree.

By contrast, Justice Stewart concluded that standardless, discretionary jury sentencing violated the eighth amendment because, in his view, no logical basis existed to distinguish between most capital offenders, who did not receive the death penalty, and the "capriciously selected random handful" who suffered the ultimate sanction.[1] Indeed, Justice Stewart likened the imposition of the death penalty in those few cases to being struck by lightning. He concluded that the eighth and 14th amendments did not permit the death penalty to be "so wantonly and freakishly imposed."

Justice White took the view that the death penalty would be constitutional if it substantially advanced some legitimate penal purpose, such as incapacitation, general deterrence, or satisfaction of society's demands for retribution. He concluded, however, that the extreme infrequency with which states actually imposed the death

---

* Baldus, Pulaski, Woodworth & Kyle, "Identifying Comparatively Excessive Sentences of Death: A Quantitative Approach" 33 *Stan.L.Rev.* 1 (Nov. 1980). © 1980 (Reprinted by permission).

1. Unlike Justice Douglas, Justice Stewart felt that the evidence concerning the impact of race on sentencing was not sufficient to prove discrimination.

penalty coupled with the usually satisfactory alternative of lengthy incarceration undercut any justification based on retribution or incapacitation. For the same reasons, Justice White also rejected the argument that discretionary death-sentencing systems were permissible as a general deterrent. He noted that, in practice, the death penalty lacked any real deterrent effect because it was impossible to determine why relatively few individuals convicted of atrocious crimes received the death penalty while many others, convicted of the same crime, did not. In Justice White's view, the death penalty could serve as a general deterrent only if regularly imposed in identifiable classes of cases.[2]

While these three Justices condemned discretionary jury sentencing for different reasons, their opinions share a common concern. They each suggest that the death-sentencing systems under scrutiny in *Furman* were unconstitutional because of two factors: (1) the infrequency with which juries actually imposed the death penalty, and (2) the lack of any legitimate explanation why some persons convicted of atrocious crimes received life sentences while others convicted of factually similar crimes were sentenced to death. For this reason, the Supreme Court has interpreted *Furman* to prohibit death-sentencing systems which permit judges or juries to impose the death penalty on the basis of constitutionally impermissible factors or which fail to provide any meaningful basis at all for discriminating between those defendants who receive the death penalty and those defendants who do not.

B. Gregg, Proffitt, and Jurek

Furman invalidated death sentences imposed on over six hundred defendants. It did not, however, abolish the death penalty altogether since only Justices Brennan and Marshall flatly condemned capital punishment under all circumstances. As a consequence, many states that wished to retain the death penalty adopted a variety of new procedures in an effort to overcome the deficiencies which made standardless, discretionary sentencing statutes unconstitutional. Some states tried to prevent abuses of sentencing discretion by making the death penalty mandatory in specified classes of cases, an approach the Supreme Court subsequently rejected.[3] Other states attempted to satisfy *Furman* while preserving some degree of sentencing discretion by enacting explicit sentencing standards and by adopting sometimes elaborate procedures to ensure that those standards were enforced.

2. Justice White did not reject the notion that capital punishment could serve as an effective general deterrent. In fact, he seemed to concede the constitutional authority of legislatures to resolve that debatable question as they deemed appropriate. However, he refused to sustain the constitutionality of death-sentencing statutes on that ground because he regarded the legislative practice of delegating the death-sentencing function to individual juries without the benefit of legislative guidance as more a legislative abdication than an exercise of legislative judgment.

3. The Court in [another case] left open the possibility of mandatory death sentences for life-term prisoners committing certain violent crimes.

In Gregg v. Georgia, Proffitt v. Florida, and Jurek v. Texas, the Supreme Court approved three different sentencing schemes of this latter type and, in the process, further clarified exactly what kind of procedures will satisfy the eighth amendment. In each case the Court emphasized the importance of certain basic safeguards.

1. *Jury Sentencing Standards and Appellate Review.*

First, the death-sentencing statutes that the Court has approved each limit capital punishment to an explicitly defined subclass of homicide cases. They do so by defining capital murder in terms of particular factual circumstances, by identifying specific aggravating circumstances the existence of which the jury must find in order to impose a death sentence, or by a combination of both methods. In this respect alone, these statutes permit one to meaningfully distinguish between cases in which the jury imposed the death sentence and at least some of the cases in which it did not.

Second, each approved statute requires that sentencing decisions be made with reference to explicit standards. These standards conform to the constitutional requirement that sentencing in capital cases must focus on the particulars of the offense and the character and background of the defendant, including any mitigating circumstances. Furthermore, these standards must be sufficiently explicit so that, assuming the jury follows them as given, the jury will not be free to determine on its own by what criteria the death penalty should be applied.

Third, each of the post-*Furman* death-sentencing statutes that the Court has approved includes a provision for appellate review by a court of statewide jurisdiction. Thus, defendants enjoy some assurance that jury findings of fact sufficient to justify imposition of the death sentence will be based upon substantial evidence. Consequently, appellate review in those states provides some check against an aberrant jury decision to impose the death sentence under circumstances which do not satisfy the legislative criteria.

Comment

The administration of capital punishment cases is in several ways different from that of other criminal prosecutions. One reason for this is that capital punishment commands far less of a consensus than does, say, imprisonment for armed robbery. Though the majority of the population favors the death penalty a very substantial number of people oppose it—and many of the others who are in principle in favor are ambivalent about the use of the death penalty in any particular case. Finally, even those who are in favor of capital punishment in a particular case recognize that the death penalty is an especially severe sanction calling for extreme care in its imposition.

The irrevocability of capital punishment is another problem. If other criminal punishments are improperly applied there are means of correcting the error eventually through habeas corpus or other post conviction remedies. Of course, this is not possible after the defendant has been executed. For this reason, too, the courts scrutinize capital punishment cases with special care.

In addition, capital punishment cases are the only cases where, after imprisonment, the defendant will continue to fight for time. In non-capital cases, the defendant will usually raise only those issues which hold some promise, however small, of causing his release from prison and are worth the time and energy which the litigation would take. The defendant under sentence of death is fighting to delay his execution, and even though his litigation eventually will lose the courts will take time to decide his questions—time during which at least he will be kept alive.

An often neglected difference between capital and other cases arises from the far greater number of federal constitutional issues in death penalty litigation. In non-capital cases, state law determines the legal issues with the exception of those protected in the Constitution such as the privilege against self-incrimination, the confrontation clause, the search and seizure rules, and the general requirements of due process. The Constitutional strictures on cruel and unusual punishment however govern the means and procedures by which the death penalty can be administered and as a result an elaborate law has developed in the Supreme Court concerning capital punishment. The importance of this is that since capital punishment cases now raise issues of Federal Constitutional law, covering virtually all aspects of the prosecution, the process of decision in capital cases will far more often involve the federal courts as the final arbitrers of federal law. This in itself will prolong and complicate the litigation. Not only will more questions, more delay and more court proceedings be necessary in capital punishment cases, but it may also be that the standards used in determining issues of federal Constitutional rights may be different as well. For instance, though the defendant's right to counsel has been interpreted in non-capital cases as requiring competent counsel, the large variations in the ability and dedication of lawyers has required that this standard be a fairly loose one, and only the most clear violations of the attorney's duty have been held to constitute incompetence of counsel.

In capital cases, however, the argument has been made that the standards should be much stricter. There are three reasons for this. First of all, it even less often can be argued in capital cases that the defendant should be stuck with the errors of the lawyer he has picked. Virtually all death penalty defendants are indigent and have their lawyer chosen by the state. Second, of course, death is a more serious and irrevocable punishment. Finally, the issue of death or life is usually closer than that of guilt or innocence and therefore smaller differences in counsel will be more important in the result. In deciding this last point, would it be important that while the prosecution wins three-quarters of the cases at trial, it loses almost two-thirds of death penalty adjudications? Would it also be important to know that when any study of the "horror cases"—those most obviously bound for death penalty—is made, it turns out that about one-third, in fact, do not receive that sentence from the jury?

In addition, issues may arise involving competence of counsel in capital cases without even any showing as to the counsel's performance. Thus, should capital punishment be allowed if the defense lawyer's first criminal case was one where the death penalty was awarded? Should it be allowed where the state paid a defense counsel for an indigent defendant $1100 for defending two capital cases? Both of these are actual cases.

C. THE REASONS FOR CAPITAL PUNISHMENT

1. DETERRENCE

a. THE DIFFICULTY OF FINDING OUT *

[T]he case against capital punishment is strengthened if it rests on moral grounds rather than if one insists, against all reason, that the threat of the ultimate punishment has no effect on behavior. In fact, capital punishment is atrociously efficient in the hands of a tyrant like Hitler. The killing of dissidents is an instrument of "horrible and tragic effectiveness"; it forces "the great majority of subjects . . . into conformance." Its very strength is an argument for denying it to governments or to judges who are merely flesh and blood.

Many studies of capital punishment, however, claim to be based on empirical data. In the last generation, capital punishment declined dramatically in the United States. Yet the murder rate remained stable. The murder rate was 4.8 per 100,000 population in 1951; in the same year, 105 persons were put to death. In 1960, the rate was 5.1 per 100,000 and fifty-six persons were executed. In 1964, the murder rate was exactly the same as in 1955 (4.8 per 100,000), but only fifteen persons were put to death, as opposed to 76. In 1966, the murder rate was 5.6 per 100,000; only one man was executed.

These figures, however, do not prove the case, one way or the other. It is clear from the data that capital punishment had gone largely out of fashion in the country. It had become a rare form of punishment—so rare that perhaps it added little or nothing to the risk a rapist or murderer ran. In 1951, about 7,500 people were murdered; yet only 105 killers were executed—about 1.4 percent. A number of states had abolished the death penalty; some had never had it; those who kept it fussed over it so, with so many appeals and delays that convicts spent ten years or more on death row. This further diluted the risk and made the condemned into objects of sympathy—victims themselves—rather than objects of hatred. Differences in risk, like differences in price, may be so

---

* Lawrence Friedman, *The Legal System,* pp. 74–75. © 1975 (Reprinted by permission). Russell Sage Foundation, New York, 1975,

small that they do not matter. If a dealer in sports cars raised the price of one model from \$7,000 to \$7,000.20, one would not expect sales to decline. Airplane passengers do not cancel a trip if the chance of a crash rises from one chance in ten billion to two. Capital punishment may have become such a rare remote risk, and so far removed in time, that it added no *significant* deterrent. Any potential murderer ran the risk of arrest, prosecution, and a long term in jail. A truly *tiny* added risk of death might not mean very much. By the late 1960s, then, it was safe to abolish the death penalty under any view of its value as a deterrent. Abolition would make only a slight difference, because the effect of the penalty was already virtually gone.

Question

Is the small size of the likely effect a reason why it is so difficult to show whether or not capital punishment has any deterrent effect? Are there any other reasons? By the way, one should mention that since 1966, the last date mentioned in the excerpt, the murder rate in the U.S. has almost doubled.

b. THE DISPUTE *

A statistical study cannot prove that executions deter murders, nor can it prove that they do not. Given a hypothesis about a causal relationship, however, a statistical analysis can determine whether that hypothesis is consistent with past experience. Both Sellin and Ehrlich tested the hypothesis that capital punishment deters murders. Both used a variable to represent the threat of capital punishment, and both compared that variable with the behavior of homicide rates in the United States. However, they used different statistical methods to make their comparisons and arrived at different conclusions.

Sellin used a "matching" technique. He selected clusters of neighboring states "closely similar" in "social organization, composition of population, [and] economic and social conditions"; in each grouping at least one state had abolished the death penalty and at least one retained it. He then compared the homicide rates for the years 1920–1955 and 1920–1962 in abolitionist and retentionist states within each group, and found that the rates in abolitionist states were not significantly or systematically different than the rates in retentionist states. From this evidence he drew the "inevitable conclusion . . . that executions have no discernible effect on homicide death rates . . ."

Ehrlich focused instead on the relationship in the nation as a whole between the homicide rate and "execution risk"—the fraction of persons convicted of murder who were subsequently executed. He compared the differences in homicide rate and execution risk for the years 1933–1969, and found a positive simple correlation between changes in the homicide

* David C. Baldus and James W.L. Cole, *A Comparison of the Work of Thorsten Sellin and Isaac Ehrlich on the Deterrent Ef-* *fect of Capital Punishment,* 85 Yale L.J. 170 (1975). © 1975 (Reprinted by permission).

rate and changes in execution risk—increases in execution risk were associated with increases in the homicide rate. However, when he controlled for the influence of other variables on the homicide rate by using a multiple regression analysis, the relationship became negative. More precisely, he estimated that the elasticity of the homicide rate with respect to the execution rate was approximately—.06—that is, a .06 percent decrease in the homicide rate was associated with a one percent increase in execution risk. This finding was the basis for his estimate that "on the average the trade off between the execution of an offender and the lives of potential victims it might have saved was of the order of magnitude of 1 for 8 for the period 1933–67 in the United States," and for his "tentative and rough calculation [that] the decline in [execution risk] alone might have accounted for about 25 percent of the increase in the murder rate between 1960 and 1967."

We believe that Sellin's work, despite its methodological shortcomings, offers a more reliable basis than Ehrlich's recent work for inferring whether the threat of capital punishment deters murders. Future studies by Ehrlich or others may weaken the credibility of work that went before him, but on the record to date Sellin makes the stronger case.

It is quite true that Ehrlich's approach is statistically more sophisticated than Sellin's. But statistical sophistication is no cure for flaws in model construction and research design. There are many questions which, because of inadequacies of data or theory, are best studied by simpler methods. The deterrent effect of capital punishment is at this point just such a question.

.   .   .

It is quite possible that because of the complexity of the social phenomenon involved, we will never know with certainty whether capital punishment does or does not deter murder. Statistical analyses can only test with the available data the hypothesis that a significant deterrent effect exists. On the basis of the work of Sellin and others who have taken his approach, we are inclined to attach more credibility to their view that capital punishment does not have a significant deterrent effect.

Comment and Questions

The debate over whether capital punishment deters is generating a great volume of writing, much of which is far too mathematically and statistically sophisticated for the student (or the authors, for that matter), to comprehend. Since there is no hope of any consensus in the foreseeable future, one of the major issues becomes "where shall the burden of proof lie." One commentator has phrased the issue this way: *

* Ernest Van Den Haag, *Punishing Criminals,* New York, Basic Books Inc.,   1975, p. 216. © 1975 (Reprinted with permission).

"In the absence of conclusive statistical proof of its effectiveness or ineffectiveness, the case for or against the death penalty as a deterrent rests on one's preference for one of two risks.

    1. If the death penalty does not add deterrence and we carry out death sentences, we lose the life of the executed convict without adding deterrence.

    2. If the death penalty does add deterrence, and we fail to pronounce and carry out death sentences for murder, we fail to deter murderers who could have been deterred had the death sentence been pronounced and carried out. We lose the lives of the victims who would have been spared had we been willing to deter their murderers by executing other murderers."

Can you guess where he comes out on the issue?

Could one also argue that the burden of proof is on the advocate of capital punishment because, before we take the life of a human being, we should at least have some evidence that it will accomplish something?

c. CAPITAL PUNISHMENT DETERS *

If [capital punishment does not deter crime] then why do criminals, even the braggadocian type, fear it most? Why does every criminal sentenced to death seek commutation to life imprisonment? Common sense alone, without the benefit of knowledge, wisdom, and experience, convinces that we are influenced to the greatest degree by that which we love, respect or fear to the greatest degree—and that we cling most tenaciously to our most valued possessions. Life is indisputably our greatest possession. Additionally, there is no definitive proof anywhere that the death penalty is not a deterrent. There are merely the gratuitous statements of wishful thinkers, some of whom, because of the responsible duties of their positions, ought not be making unprovable or misleading statements.

It is also put forth by those who would weaken our laws and, perforce, our ability to protect the innocent, that many murderers on death row claim they did not think of the death penalty when they committed their crimes. This is undoubtedly true. That is precisely the point. If they had thought of it, they would not have committed their crimes. Here we have the spectacle of a minute minority of convicted murderers convincing intelligent people that capital punishment is wrong because of their own failure to realize the consequences of their murderous conduct. Are we then to base our laws on this reasoning? What of the countless others who *were* deterred from murder through fear of the penalty? The implication is clear: even those murderers who didn't think of the death penalty would have been deterred had they given it consideration. Our laws are made for

* Edward J. Allen, "Capital Punishment,   *Chief,* Vol. 27, pp. 22 et seq., June 1960.
Your Protection and Mine," *The Police*   ©1960 (Reprinted by permission).

reasonable creatures, not to satisfy an abnormal handful. It is hardly the part of wisdom to be guided by the counsel and advice of an infinitesimally small band of bestial criminals. Further, the cunning individual and conspiratorial group who plot murder always imagine themselves too clever to get caught, or if caught, convicted.

d. DOES CAPITAL PUNISHMENT ENCOURAGE MURDER? *

I shall limit myself to two aspects of murder and capital crime: self-destructive motivations and coping devices acquired through social sanction. Both aspects have the effect of engendering killing as a result of the presence of the death penalty.

This paper shall develop a theme that murder can be committed either consciously or unconsciously in order to be killed by the state.

The other theme of this paper derives from learning theory, as well as from psychoanalytic ego psychology; namely that violence begets violence. Freud emphasized the precariousness of ego controls over the aggressive instincts, which he ultimately based on the poorly-accepted postulate of a death instinct.

Social learning theory emphasizes the importance of modeling behavior in terms of observation and imitation. Bandura and his associates have shown, in a series of studies, that children imitate specific aggressive behaviors observed in an adult (in person as well as in films and television). Children and adolescents tend to identify more with what is done by parents and other adult identification figures than with what is said by them.

The death penalty is a sanctioned mode of society's solving its problem with murderers and other perpetrators of violence. As such, society become a brutal parent and explicitly sanctions violence as a means of coping. Logically, we should expect, therefore, that those who live in a society that authorizes and inflicts the death penalty would be more likely to choose to kill as a means of problem-solving than would those who live where such a societal action example is not set. It is of note that some murderers, including some I have examined, refer to their acts as "executions."

An example of the first effect—the self destructive motivation— involved the killing of young children toward whom there was no animosity, and was the result of a conscious attempt to invoke the death penalty by means of committing a heinous act.

Patricia Wilson ** was a twenty-year-old single woman, who killed the five- and six-year-old daughters of a [woman], for whom she had served for several weeks as a live-in baby-sitter. Patricia expressed only fond feelings for the two little girls, apparently delightful, affec-

* George F. Solomon, M.D., "Capital Punishment as Suicide and Murder," 45 *Amer.Journal of Orthopsychiatry*, July 1975, p. 701, 702–706. © 1975 (Reprinted by permission).

** Names of cases are fictionalized.

tionate children quite well cared for by their mother, . . . After turning herself in, Patricia reported to the police that she had killed the children in order to be executed, believing that the death penalty would be invoked if the crime was heinous enough. She reported that she sought to be killed because she had "screwed up" many of her own suicide attempts. She had come to believe that she was incapable of killing herself.

Questions

Is it possible that studies find it so difficult to show a deterrent effect in capital punishment because the number of murders it deters is just about balanced by the number it encourages? Is there any reason to believe this?

2. RETRIBUTION *

It was the phenomenon of Simon Wiesenthal that allowed me to understand why the intellectuals were wrong and why the police, the politicians, and the majority of the voters were right: we punish criminals principally in order to pay them back, and we execute the worst of them out of moral necessity. Anyone who respects Wiesenthal's mission will be driven to the same conclusion.

Of course, not everyone will respect that mission. It will strike the busy man—I mean the sort of man who sees things only in the light cast by a concern for his own interests—as somewhat bizarre. Why should anyone devote his life—more than thirty years of it!—exclusively to the task of hunting down the Nazi war criminals who survived World War II and escaped punishment? Wiesenthal says his conscience forces him "to bring the guilty ones to trial." But why punish them? What do we hope to accomplish now by punishing SS Obersturmbannführer Adolf Eichmann or SS Obersturmbannführer Franz Stangl or someday—who knows?—Reichsleiter Martin Bormann? We surely don't expect to rehabilitate them, and it would be foolish to think that by punishing them we might thereby deter others. The answer, I think, is clear: We want to punish them in order *to pay them back*. We think they must be made to pay for their crimes with their lives, and we think that we, the survivors of the world they violated, may legitimately exact that payment because we, too, are their victims. By punishing them, we demonstrate that there are laws that bind men across generations as well as across (and within) nations, that we are not simply isolated individuals, each pursuing his selfish interests and connected with others by a mere contract to live and let live. To state it simply, Wiesenthal allows us to see that it is right, morally right, to be angry with criminals and to express that anger publicly, officially,

* Walter Berns, "For Capital Punishment," *Harpers Magazine,* April, 1979, pp. 15–20 © 1979. Reprinted with permission.

and in an appropriate manner, which may require the worst of them to be executed.

Modern civil-libertarian opponents of capital punishment do not understand this. They say that to execute a criminal is to deny his human dignity; they also say that the death penalty is not useful, that nothing useful is accomplished by executing anyone. Being utilitarians, they are essentially selfish men, distrustful of passion, who do not understand the connection between anger and justice, and between anger and human dignity.

A moral community is not possible without anger and the moral indignation that accompanies it.

Capital punishment serves to remind us of the majesty of the moral order that is embodied in our law, and of the terrible consequences of its breach. The law must not be understood to be merely a statute that we enact or repeal at our will, and obey or disobey at our convenience— especially not the criminal law. Wherever law is regarded as merely statutory, men will soon enough disobey it, and will learn how to do so without any inconvenience to themselves. The criminal law must possess a dignity far beyond that possessed by mere statutory enactment or utilitarian and self-interested calculations. The most powerful means we have to give it that dignity is to authorize it to impose the ultimate penalty. The criminal law must be made awful, by which I mean awe-inspiring, or commanding "profound respect or reverential fear." It must remind us of the moral order by which alone we can live as *human* beings, and in America, the only punishment that can do this is capital punishment. Punishment arises out of the demand for justice, and justice is demanded by angry, morally indignant men; its purpose is to satisfy that moral indignation and thereby promote the law-abidingness that, it is assumed, accompanies it.

We want to live among people who do not value their possessions more than their citizenship, who do not think exclusively or even primarily of their own rights, people whom we can depend on even as they exercise their rights, and whom we can trust, which is to say, people who, even in the absence of a policeman, will not assault our bodies or steal our possessions, and might even come to our assistance when we need it, and who stand ready, when the occasion demands it, to risk their lives in defense of their country. If we are of the opinion that the United States may rightly ask of its citizens this awful sacrifice, then we are also of the opinion that it may rightly impose the most awful penalty; if it may rightly honor its heroes, it may rightly execute the worst of its criminals. By doing so, it will remind its citizens that it is a country worthy of heroes.

Comment

Re-read Chapter II pp. 74 to 81 and ask yourself whether the material on retribution is applicable to this justification for capital punishment. By the way, can you detect a hint of a utilitarian argument in the above excerpt, despite the author's denunciation of such reasoning?

3. NOTE ON OTHER JUSTIFICATIONS FOR CAPITAL PUNISHMENT

Deterrence and retribution are the two most popular justifications for capital punishment. In addition, two other utilitarian justifications are sometimes given for the death penalty.

Incapacitation

Capital punishment is sometimes justified as a measure of extreme incapacitation. The obvious fact is that if someone is executed, he cannot commit further crimes. Nor can we answer the argument completely by pointing out that the alternative to capital punishment need not be complete freedom but rather can be life imprisonment. Unfortunately, human error being what it is, some people under sentence of life imprisonment escape or are mistakenly released on parole, and then commit further crimes—even murder. And even while still imprisoned, life termers have been known to kill other prisoners or guards.

Probably the major argument against using capital punishment as a means of preventing the murderer's repetition of his crime is that the number of murderers who do go on to repeat their crime is extremely small compared to the total number of murderers—and our predictive powers as to that few are extremely low. As a result, if we took this justification seriously, we would have to execute vastly more people than the lives we would save. Even applying a large discount, on the theory that the life of the murderer is worth far less than the life of someone else, capital punishment for this reason would involve a major net expenditure of human life.

Lower Cost

Another justification occasionally heard for capital punishment is that it is cheaper, in pure financial terms, to execute than to maintain a convict for the rest of his life—or, as is more realistic, until he is old enough to be paroled with a considerable degree of safety.

The problem with this reasoning is that what economists call the economies of scale in capital punishment are very substantial. If very large numbers were executed, the cost per execution might well be very small; but when very few people are executed, it may be more expensive to execute them than to imprison them for life. The reason is that when very few people are executed, the legal proceedings become extremely long, drawn-out and cumbersome, and the courts check with extreme care to make certain that none of the defendant's legal rights are compromised. In addition, the entire institution of capital punishment requires that a death row be maintained, that the governor have an executive clemency advisor, that special juries and rights of appeal be provided for, and the like—all of which greatly increase the cost of an execution, unless these expenses can be divided over considerably more executions than we have had for the last thirty years.

Questions

Do you find the incapacitation justification for capital punishment persuasive? What about the cost-cutting justification? What other justifications for capital punishment might there be? Are there any?

D.　OBJECTIONS TO CAPITAL PUNISHMENT

1.　IS THE DEATH PENALTY CRUEL? *

In most jurisdictions, condemned men are confined to maximum security units which they never leave, and in which their only companions are guards, occasional visitors, and each other. "Death Row" was designed to hold prisoners for what used to be the short time between pronouncement of sentence and execution; today, many inmates have spent over ten years there.

In these grim surroundings, the condemned man lives a life of extraordinary stress. In the usual case, he is fighting a legal battle for his life, and each time an appeal is turned down he faces the immediate threat of death. Then begins the agonizing wait while applications for stays are considered by the courts or the governor. Very frequently a date of execution is actually set only to be postponed. Stays have been granted when the condemned man is in the execution chamber, and it is not impossible for a prisoner to go through this experience more than once.

Prisoners on Death Row get to know each other well, and when an execution date is set, they suffer through the last days with the inmate scheduled to die. When efforts to win a reprieve fail, they watch him go to his death, and thus receive a vivid image of their own execution day. In some instances, they are housed close to the execution chamber, and sometimes can even see the death apparatus. . . .

One psychiatrist has described Death Row as a "grisly laboratory"—"the ultimate experimental stress, in which the condemned prisoner's personality is incredibly brutalized." There are occasional suicides, despite the strictest precautions, and "the strain of existence on Death Row is very likely to produce . . . acute psychotic breaks." Some inmates are driven to ravings or delusions, but the majority sink into a sort of catatonic numbness under the overwhelming stress.

A few abandon the legal battle to save their lives, preferring death itself to the torture of uncertainty and waiting. Most, however, continue to fight for life, often at severe psychological cost. A psychiatrist

---

* Working papers of the National Commission on Reform of Federal Criminal Laws, Memorandum on the Capital Punishment issue, as reported in Hearings before subcommittee No. 3, House Committee on the Judiciary, 92nd Congress Second session on HR 8414, 9486, 3243, 193, 11797 at page 300.

who came to know Caryl Chessman well reports that Chessman was able to go on only by imagining himself to be merely the lawyer in his case—by denying his identity as the condemned man. However, he could not maintain the "denial" continuously:

> "At those times . . ., Chessman would talk about the feelings of torture that he experienced waiting for death. At times he felt that he could no longer tolerate the pain, the anxiety and the fear. At such times, he expressed a wish to get the suffering over with."

When Death Row inmates do fall into psychosis, they come under that strange doctrine of our law that an insane man cannot be executed. There have been many implausible attempts to explain this doctrine, which seems in no way justified by deterrent or preventive theories of capital punishment. Many believe that one Mississippi court gave the true explanation: the insane man has "lost awareness of his precarious situation", and therefore "amid the darkened mists of mental collapse, there is no light against which the shadows of death may be cast. *It is revealed that if he were taken to the electric chair, he would not quail . . .*" (emphasis added).

The doctrine produces strange results. Henry McCracken, a condemned sex murderer, fell into a "self-induced hypnotic condition caused by fear of his impending execution. . . ." The execution was stayed, and McCracken was given electric shock treatments. He showed improvement, stopped imagining there were rabbits and cats in his cell, became neat in his personal habits, and began playing the guitar. The successful treatment meant that the stay of execution must be removed; McCracken was sane and ready to be killed. Under the interminable uncertainty of the Death Row regime, the only wonder is that more inmates do not become so obviously insane that the resources of modern psychiatry are needed to cure them for the executioner.

The long uncertainty of the wait is terrible indeed, but for many the worst time must be the last few hours, when all uncertainty is gone and the moment of death is known. Dostoevski, who actually faced a firing squad only to be reprieved at the last instant, described it thus:

> "[T]he chief and the worst pain may not be in the bodily suffering but in one's knowing for certain that in an hour, and then in ten minutes, and then in half a minute, and now, at the very moment, the soul will leave the body and that one will cease to be a man and that that's bound to happen; the worst part of it is that it's *certain*. When you lay your head down under the knife and hear the knife slide over your head, that quarter of a second is the most terrible of all."

In these last moments, men often simply disintegrate. . . .

. . . Aaron Mitchell was executed in [California] on April 12, 1967. A few hours before his execution, he took off his clothes and slashed his wrists with a hidden razor blade; he stood in the form of a crucifix, arms outstretched, with blood dripping to the floor. "This is the blood of Jesus Christ, I am the second coming," he cried. He was dragged struggling and screaming into the chamber and strapped in the chair, and was still shouting "I am Christ" when the cyanide fumes reached him. Camus has well summarized the terrible psychological cruelty of capital punishment:

> "[Execution] is not simply death. It is just as different, in essence, from the privation of life as a concentration camp is from prison . . . [I]t adds to death a rule, a public premeditation known to the future victim, an organization, in short, which is in itself a source of moral sufferings more terrible than death . . . For there to be equivalence, the death penalty would have to punish a criminal who had warned his victim of the date at which he would inflict a horrible death on him and who, from that moment onward, had confined him at his mercy for months. Such a monster is not encountered in private life."

Question

What is the relevance of cruelty to the victim or to the victim's loved ones in justifying the pain of the death penalty?

a. MAKING EXECUTION HUMANE (OR CAN IT BE?) *

As death rows around the nation swell with inmates, prison officials are grappling with a new question: How to execute a condemned criminal professionally and humanely?

States that have not inflicted the death penalty for decades say they cannot find experienced executioners. Other have trouble finding skilled technicians willing to repair electric chairs or build lethal injection systems. The need for experts has been underscored by botched executions that have caused gruesome deaths in Texas, Florida and Alabama.

Here at the Delaware Correctional Center, the state has built a gallows and a lethal-injection chamber alongside its death row. But "hangmen are a dying breed," said Fred S. Silverman, the state's Chief Deputy Attorney General.

The only experienced hangman known, said Mr. Silverman, is a backwoodsman in Canada who has not responded to notes left on a tree stump for him by the local authorities. Delaware's hanging history, between 1662 and 1946, shows that too much rope can cause decapitation and too little rope will not snap the spinal cord, leaving the inmate to strangle slowly.

---

* Michael deCourcy Hinds, "Making Execution Humane (or Can It Be?)," The New York Times, Saturday, October 13, 1990.

Americans broadly endorse capital punishment in principle. But with 2,400 people on death rows nationwide and with 23 states preparing to join the 15 that have executed prisoners since the Supreme Court reinstated the death penalty in 1976, the public is being forced to confront its grisly and brutal aspects.

As more executions occur, more problems surface. Jesse Tafero, wearing a black leather gag and mask, had flames leaping from his head when Florida's electric chair malfunctioned three times on May 5 before killing him. It took Horace F. Dunkins 19 minutes to die in the Alabama electric chair last year when it failed to deliver a single killing jolt. Raymond Landry, strapped to a gurney, waited up to 40 minutes last year while executioners in Texas repeatedly probed his veins with syringes, trying to inject a lethal dose of potassium chloride.

These are isolated events, but they throw light on a widespread problem that has gone largely unnoticed, in part because no established group is promoting execution techniques that minimize suffering. Anti-death-penalty groups like the American Civil Liberties Union say lobbying for more humane methods would undercut their fundamental opposition to the penalty; from a political perspective, they add that more humane methods would weaken their crusade by defusing public outrage. And doctors generally stay out of the debate, because their oath requires them to save lives, not take part in ending them.

The issue came into sharper focus with the recent troubles of Fred A. Leuchter Jr., who until recently was the nation's leading advisor to states on capital punishment, and who supplied lethal injection systems to four states.

In August, the Alabama Attorney General's office sent other states a memorandum raising questions about Mr. Leuchter's expertise and reliability, and a prominent Illinois physician testified in an affidavit in Federal court that use of Mr. Leuchter's injection method would paralyze inmates and cause them intense pain before they died. The system has been used so far only in Missouri and Illinois.

Mr. Leuchter, a 47-year-old former dealer in military surveillance equipment, denies that his system causes pain. "I am a proponent of capital punishment, but not a proponent of capital torture; that's why I got involved in the business," he said in an interview.

So far, Federal courts have dismissed appeals by plaintiffs who argue that methods of execution are inhumane. Still, questions persist. In Illinois and Delaware, which have Mr. Leuchter's lethal injection system, condemned inmates have gone to court, arguing that use of it would be cruel and unusual punishment, in violation of the Eighth Amendment to the Constitution. Inmates in other states challenge the states' ability to maintain execution equipment and use it properly.

Beyond that, lawyers and ethicists raise other questions: Does the constitutional guarantee against cruel punishment confer a right to a death without pain? Should physicians, who refuse on ethical grounds to take an active part in executions, share their skills to make the procedures more humane?

2. IS THE DEATH PENALTY ARBITRARY? *

[T]hese two problems—mistake and arbitrariness in death-penalty cases—are not fringe-problems, susceptible to being mopped up by minor refinements in concept and technique, but are at the very heart of the matter and are insoluble by any methods now known or now foreseeable. If we resume use of the death penalty, we will be killing some people by mistake and some without application of comprehensible standards, and we will go on doing these things until we give up the death penalty.

. . .

I will skip over the preliminary decision on arrest, and go on to the two-pronged decision made by the prosecutor. On the facts before him, he must first decide whether to *charge* an offense carrying the penalty of death, or a lesser offense. If he decides to charge the capital offense, he must quite commonly decide whether to *accept a plea of guilty* to a lesser (and therefore noncapital) offense, thus permitting the defendant to escape at this early stage the possibility of execution, at the price of going to prison without trial. . . .

If the *prosecutor,* having charged a capital crime, is nevertheless willing to accept a plea of guilty to a lesser offense, then the *defendant* has in turn the choice of accepting or rejecting this offer. This dreadful choice has to be made by a man in custody, often disoriented and frightened, and hence dependent upon advice, and susceptible to following possibly bad advice; at this point, then, the choice is partly or wholly made by the *lawyer* for the defendant. With the best of intentions, this lawyer's decision is often a difficult one.

If a "plea bargain" is not struck, then the defendant goes on trial for his life. At the end of this trial, the jury has a number of decisions or choices to make, most of them veiled by the secrecy of the jury-room. It must decide what the gross physical facts were: Did this defendant, for example, actually stab the deceased, or did somebody else do it? Did the defendant stab the victim at a time when the victim was trying to stab the defendant, or did he stab a man whose knife was sheathed? Having satisfied its mind as to the *physical* facts, the jury must then tackle the *psychological* facts. Did the defendant, who clearly (or admittedly) shot a man while that man was reaching for his handkerchief, *believe* that that man was reaching for a gun, or is the pretense that he so believed mere sham? Did the defendant *plan* this killing, or was it done in the heat of passion? Did he *intend* to kill at all?

The jury in a criminal case does not announce its decision on each of such points one by one. It simply comes in with a verdict of "not

* Charles L. Black, Jr., *Capital Punishment: The Inevitability of Caprice or Mistake* (W.W. Norton, 1974) pp. 18–20. © 1974. Reprinted with permission.

guilty," or "guilty of murder in the first degree," or of "manslaughter," or of some other offense known to the state's law. There is no question in the mind of anybody who has dealt with the criminal-law system that a jury sometimes comes in with a verdict of "guilty" of some offense lesser than the one strictly warranted by the evidence. . . .

If the jury, accepting the prosecutor's version of the facts and rejecting all defenses, convicts the defendant of an offense for which the death penalty is possible, the choice then has to be made as to *sentencing*. Under the old system, condemned in the 1972 Furman case, the usual procedure was for the jury, "in its discretion," to decide whether a death sentence was to be imposed. The form of words varied from state to state; sometimes the death sentence followed automatically unless the jury recommended mercy, while sometimes the affirmative recommendation of the jury was necessary for the sentence of death. Sometimes, indeed, the judge rather than the jury exercised this "discretion." In the newer statutes (the statutes designed to get around the 1972 Furman case) a *second* hearing on sentencing often occurs, at the end of which, on the basis of mitigating or aggravating circumstances named in the new law, the sentence of death may or may not be imposed. In this initial survey, it is enough to note that this choice must usually be made.

After conviction, sentencing, and appeal, we reach the possibility of executive clemency, or clemency exercised by a pardon board.

. . .

It becomes plainly visible that the choice of death as the penalty is the result not of just *one* choice—that of the trial judge or jury, dealt with in the Furman case—but of a *number* of choices, starting with the prosecutor's choice of a charge, and ending with the choice of the authority—the governor or a board—charged with the administration of clemency.

. . .

Regarding *each* of these choices, through all the range, one of two things, or perhaps both, may be true.

First, the choice made may be a *mistaken* one. The defendant may not have committed the act of which he is found guilty; the factors which ought properly to induce a prosecutor to accept a plea to a lesser offense may have been present, though he refused to do so; the defendant may have been "insane" in the way the law requires for exculpation, though the jury found that he was not. And so on.

Secondly, there may either be no legal standards governing the making of the choice, or the standards verbally set up by the legal system for the making of the choice may be so vague, at least in part of their range, as to be only *apparent* standards, in truth furnishing no direction and leaving the actual choice quite arbitrary.

These two possibilities have an interesting (and, in the circumstances, tragic) relationship. The concept of *mistake* fades out as the *standard* grows more and more vague and unintelligible. There is no vagueness problem about the question "Did Y hit Z on the head with a piece of pipe?" It is, for just that reason, easily possible to conceive of what it means to be "mistaken" in answering this question; one is "mistaken" if one answers it "yes" when in fact Y did not hit Z with the pipe. It is even fairly clear what it means to be "mistaken" in answering the question "Did Y *intend* to kill Z?" Conscious intents are facts; the difference here really is that, for obvious reasons, *mistake is more likely* in the second case than in the first, for it is hard or impossible to be confident of coming down on the right side of a question about past psychological fact.

It is very different when one comes to the question, "Was the action of which the defendant was found guilty performed in such a manner as to evidence an 'abandoned and malignant heart'?" (This phrase figures importantly in homicide law.) This question has the same grammatical form as a clearcut factual question; actually, through a considerable part of its range, it is not at all clear what it means. It sets up, in this range, not a standard but a *pseudo-standard*. One cannot, strictly speaking, be *mistaken* in answering it, at least within a considerable range, because to be mistaken is to be on the wrong side of a line, and there is no real line here. But that, in turn, means that the "test" may often be no test at all, but merely an invitation to arbitrariness and passion, or even to the influence of dark unconscious factors.

"Mistake" and "arbitrariness" therefore are reciprocally related. As a purported "test" becomes less and less intelligible, and hence more and more a cloak for arbitrariness, "mistake" becomes less and less possible—not, let it be strongly emphasized, because of any certainty of one's being right, but for the exactly contrary reason that there is no "right" or "wrong" discernible.

. . .

To sum up, if the nature of our institutions—and, indeed, of any institutions we can project—is such that the choice for death must often be standardless or mistaken, then the retribution question, the deterrence question, and the cruelty question all take on a different form and must be rethought. Is retribution a moral imperative when it is to fall on some persons arbitrarily chosen or chosen by mistake? Are we justified in using "deterrence" as an excuse for the execution of some persons chosen arbitrarily or by mistake when there is no affirmative case whatever for the reality of the "deterrence" effect? Are we justified in inflicting very great suffering when that suffering is to fall on some persons chosen arbitrarily or by mistake?

. . .

Comment and Questions

Does not the problem of arbitrariness also have an aspect quite apart from its relation to mistake? In the United States each year there are some 20,000 homicides that, at least at first glance, seem to be candidates for capital punishment. If public opinion and the legal system would permit the execution of all of these, or even of all those who meet any rational criterion, the problem of arbitrariness would be only that discussed in the above excerpt. The problem, however, is twofold. First, while about two thirds of Americans support capital punishment, half of these, according to the polls, do not want it applied "very often." In short, there seems to be a majority of Americans who would oppose many executions, even though a majority wants some inflictions of the death penalty. The problem is that there are so many murderers in every conceivable category to which capital punishment might be limited that the only way to avoid many executions is to pick and choose almost randomly among the appropriate class (assuming that we can determine its members). This raises not only problems of fairness to the few irrationally selected out for capital punishment, but constitutional issues as well. In the words of the attorney for the defendants in many of the death penalty cases:

> "The short of the matter, is that when a penalty is so barbaric that it can gain public acceptance only by being rarely, arbitrarily, and discriminatorily enforced, it plainly affronts the general standards of decency of the society."

3. IS THE DEATH PENALTY DISCRIMINATORY?

McCLESKEY v. KEMP

Supreme Court of the United States, 1987.
481 U.S. 279, 107 S.Ct. 1756, 95 L.Ed.2d 262.

After Gregg (see pp. 611–612) opponents of capital punishment began examining the ways capital cases were actually handled in the criminal justice system—from the initial decision to charge to the final decision to sentence. The most careful and complete such study was undertaken by Iowa law professor David Baldus and his colleagues, who found statistically significant disparities by race in the ways capital cases were handled by Georgia officials and juries. Their most striking finding was that, even when controlling for legally relevant factors, black defendants with white victims were much more likely to be convicted of capital offenses and sentenced to death than were other defendants. The study by Baldus and his colleagues was used to challenge McCleskey's sentence of death. He had been convicted of killing a white police officer.

Justice POWELL delivered the opinion of the Court.

.   .   .

.   .   . In support of his claim, McCleskey proffered a statistical study performed by Professors David C. Baldus, George Woodworth, and Charles Pulanski (the Baldus study) that purports to show a disparity in the imposition of the death sentence in Georgia based on the race of the murder victim and, to a lesser extent, the race of the defendant. The Baldus study is actually two sophisticated statistical studies that examine over 2,000 murder cases that occurred in Georgia during the 1970s. The raw numbers collected by Professor Baldus indicate that defendants charged with killing white persons received the death penalty in 11% of the cases, but defendants charged with killing blacks received the death penalty in only 1% of the cases. The raw numbers also indicate a reverse racial disparity according to the race of the defendant: 4% of the black defendants received the death penalty, as opposed to 7% of the white defendants.

Baldus also divided the cases according to the combination of the race of the defendant and the race of the victim. He found that the death penalty was assessed in 22% of the cases involving black defendants and white victims; 8% of the cases involving white defendants and white victims; 1% of the cases involving black defendants and black victims; and 3% of the cases involving white defendants and black victims. Similarly, Baldus found that prosecutors sought the death penalty in 70% of the cases involving black defendants and white victims; 32% of the cases involving white defendants and white victims; 15% of the cases involving black defendants and black victims; and 19% of the cases involving white defendants and black victims.

Baldus subjected his data to an extensive analysis, taking account of 230 variables that could have explained the disparities on nonracial grounds. One of his models concludes that, even after taking account of 39 nonracial variables, defendants charged with killing white victims were 4.3 times as likely to receive a death sentence as defendants charged with killing blacks. According to this model, black defendants were 1.1 times as likely to receive a death sentence as other defendants. Thus, the Baldus study indicates that black defendants, such as McCleskey, who kill white victims have the greatest likelihood of receiving the death penalty.

. . .

. . . [T]o prevail under the Equal Protection Clause, McCleskey must prove that the decision-makers in *his* case acted with discriminatory purpose. He offers no evidence specific to his own case that would support an inference that racial considerations played a part in his sentence. Instead, he relies solely on the Baldus study. . . .

The Court has accepted statistics as proof of intent to discriminate in certain limited contexts. First, this Court has accepted statistical disparities as proof of an equal protection violation in the selection of the jury venire in a particular district. Although statistical proof normally must present a "stark" pattern to be accepted as the sole proof of discriminatory intent under the Constitution, . . . "[b]ecause of the nature of the jury-selection task, . . . we have permitted a finding of constitutional violation even when the statistical pattern does not approach [such] extremes." . . . Second, this Court has accepted statistics in the form of multiple regression analysis to prove statutory violations under Title VII. . . .

But the nature of the capital sentencing decision, and the relationship of the statistics to that decision, are fundamentally different from the corresponding elements in the venire-selection or Title VII cases. Most importantly, each particular decision to impose the death penalty is made by a petit jury selected from a properly constituted venire. Each jury is unique in its composition, and the Constitution requires that its decision rest on consideration of innumerable factors that vary according to the characteristics of the individual defendant and the facts of the particular capital offense. . . .

Thus, the application of an inference drawn from the general statistics to a specific decision in a trial and sentencing simply is not comparable to the application of an inference drawn from general statistics to a specific venire-selection or Title VII case. . . .

. . .

McCleskey also argues that the Baldus study demonstrates that the Georgia capital sentencing system violates the Eighth Amendment . . . [and that it] is arbitrary and capricious in *application,* and therefore his sentence is excessive, because racial considerations may influence capital sentencing decisions in Georgia. We now address this claim.

. . .

At most, the Baldus study indicates a discrepancy that appears to correlate with race. Apparent disparities in sentencing are an inevitable part of our criminal justice system. The discrepancy indicated by the Baldus study is "a far cry from the major systemic defects identified in *Furman.*" . . . As this Court has recognized, any mode for determining guilt or punishment "has its weaknesses and the potential for misuse." . . . Despite these imperfections, our consistent rule has been that constitutional guarantees are met when "the mode [for determining guilt or punishment] itself has been surrounded with safeguards to make it as fair as possible." . . . Where the discretion that is fundamental to our criminal process is involved, we decline to assume that what is unexplained is invidious. In light of the safeguards designed to minimize racial bias in the process, the fundamental value of jury trial in our criminal justice system, and the benefits that discretion provides to criminal defendants, we hold that the Baldus study does not demonstrate a constitutionally significant risk of racial bias affecting the Georgia capital-sentencing process.

. . .

. . . McCleskey's arguments are best presented to the legislative bodies. It is not the responsibility—or indeed even the right—of this Court to determine the appropriate punishment for particular crimes. It is the legislatures, the elected representatives of the people, that are "constituted to respond to the will and consequently the moral values of the people." . . .

Acordingly, we affirm the judgment of the Court of Appeals for the Eleventh Circuit.

It is so ordered.

Justice BRENNAN, with whom Justice MARSHALL joins, and with whom Justice BLACKMUN and Justice STEVENS join [in part], dissenting.

.   .   .

The Court today holds that Warren McCleskey's sentence was constitutionally imposed. It finds no fault in a system in which lawyers must tell their clients that race casts a large shadow on the capital sentencing process. . . .

.   .   .

The statistical evidence in this case thus relentlessly documents the risk that McCleskey's sentence was influenced by racial considerations. . . .   In light of the gravity of the interest at stake, petitioner's statistics on their face are a powerful demonstration of the type of risk that our Eighth Amendment jurisprudence has consistently condemned.

Evaluation of McCleskey's evidence cannot rest solely on the numbers themselves. We must also ask whether the conclusion suggested by those numbers is consonant with our understanding of history and human experience. Georgia's legacy of a race-conscious criminal justice system, as well a this Court's own recognition of the persistent danger that racial attitudes may affect criminal proceedings, indicate that McCleskey's claim is not a fanciful product of mere statistical artifice.

.   .   .

The Court . . . maintains that accepting McCleskey's claim would impose a threat to all sentencing because of the prospect that a correlation might be demonstrated between sentencing outcomes and other personal characteristics. Again, such a view is indifferent to the considerations that enter into a determination of whether punishment is "cruel and unusual." Race is a consideration whose influence is expressly constitutionally proscribed. . . .

.   .   .

. . . [I]t has been scarcely a generation since this Court's first decision striking down racial segregation, and barely two decades since the legislative prohibition of racial discrimination in major domains of national life. These have been honorable steps, but we cannot pretend that in three decades we have completely escaped the grip of a historical legacy spanning centuries. Warren McCleskey's evidence confronts us with the subtle and persistent influence of the past. His message is a disturbing one to a society that has formally repudiated racism, and a frustrating one to a Nation accustomed to regarding its destiny as the product of its own will. Nonetheless, we ignore him at our peril, for we remain imprisoned by the past as long as we deny its influence in the present.

The Court's decision today will not change what attorneys in Georgia tell other Warren McCleskeys about their chances of execution. Nothing will soften the harsh message they must convey, nor alter the prospect that race undoubtedly will continue to be a topic of discussion. McCleskey's evidence will not have obtained judicial acceptance, but that will not affect what is said on death row. However many criticisms of today's decision may be rendered, these painful conversations will serve as the most eloquent dissents of all.

[Justice BLACKMUN, with whom Justice MARSHALL and Justice STEVENS joined and with whom Justice BRENNAN joined in part, also wrote a dissenting opinion.]

Question

Could the statistical disparity issue raised by McCleskey have been resolved by executing more Blacks convicted of murdering Black victims? In fact, apparently influenced by the statistical disparity argument made by McClesky, some southern states seem to have embarked on such a course of action. Do you think that is a good idea?

4. THE IRREVOCABILITY OF THE DEATH PENALTY *

The Ayatollah Khomeini sits cross-legged, and metes out justice that is cross-eyed. That twisted, fearful symmetry has condemned to death heathens, heretics, pagans, infidels, and those who play, whistle, or hum Western music. The banned Western music referred to here is not the Nashville kind, which might make the Ayatollah seem reasonable; it is, rather Beethoven, Bach, etc., the men who composed *Missa Solemnis,* the *Christmas Oratorio,* as well as other fine works. The Ayatollah, as he sits in judgment, has no doubts.

The essence of our law, on the other hand, is that everything is doubtful; all is tentative; nothing is final. Cases that are lost can be appealed up and up and up until they disappear forever in the haze of the ionosphere. And if, somehow, an appeal is finally decided, the legislature may, sooner or later, reverse the court by changing the law. And sometimes, years and years later, a court may hold that an earlier opinion that had been faithfully followed a thousand times, was wrongly decided in the first place. Nothing in the law is final or irretrievable, except death. Which brings me, finally, to the purpose of this essay: To question capital punishment.

Capital punishment requires two certainties: First, the factual certainty that the defendant is the guilty party; and second, the social-political-ethical certainty that capital punishment is the proper penalty. I suggest that our experience with the Ayatollah's certainties ought

---

* Mordecai Rosenfeld, "In Praise of the Tentative", *New York Law Journal,* Janua- ry 11, 1980, Copyright 1980, all rights reserved. (Reprinted with permission).

give us deep doubts about ever being certain enough to inflict capital punishment.

Guilty or Not

As to whether the man in the dock was the doer of the deed, errors are made more often than we dare admit. We know how unlikely it was that Nicola Sacco or Bartolomeo Vanzetti killed anyone in Braintree, Mass., on April 15, 1920. A recent book suggests strongly that Bruno Richard Hauptmann did not kidnap or kill the Lindbergh baby, and that there were officials in New Jersey who knew it. And one writer has argued that the Government's case against Ethel Rosenberg may have been somewhat less sure than the case against her husband.

Several years ago, in Brooklyn, one George Whitemore seemed to be the murderer because a certain button was found in his possession, and the victim's coat was missing a button. The case seemed simple, except that a last-minute microscopic investigation revealed that it was a different button. How many George Whitemores have been found guilty? Just last year one Edmond Jackson was found guilty of a Queens murder; his conviction was upheld, without dissent, by both New York State appellate courts. The conviction was reversed by the federal court because defendant Jackson had been pointed out to the witnesses *before* he was put into the lineup (from which he was then readily selected). It was like asking a Lilliputian to pick out which one was Gulliver.

But faulty identification is not the main reason for opposing capital punishment. Even more important is our fallible judgment. For instance, as we sputter into the 80's our economy is *still* based on the premise that the price of oil can never exceed $4.50 a barrel.

Why should we think that our judgment on capital punishment is any sounder than our judgment on Arabian crude?

The factors affecting one's judgment on the issue of capital punishment are more complicated and more subtle than the pricing of oil, f.o.b. Abadan. It is doubtful, therefore, whether any political authority (the government, judge and jury) can *always* be trusted with the power to end a life. For instance, no line can be drawn between a "pure" murder trial and a murder trial tinged with (or dominated by) political or ethnic overtones. We may be aghast because most of the 697 people (according to one count) the Ayatollah has sent before his firing squads seem guilty mainly of political opposition; one victim was charged only with having supported Israel; and several appear to have been women of the evening, who granted favors, they thought, apolitically. But even in our own country, where due process is the highest, we cannot *always* disentangle the alleged murderer from his personality and beliefs; Massachusetts v. Sacco-Vanzetti is but the most enduring example. In other murder trials, the race or sex or beliefs or appearance, both of the defendant and the victim, are unintentional but omnipresent factors. One supposes a conviction for murder would be less likely where the accused was a white, elderly, gentle lady dressed in hand-sewn gingham (remember *Arsenic and Old Lace*), and the murdered victim an alcoholic, mean, unemployed, obese Black Panther. I think it may even be fair to say that no trial can be dispassionate where capital punishment is involved.

In short, capital punishment may be too potent a weapon for any People to have, for even we, in our Country, have not *always* been able to deal with it wisely.

In Russia and China and Germany and Uganda, we note, capital punishment has been used the way we use amphetamines; pop a few, and all your problems disappear. What a better world if capital punishment could be eliminated everywhere. And what better place to start, as an example, but in America, where every known precaution is already taken to guaranty a fair trial. If even we, with all our safeguards, abolish the death sentence, it might be a faint glimmer in the long Siberian night.

E. PUBLIC OPINION AND CAPITAL PUNISHMENT

1. PUBLIC SUPPORTS DEATH PENALTY *

Public support for the death penalty is at the highest point recorded in more than half a century of polling, with almost eight Americans in 10 favoring the execution of people convicted of murder.

As recently as 1966, a 47 percent plurality opposed capital punishment for murder.

The latest Gallup Poll also reveals growing public support for the death penalty for attempting to assassinate the president (63 percent), rape (51 percent), and hijacking an airplane (49 percent). Opposition to the death penalty narrowly outweighs support, 50 percent to 42 percent, for people convicted of espionage during peacetime.

Federal Death Penalty Law

Until recently, federal law permitted executions only for espionage by military personnel and hijackings resulting in death. The 100th Congress, shortly before adjourning, completed an omnibus drug bill that includes a federal death penalty for murders committed in the course of drug-related felonies.

Attorney General Richard Thornburgh, who will retain his post in the Bush administration, has indicated his support for legislation that would expand the use of the death penalty for federal crimes, such as the assassination of government officials.

* George Gallup, Jr. and Alec Gallup, "79% of Americans Back Death Penalty," San Francisco Chronicle, Monday, December 5, 1988, Copyright 1988, L.A. Times Syndicate (Reprinted with Permission).

Affect on Presidential Vote

In a post-election poll, 57 percent of Bush voters and 38 percent of Dukakis voters described the death penalty as a very important issue in deciding which candidate to vote for.

This dichotomy is reflected in the political coloration in the public's views on capital punishment.

Majorities of Republicans, for example, favor the execution of people convicted of murder (90 percent), attempted assassination (74 percent), rape (61 percent), hijacking (54 percent), and espionage (50 percent).

Far fewer Democrats back the death penalty for these crimes: murder (69 percent), assassination (49 percent), rape (44 percent), hijacking (42 percent), and espionage (35 percent).

Comparison of the 1986 and 1988 findings on the death penalty for murder shows increases in pro-execution sentiment in all major population groups.

Death Penalty for Murder

	Favor	Oppose	No opinion
1988	79%	16%	5%
1986	70	22	8
1985	72	20	8
1981	66	25	9
1978	62	27	11
1976	65	28	7
1972	57	32	11
1971	49	40	11
1969	51	40	9
1966	42	47	11
1965	45	43	12
1960	51	36	13
1953	68	25	7
1937	65	35	*
1936	61	39	*

*Not recorded

Death Penalty for Murder

(Percent in favor)

	1988	1986
NATIONWIDE	79%	70%
Men	83	74
Women	75	67
Whites	82	73
Blacks	57	47
18–29 years	83	70

	1988	1986
30–49 years	80%	72%
50 and older	77	69
College graduates	73	67
Some college	88	73
High school graduates	81	75
Not high school graduates	73	63
Republicans	90	83
Democrats	69	62
Independents	81	69
East	78	64
Midwest	79	73
South	79	69
West	81	76

Death Penalty for Other Crimes

	Favor	Oppose	No opinion
Assassination attempt			
1988	63%	33%	4%
1985	57	37	6
Rape			
1988	51%	42%	7%
1985	45	45	10
1981	37	53	10
1978	32	56	12
Hijacking airplane			
1988	49%	45%	6%
1985	45	48	7
1981	22	68	10
1978	37	52	11
Treason			
1988	42%	50%	8%
1985	48	47	5
1981	39	49	12
1978	36	50	14

2. IS THE PUBLIC AMBIVALENT? *

Thirteen years after the United States Supreme Court restored the death penalty as the ultimate instrument of justice, the execution system has bogged down in a costly legal and emotional morass that has overloaded the courts, divided citizens and left more than 2,100 death row convicts in an agonizing and expensive legal limbo.

That 1976 decision settled the law, more or less, but it hardly settled the argument. In states without a death penalty, such as New

* Andrew H. Malcolm, "Society's Conflict on Death Penalty Stalls Procession of the Condemned," The New York Times, Monday, June 19, 1989, p. A11.

York, there are continual legislative efforts to pass one. And in states with the death penalty there is still opposition.

The debate has obscured a significant development: Although an overwhelming majority of Americans say they want capital punishment, some of their institutions show little interest in actually using it.

Yet proponents argue that a properly administered death penalty is essential to deter crime and mete out justice for heinous murders. Opponents say the death penalty is ineffective as a deterrent, is capriciously applied and is more expensive than alternatives like imprisonment with no parole.

Since 1976, when the Supreme Court began validating rewritten state death penalty laws, there have been about 240,000 murders in the United States. In those 13 years, as of midnight last night, 111 people had been executed—fewer people than die on Rhode Island's highways in one year. And while 37 states have adopted new death penalty laws, 24 have never used them.

"There's an enormous ambivalence afoot in America today," said Franklin Zimring, a criminologist at the University of California at Berkeley. "We want to have the death penalty as a statement, as the ultimate weapon like the missiles in the silo. But we really don't want to use it."

At the present rate of about 20 executions a year, it would take 108 years to handle the current death row population. Even if the rate of executions was to match the highest ever (199 were carried out in 1935), it would take 11 years to handle the backlog. But by that time about 2,420 new convicts would be awaiting execution.

But mindful of mounting concern about crime, of public-opinion polls overwhelmingly supporting executions and aware of the electoral fate last fall of Gov. Michael S. Dukakis, the Democratic Presidential nominee who opposed the death penalty, many politicians quickly embrace capital punishment.

"We have the death penalty as a political tool," said Leigh Dingerson, director of the National Coalition to Abolish the Death Penalty. "Each year we have 10 or 12 or 20 symbolic executions. But as an instrument of justice or social retribution, we really don't use the death penalty much."

3. KILL, KILL, KILL! *

The House of Representatives has passed an omnibus crime control bill that would make dozens of changes in federal laws and programs, particularly in the area of capital punishment. Other major provisions include a widening of the conditions under which illegally obtained evidence could be used in court, and expansion of crime victims' rights.

* Criminal Justice Newsletter, Vol. 21, No. 20, October 15, 1990.

H.R. 5269, the "Comprehensive Crime Control Act of 1990," came to the House floor without the support of the Bush Administration or major law enforcement organizations. At a White House meeting last month with officials of the National Association of Attorneys General and the National District Attorneys Association, the President said the bill was "tougher on law enforcement than it is on criminals."

But during several days of floor action, the House approved many amendments sought by the Administration. The debate over those changes was unusually bitter and personal. Rep. William J. Hughes, chairman of the House Subcommittee on Crime, which produced much of the bill, angrily accused his colleagues of "tearing up" the Constitution. During votes on death penalty provisions, Congressman Hughes said that Representatives were walking into the chamber at the last minute and asking colleagues "Which [amendment] is tougher?" He said colleagues showed no concern over whether the bill was fair or even Constitutional, "because we are a month away from election, and members will go back to their districts and will all say, 'I was tough, I was tough on crime.'"

At another point, a number of death penalty opponents sarcastically chanted, "Kill, kill, kill," and Rep. David Obey (D–Wis.) asked, "Would it be possible to bring the guillotines directly to the House floor, rather than bothering with courts in the future?"

Comment and Questions

Even if society accepts the eath penalty for adults, other issues remain. Should the death penalty be imposed on juveniles who have been convicted of murder? The Supreme Court has held that offenders can be executed for crimes committed while juveniles, although in *Thompson v. Oklahoma,* in a five to four decision it drew a tenuous line at imposition of the death penalty for someone under sixteen years of age. However, one of the five votes was cast by Justice Sandra Day O'Connor, who wrote that she would have voted to uphold the death penalty if the "legislature had spoken clearly" on the matter. Do you agree? Assuming that you are in favor of capital punishment would you place any age limit on it? Would you agree to the execution of a 15 year old? A 14 year old? A 12 year old? Would you impose the death penalty on someone who was mentally retarded? If not, why not?

Finally, some anti-capital punishment journalists have argued that they have a right to show executions on television, in order to inform the public of its cruel reality. Do you think the public will change its collective mind about the death penalty if its members actually witness the execution? By the way, since it is so difficult to find executioners, would you volunteer to be trained to be one?

F. RECOMMENDED READING

Bedeau, Hugo A. *The Courts, the Constitution and Capital Punishment.* Lexington Books, Lexington, Mass., 1977.

Berns, Walter F. *For Capital Punishment: Crime and Morality of the Death Penalty.* Basic Books, New York, 1979.

Black, Charles L., Jr. *Capital Punishment: The Inevitability of Caprice or Mistake.* 2d Ed. W.W. Norton, New York, 1981.

Carrington, Frank. *Neither Cruel nor Unusual Punishment: The Case for Capital Punishment.* Arlington House, New Rochelle, N.Y., 1978.

Gettinger, Stephen H. *Sentenced to Die: The People, the Crimes, and the Controversy.* MacMillan, New York, 1979.

Jayawardiene, C.H.S. *The Penalty of Death: The Canadian Experiment.* Lexington Books, Lexington, Mass., 1977.

Sellin, J. Thorsten. *The Penalty of Death.* Sage Publications, Beverly Hills, 1980.

Shin, Kilman. *Death Penalty and Crime: Empirical Studies.* Center for Economic Analysis, George Mason Univ., Fairfax, Va., 1978.

van Dine, Stephen; Conrad, John P. and Dinitz, Simon. *Restraining the Wicked: The Incapacitation of the Dangerous Criminal.* Lexington Books, Lexington, Mass., 1979.

Zimring, Franklin E. and Hawkins, Gordon. *Capital Punishment and the American Agenda.* Cambridge University Press, Cambridge, Mass., 1986.

INDEX

References are to Pages

641

†